Lecture Notes in Artificial Intelligence   3238

Edited by J. G. Carbonell and J. Siekmann

Subseries of Lecture Notes in Computer Science

Susanne Biundo   Thom Frühwirth
Günther Palm (Eds.)

KI 2004:
Advances in
Artificial Intelligence

27th Annual German Conference on AI, KI 2004
Ulm, Germany, September 20-24, 2004
Proceedings

 Springer

Series Editors

Jaime G. Carbonell, Carnegie Mellon University, Pittsburgh, PA, USA
Jörg Siekmann, University of Saarland, Saarbrücken, Germany

Volume Editors

Susanne Biundo
Thom Frühwirth
Günther Palm
Universität Ulm, Fakultät für Informatik
89069 Ulm, Germany
E-mail: {Susanne.Biundo,Thom.Fruehwirth}@informatik.uni-ulm.de
palm@neuro.informatik.uni-ulm.de

Library of Congress Control Number: 2004112071

CR Subject Classification (1998): I.2

ISSN 0302-9743
ISBN 3-540-23166-8 Springer Berlin Heidelberg New York

Springer is a part of Springer Science+Business Media

springeronline.com

© Springer-Verlag Berlin Heidelberg 2004
Printed in Germany

Typesetting: Camera-ready by author, data conversion by Olgun Computergrafik
Printed on acid-free paper   SPIN: 11318675   06/3142   5 4 3 2 1 0

Preface

KI 2004 was the 27th edition of the annual German Conference on Artificial Intelligence, which traditionally brings together academic and industrial researchers from all areas of AI and which enjoys increasing international attendance.

KI 2004 received 103 submissions from 26 countries. This volume contains the 30 papers that were finally selected for presentation at the conference. The papers cover quite a broad spectrum of "classical" subareas of AI, like natural language processing, neural networks, knowledge representation, reasoning, planning, and search. When looking at this year's contributions, it was exciting to observe that there was a strong trend towards actual real-world applications of AI technology. A majority of contributions resulted from or were motivated by applications in a variety of areas. Examples include applications of planning, where the technology is being exploited for taxiway traffic control and game playing; natural language processing and knowledge representation are enabling advanced Web-based information processing; and the integration of results from automated reasoning, neural networks and machine perception into robotics leads to significantly improved capabilities of autonomous systems.

The technical programme of KI 2004 was highlighted by invited talks from outstanding researchers in the areas of automated reasoning, robot planning, constraint reasoning, machine learning, and semantic Web: Jörg Siekmann (DFKI and University of Saarland, Saarbrücken), Malik Ghallab (LAAS-CNRS, Toulouse), François Fages (INRIA Rocquencourt), Martin Riedmiller (University of Osnabrück), and Wolfgang Wahlster (DFKI and University of Saarland, Saarbrücken). Their invited papers are also presented in this volume.

This year KI was held in co-location with INFORMATIK 2004, the German Conference on Computer Science, organized under the auspices of the German Informatics Society (GI). KI and INFORMATIK shared a joint day of invited presentations. The talks by Wolfgang Wahlster and Malik Ghallab were part of this joint programme.

A conference like KI 2004 involves the dedication of many people. First of all, there are the authors, who submitted their papers to the conference; there are the members of the program committee and the many additional reviewers, who worked hard on providing high-quality reviews in time and participated in the paper discussion process; and there is the highly supportive KI 2004 local arrangements committee. We are most grateful to all of them.

July 2004

Susanne Biundo
Thom Frühwirth
Günther Palm

Organization

General Chairs

Susanne Biundo   University of Ulm, Germany
Friedrich von Henke   University of Ulm, Germany

Program Chairs

Susanne Biundo   University of Ulm, Germany
Thom Frühwirth   University of Ulm, Germany
Günther Palm   University of Ulm, Germany

Workshop Chair

Michael Beetz   Technical University Munich, Germany

Local Arrangements Chair

Thorsten Liebig   University of Ulm, Germany

Program Committee

Slim Abdennadher	German University in Cairo, Egypt
Elisabeth André	University of Augsburg, Germany
Roman Bartak	Charles University, Prague, Czech Republic
Michael Beetz	Technical University Munich, Germany
Hans-Georg Beyer	University of Dortmund, Germany
Susanne Biundo	University of Ulm (co-chair), Germany
Gerhard Brewka	University of Leipzig, Germany
Hans-Dieter Burkhard	Humboldt University Berlin, Germany
Thomas Christaller	Fraunhofer AIS, Bonn, Germany
Henning Christiansen	Roskilde Universitym, Denmark
François Fages	INRIA, Rocquencourt, France
Thom Frühwirth	University of Ulm (co-chair), Germany
Ulrich Furbach	University Koblenz-Landau, Germany
Enrico Giunchiglia	Genoa University, Italy
Günther Goerz	Friedrich-Alexander University, Erlangen, Germany
Andreas Günter	University of Hamburg, Germany
Joachim Hertzberg	Fraunhofer AIS, Bonn, Germany
Otthein Herzog	TZI, University of Bremen, Germany

Program Commitee (cont.)

Steffen Hölldobler	University of Dresden, Germany
Werner Horn	University of Vienna, Austriy
Stefan Kirn	University of Hohenheim, Germany
Jana Koehler	IBM Zurich Research Laboratory, Austria
Gerhard Kraetzschmar	University of Ulm, Germany
Rudolf Kruse	Otto-von-Guericke-University of Magdeburg, Germany
Franz Kurfess	California Polytechnic State University, USA
Gerhard Lakemeyer	University of Aachen, Germany
Thorsten Liebig	University of Ulm, Germany
Bärbel Mertsching	University of Hamburg, Germany
Hans-Hellmut Nagel	University of Karlsruhe, Germany
Bernhard Nebel	University of Freiburg, Germany
Bernd Neumann	University of Hamburg, Germany
Heiko Neumann	University of Ulm, Germany
Günther Palm	University of Ulm, Germany (co-chair)
Frank Puppe	University of Würzburg, Germany
Martin Riedmiller	Osnabrück University, Germany
Helge Ritter	University of Bielefeld, Germany
Ulrike Sattler	University of Manchester, UK
Friedhelm Schwenker	University of Ulm, Germany
Jörg Siekmann	DFKI, Saarbrücken, Germany
Rudi Studer	University of Karlsruhe, Germany
Sylvie Thiébaux	The Australian National University, Canberra, Australia
Michael Thielscher	University of Dresden, Germany
Paolo Traverso	IRST, Trento, Italy
Wolfgang Wahlster	DFKI, Saarbrücken, Germany
Toby Walsh	University College Cork, UK
Gerhard Weiss	Technical University Munich, Germany
Stefan Wermter	University of Sunderland, UK
Herbert Wiklicky	Imperial College London, UK
Stefan Wrobel	Fraunhofer AIS and University of Bonn, Germany

Additional Reviewers

Sebastian Bader	Christian Borgelt	Jürgen Dix
Volker Baier	Olivier Bouissou	Mark Elshaw
Peter Baumgartner	Paolo Bouquet	Marc Ehrig
Berhard Beckert	Marco Bozzano	Harry Erwin
Marco Benedetti	Henrik Bulskov	Felix Fischer
Massimo Benerecetti	Philipp Cimiano	Christian Fritz
Piergiorgio Bertoli	Hendrik Decker	Tom Gedeon

Axel Grossmann
Volker Haarslev
Rémy Haemmerlé
Pascal Hitzler
Frank Hoeppner
Somboon Hongeng
Tamas Horvath
Andreas Hotho
Lothar Hotz
Gero Iwan
Lars Karlsson
Joerg Kindermann

Alexander Kleiner
Thorsten Krebs
Kai Lingemann
Yves Martin
Davide Martinenghi
Marc Meister
Matthias Nickles
Gerd Paass
Maurice Pagnucco
Yannick Pencole
Erich Rome
Michael Rovatsos

Frank Rügheimer
Wolfgang Schmidle
Olga Skvortsova
Sylvain Soliman
Nenad Stojanovic
Bernd Thomas
Sven Utcke
Raphael Volz
Stefan Wölfl
Jianwei Zhang

Local Arrangements Committee

Martin Clauß   University of Ulm, Germany
Roland Holzer   University of Ulm, Germany
Hartmut Jungholt   University of Ulm, Germany
Thorsten Liebig   University of Ulm, Germany (chair)
Marc Meister   University of Ulm, Germany

Sponsoring Institutions

University of Ulm, Germany
Microsoft Deutschland GmbH
sd&m AG
Systems, Messe München GmbH
Continental Temic Speech Dialog Systems
Projektentwicklungsgesellschaft Ulm mbH
Dresdner Bank
DaimlerChrysler
IBM Deutschland
Siemens AG

Table of Contents

Planning and Search

Neural Networks and Machine Learning

Reasoning

Robotics and Machine Perception

Author Index

Automated Reasoning Tools
for Molecular Biology

François Fages

Projet Contraintes, INRIA Rocquencourt
BP105, 78153 Le Chesnay Cedex, France
Francois.Fages@inria.fr
http://contraintes.inria.fr

In recent years, molecular biology has engaged in a large-scale effort to elucidate high-level cellular processes in terms of their biochemical basis at the molecular level. The mass production of post genomic data, such as ARN expression, protein production and protein-protein interaction, raises the need of a strong parallel effort on the formal representation of biological processes.

In this talk, we shall present the Biochemical Abstract Machine BIOCHAM and advocate its use as a formal modeling environment for networks biology. Biocham provides a precise semantics to biomolecular interaction maps. Based on this formal semantics, the Biocham system offers automated reasoning tools for querying the temporal properties of the system under all its possible behaviors. We shall review the main features of Biocham and report on our modeling experience with this language. In particular we shall report on a model of the mammalian cell cycle's control developped after Kohn's map.

Biocham has been designed in the framework of the ARC CPBIO on "Process Calculi and Biology of Molecular Networks" [1] which aims at pushing forward a declarative and compositional approach to modeling languages in Systems Biology. Biocham is a language and a programming environment for modeling biochemical systems, making simulations, and checking temporal properties. It is composed of:

1. a rule-based language for modeling biochemical systems, allowing patterns and constraints in the definition of rules;
2. a simple simulator;
3. a powerful query language based on Computation Tree Logic CTL;
4. an interface to the NuSMV [2] model checker for automatically evaluating CTL queries.

The use of Computation Tree Logic (CTL) [3] for querying the temporal properties of the system provides an alternative technique to numerical models based on differential equations, in particular when numerical data are missing. The model-checking tools associated to CTL automate reasoning on all the possible behaviors of the system modeled in a purely qualitative way. The semantics of Biocham ensures that the set of possible behaviors of the model over-approximates the set of all behaviors of the system corresponding to different kinetic parameters.

S. Biundo, T. Frühwirth, and G. Palm (Eds.): KI 2004, LNAI 3238, pp. 1–2, 2004.
© Springer-Verlag Berlin Heidelberg 2004

Biocham shares several similarities with the Pathway Logic system [4] implemented in Maude. Both systems rely on an algebraic syntax and are rule-based languages. One difference is the use in Biocham of CTL logic which allows us to express a wide variety of biological queries, and the use of a state-of-the-art symbolic model checker for handling the complexity of highly non-deterministic models.

The first experimental results of this approach for querying models of biochemical networks in temporal logic have been reported in [5, 6], on a qualitative model of the mammalian cell cycle control [7, 8] and in [6] on a quantitative model of gene expression [9]. In this talk we describe the Biocham system which provides a modeling environment supporting this methodology. The full version of this paper will appear in [10].

References

1. ARC CPBIO: Process calculi and biology of molecular networks (2002–2003) http://contraintes.inria.fr/cpbio/.
2. Cimatti, A., Clarke, E., Enrico Giunchiglia, F.G., Pistore, M., Roveri, M., Sebastiani, R., Tacchella, A.: Nusmv 2: An opensource tool for symbolic model checking. In: Proceedings of the International Conference on Computer-Aided Verification, CAV'02, Copenhagen, Danmark (2002)
3. Clarke, E.M., Grumberg, O., Peled, D.A.: Model Checking. MIT Press (1999)
4. Eker, S., Knapp, M., Laderoute, K., Lincoln, P., Meseguer, J., Sönmez, M.K.: Pathway logic: Symbolic analysis of biological signaling. In: Proceedings of the seventh Pacific Symposium on Biocomputing. (2002) 400–412
5. Chabrier, N., Chiaverini, M., Danos, V., Fages, F., Schächter, V.: Modeling and querying biochemical networks. Theoretical Computer Science **To appear** (2004)
6. Chabrier, N., Fages, F.: Symbolic model cheking of biochemical networks. In Priami, C., ed.: CMSB'03: Proceedings of the first Workshop on Computational Methods in Systems Biology. Volume 2602 of Lecture Notes in Computer Science., Rovereto, Italy, Springer-Verlag (2003) 149–162
7. Chiaverini, M., Danos, V.: A core modeling language for the working molecular biologist. In Priami, C., ed.: CMSB'03: Proceedings of the first Workshop on Computational Methods in Systems Biology. Volume 2602 of Lecture Notes in Computer Science., Rovereto, Italy, Springer-Verlag (2003) 166
8. Kohn, K.W.: Molecular interaction map of the mammalian cell cycle control and DNA repair systems. Molecular Biology of Cell **10** (1999) 703–2734
9. Bockmayr, A., Courtois, A.: Using hybrid concurrent constraint programming to model dynamic biological systems. In Springer-Verlag, ed.: Proceedings of ICLP'02, International Conference on Logic Programming, Copenhagen (2002) 85–99
10. Chabrier-Rivier, N., Fages, F., Soliman, S.: The biochemical abstract machine BIOCHAM. In Danos, V., Schächter, V., eds.: CMSB'04: Proceedings of the second Workshop on Computational Methods in Systems Biology. Lecture Notes in Computer Science, Springer-Verlag (2004)

ΩMEGA: Computer Supported Mathematics

Jörg Siekmann and Christoph Benzmüller

Saarland University, Saarbrücken, Germany,
siekmann@dfki.de, chris@ags.uni-sb.de
http://www-ags.dfki.uni-sb.de/
http://ags.uni-sb.de/~chris

Dedicated to Martin Davis

Abstract. The year 2004 marks the fiftieth birthday of the first computer generated proof of a mathematical theorem: "the sum of two even numbers is again an even number" (with Martin Davis' implementation of Presburger Arithmetic in 1954).

While Martin Davis and later the research community of automated deduction used machine oriented calculi to find the proof for a theorem by automatic means, the Automath project of N.G. de Bruijn[1] – more modest in its aims with respect to automation – showed in the late 1960s and early 70s that a complete mathematical textbook could be coded and proof-checked by a computer.

Classical theorem proving procedures of today are based on ingenious search techniques to find a proof for a given theorem in very large search spaces – often in the range of several billion clauses. But in spite of many successful attempts to prove even open mathematical problems automatically, their use in everyday mathematical practice is still limited.

The shift from search based methods to more abstract planning techniques however opened up a new paradigm for mathematical reasoning on a computer and several systems of the new kind now employ a mix of interactive, search based as well as proof planning techniques.

The ΩMEGA system is at the core of several related and well-integrated research projects of the ΩMEGA research group, whose aim is to develop system support for the working mathematician, in particular it supports proof development at a human oriented level of abstraction. It is a modular system with a central proof data structure and several supplementary subsystems including automated deduction and computer algebra systems. ΩMEGA has many characteristics in common with systems like NuPrL [ACE+00], CoQ [Coq03], HoL [GM93], Pvs [ORR+96], and ISABELLE [Pau94,NPW02]. However, it differs from these systems with respect to its focus on *proof planning* and in that respect it is more similar to the proof planning systems CLAM and λCLAM at Edinburgh [RSG98,BvHHS90].

---

[1] http://www.win.tue.nl/automath/

S. Biundo, T. Frühwirth, and G. Palm (Eds.): KI 2004, LNAI 3238, pp. 3–28, 2004.

1 Introduction

The vision of computer-supported mathematics and a system which provides integrated support for all work phases of a mathematician (see Fig. 1) has fascinated researchers in artificial intelligence, particularly in the deduction systems area, and in mathematics for a long time. The dream of mechanizing (mathematical) reasoning dates back to Gottfried Wilhelm Leibniz in the 17th century with the touching vision that two philosophers engaged in a dispute would one day simply code their arguments into an appropriate formalism and then *calculate* (Calculemus!) who is right. At the end of the 19th century modern mathematical logic was born with Frege's Begriffsschrift and an important milestone in the formalization of mathematics was Hilbert's program and the 20th century Bourbakism.

Fig. 1. Calculemus illustration of different challenges for a mathematical assistance system.

With the logical formalism for the representation and calculation of mathematical arguments emerging in the first part of the twentieth century it was but a small step to implement these techniques now on a computer as soon as it was widely available. In 1954 Martin Davis' Presburger Arithmetic Program was reported to the US Army Ordnance and the Dartmouth Conference in 1956 is not only known for giving birth to artificial intelligence in general but also more specifically for the demonstration of the first automated reasoning programs for mathematics by Herb Simon and Alan Newell.

However, after the early enthusiasm of the 1960s, in particular the publication of the resolution principle in 1965 [Rob65], and the developments in the 70s a more sober realization of the actual difficulties involved in automating everyday mathematics set in and the field increasingly fragmented into many subareas which all developed their specific techniques and systems[2]. It is only very recently that this trend is reversed, with the CALCULEMUS[3] and MKM[4] communities as driving forces of this movement. In CALCULEMUS the viewpoint is bottom-up, starting from existing techniques and tools developed in the community. MKM approaches the goal of computer-based mathematics in the new millennium by a complementary top-down approach starting from existing, mainly pen and paper based mathematical practice down to system support.

We shall provide an overview and the main developments of the ΩMEGA project in the following and then point to current research and some future goals.

2 ΩMEGA

The ΩMEGA project represents one of the major attempts to build an all encompassing assistant tool for the working mathematician. It is a representative of systems in the new paradigm of *proof planning* and combines interactive and automated proof construction for domains with rich and well-structured mathematical knowledge. The inference mechanism at the lowest level of abstraction is an interactive theorem prover based on a higher order natural deduction (ND) variant of a soft-sorted version of Church's simply typed λ-calculus [Chu40]. The logical language, which also supports partial functions, is called $\mathcal{POST}$, for **p**artial functions and **o**rder **s**orted **t**ype theory. While this represents the "machine code" of the system the user will seldom want to see, the search for a proof is usually conducted at a higher level of abstraction defined by *tactics* and *methods*. Automated proof search at this abstract level is called *proof planning* (see Section 2.3). Proof construction is also supported by already proven assertions and theorems and by calls to external systems to simplify or solve subproblems.

2.1   System Overview

At the core of ΩMEGA is the *proof plan data structure* $\mathcal{PDS}$ [CS00], in which proofs and *proof plans* are represented at various levels of granularity and abstraction (see Fig. 2). The $\mathcal{PDS}$ is a directed acyclic graph, where *open nodes* represent unjustified propositions that still need to be proved and *closed nodes* represent propositions that are already proved. The proof plans are developed

---

[2] The history of the field is presented in a classical paper by Martin Davis [Dav83] and also in [Dav01] and more generally in his history of the making of the first computers [Dav65]. Another source is Jörg Siekmann [Sie92] and more recently [Sie04].
[3] www.calculemus.org
[4] monet.nag.co.uk/mkm/index.html

and classified with respect to a taxonomy of mathematical theories in the mathematical knowledge base MBASE [FK00a,KF01]. The user of ΩMEGA, or the proof planner MULTI [MM00], or else the suggestion mechanism ΩANTS [BS00] modify the $\mathcal{PDS}$ during proof development until a complete proof plan has been found. They can also invoke external reasoning systems, whose results are included in the $\mathcal{PDS}$ after appropriate transformation. Once a complete proof plan at an appropriate level of abstraction has been found, this plan must be expanded by sub-methods and sub-tactics into lower levels of abstraction until finally a proof at the level of the logical calculus is established. After expansion of these high-level proofs to the underlying ND calculus, the $\mathcal{PDS}$ can be checked by ΩMEGA's proof checker.

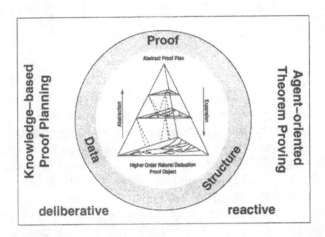

Fig. 2. The proof plan datastructure PDS is at the core of the ΩMEGA system. Proof construction is facilitated by knowledge-based proof planning (deliberative), agent-oriented theorem proving (reactive), or by user interaction.

Hence, there are two main tasks supported by this system, namely (i) to find a proof plan, and (ii) to expand this proof plan into a calculus-level proof; and both jobs can be equally difficult and time consuming. Task (ii) employs an LCF-style tactic expansion mechanism, proof search or a combination of both in order to generate a lower-level proof object. It is a design objective of the $\mathcal{PDS}$ that various *proof levels* coexist with their respective relationships being dynamically maintained.

The graphical user interface $\mathcal{L}\Omega\mathcal{UI}$ [SHB+99] (see Fig. 4) provides both a graphical and a tabular view of the proof under consideration, and the interactive proof explanation system $P.\,rex$ [Fie01b,Fie01a,Fie01c] generates a natural-language presentation of the proof.

The previously monolithic system has been split up and separated into several independent modules, which are connected via the mathematical software bus MATHWEB-SB [ZK02]. An important benefit is that MATHWEB-SB modules can be distributed over the Internet and are then remotely accessible by other research groups as well. There is now a very active MathWeb user community with sometimes several thousand theorems and lemmata being proven per day. Most theorems are generated automatically as (currently non-reusable and non-indexed) subproblems in natural language processing (see the Doris system [Dor01]), proof planning and verification tasks.

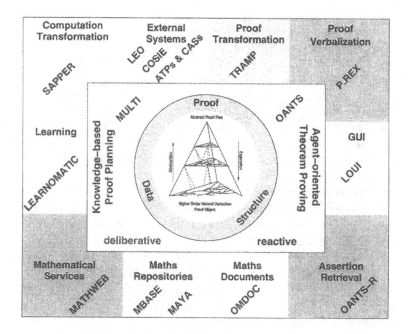

Fig. 3. The vision of an all encompassing mathematical assistance environment: we have now modularized and out-sourced many of the support tools such that they can also be used by other systems via the MATHWEB-SB software bus.

2.2 External Systems

Proof problems require many different skills for their solution. Therefore, it is desirable to have access to several systems with complementary capabilities, to orchestrate their use, and to integrate their results. ΩMEGA interfaces heterogeneous external systems such as *computer algebra systems (CASs)*, higher and first order *automated theorem proving systems (ATPs)*, *constraint solvers (CSs)*, and *model generation systems (MGs)*.

Their use is twofold: they may provide a solution to a subproblem, or they may give hints for the control of the search for a proof. In the former case, the output of an incorporated reasoning system is translated and inserted as a subproof into the $\mathcal{PDS}$. This is beneficial for interfacing systems that operate at different levels of abstraction, and also for a human-oriented display and inspection of a partial proof. Importantly, it also enables us to check the soundness of each contribution by expanding the inserted subproof to a logic-level proof and then verify it by ΩMEGA's proof checker.

Currently, the following external systems are integrated in ΩMEGA:

CASs provide symbolic computation, which can be used in two ways: first, to compute hints to guide the proof search (e.g., witnesses for existential variables), and, second, to perform some complex algebraic computation such as to normalize or simplify terms. In the latter case the symbolic computation is directly translated into proof steps in ΩMEGA. CASs are integrated via the transformation and translation module SAPPER [Sor00]. Currently, ΩMEGA uses the systems MAPLE [CGG+92] and GAP [S+95].

ATPs are employed to solve subgoals. Currently ΩMEGA uses the first order provers BLIKSEM [dN99], EQP [McC97], OTTER [McC94], PROTEIN [BF94], SPASS [WAB+99], WALDMEISTER [HJL99], the higher order systems TPS [ABI+96], and $\mathcal{LEO}$ [BK98,Ben99], and we plan to incorporate VAMPIRE [RV01]. The first order ATPs are connected via TRAMP [Mei00], which is a proof transformation system that transforms resolution-style proofs into assertion-level ND proofs to be integrated into ΩMEGA's $\mathcal{PDS}$. TPS already provides ND proofs, which can be further processed and checked with little transformational effort [BBS99].

MGs provide either witnesses for free (existential) variables, or counter-models, which show that some subgoal is not a theorem. Hence, they help to guide the proof search. Currently, ΩMEGA uses the model generators SATCHMO [MB88] and SEM [ZZ95].

CSs construct mathematical objects with theory-specific properties as witnesses for free (existential) variables. Moreover, a constraint solver can help to reduce the proof search by checking for inconsistencies of constraints. Currently, ΩMEGA employs $\mathcal{CoSIE}$ [MZM00], a constraint solver for inequalities and equations over the field of real numbers.

2.3 Proof Planning

ΩMEGA's main focus is on knowledge-based proof planning [Bun88,Bun91], [MS99], where proofs are not conceived in terms of low-level calculus rules, but at a much higher level of abstraction that highlights the main ideas and de-emphasizes minor logical or mathematical manipulations on formulae.

Knowledge-based proof planning is a new paradigm in automated theorem proving, which swings the motivational pendulum back to its AI origins in that it employs and further develops many AI principles and techniques such as hierarchical planning, knowledge representation in frames and control rules, constraint solving, tactical theorem proving, and meta-level reasoning. It differs from traditional search-based techniques in automated theorem proving not least in its level of abstraction: the proof of a theorem is planned at an abstract level where an outline of the proof is found. This outline, that is, the abstract proof plan, can be recursively expanded to construct a proof within a logical calculus provided the proof plan does not fail. The plan operators represent mathematical techniques familiar to a working mathematician. While the knowledge of such a mathematical domain as represented within methods and control rules is specific to the mathematical field, the representational techniques and reasoning procedures are general-purpose. For example, one of our first case studies [MS99] used the limit theorems proposed by Woody Bledsoe [Ble90] as a challenge to automated reasoning systems. The general-purpose planner makes use of this mathematical domain knowledge and of the guidance provided by declaratively represented control rules, which correspond to mathematical intuition about how to prove a theorem in a particular situation. These rules provide a basis for meta-level reasoning and goal-directed behavior.

Domain knowledge is encoded into methods, control rules, and strategies. Moreover, methods and control rules can employ external systems (e.g., a computer algebra system) and make use of the knowledge in these systems. ΩMEGA's multi-strategy proof planner MULTI [MM00] searches then for a plan using the acquired methods and strategies guided by the control knowledge in the control rules.

2.3.1 AI Principles in Proof Planning.
A *planning problem* is a formal description of an *initial state*, a *goal*, and some *operators* that can be used to transform the initial state via some intermediate states to a state that satisfies the goal. Applied to a planning problem, a *planner* returns a sequence of *actions*, that is, instantiated operators, which reach a goal state from the initial state when executed. Such a sequence of actions is also called a *solution plan*.

Proof planning considers mathematical theorems as planning problems [Bun88]. The initial state of a proof planning problem consists of the proof *assumptions* of the theorem, whereas the goal is the *theorem* itself. The operators in proof planning are the methods.

In ΩMEGA, proof planning is the process that computes actions, that is, instantiations of methods, and assembles them in order to derive a theorem from a set of assumptions. The effects and the preconditions of an action in proof planning are proof nodes with formulae in the higher order language $\mathcal{POST}$, where the effects are considered as logically inferable from the preconditions. A proof plan under construction is represented in the proof plan data structure $\mathcal{PDS}$ (see Section 2.5). Initially, the $\mathcal{PDS}$ consists of an open node containing the statement to be proved, and closed, that is, justified, nodes for the proof assumptions. The introduction of an action changes the $\mathcal{PDS}$ by adding new proof nodes and justifying the effects of the action by applications of the method of the action to its premises. The aim of the proof planning process is to reach a *closed* $\mathcal{PDS}$, that is, a $\mathcal{PDS}$ without open nodes. The *solution proof plan* produced is then a record of the sequence of actions that lead to a closed $\mathcal{PDS}$.

By allowing for forward and backward actions ΩMEGA's proof planning combines forward and backward state-space planning. Thus, a *planning state* is a pair of the current world state and the current goal state. The initial world state consists of the given proof assumptions and is transfered by forward actions into a new world state. The goal state consists of the initial open node and is transfered by backward actions into a new goal state containing new open nodes. From this point of view the aim of proof planning is to compute a sequence of actions that derives a current world state in which all the goals in the current goal state are satisfied.

As opposed to precondition achievement planning (e.g., see [Wel94]), effects of methods in proof planning do not cancel each other. For instance, an action with effect $\neg F$ introduced for the open node L_1 does not threaten the effect F introduced by another action for the open node L_2. Dependencies among open nodes result from shared variables for witness terms and their constraints. Constraints can be, for instance, instantiations for the variables but they can also be mathematical constraints such as $x < c$, which states that, whatever the instantiation for x is, it has to be smaller than c. The constraints created during the proof planning process are collected in a constraint store. An action introducing new constraints is applicable only if its constraints are consistent with the constraints collected so far. Dependencies among goals with shared variables are difficult to analyze and can cause various kinds of failures in a proof planning attempt. First results about how to analyze and deal with such failures are discussed in [Mei03].

Methods, Control Rules, and Strategies. *Methods* are traditionally perceived as tactics in tactical theorem proving augmented with preconditions and effects, called *premises* and *conclusions*, respectively. A method represents the inference of the conclusion from the premises. For instance, NotI-M is a method whose purpose is to prove a goal $\Gamma \vdash \neg P$ by contradiction. If NotI-M is applied to a goal $\Gamma \vdash \neg P$ then it closes this goal and introduces the new goal to prove falsity, $\bot$, under the assumption P, that is, $\Gamma, P \vdash \bot$. Thereby, $\Gamma \vdash \neg P$ is the conclusion of the method, whereas $\Gamma, P \vdash \bot$ is the premise of the method. NotI-M is a *backward* method, which reduces a goal (the conclusion) to new goals (the premises). *Forward* methods, in contrast, derive new conclusions from given premises. For instance, =Subst-m performs equality substitutions by deriving from two premises $\Gamma \vdash P[a]$ and $\Gamma \vdash a = b$ the conclusion $\Gamma \vdash P[b]$ where an occurrence of a is replaced by an occurrence of b. Note that NotI-M and =Subst-m are simple examples of domain-independent, logic-related methods, which are needed in addition to domain-specific, mathematically motivated methods. Knowledge base proof planning expands on these ideas and allows for more general mathematical methods to be encapsulated into *methods*.

Control rules represent mathematical knowledge about how to proceed in the proof planning process. They can influence the planner's behavior at choice points (e.g., which goal to tackle next or which method to apply next) by preferring members of the corresponding list of alternatives (e.g., the list of possible goals or the list of possible methods). This way promising search paths are preferred and the search space can be pruned.

Strategies employ different sets of methods and control rules and, thus, tackle the same problem in different ways. The reasoning as to which strategy to employ on a problem is an explicit choice point in MULTI. In particular, MULTI can backtrack from chosen strategies and search at the level of strategies.

Detailed discussions of ΩMEGA's method and control rule language can be found in [Mei03,MMP02]. A detailed introduction to proof planning with multiple strategies is given in [MM00].

2.4 Interface and System Support

*Ω*MEGA's graphical user interface *LΩUI* [SHB⁺99] displays the current proof
state in multiple modalities: a graphical map of the proof tree, a linearized
presentation of the proof nodes with their formulae and justifications, a term
browser, and a natural language presentation of the proof via *P.rex* (see Fig. 4
and 5).

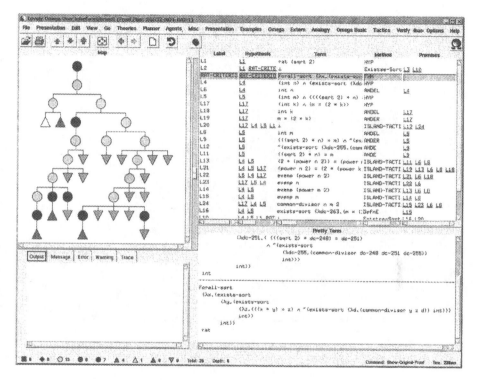

Fig. 4. Multi-modal proof presentation in the graphical user interface *LΩUI*.

When inspecting a part a proof, the user can switch between alternative levels
of abstraction, for example, by expanding a node in the graphical map of the
proof tree, which causes appropriate changes in the other presentation modes.
Moreover, an interactive natural language *explanation* of the proof is provided by
the system *P.rex* [Fie01b,Fie01a,Fie01c], which is adaptive in the following sense:
it explains a proof step at the most abstract level (which the user is assumed
to know) and then reacts flexibly to questions and requests, possibly at a lower
level of abstraction, for example, by detailing some ill-understood subproof.

Another system support is the guidance mechanism provided by the suggestion module *Ω*ANTS [BS98,BS99,BS00,Sor01], which searches pro-actively for
possible actions that may be helpful in finding a proof and orders them in a
preference list. Examples for such actions are an application of a particular cal-

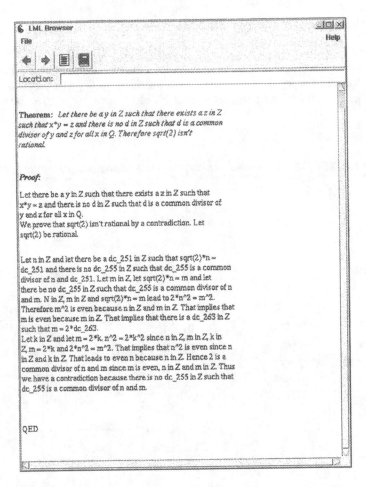

Fig. 5. Natural language proof presentation by $P.\,rex$ in $\mathcal{L}\Omega\mathcal{U}\mathcal{I}$.

culus rule, the call of a tactic or a proof method as well as a call of an external reasoning system, or the search for and insertion of facts from the knowledge base MBASE. The general idea is the following: every inference rule, tactic, method or external system is "agentified" in the sense that every possible *action* searches concurrently for the fulfillment of its application conditions and once these are satisfied it suggests its execution. User-definable heuristics select and display the suggestions to the user. ΩANTS is based on a hierarchical blackboard, which collects the data about the current proof state.

2.5   Proof Objects

The central data structure for the overall search is the proof plan data structure $\mathcal{PDS}$ in Fig. 2. This is a hierarchical data structure that represents a (partial) proof at different levels of abstraction (called partial proof plans). Technically, it is an acyclic graph, where the nodes are justified by tactic applications. Conceptually, each such justification represents a proof plan (the expansion of the justification) at a lower level of abstraction, which is computed when the tactic is executed. In *Ω*MEGA, we explicitly keep the original proof plan as well as intermediate expansion layers in an expansion hierarchy. The coexistence of several abstraction levels and the dynamical maintenance of their relationship is a central design objective of *Ω*MEGA's $\mathcal{PDS}$. Thus the $\mathcal{PDS}$ makes the hierarchical structure of proof plans explicit and retains it for further applications such as proof explanation with *P.rex* or an analogical transfer of plans. The lowest level of abstraction of a $\mathcal{PDS}$ is the ND calculus.

The proof object generated by *Ω*MEGA for example for the "irrationality of $\sqrt{2}$" theorem is recorded in a technical report [BFMP02], where the unexpanded and the expanded proof objects are presented in great detail, that is in a little less than a thousand proof steps. A general presentation of this interesting case study is [SBF+03].

2.6 Case Studies

Early developments of proof planning in Alan Bundy's group at Edinburgh used proofs by induction as their favorite case studies [Bun88]. The *Ω*MEGA system has been used in several other case studies, which illustrate in particular the interplay of the various components, such as proof planning supported by heterogeneous external reasoning systems.

A typical example for a class of problems that cannot be solved by traditional automated theorem provers is the class of ϵ–δ–proofs [MS99,Mel98a]. This class was originally proposed by Woody Bledsoe [Ble90] and it comprises theorems such as LIM+ and LIM*, where LIM+ states that the limit of the sum of two functions equals the sum of their limits and LIM* makes the corresponding statement for multiplication. The difficulty of this domain arises from the need for arithmetic computation in order to find a suitable instantiation of free (existential) variables (such as a δ depending on an ϵ). Crucial for the success of *Ω*MEGA's proof planning is the integration of suitable experts for these tasks: the arithmetic computation is done by the computer algebra system MAPLE, and an appropriate instantiation for δ is computed by the constraint solver $\mathcal{CoSIE}$. We have been able to solve all challenge problems suggested by Bledsoe and many more theorems in this class taken from a standard textbook on real analysis [BS82].

Another class of problems we tackled with proof planning is concerned with residue classes [MPS02,MPS01]. In this domain we show theorems such as: "the residue class structure $(\mathbb{Z}_5, \bar{+})$ is associative", "it has a unit element", and similar properties, where $\mathbb{Z}_5$ is the set of all congruence classes modulo 5 $\{\bar{0}_5, \bar{1}_5, \bar{2}_5, \bar{3}_5, \bar{4}_5\}$ and $\bar{+}$ is the addition on residue classes. We have also investigated whether two given structures are isomorphic or not and altogether we have proved more than 10,000 theorems of this kind (see [Sor01]). Although the problems in this domain are still within the range of difficulty a traditional automated theorem prover can handle, it was nevertheless an interesting case study for proof planning, since multi-strategy proof planning generated substantially different proofs based on entirely different proof ideas.

Another important proof technique is Cantor's diagonalization technique and we also developed methods and strategies for this class [CS98]. Important theorems we have been able to prove are the undecidability of the halting problem and Cantor's theorem (cardinality of the set of subsets), the non-countability of the reals in the interval $[0, 1]$ and of the set of total functions, and similar theorems.

Finally, a good candidate for a standard proof technique are completeness proofs for refinements of resolution, where the theorem is usually first shown at the ground level using the excess-literal-number technique and then ground completeness is lifted to the predicate calculus. We have done this for many refinements of resolution with ΩMEGA [Geb99].

However, ΩMEGA's main aim is to become a proof assistant tool for the working mathematician. Hence, it should support interactive proof development at a user-friendly level of abstraction. The mathematical theorem that $\sqrt{2}$ is not rational, and its well-known proof dating back to the School of Pythagoras, provides an excellent challenge to evaluate whether this ambitious goal has been reached. In [Wie02] fifteen systems that have solved the $\sqrt{2}$-problem show their results. The protocols of their respective sessions have been compared on a multi-dimensional scale in order to assess the "naturalness" by which real mathematical problems of this kind can be proved within the respective system.

This represents an important shift of emphasis in the field of automated deduction away from the somehow artificial problems of the past – as represented, for example, in the test set of the TPTP library [SSY94] – back to real mathematical challenges.

We participated in this case study essentially with three different contributions. Our initial contribution was an interactive proof in ΩMEGA without adding special domain knowledge to the system. For further details on this case study, which particularly demonstrates the use of ΩMEGA as a tactical theorem prover, we refer to [BFMP02]. The most important albeit not entirely new lesson to be learned from this experiment is that the level of abstraction common in most automated and tactical theorem proving environments is far too low. While our proof representation is already an abstraction (called the *assertion level* in [Hua94]) from the calculus level typical for most ATPs, it is nevertheless clear that as long as a system does not hide all these excruciating details, no working mathematician will feel inclined to use such a system. In fact, this is in our opinion one of the critical impediments for using first order ATPs and one, albeit not the only one, of the reasons why they are not used as widely as, say, computer algebra systems.

This is the crucial issue of the ΩMEGA project and our main motivation for departing from the classical paradigm of automated theorem proving about fifteen years ago.

Our second contribution to the case study of the $\sqrt{2}$-problem is based on interactive *island planning* [Mel96], a technique that expects an outline of the proof, i.e. the user provides main subgoals, called *islands*, together with their assumptions. The details of the proof, eventually down to the logic level, are postponed. Hence, the user can write down *his* proof idea in a natural way with as many gaps as there are open at this first stage of the proof. Closing the gaps is ideally fully automatic, in particular, by exploiting external systems. However, for difficult theorems it is necessary more often than not that the user provides additional information and applies the island approach recursively.

In comparison to our first tactic-based solution the island style supports a much more abstract and user-friendly interaction level. The proofs are now at a level of abstraction similar to proofs in mathematical textbooks.

Our third contribution to the case study of the $\sqrt{2}$-problem is a fully automatically planned and expanded proof of the theorem. The details of this very important case study, that shows best what (and what cannot) be achieved with current technology are presented in [SBF$^+$03], [SBF$^+$02], and [BFMP02].

The most important question to ask is: Can we find the essential and creative steps automatically? The answer is yes, as we have shown in [SBF$^+$03]. However, while we can answer the question in the affirmative, not every reader may be convinced, as our solution touches upon a subtle point, which opens the Pandora Box of critical issues in the paradigm of proof planning [Bun02]: It is always easy to write some specific methods, which perform just the steps in the interactively found proof and then call the proof planner MULTI to fit the methods together into a proof plan for the given problem. This, of course, shows nothing of substance: Just as we could write down all the definitions and theorems required for the problem in first order predicate logic and hand them to a first order prover[5], we would just hand-code the final solution into appropriate methods.

Instead, the goal of the game is to find *general* methods for a whole class of theorems within some theory that can solve not only this particular problem, but also all the other theorems in that class. While our approach essentially follows the proof idea of the interactively constructed proof for the $\sqrt{2}$-problem, it relies essentially on more general concepts such that we can solve, for example, $\sqrt[j]{l}$-problems for arbitrary natural numbers j and l.

However, this is certainly not the end of the story; in order to evaluate the appropriateness of a proof planning approach we suggest the following three criteria:

(1) How general and how rich in mathematical content are the methods and control rules?
(2) How much search is involved in the proof planning process?
(3) What kind of proof plans, that is, what kind of proofs, can we find?

These criteria should allow us to judge how general and how robust our solution is. The art of proof planning is to acquire domain knowledge that, on the one hand, comprises meaningful mathematical techniques and powerful heuristic guidance, and, on the other hand, is general enough to tackle a broad

---

[5] This was done when OTTER tackled the $\sqrt{2}$-problem; see [Wie02] for the original OTTER case study and [BFMP02] for its replay with ΩMEGA.

class of problems. For instance, as one extreme, we could have methods that encode ΩMEGA's ND calculus and we could run MULTI without any control. This approach would certainly be very general, but MULTI would fail to prove any interesting problems. As the other extreme case, we could cut a known proof into pieces, and code the pieces as methods. Guided by control rules that always pick the next right piece of the proof, MULTI would assemble the methods again to the original proof without performing any search.

The amount of search and the variety of potential proof plans for a given problem are measures for the generality of the methods and also for the appropriateness for tackling the class of problems by planning. If tight control rules or highly specific methods restrict the search to just one branch in the search tree, then the resulting proof plans will merely instantiate a pattern. In this case, a single tactic or method that realizes the proof steps of the underlying pattern is more suitable than planning. The possibility of creating a variety of proof plans with the given methods and control rules is thus an important feature.

What general lessons can we learn from small, albeit typical mathematical challenges of this kind?

1. The devil is in the detail, that is, it is always possible to hide the crucial creative step (represented as method or represented in the object language by an appropriate lemma) and to pretend a level of generality that has not actually been achieved. To evaluate a solution *all* tactics, methods, theorems, lemmata and definitions have to be made explicit.

2. The enormous distance between the well-known (top-level) proof of the Pythagorean School, which consists of about a dozen single proof steps in comparison to the final (non-optimized) proof at the ND level with 753 inference steps is striking. This is, of course, not a new insight. While mathematics can *in principle* be reduced to purely formal logic-level reasoning as demonstrated by Russell and Whitehead as well as the Hilbert School, nobody would actually want to do so *in practice* as the influential Bourbaki group showed: only the first quarter of the first volume in the several dozen volume set on the foundation of mathematics starts with elementary, logic-level reasoning and then proceeds with the crucial sentence [Bou68]: "No great experience is necessary to perceive that such a project [of complete formalization] is absolutely unrealizable: the tiniest proof at the beginning of the theory of sets would already require several hundreds of signs for its complete formalization."

3. Finally and more to the general point of interest in mathematical support systems: Now that we can prove theorems in the $\sqrt[n]{l}$-problem class, the skeptical reader may still ask: *So what?* Will this ever lead to a *general* system for mathematical assistance?

We have shown that the class of ϵ-δ-proofs for limit theorems can indeed be solved with a few dozen mathematically meaningful methods and control rules (see [MS99,Mel98b,Mei03]). Similarly, the domain of group theory with its class of residue theorems can be formalized with even fewer methods (see [MS00,MPS01,MPS02])[6]. An interesting observation is also that these methods by and large correspond to the kind of mathematical knowledge a freshman would have to learn to master this level of professionalism.

Do the above observations now hold for our $\sqrt[j]{l}$-problems? The unfortunate answer is probably *No!* Imagine the subcommittee of the United Nations in charge of the maintenance of the global mathematical knowledge base in a hundred years from now. Would they accept the entry of our methods, tactics and control rules for the $\sqrt[j]{l}$-problems? Probably not!

Factual mathematical knowledge is preserved in books and monographs, *but the art of doing mathematics* [Pol73,Had44] is passed on by word of mouth from generation to generation. The methods and control rules of the proof planner correspond to important mathematical techniques and "ways to solve it", and they make this implicit and informal mathematical knowledge explicit and formal.

The theorems about $\sqrt[j]{l}$-problems are shown by contradiction, that is, the planner derives a contradiction from the equation $l \cdot n^j = m^j$, where n and m are integers with no common divisor. However, these problems belong to the more general class to determine whether two complex mathematical objects $\mathcal{X}$ and $\mathcal{Y}$ are equal. A general mathematical principle for comparison of two complex objects is to look at their characteristic properties, for example, their normal forms or some other uniform notation in the respective theory.

And this is the crux of the matter: to find general mathematical principles and encode them into appropriate methods, control rules and strategies such that an appropriately large *class of problems* can be solved with these methods.

We are now working on formalizing these methods in more general terms and then instantiate them with appropriate parameters to the domain in question (number theory, set theory, or polynomial rings) – and the crucial creative step of the system MULTI is then to find the instantiation by some general heuristics.

3   The Future: What Next?

The vision of a powerful mathematical assistance environment which provides computer-based support for most tasks of a mathematician has stimulated new projects and international research networks across the disciplinary and systems boundaries. Examples are the European CALCULEMUS[7] (Integration of Symbolic Reasoning and Symbolic Computation) and MKM[8] (Mathematical Knowledge Management, [BGH03]) initiatives, the EU projects MONET[9], OPENMATH and MOWGLI[10], and the American QPQ[11] repository of deductive software tools.

---

[6] The generally important observation is not, of course, whether we need a dozen or a hundred methods, but that we don't need a few thousand or a million. A few dozen methods seem to be generally enough for a restricted mathematical domain.

[7] www.calculemus.org

[8] monet.nag.co.uk/mkm/index.html

[9] monet.nag.co.uk/cocoon/monet/index.html

[10] www.mowgli.cs.unibo.it/

[11] www.qpq.org

Furthermore there are now numerous national projects in the US and Europe, which cover partial aspects of this vision, such as knowledge representation, deductive system support, user interfaces, mathematical publishing tools, etc.

The longterm goal of the ΩMEGA project is the all-embracing integration of symbolic reasoning, i.e. computer algebra and deduction systems, into mathematical research, mathematics education, and formal methods in computer science. We anticipate that in the long run these systems will change mathematical practice and they will have a strong societal impact, not least in the sense that a powerful infrastructure for mathematical research and education will become commercially available. Computer supported mathematical reasoning tools and integrated assistance systems will be further specialized to have a strong impact also in many other theoretical fields such as safety and security verification of computer software and hardware, theoretical physics and chemistry and other related subjects.

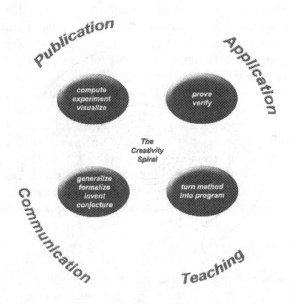

Fig. 6. Mathematical Creativity Spiral; [Buchberger, 1995].

Our current approach is strictly bottom-up: Starting with existing techniques and tools of our partners for symbolic reasoning (deduction) and symbolic computation (computer algebra), we will step by step improve their interoperability up to the realization of an integrated systems via the mathematical software bus MATHWEB-SB. The envisaged system will support the full life-cycle of the evolutionary nature of mathematical research (see Fig. 6) helping an engineer or mathematician who works on a mathematical problem in the improvement, the exploration, the distributed maintenance, the retrieval and the proving and calculation tasks and finally the publication of mathematical theories.

So what does this vision entail in the immediate future?

3.1 Formalization and Proving at a Higher Level of Abstraction

Mathematical reasoning with the *Ω*MEGA system is at the comparatively high level of abstraction of the proof planning methods. However, as these methods have to be expanded eventually to the concrete syntax of our higher order ND-calculus, the system still suffers from the effect and influence this logical representation has. In contrast, the proofs developed by a mathematician, say for a mathematical publication, and the proofs developed by a student in a mathematical tutoring system are typically developed at an argumentative level. This level has been formally categorized as *proofs at the assertion level* [Hua94] with different types of *under-specification* [ABF+03][12]. The CoRE system [Aut03] has been designed to achieve this and the goal is now to completely exchange the current natural deduction calculus by the CoRE calculus.

The proposed exchange of the logic layer in *Ω*MEGA requires the adaptation of all reasoning procedures that are currently tailored to it, including proof planning and the integration of external systems.

3.2 *Ω*ANTS: Agent-Oriented Theorem Proving

Our agent-based suggestion and reasoning mechanism is called *Ω*ANTS [BS00], whose initial motivation is to turn the hitherto passive *Ω*MEGA system into a pro-active counter-player of the user which autonomously exploits available resources. It provides societies of pro-active agents organized via an hierarchical blackboard architecture that dynamically and concurrently generate suggestions on applicable proof operators. These *Ω*ANTS agents may also call external systems or perform search for data in mathematical knowledge bases (see [BMS04]).

We will now provide improved higher order theorem proving agents based on the provers *LEO* [BK98] and TPS [ABB00], which analyze the proof context and determine promising "control settings". These higher order proof agents will work in competition with traditional first order proof agents and other "agentified" reasoning systems.

3.3 Mathematical Knowledge Representation

A mathematical proof assistant relies upon different kinds of knowledge: first, of course, the formalized mathematical domain as organized in structured theories of definitions, lemmata, and theorems. Secondly, there is mathematical knowledge on how to prove a theorem, which is encoded in tactics and methods, in *Ω*ANTS agents, in control knowledge and in strategies. This type of knowledge can be general, theory specific or even problem specific.

The integration of a mathematical proof assistant into the typical and everyday activities of a mathematician requires however other types of knowledge

---

[12] "Under-specification" is a technical term borrowed from research on the semantics of natural language. Illustrating examples and a discussion of our notion can be found in [ABF+03,BFG+03].

as well. For example, a mathematical tutoring system for students relies upon a database with different samples of proofs and proof plans linked by meta-data in order to advise the student. Another example is the support for mathematical publications: the documents containing both formalized and non-formalized parts need to be related to specific theories, lemmas, theorems, and proofs. This raises the research challenge on how the usual structuring mechanisms for mathematical theories (such as theory hierarchies or the import of theories via renaming or general morphisms) can be extended to tactics and methods as well as to proofs, proof plans and mathematical documents. Furthermore, changing any of these elements requires maintenance support as any change in one part may have consequences in other parts. For example, the validity of a proof needs to be checked again after changing parts of a theory, which in turn may affect the validity of the mathematical documents. This management of change [AHMS02,AM02,AH02,Hut00,MAH01], originally developed for evolutionary formal software engineering at the DFKI, will now be integrated into the ΩMEGA system as well.

Hierarchically structured mathematical knowledge, i.e. an ontology of mathematical theories and assertions has initially been stored in ΩMEGAs hardwired mathematical knowledge base. This mathematical knowledge base was later (end of the 90s) out-sourced and linked to the development of MBASE [FK00b]. We now assume that a mathematical knowledge base also maintains domain specific control rules, strategies, and linguistic knowledge. While this is not directly a subject of research in the ΩMEGA project, relying here on other groups of the MKM community and hence on the general development of a worldwide mathematical knowledge base ("the Semantic Web for Mathematicians"), we shall nevertheless concentrate on one aspect, namely how to find the appropriate information.

Semantic Mediators for Mathematical Knowledge Bases. Knowledge acquisition and retrieval in the currently emerging large repositories of formalized mathematical knowledge should not be based purely on syntactic matching, but it needs to be supported by semantic mediators, which suggest applicable theorems and lemmata in a given proof context.

We are working on appropriately limited HOL reasoning agents for domain- and context-specific retrieval of mathematical knowledge from mathematical knowledge bases. For this we shall adapt a two stage approach as in [BMS04], which combines syntactically oriented pre-filtering with semantic analysis. The pre-filter employ efficiently processable criteria based on meta-data and ontologies that identify sets of candidate theorems of a mathematical knowledge bases that are potentially applicable to a focused proof context. The HOL agents act as post-filters to exactly determine the applicable theorems of this set. Exact semantic retrieval includes the following aspects: (i) logical transformations to see the connection between a theorem in a mathematical knowledge base and a focused subgoal. Consider, e.g., a theorem of the form $A \Leftrightarrow B$ in the mathematical knowledge base and a subgoal of the form $(A \Rightarrow B) \land (\neg A \Rightarrow \neg B)$; they are not equal in any syntactical sense, but they denote the same assertion.

(ii) The variables of a theorem in a mathematical knowledge base may have to be instantiated with terms occurring in a focused subgoal; consider, e.g., a theorem $\forall X.is-square(X \times X)$ and the subgoal $is-square(2 \times 2)$. (iii) Free variables (meta-variables) may occur in a focused subgoal and they may have to be instantiated with terms occurring in a theorem of the mathematical knowledge base; consider, e.g., a subgoal $irrational(X)$ with metavariable X and a theorem $irrational(\sqrt{2})$.

We are investigating whether this approach can be successfully coupled with state-of-the-art search engines such as Google.

3.4 VerMath: A Global Web for Mathematical Services

The Internet provides a vast collection of data and computational resources. For example, a travel booking system combines different information sources, such as the search engines, price computation schemes, and the travel information in distributed very large databases, in order to answer complex booking requests. The access to such specialized travel information sources has to be planned, the obtained results combined and, in addition the consistency of time constraints has to be guaranteed.

We want to transfer and apply this methodology to mathematical problem solving and develop a system that plans the combination of several mathematical information sources (such as mathematical databases), computer algebra systems, and reasoning processes (such as theorem provers or constraint solvers). Based on the well-developed MATHWEB-SB network of mathematical services, the existing client-server architecture will be extended by advanced problem solving capabilities and semantic brokering of mathematical services.

The reasoning systems currently integrated in MATHWEB-SB have to be accessed directly via their API, thus the interface to MATHWEB-SB is *system-oriented*. However, these reasoning systems are used also in applications that are not necessarily theorem provers, e.g. for the semantical analysis of natural language, small verification tasks, etc. The main goal of this project[13] is therefore twofold:

Problem-Oriented Interface: to develop a more abstract communication level for MATHWEB-SB, such that general mathematical problem descriptions can be sent to the MATHWEB-SB which in turn returns a solution to that problem. Essentially, this goal is to move from a *service* oriented interface to a *problem* oriented interface for the MATHWEB-SB. This is a very old idea in the development of AI programming languages (early work included PLANNER and other languages driven by matching of general descriptions).

Advanced Problem Solving Capabilities: Typically, a given problem cannot be solved by a single service but only by a combination of several services. In order to support the automatic selection and combination of existing services, the key idea is as follows: an ontology will be used for the qualitative de-

---

[13] This is a joint project between the University of Saarbrücken (Jörg Siekmann) and the International University Bremen (Michael Kohlhase).

scription of MATHWEB-SB services and *these descriptions will then be used as AI planning operators*, in analogy to todays proof planning approach. We can then use planning techniques [CBE+92,EHN94] to automatically generate a plan that describes how existing services must be combined to solve a given mathematical problem.

3.5 Publishing Tools for Mathematics

Proof construction is an important but only a small part of a much wider range of mathematical activities an ideal mathematical assistant system should support (see Fig. 1). Therefore the ΩMEGA system is currently extended to support the writing of mathematical publications and advising students during proof construction.

With respect to the former we envision that a mathematician writes a new paper in some specific mathematical domain using a LaTeX-like environment. The definitions, lemmas, theorems and especially their proofs give rise to extensions of the original theory and the writing of some proof goes along with an interactive proof construction in ΩMEGA. As a result this allows the development of mathematical documents in a publishable style which in addition are formally validated by ΩMEGA, hence obtaining *certified mathematical documents*. A first step in that direction is currently under development by linking the WYSIWYG mathematical editor TEXMACS [vdH01] with the ΩMEGA proof assistant and other mathematical support services (see Fig. 7)

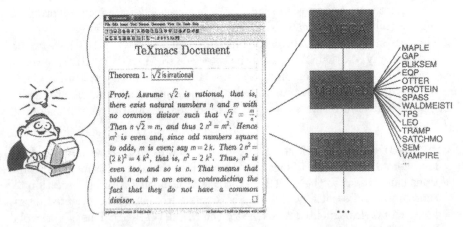

Fig. 7. Semantical documents in TeXmacs: The user will be supported in by different dynamic mathematical reasoning services that "understand" the document content.

The TEXMACS-system provides LaTeX-like editing and macro-definition features, and we are defining macros for theory-specific knowledge such as types, constants, axioms, and lemmata. This allows us to translate new textual definitions and lemmas into the formal representation, as well as to translate (partial) textbook proofs into (partial) proof plans.

As a second activity we are involved in the DFKI project ActiveMath, which develops an e-learning tool for tutoring students, in particular in advising a student to develop a proof. Thereby the interaction with the student should be conducted via a textual dialog. This scenario is currently under investigation in the DIALOG project [BFG+03] and, aside from all linguistic analysis problems, gives rise to the problem of *under-specification* in proofs.

References

[ABB00]   P.B. Andrews, M. Bishop, and C.E. Brown. System description: TPS: A theorem proving system for type theory. In *Conference on Automated Deduction*, pages 164–169, 2000.

[ABF+03] S. Autexier, C. Benzmüller, A. Fiedler, H. Horacek, and Q. Bao Vo. Assertion-level proof representation with under-specification. *Electronic in Theoretical Computer Science*, 93:5–23, 2003.

[ABI+96] P.B. Andrews, M. Bishop, S. Issar, D. Nesmith, F. Pfenning, and H. Xi. TPS: A theorem proving system for classical type theory. *Journal of Automated Reasoning*, 16(3):321–353, 1996.

[ACE+00] S. Allen, R. Constable, R. Eaton, C. Kreitz, and L. Lorigo. The Nuprl open logical environment. In McAllester [McA00].

[AH02]   S. Autexier and D. Hutter. Maintenance of formal software development by stratified verification. In M. Baaz and A. Voronkov, editors, *Proceedings of LPAR'02*, LNCS, Tbilissi, Georgia, September 2002. Springer.

[AHMS02] S. Autexier, D. Hutter, T. Mossakowski, and A. Schairer. The development graph manager MAYA. In H. Kirchner and C. Ringeissen, editors, *Proceedings 9th International Conference on Algebraic Methodology And Software Technology (AMAST'02)*, volume 2422 of *LNCS*. Springer, September 2002.

[AM02]   S. Autexier and T. Mossakowski. Integrating HOL-CASL into the development graph manager MAYA. In A. Armando, editor, *Proceedings of FROCOS'02*, volume 2309 of *LNAI*, pages 2–17. Springer, April 2002.

[Aut03]   S. Autexier. *Hierarchical Contextual Reasoning*. PhD thesis, Computer Science Department, Saarland University, Saarbrücken, Germany, 2003. forthcoming.

[BBS99]   C. Benzmüller, M. Bishop, and V. Sorge. Integrating TPS and ΩMEGA. *Journal of Universal Computer Science*, 5:188–207, 1999.

[Ben99]   C. Benzmüller. *Equality and Extensionality in Higher-Order Theorem Proving*. PhD thesis, Department of Computer Science, Saarland University, Saarbrücken, Germany, 1999.

[BF94]   P. Baumgartner and U. Furbach. PROTEIN, a PROver with a Theory INterface. In Bundy [Bun94], pages 769–773.

[BFG+03] C. Benzmüller, A. Fiedler, M. Gabsdil, H. Horacek, I. Kruijff-Korbayova, M. Pinkal, J. Siekmann, D. Tsovaltzi, B. Quoc Vo, and M. Wolska. Tutorial dialogs on mathematical proofs. In *Proceedings of IJCAI-03 Workshop on Knowledge Representation and Automated Reasoning for E-Learning Systems*, pages 12–22, Acapulco, Mexico, 2003.

[BFMP02] C. Benzmüller, A. Fiedler, A. Meier, and M. Pollet. Irrationality of $\sqrt{2}$ – a case study in ΩMEGA. Seki-Report SR-02-03, Department of Computer Science, Saarland University, Saarbrücken, Germany, 2002.

24   Jörg Siekmann and Christoph Benzmüller

[BGH03]   B. Buchberger, G. Gonnet, and M. Hazewinkel. Special issue on mathematical knowledge management. *Annals of Mathematics and Artificial Intelligence*, 38(1-3):3–232, May 2003.

[BK98]   C. Benzmüller and M. Kohlhase. LEO – a higher-order theorem prover. In Kirchner and Kirchner [KK98].

[Ble90]   W. Bledsoe. Challenge problems in elementary calculus. *Journal of Automated Reasoning*, 6:341–359, 1990.

[BMS04]   C. Benzmüller, A. Meier, and V. Sorge. Bridging theorem proving and mathematical knowledge retrieval. In Hutter and Stephan [HS04]. To appear.

[Bou68]   N. Bourbaki. Theory of sets. In *Elements of Mathematics*, volume 1. Addison-Wesley, 1968.

[BS82]   R. Bartle and D. Sherbert. *Introduction to Real Analysis*. Wiley, 2nd edition, 1982.

[BS98]   C. Benzmüller and V. Sorge. A blackboard architecture for guiding interactive proofs. In Giunchiglia [Giu98].

[BS99]   Christoph Benzmüller and Volker Sorge. Critical agents supporting interactive theorem proving. In Pedro Borahona and Jose J. Alferes, editors, *Proceedings of the 9th Portuguese Conference on Artificial Intelligence (EPIA'99)*, number 1695 in LNAI, pages 208–221, Evora, Portugal, 1999. Springer.

[BS00]   C. Benzmüller and V. Sorge. Ωants – An open approach at combining Interactive and Automated Theorem Proving. In Kerber and Kohlhase [KK00].

[Bun88]   A. Bundy. The use of explicit plans to guide inductive proofs. In Lusk and Overbeek [LO88], pages 111–120.

[Bun91]   A. Bundy. A science of reasoning. In G. Plotkin J.-L. Lasser, editor, *Computational Logic: Essays in Honor of Alan Robinson*, pages 178–199. MIT Press, 1991.

[Bun94]   A. Bundy, editor. *Proceedings of the 12th Conference on Automated Deduction*, number 814 in LNAI. Springer, 1994.

[Bun02]   A. Bundy. A critique of proof planning. In *Computational Logic: Logic Programming and Beyond*, number 2408 in LNCS, pages 160–177. Springer, 2002.

[BvHHS90]   A. Bundy, F. van Harmelen, C. Horn, and A. Smaill. The Oyster-Clam System. In M. Stickel, editor, *Proceedings of the 10th Conference on Automated Deduction*, number 449 in LNCS, pages 647–648, Kaiserslautern, Germany, 1990. Springer.

[CBE+92]   J. Carbonell, J. Blythe, O. Etzioni, Y. Gil, R. Joseph, D. Kahn, Craig. Knoblock, S. Minton, M. A. Pérez, S. Reilly, M. Veloso, and X. Wang. PRODIGY 4.0: The Manual and Tutorial. CMU Technical Report CMU-CS-92-150, Carnegie Mellon University, June 1992.

[CGG+92]   B. Char, K. Geddes, G. Gonnet, B. Leong, M. Monagan, and S. Watt. *First leaves: a tutorial introduction to Maple V*. Springer, 1992.

[Chu40]   A. Church. A Formulation of the Simple Theory of Types. *Journal of Symbolic Logic*, 5:56–68, 1940.

[Coq03]   Coq Development Team. *The Coq Proof Assistant Reference Manual*. INRIA, 1999-2003. See http://coq.inria.fr/doc/main.html.

[CS98]   L. Cheikhrouhou and J. Siekmann. Planning diagonalization proofs. In Giunchiglia [Giu98], pages 167–180.

[CS00]   L. Cheikhrouhou and V. Sorge. PDS – A Three-Dimensional Data Struc-
           ture for Proof Plans. In *Proceedings of the International Conference on Ar-
           tificial and Computational Intelligence for Decision, Control and Automa-
           tion in Engineering and Industrial Applications (ACIDCA '2000)*, Monastir,
           Tunisia, 22–24 March 2000.
[Dav65]   M. Davis, editor. *The Undecidable: Basic Papers on undecidable Propo-
           sitions, unsolvable Problems and Computable Functions.* Raven Press
           Hewlett, New York, 1965.
[Dav83]   M. Davis. The prehistory and early history of automated deduction. In
           J. Siekmann and G. Wrightson, editors, *Automation of Reasoning*, volume
           2 Classical Papers on Computational Logic 1967–1970 of *Symbolic Compu-
           tation.* Springer, 1983.
[Dav01]   M. Davis. The early history of automated deduction. In A. Robinson
           and A. Voronkov, editors, *Handbook of Automated Reasoning*, volume I,
           chapter 1, pages 3–15. Elsevier Science, 2001.
[dN99]   H. de Nivelle. Bliksem 1.10 user manual. Technical report, Max-Planck-
           Institut für Informatik, 1999.
[Dor01]   The Doris system is available at http://www.cogsci.ed.ac.uk/ jbos/doris/,
           2001.
[EHN94]   K. Erol, J. Hendler, and D. Nau. Semantics for hierarchical task network
           planning. Technical Report CS-TR-3239, UMIACS-TR-94-31, Computer
           Science Department, University of Maryland, March 1994.
[Fie01a]   A. Fiedler. Dialog-driven adaptation of explanations of proofs. In B. Nebel,
           editor, *Proceedings of the 17th International Joint Conference on Artificial
           Intelligence (IJCAI)*, pages 1295–1300, Seattle, WA, 2001. Morgan Kauf-
           mann.
[Fie01b]   A. Fiedler. P.rex: An interactive proof explainer. In Goré et al. [GLN01].
[Fie01c]   A. Fiedler. *User-adaptive proof explanation.* PhD thesis, Department of
           Computer Science, Saarland University, Saarbrücken, Germany, 2001.
[FK00a]   A. Franke and M. Kohlhase. System description: MBase, an open mathe-
           matical knowledge base. In McAllester [McA00].
[FK00b]   Andreas Franke and Michael Kohlhase. System description: Mbase, an
           open mathematical knowledge base. In David McAllester, editor, *Auto-
           mated Deduction, CADE-17 (CADE-00) : 17th International conference
           on Automated Deduction ; Pittsburgh, PA, USA, June 17-20, 2000*, volume
           1831 of *Lecture notes in computer science.* Springer, 2000.
[Gan99]   H. Ganzinger, editor. *Proceedings of the 16th Conference on Automated
           Deduction*, number 1632 in LNAI. Springer, 1999.
[Geb99]   H. Gebhard. Beweisplanung für die Beweise der Vollständigkeit ver-
           schiedener Resolutionskalküle in ΩMEGA. Master's thesis, Department of
           Computer Science, Saarland University, Saarbrücken, Germany, 1999.
[Giu98]   F. Giunchiglia, editor. *Proceedings of 8th International Conference on Arti-
           ficial Intelligence: Methodology, Systems, Applications (AIMSA '98)*, num-
           ber 1480 in LNAI. Springer, 1998.
[GLN01]   R. Goré, A. Leitsch, and T. Nipkow, editors. *Automated Reasoning –
           1st International Joint Conference, IJCAR 2001*, number 2083 in LNAI.
           Springer, 2001.
[GM93]   M. Gordon and T. Melham. *Introduction to HOL – A theorem proving
           environment for higher order logic.* Cambridge University Press, 1993.
[Had44]   J. Hadamard. *The Psychology of Invention in the Mathematical Field.*
           Dover Publications, New York, USA; edition 1949, 1944.

[HJL99]   Th. Hillenbrand, A. Jaeger, and B. Löchner. System description: Waldmeister – improvements in performance and ease of use. In Ganzinger [Gan99], pages 232–236.

[HS04]   D. Hutter and W. Stephan, editors. *Festschrift in Honour of Jörg Siekmann's 60s Birthday*, LNAI. Springer, 2004. To appear.

[Hua94]   X. Huang. Reconstructing Proofs at the Assertion Level. In Bundy [Bun94], pages 738–752.

[Hut00]   D. Hutter. Management of change in structured verification. In *Proceedings of Automated Software Engineering, ASE-2000*. IEEE, 2000.

[KF01]   M. Kohlhase and A. Franke. MBASE: Representing knowledge and context for the integration of mathematical software systems. *Journal of Symbolic Computation; Special Issue on the Integration of Computer Algebra and Deduction Systems*, 32(4):365–402, September 2001.

[KK98]   C. Kirchner and H. Kirchner, editors. *Proceedings of the 15th Conference on Automated Deduction*, number 1421 in LNAI. Springer, 1998.

[KK00]   M. Kerber and M. Kohlhase, editors. *8th Symposium on the Integration of Symbolic Computation and Mechanized Reasoning (Calculemus-2000)*. AK Peters, 2000.

[KR00]   H. Kirchner and C. Ringeissen, editors. *Frontiers of combining systems: Third International Workshop, FroCoS 2000*, volume 1794 of *LNAI*. Springer, 2000.

[LO88]   E. Lusk and R. Overbeek, editors. *Proceedings of the 9th Conference on Automated Deduction*, number 310 in LNCS, Argonne, Illinois, USA, 1988. Springer.

[MAH01]   T. Mossakowski, S. Autexier, and D. Hutter. Extending development graphs with hiding. In Heinrich Hussmann, editor, *Proceedings of Fundamental Approaches to Software Engineering (FASE 2001)*, number 2029 in LNCS, pages 269–283, Genova, April 2001. Springer.

[MB88]   R. Manthey and F. Bry. SATCHMO: A theorem prover implemented in Prolog. In Lusk and Overbeek [LO88], pages 415–434.

[McA00]   D. McAllester, editor. *Proceedings of the 17th Conference on Automated Deduction*, number 1831 in LNAI. Springer, 2000.

[McC94]   W. W. McCune. Otter 3.0 reference manual and guide. Technical Report ANL-94-6, Argonne National Laboratory, Argonne, Illinois 60439, USA, 1994.

[McC97]   W. McCune. Solution of the Robbins problem. *Journal of Automated Reasoning*, 19(3):263–276, 1997.

[Mei00]   A. Meier. TRAMP: Transformation of Machine-Found Proofs into Natural Deduction Proofs at the Assertion Level. In McAllester [McA00].

[Mei03]   A. Meier. *Proof Planning with Multiple Strategies*. PhD thesis, Department of Computer Science, Saarland University, Saarbrücken, Germany, 2003.

[Mel96]   E. Melis. Island planning and refinement. Seki-Report SR-96-10, Department of Computer Science, Saarland University, Saarbrücken, Germany, 1996.

[Mel98a]   E. Melis. AI-techniques in proof planning. In H. Prade, editor, *Proceedings of the 13th European Conference on Artifical Intelligence*, pages 494–498, Brighton, UK, 1998. John Wiley & Sons, Chichester, UK.

[Mel98b]   E. Melis. AI-techniques in proof planning. In *European Conference on Artificial Intelligence*, pages 494–498, Brighton, 1998. Kluwer.

[MM00]   E. Melis and A. Meier. Proof planning with multiple strategies. In J. Loyd, V. Dahl, U. Furbach, M. Kerber, K. Lau, C. Palamidessi, L.M. Pereira, Y. Sagivand, and P. Stuckey, editors, *First International Conference on Computational Logic (CL-2000)*, number 1861 in LNAI, pages 644–659, London, UK, 2000. Springer.

[MMP02]   A. Meier, E. Melis, and M. Pollet. Towards extending domain representations. Seki Report SR-02-01, Department of Computer Science, Saarland University, Saarbrücken, Germany, 2002.

[MPS01]   A. Meier, M. Pollet, and V. Sorge. Classifying Isomorphic Residue Classes. In R. Moreno-Diaz, B. Buchberger, and J.-L. Freire, editors, *A Selection of Papers from the 8th International Workshop on Computer Aided Systems Theory (EuroCAST 2001)*, number 2178 in LNCS, pages 494–508. Springer, 2001.

[MPS02]   A. Meier, M. Pollet, and V. Sorge. Comparing Approaches to the Exploration of the Domain of Residue Classes. *Journal of Symbolic Computation, Special Issue on the Integration of Automated Reasoning and Computer Algebra Systems*, 34(4):287–306, October 2002. Steve Linton and Roberto Sebastiani, eds.

[MS99]   E. Melis and J. Siekmann. Knowledge-based proof planning. *Artificial Intelligence*, 115(1):65–105, 1999.

[MS00]   A. Meier and V. Sorge. Exploring properties of residue classes. In Kerber and Kohlhase [KK00].

[MZM00]   E. Melis, J. Zimmer, and T. Müller. Integrating constraint solving into proof planning. In Kirchner and Ringeissen [KR00].

[NPW02]   T. Nipkow, L.C. Paulson, and M. Wenzel. *Isabelle/HOL: A Proof Assistant for Higher-Order Logic*. Number 2283 in LNCS. Springer, 2002.

[ORR+96] S. Owre, S. Rajan, J.M. Rushby, N. Shankar, and M. Srivas. PVS: Combining specification, proof checking, and model checking. In R. Alur and T. Henzinger, editors, *Computer-Aided Verification, CAV '96*, number 1102 in LNCS, pages 411–414, New Brunswick, NJ, 1996. Springer.

[Pau94]   L. Paulson. *Isabelle: A Generic Theorem Prover*. Number 828 in LNCS. Springer, 1994.

[Pol73]   G. Polya. *How to Solve it*. Princeton University Press, 1973.

[Rob65]   J. A. Robinson. A Machine-Oriented Logic Based on the Resolution Principle. J. ACM 12(1): 23-41 (1965).

[RSG98]   J. Richardson, A. Smaill, and I. Green. System description: Proof planning in higher-order logic with λClam. In Kirchner and Kirchner [KK98].

[RV01]   A. Riazanov and A. Voronkov. Vampire 1.1 (system description). In Goré et al. [GLN01].

[S+95]   M. Schönert et al. *GAP – Groups, Algorithms, and Programming*. Lehrstuhl D für Mathematik, Rheinisch Westfälische Technische Hochschule, Aachen, Germany, 1995.

[SBF+02] J. Siekmann, C. Benzmüller, A. Fiedler, A. Meier, and M. Pollet. Proof development with OMEGA: Sqrt(2) is irrational. In M. Baaz and A. Voronkov, editors, *Logic for Programming, Artificial Intelligence, and Reasoning, 9th International Conference, LPAR 2002*, number 2514 in LNAI, pages 367–387. Springer, 2002.

[SBF⁺03] J. Siekmann, C. Benzmüller, A. Fiedler, A. Meier, I. Normann, and M. Pollet. Proof development in OMEGA: The irrationality of square root of 2. In F. Kamareddine, editor, *Thirty Five Years of Automating Mathematics*, Kluwer Applied Logic series (28), pages 271–314. Kluwer Academic Publishers, 2003. ISBN 1-4020-1656-5.

[SHB⁺99] J. Siekmann, S. Hess, C. Benzmüller, L. Cheikhrouhou, A. Fiedler, H. Horacek, M. Kohlhase, K. Konrad, A. Meier, E. Melis, M. Pollet, and V. Sorge. *LOUI: Lovely ΩMEGA User Interface. Formal Aspects of Computing*, 11:326–342, 1999.

[Sie92] J. Siekmann. Geschichte des automatischen beweisens (history of automated deduction). In *Deduktionssysteme, Automatisierung des Logischen Denkens*. R. Oldenbourg Verlag, 2nd edition, 1992. Also in English with Elsewood.

[Sie04] J. Siekmann. History of computational logic. In D. Gabbay and J. Woods, editors, *The Handbook of the History of Logic*, volume I-IX. Elsevier, 2004. To appear.

[Sor00] V. Sorge. Non-Trivial Computations in Proof Planning. In Kirchner and Ringeissen [KR00].

[Sor01] V. Sorge. *ΩANTS – A Blackboard Architecture for the Integration of Reasoning Techniques into Proof Planning*. PhD thesis, Department of Computer Science, Saarland University, Saarbrücken, Germany, 2001.

[SSY94] G. Sutcliffe, C. Suttner, and T. Yemenis. The TPTP problem library. In Bundy [Bun94].

[vdH01] J. van der Hoeven. GNU TeXmacs: A free, structured, wysiwyg and technical text editor. In *Actes du congrès Gutenberg*, number 39-40 in Actes du congrès Gutenberg, pages 39–50, Metz, May 2001.

[Vor02] A. Voronkov, editor. *Proceedings of the 18th International Conference on Automated Deduction*, number 2392 in LNAI. Springer, 2002.

[WAB⁺99] C. Weidenbach, B. Afshordel, U. Brahm, C. Cohrs, Th. Engel, E. Keen, C. Theobalt, and D. Topic. System description: SPASS version 1.0.0. In Ganzinger [Gan99], pages 378–382.

[Wel94] D. Weld. An introduction to least commitment planning. *AI Magazine*, 15(4):27–61, 1994.

[Wie02] F. Wiedijk. The fifteen provers of the world. Unpublished Draft, 2002.

[ZK02] J. Zimmer and M. Kohlhase. System description: The Mathweb Software Bus for distributed mathematical reasoning. In Voronkov [Vor02], pages 138–142.

[ZZ95] J. Zhang and H. Zhang. SEM: A system for enumerating models. In C. S. Mellish, editor, *Proceedings of the 14th International Joint Conference on Artificial Intelligence (IJCAI)*, pages 298–303, Montreal, Canada, 1995. Morgan Kaufmann, San Mateo, California, USA.

An Overview
of Planning Technology in Robotics

Malik Ghallab

LAAS - CNRS, Toulouse, France
Malik.Ghallab@laas.fr

Abstract. We present here an overview of several planning techniques
in robotics. We will not be concerned with the synthesis of abstract
mission and task plans, using well known classical and other domain-
independent planning techniques. We will mainly focus on to how refine
such abstract plans into robust sensory-motor actions and on some planning techniques that can be useful for that.

The paper introduces the important and mature area of path and motion planning. It illustrates the usefulness of HTN and MDP planning
techniques for the design of a high level controller for a mobile robot[1].

1 Introduction

A robot integrates several sensory-motor functions, together with communication and information-processing capabilities into cognitive functions, in order to
perform a collection of tasks with some level of autonomy and flexibility, in some
class of environments. The sensory-motor functions in a robot are, for example:

- locomotion on wheels, legs, or wings,
- manipulation with one or several mechanical arms, grippers and hands,
- localization with odometers, sonars, laser, inertial and GPS sensors,
- scene analysis and environment modeling with a stereo-vision system on a
  pan-and-tilt platform.

A robot can be designed for tasks and environments such as:

- manufacturing: painting, welding, loading/unloading a power-press or a
  machine-tool, assembling parts,
- servicing a store, a warehouse or a factory: maintaining, surveying, or cleaning
  the area, transporting objects,
- exploring an unknown natural area, e.g., in planetary exploration: building
  a map with characterized landmarks, extracting samples and setting various
  measurement devices,
- assisting a person in an office, a public area, or at home,
- performing tele-operated surgical operations, as in the so-called minimal in-
  vasive surgery.

Robotics is a reasonably mature technology when, for example

---

[1] This article is based on a revised material from the Chapter 20 in [17].

S. Biundo, T. Frühwirth, and G. Palm (Eds.): KI 2004, LNAI 3238, pp. 29–49, 2004.

- a robot is restricted to operate within a well known and well engineered environments, e.g., as in manufacturing robotics,
- a robot is restricted to perform a single simple task, e.g., vacuum cleaning or lawn mowing.

For more diverse tasks and open-ended environments, robotics remains a very active research field.

A robot may or may not integrate planning capabilities. For example, most of the one million manufacturing robots deployed today in the manufacturing industry do not perform planning *per se*. Using a robot without planning capabilities basically requires hand-coding the environment model, and the robot's skills and strategies into a *reactive controller*. This is a perfectly sensible approach as long as this handcoding is inexpensive and reliable enough for the application at hand, which is the case if the environment is well-structured and stable and if the robot's tasks are restricted in scope and diversity, with only a limited man-robot interaction.

Programming aids such as hardware tools, e.g., devices for memorizing the motion of a pantomime, and software systems, e.g., graphical programming interfaces, allow for an easy development of a robot's reactive controller. Learning capabilities, supervised or autonomous, significantly extend the scope of applicability of the approach by allowing a generic controller to adapt to the specifics of its environment. This can be done, for example, by estimating and fine-tuning control parameters and rules, or by acquiring a map of the environment.

However, if a robot has to face a diversity of tasks and/or a variety of environments, then planning will make it simpler to program a robot. It will augment the robot's usefulness and robustness. Planning should not be seen as opposed to the reactive capabilities of a robot, handcoded or learned, neither should it be seen as opposed to its learning capabilities. It should to be closely integrated to them.

The specific requirements of planning in robotics, as compared to other application domains of planning, are mainly the need to handle:

- online input from sensors and communication channels;
- heterogeneous partial models of the environment and of the robot, as well as noisy and partial knowledge of the state from information acquired through sensors and communication channels;
- direct integration of planning with acting, sensing, and learning.

These very demanding requirements advocate for addressing planning in robotics through domain-specific representations and techniques. Indeed, when planning is integrated within a robot, it usually takes several forms and is implemented throughout different systems. Among these various forms of robot planning, there is in particular *path and motion planning*, *perception planning*, *navigation planning*, *manipulation planning*, and domain independent planning.

Today, the maturity of robot planning is mainly at the level of its domain-specific planners. Path and motion planning is a mature area that relies on computational geometry and efficiently uses probabilistic algorithms. It is already deployed in robotics and other application areas such as CAD or computer animation. Perception planning is a younger and much more open area, although some focused problems are well advanced, e.g. the viewpoint selection problem with mathematical programming techniques.

Domain-independent planning is not widely deployed in robotics for various reasons, among which are the restrictive assumptions and expressiveness of the classical planning framework. In robotics, task planning should ideally deal with time and resource allocation, dynamic environments, uncertainty and partial knowledge, and incremental planning with consistent integration to acting and sensing. The mature planning techniques available today are mostly effective at the abstract level of *mission planning*. Primitives for these plans are tasks such as "navigate to location5", "retrieve and pick-up object2". These tasks are far from being *primitive* sensory-motor functions. Their design is very complex.

Several rule-based or procedure-based systems, such as PRS, RAP, Propice, or SRCs, enable to program manually closed-loop controllers for these tasks that handle the uncertainty and the integration between acting and sensing. These high level reactive controllers permit preprogrammed goal-directed and event-reactive modalities.

However, planning representations and techniques can also be very helpful for the design of high-level reactive controllers performing these tasks. They enable to generate, off-line, several alternative complex plans for achieving the task with robustness. They are useful for finding a policy that chooses, in each state, the best such a plan for pursuing the activity.

The rest of this article presents the important and mature area of path and motion planning (Section 2). It then illustrates the usefulness of planning techniques, for the design of a high level navigation controller for a mobile robot (Section 3). The approach is not limited to navigation tasks. It can be pursued for a wide variety of robotics tasks, such as object manipulation or cleaning. Several sensory-motor functions will be presented and discussed in Section 3.1; an approach that exemplifies the use of planning techniques for synthesizing alternative plans and policies for a navigation task is described. The last section refers to more detailed and focused descriptions of the techniques presented in this overview.

2   Path and Motion Planning

Path planning is the problem of finding a *feasible geometric path* in some environment for moving a mobile system from a starting position to a goal position. A geometric CAD model of the environment with the obstacles and the free space is supposed to be given. A path is feasible if it meets the kinematics constraints of the mobile system and if it avoids collision with obstacles.

Motion planning is the problem of finding a *feasible trajectory*, in space and time, i.e., a feasible path and a control law along that path that meets the dynamics constraints (speed and acceleration) of the mobile system. If one is not requiring an optimal trajectory, it is always possible to *label* temporally a feasible path in order to get a feasible trajectory. Consequently, motion planning relies on path planning, on which we focus the rest of this section.

Fig. 1. Hilare, a car like robot with an arm and a trailer (left); HRP, a humanoid robot (right).

If the mobile system of interest is a *free-flying* rigid body, i.e., if it can move freely in space in any direction without any kinematics constraint, then six *configuration parameters* are needed to characterize its position: x, y, z and the three Euler angles. Path planning defines a path in this six-dimensional space. However, a robot is not a free-flying body. Its kinematics defines its possible motion. For example, a car-like robot has three configuration parameters, $x, y,$ and θ. Usually these three parameters are not independent, e.g., the robot may or may not be able to turn on the spot (change θ while keeping x and y fixed), or be able to move sideway. A mechanical arm that has n rotational joins needs n configuration parameters to characterize its configuration in space, in addition to constraints such as the maximum and minimum values of each angular join. The car-like robot Hilare in Figure 1 (left) has a total of 10 configuration parameters: 6 for the arm and 4 for the mobile platform with the trailer [34]. The humanoid robot HRP in Figure 1 (right) has 52 configuration parameters: 2 for the head, 7 for each arm, 6 for each leg and 12 for each hand (four finger with 3 configuration parameters each) [26, 27][2].

Given a robot with n configuration parameters and some environment, let us define:

- q, the *configuration* of the robot: an n-tuple of reals that specifies the n parameters needed to characterize the position in space of the robot,
- CS, the *configuration space* of the robot: the set of values that its configuration q may take,

---

[2] The *degrees of freedom* of a mobile system are its control variables; an arm or the humanoid robot have as many degrees of freedom as configuration parameters, a car-like robot has 3 configuration parameters but only two degrees of freedom.

- CS_{free}, the *free configuration space*: the subset of CS of configurations that are not in collision with the obstacles of the environment.

Path planning is the problem of finding a path in the free configuration space CS_{free} between an initial and a final configuration. If one could compute CS_{free} explicitly, then path planning would be a search for a path in this n-dimensional continuous space. However, the explicit definition of CS_{free} is a computationally difficult problem, theoretically (it is exponential in the dimension of CS) and practically. Fortunately, very efficient probabilistic techniques have been designed that solve path planning problems even for highly complex robots and environments. They rely on the two following operations:

- *collision checking*, which checks whether a configuration $q \in CS_{free}$, or whether a path between two configurations in CS is collision free, i.e., if it lies entirely in CS_{free},
- *kinematic steering* which finds a path between two configurations q and q' in CS that meets the kinematic constraints, without taking into account obstacles.

Both operations can be performed efficiently. Collision checking relies on computational geometry algorithms and data structures [19]. Kinematic steering may use one of several algorithms, depending on the type of kinematics constraints the robot has. For example, *Manhattan paths* are applied to systems that are required to move only one configuration parameter at a time. Special curves (called *Reed&Shepp* curves [43]) are applied to car-like robots that cannot move sideway. If the robot has no kinematic constraints, then straight line segments in CS from q to q' are used. Several such algorithms can be combined. For example, to plan paths for the robot Hilare in Figure 1 (left), straight line segments for the arm are combined with dedicated curves for the mobile platform with a trailer [34].

Let $\mathcal{L}(q, q')$ be the path in CS computed by the kinematics steering algorithm for the constraints of the robot of interest; $\mathcal{L}$ is assumed to be symmetrical.

Let $\mathcal{R}$ be a graph whose vertices are configurations in CS_{free}; two vertices q and q' are adjacent in $\mathcal{R}$ only if $\mathcal{L}(q, q')$ is in CS_{free}. $\mathcal{R}$ is called a *roadmap* for CS_{free}.

Since $\mathcal{L}$ is symmetrical, $\mathcal{R}$ is an undirected graph. Note that every pair of adjacent vertices in $\mathcal{R}$ is connected by a path in CS_{free} but the converse is not necessarily true. Given a roadmap for CS_{free} and two configuration q_i and q_g in CS_{free}, corresponding to an initial and goal configurations, a feasible path from q_i to q_g can be found as follows:

- find a configuration $q_i' \in \mathcal{R}$ such that $\mathcal{L}(q_i, q_i') \in CS_{free}$,
- find a configuration $q_g' \in \mathcal{R}$ such that $\mathcal{L}(q_g, q_g') \in CS_{free}$,
- find in $\mathcal{R}$ a sequence of adjacent configurations from q_i' to q_g'.

If these three steps succeed, then the planned path is the finite sequence of subpaths $\mathcal{L}(q_i, q_i'), \ldots, \mathcal{L}(q_g', q_g)$. In a post-processing step, this sequence is easily optimized and smoothed locally by finding shortcuts in CS_{free} between successive legs.

Given a roadmap $\mathcal{R}$, path planning is reduced to a simple graph search problem, in addition to collision checking and kinematics steering operations. There remains the problem of finding a roadmap that *covers* CS_{free}, i.e., whenever there is a path in CS_{free} between two configurations, there is also a path through the roadmap. Finding such a roadmap using probabilistic techniques turns out to be easier than computing CS_{free} explicitly.

Let us define the *coverage domain* of a configuration q to be the set:

$$\mathcal{D}(q) = \{q' \in CS_{free} | \mathcal{L}(q, q') \subset CS_{free}\}.$$

A set of configurations Q *covers* CS_{free} if:

$$\bigcup_{q \in Q} \mathcal{D}(q) = CS_{free}.$$

The algorithm Probabilistic-Roadmap (Figure 2) starts initially with an empty roadmap. It generates randomly a configuration $q \in CS_{free}$; q is added to the current roadmap $\mathcal{R}$ iff either:

- q extends the coverage of $\mathcal{R}$, i.e., there is no other configuration in $\mathcal{R}$ whose coverage domain includes q, or
- q extends the connexity of $\mathcal{R}$, i.e., q enables to connect two configurations in $\mathcal{R}$ that are not already connected in $\mathcal{R}$.

Probabilistic-Roadmap($\mathcal{R}$)
    iterate until(*termination condition*)
        draw a random configuration q in CS_{free}
        if $\forall q' \in \mathcal{R}$: $\mathcal{L}(q, q') \not\subset CS_{free}$ then add q to $\mathcal{R}$
        else if there are q_1 and q_2 unconnected in $\mathcal{R}$ such that
            $\mathcal{L}(q, q_1) \subset CS_{free}$ and $\mathcal{L}(q, q_2) \subset CS_{free}$
            then add q and the edges (q, q_1) and (q, q_2) to $\mathcal{R}$
    end iteration
    return($\mathcal{R}$)
end

Fig. 2. A probabilistic roadmap generation for path planning.

Let us assume that there is a finite set Q that covers CS_{free}[3]. Consider the roadmap $\mathcal{R}$ that contains all the configurations in Q, and, for every pair q_1 and q_2 in Q such that $\mathcal{D}(q_1)$ and $\mathcal{D}(q_2)$ intersect, $\mathcal{R}$ also contains a configuration $q \in \mathcal{D}(q_1) \cap \mathcal{D}(q_1)$ and the two edges (q, q_1) and (q, q_2). It is possible to show that $\mathcal{R}$ meets the following property: if there exists a feasible path between two configurations q_i and q_g in CS_{free}, then there are two configurations q_i' and q_g' in

---

[3] Depending on the shape of CS_{free} and the kinematics constraints handled in $\mathcal{L}$, there may or may not exist such a *finite* set of configurations that covers CS_{free} [29].

the roadmap $\mathcal{R}$ such that $q_i \in \mathcal{D}(q_i')$, $q_g \in \mathcal{D}(q_g')$, and q_i' and q_g' are in the same connected component of $\mathcal{R}$. Note that the roadmap may have several connected components that reflects those of CS_{free}.

The Probabilistic-Roadmap algorithm will not generate a roadmap that meets the above property *deterministically*, but only up to some probability value, which is linked to the termination condition. Let k be the number of random draws since the last draw of a configuration q that has been added to the roadmap because q extends the coverage of the current $\mathcal{R}$ (q meets the first if clause in Figure 2). The termination condition is to stop when k reaches a preset value k_{max}. It has been shown that $1/k_{max}$ is a probabilistic estimate of the ratio between the part of CS_{free} not covered by $\mathcal{R}$ to the total CS_{free}. In other words, for $k_{max} = 1000$ the algorithm generates a roadmap that covers CS_{free} with a probability of .999.

From a practical point of view, the probabilistic roadmap technique illustrated by the previous algorithm has led to some very efficient implementations and to marketed products used in robotics, computer animation, CAD and manufacturing applications. Typically, for a complex robot and environment, and k_{max} in the order of few hundreds, it takes about a minute to generate a roadmap on a normal desktop machine; the size of $\mathcal{R}$ is about a hundred configurations; path planning with the roadmap takes few milliseconds. This is illustrated for the Hilare robot in Figure 3 where the task is to carry a long rod that constrains the path through the door: the roadmap in this 9-dimensional space has about 100 vertices and is generated in less than one minute. The same techniques have also been successfully applied to manipulation planning problems.

3   Planning for the Design of a Robust Controller

Consider an autonomous mobile robot in a structured environment, such as the robot in Figure 1 (left), which is equipped with several sensors – sonar, laser, vision – and actuators, and with an arm. The robot has also several software modules for the same sensory-motor (sm) function, e.g., for localization, for map building and updating, or for motion planning and control. These redundant sm functions are needed because of possible failures of a sensor, and because no single method or sensor has a universal coverage. Each has its weak points and drawbacks. Robustness requires a diversity of means for achieving an sm function. Robustness also requires the capability to combine consistently several such sm functions into a plan appropriate for the current context.

The planning techniques described in this section illustrates this capability. They enables a designer to specify, off-line, very robust ways of performing a task such as "navigate to". The designer specifies a collection of Hierarchical Tasks Networks, as illustrated in Figure 4, that are complex plans, called *modes of behavior*, or *modalities* for short[4], whose primitives are sm functions. Each modality is a possible way of combining a few of these sm functions to achieve the desired task. A modality has a rich context-dependent control structure.

---

[4] *Behaviors* have generally in robotics a meaning different from our modalities.

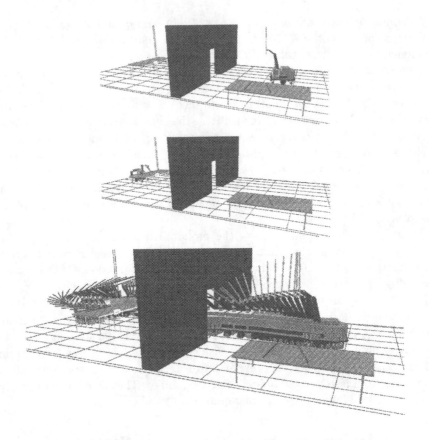

Fig. 3. Initial and goal configurations (up left and right) of a path planning problem, and generated path (down).

It includes alternatives whose selection depends on the data provided by *sm* functions.

Several modalities are available for a given task. The choice of the right modality for pursuing a task is far from being obvious. However, the relationship between control states and modalities can be expressed as a Markov Decision Process. This MDP characterizes the robot abilities for that task. The probability and cost distributions of this MDP are estimated by moving the robot in the environment. The controller is driven by policies extracted on-line from this MDP.

To summarize, this approach involves three components:
- Sensory-motor functions, which are the primitive actions.
- Modalities that are HTN plans. Alternate modalities offer different ways of combining the *sm* functions within a task,
- MDPs whose policies are used by the controller to achieve the task.

Let us describe these three levels successively.

3.1   Sensory-Motor Functions

The sensory-motor functions illustrated here and the control system itself rely on a model of the environment learned and maintained by the robot. The basic model is a 2D map of obstacle edges acquired from the laser range data. The so-called Simultaneous Localization and Mapping (SLAM) technique is used to generate and maintain the map of the environment.

A labeled topological graph of the environment is associated with the 2D map. Cells are polygons that partition the metric map. Each cell is characterized by its name and a *color* that corresponds to navigation features such as Corridor, Corridor with landmarks, Large Door, Narrow Door, Confined Area, Open Area, Open Area with fixed localization devices[5]. Edges of the topological graph are labeled by estimates of the transition length from one cell to the next and by heuristic estimates of how easy such a transition is.

An *sm* function returns to the controller a report indicating either the end of a normal execution, or giving additional information about non-nominal execution. In order to give to the reader an idea of the "low level" primitives available on a robot, of their strong and weak points and how they can be used from a planning point of view, let us discuss some of these *sm* functions.

Segment-Based Localization. This function relies on the map maintained by the robot from laser range data. The SLAM technique uses a data estimation approach called Extended Kalman Filtering in order to match the local perception with the previously built model. It offers a continuous position-updating mode, used when a good probabilistic estimate of the robot position is available. This *sm* function estimates the inaccuracy of the robot localization. When the robot is lost, a re-localization mode can be performed. A constraint relaxation on the position inaccuracy extends the search space until a good matching with the map is found.

This *sm* function is generally reliable and robust to partial occlusions, and much more precise than odometry. However, occlusion of the laser beam by obstacles gives unreliable data. This case occurs when dense unexpected obstacles are gathered in front of the robot. Moreover, in long corridors the laser obtains no data along the corridor axis. The inaccuracy increases along the corridor axis. Restarting the position updating loop in a long corridor can prove to be difficult. A feedback from this *sm* function can be a report of bad localization which warns that the inaccuracy of the robot position has exceeded an allowed threshold. The robot stops, turns on the spot and re-activates the re-localization mode. This can be repeated in order to find a non-ambiguous corner in the environment to restart the localization loop.

Localization on Visual Landmarks. This function relies on a calibrated monocular vision to detect known landmarks such as doors or wall posters. It derives

---

[5] Some environment modeling techniques that enable to automatically acquire such a topological graph with the cells and their labels exist. They are discussed in Section 4. However, in the work referred to here, the topological graph is hand-programmed.

from the perceptual data a very accurate estimation of the robot position. The setting up is simple: a few wall posters and characteristic planar features on walls are learned in supervised mode. However, landmarks are available and visible only in a few areas of the environment. Hence this *sm* function is mainly used to update from time to time the last known robot position. A feedback from this *sm* function is a report of a potentially visible landmark which indicates that the robot enters an area of visibility of a landmark. The robot stops, turns towards the expected landmark; it searches it using the pan-tilt mount. A failure report notifies that the landmark was not identified. Eventually, the robot retries from a second predefined position in the landmark visibility area.

Absolute Localization. The environment may have areas equipped with calibrated fixed devices, such as infrared reflectors, cameras, or even areas where a differential GPS signal is available. These devices permit a very accurate and robust localization. But the *sm* function works only when the robot is within a covered area.

Elastic Band for Plan Execution. This *sm* function updates and maintains dynamically a flexible trajectory as an *elastic band* or a sequence of configurations from the current robot position to the goal. Connexity between configurations relies on a set of internal forces that are used to optimize the global shape of the path. External forces are associated with obstacles and are applied to all configurations in the band in order to dynamically modify the path to take it away from obstacles. This *sm* function takes into account the planed path, the map and the on-line input from the laser data. It gives a robust method for long range navigation. However, the band deformation is a local optimization between internal and external forces; the techniques may fail into local minima. This is the case when a mobile obstacle blocks the band against another obstacle. Furthermore, it is a costly process which may limit the reactivity in certain cluttered, dynamic environments. This also limits the band length.

The feedback may warn that the band execution is blocked by a temporary obstacle that cannot be avoided (e.g. a closed door, an obstacle in a corridor). This obstacle is perceived by the laser and is not represented in the map. If the band relies on a planed path, the new obstacle is added to the map. A new trajectory taking into account the unexpected obstacle is computed, and a new elastic band is executed. Another report may warn that the actual band is no longer adapted to the planed path. In this case, a new band has to be created.

Reactive Obstacle Avoidance. This *sm* function provides a reactive motion capability towards a goal without needing a planned path. It extracts from sensory data a description of free regions. It selects the closest region to the goal, taking into account the distance to the obstacles. it computes and tries to achieve a motion command to that region.

This *sm* function offers a reactive motion capability that remains efficient in a cluttered space. However, like all the reactive methods, it may fall into local minima. It is not appropriate for long range navigation. Its feedback is a failure report generated when the reactive execution is blocked.

Finally, let us mention that a path planner (as described in Section 2) may also be seen as a *sm* function from the viewpoint of a high-level navigation controller. Note that a planned path doesn't take into account environment changes and new obstacles. Furthermore, a path planner may not succeed in finding a path. This may happen when the initial or goal configurations are too close to obstacles: because of the inaccuracy of the robot position, these configuration are detected as being outside of CS_{free}. The robot has to move away from the obstacles by using a reactive motion *sm* function before a new path is queried.

3.2 Modalities

A navigation task such as (Goto x y θ) given by a mission planning step requires an integrated use of several *sm* functions among those presented earlier. Each consistent combination of these *sm* functions is a particular plan called a *modality*. A navigation modality is a one way of performing the navigation task. A modality has specific characteristics that make it more appropriate for some contexts or environments, and less for others. We will discuss later how the controller choses the appropriate modality. Let us exemplify some of such modalities for the navigation task before giving the detail of the HTN representation for modalities and the associated control system.

Modality M_1 uses 3 *sm* functions: the path planner, the elastic band for the dynamic motion execution, and the laser-based localization. When M_1 is chosen to carry out a navigation, the laser-based localization is initialized. The robot position is maintained dynamically. A path is computed to reach the goal position. The path is carried out by the elastic band *sm* function. Stopping the modality interrupts the band execution and the localization loop; it restores the initial state of the map if temporary obstacles have been added to it. Suspending the modality stops the band execution. The path, the band, the localization loop are maintained. A suspended modality can be resumed by restarting the execution of the current elastic band.

Modality M_2 uses 3 *sm* functions: the path planner, the reactive obstacle avoidance and the laser-based localization. The path planner provides way-points (vertices of the trajectory) to the reactive motion function. Despite these way-points the reactive motion can be trapped into local minima in cluttered environments. Its avoidance capability is higher than that of the elastic band *sm* function. However, the reactivity to obstacles and the attraction to way-points may lead to oscillations and to a discontinuous motion that confuses the localization *sm* function. This is a clear drawback for M_2 in long corridors.

Modality M_3 is like M_2 but without path planning and with a reduced speed in obstacle avoidance. It starts with the reactive motion and the laser-based localization loop. It offers an efficient alternative in narrow environments like offices, and in cluttered spaces where path planning may fail. It can be preferred to the modality M_1 in order to avoid unreliable re-planning steps if the elastic band is blocked by a cluttered environment. Navigation is only reactive, hence with a local minima problem. The weakness of the laser localization in long corridors is also a drawback for M_3.

Modality M_4 uses the reactive obstacle avoidance sm function with the odometer and the visual landmark localization sm functions. The odometer inaccuracy can be locally reset by the visual localization sm function when the robot goes by a known landmark. Reactive navigation between landmarks allows to cross a corridor without an accurate knowledge of the robot position. Typically this M_2 modality can be used in long corridors. The growing inaccuracy can make it difficult to find out the next landmark. The search method allows for some inaccuracy on the robot position by moving the cameras but this inaccuracy cannot exceed one meter. For this reason landmarks should not to be too far apart with respect to the required updating of odometry estimate. Furthermore, the reactive navigation of M_2 may fall into a local minima.

Modality M_5 relies on the reactive obstacle avoidance sm function and the absolute localization sm function when the robot is within an area equipped with absolute localization devices.

Modalities are represented as Hierarchical Task Networks. The HTN formalism is adapted to modalities because of its expressiveness and its flexible control structure. HTNs offer a middle ground between programming and automated planning, allowing the designer to express the control knowledge which is available here.

An internal node of the HTN And/Or tree is a task or a subtask that can be pursued in different context-dependent ways, which are the *Or-connectors*. Each such Or-connector is a possible decomposition of the task into a conjunction of subtasks. There are two types of *AND-connectors*: with sequential or with parallel branches. Branches linked by a sequential AND-connector are traversed sequentially in the usual depth-first manner. Branches linked by a parallel AND-connector are traversed in parallel. The leaves of the tree are primitive actions, each corresponding to a unique query to a sm function. Thus, a root task is dynamically decomposed, according to the context, into a set of primitive actions organized as concurrent or sequential subsets. Execution starts as soon as the decomposition process reaches a leaf, even if the entire decomposition process of the tree is not complete.

A primitive action can be *blocking* or *non-blocking*. In blocking mode, the control flow waits until the end of this action is reported before starting the next action in the sequence flow. In non-blocking mode, actions in a sequence are triggered sequentially without waiting for a feedback. A blocking primitive action is considered ended after a report has been issued by the sm function and after that report has been processed by the control system. The report from a non-blocking primitive action may occur and be processed after an unpredictable delay.

The modality tree illustrated in Figure 4 starts with 6 Or-connectors labeled `start`, `stop`, `suspend`, `resume`, `succeed` and `fail`. The `start` connector represents the nominal modality execution; the `stop` connector the way to stop the modality and to restore the neutral state, characterized by the lack

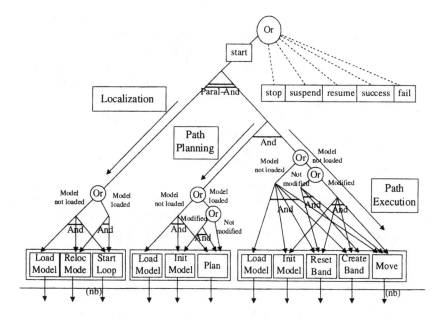

Fig. 4. Part of modality M_1.

of any *sm* function execution. Furthermore, the environment model modified by the modality execution recovers its previous form. The suspend and resume connectors are triggered by the control system described below. The suspend connector allows to stop the execution by freezing the state of the active *sm* functions. The resume connector restarts the modality execution from such a frozen state. The fail (resp. succeed) connector is followed when the modality execution reaches a failure (resp. a success) end. These connectors are used to restore the neutral state and to allow certain executions required in these specific cases.

The feedback from *sm* functions to modalities has to be controlled as well as the resource sharing of parallel activities. The control system catches and reacts appropriately to reports emitted by *sm* functions. Reports from *sm* functions play the same role in the control system as tasks in modalities. A report of some type activates its own dedicated control HTN in a reactive way. A control tree represents a temporary modality and cannot be interrupted. A nominal report signal a normal execution. Otherwise a non-nominal report signals a particular type of *sm* function execution. The aim of the corresponding control tree is to recover to a nominal modality execution. Some non-nominal reports can be non recoverable failures. In these cases, the corresponding control sends a "fail" message to the modality pursuing this *sm* function. Nominal reports may notify the success of the global task. In this case, the "success" alternative of the modality is activated.

Resources to be managed are either physical non-sharable resources (e.g. motors, cameras, pan-and-tilt mount) or logical resources (the environment model that can be temporally modified). The execution of a set of concurrent non-blocking actions can imply the simultaneous execution of different *sm* functions. Because of that, several reports may appear at the same time, and induce the simultaneous activation of several control activities. These concurrent executions may generate a resource conflict. To manage this conflict, a resource manager organizes the resource sharing with semaphores and priorities.

When a non-nominal report is issued, a control HTN starts its execution. It requests the resource it needs. If this resource is already in use by a start connector of a modality, the manager sends to this modality a suspend message, and leaves a resume message for the modality in the spooler according to its priority. The suspend alternative is executed freeing the resource, enabling the control HTN to be executed. If the control execution succeeds, waiting messages are removed and executed until the spooler becomes empty. If the control execution fails, the resume message is removed from the spooler and the fail alternative is executed for the modality.

3.3   The Controller

The Control Space. The controller has to choose a modality that is most appropriate to the current state for pursuing the task. In order to do this, a set of *control variables* have to reflect control information for the *sm* functions. The choice of these control variables is an important design issue. For example, in the navigation task, the control variables:

- The cluttering of the environment which is defined to be a weighted sum of the distances to nearest obstacles perceived by the laser, with a dominant weight along the robot motion axis. This is an important piece of information to establish the execution conditions of the motion and localization *sm* functions.

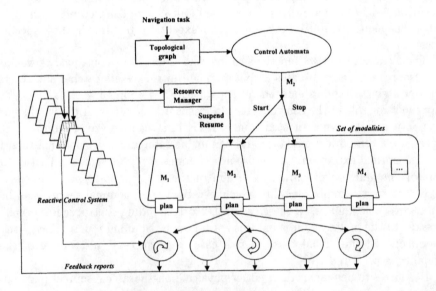

Fig. 5. The ROBEL control system.

- The angular variation of the profile of the laser range data which characterizes the robot area. Close to a wall, the cluttering value is high but the angular variation remains low. But in an open area the cluttering is low while the angular variation may be high.
- The inaccuracy of the position estimate, as computed from the co-variance matrix maintained by each localization *sm* function.
- The confidence in the position estimate. The inaccuracy is not sufficient to qualify the localization. Each localization *sm* function supplies a confidence estimate about the last processed position.
- The navigation *color* of current area. When the robot position estimate falls within some labeled cell of the topological graph, the corresponding labels are taken into account, e.g., *Corridor, Corridor with landmarks, Large door, Narrow door, Confined area, Open area, Area with fixed localization.*
- The current modality. This information is essential to assess the control state and possible transitions between modalities.

A control state is characterized by the values of these control variables. Continuous variables are discretized over a few significant intervals. In addition, there is a global failure state that is reached whenever the control of a modality reports a failure. We finally end-up with a discrete control space which enables to define a *control automaton*.

The Control Automaton. The control automaton is nondeterministic: unpredictable external events may modify the environment, e.g. someone passing by may change the value of the cluttering variable, or the localization inaccuracy variable. Therefore the execution of the same modality in a given state may lead to different adjacent states. This nondeterministic control automaton is defined as the tuple $\Sigma = \{S, A, P, C\}$:

- S is a finite set of control states,
- A is a finite set of modalities,
- $P : S \times A \times S \rightarrow [0, 1]$ is a probability distribution on the state-transition *sm* function, $P_a(s'|s)$ is the probability that the execution of modality a in state s leads to state s',
- $C : A \times S \times S \rightarrow \Re^+$ is a positive cost function, $c(a, s, s')$ corresponds to the average cost of performing the state transition from s to s' with to the modality a.

A and S are given by design from the definition of the set of modalities and of the control variables. In the navigation system illustrated here, there are 5 modalities and about a few thousand states. P and C are obtained from observed statistics during a learning phase.

The Control automaton Σ is a Markov Decision Process. As an MDP, Σ could be used reactively on the basis of a universal policy π which selects for a given state s the best modality $\pi(s)$ to be executed. However, a universal policy will not take into account the current navigation goal. A more precise approach takes into account explicitly the navigation goal, transposed into Σ as a set S_g of goal states in the control space. This set S_g is given by a look-ahead mechanism based on a search for a path in Σ that reflects a topological route to the navigation goal (see Figure 5).

Goal States in the Control Space. Given a navigation task, a search in the topological graph provides an optimal route r to the goal, taking into account estimated cost of edges between topological cells. This route will help finding in the control automaton possible goal control states for planning a policy. The route r is characterized by the pair (σ_r, l_r), where $\sigma_r = \langle c_1 c_2 \ldots c_k \rangle$ is the sequence of colors of traversed cells, and l_r is the length of r.

Now, a path between two states in Σ defines also a sequence of colors σ_{path}, those of traversed states; it has a total cost, that is the sum $\sum_{path} C(a, s, s')$ over all traversed arcs. A path in Σ from the current control state s_0 to a state s corresponds to the planned route when the path *matches* the features of the route (σ_r, l_r) in the following way:

- $\sum_{path} c(a, s, s') \geq K l_r$, K being a constant ratio between the cost of a state-transition in the control automaton to corresponding route length,
- σ_{path} corresponds to the same sequence of colors as σ_r with possible repetition factors, i.e., there are factors $i_1 > 0, \ldots, i_k > 0$ such that $\sigma_{path} = \langle c_1^{i_1}, c_2^{i_2}, \ldots, c_k^{i_k} \rangle$ when $\sigma_r = \langle c_1, c_2, \ldots, c_k \rangle$.

This last condition requires that we will be traversing in Σ control states having the same color as the planned route. A repetition factor corresponds to the number of control states, at least one, required for traversing a topological cell. The first condition enables to prune paths in Σ that meet the condition on the sequence of colors but cannot correspond to the planned route. However, paths in Σ that contain a loop (i.e. involving a repeated control sequence) necessarily meet the first condition.

Let route(s_0, s) be true whenever the optimal path in Σ from s_0 to s meets the two previous conditions, and let $S_g = \{s \in S \mid \text{route}(s_0, s)\}$. A Moore-Dijkstra algorithm starting from s_0 gives optimal paths to all states in Σ in $O(n^2)$. For every such a path, the predicate route(s_0, s) is checked in a straightforward way, which gives S_g.

It is important to notice that this set S_g of control states is a *heuristic projection* of the planned route to the goal. There is no guaranty that following blindly (i.e., in an open-loop control) a path in Σ that meets route(s_0, s) will lead to the goal; and there is no guarantee that every successful navigation to the goal corresponds to a sequence of control states that meets route(s_0, s). This only an efficient and reliable way of focusing the MDP cost function with respect to the navigation goal and to the planned route.

Finding a Control Policy. At this point we have to find the best modality to apply to the current state s_0 in order to reach a state in S_g, given the probability distribution function P and the cost function C.

A simple adaptation of the *Value Iteration* algorithm solves this problem. Here we only need to know $\pi(s_0)$. Hence the algorithm can be focused on a subset of states, basically those explored by the Moore-Dijkstra algorithm.

The closed-loop controller uses this policy as follows:

- the computed modality $\pi(s_0)$ is executed;
- the robot observes the new control state s, it updates its route r and its set S_g of goal states with respect to s, it finds the new modality to apply to s.

This is repeated until the control reports a success or a failure. Recovery from a failure state consists in trying from the parent state an untried modality. If none is available, a global failure of the task is reported.

Estimating the Parameters of the Control Automaton. A sequence of randomly generated navigation goals can be given to the robot. During its motion, new control states are met and new transitions are recorded or updated. Each time a transition from s to s' with modality a is performed, the traversed distance and speed are recorded, and the average speed v of this transition is updated. The cost of the transition $C(a, s, s')$ can be defined as a weighted average of the traversal time for this transition taking into account the eventual control steps required during the execution of the modality a in s together with the outcome of that control. The statistics on $a(s)$ are recorded to update the probability distribution function.

Several strategies can be defined to learn P and C in Σ. For example:

- A modality is chosen randomly for a given task; this modality is pursued until either it succeeds or a fatal failure is notified. In this case, a new modality is chosen randomly and is executed according to the same principle. This strategy is used initially to expand Σ.
- Σ is used according to the normal control except in a state on which not enough data has been recorded; a modality is randomly applied to this state in order to augment known statistics, e.g, the random choice of an untried modality in that state.

3.4   Analysis of the Approach

The system described here has been deployed on the Diligent robot, an indoor mobile platform, and extensively experimented with in navigation tasks within a wide laboratory environment [38, 39]. The approach is fairly generic and illustrates the use of planning techniques in robotics, not for the synthesis of mission plans but for achieving a robust execution of their high-level steps. It is not limited to navigation; it can be deployed on other robot activities.

The HTN planning technique used for specifying detailed alternative plans to be followed by a controller for decomposing a complex task into primitive actions is fairly general and powerful. It can be widely applied in robotics since it enables to take into account closed-loop feedback from sensors and primitive actions. It extends significantly and can rely on the capabilities of the rule-based or procedure-based languages for programming reactive controllers, as in the system described here.

The MDP planning technique relies on an abstract dedicated space, namely the space of control states for the navigation task. The size of such a space is just a few thousand states. Consequently, the estimation of the parameter distributions in Σ is feasible in a reasonable time: the MDP algorithms can be used efficiently on-line, at each control step. The drawback of these advantages is the *ad hoc* definition of the control space which requires a very good knowledge of the sensory-motor functions and the navigation task. While in principle the system described here can be extended by the addition of new modalities for the same task, or for other tasks, it is not clear how easy it would be to update the control space or to define new spaces for other tasks.

4   Discussion

Robot motion planning is a very advanced research field [35, 28]. The early techniques in the eighties have been mostly dedicated to deterministic algorithms [36]. They led to a good understanding and formalization of the problem, as well as to several developments on related topics such as manipulation planning [2]. More recent approaches have built on this state of the art with probabilistic algorithms that permitted a significant scale up [4]. The probabilistic roadmap techniques introduced in [30] gave rise to several successful developments [9, 29, 20, 24, 10, 32, 46] which represent today the most efficient approaches to path planning. Roadmap techniques are certainly not limited to navigation tasks; they have been deployed in other application areas, within robotics, e.g., for manipulation, or in CAD and graphics animation. The illustrations and performance figures in Section 2 are borrowed from Move3D, a state of the art system implementing roadmap techniques [45].

Sensory-motor functions are at the main core of robotics. They correspond to a very wide research area, ranging from signal processing, computer vision and learning, to biomechanics and neuroscience. Approaches relevant to the *sm* functions presented here are, for example,

- the techniques used for localization and mapping, e.g., the SLAM methods [40, 49, 14, 50],
- the methods for structuring the environment model into a topological map with areas labeled by different navigation colors [33, 48],
- the visual localization techniques, e.g., [22], and
- the flexible control techniques, e.g., [42, 44].

Several high-level reactive controllers are widely deployed in laboratory robots. They permit a preprogrammed goal-directed and event-reactive closed-loop control, integrating acting and sensing. They rely on rule-based or procedure-based systems, such as PRS, RAP, SRC and others [16, 25, 11, 15]. More recent developments on these systems, e.g., [13], aim at a closer integration to planning. The behavior-based controllers, e.g., [3], that usually focus on a more reactive set of concurrent activities, have also led to more goal-directed developments, e.g., [23].The *robot architecture*, that is the organization that enables to properly integrate the sensory-motoric functions, the reactive control system and the deliberative capabilities [1, 47] remains important issue.

The planning and robotics literature reports on several plan-based robot controllers with objectives similar to those discussed here, such as for example [5, 7, 6, 31, 8]. The approach of Beetz [6] has also been deployed for controlling an indoor robot carrying out the cores of an office courier. It relies on the SRCs reactive controllers. These are concurrent control routines that adapt to changing conditions by reasoning on and modifying plans. They rely on the XFRM system that manipulates reactive plans and is able to acquire them through learning with XFRMLEARN [7].

In addition to plan-based controllers, there is an active area of research that aims at interleaving task planning activities together with execution control and monitoring activities. Several approaches have been developed and applied, for example, to space and military applications, e.g., within the SIPE [41] or the CASPER [12] systems. Applications in robotics are for example the ROGUE system [21], and more recently the IxTeT-eXeC system [37] that integrates a sophisticated time and resource handling mechanism for planning and controlling the mission of an exploration robot.

References

1. R. Alami, R. Chatila, S. Fleury, M. Ghallab, and F. Ingrand. An Architecture for Autonomy. *International Journal of Robotics Research*, 17(4), 1998.
2. R. Alami, J. P. Laumond, and T. Siméon. *Two Manipulation Planning Algorithms*, pages 109–125. In Goldberg et al. [18], 1995.
3. R. Arkin. *Behavior-Based Robotics*. MIT Press, 1998.
4. J. Barraquand and J. C. Latombe. Robot motion planning: a distributed representation approach. *International Journal of Robotics Research*, 10(6), 1991.
5. M. Beetz. Structured reactive controllers - a computational model of everyday activity. In *3rd Int. Conf. on Autonomous Agents*, pages 228–235, 1999.
6. M. Beetz. *Plan-based control of robotics agents*, volume 2554 of *Lecture Notes in Artificial Intelligence (LNAI)*. Springer, 2002.
7. M. Beetz and T. Belker. Environment and task adaptation for robotics agents. In *Proceedings of the European Conference on Artificial Intelligence (ECAI)*, 2000.
8. M. Beetz, J. Hertzberg, M. Ghallab, and M.E. Pollack, editors. *Advances in plan-based control of robotics agents*. LNAI 2466, Springer-Verlag, 2002.
9. P. Bessiere, J. Ahuactzin, E. Talbi, and E. Mazer. The ariadne's clew algorithm: global planning with local methods. In Goldberg et al. [18], pages 39–47.
10. V. Boor, M. H. Overmars, and A. F. van der Stappen. The gaussian sampling strategy for probabilistic roadmap planners. In *IEEE International Conference on Robotics and Automation (ICRA)*, 1999.
11. John L. Bresina. Design of a reactive system based on classical planning. In *Foundations of Automatic Planning: The Classical Approach and Beyond: Papers from the 1993 AAAI Spring Symposium*, pages 5–9. AAAI Press, Menlo Park, California, 1993.
12. S. Chien, R. Knight, A. Stechert, R. Sherwood, and G. Rabideau. Using iterative repair to improve the responsiveness of planning and scheduling. In *Proceedings of the International Conference on AI Planning Systems (AIPS)*, 2000.
13. O. Despouys and F. Ingrand. PropicePlan: Toward a Unified Framework for Planning and Execution. In *Proceedings of the European Conference on Planning (ECP)*, pages 280–292, 1999.
14. M. W. M.-G. Dissanayake, P. Newman, S. Clark, H.-F. Durrant-Whyte, and M. Csorba. A solution to the simultaneous localization and map building (SLAM) problem. *IEEE Transactions on Robotics and Automation*, 17(3):229–241, 2001.

15. R. J. Firby. Task networks for controlling continuous processes. In *Proceedings of the International Conference on AI Planning Systems (AIPS)*, 1994.

16. M.P. Georgeff and F.F. Ingrand. Decision-Making in an Embedded Reasoning System. In *Proceedings of the International Joint Conference on Artificial Intelligence (IJCAI)*, 1989.

17. M. Ghallab, D. Nau, and P. Traverson. *Automated planning, theory and practice.* Elsevier, Morgan Kauffman, 2004.

18. K. Goldberg, D. Halperin, J. C. Latombe, and R. Wilson, editors. *Algorithmic Foundations of Robotics.* A K Peters, 1995.

19. J. Goodman and J. ORourke. *Handbook of discrete and computational geometry.* CRC Press, 1997.

20. K. Gupta and A. del Pobil, editors. *Practical motion planning in robotics.* Wiley, 1998.

21. K. Z. Haigh and M. M. Veloso. Planning, execution and learning in a robotic agent. In *Proceedings of the International Conference on AI Planning Systems (AIPS)*, 1998.

22. J.B. Hayet, F. Lerasle, and M. Devy. Planar landmarks to localize a mobile robot. In *SIRS'2000*, pages 163–169, 2000.

23. J. Hertzberg, H. Jaeger, U. Zimmer, and Ph. Morignot. A framework for plan execution in behavior-based robots. In *Proc. of the 1998 IEEE Int. Symp. on Intell. Control*, pages 8–13, 1998.

24. D. Hsu, L. Kavraki, JC. Latombe, R. Motwani, and S. Sorkin. On finding narrow passages with probabilistic roadmap planners. In P. Agarwal et al., editor, *Robotics: The Algorithmic Perspective (WAFR98)*, 1998.

25. F.F. Ingrand and M.P. Georgeff. An Architecture for Real-Time Reasoning and System Control. *IEEE Expert*, 6:33–44, 1992.

26. H. Inoue, S. Tachi, Y. Nakamura, K. Hirai, N. Ohyu, S. Hirai, K. Tanie, K. Yokoi, and H. Hirukawa. Overview of humanoid robotics project of METI. In *32nd International Symposium on Robotics*, 2001.

27. F. Kanehiro, M. Inaba, H. Inoue, H. Hirukawa, and S. Hirai. Developmental software environment that is applicable to small-size humanoids and life-size humanoids. In *IEEE International Conference on Robotics and Automation (ICRA)*, 2001.

28. L. Kavraki. Algorithms in robotics: The motion planning perspective. In *Frontiers of Engineering Publication*, pages 90–93. National Academy of Engineering, 1999.

29. L. Kavraki, M. Kolountzakis, and J.C. Latombe. Analysis of probabilistic roadmaps for path planning. *IEEE Transactions on Robotics and Automation*, 14(1):166–171, 1998.

30. L. Kavraki, P. Svestka, J.C. Latombe, and M.H. Overmars. Probabilistic roadmaps for path planning in high-dimensional configuration spaces. *IEEE Transactions on Robotics and Automation*, 12(4):566–580, 1996.

31. D. Kortenkamp, R.P. Bonasso, and R.R. Murphy, editors. *AI-based Mobile Robots: Case studies of successful robot systems.* MIT Press, 1997.

32. J. Kuffner and S. Lavalle. RRT-connect: an efficient approach to single-query path planning. In *IEEE International Conference on Robotics and Automation (ICRA)*, 2000.

33. S. Lacroix and R. Chatila. Motion and perception strategies for outdoor mobile robot navigation in unknown environments. In O. Khatib and J. K. Salisbury, editors, *International Symposium on Experimental Robotics*, pages 538–547. LNCIS 223, Springer-Verlag, 1997.

34. F. Lamiraux, S. Sekhavat, and J.P. Laumond. Motion planning and control for hilare pulling a trailer. *IEEE Transactions on Robotics and Automation*, 15(4), 1999.
35. J. C. Latombe. Motion planning: A journey of robots, molecules, digital actors, and other artifacts. *International Journal of Robotics Research*, 18(11):1119–1128, 1999.
36. J.C. Latombe. *Robot Motiton Planning*. Kluwer Academic Publishers, 1991.
37. S. Lemai and F. Ingrand. Interleaving temporal planning and execution in robotics domains. In *Proceedings of the National Conference on Artificial Intelligence (AAAI)*, 2004.
38. B. Morisset and M. Ghallab. *Learning how to combine sensory-motor modalities for a robust behavior*, pages 157–178. In Beetz et al. [8], 2002.
39. B. Morisset and M. Ghallab. Synthesis of supervision policies for robust sensory-motor behaviors. In *7th International Conference on Intelligent Autonomous Systems*, pages 236–243, 2002.
40. P. Moutarlier and R. G. Chatila. Stochastic Multisensory Data Fusion for Mobile Robot Location and Environment Modelling. In *Proc. International Symposium on Robotics Research*, 1989.
41. K. L. Myers. A Continuous Planning and Execution Framework. *AI Magazine*, pages 63–69, 1999.
42. S. Quinlan and O. Khatib. Towards real-time execution of motion tasks. In R. G. Chatila and G. Hirzinger, editors, *Experimental Robotics 2*. Springer-Verlag, 1992.
43. J. A. Reed and R. A. Shepp. Optimal paths for a car that goes both forward and backwards. *Pacific Journal of Mathematics*, 145(2):367–393, 1990.
44. A. Saffiotti. Handling uncertainty in control of autonomous robots. In Wooldridge and Veloso, editors, *Artificial Intelligence Today*, pages 381–408. LNAI1600, Springer-Verlag, 1999.
45. T. Siméon, J.P. Laumond, and F. Lamiraux. Move3d: a generic platform for path planning. In *4th International Symposium on Assembly and Task Planning*, 2001.
46. T. Siméon, J.P. Laumond, and C. Nissoux. Visibility based probabilistic roadmaps for motion planning. *Advanced Robotics Journal*, 14(6), 2000.
47. R. Simmons. Structured control for autonomous robots. *IEEE Transactions on Robotics and Automation*, 10(1):34–43, 1994.
48. S. Thrun. Learning metric-topological maps for indoor mobile robot navigation. *Artificial Intelligence*, 99(1):21–71, 1998.
49. S. Thrun, A. Bücken, W. Burgard, D. Fox, T. Frölinghaus, D. Hennig, T. Hofmann, M. Krell, and T. Schmidt. *Map learning and high-speed navigation in RHINO*. In Kortenkamp et al. [31], 1997.
50. S. Thrun, W. Burgard, and D. Fox. A probabilistic approach to concurrent mapping and localization for mobile robots. *Machine Learning*, 31:29–53, 1998.

SmartWeb: Mobile Applications of the Semantic Web

Wolfgang Wahlster

Deutsches Forschungszentrum für Künstliche Intelligenz (DFKI)
Stuhlsatzenhausweg 3, 66123 Saarbrücken, Germany
wahlster@dfki.de
http://www.dfki.de/~wahlster

Extended Abstract

Recent progress in *mobile broadband communication* and *semantic web technology* is enabling innovative internet services that provide advanced personalization and localization features. The goal of the SmartWeb project (duration: 2004–2007) is to lay the foundations for multimodal user interfaces to distributed and composable semantic Web services on mobile devices. The SmartWeb consortium brings together experts from various research communities: mobile services, intelligent user interfaces, language and speech technology, information extraction, and semantic Web technologies (see www.smartweb-project.org).

SmartWeb is based on two parallel efforts that have the potential of forming the basis for the next generation of the Web. The first effort is the *semantic Web* [1] which provides the tools for the explicit markup of the content of Web pages; the second effort is the development of *semantic Web services* which results in a Web where programs act as autonomous agents to become the producers and consumers of information and enable automation of transactions.

The appeal of being able to ask a question to a mobile internet terminal and receive an answer immediately has been renewed by the broad availability of information on the Web. Ideally, a spoken dialogue system that uses the Web as its knowledge base would be able to answer a broad range of questions. Practically, the size and dynamic nature of the Web and the fact that the content of most web pages is encoded in natural language makes this an extremely difficult task. However, SmartWeb exploits the machine-understandable content of semantic Web pages for intelligent question-answering as a next step beyond today's search engines. Since semantically annotated Web pages are still very rare due to the time-consuming and costly manual markup, SmartWeb is using advanced language technology and information extraction methods for the automatic annotation of traditional web pages encoded in HTML or XML.

But SmartWeb does not only deal with information-seeking dialogues but also with task-oriented dialogues, in which the user wants to perform a transaction via a Web service (e.g. buy a ticket for a sports event or program his navigation system to find a souvenir shop).

SmartWeb is the follow-up project to SmartKom (www.smartkom.org), carried out from 1999 to 2003. SmartKom is a multimodal dialog system that combines speech, gesture, and facial expressions for input and output [2]. Spontaneous speech understanding is combined with the video-based recognition of natural gestures and facial

S. Biundo, T. Frühwirth, and G. Palm (Eds.): KI 2004, LNAI 3238, pp. 50–51, 2004.

expressions. One version of SmartKom serves as a mobile travel companion that helps with navigation and point-of-interest in-formation retrieval in location-based services (using a PDA as a mobile client). The SmartKom architecture [3] supports not only simple multimodal command-and-control interfaces, but also coherent and cooperative dialogues with mixed initiative and a synergistic use of multiple modalities. Although SmartKom works in multiple domains (e.g. TV program guide, tourist information), it supports only restricted-domain question answering. SmartWeb goes beyond SmartKom in supporting *open-domain question answering* using the entire Web as its knowledge base.

SmartWeb provides a *context-aware user interface*, so that it can support the user in different roles, e.g. as a car driver, a motor biker, a pedestrian or a sports spectator. One of the planned demonstrators of SmartWeb is a personal guide for the 2006 FIFA world cup in Germany, that provides mobile infotainment services to soccer fans, anywhere and anytime. Another SmartWeb demonstrator is based on P2P communication between a car and a motor bike. When the car's sensors detect aquaplaning, a succeeding motor biker is warned by SmartWeb "Aqua-planing danger in 200 meters!". The biker can interact with SmartWeb through speech and haptic feedback; the car driver can input speech and gestures.

SmartWeb is based on two new W3C standards for the semantic Web, the *Resource Description Framework* (RDF/S) and the *Web Ontology Language* (OWL) for representing machine interpretable content on the Web. OWL-S ontologies support semantic service descriptions, focusing primarily on the formal specification of inputs, outputs, preconditions, and effects of Web services. In SmartWeb, multimodal user requests will not only lead to automatic Web service discovery and invocation, but also to the automatic composition, interoperation and execution monitoring of Web services.

The academic partners of SmartWeb are the research institutes DFKI (consortium leader), FhG FIRST, and ICSI together with university groups from Erlangen, Karlsruhe, Munich, Saarbrücken, and Stuttgart. The industrial partners of SmartWeb are BMW, DaimlerChrysler, Deutsche Telekom, and Siemens as large companies, as well as EML, Ontoprise, and Sympalog as small businesses. The German Federal Ministry of Education and Research (BMBF) is funding the SmartWeb consortium with grants totaling 13.7 million euros.

References

1. Fensel, D., Hendler, J.A., Lieberman, H., Wahlster, W. (eds.): Spinning the Semantic Web: Bringing the World Wide Web to Its Full Potential, MIT Press, Boston (2003)
2. Wahlster, W.: Towards Symmetric Multimodality: Fusion and Fission of Speech, Gesture, and Facial Expression. In: Günter, A., Kruse, R., Neumann, B. (eds.): KI 2003: Advances in Artificial Intelligence, Lecture Notes in Artificial Intelligence, Vol. 2821, Springer-Verlag, Berlin Heidelberg New York (2003) 1-18
3. Wahlster, W. (ed): SmartKom: Foundations of Multimodal Dialogue Systems. Springer-Verlag, Berlin Heidelberg New York (2004)

Machine Learning for Autonomous Robots

Martin Riedmiller

University of Osnabrück, Neuroinformatics Group

Abstract. Although Reinforcement Learning methods have meanwhile been successfully applied to a wide range of different application scenarios, there is still a lack of methods that would allow the direct application of reinforcement learning to real systems. The key capability of such learning systems is the efficency with respect to the number of interactions with the real system. Several examples are given that illustrate recent progress made in that direction.

1 Introduction

In recent years, many successful (real world) applications of machine learning methods have been developed, e.g. in classification, diagnosis or forecasting tasks. However, for a broad acceptance of learning methods as a standard software tool, still many theoretical and practical problems have to be solved. This is especially true for Reinforcement Learning scenarios, where the only training signal is given in terms of success or failure. Although this paradigm is in principle very powerful due to the minimal requirements on training information, today's real world applications often fail due to the large amount on training experiences, until a task is successfully learned. Our research effort lies in narrowing this gap by developing methods for data-efficient and robust machine learning. Autonomous robots - some of them with the ability to play soccer - are one of our favorite testbeds. Examples of efficient machine learning methods and their integration into large software systems are given by several (real world) tasks.

2 Basic Idea of Reinforcement Learning

The framework we consider in Reinforcment Learning (RL) is a standard Markov Decision Process (MDP) [10]. An MDP is a 4-tuple, (S, A, T, r), where S denotes a finite set of states, A denotes the action space, T is a probabilistic transition function $T : S \times A \times S \rightarrow [0, 1]$, that denotes the probability for a transition from state s to state s' when a certain action a is applied. Finally, $r : S \times A \rightarrow \Re$ is a reward function, that denotes the immediate reward for applying a certain action a in a certain state s. We are looking for an optimal policy $\pi^*(s) = \min_\pi J^\pi(s)$ that minimizes the expected path costs $J^\pi(s) = \sum_t r(s_t, \pi(s_t)), s_0 = s$. The *value iteration* procedure is given by the following recursive equation: $J_k(s) = \min_{a \in A} E\{r(s, a) + J_k(s')\}$, where s' is the

S. Biundo, T. Frühwirth, and G. Palm (Eds.): KI 2004, LNAI 3238, pp. 52–55, 2004.

successor state that is reached with probabilty $T(s, a, s')$, and E denotes the expectation. Value iteration can be shown to reach the optimal path costs $J^*(s)$ in the limit under certain assumptions. The optimal policy is then given by greedily exploiting the optimal value function: $\pi^*(s) \in \arg\min_{a \in A} E\{r(s, a) + J^*(s')\}$.

In case of a finite state space, incrementally updating the value function for every state finally approaches the optimal value function and therefore yields the optimal policy.

3   Enhancing the Basic Framework

When it comes to real world applications, the assumption of a finite state space is often not met. Especially in control applications, state variables are continuous, and often state spaces are of dimension 4, 5 or higher. Function approximators such as CMAC, feedforward neural networks or grid-based approaches have to be applied in case of continuous state variables in order to represent the value function. Also, instead of an idividual update of each state (which is not feasible in case of an infinte state space), the value function is updated at certain points only, e.g. along concrete trajectories [9]. Due to the different behaviour of function approximators compared to a tabular based value function, also the reinforcement learning process itself has to be adapted: whereas in case of a table the order of the updates is uncritical as long as some fairness conditions are met, the careful choice of training experiences plays an important role when function approximators are used, since every update in parameters can change the value function at many other places.

3.1   Example Applications

One of the first big successes in RL was Tesauro's TD-gammon system that used a neural network to represent the value function. By pure self-play it was finally able to play Backgammon at a grandmaster level. Further examples reach from elevator control [7], scheduling [8], to helicopter control.

Our research group has a special focus on learning of closed loop control systems for technical applications. Among the successful applications are the control of a chemical plant (2 state variables, strongly nonlinear), control of a single and double inverted pendulum (4 and 6 state variables, strongly instable) [2], control of a combustion engine (industrial project, 4 state variables, 2 control inputs) [1], thermostat control (industrial project, strongly varying time scales) [5].

In our Brainstormers project, we follow the approach of integrating learning and other AI techniques in a large software system, using the strengths of the individual methods and plugging them together. The Brainstormers are a team of virtual soccer playing robots, that compete in the RoboCup international competitions. Our goal is to show, that learning techniques can be successfully applied in very complex environments and are able to compete with other approaches. Year by year, we increase the amount of learned behaviour, starting with basic skills (1999 and 2000), via positioning (2001) to multi-agent attack behaviour (2002–2004). In the last five world championships, we won three second prices and two third prices [3].

4   Learning in Real Systems

Despite the considerable successes of learning in complex and non-trivial tasks, the direct application of RL to real world systems is still an open problem. While this can be explained to some extent by the really sparse training information (success or failure), which intrinsically requires exploration and experimentation, the typical amount of some 10,000 trajectories or even more to learn a desired behaviour is not acceptable for many real world systems.

One common way to go is to build a simulation of the real system first and the to learn in simulation. If the simulation is accurate enough, the learned controller can be directly applied to the real system. This often is sufficient, since the closed loop nature of the overall system can deal with smaller inaccuracies between simulated and real plant. An example of this is the learning of a positioning with obstacles for our omnidirectional soccer playing robot [6]. However, the method of simulation requires the additional effort of modelling the real plant first, and this is often either costly and sometimes even infeasible.

Therefore, an urgent need for efficient learning methods exists. We understand 'efficiency' here in the sense that only a low number of interactions with the real system occurs during the learning phase. Efficiency does not necessarily mean, that the overall learning process is fast, e.g. there might well be time-consuming offline phases to adapt internal parameters.

One promising direction to go is to consider the problem on a coarser level. More precisely, the idea is to construct so-called abstract states, that themselves contain a huge number of states of the original problem. Therefore, fixing the right policy for such an abstract state immediately defines the policy for a huge number of original states. This could vastly improve learning speed. However, there are two problems with this idea: One is to find the correct state space abstraction. At the moment, we rely on human intuition to solve that part of the problem, although we expect to come up with algorithmic solutions for this task. The other problem is, that the original value iteration method can be shown to fail in general, even if a policy for the abstract state space exists in principle. We recently came up with several algorithms that are based on both search and ideas from Dynamic Programming and that can be guaranteed to find solutions under certain assumptions [4]. First results are promising, allowing for example to learn a policy to swing up a pole in a few hundred trials instead of some tenthosand trials.

5   Future Work

Our current research concentrates on the development of better, i.e. more efficient methods for RL, but also on the embedding of such learning methods in larger software systems. We also started an effort to establish a benchmark suite, that allows to compare various algorithms and methods with respect to figures relevant for learning real system's control, like e.g. the number of interactions with the real system or the quality of the learned control policy.

References

1. R. Schoknecht, M. Riedmiller Using reinforcement learning for engine control in Proc. of ICANN'99 (1999)
2. M. Riedmiller Concepts and facilities of a neural reinforcement learning control architecture for technical process control Journal of Neural Computing and Application (2000)
3. Riedmiller, M., Merke, A.: Using Machine Learning Techniques in Complex Multi-Agent Domains in I. Stamatescu, W. Menzel, M. Richter and U. Ratsch (eds.), Perspectives on Adaptivity and Learning (2002), LNCS, Springer
4. M. Lauer, M. Riedmiller: Generalisation in Reinforcement Learning and the Use of Observation-Based Learning in Gabriella Kokai, Jens Zeidler: Proc. of the FGML Workshop (2002)
5. R. Schoknecht, M. Riedmiller Learning to Control at Multiple Time Scales in O. Kaynak, E. Alpaydin, E. Oja and L. Xu: Proc. of ICANN (2003), LNCS Springer
6. R. Hafner, M. Riedmiller Reinforcement Learning on an omnidirectional mobile robot in: Proc. IROS 2003
7. A. G. Barto, R. H. Crites Improving Elevator Performance using Reinforcement Learning, in Proc. NIPS 1996
8. S. Mahadevan and G. Theocharous Optimization production manufacturing using reinforcement learning in Proc. FLAIRS (1998)
9. A. G. Barto, S. J. Bradtke and S. P. Singh Learning to Act using Real-Time Dynamic Programming Artificial Intelligence, Vol. 72 (1995)
10. R. S. Sutton, A. G. Barto Reinforcement Learning, MIT Press (1998)

Generation of Sentence Parse Trees
Using Parts of Speech

Tunga Güngör

[1] Boğaziçi University, Computer Engineering Department, Bebek,
34342 İstanbul, Turkey
Gungort@boun.edu.tr

Abstract. This paper proposes a new corpus-based approach for deriving syntactic structures and generating parse trees of natural language sentences. The parts of speech (word categories) of words in the sentences play the key role for this purpose. The grammar formalism used is more general than most of the grammar induction methods proposed in the literature. The approach was tested for Turkish language using a corpus of more than 5,000 sentences and successful results were obtained.

1 Introduction

In this paper, we propose a corpus-based approach for deriving the syntactic structures of sentences in a natural language and forming parse trees of these sentences. The method is based on a concept which we name as *proximity*. The parts of speech (word categories) of words in the sentences play the key role in determining the syntactic relationships within sentences. The data about the order and frequency of word categories are collected from a corpus and are converted to proximity measures for word categories and sentences. Then these data are used to obtain probable parse trees for a given sentence.

It is well-known that grammars of natural languages are highly complicated and powerful. There have been several efforts for obtaining suitable grammars for particular languages that can generate most (if not all) of the sentences in those languages. The grammars defined manually for this purpose have limited success. The difficulty lies in the resistance of natural languages against syntactic formalizations. It is not known exactly what are the syntactic hierarchies inherent in the sentences. In fact, it is very easy to define a grammar that can generate all sentences in a language, but such a "general" grammar also generates non-sentences. Thus, forming grammars that can include sentences and at the same time exclude non-sentences is the difficult part of this task.

In order to overcome the difficulties posed by such rule-based approaches in processing natural languages, corpus-based approaches (collected under the name "statistical natural language processing") have begun to emerge recently [1,2]. They embody the assumption that human language comprehension and production works with representations of concrete past language experiences, rather than with abstract grammatical rules. There are several studies on statistical natural language processing. A nice approach is *data oriented parsing* model [3,4,5]. This model necessitates annotated corpora in which parse trees of sentences are explicit. The idea is building new sentences by composing fragments of corpus sentences.

S. Biundo, T. Frühwirth, and G. Palm (Eds.): KI 2004, LNAI 3238, pp. 56–66, 2004.

An interesting field where corpus-based approaches are used is grammar induction (learning). This usually means in the literature learning probabilistic context-free grammars (PCFGs). As stated in [1], the simplest method (and the basic idea) is generating all possible rules, assigning them some initial probabilities, running a training algorithm on a corpus to improve the probability estimates, and identifying the rules with high probabilities as the grammar of the language. However, this method is unrealistic as there is no bound on the number of possible rules, and even with constraints on the number of rules, often the number is so large that it becomes impractical in terms of computation time. The solution usually applied is restricting the rule types. In [6,7,8,9], some methods which use dependency grammars or Chomsky-normal-form grammars are presented.

2 Outline of the Method

Given a sentence, first the categories of the words in the sentence are determined. The sentence is at first considered as a single unit, which is formed of the sequence of these categories. It is then analyzed how this sequence can be divided into subsequences. For nontrivial sentences, the number of possible subsequences is quite large, and in general it grows exponentially with the length of the sentence. Among the possible subsequences, the best one is found according to the data in the corpus. The result is a set of smaller sentences. For each sentence in this set, the same process is repeated until the original sentence is partitioned into single categories.

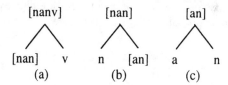

Fig. 1. Partitions for the sentence "adam siyah şapkayı beğendi"

The process is illustrated for the following simple Turkish sentence in Figure 1:

adam   siyah   şapkayı   beğendi
 (n)   (a)   (n)   (v)
man   black   hat+acc   like+pst+3sg
(the man liked the black hat)

(The word categories that appear in this work are: a for adjective, d for adverb, n for noun, and v for verb.) We represent the sentence as [nanv] in the form of a single sequence of word categories. Suppose that, after all alternative subsequences are evaluated, dividing into two groups as [nan] and v yields the best result, as shown in Figure 1.a. These two subsequences are considered as new (smaller) sentences. The process is over for the second one since it is formed of a single category. The other sentence ([nan]) is analyzed and divided into subsequences n and [an] (Figure 1.b). Finally, the only subsequence left ([an]) is partitioned into a and n, as shown in Figure 1.c. (In fact, an analysis need not be performed for a subsequence of length two, since there is only one way it can be partitioned.) The process ends up with all the subsequences having a single category. By combining the phases of this process, we can obtain a tree structure as the result of the analysis of the sentence. This is shown in Figure 2.

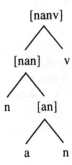

Fig. 2. Combination of partitions for the sentence "adam siyah şapkayı beğendi"

As can be seen, the tree formed after the analysis of a sentence is very similar to a parse tree of the sentence. By denoting the root node with S and the intermediate nodes with special symbols X_i, $i \geq 1$, and extending the leaf nodes with the words in the sentence, it is converted to a parse tree. The symbols X_i denote syntactic constituents like NP, VP. Since the parse tree of a sentence is built with respect to a grammar for the language, it is possible to extract the grammatical rules inherent in the tree. This grammar induction process is beyond the scope of this research. But, it can be solved with a simple mechanism when the parse trees are already available. Our aim here is limited to obtaining probable parses for sentences.

3   The Grammar Formalism

The grammar type underlying the parse trees in this research is a restricted context-free grammar: Each rule is in the form $N \rightarrow \alpha$, where N is a nonterminal symbol, α is a string of nonterminal and terminal symbols, and the number of symbols in α is greater than one. The only restriction we impose on a context-free grammar comes from the last part of this definition; a rule can not derive a single nonterminal or terminal symbol. We call a rule $N \rightarrow A$, where N is a nonterminal and A is a nonterminal or terminal, a *1-1 rule* and the corresponding derivation a *1-1 derivation*. In our grammar, 1-1 rules are not allowed. Note that the grammar type we employ is more general than those in [6,8,9], which restrict themselves to dependency and Chomsky-normal-form grammars.

The number of parse trees that can be generated by this grammar is exponential in nature. For a sentence formed of n words (categories), there are $2^{n-1}-1$ alternative derivations in the first level. If we continue enumerating the alternative derivations until each category is a leaf node, we obtain a large number of parse trees.

A few words are in order about the restriction we impose on the grammar. The reason of this restriction is to limit the number of parse trees that can be generated to a finite (albeit, very large) number and also to decrease the computation time. If 1-1 derivations are allowed when enumerating all the parse trees of a sentence, there will obviously be an infinite number of trees. However, in the case that 1-1 derivations are not used, the number of categories in a node will always be less than that of its parent node, and thus the depth of the tree will be finite.

4 Parse Tree Generation

The method makes use of a corpus containing individual sentences. For each sentence, the categories of the words in the sentence are found first and then the number of each consecutive two-category, three-category, etc. combinations are stored. We call each such category combination a *category string*. In other words, for a sentence of n categories $[c_1c_2...c_n]$, the category strings are as follows: $[c_1c_2]$, $[c_2c_3]$, ..., $[c_{n-1}c_n]$, $[c_1c_2c_3]$, $[c_2c_3c_4]$, ..., $[c_{n-2}c_{n-1}c_n]$, ..., $[c_1c_2...c_{n-1}]$, $[c_2c_3...c_n]$, $[c_1c_2...c_n]$. This calculation is performed for each sentence in the corpus and the numbers are totalled. The result gives us an indication about the frequency of consecutive use of word categories. As can be guessed, the frequencies of short category strings are usually greater than those of long category strings, since short category strings already appear within some long ones. We will denote the frequency of a category string $[c_ic_{i+1}...c_j]$, i<j, with $Freq(c_i,c_{i+1},...,c_j)$.

Definition: Given a sentence of n words $[c_1c_2...c_i...c_j...c_n]$, n>1, $1 \le i,j \le n$, i<j, the *category proximity* of the category string $[c_ic_{i+1}...c_j]$, $CP(c_i,c_{i+1},...,c_j)$, indicates the closeness of the categories c_i, c_{i+1}, ..., c_j to each other and is defined as follows:

$$CP(c_i,c_{i+1},...,c_j) = \frac{Freq(c_1,c_2,...,c_n)}{Freq(c_i,c_{i+1},...,c_j)}. \tag{1}$$

$CP(c_i,...,c_j)$ is a measure of the strength of the connection between the categories c_i, ..., c_j when considered as a single group. Small value of CP indicates stronger connection. If $CP(c_i,...,c_j)$ is small, it is more likely that $[c_i...c_j]$ forms a syntactic constituent.

Figure 3 compares a small CP value with a large CP value. For visualization, we represent CPs as distances between relevant nodes on a tree; that is, $CP(c_i,...,c_j)$ is the distance between nodes c_i and c_j. In Figure 3.a, $CP(c_i,...,c_j)$ is a small number (relative to Figure 3.c), which means that the categories c_i, ..., c_j are close to each other (i.e. this category combination is a frequently occurring one). Thus they have a tendency to form a syntactic constituent, as shown in Figure 3.b. (Note that the branches in Figure 3.a do not indicate a derivation – this is emphasized by using dotted lines. They are used only to visualize the CPs on a figure. Also note that, since the situation is explained for one group of categories c_i, ..., c_j, we do not take the other categories $(c_1, ..., c_{i-1}, c_{j+1}, ..., c_n)$ into account. The CP values of other categories will in fact affect the partitioning in Figure 3.b.) On the other hand, Figure 3.c shows a case where $CP(c_i,...,c_j)$ is large. In this case, we say that the category combination c_i, ..., c_j does not occur frequently. They do not tend to form a syntactic constituent; rather they tend to be partitioned as separate branches in the tree, as shown in Figure 3.d.

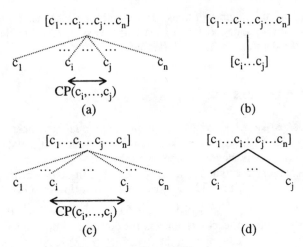

Fig. 3. Comparison of CP values

As an example, consider the following sentence:

birdenbire   odaya   girdi
   (d)   (n)   (v)
suddenly   room+dat   enter+pst+3sg
(he/she suddenly entered the room)

Suppose that Freq(d,n)=100, Freq(n,v)=1000, and Freq(d,n,v)=50. That is, the adverb-noun combination is followed by a verb half of the time, and the noun-verb combination occurs frequently but it is rarely preceded by an adverb. Then, the category proximity measures are as follows: CP(d,n)=0.5, CP(n,v)=0.05. We see the situation in Figure 4. The figure suggests that the noun and the verb can form a syntactic constituent.

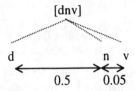

Fig. 4. CP values for the sentence "birdenbire odaya girdi"

Definition: Given a sentence of n words $[c_1c_2...c_n]$, n>1, the *sentence proximity* of the sentence, $SP(c_1,c_2,...,c_n)$, indicates the overall closeness of the categories in the sentence and is defined in terms of category proximities:

$$SP(c_1,c_2,...,c_n) = \sum_{i=1}^{n-1} CP(c_i,c_{i+1}) . \qquad (2)$$

Similar to category proximity, $SP(c_1,...,c_n)$ is a measure of the strength of the connection between the categories in the sentence. The difference lies in the range of categories it affects. Instead of determining how probable it is for a particular group of categories $c_i, \ldots, c_j$ within the sentence to form a syntactic constituent, it increases or decreases these probabilities for all category combinations in the sentence. Small value of SP is a bias in favour of more syntactic constituents.

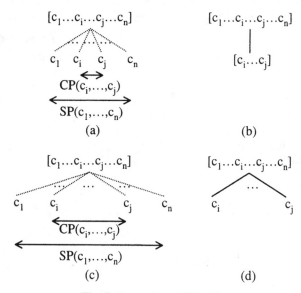

Fig. 5. Comparison of SP values

Figure 5 compares a small SP value with a large SP value. Assume that the ratio $\dfrac{CP(c_i,\ldots,c_j)}{SP(c_1,\ldots,c_n)}$ (and the ratios for category strings other than $[c_i\ldots c_j]$) are the same in Figures 5.a and 5.c. In this case, the category proximity measure is not sufficient to differentiate the different syntactic relationships among the categories (as will be clear later) – it will force the same syntactic constituents to be built in both sentences. However, in reality, the fact that category combinations occur more frequently is a sign of more syntactic relationships (since they did not occur in that sentence "by chance"). This effect is provided by the sentence proximity measure. Figure 5.b shows that the categories $c_i, \ldots, c_j$ of Figure 5.a form a syntactic constituent, whereas Figure 5.d shows that the categories $c_i, \ldots, c_j$ of Figure 5.c tend to be partitioned as separate categories.

The two proximity concepts are used together in order to produce a parse tree for a sentence. Suppose that we have a sentence of n words $[c_1c_2\ldots c_n]$, $n>1$. The category proximity values for all category strings in the sentence (except $CP(c_1,\ldots,c_n)$) are calculated. These values may be in conflict with each other. For instance, $CP(c_1,c_2)$ and $CP(c_2,c_3)$ may be small, forcing the corresponding categories to make a group, but $CP(c_1,c_2,c_3)$ may be large, having an opposite effect. The idea is extracting the real (or, best) proximity figures inherent in these data. This is accomplished by taking the initial CP values of category strings of length two (i.e. $CP(c_i,c_{i+1})$, $1 \leq i < n$) into

62   Tunga Güngör

consideration, applying the effects of other CP values on these, and arriving at final
CP values of category strings of length two. These values denote the real proximities
for each pair of categories.

For this purpose, the following linear programming problem is formulated and
solved: (The equations have n-1 variables $x_1, x_2, ..., x_{n-1}$ whose values are sought. x_i,
$1\le i<n$, corresponds to $CP(c_i,c_{i+1})$. $p_{i,j}$ and $n_{i,j}$, $1\le i\le n-2$, $1\le j\le n-1$, $i+j\le n$, stand for positive and negative slack variables, respectively. The goal is obtaining actual $CP(c_i,c_{i+1})$
values (i.e. x_i's) such that the sum of the slack variables is minimum.)

$$\min p_{1,1}+...+p_{1,n-1}+p_{2,1}+...+p_{2,n-2}+...+p_{n-2,1}+p_{n-2,2}+$$
$$n_{1,1}+...+n_{1,n-1}+n_{2,1}+...+n_{2,n-2}+...+n_{n-2,1}+n_{n-2,2}$$
subject to
$$x_1+p_{1,1}-n_{1,1} = CP(c_1,c_2)$$
$$x_2+p_{1,2}-n_{1,2} = CP(c_2,c_3)$$
$$\vdots$$
$$x_{n-1}+p_{1,n-1}-n_{1,n-1} = CP(c_{n-1},c_n)$$
$$x_1+x_2+p_{2,1}-n_{2,1} = CP(c_1,c_2,c_3)$$
$$\vdots$$
$$x_{n-2}+x_{n-1}+p_{2,n-2}-n_{2,n-2} = CP(c_{n-2},c_{n-1},c_n)$$
$$\vdots$$
$$x_1+...+x_{n-2}+p_{n-2,1}-n_{n-2,1} = CP(c_1,...,c_{n-1})$$
$$x_2+...+x_{n-1}+p_{n-2,2}-n_{n-2,2} = CP(c_2,...,c_n)$$

Let $CP'(c_i,c_{i+1})$, $1\le i<n$, denote the actual category proximity values obtained and
$SP'(c_1,...,c_n)$ $(= \sum_{i=1}^{n-1} CP'(c_i,c_{i+1}))$ the actual sentence proximity value. The tree structure formed with these actual values will be called the *actual tree*. As mentioned in
Section 3, the category string $[c_1...c_n]$ can be partitioned in $2^{n-1}-1$ ways. We call each
such partition a *partition tree*. The task is finding the most probable partition tree. To
this effect, the actual tree is compared with each partition tree, a score is calculated
for each, and the one with the smallest score is chosen.

Definition: Given an actual tree and a partition tree P of n words $[c_1c_2...c_n]$, $n>1$, the
sentence proximity of the partition tree, $SP_P(c_1,c_2,...,c_n)$, is equal to the sentence proximity of the actual tree. That is,

$$SP_P(c_1,c_2,...,c_n) = SP'(c_1,c_2,...,c_n). \tag{3}$$

Definition: Given a partition tree P of n words $[c_1c_2...c_n]$, $n>1$, let the m partitions,
$1<m\le n$, be $(c_1,...,c_{i_1})$, $(c_{i_1+1},...,c_{i_2})$,..., $(c_{i_{m-1}+1},...,c_{i_m})$ $(1\le i_1<i_2<...<i_m=n)$. Then, the
category proximity of two consecutive categories, $CP_P(c_i,c_{i+1})$, $1\le i<n$, in the tree, is
defined as follows:

$$CP_P(c_i, c_{i+1}) = \begin{cases} 0 & \text{, if } c_i \text{ and } c_{i+1} \text{ are in the same partition} \\ \dfrac{SP_P(c_1,...,c_n)}{m-1} & \text{, otherwise} \end{cases} \qquad (4)$$

Intuitively, we consider the distance (proximity value) between the first and last branches of a partition tree as equal to the same distance in the actual tree and then divide this distance to the number of branches minus one to obtain an equal distance between each pair of branches.

Having obtained the actual tree, it is compared with each possible partition tree in order to find the most similar one. In fact, the actual tree is the most realistic tree in terms of showing the syntactic relationships in the sentence. However, since such "fuzzy" derivations can not take part in sentence parse trees, we must represent it with a suitable partition tree.

Definition: Given an actual tree of n words $[c_1c_2...c_n]$, $n>1$, the *cumulative category proximity* of a category c_i, $1<i<n$, $CCP'(c_i)$, is the total of the category proximity values between the first and the c_i^{th} categories. That is,

$$CCP'(c_i) = \sum_{j=1}^{i-1} CP'(c_j, c_{j+1}) . \qquad (5)$$

The cumulative category proximity for a partition tree P, $CCP_P(c_i)$, is defined analogously. Note that $CCP'(c_1)=0$ and $CCP'(c_n)=SP'(c_1,...,c_n)$; but these border values will not be used in the following derivations.

Definition: Given an actual tree and a partition tree P of n words $[c_1c_2...c_n]$, $n>2$, the *similarity score* between the two trees, SS_P, is defined as follows:

$$SS_P = \sum_{i=2}^{n-1} abs[CCP'(c_i) - CCP_P(c_i)] * cg(c_i) . \qquad (6)$$

where *abs* is the absolute value function and $cg(c_i)$ is the category grouping value:

$$cg(c_i) = \begin{cases} 1 & \text{, if } c_i \text{ forms a partition by itself} \\ SP'(c_1,...,c_n) & \text{, otherwise} \end{cases} \qquad (7)$$

Intuitively, the similarity score between an actual tree and a partition tree indicates the total of the amount of the distances traversed when "moving" the branches of the actual tree in order to make the actual tree identical to the partition tree. Small value of SS_P means more similarity between the trees, as the distance traversed will be less.

The category grouping value serves for the effect of sentence proximity mentioned before (Figure 5). Suppose that a category c_i is included within a partition of length greater than one, as in Figure 5.b, so $cg(c_i)=SP'(c_1,...,c_n)$. Then, an actual tree with a smaller SP' value (Figure 5.a) than another actual tree with a larger SP' value (Figure 5.c) will be more similar to that partition tree, since $cg(c_i)$ is a multiplicative factor in equation (6). In other words, the former one will bias in favour of those partition trees in which c_i appears within a group among all the possible partition trees, whereas the latter one will bias in favour of partition trees in which c_i forms a separate partition.

After the most similar partition tree is chosen, each partition with length greater than two is considered as a new sentence and the whole process is repeated. As explained in Section 2, the collection of all the most similar partition trees then forms the parse tree of the sentence.

5 Implementation of the Method

The proposed approach was implemented for Turkish. A corpus of general text containing about 5,700 sentences was compiled. The average length (number of words) of the sentences is 18.6. The corpus includes long sentences having as many as 50 words. Word categories are derived by using the spelling checker program explained in [10]. The frequencies of all category strings in the corpus are collected and stored in a database.

The method was applied to several sentences and parse trees were generated. Below we present the details of a short sentence only due to lack of space. The sentence was taken from a newspaper:

    ülkedeki   demokratik gelişmeler   yetersizdir
      (n)   (a)   (n)   (v)
    country+loc democratic progress+pl adequate+neg+cop
    (democratic progresses in the country are not adequate)

Table 1. Calculations for the example sentence (first iteration)

Freq(n,a) = 5,992 Freq(a,n) = 6,973 Freq(n,v) = 6,639 Freq(n,a,n) = 3,036 Freq(a,n,v) = 865 Freq(n,a,n,v) = 367 (a)	CP(n,a) = 0.061 CP(a,n) = 0.053 CP(n,v) = 0.055 CP(n,a,n) = 0.121 CP(a,n,v) = 0.424 SP(n,a,n,v) = 0.169 (b)

min p1+n1+p2+n2+p3+n3+p4+n4+p5+n5
subject to
x1+p1-n1=0.061
x2+p2-n2=0.053
x3+p3-n3=0.055
x1+x2+p4-n4=0.121
x2+x3+p5-n5=0.424
(c)

CP'(n,a) = 0.061 CP'(a,n) = 0.060 CP'(n,v) = 0.365 SP'(n,a,n,v) = 0.486 (d)	CP$_P$(n,a) = 0 CP$_P$(a,n) = 0 CP$_P$(n,v) = 0.486 SP$_P$(n,a,n,v) = 0.486 (e)	CCP'(a) = 0.061 CCP'(n) = 0.121 CCP$_P$(a) = 0 CCP$_P$(n) = 0 SS$_P$ = 0.088 (f)

Table 2. Calculations for the example sentence (second iteration)

Freq(n,a) = 5,992 Freq(a,n) = 6,973 Freq(n,a,n) = 3,036 (a)	CP(n,a) = 0.507 CP(a,n) = 0.435 SP(n,a,n) = 0.942 (b)	
min p1+n1+p2+n2 subject to x1+p1-n1=0.507 x2+p2-n2=0.435 (c)		
CP′(n,a) = 0.507 CP′(a,n) = 0.435 SP′(n,a,n) = 0.942 (d)	CPₚ(n,a) = 0.471 CPₚ(a,n) = 0.471 SPₚ(n,a,n) = 0.942 (e)	CCP′(a) = 0.507 CCPₚ(a) = 0.471 SSₚ = 0.036 (f)

For each iteration of the process, we give the calculations in a table. The calculations involve the actual tree and the most probable partition tree P. Calculations for other partition trees are not shown due to the large number of possible trees. Each table consists of the following data: category string frequencies (part a), initial category proximities and sentence proximity (part b), linear programming problem (part c), actual category proximities and sentence proximity (part d), category proximities and sentence proximity for the partition tree P (part e), and cumulative category proximities and the similarity score between the actual tree and the partition tree P (part f).

Table 1 contains the data and the results for the category string [nanv] and Table 2 for the category string [nan]. The final parse tree is shown in Figure 6.

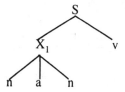

Fig. 6. Parse tree for the example sentence

An observation about the computational complexity of the method is worth mentioning here. The program was executed on a Pentium 4 1.3 Ghz machine. The execution time is very low for sentences containing at most 15-20 words. It takes about 4-5 seconds parsing such sentences. The computation time seems very promising when we consider the size of the search space – that is, we are working with a nearly unrestricted context-free grammar formalism. The reason is pruning the search space at each iteration and taking only the best partitioning into account.

6 Conclusions

In this paper, we proposed a new method for generating parse trees of natural language sentences. Due to the limitations of rule-based techniques in formalizing natu-

66   Tunga Güngör

ral languages, statistical techniques are gaining popularity. This was the direction pursued in this research. The method is based on the information inherent in the word categories (parts of speech) of words within the sentences. By using the frequency and order of these categories, a method was formulated to make the syntactic relationships in sentences explicit.

The parse trees that the method produces are equivalent to those that can be generated by a little restricted context-free grammar. The grammar formalism used is more general than those used by other similar approaches.

The approach was tested for Turkish using a corpus of about 5,700 sentences. Although an exact evaluation is not possible since there does not exist a complete grammar for the language, the results are successful. The parse trees produced by the program for about half of the sentences seem correct. One strength of the method is its ability to generate plausible parses for complex sentences. But parses which can not capture the syntactic relationships inside the sentences or that result in slightly misplaced constituents were also produced. As the size of the corpus increases, we may expect better results.

An attractive area for future research is extracting a grammar using these parse trees. This will be an important contribution if it becomes possible to obtain a robust grammar, since no comprehensive grammars have been written yet. It may also provide feedback to rule-based grammar studies.

Acknowledgement

This work was supported by the Boğaziçi University Research Fund, Grant no. 02A107.

References

1. Charniak, E.: Statistical Language Learning. MIT, Cambridge MA (1997)
2. Manning, C.D., Schütze, H.: Foundations of Statistical Natural Language Processing. MIT, Cambridge MA (2002)
3. Bod, R.: Data Oriented Parsing. In: Computational Linguistics in the Netherlands. Amsterdam The Netherlands (1991) 26-39
4. Bod, R.: Beyond Grammar: An Experience-Based Theory of Language. CSLI Publications, Stanford (1998)
5. Kaplan, R.: A Probabilistic Approach to Lexical-Functional Analysis. In: Conference and Workshop on Lexical Functional Grammar. CSLI Publications, Stanford (1996)
6. Carroll, G.: Learning Probabilistic Grammars for Language Modelling. Ph.D. Thesis. Brown University, Providence RI (1995)
7. Carroll, G., Charniak, E.: Learning Probabilistic Dependency Grammars from Labelled Text. AAAI Fall Symposium on Probabilistic Approaches to Natural Language. Cambridge MA (1992) 25-32
8. Pereira, F., Schabes, Y.: Inside-Outside Reestimation from Partially Bracketed Corpora. In: Annual Meeting of the Association for Computational Linguistics. Newark Deleware (1992) 128-135
9. Briscoe, T., Waegner, N.: Robust Stochastic Parsing Using the Inside-Outside Algorithm. AAAI Workshop on Statistically-Based NLP Techniques. San Jose California (1992) 30-53
10. Güngör, T.: Computer Processing of Turkish: Morphological and Lexical Investigation. Ph.D. Thesis. Boğaziçi University, İstanbul Turkey (1995)

Application of Machine Learning Techniques to the Re-ranking of Search Results

Martin Buchholz[1,2], Dirk Pflüger[1,2], and Josiah Poon[2]

[1] Fakultät IEI, Universität Stuttgart, Germany
[2] School of Information Technologies, University of Sydney, Australia

Abstract. Even though search engines cover billions of pages and perform quite well, it is still difficult to find the right information from the returned results. In this paper we present a system that allows a user to re-rank the results locally by augmenting a query with positive example pages. Since it is not always easy to come up with many example pages, our system aims to work with only a couple of positive training examples and without any negative ones. Our approach creates artificial (virtual) negative examples based upon the returned pages and the example pages before the training commences. The list of results is then re-ordered according to the outcome from the machine learner. We have further shown that our system performs sufficiently well even if the example pages belong to a slightly different (but related) domain.

1 Introduction

Finding information has always been one of the popular tasks in the Internet. Whereas human-maintained web directories seemed capable of providing access to all interesting information in the beginning, they were not able to keep up with the exponential growth of web pages over the Internet. Nowadays general purpose search engines seem to provide acceptable results, but their greatest strength – their generality, i.e. their capability to retrieve information for any kind of search – is at the same time their greatest weakness.

Danny Sullivan from http://searchenginewatch.com estimated that on September 2nd, 2003, the search engine with the biggest index of web pages was Google with about 3.3 billions of textual documents indexed ([11]). This means that a vast amount of data is available to the user. The main problem for a user is to specify a query for a search engine to retrieve the documents she is looking for. It is often hard to specify search queries – a survey by the NEC Research Institute in Princeton, New Jersey, revealed that "up to 70% of web users typically type in only one keyword or search term" ([3]). This seems to be a wide-spread phenomena. They also found that almost 50% of the queries contained just one word and a mere 30% contained two key words, even amongst the queries made by their own staff.

We try to look at the search problem from a user's psychological perspective (while she is sitting in front of a terminal to conduct a search), and we will address two specific areas, namely, *query formulation* and *ranking*. To express

S. Biundo, T. Frühwirth, and G. Palm (Eds.): KI 2004, LNAI 3238, pp. 67–81, 2004.

what one wants is not always easy. Although a query may look trivial, there are a lot of subtlies in one's intention that are difficult to make explicit. In the research paradigm of case-based reasoning [7], people usually apply some of their past cases/experience to solve the current problem. Hence, it is hypothesized that the formulation of a search query may become easier if the user can provide some example pages that she believes to be similar/relevant. Another area of concern in a search process is the ordering of the information from a general purpose search engine. Most of the powerful engines nowadays can find useful information, but the returned documents are only ranked according to a universal formula that may not accommodate to individual needs. The user has to further identify the web pages that satisfy her current needs; this may require a user to flip through many pages of search results and to go through the details of each and every returned document. In other words, the user still has to find the needle albeit in another haystack, and this can be quite discouraging. The ordering of the results is very important. When a user performs a search in the Internet, it does not help if a search engine returns plenty of positive documents but none of them appears within the top 50 search results. Users are generally unwilling to flip through many negative documents to find the first positive one.

Our aim is to create a system that re-ranks the pages locally on the client machine according to the implicit constraints inherent in the positive example pages provided by the user. Even if the list of documents returned by the general search engine contains a very low percentage of relevant documents, they will be rearranged to the top of the list. Another reason of leaving the re-ranking in the client machine rather than at the server side is to enable the privacy of the user. A user can now do more specific search without exposing herself too much to the search engine providers.

The rest of this paper is organized as follows. A brief overview of related work is described in Sect. 2. The design of the system can be found in Sect. 3 where we will pay specific attention to the feature selection, the creation of artificial negative examples and our methodology of cost-benefit assessment. Three experiments with different aims are reported and discussed in Sect. 4. Section 5 summarises the work and contains future enhancements.

2   Related Work

Current research dealing with information retrieval in the internet often tries to overcome weaknesses of general purpose search engines. For example, lots of domain specific search engines have been developed. [5] proposed the use of AI-techniques to improve the results of general search engines and discussed different approaches to get better results in specific domains. They discuss systems like Ahoy!, which uses heuristics to find homepages, or ShopBot, which tries to assist users doing online-shopping. [13] built a search engine for abstracts of papers of IEEE Transactions. The system responds to a query with results that are linked to other related documents and a set of suggestions for query refinements. The authors used an ontology that was previously derived from the collection with the help of other resources like WordNet. [8] developed a system that automatically constructs hierarchies for small domains, for example intranets or local web sites. We were not able to adopt these approaches for our system as our aim was not to create a search engine for one single domain but a search engine that can be used in any domain. The creation of an ontology that covers every single topic in the whole internet is not feasible.

Some systems use general purpose search engines and try to improve a user's query to get better results. The system in [6] tries to select few features out of a set of documents which are then used to modify a search query. This approach is quite similar to the approach in [9] which is to generate keyword spices, which are keywords that can be added to any query to restrict the query to a certain domain. Both require a lot of preliminary human work to find positive and negative examples. Once done, their system is an easy implementable and fast domain specific search engine. Some of the systems are not absolutely fixed on one domain, but in most of them a lot of work has to be done to adapt them to a new domain and they are usually only functional if much more example documents are available then we have.

A completely different approach which has some similarities with our system is discussed in [4]. The authors try to make use of the processing power of the user's computer. After extracting all noun phrases from a set of documents, the user has to select some of those phrases. As a final step a Kohonen Self-Organizing Map (SOM) is used to cluster the web pages into a two dimensional map according to the selected noun phrases. Their feature selection process is similar to ours. Instead of a clustering we wanted to achieve a good ranking from the users point of view.

Other papers deal with creating artificial or virtual examples. [10] incorporates transformation invariances by creating artificial examples, for example. They have in common that they use some domain-specific knowledge to create new training samples by modifying classified training data. We do not have enough classified – and especially no negative – documents available. We had to find a new way to create negative examples.

In contrary to some similar attempts to re-rank results of search engines we put our focus on the optimization of the ranking for the first few results: Users of search engines usually scan only the top results and skip the search if they cannot find any positive documents. This led us to the use of example documents and the creation of artificial negative examples.

3   Design

In our proposed system, the user specifies a general query that covers her domain roughly and, in addition, she also provides a set of example pages within her domain of interest. As we understand that it is an expensive activity to turn up with many training cases, our system is able to cope with *very few* example pages to minimize the tedious workload for the user. The system is also designed to cope with only positive example documents and no negative ones. For exam-

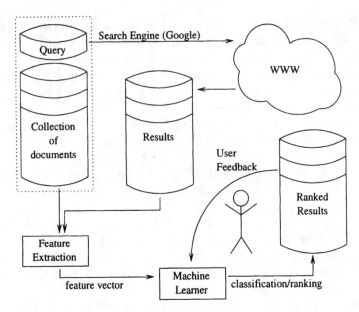

Fig. 1. System Design.

ple, we used just three positive and no negative example documents in all our experiments.

Figure 1 illustrates the different components of our system. Starting with the provided query, the system uses a general purpose search engine to retrieve a list of documents for the given query. It downloads a number of them and uses them together with the initial example documents in the feature extraction process to produce feature vectors for all documents.

The system creates artificial (virtual) negative training samples to augment the existing pages to create the training set for the Machine Learner (ML). The confidence of the ML in each classification is used to re-rank the results. The results are further fine tuned to provide a better ranking than a random ordering.

The computed ranking is presented to the user. The user can look at the corresponding web pages and provide feedback by specifying the correct classification. This feedback can be used to further refine the ranking. While it is desirable to minimize the user involvement, we assume that it requires significantly less effort from the user to give some feedback to a ranked list of relatively filtered pages than to look at a vast number of irrelevant web pages.

3.1   Feature Extraction

To make the learning more efficient, only a subset of words in the documents is used. In our experiments we focused mainly on nouns because this can decrease the number of features significantly while still providing sufficient information for our task. We also applied simple stemming and the system is case-insensitive to further reduce the number of features.

We can constrain the number of features to a reasonably small size if we extract them from the training documents provided by the user. But if we select our features only from the few positive example documents, those features are not adequate to represent the negative documents. We have to select other features from the documents in the list offered by the search engine to overcome this problem. However, the total number of returned documents can be quite high so we need to restrict the total number of features to be under a threshold. In most of our experiments, this limit was set to around 300 words with about half of them selected from the example documents.

Tf-idf is a way to represent the significance of a feature in the concerned corpus. It is determined by the term frequency (tf) as well as the inverse of the document frequency (df), i.e. the number of documents in which a term occurs. We have also taken into account that the length of a document has its role in the calculation of the weight value of each feature. The basic philosophy is: If a word occurs several times in a short document, it is more important than the same absolute frequency in a larger document. We finally calculated the values using the following formula:

$$y = (1 + log(\frac{tf * maxsize}{docsize})) * log(\frac{n}{df})$$

where n is the total number of documents, $maxsize$ is the size of the largest document and $docsize$ is the size of the document for which the current feature value is calculated.

3.2 Fine Ranking

When there are documents sharing the same confidence level, they will be presented in a random order within this group. A fine ranking is applied to the documents within such a collection so that the ordering is better than a random ordering. The ordering scheme is based on Euclidian distances of the feature vectors in a subspace of the feature space.

The idea was to restrict our feature space for distance calculations to features (attributes) that are most important for the set of positive documents. We select the attributes that occur in at least

$$\sqrt{\# \text{ positive documents}}$$

positive documents (and at least 10 attributes). Then we compute the mean value of the shortened feature vectors of the positive documents in the current training set and rank the documents within one plateau according to the Euclidian distance of their feature vector from the mean vector.

Even if this method of fine ranking may not be optimal, it performs better than average in all our test cases. If one of the more sophisticated MLs (e.g. Support Vector Machine) is used or the training set increases, the confidence value for each single document offered by the classifier usually differs enough to leave out the application of fine ranking.

3.3   Cost-Benefit Analysis

The standard evaluation measurements for an information retrieval system are usually precision, recall and the F-value, a combination of them. In our case, they do not necessarily reflect the performance perceived by the user of our system: the ranking is more important than the actual classification. Another thorny issue in our design is to cater for the limited number of documents available for training.

The main interest of a user is to have as many positive results as possible to be ranked to the topmost of the list. The application of a threshold value to one of the standard measurements as a ranking measurement is not meaningful because it does not capture the essence of the overall ranking. We created an alternative visualisation scheme that is similar to the ROC (Receiver Operating Characteristcs) curve[1]. This measure covers the whole ranking and corresponds to a user's interest. We call the number of negative documents a user has to look at before she gets the next positive document the "cost", and the number of positive documents the user gets before she has to look at the next negative document as "benefit". We plot the (maximum) benefits (vertical axis) one can get against the costs (horizontal axis) it takes to reach them.

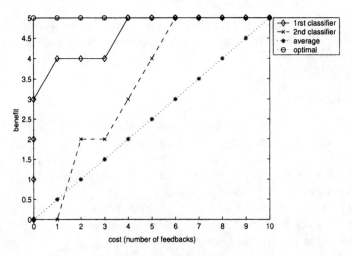

Fig. 2. An example plot showing the properties of our evaluation method. The set of 15 documents consists of 5 positive and 10 negative documents.

A user starts looking at the documents, beginning with the first one. As soon as she encounters a negative document, she gives feedback to the system by classifying the new document as negative and all previous positive documents she looked at since the last negative document as positive. After reclassifying the remaining documents, the user continues to examine the results. In the optimal case all positive documents come before all the negative documents in

---

[1] A ROC curve shows the relationship between false positives and true positives, or the recall versus fallout.

the ranking, which is maximum benefit at no costs. The documents retrieved by the query are independent of the set of sample documents. We regard the ranking of documents in Google to be just "random". Google somehow sorts on the importance of the pages, but the sorting is for the whole web community, not specialized for a single user (for Google's PageRank technology see [2]). In the evaluation of our re-ranking, we aim to get a ranking better than Google's (or basically a random ranking). We consider the Google ranking as the lower bound of our performance criterion.

The average curve in Fig. 2 represents the performance obtained by the underlying Google query. In this example setting we show the performance of two fictive classifiers. Let's look at the 1st classifier. The first three documents (in this example) are positive documents $(+)$, i.e. no negative document $(-)$ has been seen yet. We have a point at $(0,3)$ because the next document is negative, which means that we have to look at zero negative documents to get a maximum of three positive ones. After the first negative document (and therefore the first feedback), there is exactly one positive document before the next negative one, so we have to look at one negative document to get a total maximum of four positive ones (point $(1,4)$). According to the arrival pattern of this set of documents for the 1st classifier, we should have the points $(0,3)$, $(1,4)$, $(2,4)$ etc. plotted on the chart. The chart shows that our performance measurement is quite intuitive: The first classifier is closer to the optimum than the second one and therefore it has a better performance. For the first classifier you get three positive documents before you have to look at the first negative one. The ranking for the whole set of documents for the first classifier – including feedback – is

$$[\ + \ \ + \ \ + \ \ - \ \ + \ \ - \ \ - \ \ - \ \ + \ \ - \ \ - \ \ - \ \ - \ \ - \ \ - \ ].$$

3.4   Creating Artificial Negative Examples

The most challenging requirement for our system is to cope with only a very small training set. This set is not only small, but it contains only positive sample documents and no negative ones at all. This makes the training difficult because a classification task generally anticipates two distinct classes of labelled data.

Our system works with feedback on each negative document observed. For example, our system starts training with three documents and the first document the user looks at is a negative one. As soon as the user communicates her observation to the system, the training set becomes a set of three positive and one negative documents. Although the size has increased, this is still not big enough to get a useful training process for most of the MLs, and this has led us to the creation of artificial negative documents.

After normalization the values for all features are $\in [0, 1]$. The three positive sample documents are somewhere in a unit hypercube. If we just create documents within this hypercube we could end up creating a negative document within a cluster of positive documents.

We hold an assumption that there are two points in the hypercube that will not be present in the set of positive documents; they are the points zero

$(0\ 0\ 0\ \dots\ 0)^T$ (Artificial Document 0, *AD0*) and one $(1\ 1\ 1\ \dots\ 1)^T$ (Artificial Document 1, *AD1*). A document which is very close to zero has nothing to do with the domain our user is interested in. The feature vector contains the attributes that are most common for the example set. We assume that other documents within our target domain will have at least some of these attributes in common. A document located at *AD1* will have the highest document frequency for all the attributes, but it is practically impossible to have such a document. This is because the feature vector contains high frequency features from the positive documents as well as from some of the negative documents.

We create further nondeterministic negative documents. First, the subset of features that are insignificant for all currently known positive documents is computed. These are mainly attributes that do not occur in any of the known positive documents. They are probably characteristic for some cluster of negative documents. We use this set of features to compute new artificial instances:

- For each new artificial negative document construct a feature vector that has a value of zero for all features.
- For a certain percentage p of features out of the subset that was computed previously, set the value to a random number $\in [0, 1]$.

Empirical evaluations showed that it is reasonable to choose $0.1 \le p \le 0.4$. For the experiments in Section 4, we chose $p = 0.4$.

We are unsure about the usefulness of *AD1* in our classification task. For some combinations of scenarios and machine learners we got a better performance by using both *AD0* and *AD1*, for others the performance was better without *AD1*. We have not yet been able to find out whether it is better to omit *AD1* or not. However, the performance due to *AD0* is more obvious. If a document is completely off-topic and has nothing to do with any other document it is located at point zero or at least close by. It is likely that a bigger set of documents (e.g. 300) contains a few of such documents. Experiments showed that using the *AD0* can improve the performance. Therefore, we finally decided to use just *AD0* and random documents in all our experiments.

In Fig. 3 we show some typical observations. As we expected, the performance without any artificial training examples is worst at the beginning. After the user has given feedback 15 times it outperforms the runs with artificial examples. This is because the system has gained enough "real" examples to train on and they are better than the artificial ones. But about 15 steps later the other runs take over again, the collected "real" documents do not represent all negative examples. The runs with more random examples perform slightly better in the beginning. Later on those with less random examples are better. Similar behaviour can be observed in other examples. Unfortunately this is not valid for all combinations of machine learners and scenarios. More indepth research is required to identify the relationship among ML, data profile and the artificial data. But in any case it is useful to create some artificial negative documents. It offers better results, especially for the first places in the ranking – and they are the most important ones in the eyes of the normal average user.

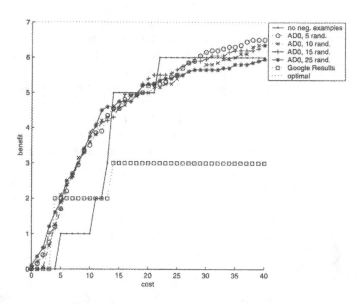

Fig. 3. Performance of different amounts of random examples, overlay scenario, averaged over 20 runs, 91 documents.

4   Experiments and Evaluation

Our architecture is generic and it is independent of any specific search engine. There are many general purpose search engines available in the internet, and we just chose Google to be the search engine to which the queries were sent in the current experiment. We have built a few scenarios of different kinds of domains to test if the system is able to cope with any domain as specified through the queries and the example documents provided by the user. We looked at either the first 100 or 500 results returned by Google. As we evaluated only html-pages (and not pdf, ps or ppt documents, for example), the actual size of our test set is usually a bit smaller.

The results from the various queries are fed to a few MLs. We use tf-idf (normalized by document length), simple stemming, a stop list and only nouns and proper nouns (NN, NNS, NNP and NNPS). For all the runs we use six artificial negative documents ($AD0$ plus 5 randomly created documents within the hypercube).

Our system has a choice of classifiers, but for clarity we focus on three basic machine-learning algorithms and three meta-learning schemes. The classifiers were obtained from WEKA [12] and they are: (1) J48, a decision tree learner which is an implementation of the popular C4.5, (2) IB1, which is a nearest neighbour machine learner and (3) SMO, an implementation of the Sequential Minimal Optimization algorithm – one of the fastest methods for Support Vector Machines (SVM).

We have also applied three different schemes to boost the performance, namely bagging and boosting for the J48 learner and co-training for the J48 and SMO classifiers. Co-Training [1] is an algorithm that uses unlabeled data to augment a much smaller set of labelled data. In particular, it uses two distinct views on the same data to train two classifiers, uses the most confident predictions of both to augment the labelled data and repeats this process a number of iterations. In our current co-training implementation, we did a split on the attributes: One machine learner uses all the attributes at the even numbered positions (attributes number 0, 2, 4, 6, ...) while the other one uses the odd numbered attributes.

We evaluated different settings on the number of artificial examples; especially whether to use *AD0* and *AD1*. Since a test run which involves randomly generated instances will have non-determinstic performance, the charts we plotted are the average performance over several (a minimum of 20) runs.

4.1 Scenario 1

The aim of this experiment is to see if the system can cope with the situation that only very few documents are actually positive documents.

Imagine a search made by a tourist looking for information about Australia. As already mentioned in the introduction, many users usually type in only one keyword. It will be "Australia" in this scenario. Naturally, most of the results that are returned from Google will not contain any useful information. Many returned pages are about the government, newspapers, commerce, education etc. One problem inherent in this classification is that the amount of positive documents is very small. The negative documents come from a diverse set of domains. This makes it difficult for our ML to identify the very small subdomain the user is interested in. Another problem is that many of these pages are the Welcome pages of some bigger websites. The documents have void contents, i.e. they are only some kind of menu.

If you just search for "australia travel" you will neglect pages about accommodation and so on. Hence, the three initial documents for this example were created by three specialised queries. Each of these special queries contained two keywords; the first one was "australia" and the second keyword was either "travel", "tourist" or "accommodation". Out of the three Google results (first ten documents) we selected one document that is – in our opinion – of interest to a tourist.

In this scenario, the number of useful pages among the first 100 results returned by Google is very small. It can be observed in Fig. 4 that most of the MLs can deliver the positive pages (the right kind of information) much earlier than the original ranking as offered by the underlying search engine. In other words, the user can find the information much quicker and she does not have to flip through many screens and to read many irrelevant documents. The SMO fares best among all the MLs, which is followed by the boosting and bagging of J48. The two co-training learning schemes did not pay off, which might be due to the reason that the total numbers of positive cases in this scenario is too small and

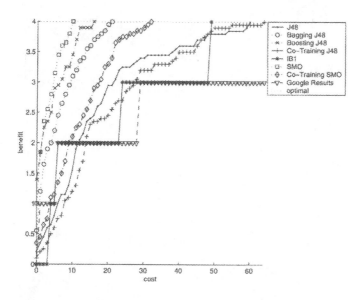

Fig. 4. Performance of different machine learners for the Australia query example (**Scenario 1**). Ranking of the first 87 Google results.

is not sufficient to enable the co-trainer to take advantage of. The IB1 is worse than Google until the cost reaches five but eventually surpasses Google. As there are only four positive documents in this analysis, the differences in performance are very small – but all MLs outperform Google as a whole.

4.2   Scenario 2

In this scenario, the user has a better idea of what she is looking for. The aim of Scenario 2 is to find out how well the system can cope with a situation where all documents are somehow in the same domain – the vocabulary is similar for (almost) all documents. The target set is a very specialized subdomain.

This scenario is, in fact, based on a real world problem we encountered. We wanted to connect a laptop over its TV-out-socket to a TV and watch a video. While we had no problem to see all "normal" graphics (windows, ...) on the TV, we only saw a black box where the video should have been. In our search, we got the first positive results with a very specific query containing four words: "laptop tv video overlay". As there are several different solutions to this problem, it wasn't necessarily sufficient to find only one solution. We used three pages of the Google results as our example documents and the task for our system was to identify all the other ones. The demands on the system are very different from the first example. The query is already very specialized (there are four terms in the search query), the domains of many of the documents are closely related to each other. Most of the good results are FAQ's or questions/answers found in forums. These pages often contain lots of advertisement, menus and other things that don't have anything to do with the domain we are looking for – the

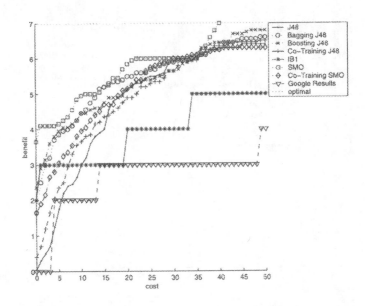

Fig. 5. Performance of different machine learners for the overlay query example (**Scenario 2**). Ranking of the first 91 Google results.

proportion of text on the page that deals with the interesting topic is often very low. The returned pages in Scenario 1 could be classified relatively fast by a human user. In this scenario, the classification is difficult, even for a human.

We used 91 pages from Google for our analysis. According to Fig. 5, all the MLs perform better than the original ranking made by Google. The IB1 learner fares well and it uses another distance measurement (distances to neighbours) than our fine ranking; its performance is still a good indication that distances can be used to generate a simple ranking. The behaviour of the J48 depends on our fine ranking scheme and it has delivered a good performance. All meta-learning mechanisms (bagging, boosting and co-training), when applied to J48, further improve the performance of the J48. The SMO outperforms all the other classifiers, even co-training does not improve the results for the SMO. Co-training algorithms need plenty of both positive and negative instances within the unlabeled set, otherwise they are unable to assign a high confidence in the unlabeled documents to boost the labelled set. And in Scenario 2 we have only seven positive documents out of 91 test instances, which is quite insufficient to facilitate co-training.

4.3   Scenario 3

A user does not necessarily have any sample pages from the domain of interest, but she may have some documents from a related domain. This last scenario aims to test the generalisation ability of our system.

The user in this example is interested in a recipe for baking apple pie. She hasn't got any apple pie recipes but she has other recipes and can give them as input for our system to identify similar pages which contain the recipe she is interested in. One of the sample documents she provides is about cooking fish, one about baking bread and one about baking some other pie – the query she provides is "apple pie". Here the sample pages are not directly from the domain of interest but rather from similar domains. Our system has to generalize from the given data to be able to identify new pages from the related domain.

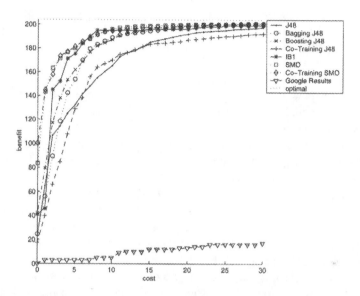

Fig. 6. Performance of different machine learners for the apple pie (recipe) query example **(Scenario 3)**. Ranking of the first 462 Google results.

In this scenario, we used the top 462 pages returned by Google for analysis and there are about 40% positive documents. This situation is better than in the previous two scenarios where we had only 5% to 8% of positive test instances. The scale of usefulness has exceeded the user's expectation – who is interested in reading 204 different recipes of apple pies? In Fig. 6, all MLs perform much better than Google and the SMO shows superior results. The SMO-class MLs continue to excel in the performance league. The SMO ranks more than 80 positive pages and its co-training version even has 100 positive documents on top of the list in the first step. The results delivered by the IB1 are better than those of the J48 and all its meta-learners. The J48 and its co-training counterparts produce the second and third weakest ranking. Bagging and boosting improve the performance of the J48 and boosting is, once more, better than bagging.

This scenario has demonstrated the generalization capabilities of this system. The three sample documents are related to but do not belong to the target domain. The system has even achieved a good performance when it was only the fish recipe provided as a single positive example. Co-training is only useful if there are enough positive documents in the data set (negative ones are normally abundant). But even without co-training: The SMO classifier shows a very good performance even on extreme data and small training sets.

5   Conclusions and Future Work

In Sect. 2 we have already looked at different systems which try to solve similar problems. All of them either concentrate only on one specific domain or they have to be adapted to work in a new area. We tried to design our system to eliminate these limitations and be as general as possible without concentrating on special domains, so no adaptation is required. Another assumption of these related systems is the availability of lots of preclassified training pages, but this is practically infeasible as we are not limited to one domain. We have demonstrated that our new approach is able to cope with a *very* small size of training examples. This includes the generation of artificial examples to cope with the lack of negative instances.

From a user's point of view, the time it takes to re-rank a few hundreds of documents can be neglected. The main bottleneck, as in similar systems, is the time it takes to download all the documents.

Our system cannot always perform as good under the extreme conditions we examined as a search engine developed exclusively for a specific domain. It would be resource-expensive and time-consuming to create domain-specific search engines for any arbitrary domain. Hence, from the perspective of a user who is searching information in the web, our system performs quite well by always re-ranking relevant pages to the top of the list regardless whether it is a very general query (Scenario 1) or a very specialized one (Scenario 2), and the system is also able to generalise from one domain to a related one (Scenario 3).

In spite of our good results there is still room for improvement. Currently we use only the content of a document but not the structure. The information contained in headings is usually more important than normal text. The feature selection can be modified to reflect the different importance of different parts of a document. Feature selection can also be performed after every user feedback to capture the very specific knowledge pertained in the new classification step provided by the user. In our experiments, we mainly chose five random artificial examples. It will be useful to find out a trade-off for the number of artificial instances that are used. Another possible extension will be related to co-training. For test sets with a limited amount of positive documents, this technique can not work properly and the performance suffers. If it is somehow possible to coarsely estimate the percentage of positive documents, we can adapt the number of runs adequately to improve the overall performance.

References

1. Avrim Blum, Tom Mitchell: Combining Labeled and Unlabeled Data with Co-training. In Proceedings of the Workshop on Computational Learning Theory, Morgan Kaufmann Publishers, 1998.

2. S. Brin and L. Page: The Anatomy of a Large-Scale Hypertextual Web Search Engine. Proc. of 1998 WWW Conference, 1998
3. Decan Butler: Souped-up search engines. In Nature, Vol. 405, pp. 112-115, 2000.
4. Michael Chau, Daniel Zeng, Hsinchun Chen: Personalized Spiders for Web Search and Analysis. In Proceedings of the First ACM/IEEE-CS Joint Conference on Digital Libraries (JCDL'01), pp. 79-87, Roanoke, Virginia, June 24-28, 2001.
5. Oren Etzioni: Moving Up the Information Food Chain: Deploying Softbots on the World Wide Web, 1996.
6. Eric J. Glover, Gary W. Flake, Steve Lawrence, William P. Birmingham, Andries Kruger, C. Lee Giles, David M. Pennock: Improving Category Specific Web Search by Learning Query Modifications. In Symposium on Applications and the Internet, SAINT 2001, San Diego, California, January 8–12, 2001.
7. J. Kolodner: Case-Based Reasoning. Morgan Kaufmann. 1993.
8. Udo Kruschwitz: A Rapidly Acquired Domain Model Derived from Markup Structure. In Proceedings of the ESSLLI'01 Workshop on Semantic Knowledge Acquisition and Categorisation, Helsinki, 2001.
9. Satoshi Oyama, Takashi Kokubo and Toru Ishida: Domain-Specific Web Search with Keyword Spices. In IEEE Transactions on Knowledge and Data Engineering, 2003 (to appear).
10. Bernhard Schölkopf, Chris Burges, Vladimir Vapnik: Incorporating Invariances in Support Vector Learning Machines. ICANN 96; Springer Lecture Notes in Computer Science, Vol. 1112
11. Danny Sullivan, Search Engine Sizes. http://searchenginewatch.com/reports/article.php/2156481, September 2nd, 2003.
12. I. H. Witten, E. Frank: Data Mining: Practical Machine Learning Tools with Java Implementations. Morgan Kaufmann. 1999.
13. Dwi H. Widyantoro, John Yen: A Fuzzy Ontology-based Abstract Search Engine and Its User Studies. In Proceedings of the 10th IEEE International Conference on Fuzzy Systems, pp. 1291-1294 vol.2, 2001.

A Pragmatics-First Approach
to the Analysis and Generation of Dialogues

Bernd Ludwig

Bavarian Research Cooperation for Situated,
Individualized, and Personalized Human-Computer Interaction
University of Erlangen-Nürnberg
Haberstraße 2, D-91058 Erlangen
bernd.ludwig@forsip.de

Abstract. Integration of new utterances into context is a central task in any model for rational (human-machine) dialogues in natural language. In this paper, a pragmatics-first approach to specifying the meaning of utterances in terms of plans is presented. These plans are computed during a dialogue on the basis of information about the current situation that is updated continually. New contributions are integrated into a dialogue if they help in establishing a new plan, or if they deliver important information for executing an already established plan.

1   Introduction

Complex computer based systems are getting more and more important in everyday life. Such systems should provide natural language interaction to users as this is the most convenient way to control a complex system. Many users are overwhelmed when they have to learn all the functions a specific device offers. However, it is easy to express individual wishes that the system should process.

1.1   A Pragmatics-First View on Rational Dialogues

Rational dialogues that are based on Grice's maxims of conversation serve as a communicative tool in jointly executing a task in the domain of discourse (called *the application domain*) by following a plan that could solve the task assigned to the participants of the dialogue. Therefore, the interpretation of new contributions and their integration into a dialogue is controlled by global factors (e.g. the assumption that all dialogue participants behave in a cooperative manner and work effectively towards the completion of a joint task) as well as by local factors (e.g. how does the new contribution serve in completing the current shared plan?). Within this framework, the paper focuses on two issues:

- How can we determine whether a new contribution is related to executing the current step in a shared plan?
- What is the influence of the computed relation on the dialogue structure and how does this affect the reaction of the hearer?

S. Biundo, T. Frühwirth, and G. Palm (Eds.): KI 2004, LNAI 3238, pp. 82–96, 2004.

In this respect, we have to distinguish between the *dialogue situation* and the *application situation*: The dialogue situation is modified whenever speech acts are performed, whereas the application situation changes according to the effects of each action being executed.

The main hypothesis of this paper is that modifications of the dialogue situation are triggered by changes of the application situation. As a response to a speech act, dialogue participants perform a series of actions aiming at achieving some goal. If these actions can be executed, the reaction can signal success. At this point, our understanding of the role of shared plans exceeds that of [1]: GROSZ and KRAUS define an action to be *resolved* if it is assumed that an agent is able to execute the action. However, in order to understand coherence relations in complex dialogues, it is important to know whether an action has actually been executed and – if this is the case – what effect it has produced. Consider the following excerpt from a MapTask dialogue (quoted from [2]):

MAP 9
R: ++ and ++ you are not quite
horizontal you are taking a slight
curve up towards um the swamp ++
not obviously going into it

G: well sorry I have not got a swamp
R: you have not got a swamp?
G: no
R: OK
G: start again from the palm beach

Obviously, *G* has failed to find the swamp, which means *G* has failed to perform the action necessary to perform the next one (take a slight curve) in *R*'s previous utterance. Such cases, when the system acting as a dialogue participant notices that a necessary step has not been reached, are not covered sufficiently by current approaches to dialogue understanding, although they occur very often. In communication between humans, an analysis depending on the current dialogue and application situation serves as the basis for continuing a dialogue in such a way that misunderstandings can be clarified. An example from the TRAINS corpus [3] illustrates a typical human reaction:

9.1 M: so we should
9.2 : move the engine
9.3 : at Avon
9.4 : engine E
9.5 : to

10.1 S: engine E1
11.1 M: E1
12.1 S: okay
13.1 M: engine E1
13.2 : to Bath

This excerpt is a subdialogue to clarify a misunderstanding in identifying an object (engine E vs. E1). Finite state approaches cannot foresee all repair states for every combination of an assumed engine and the one actually at the mentioned location. Even worse, eventually the location is wrong and has to be repaired. How to decide that a priori?

This paper elaborates an approach to plan based dialogue understanding that relies on an efficient planning algorithms: We use the Planning Domain Definition Language (PDDL) to model actions. The meaning of an utterance is specified in terms of a satisfiable plan whose execution is monitored. The convergence or divergence between the observed effects and the expected ones determines the content and the function of the future speech acts. We use such information in order to diagnose and clarify misunderstandings as it is the case in human-human-interaction.

1.2 Organisation of the Paper

In section 2 we describe how knowledge is represented in our system. Section 3 sketches how user intentions are recognized by analyzing natural language input. In section 4, we discuss the distinction between global and local factors. Section 5 focuses on how follow-up contributions to the initial one may influence the update of a shared plan, and how this affects the relation between the new contribution and the previous dialogue. In section 6, we show that if the discourse relation of a new contribution is unclear, the dialogue can be continued by focusing on a clarification. We claim in section 7 that decision procedures choose from several options that determine how the dialogue should be continued in such a situation. Finally, related work and conclusions are presented.

1.3 An Example Dialogue

The scenario type we are currently using is an online B2B shop in the internet (see [4]) where one can buy boxes of different types, sizes, colors, and materials. The shop offers various functions to the user: one can search the data base, select articles and move them to the basket, request an offer and negotiate the price, and finally accept or reject the offer. A typical dialogue between a user and system looks as in figure 1. Turn $System_2$ results from the pragmatic information that the product specification given by the user was not completely matched.

$System_1$: Guten Tag und willkommen in unserem Shop! Was kann ich für Sie tun? (Hello and wellcome to our shop! How may I help you?)
$User_1$: Ich würde gerne 100 Boxen in Rot kaufen. (I want to buy 100 red boxes.)
$System_2$ (highlights an item in a list of proposed products): Ich empfehle Ihnen diesen Artikel, denn er kommt Ihren Präferenzen am nächsten. (I recommend this products, as it matches your preferences best.)
$User_2$: Okay.
$System_3$: Hier sehen Sie ihren Warenkorb. Soll ich Ihnen dafür ein Angebot erstellen? (Here is your basket? Shall I present you an offer for it?)

$User_3$: Ich möchte meine alten Aufträge sehen. (I want to see my previous orders.)
$System_4$: Bitte schön. (Here you are.)
$User_4$: Bitte mach mir ein Angebot! (Present me an offer, please!)
$System_5$: Ich kann Ihnen die Waren für 734 Euro 90 anbieten. Der Rabatt beträgt 6%. (May I offer you the basket for 734 Euro 90? The price is 6% off the retail price.)
$User_5$: Das ist mir zu teuer.
$System_6$: Ich kann Ihnen noch um 20 Euro entgegenkommen. (I can give you 20 Euro additional discount.)
$User_7$: Ich nehme das Angebot an. (I accept your offer.)
$System_8$: Sie haben einen guten Kauf getätigt. Vielen Dank. (This is a good deal for you. Thank you.)

Fig. 1. An example dialogue.

This influences the text generator's decision on how to verbalize a response that does not affect the proposed offer negatively. In turn $System_3$, the system initiative is motivated by the fact that the execution of the next step in the plan that satisfies $User_1$ depends on the user's willingness to continue the negiotation. In turn $User_3$, the user does not respond directly to the question. However, the dialogue system realizes that in the current application situation there is no conflict between the goals of $User_3$ and $User_1$. Therefore, the focus of the dialogue is shifted to the new goal. $User_4$'s utterance returns to the previous goal and the focus is shifted back again after the temporary parallel goal has been achieved. $User_5$ is an indirect speech act by which the user starts negotiating the price. The system realizes that the goal expressed by the utterance can be reached if it is possible to modify the offer appropriately. This leads to turn $System_6$. $User_7$ allows the conclusion that the plan has been executed successfully. $System_8$ signals that the plan for $User_1$ has been completed as well.

2 A Domain Model for the Application

Before explaining details of how dialogues like the one in figure 1 are processed, this section gives an overview of how linguistic and application specific knowledge is represented in the system.

In order to be able to refer to functions and objects of the application in natural language, we need a domain model. It is generated semi-automatically from the specification of a Java API. This programming interface to the B2B online shop defines classes and methods that can be accessed, instantiated, and executed from outside the application. They are translated to concept definitions in the Description Logic language $\mathcal{ALC}$ [5] and incorporated in the SUMO (Suggested Upper Merged Ontology – see [6]) as shown in the following example for the class offer:

```
class offer {
       T_NEW_CATALOG has-catalog;
       DISCOUNT has-discount;
       PRICE has-price;
       OfferStatus has-status;

       PRICE offer();
       void offerconfirmation(DISCOUNT has-discount,PRICE has-price); };
```

The fields of the class are translated into role restrictions of the concept which stands for the class itself. The translation is recursive for the classes that serve as data types of the translated fields. The concept for offer is a subconcept of the SUMO concept Requesting in the following concept definition:

```
(define-primitive-concept
  offer (and Requesting
                (all has-catalog T_NEW_CATALOG)
                (all has-discount DISCOUNT)
                (all has-price PRICE)
                (all has-status OfferStatus)))
```

Methods, in turn, are translated into planning operators in the PDDL planning language, as it is shown below:

```
(:action offerconfirmation
  :parameters (?t - T_NEW_CATALOG  ?p - PRICE  ?o - offer)
  :precondition (and (has-catalog ?o ?t) (has-price ?o ?p)
                     (not (has-status ?o confirmed)))
  :effect (has-status ?o confirmed))
```

This method offerconfirmation changes the status of an offer to confirmed if this has not been done already. A domain model of this kind allows for simulation of the effects of a natural language utterance as will be discussed below.

3 Interpretation of Natural Language Utterances

The interface between the shop and the user is implemented by configuring a natural language dialogue system to meet the needs of the class of dialogues that can be conducted with the online shop. Natural language input (either via speech or via keyboard) is parsed by the system described in [7]. The parser's output – a discourse representation structure (DRS) – is interpreted by the dialogue system as a description of the goal the user wants to reach. Guided by the principle of cooperativity, the dialogue system tries to compute a shared plan for that goal. For that purpose, the planner described in [8] is applied to find out whether it is generally possible to find a plan for the user's goal. For the user utterance

> **User:** *I want to buy 100 red boxes.*

the plan in figure 4 is computed. The associated goal is shown in figure 2. It encodes the functional semantics of *buy*. If something is to be bought, an offer for it has to be accepted. This commonsense meaning of *buy* is the illocutionary force of the verb; the most important consequence of this observation is that any user utterance only indicates and describes transactions, but does not perform them. All information in an utterance is considered to be hypothetical; for it has to be verified that boxes can be bought at the shop, that boxes in red are available, and that the required quantity does not exceed the number of currently available boxes.

Furthermore, the commonsense meaning has to be interpreted in terms of the application domain model. This is done firstly by deriving a formal description from the hypotheses indicated by the utterance (see the already mentioned goal in figure 2). Secondly, a plan for that goal has to be found. If this can be achieved, it is in principle possible to get the effects indicated by the user's utterance, which implies that each step of the plan has to be carried out sucessfully.

For planning, an initial situation is needed as a representation of the current state of affairs. In the interactive environment, there are three sources of information that add facts to the initial situation:

$$\Delta: \begin{array}{|l|}
\hline
o\ s\ t\ p\ q\ f\ a \\
\hline
\text{Offer}(o) \\
\text{has-status}(o,s)\ \text{Confirmation}(s) \\
\text{has-catalog}(o,t)\ \text{T-New-Catalog}(t) \\
\text{has-product}(t,p)\ \text{Product}(p) \\
\text{has-quantity}(p,q)\ \text{Quantity}(q)\ \text{value}(q,100)\ \text{Number}(100) \\
\text{has-article}(p,a)\ \text{Article}(a)\ \text{has-feature}(a,f)\ \text{feature}(f) \\
\text{has-FNAME}(f,\texttt{CAA074001})\ \text{fname}(\texttt{CAA074001}) \\
\text{has-FVALUE}(f,\textbf{red})\ \text{fvalue}(\textbf{red}) \\
\hline
\end{array}$$

Fig. 2. DRS for the goal derived from the utterance *I want to buy 100 red boxes*.

```
(define (problem transaction342)
  (:objects u1 - T_NEW_CATALOG t - T_NEW_CATALOG a - article
            ba342 - Basket o - Offer b342 - BMOResult n342 - UM-Need
            p - product q - quantity p342 - price s - Confirmation
            f - feature)
  (:init (has-content n u1) (has-product u1 p)
         (has-quantity p q) (value q 100) (has-article p a)
                                          (has-feature a f)
         (has-FNAME f CAA074001) (has-FVALUE f red)))
```

Fig. 3. Initial situation for the utterance *I want to buy 100 red boxes*.

- The current state can be determined by the actions executed so far.
- The user's utterance contains hypothetical propositions about the state of the shop that have to be consistent with what is known from the record of the previous actions.
- The plan for reaching the indicated goal contains hypothetical objects and assertions about them whose existence or correctness cannot be proven until the plan is (at least partially) executed.

The last point implies that a violation of the closed world assumption normally made by PDDL planners can arise: first, since new objects can be introduced in the course of the negotiation, not all objects exists in the initial situation. Second, as a consequence, missing information cannot be considered wrong (by negation as failure). Therefore, the initial situation for the planning will contain hypothetical objects and assertions to be validated later. The initial situation for the example above in shown in figure 3.

Since the information about the user's intentions is underspecified at the moment when a plan is computed, the dialogue system interleaves the transactions which have to be performed by the online shop (steps 1, 3, 5) with interactive tasks (step 2, 4, 6). When they are performed by the dialogue system itself, system utterances that are expected to achieve the current interactive task are produced (e.g. in step 2: obtaining a selection of articles that will be added to the user's shopping cart in step 3). During the plan execution, the dialogue system verifies whether the current situation allows the next step in the plan. For that purpose, it distinguishes between an interactive and an application-oriented (i.e.

```
1: PRODUCTSEARCH N U1 TB B SVEN
2: REQUEST S SVEN TS1
3: ADDTOBASKET S SVEN TB TS1 BA
4: QUERY-IF R YES SVEN
5: OFFERREQUEST N TS1 O1 SVEN
6: OFFERACCEPTANCE N TS1 O1
```

Fig. 4. Shared plan for the utterance *I want to buy 100 red boxes*. This plan is the situation dependent meaning of the utterance.

```
(:action request
 :parameters (?st - SystemTurn ?n - UM-Selection
              ?u - SIKOWO-DiscretePerson ?tn - T_NEW_CATALOG)
 :precondition (and (about ?st ?n)
                    (has-content ?n ?tn)
                    (evoc-fun ?st doaction))
 :effect (when (evoc-fun ?st doaction)
              (exists (?ut - UserTurn)
                  (and (expr-fun ?ut doaction)
                       (expressed ?ut ?u)
                       (coherent ?ut ?n)))))
```

Fig. 5. Definition of the interactive task REQUEST in PDDL.

a transaction) task, because either the state of the transaction or that of the dialogue has to be consulted for the verification.

4   Discourse and Application Pragmatics

The plan in figure 4 highlights the fact that the dialogue model presented here draws a clear distinction between transactional and interactive tasks. While the first type of tasks aims to an explicit symbolic representation of transactions to be executed by the shop, the second type represents requests to the dialogue system for the interaction with the user during the execution of a shared plan. The transactional tasks are formalized in terms of PDDL plan operators; as a consequence, all applications whose functionality can be expressed in PDDL are suited for integration into the outlined dialogue model. Interactive tasks are represented in PDDL as well and therefore can be integrated into planning. The specification of REQUEST that is used in figure 4 is shown in figure 5. The effects of interactive tasks are taken into account by referring to the information state of the current interaction between user and system. For this purpose, a-modal constraints as (expressed ?ut ?u) and (coherent ?ut ?n) are used to verify that the necessary information is available for planning the next step towards the user goal as in the following excerpt of the preconditions for ADDTOBASKET:

```
:precondition
   (and (coherent ?ut ?n)
        (has-catalog ?n ?ts)
        (expressed ?ut ?u))
```

4.1 Constructing Meaning

The interactive tasks are executed by the dialogue system itself; they can be specified in detail in a proprietary programming language. It allows for mapping of tasks to speech acts that depends on the current dialogue situation (see section 4.2). Interactive tasks determine the way in which the user contributes to the construction or execution of a shared plan. In general, there are three different types of contributions and therefore three classes of interactive tasks:

- *Modification* of information
- *Querying* of information
- *Execution* of actions

In cooperative dialogues, interactive tasks are completed when certain expectations are met – according to the class a task belongs to:

- *Modification*: Can the modification be performed without conflicts with the available knowledge?
- *Querying*: The queried information has to be computed.
- *Execution*: Can a shared plan be found and executed?

Depending on the type of information that forms the content of the interactive task – e.g. the intensional or extensional knowledge a task refers to – the knowledge about plan operators, terminological definitions, linguistic (lexical, grammatical) information, or the knowledge of the current dialogue and application situation is a subject to interactive tasks. In the class of dialogues discussed in this paper, interaction with the user can only be about the current situation. In such an approach to dialogue, natural language utterances fulfill two functions:

- They indicate an interactive task (e.g. by cue phrases and syntactic means as questions or imperatives).
- They indicate transactional tasks or information about the current application situation.

On this basis utterances and dialogues can be analyzed by determining hypotheses for the situation based functions of each new utterance. In order to decide whether an utterance can be incorporated into a dialogue, the preconditions for a hypothesis are to be verified in the dialogue situation for the interactive task and in the application situation for the transactional task. In the example above, *buy 100 red boxes* indicates a transaction, while *I want to* does communicates new information about the speaker's intention. This leads to the DRS in figure 6: In this DRS, intention(i) captures the meaning of the modal verb *want*.

4.2 Acting and Reacting in a Dialogue

As a consequence of the described approach to semantics, plans have to be computed for discourse-pragmatic goals as well as for transactional goals. Possible goals are specific for each class of interactive tasks and defined by the

$$\left[\begin{array}{l} i \\ \hline \text{intention}(i) \\ \text{content}(i, \Delta) \end{array} \right]$$

Fig. 6. Formal meaning of the utterance *I want 100 red boxes*. Δ is defined in figure 2.

expectations listed above. To meet the goal assigned to the example utterance, intention(i) needs to be verified in the current dialogue situation.

For that purpose, a plan that determines the *reaction* to the new contribution has to be computed (see figure 7): for building the plan, operators are applied that encode the global factors mentioned in the introduction. The most important one is cooperativity. To verify whether the new intention is satisfiable, a shared plan is constructed for the user action *buy*. The user can buy something at the online shop, if in the current application situation a plan can be found for the presentation of an offer about the requested products (see figure 4). This means that the dialogue system tries to find a plan (in the application domain) that satisfies the transactional task indicated in the user utterance. The next step in reacting to the user utterance is to execute the plan. Finally, if the execution succeeded, the completion of the reaction is signaled by ACCEPT. ACCEPT is – as REQUEST and QUERY-IF in figure 4 are – a basic dialogue operation that maps interactive tasks to (sequences of) speech acts. Which speech acts are generated in order to verbalize the interactive task depends on the requirements of the current dialogue situation. In human communication, the decomposition of discourse pragmatic goals into speech acts and their verbalization is influenced to a large extent by a number of factors like (see [9, 10]): e.g. topicalization, stylistic variability, relations between dialogue participants, availability and limitations of resources, or ognitive capacity and personality of the dialogue participants. To enable interactive tasks to consider these factors in generation of speech acts, all basic dialogue operations are programmable and in this way can take the current dialogue situation into account.

The implementation of ACCEPT in figure 8 considers limitations of the cognitive capacity of the hearer: by summing up all discourse referents t in contribution, it computes the relevance of the contribution's content and its amount. By relating it to the temporal distance to the last utterance in the dialogue, a "speed of information" is calculated. If it is too high, a speech act is generated only if ACCEPT is important enough.

The example shows that utterances are not directly related to interactive tasks. In order to reach a discourse pragmatic goal, factors not determined by the content of a task have to be taken into account.

```
1: FIND-PLAN BUY P
2: EXECUTE-PLAN P
3: ACCEPT BUY
```

Fig. 7. Discourse plan for the utterance *I want to buy 100 red boxes*.

```
proc ACCEPT(task contrib);
drs utterance = content(contrib); float rel = 0.0, vol = 0.0, speed, dist;
begin
    forall referent t in utterance do
        vol += consumption(utterance,t), rel += priority(utterance,t);

    dist := time() - last_time; last_time := curr_time;
    speed := vol/dist; old_speed := speed
    if speed < 0.25 then utter contrib;
    else if rel > 4.0 then utter contrib;
end;
```

Fig. 8. Implementation of the dialogue operation `ACCEPT`.

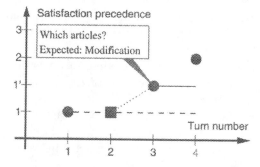

Fig. 9. Chart of discourse relations after new turn has been shown irrelevant to the current focus.

5 Building up the Discourse Structure

The preceeding section explained that discourse structures are built during the execution of discourse pragmatic plans. The discourse structure is a graph whose edges relate interactive tasks (the nodes of the graph). An edge between two nodes determines in which way the later interactive task contributes to the completion of the earlier one as in [11]. From the viewpoint of the discourse model presented in this paper, the relation of *satisfaction-precedence* holds between two tasks if they are subsequent steps in a plan (e.g. QUERY-IF (step 4) in figure 4 is *satisfaction-preceded* by REQUEST (step 2): after the online shop finds articles in its data base and presents them to the user (step 1), it requests the user to select some of them for the shopping cart (step 2). The shop cannot ask the user if he wants an offer (step 4) until step 2 and 3 are completed. The relation of *dominance* holds between two tasks if the dominated task contributes to the completion of the dominating one. For example, all user responses are dominated by interactive tasks initiated by the system. Figure 9 shows the discourse structure after step 2. Satisfaction-precedence is visualized by going up the y axis, while dominance holds between tasks if they appear along a horizontal line.

The goal of an interactive task is achieved if it dominates another interactive task. In this case, its expectation is met. For the case when the expectations of an interactive task are not met, consider the continuation of the dialogue in section 2:

User: *I want to buy 100 red boxes.*
System: You may now choose from the articles in the presented selection. Which of them would you like?
User: *I need containers.*

In this example, even the reaction of the dialogue system (step 2) violates the expectation assigned to the interactive task (step 1) that has been initiated by the user. In order to react appropriately, the user has to analyze the system's utterance and understand that it indicates an admissible step in a plan for the request. Analogously, the system has to analyze user utterances whether they constitute expected reactions that allow the next step in the shared plan to be executed.

On the assumption that boxes and containers are two different types of articles and therefore with the utterance *"I need containers."* the user does not choose any article from the proposed selection, the goal for the second user utterance is incompatible with the shared plan for the first utterance. Neither satisfaction-precedence nor dominance holds between the system's and the user's second utterance. What else discourse relation holds between them?

6   Logical and Discourse Relations

For an answer to the above question, it is useful to analyze relations that eventually hold between the transactional tasks assigned to the both utterances. The implementation of the online shop may allow other relations than satisfaction-precedence that implies the first task to be completed before the second one can start. If the shop is capable to present multiple windows for selections at the same time, it can handle two transactions concurrently.

Concurrent execution of plans can be modeled with the help of the planner presented in section 2. The planner computes a partial order of the actions to be executed for a goal: if in a step there is more than one action specified, all actions in this step may be executed in parallel. Consequently, if one wants to test whether two interactive tasks are related by *in-parallel*, one has to compute a plan for the conjunction of the associated transactional tasks. If there is a plan, *in-parallel* eventually holds (see section 7).

If no plan for execution in parallel can be found, the second utterance (*"I need containers."*) *blocks* the execution of the current shared plan (see figure 4). In this case, as with *in-parallel* neither *satisfaction-precedence* nor *dominance* correctly express the relationship between interactive tasks. As [12] observes, additional discourse relations are necessary to adequately describe the discourse structure if a conflict occurs when an utterance is integrated into the discourse structure.

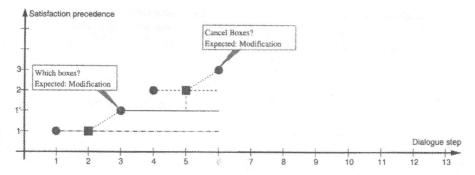

Fig. 10. Discourse structure resulting from a *block* relation between the last utterances.

In contrast to [12], this approach distinguishes between discourse relations – which statically describe a state of affairs – and discourse pragmatic plans – which devise a way to continue a dialogue: if – during the analysis of the second user utterance (*"I need containers."*) – it turns out that the new contribution blocks the completion of the current shared plan, some way out of this conflict must be found. In figure 10, the discourse structure is shown for the following continuation of the dialogue:

System: You cannot browse boxes and containers at the same time.
System: Do you want to stop selecting boxes?

In our analysis the first utterance is dominated by the user request as it completes the associated interactive task (by indicating failure). The second utterance satisfaction precedes everything else, as without an answer, the system cannot decide how to complete the pending transactions. In Asher's terms a *correction* relation would hold between dialogue step 4 and 5, while in our view CORRECTION is the interactive task that was performed and resulted in the discourse structure of figure 10. CORRECTION can be performed because a discourse pragmatic plan was found that allowed the dialogue system to ask the user for information *in parallel* to the pending query to choose items from the selection for the basket.

In substance, Asher's and our analysis do not differ; however, the distinction between relations and tasks is better suited for an efficient implementation of a dialogue model that allows for analysis *and* generation of dialogue turns.

The user can react to the system's attempt to resolve the blocking of the shared plan by

User: Yes.

In this case, the dialogue system can complete its plan and resolve the blocking by canceling the blocked shared plan. Now, a plan for satisfying the transactional task associated with dialogue step 4 can be found and executed.

$$V(\text{in-parallel}|H, A) = V(\text{expr}(H) \neq \text{evoc}(A)|H, A) \cdot \quad \textit{Does task type match expectations?}$$
$$V(\text{parallel}(A, H)|H, A) \cdot \quad \textit{Can transactions run in parallel?}$$
$$V(\text{anchor}(A, H)|H, A) \quad \textit{Is A a good anchor for H?}$$
$$V(\text{Blocking}|H, A) = V(\text{expr}(H) \neq \text{evoc}(A)|H, A) \cdot$$
$$V(\text{blocked}(A, H)|H, A) \cdot$$
$$V(\text{anchor}(A, H)|H, A)$$

Fig. 11. Valuation of discourse relations.

7 Deciding How to React

Depending on certain constraints in the application situation, when expectations of interactive tasks are not met, the logical relation between the associated transactional tasks may lead to an ambiguous discourse relation between a new contribution and the previous dialogue.

In this case, a decision has to be made which of the possible interpretations to choose. This decision is based on a valuation of each option in the current situation. Figure 11 shows how the options under consideration (*in-parallel* and *blocking*) are scored. Three factors are taken into account: First, the type of the interactive task expr(H) should not meet the expectation evoc(A) of the task A whose shared plan is executed currently. Second, the transactional tasks associated with A and H can be executable concurrently, and, third, A should be a good anchor for H (ideally, A is the current focus). On the basis of this valuation, the following decision rule is applied:

$$\text{relation}(H, A) = v \leftrightarrow v = \text{argmax}_x V(x|H, A)$$
$$x \in \{\text{in-parallel}, \text{Blocking}\}$$

This rule selects the hypothesis with the best valuation. If there is no unique v, then a CLARIFICATION is started which generates a query to the user to choose an alternative:

System: Do you want to browse boxes and containers as well?

This example shows that blocking in a discourse pragmatic plan is handled as well as the blocking of a transactional task. The dialogue model allows user and system to start negotiating propositions about dialogue situation that is viewed as a cause for a discourse pragmatic plan to be blocked.

8 Related Work and Conclusions

Theoretical foundations for our work are the results in discourse analysis presented in [13] on the influence of plans on discourse structure. [14, 15] show that the interactive nature of dialogues makes it necessary to coordinate plans of all participants involved in the dialogue. However, the conversational principles a participant is obliged to and the knowledge he has about the application domain as well as about the current situation is not accessible to the discourse pragmatic reasoning of other dialogue participants. It can only be reconstructed partially from utterances. In order to enable collaboration, the reconstructed information must be aligned with the information in knowledge base of the system. The alignment is achieved by continuously comparing expectations in plans with observations derived from utterances and the execution of actions. When a mismatch is found, plans for interactive tasks are constructed to obtain information that is sufficient to decide whether a realignment is possible or not. From this abstract point of view, it does not make difference whether a task is related to application or discourse pragmatics. This advantage follows from the distinction between application and dialogue domain and the observation that the same planning and plan execution approach can be applied to both domains.

The described approach is implemented in a dialogue system for spoken language that works in real-time. The system was presented to the public during SYSTEMS in October 2003. The implementation shows the tractability of the outlined approach; the prototype system performs in real-time. For the future, recovery from failed plans has to be studied in more detail. As corpus analyses show, repair strategies are influenced by application specific knowledge. We will explore how such strategies can be specified for various dialogue applications.

[16] presents a detailed analysis of the dialogue engine used in the TRINDI and TALK projects. LARSSON's notion of *accommodation* is similar to what was called alignment above. However, recovery from critical situations is not discussed. Dialogue and application domain remain undistinguished.

[17] focuses on the issue of system architecture; a detailed theoretical model for dialogues is not in the scope of Allen's paper.

A logic-based approach to dialogue understanding is presented in [18]. Our approach differs from BOS' and OKA's one by separating between dialog and application situation instead of relying on a discourse memory only. Beyond that, by incorporating a planner as an reasoning mechanism additional to model building, we can handle different reasoning problems with the help of appropriate tools. Finally, we discuss the selection among and execution of interactive configurable strategies when expectations of dialogue participants are violated.

Acknowledgements

H. Niemann, G. Görz, M. Klarner, Y. Lierler, P. Reiß, and I. Thabet provided valuable support for the presented research. It has been done within the Bavarian Research Cooperation for Situated, Individualized and Personalized Human-Computer Interaction which is funded by the Bavarian State Ministry for Science, Research and Art.

References

1. Grosz, B.J., Hunsberger, L., Kraus, S.: Planning and acting together. AI Magazine **20** (1999) 23–34
2. Carletta, J.: Risk-Taking and Recovery in Task-Oriented Dialogue. PhD thesis, University of Edinburgh (1992)

3. Heeman, P.A., Allen, J.: The trains 93 dialogues. Technical report, Computer Science Dept., University of Rochester (1995) Trains Technical Note 94-2.
4. Fischer, S., Kießling, W., Holland, S., Fleder, M.: The cosima prototype for multi-objective bargaining. In: Proceedings of the 1st International Joint Conference on Autonomous Agents and Multiagent Systems, Bologna, Italy (2002) 1364–1371
5. Baader, F., Nutt, W.: Basic description logics. In Baader, F., Calvanese, D., McGuinness, D.L., Nardi, D., Patel-Schneider, P.F., eds.: The Description Logic Handbook – Theory, Implementation, and Applications. Cambridge University Press (2003) 41–95
6. Pease, A., Niles, I.: Ieee standard upper ontology: A progress report. Knowledge Engineering Review **17** (2002) 65–70
7. Bücher, K., Knorr, M., Ludwig, B.: Anything to clarify? report your parsing ambiguities! In: Proceedings of the 15th European Conference on Artifical Intelligence. (2002) 465–469
8. Hoffmann, J., Nebel, B.: The ff planning system: Fast plan generation through heuristic search. Journal of Artificial Intelligence Research **14** (2001) 253–302
9. Carolis, B.D., Pelachaud, C., Poggi, I.: Verbal and non verbal discourse planning (2000)
10. Cassell, J., Stone, M., Yan, H.: Coordination and context-dependence in the generation of embodied conversation (2000)
11. Grosz, B.J., Sidner, C.L.: Attention, intentions, and the structure of discourse. Computational Linguistics **12** (1986) 175–204
12. Asher, N., Gillies, A.: Common ground, corrections and coordination. Argumentation **17** (2003) 481–512
13. Chu-Carroll, J., Carberry, S.: Conflict detection and resolution in collaborative planning. In: Intelligent Agents: Agent Theories, Architectures, and Languages. Volume 2 of Lecture Notes in Artificial Intelligence. Springer Verlag (1996) 111–126
14. Cohen, P.R., Levesque, H.J.: Communicative actions for artificial agents. In: Proceedings of the First International Conference on Multi-Agent Systems, San Francisco, CA (1995) 65–72
15. Allwood, J.: An activity based approach to pragmatics. In Bunt, H.C., Black, B., eds.: Abduction, Belief, and Context in Dialogue. Studies in Computational Pragmatics. John Benjamins, Amsterdam (2000)
16. Larsson, S.: Issue-based Dialogue Management. PhD thesis, Department of Linguistics, Göteborg University, Göteborg, Sweden (2002)
17. Allen, J.F., Byron, D., Dzikovska, M., Ferguson, G., Galescu, L., Stent, A.: Towards conversational human-computer interaction. AI Magazine (2001)
18. Bos, J., Oka, T.: An inference-based approach to dialogue system design. In: Proceedings of the 19th International Conference on Computational Linguistics. (2002) 113–119

Hybrid Natural Language Generation in a Spoken Language Dialog System

Martin Klarner[1] and Bernd Ludwig[2]

[1] University Erlangen-Nuremberg, Chair for Computer Science 8
Haberstaße 2, D-91058 Erlangen, Germany
[2] University Erlangen-Nuremberg, Chair for Computer Science 8
Am Weichselgarten 9, D-91058 Erlangen, Germany

Abstract. Natural Language Generation (NLG) systems have almost reached the state of "market-readiness" now, mostly because hybrid systems of different types have emerged as a de-facto standard. But still relatively few dialog systems make use of NLG techniques.
In this paper, we discuss the output part of our spoken language dialog system by presenting an example scenario including dialog management, NLG, and speech synthesis. Our approach to hybrid NLG couples shallow and deep processing with respect to the linguistic and pragmatic system resources and also on the architectural level and thus increases processing efficiency (compared to pure deep generation) as well as generative power (compared to pure shallow generation). Our system has been applied to three different domains, namely home A/V management, model train controlling, and B2B e-procurement.

Keywords: Hybrid Natural Language Generation, Spoken Language Dialog System, Bottom-up Generation

1   Introduction

There are different ways of realizing the system output part of a human-computer interface, including mail-merge, human authoring and graphics (cf. [1]). Among these, we think NLG, and, more specifically, hybrid NLG is the most promising approach for dialog systems, because it can provide a unique combination of processing efficiency and linguistic coverage.

In this paper, we discuss our variant of hybrid NLG which is embedded in our spoken language dialog system. The paper is organized as follows: In sect. 2, we will introduce our notion of hybrid NLG which is somewhat different from current approaches. Sect. 3 deals with the system core of HYPERBUG, our hybrid NLG system which couples and interleaves shallow and deep processing with respect to system resources and architecture to increase processing efficiency as well as generative power. The part of dialog management which is relevant for system output specification is described in sect. 4. In sect. 5, we discuss a relatively simple, but nevertheless illustrative example to demonstrate how system output is accomplished in our system; we will also describe the system components involved in more detail there. Finally, we address relevant work in the field of hybrid approaches for NLG and future work for our NLG system in sect. 6.

S. Biundo, T. Frühwirth, and G. Palm (Eds.): KI 2004, LNAI 3238, pp. 97–111, 2004.

2   Hybrid NLG Systems

Several notions of hybridism in the context of NLG systems exist, including stochastic approaches [2], usage of machine learning (ML), as in [3] and lately in [4], and generation using XSLT[5]. We will use a rather traditional notion of hybridism instead: Our definition concentrates on a mixing strategy for the two classical approaches, shallow and deep generation. [6] describes two types of such hybrid NLG systems: Type I consists of shallow generation with deep elements, type II of deep generation with shallow elements. We want a third type to be added to this typology: This type III uses separate shallow and deep processing branches and combines the results appropriately, in analogy to the approach taken in VERBMOBIL [7] for the language analysis part of the system. This analogy is certainly not complete: In VERBMOBIL, several different analysis branches process the input simultaneously. *After that*, a module called Integrated Processing combines the results to obtain a single semantic representation, the VERBMOBIL Interface Term (VIT), for further processing. In our system, as we will describe further in sect. 3, the decision between the different generation branches is made *before* actual processing is done.

However, if you model analysis and generation as inverse operations[1], you can motivate the different positions of the decision module in the VERBMOBIL analysis part and our generation system by saying that we just *mirror* the VERBMOBIL architecture: What comes last in analysis (combining several syntactic and semantic representations into one single structure) must come first in generation (expanding one single semantic structure into several output specifications for the different processing branches). But there is, of course, a different, more obvious, and more practical argument for putting the decision module in front of the generation process: We want to save processing time by feeding the same input structure into different processing branches which are essentially capable of producing the same results.

On a theoretical level, shallow and deep processing are not far apart: Basically a template system allowing recursive templates has the same expressive power as a context-free grammar. On the other hand, if you restrict a grammar to non-recursive rules, you can compile grammar and lexicon into a single template system. But in practice, both these extreme approaches are normally not taken: There are situations when fast and simple system answers are needed, and there are also situations which require more elaborated answers. In a standard hybrid approach, the *discourse and application domains* determine which mixture between shallow or deep generation techniques is most appropriate. But it would be more desirable to allow this mixing strategy to be tailored to the specific *dialog situation* at hand.

Hence, our approach to NLG is to build a system that involves all three types of hybridism and decides at runtime, given a specific dialog situation, which one to choose for the current utterance. After the utterance has been generated,

---

[1] Which is at least true on a sufficiently abstract level, as the input of language analysis is the output of language generation and vice versa.

a feedback loop tries to determine whether the chosen processing branch has produced the desired result and updates the decision strategy accordingly. We will provide a more detailed description of our NLG system in the following section.

3   NLG System Core

In our generation system HYPERBUG, the three types of hybrid NLG approaches introduced in sect. 2 are all encompassed: The system utilizes canned text, templates, and deep NLG not only in concurring processing branches, but combines shallow processing with deep elements, deep processing with shallow elements, and concurring shallow and deep processing in one single system. The system core is displayed in fig. 1.

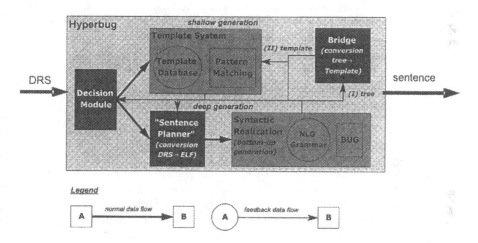

Fig. 1. System Core.

When an utterance has to be generated, the dialog manager sends a discourse representation structure (DRS) [8], a semantic representation of the utterance content, to the **Decision Module** which determines whether shallow or deep generation is more appropriate to produce the desired output. The decision module maintains an index table of available templates and canned text sentences. Deep generation is used only if canned text and shallow generation are unavailable, i. e. if no pointer to an appropriate template in the index table is found. This way, the more complex pattern matching algorithm used by the shallow generation branch is not needed in the decision module: We want to avoid using any computational resources needed only for deep *or* shallow generation here. The decision is rather based on values for certain XPath variables, resulting in a shallow but still sufficient analysis. The XPaths are potentially domain-specific and may have to be replaced when a domain change is envisaged, but only if the interface specifications are modified[2]. Concurring shallow and deep process-

---

[2] Such modifications have already proved necessary in the transition between two of our domains, cf. sect. 6.

ing branches combined with the decision module result in our system becoming hybrid type III in our classification.

If shallow generation is selected, a **Template System** with an advanced pattern matching algorithm which uses a database with multipart templates[3] further processes the input. The template database entries are modular (by inclusion of other entries), they contain subparts and repeatable sections (for enumerations), syntactic features like category and agreements (for lexicon and morphology access)[4], and prosodic markers and pointers to wave files (for speech synthesis). By this enriched template system our NLG approach becomes type I in our classification in sect. 1.

If the decision module opts for deep generation, a **Sentence Planner** converts the input DRS into an extended logical form (ELF). In addition to to a conventional LF the ELF may contain syntactic features like number, tense, mode, and subordination clause type. Surface forms like proper nouns are also allowed; hence the deep generation module is of hybrid type II. The ELF is processed by the deep syntactic realization module: As the acronym HYPERBUG[5] suggests, we have implemented an extended version of the Bottom-up Generation algorithm presented in [9] as our deep generation component. This component uses a unification grammar and re-uses our system lexicon and morphology component which were initially developed for parsing. During the generation process the surface structure is produced and, at the same time, syntactic information is gathered by the unification algorithm and stored in an extended derivation tree. Its leaves contain the surface structures of the words which make up the generated sentence, their syntactic categories, and optionally subtype and agreement features.

After deep generation is complete, a module called **Bridge** generates a new template out of the derivation tree and feeds it back to the shallow generation branch for further use in subsequent dialogs. The decision module is also requested to update its index table of available templates; thus, the deep processing branch is not needed for generating utterances of the same type any longer. This way, the workload on deep generation is consistently reduced at runtime.

With any of the two processing branches, HYPERBUG produces a natural language sentence specification which is sent to the speech synthesis agent which converts it into a wave file and utters it to the user.

4   Dialog Management and System Output Specification

Our NLG system is not implemented as a stand-alone software module, but integrated into a generic multi-agent spoken language dialog system which contains

---

[3] Sect. 5 will give an example.

[4] Note that lexicon and morphology component are linguistic resources not normally used in templates, but rather reserved for deep generation.

[5] It stands for **Hybrid Pragmatically Embedded Realization** using **Bottom-Up Generation**.

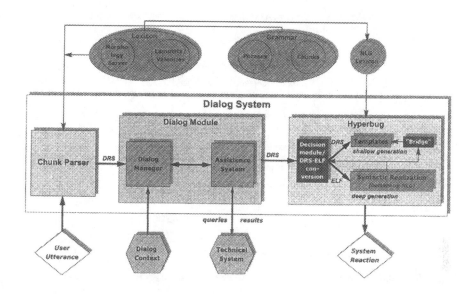

Fig. 2. Distributed System Architecture.

agents for speech analysis, parsing and semantic construction, dialog management, speech output, and for the (domain-specific) technical system which encapsulates application information and control. This technical system can range from a simple database querying interface in a slot-filling domain to a complex planner and problem solver in a more sophisticated domain such as electronic device management.

Fig. 2 sort of zooms out of fig. 1 and shows the distributed architecture of the dialog system in which the generation module is integrated. In this system, content for utterances can be determined in two places: On the one hand, pragmatic feedback to user requests is generated within the **Technical system**; it is responsible for content generation in cases when system initiative is required as well. On the other hand, the **Dialog Manager** (DM) itself can generate content for utterances if the current dialog situation requires it to do so (e. g. for the clarification of syntactic ambiguities in a previous user utterance).

The DM is responsible for the integration of user and system utterances into the discourse context. From the NLG perspective, it also provides *content determination* (either on its own or with the help of the technical system, as stated above): It provides the generation module with a semantic specification for an utterance to be generated which, however, lacks any form of linguistic knowledge: The DM is *amodal*, i. e. the language output part of the system is just another application for the DM, similar to the technical system. In our dialog system, the output specification is written in a DRS and encoded in XML[6].

---

[6] Technically, the XML structure is the content part of a message in the agent communication language KQML, but this is not in our focus here.

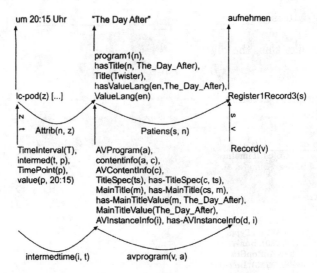

Fig. 3. Translation from the application to natural language via the semantic level.

The two-stage translation process from the application domain to natural language in our dialog system is shown in fig. 3: The application domain concepts on the level of the technical system are shown in the bottom of the figure; they are mapped to linguistic concepts on the semantic level (depicted in the middle of the figure) by the dialog manager (DM), and these in turn are verbalized by the NLG module, i. e. translated to surface strings (shown on top of fig. 3). The second stage of this translation process will be covered by our example in the next section.

The DM also makes an important decision in terms of discourse pragmatics, namely which speech act is most appropriate for the integration of the utterance to be generated into the current dialog context[7]. For planning and realizing the utterance in detail, this information is passed to the generation module as well, because it has to decide how the speech act and the content of the utterance can be verbalized best.

5   Example Output Scenario

In this section, we will give an overview of the output part of our dialog system by using an example in a home A/V management domain. This example itself is simple but nevertheless points to some interesting linguistic and implementation problems. In our example scenario, the user has just requested a VCR recording of the program "The Day After" tonight (on July 3rd, 2004) at 08:15 PM, and the system wants to inform the user that the request has been processed successfully (i. e. that the VCR has been programmed accordingly).

---

[7] This decision procedure is described in [10] and cannot be further discussed here.

5.1   Dialog Manager

In a situation like this, the dialog manager (DM) receives a message from the technical system; its content is shown in the DRS in fig. 4[8]. The concepts contained in the DRS in fig. 4 are defined in the domain model whose organization is described in more detail in [11].

$$
\begin{array}{|l|}
\hline
a\ t\ s\ p\ c\ ts\ m\ at\ as \\
\hline
\text{ApplicationStatusInfo}(a),\ \text{TimeInterval}(t),\ \text{has-TimeInterval}(a,t), \\
\text{StartTime}(s),\ \text{has-StartTime}(a,s), \\
\text{StartTimeValue(2004-07-03 20:15:00)},\ \textbf{has-StartTimeValue(s, 2004-07-03 20:15:00)}, \\
\text{AVProgram}(p),\ \textbf{has-AVProgram(a, p)},\ \text{AVContentInfo}(c),\ \text{TitleSpec}(ts),\ \text{has-TitleSpec}(c,ts), \\
\text{MainTitle}(m),\ \text{has-MainTitle}(ts,m), \\
\text{MainTitleValue(The Day After)},\ \textbf{has-MainTitleValue(ts, The Day After)}, \\
\text{ValueLang(en)},\ \textbf{has-ValueLang(ts, en)}, \\
\text{ActionType}(at),\ \text{has-ActionType}(a,at), \\
\text{ActionTypeValue(RECORD)},\ \textbf{has-ActionTypeValue(at, RECORD)}, \\
\text{ActionStatus}(as),\ \text{has-ActionStatus}(a,as), \\
\text{ActionStatusValue(WAITING)},\ \textbf{has-ActionStatusValue(a, WAITING)} \\
\hline
\end{array}
$$

Fig. 4. DRS representation of the system response to a user request.

In addition to the DRS, the input structure contains the information that the message is a response to a request and that a positive reaction to the request has taken place (the request is satisfied). The effects of the reaction are described in the content of the message. From this information, the DM concludes that it can update the dialog situation: This implies that the pending user request needs a response about the successful outcome of the related system activities and that the information in the system message must be communicated to the user. According to the current state of the interaction between user and system, the DM decides how both update requirements can be satisfied. For an utterance that serves as a correct and useful response a decision has to be made about the speech act and the content for a new utterance. In our example, all information contained in the system message is relevant. The DM encapsulates it in a `message_inform` speech act that is used for communicating information without expecting a reaction and therefore meets the needs in the current dialog situation.

Therefore, the DM requests the NLG system to produce an output with the DRS semantics given above (see fig. 4) which will result in the generation of the German sentence "Ich werde heute Abend um 20:15 Uhr die Sendung 'The Day After' aufnehmen." ("I'm going to record the program 'The Day After' tonight at 08:15 PM.")[9]. To this end, the DRS in fig. 4 is transformed by the DM into the XML structure displayed in fig. 5, which serves as input for our generation system.

---

[8] The relevant parts for processing the example are marked **bold** in fig. 4.

[9] From the linguistic point of view, the example sentence is simple enough, but still contains two interesting features: An analytical tense form (future tense) and a proper noun as an apposition to the direct object noun phrase.

```
<SystemDialogAct status="ok" speechact="message_inform" ID="1701">
<Information><ApplicationStatusInfo><TimeInterval>
  <StartTime><StartTimeValue>2004-07-03 20:15:00</StartTimeValue></StartTime>
</TimeInterval>
<AVProgram><AVContentInfo><TitleSpec><MainTitle>
  <MainTitleValue>The Day After</MainTitleValue><ValueLang>en</ValueLang>
</MainTitle></TitleSpec></AVContentInfo></AVProgram>
<ActionType><ActionTypeValue>RECORD</ActionTypeValue></ActionType>
  <ActionStatus><ActionStatusValue>WAITING</ActionStatusValue></ActionStatus>
</ApplicationStatusInfo></Information></SystemDialogAct>
```

Fig. 5. XML input structure for the system response.

5.2 Preprocessing: The Decision Module

As a first step in our NLG component, the XML input is analyzed and information relevant to determine the appropriate generation branch is extracted. This is done using XPath expressions, like the following determining the action type of the current sentence:

`/Information/ApplicationStatusInfo/ActionType/ActionTypeValue/text()`

In our example, the XML input indicates that the desired action is of type RECORD with status WATTING. If we have not yet generated a sentence of this type before in our current dialog, the decision module cannot find an appropriate entry in its index table of templates and must pass the task of generating the sentence to the deep generation branch.

5.3 Deep Generation

The Sentence Planner converts the DRS contained in the input XML structure in fig. 5 into an ELF which looks like follows:

`(TONIGHT (AT 20:15:00 (FUT (RECORD SYSTEM (T_D_A (DEF AVPROGRAM))))))`

To accomplish this, the sentence planner completes the analysis performed by the decision module and extracts the relevant XPaths needed for conversion. These paths are stored for further use in the "Bridge" template generation component. The relative date specification TONIGHT can be derived from the absolute date given in the XML input structure, whereas the fact that "The Day After" is an AVPROGRAM is already contained in the encompassing bracket structure for the program. The future tense in the sentence is inferred from the ActionStatusValue (WAITING) in the XML structure.

The core of the bottom-up generation algorithm in Java which is used by BUG for deep generation is depicted in fig. 6. The algorithm takes an input structure, usually a node with the main category and an LF of the whole sentence to be generated, and *predicts a word* out of the lexicon from it, a usually smaller node which shares its LF (i. e. the LFs of the two nodes must be unifyable). While this is a top-down step, the following *connection* works bottom-up: It determines if the small and the big node are unifyable which means that the algorithm is finished. Normally, this requires *predicting a rule* which is (directly or

```
Node BUG(Node n) { return connect(predictWord(n), n); }
Node connect(Node small, Node big) {
  if (small == big) return small;
  else return generateDaughters(predictRule(small), big);
}
Node generateDaughters(Rule r, Node big) {
  foreach daughter in r { daughter = BUG(daughter); }
    return connect(getMother(r), big);
}
Node predictWord(Node n) { ... }    // searches terminal rule with LF of n
Node predictRule(Node n) { ... }    // searches rule with LF and category of n in its head
Node getMother(Rule r) { }          // returns the left side of r
```

Fig. 6. Core parts of the BUG algorithm in Java.

indirectly) linked to the big node in the grammar, i. e. which has the small node as its semantic head. If this rule has other daughters, they must be generated recursively using the predict/connect method just described. If the predicted rule cannot be connected to the initial node yet does (which means that there is no direct link between the two nodes in question), the new node is used for rule prediction, until the connection eventually succeeds.

After processing the given ELF input in this way, BUG produces the (slightly shortened) derivation tree depicted in fig. 7. Its leaves contain not only the words of the generated sentence, but also their syntactic categories, the subtype (in the case of the auxiliary verb), and agreement features with their values (for flectional categories like nouns and verbs). This information is used to generate a template in the "bridge" module, which is described in the next section.

```
[MAIN,
  [NP, [PRON, "ich", [gender MASC, case NOM, number SG, person 1]]],
  [VO, "werde", AUX, [number SG, person 1, type FIN]],
  [S,
    [VP,
      [ADV, "heute Abend"],
      [VP,
        [PP, [PREP, "um"],
             [NP, [EN, "20:15 Uhr", [gender FEM, case ACC, number SG]]]],
        [VP, [NP, [NP, [DET, "die"],
                       [N1, [N, "Sendung", [gender FEM, case ACC, number SG]]]],
                  [EN, "'The Day After'", [gender MASC, case ACC, number SG]]],
             [V1, [V1, [V, [VO, "aufnehmen", [type INFIN]]], [V, VGAP]]]]]],
  [INTPKT, "."]]
```

Fig. 7. Derivation tree for our example.

5.4   Post-processing: The "Bridge"

Combining deep and shallow processing in HYPERBUG is completed by the "Bridge" between deep and shallow generation. This module uses the deep generation output to generate a template which is then passed on to the shallow generation branch where it is stored and can be used later for generating similar sentences.

The resulting generated template (shown in fig. 8) contains tokens with XPaths and syntactic features (category and agreements), several constant and

```
DialogAct: message_inform
Status:    ok
Token #1:  ".//TimeInterval/StartTime/StartTimeValue/text()"
Token #2:  ".//AvContentinfo/TitleSpec/MainTitle/MainTitleValue/text()"#N.case_ACC_number_SG
Token #3:  ".//ActionType/ActionTypeValue/text()"
Template #1:
  TempStr: "Ich werde (um %1 die Sendung %2) %3."
  TempPart #1: "Ich werde (um"
  TempPart #2: "%1"              // reference to token #1 (StartTimeValue)
  TempPart #3: "die Sendung %2)" // reference to token #2 (MainTitleValue)
  TempPart #4: "%3."             // reference to token #3 (ActionTypeValue)
```

Fig. 8. Template for our example.

variable parts[10], and two interesting generalization features: First, the brackets
() indicate a potential enumeration (in our example, this is useful if more than
one program will be processed). And second, the main verb RECORD has been
generalized to enable expressing other action types (like SHOW or PLAY) as well.
The adverbial phrase "heute Abend" is omitted because of lacking generalization potential; this demonstrates the advantage of deep generation over shallow
generation in terms of linguistic expressivity in a nutshell.

Our template generation algorithm works as follows:

1. At first, the dialog act and status for the template entry are taken from the
   initial XML input structure.
2. The generated surface structure of BUG which is canned text without any
   generalization is used as an initial template string.
3. Then, the derivation tree produced by BUG is analyzed.
   (a) Candidates for generalization are determined by matching the syntactic
       categories in the leafs of the derivation tree against a stored list of con-
       tent word categories (such as nouns, especially proper nouns, date/time
       specifications, and verbs). Function words are generally considered as
       candidates for constant positions in the template string.
   (b) If no candidates for generalization are found, a heuristic is applied to
       determine whether the sentence is important enough to be stored in the
       canned text table of the decision module[11]. If so, this is done, and the
       algorithm is finished.
   (c) Aggregation marks are inserted in the template string. These are deter-
       mined by scanning the derivation tree for phrases suitable for enumera-
       tion (such as noun phrases, adjective phrases, and prepositional phrases,
       especially with date/time specifications).
4. The XPath entries leading to the content words in the initial XML input
   structure which were stored by the "sentence planner" are retrieved and
   combined to generate the appropriate token entries for the variables in the
   template string.
5. The categories and agreement features (taken from the leafs in the derivation
   tree) are appended to the token lines in the template entry.

---

[10] This distinction between constant and variable parts is important for the speech
synthesis agent, see below.
[11] This heuristic is based on the dialog act and the main action type.

6. Finally, the template string is split into constant and variable parts for speech synthesis. This is particularly tricky for enumerations, which are currently treated as variable parts altogether and thus always completely synthesized.

5.5 Shallow Generation

After inserting the generated template in the database and updating the index table, the next time a sentence comparable to our example must be generated, the decision module will be able to find an appropriate entry for it. Therefore the shallow generation branch will be selected this time. As a matching template, the one depicted in fig. 8 will be found and instantiated, producing the sentence mentioned above.

But our templates provide significantly more flexibility than the example suggests. Fig. 9 shows the (somewhat abridged, for clarification purposes) specification of a template entry. We will now give a short overview of our template entry specification language and how it is interpreted by our template replacing and instantiating algorithm.

If more than one template is applicable, the one with the highest Priority is selected; if several templates with the same priority setting (or with no priority setting at all) are available, one is selected at random. This way, setting of the priority does not prevent output variability. The Status line further specifies the DialogueAct by revealing its success state. A Hint gives information about lexical choice and referring expressions: An item can be referenced by name, category, cardinality, and other (domain-specific) ways, such as starting time. More than one Template string can be specified; if so, the first one which can be fully instantiated is used, i.e. where all references to tokens and includes can be resolved. In a <TEMPLATE> string, a %n/m indicates that the mth matching instance of the nth token is replaced (the so-called *single mode*), whereas a single %n is replaced by the enumeration of all matches of the mth token (the so-called *aggregate mode*). In this mode, the type of enumeration (conjunction and disjunction) is triggered by surrounding <AND> and <OR> tags in the XML input structure. Each $n in a template string is replaced by the number of matches for the nth token, and every §n is replaced by the template string of the template marked by its Label in the nth Include line. If this mechanism is used recursively, the template language becomes as expressive as a context-free grammar, but we restrict it to a macro-expansion technique, i. e. we never use the same template for inclusion, not even indirectly.

5.6 Speech Synthesis

Finally, the generated sentence is sent to the speech synthesis agent which is basically a wrapper agent around the open-source synthesizer MBROLA [12]. The agent checks for each constant part of the sentence whether it has been synthesized before. If so, it uses pointers to previously stored wave files; if not, the newly synthesized constant parts are stored for further use. This is similar to the approach used in the core generation system; it considerably reduces the

```
[Label:       <LABEL>]
[Include:     <INCLUDE>]
[Priority:    <INT>]                          (increasing priority; default: 0)
DialogueAct: message_greeting|message_closing|message_inform|...
[Status:     error|warning|ok|busy|idle|failed|offer]
[Hint:       useCategory|useNames|useStartTime|useCardinality|useNumerals|
             none]                       ("none" is the same as no hint given!)
[Token:      [\[XPATH[#<KAT>[\.<AGR>]][<NUM>][\]]]*
                              ([...] around a token indicate that it is optional)
Template:    "<TEMPLATE>"           (the actual template string with variables)
[Template:   "<TEMPLATE>"]*         (template string(s) for optional token(s))
```

Fig. 9. Specification of a template entry.

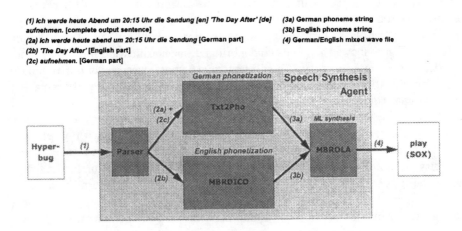

Fig. 10. Bilingual Synthesis Agent.

processing time in the synthesis module and thus contributes to the real-time capability of the whole dialog system. After processing the constant parts, the variable parts are synthesized as well, the wave file is concatenated and uttered.

An overview of our speech synthesis agent is displayed in fig. 10. Certain domain requirements for bilinguality (proper nouns in English, whereas German is used otherwise) led us to build in an intrasentential bilingual capacity: This is accomplished by parsing language switching commands in the output of the NLG component ([en] for English and [de] for German) and invoking the appropriate phonetization module, txt2pho for German and mbrdico for English sentence parts. These different phonetizations are synthesized by MBROLA, concatenated to wave files afterwards, and uttered using the SOX play command. In our example sentence two language switchings occur: The first one before "The Day After" (from German to English) and the second one after this program title (back to German again). These switchings and the corresponding signal flow through our speech synthesis agent are shown in fig. 10 as well.

Our speech synthesis method is admittedly rather naive, since our approach does not account for content-to-speech issues, especially prosodic features. Aside from some basic hints about the sentence accent, processing prosodic marks is outsourced to the synthesizer, which suits our needs as speech synthesis itself is not in the focus of our work. However, our approach is still preferable over synthesizing English parts with a German phoneme set and phonetization algorithm. Moreover, since the variable parts in our wave files always realize the same syntactic functions, we simply assume that prosodic marking is not affected by filling in different instances.

6 Conclusion

We have presented a hybrid NLG approach embedded in a natural language dialog system. The NLG system is implemented in Java and used in three different domains, namely home A/V management [13], model train controlling [14], and B2B e-procurement [15]. Domain shifts were carried out without major problems, but not completely automatically. The reasons for this are primarily differences in the semantic representations of the domain concepts, resulting in different specifications for the XML structure used as input for the NLG component. Hence especially the Sentence planner had to undergo significant adaptations when the domain was shifted from the A/V management to the B2B e-procurement scenario. Moreover, the system was developed further during the various domain changes, so the system ability to (semi-)automatically adapt to new domains could not be tested under realistic conditions.

For similar reasons, we have no end-to-end evaluation of our system in terms of user acceptance so far: In the home A/V domain, this type of evaluation was not carried out in the whole project, only a study to determine increases in the dialog success rate was committed. And the other two domains are applications in ongoing projects; the system has therefore not been end-to-end evaluated in these domains yet.

6.1 Related Work

Explanation-based generalization or explanation-based learning (EBL), an approach known from Machine Learning (ML), contains ideas similar to the ones described here and has already been applied to NLG: In [3], templates for subgrammars are generated from a corpus using EBL techniques. However, normally a training phase, a running phase, and a separate training corpus are needed in EBL, which is not the case in our approach: We just process our dialogs directly, generating everything on-the-fly.

[4] uses a statistical learning approach to train a grammar from a given corpus to realize a certain type of LF in the AMALGAM generation system. Comparable to our ELF, the LF mentioned in [4] contains syntactic features, but it also includes lexical entries (agreement features and surface structures). The system lexicon is therefore not accessed within the realization algorithm of AMALGAM, but it has to be consulted beforehand to perform lexical choice and to construct its LF type. Hence, AMALGAM itself cannot generate synonyms for semantic concepts, but is always restricted to a single word or phrase.

In [16] BUSEMANN presents the generator TG/2 which is used in his TEMSIS system [6]. In TG/2, canned text, templates, and deep generation are integrated in a single framework, the Template Generation Language (TGL). TG/2 is nevertheless not a system of type III, because there are no concurring processing branches for a given semantic representation. The TGL is basically a phrase structure grammar with a context-free skeleton which allows additional applicability tests and feature percolation using constraint equations. As TGL rules can also contain words (which is trivially true for canned text, of course), a separate lexicon access becomes, once again, superfluous, like in AMALGAM. All in all, TG/2 is a type II system which lacks the concurring processing branches and, consequently, the feedback loop provided by our Bridge and thus the learning capacity built into HYPERBUG.

As we use XML as input structure, generation from XSLT [5] can be seen as an alternative to our approach, albeit without ML ideas and deep processing. Therefore XSLT generation is rather shallow and static in our point of view.

6.2   Future Work

We are going to introduce deep processing into our Sentence Planner in the near future using the DL inference engine RACER [17]. This will be even more necessary when we use the DIG standard [18] in our XML input structures and XPATH will no longer be usable to extract the relevant information out of these DIG-based XML structures. RACER might be able to replace XPATH here and enable us to retain the internal organization of our template database entries.

Furthermore, we want to improve the decision module by a planning procedure using the speech act, the discourse situation, and the user model to ensure that the most appropriate processing branch is selected, which means that deep generation can be used even if a template is already available.

References

1. Reiter, E., Dale, R.: Building Natural Language Generation Systems. Cambridge (2000)
2. Oh, A., Rudnicky, A.: Stochastic language generation for spoken dialogue systems. In: Proc. ANLP/NAACL 2000 Workshop on Conversational Systems, Seattle (2000)
3. Neumann, G.: Applying explanation-based learning to control and speeding-up natural language generation. In: Proc. ACL/EACL-97, Madrid (1997)
4. Corston-Oliver, S.: An overview of amalgam: A machine-learned generation module. In: Proc. INLG-2002, New York (2002)
5. Wilcock, G.: Integrating natural language generation with xml web technology. In: Proc. EACL-2003 Demo Sessions, Budapest (2003)
6. Busemann, S.: A flexible shallow approach to text generation. In Hovy, E., ed.: Proc. INLG-98, Niagara-on-the-Lake (1998)
7. Wahlster, W.: Verbmobil: Foundations of Speech-to-Speech Translation. Berlin, Heidelberg, New York (2000)

8. Kamp, H., Reyle, U.: From Disourse To Logic. Dordrecht (1993)
9. van Noord, G.: An overview of head-driven bottom-up generation. In Dale, R., Mellish, C., Zock, M., eds.: Current Research in Natural Language Generation, Berlin, Heidelberg, New York (1990)
10. Ludwig, B.: Dialogue understanding in dynamic domains. In Kühnlein, P., Rieser, H., Zevat, H., eds.: Perspectives on Dialogue in the New Millennium. John Benjamins Publishing Company (2003)
11. Forkl, Y., Hellenschmidt, M.: Mastering agent communication in embassi on the basis of a formal ontology. In: ISCA Tutorial and Research Workshop on Multi-Modal Dialogue in Mobile Environments, Kloster Irsee (2002)
12. Dutoit, T.: Euler: An open, generic, multi-lingual and multi-platform text-to-speech system. In: Proc. LREC-2000, Athen (2000)
13. Bücher, K., Forkl, Y., Görz, G., Klarner, M., Ludwig, B.: Discourse and application modeling for dialogue systems. In: Proc. KI-2001 Workshop on Applications of Description Logics, Wien (2001)
14. Huber, A., Ludwig, B.: A natural language multi-agent system for controlling model trains. In: Proc. AI, Simulation, and Planning in High Autonomy Systems (AIS-2002), Lissabon (2002)
15. Kießling, W.: Design and implementation of cosima - a smart and speaking e-sales assistant. In: Proc. 3rd International Workshop on Advanced Issues of E-Commerce and Web-Based Information Systems (WECWIS '01), San Jose, CA (2001)
16. Busemann, S.: Best-first surface realization. In Scott, D., ed.: Proc. INLG-96, Brighton (1996)
17. Möller, R., Haarslev, V.: Description logics for the semantic web: Racer as a basis for building agent systems. KI - Zeitschrift für Künstliche Intelligenz (special issue on Semantic Web), No. 3 (2003)
18. Bechhofer, S., Möller, R., P. Crowther, P.: The dig description logic interface. In: Proc. 2003 Int. Workshop on Description Logics (DL2003), Rom (2003)

Error-Tolerant Finite-State Lookup
for Trademark Search

Andreas Eisele[1] and Tim vor der Brück[2]

[1] Computational Linguistics, Saarland University, D-66123 Saarbrücken
eisele@coli.uni-sb.de
[2] German Meteorological Service, Kaiserleistraße 35, D-63067 Offenbach
tim.brueck-vor-der@dwd.de

Abstract. Error-tolerant lookup of words in large vocabularies has many potential uses, both within and beyond natural language processing (NLP). This work[1] describes a generic library for finite-state-based lexical lookup, originally designed for NLP-related applications, that can be adapted to application-specific error metrics. We show how this tool can be used for searching existing trademarks in a database, using orthographic and phonetic similarity. We sketch a prototypical implementation of a trademark search engine and show results of a preliminary evaluation of this system.

1 Introduction

Many applications of NLP have to deal with some kind of deviation of observed input from the theoretically correct form. Sources for such deviations may include human performance (typing) and competence (spelling) errors as well as technical inaccuracies of transmission and recognition, especially in cases involving speech or character recognition. An ideal NLP system should be able to guess a correction of deviating parts of the input and find an interpretation that is compatible with the user's intent.

Besides correction of errors, there are many other applications where the focus is to find terms that are similar to a given query. These include retrieval of person or product names from databases, or documents from text repositories[2] as well as cross-lingual applications, e.g. for finding likely transcriptions of names in different writing systems or for the alignment of words and phrases in translation memories.

---

[1] The work described here was done while the authors were at Language Technology Lab, German Research Center for Artificial Intelligence (DFKI GmbH), Stuhlsatzenhausweg 3, D-66123 Saarbrücken, Germany.

[2] See http://www.google.com/jobs/britney.html for a list of 593 query types for which the google search engine proposed "Britney Spears" as correction. More than 23% of the queries were misspelled.

S. Biundo, T. Frühwirth, and G. Palm (Eds.): KI 2004, LNAI 3238, pp. 112–126, 2004.

The concept of similarity depends strongly on the input modalities and other properties of the application, as will be explained in more detail in Sect. 4. In order to be able to address the wide range of applications in a generic way, we implemented a library, called SILO, for error-tolerant or similarity-based lookup from a set of strings which is given in the form of a finite-state device.

This papers focuses on a innovative use of SILO in a specialized search engine for trademarks, where the goal is to test whether a potential brand or product name conflicts with existing trademarks that look or sound similar.

2   Requirements for Trademark Search

The main purpose of trademark law is to protect the public from being confused or deceived about the origin and quality of a product. This is accomplished by the trademark owner preventing competitors from using a mark that the consuming public is likely to confuse with theirs, whether because it is identical (such as another computer manufacturer calling themselves "Apple") or sufficiently similar (such as a soft drink called "Popsi", to mimic "Pepsi"). See [Wil98] for an easy-to-read introduction to the subject.

When a company registers a new trademark at one of the national or international authorities, it must check whether this or a similar trademark already exists in the same industry sector[3]. Infringement of an existing trademark may cause very high costs, including the need to destroy products already manufactured, or to suspend expensive marketing campaigns. Manual search for existing trademarks has several obvious disadvantages, including the high cost of manual labour, potential incompleteness of the results and the need to redo the search after a change in the database. Therefore an automatic approach would be much preferable. Trademark search needs to be aware of several types of similarity, which can be character-based, phonetic or semantic. The most obvious form of similarity between two terms consists in the use of letters in a similar order. Especially the insertion or omission of repeated characters is very hard to notice (compare Alibert vs. Allibert) and therefore leads to a high confusability of the names.

Two trademarks can be pronounced similarly even if the orthography is quite different. For instance, the German optician Fielmann could be spelled as Viehlman, Philmahn, etc. without noticeable difference in pronunciation. Given our machinery for error-tolerant lookup, one might be tempted to translate knowledge about phonetic similarity between strings of characters into substitutions for the error metric. However, the large resulting number of substitutions would be inconvenient to specify and would make lookup unnecessarily slow. Instead, it appears much more adequate to transcribe strings into phonetic representations and determine similarity scores on that level. Fortunately, we could make use of existing software from the MARY project [ST01] for the transcription into phonetic representations, assuming phonetic rules for German or

---

[3] This is in contrast to the case of patents, where the authorities are responsible for the evaluation of novelty before registration.

English[4]. We can then look for similarities on the phonetic level, using a much smaller set of possible confusions. Current leading trademark search engines like Eucor [EUC04] or Compumark [Com04] also use orthographic and phonetical similarity. However, technical information about the inner workings of these engines is rather sparse.

Words can also be semantically similar, i.e. they can be near synonyms, one can be a special case of the other, or they can be translations of each other. Although one could try to tackle semantic similarity with a resource like Wordnet, coverage may not be sufficient for the very large vocabulary used in the trademark domain. The current implementation does not take semantic similarity into account.

The proper treatment of trademarks composed of multiple words requires the assignment of weights to the constituents. Ideally, one would like to give a high weight to specific words and names, whereas generic or descriptive parts of the names should have a lower weight. Attempts to infer good weights from the frequencies of words in the database have had mixed results so far, so the current implementation supports the interactive specification of weights for the parts of multi-word trademarks.

3   Finite-State-Based Lexical Lookup

Our implementation is based on a generic toolkit that aims at a much broader scale of tasks related to robust and multilingual natural language processing. Especially when languages are richly inflected or involve compositional morphology, a full enumeration of all possible word forms gives rise to prohibitive storage requirements or is plainly impossible.

In order to be useful even in these cases, the implementation of the lookup is based on a representation of the relevant data in the form of finite-state acceptors (FSA) or transducers (FST) in the style of [KK94] and [Kar94]. FSAs can be seen as improved versions of letter trees or tries [Fre60] to regular languages [HU79], in which the possibility to share trees of suffixes can make the representation exponentially more compact and even encode infinite vocabularies. FSTs describe regular relations between strings in a declarative way. Their mathematical properties are simple and well understood, and they can be used for generation of surface forms as easily as for morphological analysis. They generalize finite-state acceptors to multiple tapes, where transitions between states simultaneously affect several levels of string representation. Applications for morphological lookup use one of these tapes for the surface string, and another for the underlying linguistic analysis. Since FSTs factor out independent sources of variation, exponential or infinite numbers of forms with all morphological

---

[4] A proper assessment of trademark similarity in a multilingual context needs to address potential confusions of many different types, such as: "Does word X (which is really from language Y), when pronounced in language Z, sound similar to word U (which is really from language V),...", which is further complicated by neologisms and trademarks composed from multilingual pieces.

readings can be represented very compactly. The clear separation between compilation of the FST and transduction of strings nicely accommodates different requirements for off-line and on-line processing of the linguistic specification and makes it easy to embed morphological processors for different natural languages into larger systems.

The compiled FST representations can then be interpreted by existing implementations of exact and error-tolerant finite-state lookup implemented at the German Research Center for Artificial Intelligence (DFKI). In order to accommodate different requirements for functionality, speed and compatibility, there are two implementations of the lookup routine that can work with the same binary representations. The Java implementation focuses on simplicity and reliability and can be included in multi-threaded applications. The C implementation is significantly faster and allows for the search of a set of most similar strings under a given distance metric, as described below. Programming interfaces to several host languages exist. Using this generic framework, robust morphological analysis and generation can be embedded quite flexibly into various platforms for NLP and into other applications.

4   Lookup with Application-Specific Error Tolerance

The concept of similarity most suitable for robust lookup and error correction depends strongly on the sources of deviations such as the modalities of textual input. If text is typed, confusions of keys nearby on the keyboard are much more likely than others, and the keyboard layout also influences the likelihood of swapping adjacent characters. If text is decoded from document images by an OCR system, similarities in visual appearance are important; typical confusions involve the sets {I,l,1}, {e,c}, {m, rn}, {d,cl}, and so on. Phonetic similarity plays a crucial role both for the correction of spelling errors and of errors in the result of automated speech recognition.

For the application in trademark search, the latter two kinds of similarity are also immediately applicable, as will be explained below. Keyboard layout, however, does not matter in this case.

As we want to support cases where the vocabulary is specified as a finite-state device, we needed a way to incorporate application-specific error tolerance into a finite-state lookup algorithm. Such mechanisms have been described in the literature [OG94,Ofl96,SM01], but these approaches are based on uniform costs for all kinds of errors, i.e. the error model is built into the search algorithm and cannot be parametrized according to the needs of the application. [KCG90,BM00] describe the use of application-specific probability distributions for the correction of typing and spelling errors, but the method they give for efficient lookup does not seem to be immediately applicable to infinite vocabularies, encoded in cyclic FSMs. Our error-tolerant lookup follows roughly the approach of [Ofl96], but furthermore allows to specify the likelihood of deviations (such as typing/spelling/OCR errors or phonetic similarity) in an application-specific error metric.

Error metrics consist of parameters that specify the cost of generic edit operations such as deletion, reversal, substitution, and insertion, where the latter can be further differentiated according to the place of the insertion (initial vs. inner vs. final position). Furthermore, we allow to list specific substitutions in the form of 4-tuples $\langle w_i, w_{d_i}, w_{c_i}, s \rangle$ with $w_i, w_{d_i}, w_{c_i} \in \Sigma^*, s \in R^+$, where Σ is the set of characters, w_i and w_{d_i} stand for possible substrings of the query and the target string that are matched with error cost s, and where w_{c_i} specifies a (potentially empty) left context, to which this replacement is constrained. Whereas this definition may not satisfy all wishes for generality or elegance, it has proven flexible enough to deal with many important classes of phenomena. For the trademark search, the possibility to make edit costs dependent on the position within a word and to penalize the insertion of whitespace that would break words have proven especially useful.

The lookup happens in two steps. In a preprocessing step, substrings of the given query are enriched with potential alternatives according to the list of 4-tuples, whenever the left context given in the substitution matches. Conceptually, this transforms the given query into a weighted graph, specifying a set of variants of the query modulo the substitutions. The main lookup routine now performs a backtracking search for compatible paths through the expanded query graph and the lexicon FSM, where the use of generic edit operations is taken into account as well as the possibility and costs of picking variants of the query.

While traversing the pair of FSMs, costs for the edit operations or variant branches are cumulated, and branches that exceed a given upper limit (tolerance) are abandoned. In this way, the backtracking search enumerates all matches that are possible within the initial tolerance. This limit is increased by iterative deepening, until a pre-specified minimal number of matches has been found.

5   Trademark Search Algorithm

The following section specifies the principles discussed in the previous section in a more formal and detailed manner.

5.1   Similarity Comparison

The lexicon which is used for similarity comparison is stored in a finite state machine, which is a popular, efficient and memory-saving mechanism to store large numbers of strings. In order to simplify the presentation and because it does not make a difference for the purpose of the paper, we restrict the examples to the special case of letter trees, such as in Fig. 1, which are finite state machines where each node has maximally one ingoing arc. The word entries of the lexicon are the concatenation of the letters from the tree root to a leaf node.

In the example in Fig. 1 the lexicon would consists of the words

- ab
- au
- b

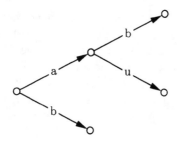

Fig. 1. Letter Tree.

The input word consists of letters of some alphabet Σ such that $w \in \Sigma^*$. The similarity algorithm now returns all entries of the lexicon d for which similarity to some input w is below some given threshold t.

$$similar\_words_d(w, t) = \{(w_d, sim) | w_d \in d \wedge sim_{total}(w_d, w) < t\}$$

This is done by recursively examining all routes of the tree from the root until it reaches a leaf node or the similarity is already higher than the given threshold using a depth-first search. The search can be aborted if the threshold is exceeded since the cost (similarity value) of choosing some arc depending of some letter of the input w is always positive or zero. The similarity function is defined as follows

$$sim : \Sigma^* \times \Sigma^* \times \Sigma^* \to \Re_{+0} : sim(w_i, w_{d_i}, w_{c_i}) = s$$

with

- w_i: some part of the input
- w_{d_i}: concatenations of arcs in the tree
- w_{c_i}: context: some part of the input directly in front of w_i: $w = a w_{c_i} w_i b$ where $a, b \in \Sigma^*$.

This function is partial and does not have to be defined for all possible input words. However it should at least be defined for all $w_i, w_{d_i} \in \Sigma$. The similarity for the whole word is the sum of the similarities for the word parts.

$$sim_{total}(w, w_d) := \min\{\sum_{i=1}^{n} sim(w_i, w_{d_i}, w_{c_i}) \mid w_d = w_{d_1} \bullet ... \bullet w_{d_n} \in d \wedge$$
$$w = w_1 \bullet ... \bullet w_n \wedge$$
$$w = v \bullet w_{c_i} \bullet w_i \bullet ... \bullet w_n\}$$

This basic algorithm is already quite useful for similarity determination. But there are also some cases where no comparison would be possible. Consider the input string "Pateck Phillip" and the entry "Patek Phillip" in the database. The algorithm described above could only determine the similarity between both strings if the value of $sim(ck, k, \varepsilon)$ (or alternatively $sim(c, \varepsilon, \varepsilon)$) would be explicitly defined.

Therefore additionally to the algorithm stated above we introduce the possibility to leave out one character of the input string without changing the state in the tree. Furthermore we have to define how much the costs determining the similarity value between the input string and a tree node is raised by this action. Especially in connection with trademark names it makes a difference whether characters are left out at the beginning, in the middle or at the end of the input sentence e.g. "Gosun" would be considered less similar to the mark name "SUN" than "Sungo".

Similar to this case it can also be useful to change the state in the tree without going to another character in the input sentence. Generally we can define a second similarity function as follows

$$sim' : Op \times Loc \rightarrow \Re_{0+}$$

where

$$Op \in \{Jump, Stay\}, Loc \in \{Beginning, Middle, End\} \ .$$

So the first similarity function sim can be extended in the following way:

$$sim(w, \varepsilon, w_c, loc) = sim'(Stay, loc)$$
$$sim(\varepsilon, w_d, w_c, loc) = sim'(Jump, loc) \ \forall w, w_d, w_c \in \Sigma^*$$

Note that the parameter list of sim_{total} has to be extended for an additional parameter indicating the current location inside the query term.

5.2   Weighted Merge

The proposed algorithm tends to return too small similarity values when used for trademarks which consists of several words. Consider the trademark SUN and the two strings "Gesund" and "Ge sun d". Although the latter two strings both contain the word sun and are written using the same letters in the same sequence only the last one would conflict with the trademark SUN because by using a blanks before and after the substring "sun" it becomes obvious that "sun" is part of "Ge sun d".

Therefore the base algorithm was extended for multi-word trademarks to compare not only the whole expression but also every word separately with the words from the database. Now we use the individual rankings of the word for word comparison to compute a global ranking. To do this we use the condition that if every word-for-word similarity calculation for some search string would result in the same similarity value then the global similarity should be equal to this value.

Additionally there should be a possibility to use weights for the words of the input strings, e.g. in the upper example string "ge sun d", "sun" could be weighted more (or less) important than the token "ge".

Let sim_i denote the similarity of the i'th token with some word w_d from the database. sim_i is constraint from 0 (total identical) to ∞ (maximal difference) Let w_i denote the weight of the i'th token in the input string w. For better computation we first shift the rating sim_i in the interval from 0 (least similar) to 1 (identical). The conversion formula is easily given by $sim'_i = 1/(sim_i + 1)$. The global similarity is calculated by

$$g = (\sum_{i=1}^{\sharp Tokens(s)} w_i * sim'_i)/ \sum_{i=1}^{\sharp Tokens(s)} w_i .$$

Afterwards the similarity must be reconverted to the scale from 0 to infinity which is done by: $g' = (1/g) - 1$.

5.3   Automatically Determined Weights

If some query term consists of more than one word, weights can be assigned to each singular word. Sometimes such multi-word expressions includes class names (e.g. "Cafe" in "Cafe Karlo") or corporation abbreviations like ("Deutsche Telekom AG" or "IBM Corp."). A different trademark should not be considered similar to IBM Corp. only because the other company trademark also includes the word "Corp". One approach we followed here is doing a frequency analysis to count how often a word appears. The probability is high that a word like 'AG', 'GmbH' or 'Corp' appears quite often. So if a word is appearing often, the weight used for this word should be low (near to zero). Unfortunately, this approach turned out to be too simple and leads to wrong results in some situations. So it is assumed that also the position of the word should be considered, so 'AG' or 'Corp' should only be weighted low if it appears at the end of the expression.

6   Implementation and First Results

The program for trademark comparison is implemented as a web server application with Java Server Pages and Servlets. The trademarks are stored in a MySQL database and are accessed via JDBC. The user can chose between different views, including a compact view with only one score per result or a detailed view where scores of textual similarity, phonetical similarity for English and German and weighted combinations of metrics are given. Hyperlinks allow to obtain more detailed information on each trademark in a separate frame (see Fig. 2 and 3).

During the construction of the trademark database, phonetic transcriptions of the trademarks are generated according to German and English pronunciation rules[5], and the resulting strings are stored in additional fields of the trademark database. Finite-state encodings are then generated both for the relevant orthographic and phonetic representations found in the database.

When a query is entered into the system, transcriptions are generated for the query term in all relevant languages. For the set of representations obtained in this way, similarity searches are performed in the respective parts of the database, and the results are merged into one unified ranking according to the lowest distance across all types of similarities that are computed.

---

[5] Transcriptions for more languages are under preparation.

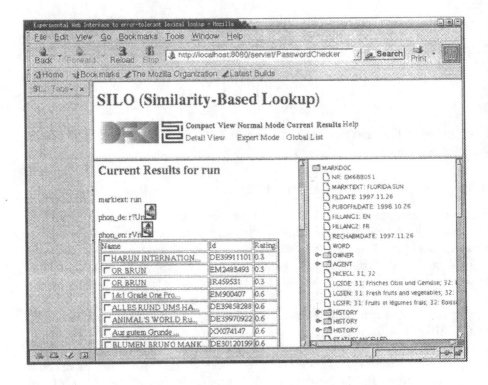

Fig. 2. Silo.

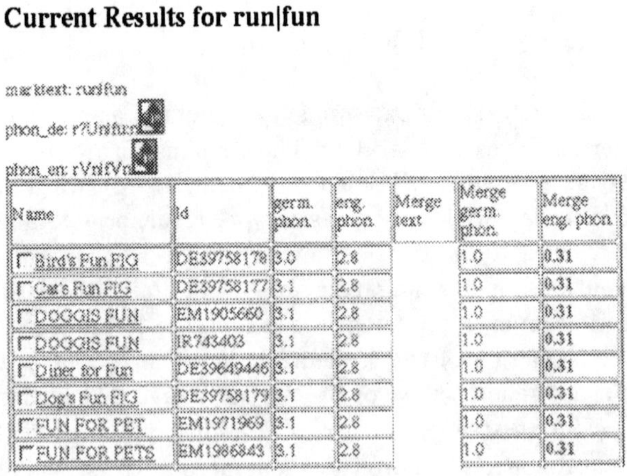

Current Results for run|fun

marktext: run|fun

phon_de: r?Un|fun

phon_en: rVn|fVn

Name	Id	germ. phon.	eng. phon.	Merge text	Merge germ. phon.	Merge eng. phon.
Bird's Fun FIG	DE39758178	3.0	2.8		1.0	0.31
Cat's Fun FIG	DE39758177	3.1	2.8		1.0	0.31
DOGGIS FUN	EM1905660	3.1	2.8		1.0	0.31
DOGGIS FUN	IR743403	3.1	2.8		1.0	0.31
Diner for Fun	DE39649446	3.1	2.8		1.0	0.31
Dog's Fun FIG	DE39758179	3.1	2.8		1.0	0.31
FUN FOR PET	EM1971969	3.1	2.8		1.0	0.31
FUN FOR PETS	EM1986843	3.1	2.8		1.0	0.31

Fig. 3. Silo - Detailed View.

The system also includes an interface to the MBROLA-based speech synthesizer of the Mary system[ST01]. This was motivated by imperfections in the phonetic transcription for unknown words, which however constitute an important subset of the trademark vocabulary. As the system can provide audible feed-back, users who are not familiar with the encoding of the phonetic transcription are still able to spot mistakes in the automatically computed transcriptions of the query, and can alleviate these errors by entering "hints" in the form of vari-ants of the query that lead to pronunciations that are closer to the intended outcome.

A first round of evaluation has been performed by BOEHMERT & BOEHMERT, a law firm specialized in trademarks and intellectual property rights from which this project originated. Results of the search engine were com-pared with the outcome of manual searches and of search engines by commercial service providers. The recall of our implementation turned out to be very promis-ing, compared to the alternatives. The precision of the results was a bit lower than that of manual search agents, which apparently make use of certain "intu-itive" notions of relevance that are difficult to capture formally. However, so far the distance metrics used in the experiments have been rather simple, and we hope to further improve the precision (i.e. shorten the result lists without losing too many relevant hits) by a somewhat more careful design of the metrics. More details of the evaluation are given in the following section.

7   Evaluation

Section 7.1 gives an evaluation of the basic algorithm which shows how the sys-tem performed with respect to precision, recall and f-measure, which trademarks were missing, and compares this with the performance of a human researcher, and also gives an interpretation of the results. Section 7.2 shows results of the weighted merge extension to the algorithm, which we did ourselves and also discusses these findings.

7.1   Results of the Basic Algorithm

The following examples show that SILO had quite good results in the recall but sometimes poor results in precision. The fact that precision scores are not very good is based partly on technical issues. SILO requires the user to select the number of trademarks it should return and always returns that number of trademarks even if only one single trademark in the database is really similar. To overcome this problem one could only select trademarks up to a predefined max-imal distance. But such a limit would have to be determined using psychological experiments to determine the level of similarity people consider as significant for this application. Such data could in principle be collected using a suitable extension of the system for collecting user feed-back. However, such a module has not yet been implemented.

QUERY STRING: PERFECT FIT

Value	Silo	human researcher
Precision	0.02	0.125
Recall	1.0	1.0
F-Value	0.03	0.22

QUERY STRING: CREMISSIMA

Value	Silo	human researcher
Precision	0.31	0,5
Recall	1.0	0.33
F-Value	0.47	0.19
Missing trademark	-	KäsEmilia Carnissimo PETISSIMO ledissimo

QUERY STRING: LAITANA

Value	Silo	human researcher
Precision	0.06	0.75
Recall	0.5	0.5
F-Value	0.1	0.6
Missing trademarks	Lactina Lacsana	MULTANA altina

QUERY STRING: CURLIES

Value	Silo	human researcher
Precision	0.2	-
Recall	0.42	-
F-Value	0.15	-
Missing trademarks	JERKIES URVIS Cultaris LIS Lis ULIS FORLYSE CORALISE BURGYS CHRYSALIS CEREALIS	

One can further see in the statistics that SILO sometimes does not recognize words which appear in the middle of some trademark in the database. This problem could be removed by finetuning or automatically learning the costs for leaving out letters at the beginning or at the end.

7.2   Evaluation of Weighted Merge

This section describes how the evaluation for the "weighted merge"-algorithm was done. First the 50 most similar words to the given query were retrieved using both the "weighted merge" and the basic algorithm. Now we subjectively selected from this set the 10 words most similar to the query and compared how many of them were contained in the 10 topmost ranking entries of the respective result lists found by either algorithm. To ensure that the selection was not influenced by the initial ranking within the result lists, these lists were first shuffled, which made sure that the similarity rating the algorithms assigned to the terms were not visible. Since the number of terms found by the algorithm used for the evaluation and of the manually selected terms are both 10, recall, precision and f-measure all have the same value. Therefore only the value of the recall is given in the tables.

QUERY STRING: High Meyer

Value	Normal	Weighted Merge
Recall	0.1	0.1
Missing trademarks	HAI PRO-FIT Meyer MEYER FIG Heinrich Liesmeyer Metzger Meier Fleischermeister KEINE FEIER OHNE MEYER High Tech mit gutem Gewissen hy Herrman Meyer	HAI PRO-FIT Meyer MEYER FIG Heinrich Liesmeyer Metzger Meier Fleischermeister KEINE FEIER OHNE MEYER High Tech mit gutem Gewissen hy Herrman Meyer

QUERY STRING: Maut Champion

Value	Normal	Weighted Merge
Recall	0.7	0.7
Missing trademarks	HAI Frolic Champion FIG Mr. Champ UEFA European Football Champion	HAI Frolic Champion FIG Mr. Champ UEFA European Football Champion

QUERY STRING: Power Flip

Value	Normal	Weighted Merge
Recall	0.3	0.2
Missing trademarks	Flip	PowerVit
	Preis Power FIG	Preis Power FIG
	STOPY FLIPS	STOPY FLIPS
	UEFA European Football Champion	UEFA European Football Champion
	POWER	POWER
	NP National Power FIG	power POOL FIG
	Power Pur FIG	Power Pur FIG
		PowerFlakes

This experiment shows that the "weighted merge"-algorithm can retrieve terms that would not be found using only the standard algorithm (e.g. "Flip" for the query term "Power Flip". Actually this term does not even appear at the first 50 terms found by the ordinary algorithm)). The "Weighted Merge"-algorithm is especially useful if only one word of the query term is appearing in the database. On the other hand the overall performance of the "weighted merge"-algorithm is not significantly better than that of the ordinary algorithm. We expect that the results can be improved by additional fine-tuning of the weighting scheme.

8   Other Applications of SILO

The advantages of FST-based morphology motivated the transformation of existing resources for 5 European languages [PR95,BLMP98] into FST representations, where e.g. over 6.5 million different analyses of German full forms could be represented in only 1.2 MB. In the case of a resource currently under construction for Arabic [SE04], the restoration of missing vowels, tightly integrated into the lookup operation, comes as a free extra feature without additional implementation work[6].

Using the generic framework on which SILO is built, robust morphological analysis and generation can also be embedded quite flexibly into various platforms for NLP. Several design studies and demonstrators have been built, including on-line correction of typing errors in a dialogue system, OCR correction for financial documents transmitted via FAX, and the correction of typing errors in a database of job offers. Current activities include the integration of SILO into the platforms LKB [Cop01] or PET [Cal00] for deep, HPSG-based syntactic analysis and generation, which are used in the project Deep Thought [CESS04], and many related activities.

---

[6] As long as we want to have *all* readings. Selecting the *correct* interpretation in ambiguous cases is of course much more difficult.

9   Conclusion and Outlook

We have shown how a generic toolkit for similarity-based lookup of strings in finite-state devices can be used for searching existing trademarks in a database, using orthographic and phonetic similarity. First evaluation results of the system look quite promising, but a lot of possibilities for fine-tuning the parameters of the system have not yet been explored. In order to support this kind of optimization, it would be very helpful if judgements of users about relevance or similarity of the proposed trademarks could be collected in a lightweight, semi-automatic way, so that machine learning methods could then turn the collected judgements into optimal weights for a significant set of tunable parameters.

Acknowledgements

We would like to thank Dr. Detmar Schäfer from the law firm BOEHMERT & BOEHMERT for the original idea, development data, and for valuable feed-back, Marc Schröder for the transcription of words into phonetic representations and many helpful advices, Stephan Busemann for keeping the project going and a tremendous amount of supporting work, and an anonymous reviewer for spotting errors in the draft version of this paper.

References

[BLMP98] P. Bouillon, S. Lehmann, S. Manzi, and D. Petitpierre. Développement de lexiques à grande échelle. In *Actes du Colloque des journées LTT de TUNIS*, pages 71–80, 1998.

[BM00] E. Brill and R. C. Moore. An improved error model for noisy channel spelling correction. In *Proceedings of the ACL*. ACL, 2000.

[Cal00] U. Callmeier. PET — A platform for experimentation with efficient HPSG processing techniques. *Natural Language Engineering*, 6 (1):99–108, 2000.

[CESS04] Ulrich Callmeier, Andreas Eisele, Ulrich Schäfer, and Melanie Siegel. The DeepThought core architecture framework. In *Proceedings of LREC*, Lisbon, Portugal, 2004.

[Com04] Compumark, 2004. http://www.compumark.com.

[Cop01] A. Copestake. *Implementing Typed Feature Structure Grammars*. CSLI Lecture Notes. Center for the Study of Language and Information, Stanford, 2001.

[EUC04] Eucor, 2004. http://www.eucor.de.

[Fre60] E. Fredkin. Trie memory. *Communications of the ACM*, 3(9):490–499, 1960.

[HA01] V. J. Hodge and J. Austin. An evaluation of phonetic spell checkers. Technical report, Department of Computer Science, University of York, 2001. Technical report YCS 338.

[HU79] J. E. Hopcroft and J. D. Ullman. *Introduction to Automata Theory, Languages, and Computation*. Addison-Wesley, Reading, MA, 1979.

[Kar94] L. Karttunen. Constructing lexical transducers. In *COLING-94*, pages 406–411, Kyoto, Japan, 1994.

126   Andreas Eisele and Tim vor der Brück

[KCG90]   M. D. Kernighan, K. W. Church, and W. A. Gale. A spelling correction program base on a noisy channel model. In *COLING-90*, volume II, pages 205–211, Helsinki, 1990.

[KK94]   R. M. Kaplan and M. Kay. Regular models of phonological rule systems. *Computational Linguistics*, 20(3):331–378, 1994.

[Ofl96]   K. Oflazer. Error-tolerant finite state recognition with applications to morphological analysis and spelling correction. *Computational Linguistics*, 22(1), 1996.

[OG94]   K. Oflazer and C. Güzey. Spelling correction in agglutinative languages. In *4th ACL Conference on Applied NLP, Stuttgart*, Stuttgart, Germany, 1994. Association for Computational Linguistics.

[PR95]   D. Petitpierre and G. Russell. MMORPH - the Multext morphology program. Technical report, ISSCO, CH-1227 Carouge, Switzerland, October 1995.

[SE04]   A. Soudi and A. Eisele. Generating an Arabic full-form lexicon for bidirectional morphology lookup. In *Proceedings of LREC*, Lisbon, Portugal, 2004.

[SM01]   K. U. Schulz and S. Mihov. Fast string correction with Levenshtein-automata. Technical report, CIS, Universität München, 2001. CIS-Bericht-01-127.

[ST01]   M. Schröder and J. Trouvain. The german text-to-speech synthesis system MARY: A tool for research, development and teaching. In *4th ISCA Workshop on Speech Synthesis*, Blair Atholl, Scotland, 2001.

[Wil98]   L. Wilson. *The Trademark Guide*. Allworth Press, New York, 1998.

[ZD95]   J. Zobel and P. Dart. Finding approximate matches in large lexicons. *Software - Practice & Experience*, 25(3):331–345, March 1995.

Mining Hierarchical Temporal Patterns in Multivariate Time Series

Fabian Mörchen and Alfred Ultsch

Data Bionics Research Group
University of Marburg, D-35032 Marburg, Germany

Abstract. The *Unification-Based Temporal Grammar* is a temporal extension of static unification-based grammars. It defines a hierarchical temporal rule language to express complex patterns present in multivariate time series. The *Temporal Data Mining Method* is the accompanying framework to discover temporal knowledge based on this rule language. A semiotic hierarchy of temporal patterns, which are not a priori given, is built in a bottom up manner from static logical descriptions of multivariate time instants. We demonstrate the methods using music data, extracting typical parts of songs.

1 Introduction

Knowledge Discovery is the mining of previously unknown rules that are useful, understandable, interpretable, and can be validated and automatically evaluated [1]. There are few approaches for mining rules from time series, even less for multivariate time series. Some mining techniques are based on data models that can be obtained from time series by clustering [2], segmentation [3] or discretization [4]. Most methods concentrate on a single data model and their rules represent only one or very few temporal concepts, e.g. coincidence [5].

Our rule language, called *Unification-Based Temporal Grammar* (UTG), is based on multiple data models. The problem is decomposed into the mining of single temporal concepts. The resulting rules have a hierarchical structure that opens up unique possibilities in relevance feedback during the knowledge discovery process and in the interpretation of the results. An expert can focus on particularly interesting rules and discard valid but known rules before the next level constructs are searched. After obtaining the final results, an expert can zoom into each rule to learn about how it is composed and what its meaning and consequences might be. The decomposition is also of advantage for the mining algorithms, because the hypothesis space for a single mining step is smaller. We will give a detailed description of the UTG and explain the temporal concepts expressible with this language. The accompanying time series data mining framework, called *Temporal Data Mining Method*, will be briefly described and applied to music data.

In Section 2 we mention some alternative methods. Section 3 describes our rule language in detail and Section 4 outlines the mining framework. The use of

S. Biundo, T. Frühwirth, and G. Palm (Eds.): KI 2004, LNAI 3238, pp. 127–140, 2004.

the UTG and TDM is demonstrated in Section 5. The results of the application are discussed in Section 6. Section 7 summarizes the paper.

2   Related Work

We know of two approaches that extract rules from multivariate time series. Both convert the time series to labeled intervals using segmentation and feature extraction. Höppner [6] mines temporal rules expressed with Allen's [7] interval logic and a sliding window to restrict the pattern length. The patterns are mined with an *a priori* algorithm using support and confidence and ranked by an interestingness measure afterwards. Last *et al.* [3] mine association rules on adjacent intervals using the Info-Fuzzy Network (IFN). The rule set is reduced using Fuzzy theory.

The next two methods also work on interval sequences, that could be obtained from time series in analogy to the approaches above. Villafane *et al.* [5] search for containments of intervals. A containment lattice is constructed from the intervals and rules are mined with the so called Growing Snake Traversal to reduce the storage space required by the naive algorithm. Kam and Fu [8] use Allen's interval operators to formulate patterns. The rules are restricted to so called A1 patterns, that only allow concatenation of operators on the right hand side. The patterns are mined with an *a priori* algorithm.

The remaining approaches work on symbol sequences possibly obtained from time series. Mannila *et al.* discover frequent Episodes [9] using an *a priori* style algorithm. Das *et al.* [2] use clustering of short time series segments extracted with a sliding window to produce a sequence of cluster labels. The symbol sequence is mined for association rules within a time window interpreted as *if-then* rules. An extensions to multivariate time series is proposed. Recently, Saetrom and Hetland [4] criticized the restrictive rule languages (e.g. for Episodes) needed to make many mining approaches feasible. A general rule language, that includes many others as special cases, is proposed. The patterns are mined using Genetic Programming [10]. The candidate patterns are evaluated using special hardware to speed up the search.

3   Unification-Based Temporal Grammar

The *Unification-Based Temporal Grammar* (UTG) is a rule language developed especially for the description of patterns in multivariate time series [11]. Due to the lack of space we will only describe the concepts here, for more technical details see [12].

Unification-based Grammars are an extension of context free grammars with side conditions. They are formulated with first order logic and use unification. The use of Definite Clause Grammars over Context Free Grammars makes it possible to formulate semantic side conditions. The conditions are checked while the rules are evaluated and they can also be used to interpret the semantics of the rules.

The UTG offers a hierarchical description of temporal concepts. With a hierarchy of semiotic levels complex patterns are successively built from lower level constructs. Starting with simple patterns, called *Primitive Patterns*, and using intermediate concepts called *Successions*, *Events*, and *Sequences*, the final rules, called *Temporal Patterns* are created (see Figure 1).

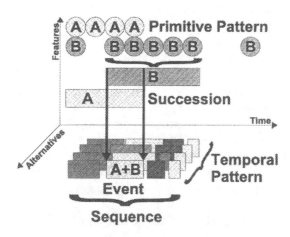

Fig. 1. Unification-Based Temporal Grammar.

At each hierarchical level the grammar consists of semiotic triples: a unique symbol (syntax), a grammatical rule (semantic), and a user defined label (pragmatic). The grammatical rule is produced by a mining algorithm for this hierarchy level (see Section 4). An expert is needed to interpret the rule and complete the triple with a meaningful label. Optionally, the symbol can also be set to a meaningful abbreviation. An example of such a semiotic triple is shown in Figure 2. The generated rule describes a Primitive Pattern (a state assignment for a time point) by two interval conditions. An expert could diagnose this as a beat from a *bass drum*, assign the appropriate label and choose e.g. *BD* as a symbol.

```
symbol: BD
rule: A PrimitivePattern is a 'BD'
if
        'energy-630-770Hz'    in       [-6908.37, 15860.27]
and
        'energy-770-920Hz'    in       [-2079.46, 17153.04]
.
label: bassdrum
```

Fig. 2. A semiotic triple.

In absence of a domain expert, the unique symbols and labels can be generated automatically during the mining process, but they should be adjusted later for better interpretation. One semiotic triple describes a class of constructs, each class usually has many instances occurring at certain time points or during certain intervals.

On each level we allow a special blank symbol, called *Tacet*[1], to express the fact, that there is no UTG construct for a time point or interval. Short, not plausible interruptions of an otherwise persisting state are called *Transients*. The maximum length for Transients is application and level dependent. A group of related time series is called *Aspect*.

A *Primitive Pattern* describes a single point in time. It represents a temporal atom, because it has unit duration. Not every time point needs to represent a state, points can be labeled as Tacets. We allow all rules that map the data space of an Aspect to a symbol representing a class or to the complement of the class, i.e. classification rules, not temporal rules. This very general definition is informally constrained as follows: The classification rules should be given in first order logic (FOL), possibly extended by an estimation calculus, for example a conjunction of interval conditions. This ensures that the rules can be automatically evaluated by an expert system. The resulting data model for each Aspect on this hierarchy level is a sequence of discrete symbols including the Tacet label.

A *Succession* introduces the temporal concepts of duration and persistence. It represents a time interval where nearly all time points have the same Primitive Pattern label. The data model for each Aspect on this hierarchy level is a sequence of labeled intervals, including Tacet intervals.

An *Event* represents the temporal concepts of coincidence and synchronicity. It represents a time interval where several Successions overlap. If the distances between the first and last start point and between the first and the last end point of all Successions are below a threshold, the Event is called *synchronous*. Note, that only Events work on multivariate input data in form of several Succession series, the other hierarchy levels have univariate input data. The user interaction, in form of an expert choosing a label, is very important for Events. While a label can be generated from the Succession labels and durations involved, a short and precise label based on application insight will be easier to grasp in higher level constructs. The common data model for all Aspects on this hierarchy level is a single sequence of labeled intervals, including Tacet intervals, where no Events were found.

A *Sequence* introduces the temporal concept of order. A Sequence is composed of several Events occurring sequentially, but not necessarily with meeting end and start points. A Sequence is thus a typical subsequence of the Event sequence ignoring Event and Tacet durations. The common data model for all Aspects on this hierarchy level is a set of labeled intervals.

A *Temporal Pattern* is the abstraction of several Sequences based on alternatives. Several similar Sequences, differing in only a few Events, form a Temporal Pattern.

---

[1] A Tacet is the pausing of an instrument or voice in a musical piece.

4   Temporal Data Mining Method

The time series Knowledge Discovery framework *Temporal Data Mining Method* (TDM) is described briefly. For more details, e.g. on alternative algorithms, see [13].

The starting point of the TDM is a multivariate time series, usually but not necessarily uniformly sampled. The knowledge discovery steps of the TDM are shown in Figure 3. First, preprocessing and feature extraction techniques should be applied where necessary. An expert should group the set of time series into possibly overlapping subsets, the Aspects. The series within an Aspect should be related w.r.t. the investigated problem domain. In the absence of such prior knowledge, one Aspect per time series can be used. The remaining steps correspond to the hierarchy levels of the UTG and are described below.

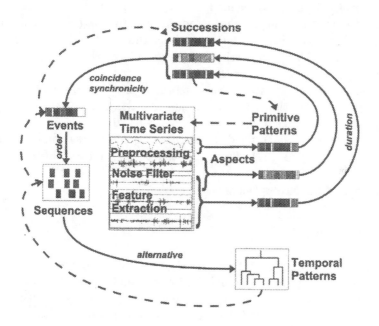

Fig. 3. Temporal Data Mining Method.

Since the amount of data in multivariate time series is usually very large some abstraction mechanism is necessary to make the detection of regularities possible. Finding Primitive Patterns, i.e. reducing the large amount of distinct high dimensional values in a (multivariate) time series to a limited number of state labels provides such an abstraction. Each Aspect is treated individually to produce a discrete state sequence, possibly containing gaps in the form of Tacets.

For univariate Aspects many existing unsupervised discretization techniques can be used, e.g. [14] [15] [16] [17] [18] [19]. It is important, that the symbols are accompanied by a rule and a linguistic description like *high* or *convexly increasing*.

For Aspects spanning several time series, it is often better to use clustering and rule generation of the instantaneous attribute vectors. If the process alternates between several regimes or states, these regions should form clusters in the space spanned by the spatial attributes. In [20] we used Emergent Self-Organizing Maps [1] to identify clusters in the dataset. The rules for each class were generated using the Sig* Algorithm [21], that extracts understandable rules from the sub-symbolic neural model. Other combinations of clustering and rule generation algorithms can be used as well.

A simple, straightforward algorithm is used to create Successions of Primitive Patterns. Transients are filtered out in a post-processing step. For this filter, the user needs to specify the maximum length of an interruption.

All Events maximal w.r.t the number of aspects involved and the length of the interval can be found with a linear time algorithm. For aspects containing k time series, $k-1$ sweeps are made to successively identify Events spanning k, $k-1$, ..., 2 Events. Any time position already covered by a larger Event is ignored. Synchronous Events are identified, given a range threshold. The resulting Events are usually filtered by an interestingness measure, e.g. by length or frequency. Additionally, Transients can be filtered out.

A rather difficult step of the conversion process is the discovery of Sequences. We are using an algorithm based on Sequitur [22], that builds a hierarchical grammar from a sequence of discrete symbols in linear time.

Since sequences can and often do overlap, the last step tries to find generalized Sequences, call Temporal Patterns. The distance between two Sequences can be calculated with a string distance metric and hierarchical clustering can be used to find groups of similar sequences.

5 Application

We applied the TDM to a multivariate time series extracted from audio data. Sound in audio CD quality is sampled at 44kHz and not multivariate at first sight. For stereo sound there are two channels, usually highly correlated. This essentially univariate time series does contain a lot of information, though. Many sounds, that can be modelled as combinations of sine waves, are overlayed. We therefore extract multiple channels from the univariate time series to describe different features.

A straightforward way to obtain a multivariate series is to calculate the loudness in different frequency bands using the Short Time Fourier Transform (STFT). The frequency bands and some weighting factors were chosen according to psychoacoustic models as used by Pampalk et al. [23]. Nine frequency bands were placed between 1.5kHz and 6.4kHz, because these frequencies are most relevant for the human auditory perception [23]. Two more bands cover the remaining low and high frequencies. We are also experimenting with more complex features describing the current pitch and beat content [24]. For this analysis, only the loudness features were used.

We selected the following 11 songs to test the performance with different genres: *Beatles - Octopuses' Garden* (Classic Rock), *Black Eyed Peas - Que Dices* (Hip-hop), *Buena Vista Social Club - Chan Chan* (Cuban), *Herbie Hancock - Cantaloup Island* (Jazz), *Bob Marley - I Shot the Sheriff* (Reggae), *Metallica - Harvester of Sorrow* (Heavy Metal), *Offspring - Bad Habit* (Punk), *Rage Against The Machine - Bullet In The Head* (Crossover), *Frank Sinatra - My Way* (Oldies), *Weezer - Island In The Sun* (Alternative Rock), *White Stripes - Seven Nation Army* (Rock).

One Aspect per frequency band was created. Alternatively, groups of correlated neighboring frequency bands could be merged into larger Aspects. The windows size for the STFT was about 0.1 seconds with 50% overlap. This produces a time series with about 5k samples for a typical 4 minute song. The series was smoothed with a weighted moving average using a window of width 10.

Each univariate aspect was discretized using a histogram with percentile based bins corresponding to the labels *low* (40%), *medium* (20%), and *high* (40%). See Figure 4 for a typical plot of the Pareto Density Estimation [25] with the histogram bins. Figure 5 shows one of the semiotic triples created.

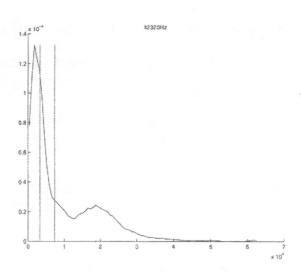

Fig. 4. Loudness probability density.

```
symbol: M
rule: A PrimitivePattern is a 'M'
if
        'energy-3700-4400Hz'    in        [3244.18, 7328.63]
.
label: medium
```

Fig. 5. A Primitive Pattern triple.

Only very short Successions were filtered out, to keep a high level of detail corresponding to elementary sounds. Figure 6 shows the Primitive Patterns and Successions of one frequency band over a time window of 45 seconds. A typical semiotic triple is listed in Figure 7. Note, that the label is inherited from the underlying Primitive Pattern. The minimum and maximum duration is annotated. There are several Transients removed around the sample indices 800 and 1600.

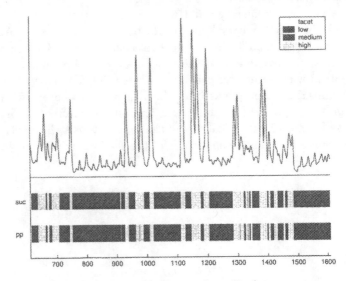

Fig. 6. Successions in 45 seconds audio data.

```
symbol: L
A Succession is a 'L'
if
        'L' lasts [2, 15]
.
label: low
```

Fig. 7. A Succession triple.

Since the exact length of elementary sounds present in the audio files was not known, the minimum length for Events was set to only 2 sample indices, i.e. roughly 0.1s. This resulted in a large number of Events e.g. 2582 Events in 2016 classes for the Hip-hop song. The fact that the number of instances is not much larger than the number of classes already suggests, that there are many rare Events. Filtering the Events by a frequency threshold of 10, reduced the result to 244 Event instances in 11 classes. The results for the other songs are comparable (see Table 1), the number of classes is reduced by over 99% in all cases. Note, that the most frequent, i.e. most repetitive Events are the most interesting in this application.

Table 1. Events.

Artist	all Events		frequent Events		Reduction	
	Instances	Classes	Instances	Classes	Instances	Classes
Black Eyed Peas	2582	2016	244	11	90.5%	99.5%
Buena Vista Social Club	2372	1879	318	13	86.6%	99.3%
Bob Marley	2875	2306	297	12	89.7%	99.5%
The Offspring	1713	1361	163	7	90.5%	99.5%
Rage Against the Machine	2415	1852	363	12	85.0%	99.4%
The White Stripes	1841	1149	459	10	75.1%	99.1%
Metallica	3514	2561	488	12	86.1%	99.5%
Herbie Hancock	2932	2302	362	15	87.7%	99.4%
Weezer	1668	1348	137	5	91.8%	99.6%
The Beatles	1762	1521	108	6	93.9%	99.6%
Frank Sinatra	1390	1116	127	6	90.9%	99.5%

Most Events lasted less than a second, thus representing elementary sounds. The interpretation of Events is relatively easy, because the original audio data is available. By listening to all instances of an Event labels like *guitar riff, bass drum, scream* etc. can be assigned. The bottom row of Figure 8 shows some Event instances found in 37 seconds of the Weezer song. The high activity over all frequency bands from sample index 2000 to 2350 with several Events found corresponds to the chorus of this song. In Figure 9 you can see part of the triple for a typical scream present in the Offspring song.

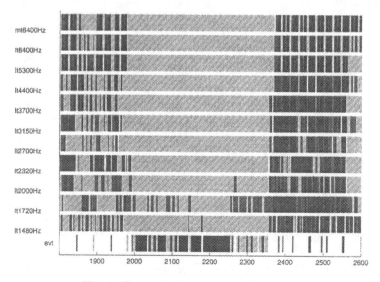

Fig. 8. Events in 90 seconds audio data.

```
symbol: S
An Event is a 'S'
if
        'lt1480Hz high'
coincides with
        'lt1720Hz low'
...
coincides with
        'lt6400Hz high'
coincides with
        'mt6400Hz high'
lasts
        [3,26]
.
label: scream
```

Fig. 9. An Event triple.

The minimum length for sequences was set to 5 Events and accordingly the Sequences found usually lasted between 5 and 10 seconds, representing typical parts of the song. The minimum count was also set to 5, the reduction of the Sequence instances and classes is listed in Table 2. Note, that for the last three songs no numerosity reduction was necessary.

Table 2. Sequences.

Artist	all Sequences Instances	Classes	frequent Sequences Instances	Classes	Reduction Instances	Classes
Black Eyed Peas	120	27	74	9	38.3%	66.7%
Buena Vista Social Club	182	36	124	13	31.9%	63.9%
Bob Marley	176	38	109	13	38.1%	65.8%
The Offspring	100	18	78	8	22.0%	55.6%
Rage Against the Machine	243	36	203	20	16.5%	44.4%
The White Stripes	368	40	334	26	9.2%	35.0%
Metallica	327	50	253	24	22.6%	52.0%
Herbie Hancock	226	39	164	17	27.4%	56.4%
Weezer	55	10				
The Beatles	22	11				
Frank Sinatra	77	13				

Again, interpretation is fairly easy. Figure 10 shows the most frequent Sequences found in the song by Weezer. Sequence 9 in the second row corresponds to the chorus mentioned above. Figure 11 lists the semiotic triple.

The Sequences 2, 0, 11, and 3 occur partly during the same time intervals and partly during adjacent intervals at the beginning of the song. A closer look at a more compact representation in Figure 12 reveals a high similarity between them. These Sequences should thus be merged into a Temporal Pattern, the final form of the UTG representation.

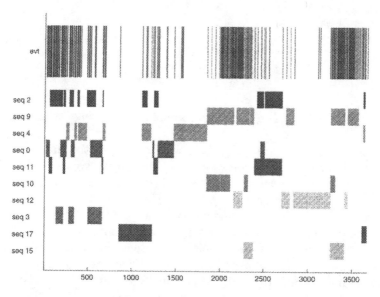

Fig. 10. Sequences in a song.

```
symbol: C
A Sequence is a 'C'
if
        'almost all high energy' lasts [5, 10]
followed after [2, 4] by
        'all high energy' lasts [4, 12]
...
lasts
        [53, 200]

label: chorus
```

Fig. 11. A Sequence triple.

6 Discussion

The results on audio data are promising. The TDM found typical parts in 11 songs of from different genres. These typical parts could be used for further analysis and feature extraction [24]. Determining the similarity of different songs based on a typical part of each should give better results than using an arbitrarily placed window. Compared to using the whole song, the storage and computational effort is tremendously reduced.

A validation of the results other than listening to the extracted samples is difficult, but for the above mentioned application it should be enough to have some typical part, not the most typical.

The discretization of the loudness into Primitive Patterns leaves room for improvements. Instead of percentile based bin boundaries, the modes of the

```
seq  2: 3 -> 3 -> 3 -> 3 -> 3 -> 3 -> 3 -> 3
seq  0: 3 -> 4 -> 3 -> 4
seq 11: 4 -> 3 -> 3
seq  3: 3 -> 3 -> 3 -> 3 -> 3 -> 4
```

Fig. 12. Similar Sequences.

energy distribution should be taken into account, e.g. by using Gaussian mixture models.

Note, that Sequences are very robust with respect to the single Event durations and the length of the gaps between consecutive Events. Grounded on the underlying Event instances, a Sequence bridges the gaps by including the Tacet intervals in the final Sequence interval. This is especially helpful for audio data, because longer consecutive audio samples are extracted. While we see this robustness and completion as an advantage of our method, for some applications constraints on the length of the gaps might be needed. The instance of Sequence 2 in Figure 11 at the sample index 2500 seems to span too large gaps.

Many parameters need to be adjusted manually for our mining method. Based on the intermediate results, decisions have to be revised and previous mining steps have to be rerun. Automating the actual Knowledge Discovery step is not advisable, because (partial) results should always be carefully validated. The hierarchical structure of the Unification-Based Temporal Grammar offers unique possibilities for the expert to interpret, investigate and validate the discovered rules at different abstraction levels and change parameters based on this analysis. The application of the temporal rules to new, larger data set can be automated using an expert system interpreting the logical UTG rules. We are working on finding a robust set of parameters for audio data, to automate the location of typical song elements.

A detailed analysis of Successions indicated, that allowing the concept of order on the Succession level, might improve the results. This way Events would be more robust towards little time shifts and varying durations of typical Succession patterns. While the data model for Events is currently univariate, we are experimenting with algorithms allowing overlapping Events. However, this increases the number of Events found and makes mining Sequences more problematic.

7 Summary

We have described our temporal rule language and the accompanying time series knowledge extraction framework. Many methods and algorithms can and need to be combined to mine rules in UTG notation. The UTG builds up a hierarchy of concepts that introduces the temporal concepts *duration, coincidence, synchronicity* and *order* at successive levels. Rules from each level are accompanied by linguistic descriptions, thus partial results can be interpreted and filtered by experts. All mining steps were demonstrated using audio data. We were able to find typical parts in songs from different genres. An experimental comparison to other rule finding algorithms is ongoing research.

Acknowledgements

We thank Niko Efthymiou, Ingo Löhken, and Michael Thies for programming the audio feature extraction.

References

1. Ultsch, A.: Data mining and knowledge discovery with emergent self-organizing feature maps for multivariate time series. In: Oja, E., Kaski, S. (Eds.): Kohonen Maps. (1999) 33–46
2. Das, G., Lin, K.I., Mannila, H., Renganathan, G., Smyth, P.: Rule discovery from time series. In: Knowledge Discovery and Data Mining. (1998) 16–22
3. Last, M., Klein, Y., Kandel, A.: Knowledge discovery in time series databases. IEEE Transactions on Systems, Man, and Cybernetics 31B(2001). (2001)
4. Saetrom, P., Hetland, M.L.: Unsupervised temporal rule mining with genetic programming and specialized hardware (2003)
5. Villafane, R., Hua, K.A., Tran, D., Maulik, B.: Mining interval time series. In: Data Warehousing and Knowledge Discovery. (1999) 318–330
6. Höppner, F.: Learning dependencies in multivariate time series. Proc. of the ECAI'02 Workshop on Knowledge Discovery in (Spatio-) Temporal Data, Lyon, France (2002) 25–31
7. Allen, J.F.: Maintaing knowledge about temporal intervals. Comm. ACM, 26(11) (1983) 832–843
8. Kam, P.S., Fu, A.W.C.: Discovering temporal patterns for interval-based events. In Kambayashi, Y., Mohania, M.K., Tjoa, A.M., eds.: Second International Conference on Data Warehousing and Knowledge Discovery (DaWaK 2000). Volume 1874., London, UK, Springer (2000) 317–326
9. Mannila, H., Toivonen, H., Verkamo, A.I.: Discovery of frequent episodes in event sequences. Data Mining and Knowledge Discovery 1 (1997) 259–289
10. Koza, J.R.: Genetic programming. In Williams, J.G., Kent, A., eds.: Encyclopedia of Computer Science and Technology. Volume 39., Marcel-Dekker (1998) 29–43
11. Ultsch, A.: A unification-based grammar for the description of complex patterns in multivariate time series (german) (1996)
12. Ultsch, A.: Unification-based temporal grammar. In: Technical Report No. 37, Philipps-University Marburg, Germany. (2004)
13. Mörchen, F., Ultsch, A.: Discovering temporal knowlegde in multivariate time series. In: submitted to Proc. GfKl 2004, Dortmund, Germany. (2004)
14. Geurts, P.: Pattern extraction for time series classification. Lecture Notes in Computer Science **2168** (2001) 115–127
15. Lin, J., Keogh, E., Lonardi, S., Chiu, B.: A symbolic representation of time series, with implications for streaming algorithms (2003)
16. Agrawal, R., Psaila, G., Wimmers, E.L., Zaot, M.: Querying shapes of histories. In Dayal, U., Gray, P.M.D., Nishio, S., eds.: Twenty-first International Conference on Very Large Databases (VLDB '95), Zurich, Switzerland, Morgan Kaufmann Publishers, Inc. San Francisco, USA (1995) 502–514
17. Rodriguez, J.J., Alonso, C.J., Bostroem, H.: Learning first order logic time series classifiers (2000)
18. Kadous, M.W.: Learning comprehensible descriptions of multivariate time series. In: Proc. 16th International Conf. on Machine Learning, Morgan Kaufmann, San Francisco, CA (1999) 454–463

140   Fabian Mörchen and Alfred Ultsch

19. Höppner, F.: Discovery of temporal patterns – learning rules about the qualitative behaviour of time series. In: Proc. of the 5th European Conference on Principles and Practice of Knowledge Discovery in Databases, Lecture Notes in Artificial Intelligence 2168, Springer. (2001)
20. Guimaraes, G., Ultsch, A.: A method for temporal knowledge conversion. In: D. J. Hand, J. N. Kok, and M. R. Berthold, editors, Advances in Intelligent Data Analysis, Proc. of the 3rd Int. Symp., Amsterdam, The Netherlands, Sprginer, Berlin. (1999) 369–380
21. Ultsch, A.: Connectionistic models and their integration in knowledge-based systems (german) (1991)
22. Nevill-Manning, C., Witten, I.: Identifying hierarchical structure in sequences: A linear-time algorithm. Journal of Artificial Intelligence Research, 7 (1997) 67–82
23. Pampalk, E., Rauber, A., Merkl, D.: Content-based Organization and Visualization of Music Archives. In: Proceedings of the ACM Multimedia, Juan les Pins, France, ACM (2002) 570–579
24. Tzanetakis, G., Essl, G., Cook, P.: Automatic musical genre classification of audio signals (2001)
25. Ultsch, A.: Pareto density estimation. In: Proc. GfKl 2003, Cottbus, Germany. (2003)

Using Behavioral Knowledge for Situated Prediction of Movements

Michael Arens, Artur Ottlik, and Hans-Hellmut Nagel

Institut für Algorithmen und Kognitive Systeme
Fakultät für Informatik der Universität Karlsruhe (TH)
76128 Karlsruhe, Germany
{arens,ottlik,nagel}@iaks.uni-karlsruhe.de

Abstract. The textual description of video sequences exploits conceptual knowledge about the behavior of depicted agents. An explicit representation of such *behavioral knowledge* facilitates not only the textual description of video evaluation results, but can also be used for the inverse task of generating synthetic image sequences from textual descriptions of dynamic scenes. Moreover, it is shown here that the behavioral knowledge representation within a cognitive vision system can be exploited even for prediction of movements of visible agents, thereby improving the overall performance of a cognitive vision system.

1 Introduction

Artificial cognitive vision systems are supposed to analyze single video frames or entire video sequences in order to construct a conceptual representation of the depicted scene [12, 7]. Based on such a conceptual scene description, natural language descriptions can be derived [15, 19, 3, 6].

It has been shown that encompassing natural language descriptions of image sequences from innercity intersections can be generated by employing explicitly formulated knowledge about the discourse in question [11, 6]. Especially the explicit representation of *behavioral knowledge* in form of so-called *situation graph trees* (SGTs) enables the cognitive vision system to aggregate conceptual primitives derived from quantitative vision results to complex, context-dependent concepts (compare [11, 1]).

In [19, 3] the authors pointed out that by solving the inverse task of creating a synthetic video sequence from textual descpritions of a time-varying scene (see, too, [4]), the performance of the overall system can be improved: the generated text is analyzed in order to re-create the initial scene which led to the given textual description. Supposing that original and synthetic image sequence can be compared, significant differences between original and synthetic image sequence can point to details which need to be incorporated into the textual description of the initial scene. The differences are analyzed in order to come up with a better textual description, i. e., one that minimizes the differences between the original sequence and the synthetic sequence which one might create as a *'mental image'* when reading the textual description.

S. Biundo, T. Frühwirth, and G. Palm (Eds.): KI 2004, LNAI 3238, pp. 141–155, 2004.

The authors of [20] use conceptual knowledge employed within a surveillance system to create test sequences for their vision system. This usage of background knowledge normally employed within a vision system is an elegant way to test the completeness of the overall system in two senses: can every (visual) behavior, which the surveillance system is supposed to detect, be modelled by this knowledge? And, moreover, is every behavior modelled within the knowledge base also detectable by the vision system?

In [9], still another use of conceptual knowledge employed in a vision context has been presented: behavioral knowledge in form of *situation graph trees* (SGTs) was not only used to link quantitative vision results with complex concepts in order to generate textual descriptions of a scene. In addition to this, the knowledge represented as SGTs was employed to generate *quantitative predictions* of *where* an agent recognized by the vision system would be positioned in the future, e.g., in the next frame of the video sequence.

This leaves the conceptual knowledge employed within a cognitive vision system with (at least) three main purposes it should be solving or enabling: first, the most obvious purpose of behavioral knowledge within a vision context is to link quantitative vision results to complex *concepts*. Second, the same knowledge should be usable to generate synthetic video sequences from conceptual or textual descriptions of scenes. And last, the behavioral knowledge represented within the vision system should be capable of *predicting* the behavior of agents not only in a conceptual, but also in a *quantitatively exploitable* way.

In the sequel, we will show that, in principle, SGTs as a representational form for behavioral knowledge satisfy all three demands mentioned above: in Section 2 we will first briefly recapitulate SGTs as such and how they can be of benefit in conceptualizing video sequences of, e.g., innercity road traffic. Section 3 will be concerned with the generation of synthetic video sequences based on SGTs. In the present contribution, we will extend the work presented in [1] by showing how conceptual representations of a certain behavior can be linked to quantitative movements. Section 4 will then demonstrate how this linkage can also be used for the situated prediction of movements within the quantitative processes implementing computer vision approaches towards vehicle tracking in real-world image sequences.

2   Cognitive Vision

XTRACK (compare [10, 13]) is a *model-based* vision system capable of detecting and tracking vehicles in image sequences of innercity road traffic. *Model-based* in this context means that the system comprises explicit representations of several pieces of background knowledge. These include geometric models of vehicles and other scene components like lane models. Additionally, an algebraic vehicle motion model is used within a Kalman filter approach [5, 8] to describe the systematic changes which vehicle *poses* undergo during vehicle motion. Such a pose is called the state of a vehicle and is to be estimated by XTRACK for each recognized vehicle for each video frame. As a result of the tracking process conducted by XTRACK, the system derives a *geometric scene description* (GSD) [17] for each image frame, comprising both the static scene components and the time-varying *states* of recognized vehicles.

The GSD is imported into a conceptual inference system based on the *fuzzy metric temporal Horn logic* (FMTHL) introduced by [18], which facilitates logic inference on *time-varying* and *fuzzy* facts and rules. Based on the state vectors and other scene descriptions imported as facts into this inference system, the system uses additional background knowledge – this time in form of logic rules – to derive *conceptual primitives* from the imported facts. This knowledge is called the *terminology* and defines, e.g., which velocity of a vehicle should be labeled with the concept fast or which constellation of positions of two vehicles should be denoted as in_front_of. Note that both terms are *vague* and thus are modelled as fuzzy predicates within FMTHL [7].

Defining more complex concepts in terms of a terminology quickly becomes infeasible, because the same value (or change in values) of vehicle states are combined with the same conceptual primitives all the time. No difference is made by terminologic rules between, e.g., a vehicle changing_the_lane while starting to overtake another car and changing_the_lane after finishing the process of overtaking. We employ *situation graph trees* (SGTs) in order to express such more complicated dependencies of concepts on the *context* in which a certain value (change) should be labeled with that concept.

SGTs are graphs whose nodes are given by *situation schemes*. A situation scheme combines the description of the *state* of an agent (e.g., a vehicle) in terms of conceptual primitives with the description of the actions this agent might perform whenever it is in that situation. Situation schemes build *situation graphs* by connecting single schemes by so-called *prediction edges*. These directed edges define a temporal successor relation on situation schemes, i.e., whenever a scheme was instantiated by a vehicle, all those schemes describe plausible successor situations which can be reached from the present scheme by following a prediction edge. A second type of directed edges – called *particularization edges* – connect situation schemes with situation graphs. These edges represent the fact that a single situation can be described in more detail by a whole sequence of other situations. Thus, particularization edges connect situation schemes with those graphs comprising such detailing sequences. In summary, an SGT describes the state of an agent as it is embedded into the context of past and possible future states and possible actions of this agent together with more detailed or more general possible descriptions (compare, e.g., [1]).

The question which vehicle recognized by XTRACK instantiates which situation of the employed SGT can be answered by traversing the SGT along prediction- and particularization edges. SGTs can therefore be transformed into logic programs within FMTHL (compare [18]). Thus, they perfectly fit to the conceptual primitives derived in our conceptual inference system. Such an SGT-traversal results in a *conceptual scene description* (CSD) comprising complex concepts, e.g., – to stay with the example mentioned above – starting_to_overtake, finished_overtaking, and overtaking in general. These concepts can then be further transformed by a natural language generation system into natural language text. For details on this transformation see [6].

3   Controlled Imagery Generation

In [16] (see also [14]) it has been described how conceptual primitives – as derived by the inference subsystem of a cognitive vision system – can be (re-)visualized. In [2] first results have been presented on how such a visualization can be performed on natural language input texts, again, using texts previously produced by a combination of a vision system together with an inference- and a natural language sub-system. However, this approach did not exploit exactly the same knowledge (i.e., the SGTs) which was originally employed to produce the texts. Such a procedure is, however, a prerequisite to test the knowledge base for completeness as has been motivated in Section 1.

SGTs can be used to solve certain problems arising due to the inherent incompleteness of natural language texts [1]: because these texts are normally aimed at human readers, these readers are assumed to be able to use their commonsense knowledge in order (i) to *embed* given information into a plausible context and (ii) to *detail* general information to a degree sufficient for imagining what is going on in the scene decribed by the text.

For both tasks, context-embedding and information-detailing, an algorithm based on the structure of SGTs and the behavioral knowledge stored therein has been presented in [1]. Given a sequence of situations, e.g., derived from a natural language input text, the algorithm returned so-called *maximized SGT-compatible behaviors*. These behaviors comprised the information given by the initial situation sequences, but described in the most detailed way possible based on the knowledge represented by the SGT and embedded into a context also compatible with that SGT (for details, see [1]). What remained to be done at that point was to transform such an SGT-compatible behavior – a situation sequence itself – into an actual video sequence visualizing this behavior.

It turned out that the visualization of situation sequences can be facilitated by defining suitable *action schemes* within situation schemes. The connection between these action schemes and the states of vehicles in a scene to be visualized is established by the motion model already defined within the vision system XTRACK. This motion model had to be extended, however.

3.1   From Action Predicates to Vehicle States

The action scheme of a situation scheme defines actions to be performed either by the vision system itself or by the agent vehicle in question in terms of action predicates. The vision system might, e.g., print out a string announcing the corresponding situation scheme to be instantiated. The vehicle itself might be expected, e.g., to follow_the_lane. In the *descriptive* system approach sketched in Section 2, however, the action scheme was exclusively used for the former purpose. The latter can, however, be facilitated by defining complex action predicates in terms of a so-called *action terminology*.

An action terminology describes each complex action predicate in terms of more simple actions. Basic actions or *action-primitives* in the case of vehicles are acceleration ('longitudinal control') and steering commands ('lateral control'). The action terminology can – as the terminology which defined complex concepts on conceptual primitives – be expressed in form of logic rules within FMTHL. Thus, the background knowledge accessible during the vision task described in Section 2 can also be used within this action terminology. For example, an action predicate like follow_lane – which should cause a vehicle to stay on the lane it is presently driving on – can use the geometric information stored about the lane structure of a road scene together with the present position and speed of the vehicle in question to break down this action predicate into steering commands. These steering commands together with commands concerning the acceleration of an agent result in desired values for the speed and heading of each vehicle to be visualized. By feeding these desired values for speed and heading of vehicles into a *controllable vehicle motion model* (see Appendix A), a sequence of situations results in a sequence of vehicle states compatible with the situation sequence – the behavior. The resulting vehicle states can then be visualized by using standard graphic algorithms.

3.2 Results

Based on an SGT describing the (expected) possible behavior of vehicles at an intersection, we selected one situation scheme to be comprised in the behaviors we want to visualize, namely driving_towards_intersection. Notice that this selection process might be initialized by the analysis of a natural language text as suggested in [2] or, as presented here, by interactively selecting a scheme directly from within an SGT in order to view all behaviors compatible with this scheme.

Using the algorithm proposed in [1], we derived all maximized SGT-compatible behaviors with respect to the given SGT and the selected scheme. These behaviors themselves are sequences of situation schemes, as can examplarily be seen in Figure 1. Notice that the depicted behavior is only one of six behaviors which have been created, reflecting the fact that more than one behavior represented by the SGT is conceptually compatible with the situation scheme initially selected: several created behaviors comprise the notion of an additional vehicle, i.e., a vehicle to which the agent (whose behavior is modelled) would have to give way while crossing the intersection. From the six behaviors compatible with the selected scheme, we manually selected one to be visualized.

Each situation scheme comprised in that behavior contains action predicates. These are (i) follow_lane(Agent), which causes the agent to stay on the lane it is presently driving on, (ii) follow_lseg(Agent) by which the agent is caused to stay on the centerline of the present segment of the lane he is driving on, and (iii) accelerate_to(Agent,normal), which results in the agent accelerating to a velocity which is given by the conceptual value of normal. These action predicates are translated into action-primitives on the basis of the action terminology: the definition of follow_lane takes the present position of the agent and additional knowledge about the lane structure into account to result in the

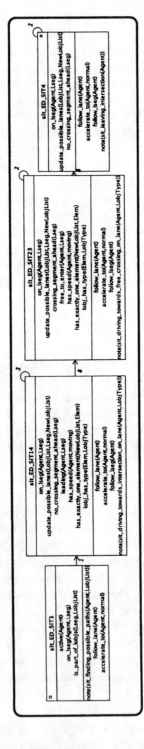

146   Michael Arens, Artur Ottlik, and Hans-Hellmut Nagel

Fig. 1. One of the maximized SGT-compatible behaviors created on the basis of an SGT describing the behavior of vehicles at an intersection. The created behavior is depicted as a linear sequence of situation schemes. A situation scheme corresponding to the concept driving_towards_intersection comprised in the SGT had been selected interactively. Given this scheme, six behaviors have been found to be compatible with this concept. The depicted behavior was interactively selected from those six. Notice that the initially selected scheme itself is not comprised in the behavior shown. Instead, the behavior replaced this scheme by the more detailed description driving_towards_intersection_on_lane. See [1] for details.

action-primitive steer_to(Agent,<num>) where <num> denotes the *absolute* numerical value for the resulting steering angle. In the same way, follow_lseg results in the action-primitive steer(Agent,<num>). Here, <num> denotes a *relative* steering angle the agent vehicle is supposed to employ. The definition of the predicate accelerate_to translates the conceptual value normal into a numerical value <num> for the velocity the agent vehicle is supposed to reach. This results in the action-primitive accelerate_to(Agent,<num>). These action-primitives are used to control the agent vehicle motion model described in Appendix A.

By manually selecting an initial vehicle state, the created behavior can be traversed like a normal SGT: the initial vehicle state leads to the instantiation of the first situation scheme within the behavior. The action-primitives resulting from this scheme create a new vehicle state based on the controllable motion model. This state again leads to the instantiation of the same or the next scheme in the behavior, and so on. The trajectory, i.e. the sequence of vehicle states, created from the behavior selected from Figure 1 is depicted in Figure 2. Notice that the created image sequence used a single image frame from a video sequence of an intersection as background. The trajectory data was superimposed to this image, but could also have been used to create any other *view* on the 3D-scene represented by the trajectory data created from within the SGT and the geometric background knowledge about the static scene components. For one such different view see, too, Figure 2.

4 Cognitive Vision with Situated Prediction of Movements

As has been shown in the preceding section, each situation scheme comprised in a maximized SGT-compatible behavior contained action predicates which could be translated into action-primitives. These primitives were *executed* by a motion model, resulting in time-varying state vectors of agent vehicles.

Obviously, the action schemes defined in situation schemes are not only accessible via the creation of maximized SGT-compatible behaviors, but via the SGT-traversal performed during the vision task, too. How these action schemes can be used in the quantitative vision process will be described in the sequel.

Remember that XTRACK employs a Kalman filter approach to estimate the state of vehicles to be tracked. This approach relies on a measurement at each video frame, but also on a *prediction* of the state to be expected in that frame. This prediction is generated with the help of a motion model accessible to XTRACK. This motion model normally assumes – due to the lack of better assumptions – a constant steering angle and constant speed of observed vehicles. This – obviously not correct – assumption can be refined by the knowledge represented in SGTs.

Once XTRACK has estimated the state of a vehicle and the conceptual subsystem has instantiated a situation scheme for that vehicle, action predicates defined in that scheme can be executed employing the controllable motion model described in Appendix A. This leads to an updated state vector of that vehicle.

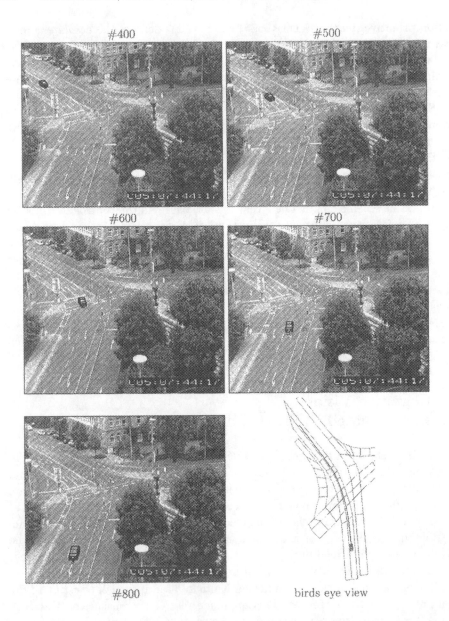

Fig. 2. Representative frames of the visualization of the behavior given in Figure 1. All agent vehicle states have been superimposed to a single frame of an intersection video sequence. The bottom-right figure shows a birds eye view onto the lane model with the synthetically created vehicle trajectory superimposed.

By using this state vector as a prediction within the Kalman filter, XTRACK can profit from the knowledge about the expected behavior of vehicles concerning steering and acceleration.

SGTs have been used already to predict the movement of agents [9]. This was only done, however, under certain circumstances (at least 80% of occlusion of a vehicle due to static scene components) and for a few selected situations. In addition to these restrictions, the actions to be performed by a *simulated* agent – i.e., the internal representation of the vehicle recognized in the scene – were tied closely to situations, i.e., one situation corresponded to one action implemented directly as a procedure of the core vision system. The approach described here instead defines complex actions in terms of an action terminology. This leads to action-primitives which always have the same form (acceleration and steering commands). The overall conceptual sub-system, therefore, is much more flexible with respect to extensions: new situations can define their action scheme in terms of the action terminology, while the motion model controlled by the resulting action-primitives remains unchanged once it has been fully implemented.

4.1   Results

Figure 3 shows tracking results obtained with XTRACK on a video sequence of an innercity intersection. For this experiment, four vehicles were initialized interactively and then tracked by XTRACK automatically: The left column of Figure 3 show the results obtained using the original motion model which assumes a constant steering angle and velocity of vehicles. This assumption is accurate enough for XTRACK to track vehicles under optimal measurement condition, i.e., when the vehicles are not occluded by other scene components. Under such conditions, the vision system can adapt to subtle changes in steering angle or velocity simply during the updating step of the prediction/update cycle realized by the Kalman filter. In the sequence depicted in Figure 3, however, all four vehicles become partially or totally occluded by a tree *and* change both their steering angle and velocity during this period. As a consequence, two of the four vehicles cannot be tracked correctly and *get lost*.

The right column depicts results on the same vehicles obtained with the new controllable motion model. Steering and acceleration action-primitives were derived by an SGT-traversal in this case. In contrast to the tracking results obtained with XTRACK alone, the *situated prediction* of movements leads to more realistic expectations about the change in steering angle and velocity. Thus, all four cars can be tracked correctly throughout the whole sequence.

Figure 4 summarizes similar results obtained for a vehicle which approaches a red traffic light where a transporter already stands waiting. While the approaching vehicles stops behind the transporter it gets occluded by a large traffic sign. XTRACK again cannot cope with the change in velocity of the *occluded* vehicle. Thus, as the actual car reappears from behind the sign, it is already lost by XTRACK. In contrast, by employing SGT-traversal and the action commands following from this traversal, the vehicle is smoothly stopped behind the traffic sign, because the SGT comprises the knowledge that a vehicle usually stops in front of a stationary obstacle. As the transporter begins to accelerate again, this leads to a change in situation instantiation of the trailing vehicle, too. Therefore,

XTRACK alone   XTRACK with SGT

Fig. 3. Representative frames of a video sequence showing an innercity intersection (rows from top to bottom: frames #1400, #1650, and #1900) with superimposed state estimates for four vehicles. The left column shows the tracking results obtained by XTRACK alone. The right column shows tracking results for the same vehicles, but this time with state predictions obtained by SGT–traversal. Note that two vehicles were lost in the left column due to the occluding tree, whereas these vehicles could be tracked successfully with the help of SGT–traversal–based state prediction.

this vehicle is expected to accelerate as the preceding transporter does. As can be seen in Figure 4, this more elaborated assumption about the acceleration of vehicles leads to successful tracking.

Fig. 4. Clippings from representative frames of the same video sequence as in Figure 3 (rows from top to bottom: frames #1200, #1400, and #1600). The clippings show the tracking results for a vehicle which arrives at a red traffic light, where a waiting transporter is already standing. In the left column, tracking results of XTRACK alone can be seen: here, the vehicle was lost during an occlusion. The right column shows tracking results obtained by XTRACK with the help of SGTs. In this case, the vehicle was tracked correctly.

5   Conclusion

It has been shown that *situation graph trees* (SGTs), originally introduced as representation formalisms within a cognitive vision system, fulfill two other demands which might be imposed on formalisms capable of representing behavioral knowledge: the generation of synthetic video sequences and the quantitative exploitation of behavioral knowledge in a predictive manner already *during* the performance of a computer vision task. The former usage of SGTs could be demonstrated by extending work already presented in [1]. Maximized SGT-compatible behaviors can now be visualized in form of a synthesized video sequence by linking these situation sequences to quantitative vehicle states via a controllable motion model. For the latter usage of SGTs, namely the situated prediction of movements during model-based tracking, the controllable motion model was used again. It has been shown here that the quantitative exploitation of conceptual knowledge about the *expected* behavior leads to better performance of model-based vehicle tracking.

6   Future Work

For the investigations presented here, we assumed that the successor situation of the current agent vehicle situation is always uniquely determinable. This is, however, a very strong and often not satisfied assumption. Future work will concentrate on how *competing hypotheses* about the successor situation can be modelled and tested for compatibility with the model-based tracking results. This requires a *fuzzy* traversal of SGTs on the one hand and a function which evaluates and compares the fitting of different vehicle states – following from different hypotheses – to the data estimated by state-of-the-art model-based tracking approaches.

Acknowledgements

The authors gratefully acknowledge support for this work by the European Union under contract No. IST-2000-29404 (CogViSys).

References

1. M. Arens and H.-H. Nagel: *Behavioral Knowledge Representation for the Understanding and Creation of Video Sequences.* In: A. Günter, R. Kruse, and B. Neumann (Eds.): Proc. of the 26th German Conf. on Artificial Intelligence (KI-2003), 15–18 September 2003, Hamburg, Germany, (LNAI) **2821**, Springer-Verlag, Berlin u.a. 2003, pp. 149–163.
2. M. Arens, A. Ottlik, and H.-H. Nagel: *Natural Language Texts for a Cognitive Vision System.* In: F. van Harmelen (Ed.): Proc. of the 15th European Conf. on Artificial Intelligence (ECAI-2002), 21–26 July 2002, Lyon, France, IOS Press, Amsterdam 2002, pp. 455–459.

3. A. Blocher and J. R. J. Schirra: *Optional Deep Case Filling and Focus Control with Mental Images: ANTLIMA-KOREF.* In: C. S. Mellish (Ed.): Proc. of the 14th Int. Joint Conf. on Artificial Intelligence (IJCAI-95), 20–25 August 1995, Montréal, Canada, Morgan Kaufmann, San Mateo, CA, USA 1995, pp. 417–423.

4. A. Egges, A. Nijholt, and P. Nugues: *Generating a 3D Simulation of a Car Accident from a Formal Description: the CarSim System.* In: V. Giagourta and M. G. Strintzis (Eds.): Proc. of the Int. Conf. on Augmented, Virtual Environments and Three-Dimensional Imaging (ICAV3D), 30 May – 1 June 2001, Mykonos, Greece, pp. 220–223.

5. A. Gelb (Ed.): *Applied Optimal Estimation.* The MIT Press, Cambridge/MA, USA, London/UK, 1974.

6. R. Gerber: *Natürlichsprachliche Beschreibung von Straßenverkehrsszenen durch Bildfolgenauswertung.* Dissertation, Fakultät für Informatik, Universität Karlsruhe (TH), Januar 2000 (in German); see:
http://www.ubka.uni-karlsruhe.de/cgi-bin/psview?document=2000/informatik/8.

7. R. Gerber and H.-H. Nagel: *Occurrence Extraction from Image Sequences of Road Traffic Scenes.* In: L. van Gool and B. Schiele (Eds.): Proc. of the Workshop on Cognitive Vision, 19–20 September 2002, ETH Zurich, Switzerland; pp. 1–8, see:
http://www.vision.ethz.ch/cogvis02/finalpapers/gerber.pdf.

8. M. S. Grewal and A. P. Andrews: *Kalman Filtering: Theory and Practice.* Prentice Hall, Englewood Cliffs, NJ, USA, 1993.

9. M. Haag und H.-H. Nagel: *'Begriffliche Rückkopplung' zur Behandlung temporärer Verdeckungssituationen in der Bildfolgenauswertung von Strassenverkehrsszenen.* In: J. Dassow und R. Kruse (Hrsg.): Informatik'98, Informatik zwischen Bild und Sprache, 28. Jahrestagung der GI, 21–25 September 1998, Magdeburg, Deutschland, Informatik aktuell, Springer-Verlag, Berlin u.a. 1998, pp. 13–22 (in German).

10. M. Haag and H.-H. Nagel: *Combination of Edge Element and Optical Flow Estimates for 3D-Model-Based Vehicle Tracking in Traffic Image Sequences.* International Journal of Computer Vision **35**:3(1999) 295–319.

11. M. Haag and H.-H. Nagel: *Incremental Recognition of Traffic Situations from Video Image Sequences.* Image and Vision Computing **18**:2 (2000) 137–153.

12. R. J. Howarth and H. Buxton: *Conceptual Descriptions from Monitoring and Watching Image Sequences.* Image and Vision Computing **18**:2 (2000) 105–135.

13. H. Leuck: *Untersuchungen zu einer systematischen Leistungssteigerung in der modellbasierten Bildfolgenauswertung.* Dissertation, Fakultät für Informatik, Universität Karlsruhe (TH), Juli 2000; Berichte aus der Informatik; Shaker-Verlag Aachen 2001 (in German).

14. A. Mukerjee, K. Gupta, S. Nautiyal, M.P. Singh, and N. Mishra: *Conceptual Description of Visual Scenes from Linguistic Models.* Image and Vision Computing **18**:2 (2000) 173–187.

15. H.-H. Nagel: *From Image Sequences towards Conceptual Descriptions.* Image and Vision Computing **6**:2 (1988) 59–74.

16. H. H. Nagel, M. Haag, V. Jeyakumar, and A. Mukerjee: *Visualisation of Conceptual Descriptions Derived from Image Sequences.* 21st DAGM-Symposium, 15–17 September 1999, Bonn, Springer-Verlag, Berlin u.a 1999, pp. 364–371.

17. B. Neumann: *Natural Language Description of Time-Varying Scenes.* In D. Waltz (Ed.): Semantic Structures: Advances in Natural Language Processing, Lawrence Erlbaum Publishers, Hillsdale/NJ · Hove and London/UK 1989, pp. 167–206.

18. K. H. Schäfer: *Unscharfe zeitlogische Modellierung von Situationen und Handlungen in Bildfolgenauswertung und Robotik.* Dissertation, Fakultät für Informatik, Universität Karlsruhe (TH), Juli 1996; Dissertationen zur Künstlichen Intelligenz (DISKI) **135**; infix-Verlag: Sankt Augustin 1996 (in German).
19. J. R. J. Schirra: *Bildbeschreibung als Verbindung von visuellem und sprachlichem Raum.* Dissertation, Fakultät für Informatik, Universität des Saarlandes, Saarbrücken, April 1994; Dissertationen zur Künstlichen Intelligenz (DISKI) **71**; infix-Verlag: Sankt Augustin 1994 (in German).
20. V. T. Vu, F. Brémond, and M. Thonnat: *Human Behaviour Visualisation and Simulation for Automatic Video Understanding.* In V. Skala (Ed.): Proc. of the 10th Int. Conf. in Central Europe on Computer Graphics, Visualization and Computer Vision (WSCG-2002), Plzen-Bory, Czech Republic, 2002; see Journal of WSCG **10**:2 (2002) 485–492, ISSN 1213–6972.

A   Externally Controlled Vehicle Motion Model

The state of a vehicle at a time point k shall be given as:

$$\mathbf{x}_k = (x_k, y_k, \theta_k, v_k, \psi_k,)^T ,\tag{1}$$

where x and y denote the X- and Y-position of the reference point of the vehicle. θ stands for the orientation of the vehicle in the ground plane. v denotes the velocity in the direction of that orientation. ψ, finally, represents the steering angle of the vehicle. The movement of a vehicle is assumed to be acceptably modelled as:

$$\mathbf{x}_k = \begin{pmatrix} x_{k-1} \\ y_{k-1} \\ \theta_{k-1} \\ v_{k-1} \\ \psi_{k-1} \end{pmatrix} + \begin{pmatrix} v_{k-1}\Delta t \cos(\theta_{k-1} + \psi_{k-1}) \\ v_{k-1}\Delta t \sin(\theta_{k-1} + \psi_{k-1}) \\ \arctan(\frac{v_{k-1}\Delta t \sin(\psi_{k-1})}{\mathcal{L}}) \\ \Delta v_k e^{-\Delta t D_v} \\ \Delta \psi_k e^{-\Delta t D_\psi} \end{pmatrix} ,\tag{2}$$

where Δt is the time increment from time point $k - 1$ to time point k. With $\mathcal{L}$ we denote the length of the vehicle currently modelled. Δv_k and $\Delta \psi_k$ are the velocity and steering angle increments, respectively, following from external control inputs at time point k. D_v and D_ψ are parameters defining the damping of changes forced onto the velocity and the steering angle. We assume that – given a desired speed value $\bar{v}_k$ – the speed increment for time point k is simply defined as $\Delta v_k = \bar{v}_k - v_{k-1}$. Similarly assuming that a desired orientation of $\bar{\theta}_k$ is given, we define the desired steering angle $\bar{\psi}_k$ which would lead to such a desired orientation $\bar{\theta}_k$ (compare [13]) as:

$$\bar{\psi}_k = \arcsin\left(\frac{\mathcal{L}\tan(\bar{\theta}_k - \theta_{k-1})}{v_{k-1}\Delta t D_\psi} \right).\tag{3}$$

Thus, the steering angle increment follows from $\Delta \psi_k = \bar{\psi}_k - \psi_{k-1}$. We assume the system under observation to be excited by a deterministic control input

Table 1. Kalman filter equations according to the notation from [8]. F denotes the Jacobian of the system function f, whereas H stands for the Jacobian of the measurement function h. Both are needed for linearization of the non-linear system and measurement function, respectively. $\mathbf{x}$ denotes the *real* system state, while P denotes the error covariance matrix with which this state is estimated.

System Model	$\mathbf{x}_k = f(\mathbf{x}_{k-1}, \mathbf{u}_{k-1}) + \mathbf{w}_{k-1}$, where $\mathbf{w}_{k-1} \sim N(\mathbf{0}, Q)$
Measurement Model	$\mathbf{z}_k = h(\mathbf{x}_k) + \mathbf{v}_k$, where $\mathbf{v}_k \sim N(\mathbf{0}, R)$
Initial Conditions	$E[\mathbf{x}_0] = \hat{\mathbf{x}}_0, E\left[(\mathbf{x}_0 - \hat{\mathbf{x}}_0)(\mathbf{x}_0 - \hat{\mathbf{x}}_0)^T\right] = P_0$
Other Assumptions	$E\left[\mathbf{w}_j \mathbf{v}_k^T\right] = 0$ for all j, k
Estimate Prediction	$\hat{\mathbf{x}}_k^- = f(\hat{\mathbf{x}}_{k-1}^+, \mathbf{u}_{k-1})$
Covariance Prediction	$P_k^- = F_k(\hat{\mathbf{x}}_{k-1}^+)P_{k-1}^+ F^T(\hat{\mathbf{x}}_{k-1}^+) + Q$
Kalman Gain Matrix	$K_k = P_k^- H_k^T(\hat{\mathbf{x}}_k^-) \left[H_k(\hat{\mathbf{x}}_k^-)P_k^- H_k^T(\hat{\mathbf{x}}_k^-) + R\right]^{-1}$
Estimate Update	$\hat{\mathbf{x}}_k^+ = \hat{\mathbf{x}}_k^- + K_k\left[\mathbf{z}_k - h(\hat{\mathbf{x}}_k^-)\right]$
Covariance Update	$P_k^+ = \left[I - K_k H_k(\hat{\mathbf{x}}_k^-)\right]P_k^-$

$\mathbf{u}$ which shall not affect the state measurement. The system function f and measurement function h are assumed to be constant with respect to time. In the same way, we assume $\mathbf{w}$ and $\mathbf{v}$ to be white noise with time-independent covariances. The Kalman filter equations are summarized in Table 1. For details about the measurement function see [13]. The Jacobian F of the system function f, which is needed to *linearize* the non-linear system function, follows from

$$F = \begin{pmatrix} 1 & 0 & -v\Delta tS & \Delta tC & -v\Delta tS \\[1.2em] 0 & 1 & v\Delta tC & \Delta tS & v\Delta tC \\[1.2em] 0 & 0 & 1 & \frac{\Delta t \sin(\psi)}{\mathcal{L} + \frac{v^2 \Delta t^2 \sin^2(\psi)}{\mathcal{L}}} & \frac{v\Delta t \cos(\psi)}{\mathcal{L} + \frac{v^2 \Delta t^2 \sin^2(\psi)}{\mathcal{L}}} \\[1.2em] 0 & 0 & 0 & 1 + (\frac{\partial \bar{v}}{\partial v} - 1)e^{-\Delta t D_v} & 0 \\[1.2em] 0 & 0 & -\frac{\mathcal{L}e^{-\Delta t D_\psi}}{v\Delta t \cos^2(\bar{\theta}-\theta)\sqrt{1 - \frac{\mathcal{L}^2 T^2}{v^2 \Delta t^2 D_\psi^2}}} & -\frac{\mathcal{L}T e^{-\Delta t D_\psi}}{\Delta t D_\psi \sqrt{1 - \frac{\mathcal{L}^2 T^2}{v^2 \Delta t D_\psi}}} & 1 + (\frac{\partial \bar{\psi}}{\partial \psi} - 1)e^{-\Delta t D_\psi} \end{pmatrix} \quad (4)$$

with the abbreviations $S = \sin(\theta + \psi)$, $C = \cos(\theta + \psi)$, and $T = \tan(\bar{\theta} - \theta)$.

Integration of Manual and Automatic Text Categorization. A Categorization Workbench for Text-Based Email and Spam

Qin Sun[1], Christoph Schommer[1], and Alexander Lang[2]

[1] Department of Biology and Computer Science,
Johann Wolfgang Goethe-University Frankfurt am Main, Germany
{sun,schommer}@informatik.uni-frankfurt.de
[2] Data Management Development,
IBM Development Laboratory Boeblingen, Germany
alexlang@de.ibm.com

Abstract. As a method structuring information and knowledge contained in texts, text categorization can be to a great extend automated. The automatic text classification systems implement machine learning algorithms and need training samples. In commercial applications however, the automatic categorization appear to come up against limiting factors. For example, it turns out to be difficult to reduce the sample complexity without the categorization quality in terms of recall and precision will suffer. Instead of trying to fully replace the human work by machine, it could be more effective and ultimately efficient to let human and machine cooperate. So we have developed a categorization workbench to realise synergy between manual and machine categorization. To compare the categorization workbench with common automatic classification systems, the automatic categorizer of the IBM *DB2 Information Integrator for Content* has been chosen for tests. The test results show that, benefiting from the incorporation of user's domain knowledge, the categorization workbench can improve the recall by a factor of two till four with the same number of training samples as the automatic categorizer uses. Further, to get a comparable categorization quality, the categorization workbench just needs an eighth till a quarter of the training samples as the automatic categorizer does.

Keywords: Knowledge-Based Systems, Machine Learning, Document Classification, Concept Learning.

1 Introduction

In this paper, we are considering text-based email and spam. Since spam needs to be recognized firstly in order to be stopped, distinguishing between useful email and spam is to a certain extent a task of text classification. In the case of email, we can classify it on the basis of its syntactic features such as size, priority, existence and format of attachment etc., as well as to focus on its semantic related to main text, subject, sender's address and date. Here, we are addressing techniques for the latter one. According to the content of spam, we can define various categories for spam and let it be recognized and categorized automatically.

S. Biundo, T. Frühwirth, and G. Palm (Eds.): KI 2004, LNAI 3238, pp. 156–167, 2004.
© Springer-Verlag Berlin Heidelberg 2004

After describing automatic text classification systems and their problems in Section 2, we will explore the differences between automatic and manual categorization in Section 3. To integrate advantages of automatic and manual text classification we have developed a Categorization Workbench that will be described in Section 4. In order to prove whether our Categorization Workbench can solve the problems that automatic categorizers generally have, we carried out a comparative analysis of the Categorization Workbench and an automatic categorizer which implements a decision-tree-based symbolic rule induction system. Section 5 shows the result of the comparison.

2 Automatic Text Categorization and Its Limits

Automatic text classification systems implement machine learning methods[1] such as decision trees (with or without boosting) [1, 12], naive Bayes classifiers [9, 10], nearest neighbour methods and centroid model [11, 13], support vector machines [6, 5, 4] and various kinds of direct symbolic rule induction [2]. Since human comprehensible rules often provide valuable insights in many practical problems, among all these methods, we are particularly interested on a decision-tree-based symbolic rule induction system [7].

In this paper, we are focussing on an automatic categorizer that implements the decision-tree-based symbolic rule induction system, and that is a component of the IBM product *DB2 Information Integrator for Content* (II4C). The following figure illustrates a use case of this kind of automatic categorizers in general:

Initially, there is a taxonomy of categories that is and should be built by the user. Depending on the machine learning method used and linguistic preprocessing (such as tokenization and lemma lookup) done, automatic categorizer need between tens and thousands of training documents for each category, in order to build a categorization model with acceptable categorization quality[2]. The categorization model built by various machine learning methods can be mathematically formalized in different ways. The categorization model of the categorizer used in our experiments is a symbolic rule set. For example, rule "now $> 0 \rightarrow$ B." means that a document will be assigned to the category "Brain Science" if the term "now" occurs in this document at least once. These rules will then be applied on a set of documents to assign them to the existing categories.

In real world applications, users of automatic categorization are confronted with two problems:

1) Getting the needed quantity of training samples for a taxonomy can be a quite laborious task, especially for category topics chosen which are semantically close to each other.

2) Though using automatic categorization, some customers wish to keep control of the assignment of certain documents. Just as many other text categorization methods, the document assignment is determined by the categorization model gener-

---

[1] Compared with manual categorization, the pros and cons of automatic categorization depend less on the choice of these methods, so we will not go into individual method in this paper.

[2] In Section 3, we will go into the details about the issue how categorization quality will be measured.

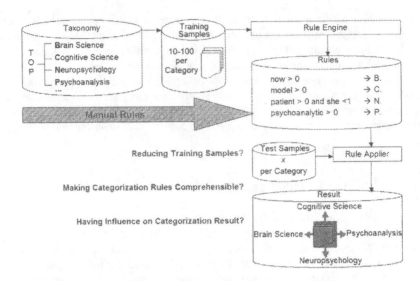

Fig. 1. Automatic categorizer of II4C and its problems

ated on the basis of training samples. So the customer can only let the model be modified indirectly by altering the training set. Additionally, as most of the categorization models are hardly human comprehensible, modifying the categorization model is more or less haphazardly.

These problems awake the need for an integration of manual categorization rules into the overall categorization process with which the sample complexity should be reduced, and the user should be enabled to influence the categorization result more directly and effectively. However, letting user build some categorization rules as showed above and then adding them to automatic rules is trivial. The question is how to help the user with building rules so that problems mentioned above can be solved, and the categorization quality will not deteriorate.

3   Automatic vs. Manual Categorization

Firstly, we have to introduce two common quantities with which the categorization quality can be measured: recall and precision.

Table 1 shows the structure of a *Document Target Current Comparison Table* and the mathematical definition of the recall and precision. The recall and precision of a category are calculated on a pre-classified document set. n is the number of categories. A target category C_i of a document is the category from pre-classification, and a current category C_j is the category currently assigned by the categorizer as categorization result. C_0 is a so-called null category for documents that cannot be assigned to any category by the categorizer. D_{ij} is the number of documents that are pre-classified to the target category C_i, but now assigned to the current category C_j. As defined in Table 1, the recall measures the completeness of the categorization related to a certain category, and the precision expresses the accuracy.

Table 1. Categorization quality and *Document Target Current Comparison Table*

		Current Category					
		C_1	$\cdots$	C_j	$\cdots$	C_n	C_0	Recall
Target Category	C_1	D_{11}		D_{1j}		D_{1n}	D_{10}	
	$\vdots$							
	C_i	D_{i1}		D_{ij}		D_{in}	D_{i0}	$\dfrac{D_{ii}}{\sum\limits_{j=0}^{n} D_{ij}}$
	$\vdots$							
	C_n	D_{n1}		D_{nj}		D_{nn}	D_{n0}	
Precision				$\dfrac{D_{jj}}{\sum\limits_{i=1}^{n} D_{ij}}$				

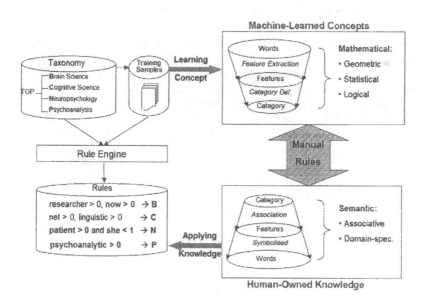

Fig. 2. Differences between automatic and manual text categorization

With Fig. 2, we try to illustrate the difference between both ways of categorization.
In most of the automatic text categorization methods, the word frequency plays a central role in concept learning. Learning from the training set, characteristic words and features respectively will be "calculated" and formalized by geometrical, statistical or logical approaches as mentioned in Section 2, in order to define individual category. In case of symbolic rule induction, the categorization rules can discriminate

between categories with relative high precision [7], but not all of them are also logically comprehensible to us.

However, the quality of the categorization model can only be as good as the training documents chosen. To avoid overfitting on the training set, decision-tree based categorizers prune the rule set to include only rules that are able to classify the training set with a certain degree of precision. As there are then fewer rules remaining, the pruning process leads often to a lower recall. The pruning factor can be adjusted in order to include more categorization rules what may lower the precision, because each additional rule may be applied to documents outside the target category as well.

Unlike automatic categorizers, the manual categorization performed by human beings is based on the semantic of words. Usually, human beings associate each category with its characteristics that can be symbolised by and embodied in words. So categories can be discriminated by domain-specific lexicon. Compared with automatic categorizer, human beings have lower precision [7]. But we might assume that manual categorization will achieve higher recall, since a domain expert has over those of the training set more extensive domain-specific vocabulary.

4   Categorization Workbench as an Integration

After identifying the advantages of automatic and manual categorization, we have developed a Categorization Workbench to realise the synergy of both of them. Fig. 3 shows a use case of the workbench.

Except from the *Rule Engine*, *Feedback* and *Optimizer*, the categorization process is in principle the same as in the automatic categorizer described in Section 2. The *Rule Engine* of the categorization workbench is the component where user's domain knowledge can be incorporated into the automatic categorization process. After one iteration of categorizing pre-classified test samples and on the base of information generated by the *Feedback* component, the *Optimizer* component provides the user with various possibilities to optimize the categorization model on demand. According to the result of experiments which will be reported in Section 5, the problems of automatic categorization mentioned in Section 2 could be solved already after the first categorization iteration. So in this section, we will focus on the *Rule Engine* component and the feature selection model respectively.

As mentioned above, machine learning methods are not able to choose features according to their semantic relevance like human beings do. A study on automatic feature selection shows that in order to achieve a precision of more than 90% with decision tree method C4.5, either at least ca. 200 training samples are needed, or the applied algorithm is able to determine an appropriate subset with few features [8]. As stated otherwise as well, the optimal number of features automatically chosen ranges from 10 to 15 [9]. However, it also has been shown that searches for smallest possible feature sets are NP-complete [3]. So we might infer that real world applications of automatic feature selection have options between a high sample complexity and an even higher computational complexity, in order to get a certain acceptable categorization quality.

To solve this problem, we have designed a feature selection model that can incorporate user's background knowledge to reduce the sample complexity, improve the recall and keep up the precision at the same time. In Step 1 text analysis of the use

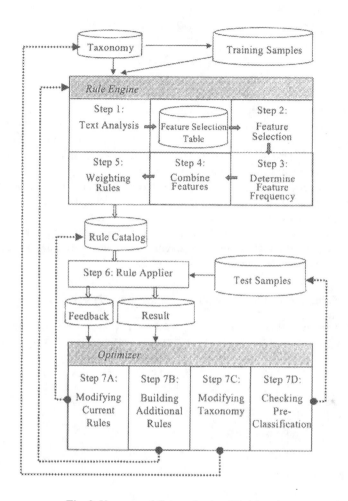

Fig. 3. Use case of Categorization Workbench

case (Fig. 3), we let a feature selection table be generated with Information Gain (IG), Document Frequency Distribution (DFD) and Term Category Distribution (TCD) for each term t of the training set. In contrast with IG, DFD and TCD are category-specific quantities. With the same meaning of the symbols n and C_i in Table 1, they are defined as the following:

$$\mathbf{IG}\ (t) =$$

$$\underbrace{-\left[\sum_{i=1}^{n} \Pr\ (C_i)\cdot \log\ (\Pr\ (C_i))\right]}_{CategoryEn\ tropy} -$$

$$\underbrace{\left\{-\left[\Pr\ (t)\cdot \sum_{i=1}^{n} \Pr\ (C_i\mid t)\cdot \log\ (\Pr\ (C_i\mid t)) + \Pr\ (\bar{t})\cdot \sum_{i=1}^{n} \Pr\ (C_i\mid \bar{t})\cdot \log\ (\Pr\ (C_i\mid \bar{t}))\right]\right\}}_{TermEntrop\ y}$$

$$[1, 14]$$

$$\mathbf{DFD}\,(t, C_i) = \Pr\,(C_i \mid t),$$
$$\mathbf{TCD}\,(t, C_i) = \Pr\,(t \mid C_i).$$

Table 2 shows a feature selection table generated on the base of a training set with 10 samples for each category. Term names in this table[3] are sorted by IG. At Step 2 feature selection, if the user only chooses terms with DFD = 1[4], a precision of 100% on the training set can be guaranteed what could be more than keeping up with the precision of the automatic categorizer. As illustrated in Table 2, our feature selection model provides a certain access to features that would be used by the automatic cate- gorizer to build rules working on the same training set, because decision-tree-based automatic categorizer uses IG either. Beyond these terms, more domain-specific terms can be selected by the user. For example, user with background knowledge would also select "neurons" as a feature for brain science. Building more categorization rules with more features can often cause a higher recall.

Table 2. Access to features of automatic generated rules and more

Term Name	IG	Brain Science		Cognitive Science		Neuropsychology		Psychoanalysis	
		DFD	TCD	DFD	TCD	DFD	TCD	DFD	TCD
the	0.597	0.25	1.00	0.25	1.00	0.25	1.00	0.25	1.00
researcher	0.554	1.00	0.90	-	-	-	-	-	-
representation	0.481	-	-	1.00	0.50	-	-	-	-
university	0.481	1.00	0.50	-	-	-	-	-	-
⋮									
psychoanalytic	0.481	-	-	-	-	-	-	1.00	0.50
⋮									
neurons	0.481	1.00	0.50	-	-	-	-	-	-
⋮									
brain	0.472	0.40	-	-	-	-	-	-	1.00
⋮									
Rules of Automatic Categorizer:		researcher > 0		representation > 0		patient > 2 and this < 1		psychoanalytic > 0	

---

[3] As the documents chosen for the experiments were in German, term names in Table 2 are the translations. The original German terms in turn are: "der", "Forscher", "Repräsentation", "U- niversität", "psychoanalytisch", "Nervenzellen", "Gehirn", "Patient" and "dieser".

[4] For the sake of the clarity, zeros in the table are substituted by hyphens.

5 Comparative Analysis

To prove whether our approach of integrating manual rules into automatic categorization can yield better results, we carried out several comparisons between the Categorization Workbench and the automatic categorizer used in II4C. In the sample tests, we let the automatic categorizer focus on rules with high precision, and tried to find manual rules to enhance the recall with the workbench.

Tables 3 and 4 describe the conditions of the comparative analysis related to structure of taxonomies, choice of samples and conception of the tests. Categories in taxonomy A are more common topics, while categories in taxonomy B are of a more specific scope. They are all German texts chosen. In all tests, training samples are subsets of test samples. The same number of samples indicates the same document set.

Table 3. Conditions of comparison (1)

Taxonomy	Categories	Text Source
A	Culture	Journal: Spiegel etc.
	Politics	Newspapers: Die Welt, Süddeutsche Zeitung
	Sport	Die Welt, www.yahoo.de
	Science	Journal: Bild der Wissenschaft, www.geo.de, www.chemiewelt.de etc.
B	Brain Science	www.hirnforschung.de
	Cognitive Science	Journal: Kognitionswissenschaft
	Neuropsychology	Journal: Zeitschrift für Neuropsychologie
	Psychoanalysis	Journal: Forum der Psychoanalyse

Table 4. Conditions of comparison (2)

Test	Categorizer	Number of Training Samples	Number of Test Samples
1	Automatic Categorizer	10	40
2		40	40
3	Categorization Workbench	5	40
4		10	40

5.1 Improvement of Categorization Quality

Using 10 training samples for both categorizers, the average precisions are all square over both taxonomies, while Categorization Workbench achieves here a higher average recall by a factor of two till four. Using 40 training samples for automatic categorizer and only 10 for the workbench, the average precision of each taxonomy is similar, and the latter shows a slight improvement in average recalls. (Fig. 4)

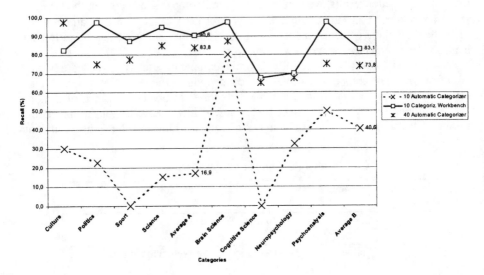

• with 10 training samples: 40 – 70 percentage points higher

• with 40 training samples: 5 – 10 percentage points higher

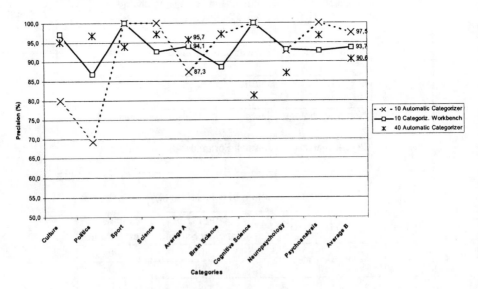

• with both sample sizes: similar

Fig. 4[5]. Recall and precision of test 1, 2 and 4

---

[5] In the following figures, lines connecting point series are intended to show the most characteristic comparison result rather than to indicate any trends.

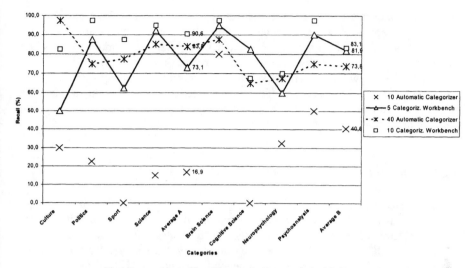

- with 1/2 samples: 40 – 60 procentage points higher
- with 1/4 samples: 5 – 10 procentage points higher
- with 1/8 samples: similar

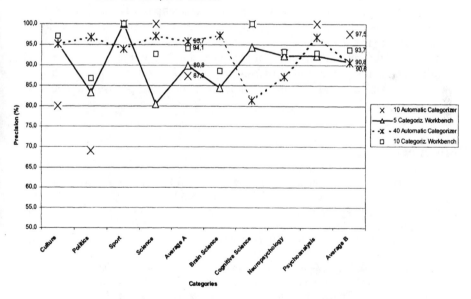

- after sample reduction by a factor of 2, 4 and 8: similar

Fig. 5. Recall and precision of test 1, 2, 3 and 4

5.2 Reduction of Sample Complexity

Using 10 training samples for automatic categorizer and 1/2 of it for the workbench, the average precision in each taxonomy remains similar, and Categorization Workbench even achieves a higher average recall by a factor of two till four. Using 40 training samples for automatic categorizer and 1/4 of it for the workbench, the average precision in each taxonomy is still similar, and Categorization Workbench shows a slight improvement in average recalls. Using 40 training samples for automatic categorizer and only 1/8 of it for the workbench, Categorization Workbench can keep up with its competitor in both average recalls and precisions. (Fig. 5)

Above figures show that the combination of automatic and manual rules facilitated by our Categorization Workbench could achieve better categorization quality than the automatic categorizer: maintaining the good precision of the automatic rules, while increasing the recall using the manual rules.

6 Conclusion and Future Work

The feature selection model constitutes the gist of our approach to integrate advantages of automatic and manual text categorization with each other. Benefiting from the incorporation of user's domain knowledge, the categorization workbench can improve the recall and reduce the sample complexity remarkably. With calculated Information Gain (IG) and Document Frequency Distribution (DFD) of each term, the user has possibilities to choose features and build rules in such a manner as to let the Categorization Workbench's precision be all square with that of the automatic categorizer.

As future work, methods of natural language processing (NLP) and pattern detection can be exploited to make feature selection more effective. So NLP-approaches on ambiguity, synonyms, lexical affinity, co-reference resolution will be needed in order to better model the cognitive process of text analysis. Data mining methods such as finding collocation of words and clustering can be useful to track down hitherto unknown connections between features in order to build more precise categorization rules.

References

1. Apte, C.; Damerau, F. and Weiss, S. M. (1994). Towards language independent automated learning of text categorization models. *Proceedings of ACM SIGIR '94*.
2. Apte, C.; Damerau, F. and Weiss, S. M. (1994). Automated learning of decision rules for text categorization. *ACM Transactions on Information Systems*, 12: 233-251.
3. Davies, S. and Russell, S. (1994). NP-completeness of searches for smallest possible feature sets.
   http://www.cs.berkeley.edu/~russell/papers/mini94f-relevance.ps (11.5.2003).
4. Dumais, S.; Platt, J.; Heckerman, D. and Sahami, M. (1998). Inductive learning algorithms and representations for text categorization. *Proceedings of the 1998 ACM 7th International Conference on Information and Knowledge Management*, 148-155.
5. Joachims, T. (1998). Text categorization with support vector machines: learning with many relevant features. *European Conference on Machine Learing, ECML-98*, 137-142.
6. Joachims, T. (1999). Making large-scale svm learning practical. Advances in kernel methods. *MIT-Press*.
7. Johnson, D. E.; Oles, F. J.; Zhang, T. and Goetz, T. (2001). A decision-tree-based symbolic rule induction system for text categorization.
   http://www.research.ibm.com/dssgrp/Papers/kitcat-ibmj.ps (29.2.2004).
8. Koller, D. and Sahami, M. (1996). Toward optimal feature selection. *Machine Learning: Proceedings Conference*. Morgan Kaufmann.

9. Lewis, D. D. (1992). Feature selection and feature extraction for text categorization. *Proceedings of the Speech an Natural Language Workshop*, 212-217.
10. McCallum, A. and Nigam, K. (1998). A comparison of event models for naive bayes text classification. *AAAI/ICML-98 Workshop on Learning for Text Categorization*, 41-48.
11. Rocchio, J. (1971). The smart retrieval system: Experiments in automated document processing. *Prentice Hall*, 313-323.
12. Weiss, S. M.; Apte, C.; Damerau, F.; Johnson, D. E.; Oles, F. J.; Goetz, T. and Hampp, T. (1999). Maximizing text-mining performance. *IEEE Intelligent Systems*, 14: 63-69.
13. Yang, Y. (1999). An evaluation of statistical approaches to text categorization. *Information Retrieval Journal*, 1: 69-90.
14. Yang, Y. and Pedersen, J. O. (1997). A comparative study on feature selection in text categorization.
   http://citeseer.nj.nec.com/yang97comparative.html (11.5.2003)

Model Based Deduction for Database Schema Reasoning

Peter Baumgartner[1], Ulrich Furbach[2], Margret Gross-Hardt[2], and Thomas Kleemann[2]

[1] MPI Informatik, D-66123 Saarbrücken, Germany
baumgart@mpi-sb.mpg.de
[2] Universität Koblenz-Landau, D-56070 Koblenz, Germany
{uli,margret,tomkl}@uni-koblenz.de

Abstract. We aim to demonstrate that automated deduction techniques, in particular those following the model computation paradigm, are very well suited for database schema/query reasoning. Specifically, we present an approach to compute completed paths for database or XPath queries. The database schema and a query are transformed to disjunctive logic programs with default negation, using a description logic as an intermediate language. Our underlying deduction system, *KRHyper*, then detects if a query is satisfiable or not. In case of a satisfiable query, all completed paths – those that fulfill all given constraints – are returned as part of the computed models.

The purpose of computing completed paths is to reduce the workload on a query processor. Without the path completion, a usual XPath query processor would search the whole database for solutions to the query, which need not be the case when using completed paths instead.

We understand this paper as a first step, that covers a basic schema/query reasoning task by model-based deduction. Due to the underlying expressive logic formalism we expect our approach to easily adapt to more sophisticated problem settings, like type hierarchies as they evolve within the XML world.

1 Introduction

Automated theorem proving is offering numerous tools and methods to be used in other areas of computer science. An extensive overview about the state of the art and its potential for applications is given in [7]. Very often there are special purpose reasoning procedures which are used to reason for different purposes like knowledge representation [1] or logic programming [10].

The most popular methods used for practical applications are resolution-based procedures or model checking algorithms. In this paper we want to demonstrate that there is a high potential for model based procedures for database schema reasoning. Model based deduction can be based very naturally on tableau calculi [12], and in particular on the developments that started with the *SATCHMO* approach [16], which was refined later and extended in the hyper tableau calculus [6].

We start with the idea of representing a database schema as a description logic knowledge base. This idea as such is not new and has been put forward in [8, 9]. However, we found that the services usually available in description logic reasoners do not allow to express all constraints imposed by the schema in order to solve the tasks we

S. Biundo, T. Frühwirth, and G. Palm (Eds.): KI 2004, LNAI 3238, pp. 168–182, 2004.

are looking at. Indeed, the work in [8,9] aims at different purposes, where schema reasoning tasks can be reduced to *satisfiability* of description logic knowledge bases.

We are considering the tasks of testing and optimizing certain forms of database queries as they arise in the XML world. To this end, a "pure" description logic approach was proposed before in [4]. In the present paper, the limitations of that approach are overcome by translating a schema and a given XPath like query into a disjunctive logic program (with default negation). The *KRHyper* system then detects if a query is satisfiable or not. In case of a satisfiable query, all completed paths – those that fulfill all given constraints – are returned as part of the computed models. The purpose of computing completed paths is to reduce the workload on a query processor. Without the path completion, a usual XPath query processor would search the whole database for solutions to the query, which need not be the case when using completed paths instead. The usage of a *model generation* theorem prover thus is motivated by the applications requirement to enumerate models/answers rather than querying the existence of a model.

We start with a brief review of the hyper tableau prover.

2   Theorem Proving with Hyper-tableau

Features. The Hyper Tableau Calculus is a clause normal form tableau calculus [6], which can be seen as a generalization of the SATCHMO-procedure [16]. Hyper tableau have been used in various applications (for examples see [3,5]), where two aspects turned out to be of importance: The result of the theorem prover is a model (if the specification is satisfiable) and this model can be seen as the result of the prover's "computation"; it can be used by the system, where the prover is embedded, for further computation steps. The second aspect is concerned with default negation. Although an entire discipline, namely knowledge representation, is emphasizing the necessity of non-monotonic constructs for knowledge representation, there are only very few sophisticated systems dealing with such constructs [17,11].

The hyper tableau theorem prover *KRHyper* allows application tasks to be specified by using first order logic – plus possibly non-monotonic constructs – in clausal form. While *KRHyper* can be used straightforwardly to prove theorems, it also allows the following features, which are on one hand essential for knowledge based applications, but on the other hand usually not provided by first order theorem provers:

1. Queries which have the listing of predicate extensions as answer are supported.
2. Queries may also have the different extensions of predicates in alternative models as answer.
3. Large sets of uniformly structured input facts are handled efficiently.
4. Arithmetic evaluation is supported.
5. Default negation is supported.
6. The reasoning system can output proofs of derived facts.

More details about these features can be found in [22]. Also, we only note that with a simple transformation of the given rule set, *KRHyper* is sound, complete and terminating with respect to the *possible models* [18] of a stratified disjunctive logic program without function symbols (except constants).

A Small Example. Hyper tableau is a "bottom-up" method, which means that it generates instances of rule[1] heads from facts that have been input or previously derived. If a hyper tableau derivation terminates without having found a proof, the derived facts form a representation of a model of the input clauses.

The following example illustrates how our hyper tableau calculus based system, *KRHyper*, proceeds to generate models. Figure 1 shows four subsequent stages of a derivation for the following input clauses[2]:

$$p(a) \leftarrow \tag{1}$$
$$q(x,y) \vee r(f(z)) \vee r(x) \leftarrow p(x) \tag{2}$$
$$\leftarrow q(x,x) \tag{3}$$
$$s(x) \leftarrow p(x), \text{ not } r(x) \tag{4}$$

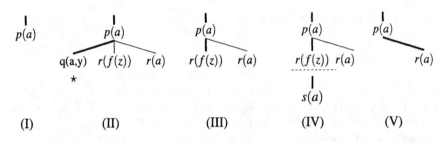

Fig. 1. Stages of a *KRHyper* derivation.

KRHyper provides stratified default negation. The set of input clauses is partitioned into *strata*, according to the predicates in their heads: if a clause c_1 has a head predicate appearing in the scope of the negation operator "not" in the body of c_2, then c_1 is in a lower stratum than c_2. In the example, we have two strata: the lower one containing clauses (1), (2) and (3), the higher one clause (4).

As noted, a rule head may be a disjunction. In hyper tableau, disjunctions are handled by exploring the alternative branches in a systematic way. This explains the tree structure in Figure 1. Backtracking can be used to generate one model after the other.

Stage (I) shows the data structure maintained by the method, also called *hyper tableau*, after the input fact (1) has been processed. One can view the calculus as attempting to construct the representation of a model, the *active branch*, shown with bold lines in the figure. At step (I), this model fragment contradicts for example with clause (2): a model containing $p(a)$ must also contain all instances of $q(a,y)$ or of $r(f(z))$ or $r(a)$. The model fragment is "repaired" by derivating consequences and attaching them

---

[1] We use an implication-style notation for clauses throughout this paper: A clause is viewed as rule *Head* ← *Body*, where *Head* consists of its positive literals, combined by "∨", and *Body* consists of its negative literals, combined by "," (*and*). Both the head and the body may be empty.

[2] Here and below, the letters x, y, z denote variables, while a, b denote constants.

to the hyper tableau: The corresponding instance of clause (2) is attached to the hyper tableau. Since it has a disjunctive head, the tableau splits into three branches. The first branch is inspected and proved contradictory with clause (3) (the branch is said to be *closed*). This state is shown in (II).

Computation now tracks back and works on the second branch. With the clauses of the lower stratum, no further facts can be derived at this branch, which means that a model for the stratum has been found, as shown in step (III). Computation then proceeds with the next higher stratum: $s(a)$ can be derived by clause (4). Since no further facts can be derived, a model for the whole clause set has been found, represented by the facts on the active branch: $\{p(a), r(f(z)), s(a)\}$, as shown in (IV).

If desired, the procedure can backtrack again and continue to find another model, as shown in state (V). Another backtracking step then finally leads to the result, that there is no further model.

We conclude by noting that the *KRHyper* system implements the calculus by a combination of semi-naive rule evaluation with backtracking over alternative disjuncts and iterative deepening over a term weight bound. It extends the language of first order logic by stratified default negation and built-ins for arithmetic.

3   Flexible Database Queries for XML Data

Querying databases requires that users know the structure of a database. In fact, they have to know the *database schema* in order to formulate valid queries. In the context of complex structured data and large database schemas, knowing the complete schema is not always possible. Querying data, therefore, may be a tedious task. This section describes the application of the *KRHyper* System in order to enhance the flexibility of database queries. In particular, we focus on XML databases and address the following issues in querying XML databases:

- XML documents contain complex structured data, often rather nested. Users therefore have to navigate through these data.
- XML data usually is described by Document Type Definitions (DTDs) and more recently, XML Schema is used. Different from DTDs, XML Schema offers in some sense object oriented concepts as user defined types and aggregation as well as specialization relationships between them. During query processing and optimization this schema knowledge may be used, e.g. in order to avoid evaluation of unsatisfiable queries.
- In an XML Schema[20] so called *substitution groups* define types that can be substituted for each other, comparable to union types in other (programming) languages, though, with the difference that types which are substitutes for each other have to be related via specialization.
- Existing querying languages like XQuery [21] offer navigational expressions on the document level in order to access parts of an XML document. These languages do not cope with type expressions. Type expressions may be helpful in order to query instances of some *general* type T, resulting in instances of type T as well as of all subtypes for T.

172   Peter Baumgartner et al.

Let us consider an example XML document representing a university with a library and researchers working in the university. A library consists of books where each book has a title, an author and an ISBN. Researchers have a name and an associated set of publications e.g. articles, monographs or some general kind of publication.

An XML Schema itself also is an XML document listing the complex types together with their elements referring to other (complex) types. Furthermore by means of a so called restriction expression, it is possible to represent specialization relationships between types. Instead of the linear, XML based description of an XML Schema, we use a more illustrative, graphical representation for the types and their relationship in a schema. An XML Schema is represented by a schema graph, where nodes represent the types and substitution groups of the schema and edges represent aggregation and specialization relationships between types. Starting from such a schema graph, we present an approach that allows a user to query the data, even if only parts of a database schema are known. Figure 2 shows an example schema graph.

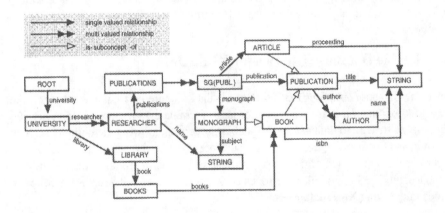

Fig. 2. Example schema graph.

This schema shows types like UNIVERSITY, PUBLICATION, AUTHOR etc. with their elements referring to other types as well as specialization relationships between types. For instance, the type UNIVERSITY has an element researcher of type RESEARCHER and an element library of type LIBRARY. Furthermore, PUBLICATION is a general type with specializations BOOK and ARTICLE. There is one substitution group SG(PUBL) contained in this schema whose general type is PUBLICATION and potential substitutes are ARTICLE and MONOGRAPH, actually specializations of PUBLICATION. In the transformation given below, we will see that substitution groups are a means to express a disjunction of disjoint concepts.

To keep the representation of schema graphs as well as the query processing simple, we only consider (XML-)*elements* describing complex data structures but do not cope with the term of (XML-)*attributes*. Nevertheless, we will use both terms in order to refer to properties of data items.

3.1 From XML Schema to Description Logics

An XML database is described by an XML Schema. The schema is represented by a graph. The nodes of the graph are the complex type identifiers; relationships between elements and their corresponding subelement types are represented by aggregation edges and "extension"-relationships, describing the generalization relationship between complex types, are represented by so called is-a edges. XML Schema supports the modelling of multiple complex types, that are extensions of the same general complex type within a substitution group, comparable to a union type in other languages.

In the following we assume a possibly infinite set L of labels.

Definition 1 (XML Schema). *Let C be a set of type names and SG be a disjoint set of substitution group identifiers. An XML Schema (or schema for short) is a graph $S = (C \cup SG, E_{rel} \cup E_{isa} \cup E_{SG\text{-}in} \cup E_{SG\text{-}out}, r)$ where C and SG are the nodes, E_{rel}, E_{isa}, $E_{SG\text{-}in}$, $E_{SG\text{-}out}$ are disjoint sets of edges (representing attributes/elements edges, inheritance edges, incoming edges to SG nodes, outgoing edges from SG nodes, respectively), and $r \in C$ represents the root of the schema. Every schema must satisfy the following properties:*

1. *$(v,v) \notin E_{rel} \cup E_{isa} \cup E_{SG\text{-}in} \cup E_{SG\text{-}out}$, for any node v.*
2. *Each edge in E_{rel} and each edge in $E_{SG\text{-}out}$ is labeled with an element from L. All other edges are not labeled.*
3. *$(v,v') \in E_{SG\text{-}in}$ if and only if $v' \in SG$ (incoming edges to nodes in SG are precisely those in $E_{SG\text{-}in}$).*
4. *$(v,v') \in E_{SG\text{-}out}$ if and only if $v \in SG$ (outgoing edges from nodes in SG are precisely those in $E_{SG\text{-}out}$).*

The schema can be translated in a straightforward way to description logics as follows[3]:

Definition 2 (Schema to Description Logic). *Let $S = (C \cup SG, E_{rel} \cup E_{isa} \cup E_{SG\text{-}in} \cup E_{SG\text{-}out}, r)$ be a schema. The TBox for S, $T(S)$, is defined as the smallest set of inclusion statements satisfying the following properties:*

Translation of is-a links. *If $c \in C$ and $\{d \mid (c,d) \in E_{isa}\} = \{d_1, \ldots, d_n\}$, for some $n \geq 1$, then $T(S)$ contains the inclusion $c \sqsubseteq d_1 \sqcup \cdots \sqcup d_n$.*
Translation of elements/attributes. *If $(c,d) \in E_{rel}$ and (c,d) is labeled with l, then $T(S)$ contains the inclusion $c \sqsubseteq \exists l.d$.*
Translation of substitution groups. *If $(c,v) \in E_{SG\text{-}in}$ then $T(S)$ contains the inclusion $c \sqsubseteq v$. If $v \in SG$ and $\{d \mid (v,d) \in E_{SG\text{-}out}\} = \{d_1, \ldots, d_n\}$, for some $n \geq 1$, then $T(S)$ contains the inclusion $v \sqsubseteq d_1 \sqcup \cdots \sqcup d_n$ and the inclusions $d_i \sqcap d_j \sqsubseteq \bot$, for all i, j with $1 \leq i, j \leq n$ and $i \neq j$.*

This translation conforms to concept and role formations found even in basic description logic languages like $\mathcal{ALC}$. Although the translation does *not* result in an $\mathcal{ALC}$ TBox ($T(S)$ might contain several inclusion statements with the same concept at the left hand side), it is easy to see that the result of the transformation can easily be brought to an $\mathcal{ALC}$ conforming TBox (possibly cyclic).

---

[3] We use standard description logic notation, see [1].

At this point we will not discuss how to employ description logic reasoners to solve the tasks we are interested in. This discussion will be postponed after our approach based on model computation has been described.

3.2   From Description Logics to Model Computation

The following translation is the standard relational translation from description logics to predicate logic. For our purpose, it is enough to work in a restricted setting, where all inclusions in a TBox are of a particular form, which is obtained as the result of the transformation in Definition 2.

Definition 3 (Description Logic to Rules – Basic Version). *Let S be a schema. The rules for S, $R(S)$, are defined as the smallest set of rules satisfying the following properties:*

1. *if $c \sqsubseteq c_1 \sqcup \cdots \sqcup c_n \in T(S)$ then $R(S)$ contains the rule $c_1(x) \vee \cdots \vee c_n(x) \leftarrow c(x)$*
2. *if $c \sqsubseteq \exists l.d \in T(S)$ then $R(S)$ contains the rules $l(x, f_{c,l,d}(x)) \leftarrow c(x)$ and $d(f_{c,l,d}(x)) \leftarrow c(x)$. ($f_{c,l,d}$ is a unary function symbol whose name contains c, l and d, as indicated.)*
3. *if $c \sqcap d \sqsubseteq \bot \in T(S)$ then $R(S)$ contains the rule* false $\leftarrow c(x), d(x)$.

Using this transformation, simple graph reachability problems can be reduced easily to model computation problems. Speaking in terms of the schema graph, to compute a path, say, from a node c to a node d in a schema S, it suffices to add to $R(S)$ the fact $c(a) \leftarrow$ (for some constant a) and the rules found $\leftarrow d(x)$ and false $\leftarrow$not found, where found is a predicate symbol not occuring in $R(S)$. Each model of the thus obtained program corresponds to exactly one path from c to d in S. However, this approach works only in a satisfactory way if the schema does not contain any circle.

Example 1 (Cycle). Consider a TBox consisting of the two inclusions $c \sqsubseteq \exists l.d$ and $d \sqsubseteq \exists k.c$. It can be obtained by translating a suitable schema containing a circle. Its translation to rules gives the following program:

$$l(x, f_{c,l,d}(x)) \leftarrow c(x) \qquad\qquad d(f_{c,l,d}(x)) \leftarrow c(x)$$
$$k(x, f_{d,k,c}(x)) \leftarrow d(x) \qquad\qquad c(f_{d,k,c}(x)) \leftarrow d(x)$$

Now, any Herbrand model as computed by bottom-up procedures will be infinite and contains $c(a)$, $c(f_{d,k,c}(f_{c,l,d}(a)))$, $c(f_{d,k,c}(f_{c,l,d}(f_{d,k,c}(f_{c,l,d}(a)))))$ and so on. Therefore, *KRHyper* and related procedures will not terminate.

3.3   Blocking by Transformation

In this section we give an improved transformation in order to guarantee termination of the model computation. This will be achieved by a "loop check" similar to the blocking technique known from the description logic literature [14, e.g.]. The idea is to re-use an individual already known to belong to a certain concept instead of adding a new individual to it in order to satisfy an existentially quantified role constraint. In the example, the individual a can be re-used instead of $f_{d,k,c}(f_{c,l,d}(a))$ in order to put $f_{c,l,d}(a)$ into the k-relation to some individual belonging to c. This re-use technique will be described now. It will guarantee the termination of our reasoning algorithm.

Definition 4 (Description Logic to Rules – Improved Version). *Let S be a schema. The rules for S, R(S), are defined as the smallest set of rules satisfying the following properties:*

1. *if* $c \sqsubseteq c_1 \sqcup \cdots \sqcup c_n \in T(S)$ *then* $R(S)$ *contains the rule* $c_1(x) \vee \cdots \vee c_n(x) \leftarrow c(x)$
2. $R(S)$ *contains the fact* $\mathsf{equal}(x,x) \leftarrow .$
3. *if* $c \sqsubseteq \exists l.d \in T(S)$ *then* $R(S)$ *contains the following rules:*

$$\mathsf{new}_{c,l,d}(x) \vee \mathsf{old}_{c,l,d}(x) \leftarrow c(x) \tag{1}$$
$$\mathsf{false} \leftarrow \mathsf{new}_{c,l,d}(x), \mathsf{old}_{c,l,d}(x) \tag{2}$$
$$l(x, f_{c,l,d}(x)) \leftarrow \mathsf{new}_{c,l,d}(x) \tag{3}$$
$$d(f_{c,l,d}(x)) \leftarrow \mathsf{new}_{c,l,d}(x) \tag{4}$$
$$l(x,z) \leftarrow \mathsf{old}_{c,l,d}(x), c(y), l(y,z), d(z) \tag{5}$$
$$\mathsf{false} \leftarrow \mathsf{old}_{c,l,d}(x), \mathsf{not}\ \mathsf{some}_{c,l,d} \tag{6}$$
$$\mathsf{some}_{c,l,d} \leftarrow c(x), l(x,y), d(y) \tag{7}$$
$$\mathsf{false} \leftarrow \mathsf{new}_{c,l,d}(x), \mathsf{new}_{c,l,d}(y), \mathsf{not}\ \mathsf{equal}(x,y) \tag{8}$$

4. *if* $c \sqcap d \sqsubseteq \bot \in T(S)$ *then* $R(S)$ *contains the rule* $\mathsf{false} \leftarrow c(x), d(x)$.

Some comments are due. The difference to the previous version is the translation of inclusions of the form $c \sqsubseteq \exists l.d$. In order to explain it, suppose that the concept c is populated with some individual, say, a. That is, when constructing a model, $c(a)$ already holds true. Now, the program above distinguishes two complementary cases to satisfy the constraint $\exists l.d$ for a: either a new l-connection is made between a and some new individual in d, or an existing ("old") l-connection between some individual from c and from d is re-used. That exactly one of these cases applies is guaranteed by the rules (1) and (2). The rules (3) and (4) are responsible to establish a new connection, while the rule (5) is responsible to re-use an existing connection. To achieve the desired effect, some more constraints are needed: as said, re-using an existing connection is realized by applying the rule (5). It establishes the connection $l(x,z)$, where x stands for the object the connection is to be established from (a in the example), and z stands for the re-used object from d. However, there is no guarantee per se that the rule's subgoals $c(y)$, $l(y,z)$ and $d(z)$ are satisfied. This, however, is achieved by the rules (6) and (7): whenever the program chooses to re-use an old connection, i.e. to build a model containing this choice, by (6) and (7) this can succeed only if the mentioned subgoals are satisfiable. Finally, the rule (8) acts as a "loop check": with it, it is impossible that between individuals belonging to the concepts c and d more than one new l-connection is made. Only new l-connections cause insertion of more complex atoms[4] and thus are the only source for non-termination. With the rule (8) there is a finite bound on the complexity then for a given program.

The program above is intended to be run by a bottom-up model computation procedure like *KRHyper* (Section 2). Together with some more rules and facts obtained by further transformation steps this yields an algorithm that is similar to usual tableau algorithms developed for description logics. On the one side, our translation and the

---

[4] Complexity being measured as the tree depth of the atoms.

reasoning tasks to be solved do not quite match those in existing algorithms. This is because of the use of default negation to filter out nonintended models (see Section 3.5). Another difficulty we encountered with existing systems is their inability to actually output the computed models. From our application point of view this is problematic, as the answer to the tasks to be solved *is* the model (see again Section 3.5).

On the other side, it suffices for our purpose to work with TBoxes that are quite simple and do not involve constructs that are notoriously difficult to handle (like the combination of inverse roles, transitive roles and number restrictions). This allows us to use the above rather simple "loop checking" technique, which is inspired by the blocking technique developed for an ABox/TBox reasoner in [14].

3.4 Query Language

Existing query languages use path queries that navigate along the structures of the XML data. For instance, in order to access the name of all researchers of a university in *XPath* [19] one may use the XPath expression `/university/researcher/name`. Path queries usually allow some form of "abbreviation". For instance, with `//researcher/name` one addresses all descendants of the "root" that are *researcher*-elements and navigate to their names. However, because path queries work directly on the XML data and not on the schema, it is not possible to query those elements from a data source that belongs to the same type or concept. In particular, in order to ask e.g. for all kinds of publications, one would have to construct the union of path queries navigating to publication, book, article and monograph, explicitly.

This problem has been addressed in [13] where concepts or type expressions, respectively, have been added to the query language. Querying instances of types or concepts is well known in object oriented databases. Furthermore, path expressions allow to navigate through the nested structure of the data. We assume a syntax similar to that applied in object oriented databases [15]. We aim at a query language that combines schema expressions as used in object oriented query languages with a flexible navigation mechanism as given by "abbreviated" path expressions as e.g. provided by XPath.

Let A denote a set of attribute names.

Definition 5 (Query Syntax). *A* path term *is an expression of the form* $c[x]\ op_1\ a_1[x_1]$ $\dots op_m\ a_m[x_m]$, *where* $m \geq 0$, c *is a type name, a substitution group identifier (cf. Def. 1) or the symbol* $\top$, $op_i \in \{.,!\}$, $a_i \in A$, *and* x, x_i, *for* $i = 1, \dots, m$ *are variables.*

A conjunctive query expression *is a conjunction of path terms* $p_1 \wedge \dots \wedge p_n$, *where* $n \geq 1$. *A* disjunctive query expression *is a disjunction of conjunctive query expressions* $e_1 \vee \dots \vee e_n$, *where* $n \geq 1$.

By simply a *query expression* we mean a disjunctive query expression, which includes the case of a conjunctive query expression as a disjunction with one element.

A path term is an expression that starts in a concept and navigates through a schema by a sequence of attributes. Variables are used to "hold" the spots during this navigation. At the instance level, a path term describes a set of paths in a data source. The result of a path term basically is a relationship, where all variables occuring in a path term are bound to elements in the XML document. Actually, there are two possibilities to traverse a schema. First, by explicit navigation that specifies a path step by step. We use the "!" operator for this kind of navigation. Second, a path term may specify only some attributes occuring on one or several paths in a schema; then the "." operator is used.

For instance, BOOK$[b]$!title$[t]$ describes all instances b of type BOOK, with a title t as subelement. The result, basically, is a binary relation containing values for b and t. Compared to an XPath-expression, the "!" operator matches "/" and the "." operator can be compared to "//". Different from an XPath expression, in our query syntax variables can be specified and type expressions are possible. If a user does not want to specify an explicit type, the most general type $\top$ can be taken. As will be shown below (see Section 3.5), using type expressions in a query allows a user to query for different elements described by the same general type in one simple expression. For instance, BOOK$[b]$!title$[t]$ retrieves all BOOK elements with their titles as well as all MONO-GRAPH elements, because of the underlying specialization/subsumption relationship.

Furthermore, using type expressions in a query provides a query processor with a possibility to validate purely by means of the schema if a query is satisfiable. Consider another query: PUBLICATION$[p]$.isbn$[i] \wedge \top[p]$.proceedings$[x]$. This query asks for all instances p of PUBLICATION with their isbn and their proceedings. Actually, there are no such instances. This fact can be established automatically, as will be shown below. This means it is useless to try this query on any concrete database satisfying the schema, as the result will be empty anyway.

We conclude this section by informally describing the semantics of queries: we say a query expression $q = e_1 \vee \cdots \vee e_n$ (cf. Definition 5) is *satisfiable in a schema* S (cf. Definition 1) iff there is a conjunctive query expression e_i, $(1 \leq i \leq n)$, and a substitution σ mapping each variable in e_i to a type name or a substitution group identifier, such that (i) S satisfies each path term in $e_i\sigma$ according to the just indicated semantics of the operators "!" and ".", and (ii) no type name or substitution group identifier is visited more than twice on the traversal of S as specified by $e_i\sigma$. Any such substitution is called a *solution for q*.

The rationale behind condition (ii) is to allow queries admitting solutions representing circles in the schema graph, but no circle should be followed more than once.

3.5   Translating Queries to Rules

The translation of a path term p of the form $c[x]\ op_1\ a_1[x_1] \cdots op_m\ a_m[x_m]$ (cf. Definition 5) is the following list of atoms $tr(p)$:

$$c(x),\ tr_{sel}(x, op_1\ a_1[x_1]),\ tr_{sel}(x_1, op_2\ a_2[x_2]), \ldots, tr_{sel}(x_{m-1}, op_m\ a_m[x_m])\ ,$$

where

$$tr_{sel}(x, op\ a[y]) = \begin{cases} a(x,y) & \text{if } op = \text{!} \\ \text{role\_filler\_ref\_trans}(x,z), a(z,y) & \text{if } op = \text{.} , \\ & \text{where } z \text{ is a fresh variable} \end{cases}$$

The purpose of $tr(p)$ is to translate the path term p into a sequence of subgoals that correspond to traversing the schema as prescribed by p and thereby assigning values to the variables mentioned in p. Notice the translation distinguishes between the operators

".” and “!”. The former stands for the presence of an attribute immediately at the current point of the traversal and thus translates into a corresponding role filler subgoal. The latter is similar, but it allows to follow an arbitrary number of attributes first, by means of the role_filler_ref_trans relation. A query is translated into rules as follows:

(1) The translation of a conjunctive query expression $p_1 \wedge \ldots \wedge p_n$, where $n \geq 1$ and each p_i (for $i = 1, \ldots, n$) is of the form just mentioned and written as $p_i = c^i [x^i] op_1{}^i a_1^i [x_1^i] \cdots op_{m_i}^i a_{m_i}^i [x_{m_i}^i]$ consists of the following rules:

$$\text{solution\_path}(x^1, (x_{m_1}^1, \ldots, x_{m_n}^n)) \leftarrow \text{role\_filler\_ref\_trans}(\text{init}, x^1), \ c^1(x^1),$$
$$tr(p_1), \ldots, tr(p_n)$$

Observe that the selector x^1 mentioned in the first path term p_1, is treated in a special way. Its type c^1 is treated as the “start type”, and a path from the root to it is computed in the first argument of the solution_path predicate.

The translation of a disjunctive conjunctive query expression $e_1 \vee \ldots \vee e_n$ is the union of the translation of each e_1, for $i = 1, \ldots, n$.

(2) The following rules constrain the admissible models to those that contain at least one “solution path”:

$$\text{false} \leftarrow \text{not some\_solution\_path}$$
$$\text{some\_solution\_path} \leftarrow \text{solution\_path}(x, y)$$

(3) Let E_{rel} be a set of attribute names as mentioned in Definition 1. The set E_{rel} is reified by the set of rules

$$T(E_{\text{rel}}) = \{\text{role\_filler}(x, y) \leftarrow l(x, y) \mid l \text{ is the label of some attribute in } E_{\text{rel}}\}$$

The reflexive-transitive closure of $T(E_{\text{rel}})$ is obtained as follows:

$$\text{role\_filler\_ref\_trans}(x, x) \leftarrow$$
$$\text{role\_filler\_ref\_trans}(x, z) \leftarrow \text{role\_filler}(x, y), \ \text{role\_filler\_ref\_trans}(y, z)$$

In the following definition all transformations introduced so far are collected and combined. It states the complete transformation applied to a schema and a query.

Definition 6 (Transformation of a Schema and a Query). *Let* $S = (C \cup SG, E_{\text{rel}} \cup E_{\text{isa}} \cup E_{\text{SG-in}} \cup E_{\text{SG-out}}, r)$ *be a schema as in Definition 1 and* q *a query expression. The transformation of* S *and* q *consists of the union of* $R(S)$ *of Definition 4, the result of the transformation step (1) applied to* q, *the rules from (2), the rules from (3) (both* $T(E_{\text{rel}})$ *and the rules for the reflexive-transitive closure of* $T(E_{\text{rel}})$), *and the facts*

$$\top(x) \leftarrow \qquad\qquad\qquad \text{root}(\text{init}) \leftarrow$$

As said earlier, the purpose of our model based approach is to detect if a XPath like query is satisfiable or not. In case of a satisfiable query, a fully completed path – one that fulfills all given constraints – is returned as part of the model. Furthermore, every such fully completed path will be computed. The following theorem states this result more formally and summarizes important properties of our transformation.

Theorem 1 (Soundness and Solution Completeness). *Let S be a schema as in Definition 1 and q a query expression. Let T be a tableau derived by KRHyper applied to the transformation of S and q. Then the following holds:*

1. *Every open branch in T contains an (at least one) atom of the form* solution_path(t, $(t_1, \ldots, t_n)$)) *and it denotes a solution for q, by means of the substitution* $\{x/t, x_1/t_1, \ldots, x_n/t_n\}$, *where* $x_1, \ldots, x_n$ *are the variables occuring in some conjunctive query expression of q, in this order.*
2. *For every solution* $\{x/t, x_1/t_1, \ldots, x_n/t_n\}$ *for q there is an open branch in T containing the atom* solution_path(t, $(t_1, \ldots, t_n)$).

From the theorem it follows easily that T does not contain an open branch (i.e. T is closed) iff q is not satisfiable in S, as expected.

In the statement of the theorem it is implicitly assumed that the tableau construction by *KRHyper* terminates. That this is indeed the case was argued for in Section 3.3. The other properties stated can be shown with a careful analysis of the properties of the transformation of S and q. The idea is to show that traversing the schema according to a given solution is simulated by the model construction, and vice versa. An important detail concerns solutions representing circles in the schema graph. As explained at the end of Section 3.4, following circles *once* is admissible, which matches exactly with what the blocking technique in Section 3.3 achieves.

3.6   Example

The query expression BOOK[b]!title[t] from above translates into the following program:

$$\top(x) \leftarrow \tag{1}$$
$$\text{root}(\text{init}) \leftarrow \tag{2}$$
$$\text{solution\_path}(b,t) \leftarrow \text{role\_filler\_ref\_trans}(\text{init}, b), \tag{3}$$
$$\text{BOOK}(b), \text{role\_filler\_ref\_trans}(b,z), \text{title}(z,t)$$
$$\text{false} \leftarrow \text{not some\_solution\_path} \tag{4}$$
$$\text{some\_solution\_path} \leftarrow \text{solution\_path}(x,y) \tag{5}$$
$$\text{role\_filler\_ref\_trans}(x,x) \leftarrow \tag{6}$$
$$\text{role\_filler\_ref\_trans}(x,z) \leftarrow \text{role\_filler}(x,y), \tag{7}$$
$$\text{role\_filler\_ref\_trans}(y,z)$$
$$\text{role\_filler}(x,y) \leftarrow \text{university}(x,y) \tag{8}$$
$$\vdots \qquad \vdots \tag{9}$$
$$\text{role\_filler}(x,y) \leftarrow \text{isbn}(x,y) \tag{10}$$

Notice the rule (3) is the translation of the given (single conjunct) query expression according to the scheme (1) above. The rules starting from (6) stem from the translation of the schema graph in Figure 2 according to the scheme (3).

Now, suppose that this rule set is combined with the translation of the schema graph in Figure 2 according to Definitions 2 and 3 (or Definition 4 instead). The unique model contains

$$\text{solution\_path}(f_{\text{BOOKS,books,BOOK}}(f_{\text{LIBRARY,book,BOOKS}}(\\
f_{\text{UNIVERSITY,library,LIBRARY}}(f_{\text{ROOT,university,UNIVERSITY}}(\text{init})))),\\
f_{\text{PUBLICATION,title,STRING}}(f_{\text{BOOKS,books,BOOK}}(f_{\text{LIBRARY,book,BOOKS}}(\\
f_{\text{UNIVERSITY,library,LIBRARY}}(f_{\text{ROOT,university,UNIVERSITY}}(\text{init}))))))$$

Observe that the path from the ROOT concept to the BOOK concept is coded in the names of the Skolem function symbols in the first argument of solution_path. This path is extended towards a path to the title attribute in the second argument; this extension encodes, in terms of the schema graph, moving from the BOOK type to its supertype PUBLICATION and then moving to the title attribute. We note that the query expression BOOK[b].title[t] would have given the same result.

As a second example consider PUBLICATION[p].isbn[i] $\wedge$ $\top$[p].proceedings[x] from above. Its translation according to scheme (1) is

$$\text{solution\_path}(p,(i,x)) \leftarrow \text{role\_filler\_ref\_trans}(\text{init},p), \qquad (3)\\
\text{PUBLICATION}(p), \text{isbn}(p,i),\\
\top(p), \text{proceedings}(p,x)$$

The rest of the transformation is the same as in the previous examples and is omitted. This time, the solution_path relation is empty, as the body of rule (3) cannot be satisfied. But then, with rules (4) and (5) this rule set is unsatisfiable. This is the expected result, because, as mentioned above, the query expression is unsatisfiable (in terms of the schema graph)[5].

4 Conclusion

In this paper we aimed to demonstrate that automated deduction techniques, in particular those following the model computation paradigm, are very well suited for database schema/query reasoning. We started by showing how to represent an XML Schema graph in basic description logic. This representation then is transformed into the predicate logic language of the first order theorem prover *KRHyper*. We also proposed a flexible query language containing constructs for path specification similar as in the XPath query language, and we showed how to transform the query language into *KRHyper*'s input language. The models computed by *KRHyper* then encode fully specified XML path queries. The purpose of computing fully specified XML path queries is to reduce the workload on a query processor, because, in general, fully specified queries involve much less search on the database than XPath queries. To our knowledge an approach comparable to ours, based on model based deduction, has not been considered before.

An obvious question concerns the correctness of our approach, i.e. termination, soundness and completeness of the combination of *KRHyper* and the transformed

---

[5] The runtime of *KRHyper* on both examples is negligible.

database schema and query. While termination has been argued for in Section 3.3, it is hardly possible to establish the other two properties: there is no formal semantics of XML path queries in the literature.

We found description logic to be helpful as an intermediate language to represent XML Schema graphs. Moreover, our transformation includes a blocking technique comparable to those used in description logic reasoners [14, e.g.]. However, we went beyond the "classical" description paradigm in two aspects. The first aspect concerns the use of *models* to represent the solutions of the given problem of computing paths (as explained). As a second aspect, we found *default negation* very helpful to formulate constraints on acceptable models. From this point of view, we believe having shown there are applications for description logics where model computation and default negation is an issue. We perceive our approach to knowledge representation also as an original contribution of our work. A similar direction was proposed only recently in [2], where related ideas as presented here are exploited in the context of natural language processing. In a wider context, we speculate that *Semantic Web* applications would profit from knowledge representation languages as discussed here.

We understand this paper as a first step, that covers a basic schema/query reasoning task by model-based deduction. Due to the underlying expressive logic formalism we expect our approach to easily adapt to more sophisticated problem settings, like type hierarchies as they evolve within the XML world. One big advantage of such a declarative approach over, say, explicitly programmed algorithms is the possibility to easily add further constraints. We intend to explore this potential in future work.

References

1. F. Baader, D. Calvanese, D. McGuinness, D. Nardi, and P. Patel-Schneider, editors. *Description Logic Handbook*. Cambridge University Press, 2002.
2. P. Baumgartner and A. Burchardt. Logic Programming Infrastructure for Inferences on FrameNet. In *The European Conference on Logics in Artificial Intelligence*, LNAI. Springer Verlag, Berlin, Heidelberg, New-York, 2004. To appear.
3. P. Baumgartner, P. Fröhlich, U. Furbach, and W. Nejdl. Semantically Guided Theorem Proving for Diagnosis Applications. In M. E. Pollack, editor, *15th Int. Joint Conf. on Artificial Intelligence (IJCAI 97)*, pages 460–465, Nagoya, 1997. Morgan Kaufmann.
4. P. Baumgartner, U. Furbach, M. Gross-Hardt, and T. Kleemann. Optimizing the Evaluation of XPath using Description Logics. In *Proc. INAP2004, 15th Int. Conf. on Applications of Declarative Programming and Knowledge Management*, Potsdam, 2004.
5. P. Baumgartner, U. Furbach, M. Gross-Hardt, and A. Sinner. `'Living Book'` : - `'Deduction'`, `'Slicing'`, `'Interaction'`. – system description. In F. Baader, editor, *CADE-19 – The 19th Int. Conf. on Automated Deduction*, LNAI. Springer, 2003.
6. P. Baumgartner, U. Furbach, and I. Niemelä. Hyper Tableaux. In *Proc. JELIA 96*, number 1126 in LNAI. European Workshop on Logic in AI, Springer, 1996.
7. W. Bibel and P. H. Schmitt, editors. *Automated Deduction. A basis for applications*. Kluwer Academic Publishers, 1998.
8. D. Calvanese, G. D. Giacomo, and M. Lenzerini. Answering queries using views in description logics. In *Proc. DL'99, Description Logic Workshop*, 1999.
9. D. Calvanese, G. D. Giacomo, and M. Lenzerini. Representing and reasoning on XML documents: a description logic approach. *J. of Logic and Computation*, pages 295–318, 1999.

10. J. Dix, U. Furbach, and I. Niemelä. Nonmonotonic Reasoning: Towards Efficient Calculi and Implementations. In A. Voronkov and A. Robinson, editors, *Handbook of Automated Reasoning*, pages 1121–1234. Elsevier-Science-Press, 2001.
11. T. Eiter, W. Faber, N. Leone, and G. Pfeifer. Declarative problem-solving using the DLV system. In *Logic-based artificial intelligence*, pages 79–103. Kluwer Academic Publishers, 2000.
12. U. Furbach. Automated deduction. In W. Bibel and P. Schmitt, editors, *Automated Deduction. A Basis for Applications*, volume I: Foundations. Calculi and Refinements. Kluwer Academic Publishers, 1998.
13. M. Gross-Hardt. Querying concepts – an approach to retrieve xml data by means of their data types. In *17. WLP - Workshop Logische Programmierung*, Technical Report. Technische Universität Dresden, 2002.
14. V. Haarslev and R. Möller. Expressive ABox Reasoning with Number Restrictions, Role Hierarchies, and Transitively Closed Roles. In *KR2000: Principles of Knowledge Representation and Reasoning*, pages 273–284. Morgan Kaufmann, 2000.
15. M. Kifer, W. Kim, and Y. Sagiv. Querying object-oriented databases. In *SIGMOD*, 1992.
16. R. Manthey and F. Bry. SATCHMO: a theorem prover implemented in Prolog. In E. Lusk and R. Overbeek, editors, *Proc. of the 9th Conf. on Automated Deduction, Argonne, Illinois, May 1988*, volume 310 of *LNCS*, pages 415–434. Springer, 1988.
17. I. Niemelä and P. Simons. Efficient implementation of the well-founded and stable model semantics. In *Proc. of the Joint Int. Conf. and Symposium on Logic Programming*, Bonn, Germany, 1996. The MITPress.
18. C. Sakama. Possible Model Semantics for Disjunctive Databases. In W. Kim, J.-M. Nicholas, and S. Nishio, editors, *Proc. First Int. Conf. on Deductive and Object-Oriented Databases (DOOD-89)*, pages 337–351. Elsevier Science Publishers B.V. (North–Holland) Amsterdam, 1990.
19. W3C. XPath specification. http://www.w3.org/TR/xpath, 1999.
20. W3C. XML Schema - part 0 to part 2. http://www.w3.org/TR/xmlschema-0, -1, -2, 2001.
21. W3C. XQuery 1.0: An XML query language. http://www.w3.org/TR/xquery/, 2001.
22. C. Wernhard. System Description: KRHyper. Fachberichte Informatik 14–2003, Universität Koblenz-Landau, Institut für Informatik, 2003.

Applying Automatic Planning Systems to Airport Ground-Traffic Control – A Feasibility Study

Sebastian Trüg, Jörg Hoffmann, and Bernhard Nebel

Institut für Informatik
Universität Freiburg
79110 Freiburg, Germany
{trueg,hoffmann,nebel}@informatik.uni-freiburg.de

Abstract. Planning techniques have matured as demonstrated by the performance of automatic planning systems at recent international planning system competitions. Nowadays it seems feasible to apply planning systems to real-world problems. In order to get an idea of what the performance difference between special-purpose techniques and automatic planning techniques is, we applied these techniques to the airport traffic control problem and compared it with a special purpose tool. In addition to a performance assessment, this exercise also resulted in a domain model of the airport traffic control domain, which was used as a benchmark in the 4th International Planning Competition.

1   Introduction

Planning techniques have matured as demonstrated by the performance of automatic planning systems at recent international planning system competitions [1, 12]. Current planning systems are able to generate plans with hundred steps and more compared with ten steps or less ten years ago. Given the inherent complexity of the planning problem, this is a dramatic improvement. The reason for this performance boost is the use of new algorithms and the development of powerful heuristics [2, 3].

In order to assess how feasible it is to apply automatic planning systems to real-world problems, we used these techniques to solve the operational airport ground-traffic control problem [8]. This is an NP-complete problem that can be characterized as a job-shop scheduling problem with blocking. Using special-purpose techniques, it can be solved approximately for a realistic number of airplanes (roughly 50) on realistic airports (such as Frankfurt airport).

So how far do we get with planning techniques for this problem? As our experiments indicate, the *expressiveness* of current planning systems approaches the point where one can formulate the traffic problem as a planning problem. From a *performance* point of view, the results are less encouraging. The planners we evaluate in our experiments are only good enough for small airports with few airplanes. One has to put this result into perspective, however. Special-purpose

S. Biundo, T. Frühwirth, and G. Palm (Eds.): KI 2004, LNAI 3238, pp. 183–197, 2004.

scheduling techniques are, of course, highly optimized for the particular scheduling problem. Furthermore, the performance penalty to be expected for general-purpose solutions is always quite high and often prohibitive. On the positive side, the exercise of formalizing the traffic problem has led to a new challenging, real-world benchmark problem for automatic planning systems[1]. Indeed, the domain was used as a benchmark in IPC-4, the 4th International Planning Competition. The results obtained by the competitors in IPC-4 are somewhat more encouraging than our own results. The IPC-4 results were available just a few days before the deadline for the conference version of this paper. We provide a short summary of the results.

The rest of the paper is structured as follows. In Section 2, we give a description of the airport ground-traffic control problem. Section 3 describes then the formalization using PDDL [11], the *de facto* standard for planning systems. In order to allow existing planning systems to be used, we also describe how to compile the PDDL specification into basic STRIPS. Based on that, in Section 4, the results of our experiments, and a summary of the IPC-4 results, are given. Section 5 summarizes and concludes.

2   The Airport Ground-Traffic Control Problem

In a nutshell, the airport ground-traffic control problem consists of coordinating the movements of airplanes on the airport so that they reach their planned destinations (runway or parking position) as fast as possible – whereby collisions shall be, of course, avoided.

The airplanes move on the airport *infrastructure*, which consists of *runways, taxi ways,* and *parking positions.* Airplanes are generally divided into the three 'Wake Vortex Categories': *light, medium,* and *heavy,* which classify them according to their engine exhaust. A moving airplane can either be *in-bound* or *out-bound.* In-bound airplanes are recently landed and are on their way from the runway to a parking position, usually a gate. Out-bound airplanes are ready for departure, meaning they are on their way to the departure runway. Since airplanes are not able to move backwards, they need to be pushed back from the gate on the taxiway where they start up their engines. Some airports provide different park positions that allow an airplane to start its engines directly but to simplify the situation we assume that an airplane always needs to be pushed back.

The ground controller has to communicate to the airplanes which ways they shall take and when to stop. While such guidance can be given purely reactively, it pays off to base decisions on anticipating the future. Otherwise it may happen that airplanes block each other and need more time than necessary to reach their destinations on the airport. The objective is to minimize the overall summed up traveling times of all airplanes.

---

[1] The full encoding of the problem can be found in the technical report version of this paper [14].

From a formal point of view, one considers the problem with a time horizon of say one hour and schedules all movements, minimizing the movement times of the planes. Of course, because the situation changes continually (new planes arrive and schedules cannot be executed as planned), continuous rescheduling is necessary. We will consider, however, only the static optimization problem with a given situation on the airport and a time horizon of a fixed time span.

Our domain representation and implementation is based on software by Wolfgang Hatzack, namely on a system called *Astras*: Airport Surface ground TRAffic Simulator. This is a software package that was originally designed to be a training platform for airport controllers. Astras provides a two-dimensional view of the airport, allowing the user to control the airplanes by means of point and click. Astras also includes features for simulating the traffic flow on an airport over the course of a specified time window, as well as an automated controller (named *Acore*) driven by a greedy re-scheduling approach [8]. Our PDDL domain encoding is based on Astras's internal representation of airports. We generated our test instances by software that is integrated with Astras. During an airport simulation, if desired by the user our software exports the current traffic situation in various PDDL encodings.

3   The PDDL Encoding of the Airport Domain

The central object in the PDDL encoding of the airport domain is the airplane that moves over the airport infrastructure. The airport infrastructure is built out of segments. An airplane always occupies one segment and may block several others depending on its type. Our assumption here is that medium and heavy airplanes block the segment behind them whereas light airplanes only block the segment they occupy. Blocked segments cannot be occupied by another airplane. To handle terms like *behind* we need to introduce direction in segments. Since our segments are two-dimensional objects we need exactly two directions which we quite inappropriately call north and south. Every segment has its north end and its south end so it becomes possible to talk about direction in a segment.

To model the airplane movement we need at least two actions. The *move* action describes the normal forward movement of an airplane from one segment to another. The *pushback* action describes backward movement when an airplane is being pushed back from its park position.

We also introduce an airplane state. An airplane can either be moving, be pushed, be parked, or be airborne. We want to make sure that an airplane only moves backwards while being pushed from its park position and only moves forward if not. The parked state is necessary since a parked airplane's engines are off and thus the airplane does not block any segments except the one it occupies unlike when moving. If a plane is airborne, i.e. the plane took off already, then that means that the plane is not relevant to the ground traffic anymore.

The actions *park* and *startup* describe the transitions between the different states. As one may expect the park action makes sure the airplane only blocks the occupied segment while the startup action does the exact opposite. It initially blocks segments depending on the airplane type.

A last action is needed to completely remove the airplane from the airport after takeoff. This action is called *takeoff* and makes sure the airplane does not block or occupy any segment anymore.

In the following we describe our different encodings of the airport domain: a durative and non-durative ADL [13] encoding, a STRIPS [6] encoding where the ADL constructs were compiled out, finally a means to model runway blocking for landing airplanes.

3.1   ADL Encoding

Our domain has four types of objects: *airplane, segment, direction,* and *airplanetype.*

The airplane type (its Wake Vortex Category) is described with the *has-type* predicate:

```
(has-type ?a - airplane ?t - airplanetype)
```

The airplane state is described with four predicates:

```
(airborne ?a - airplane ?s - segment)
(is-moving ?a - airplane)
(is-pushed ?a - airplane)
(is-parked ?a - airplane ?s - segment)
```

The *is-parked* predicate has a second parameter stating the park position the airplane is parked at. The second parameter of the *airborne* predicate just states from which segment the airplane took off. This is useful in case an airport provides several departure runways and we want to force an airplane to use a specific one. Apart from the airplane state we also need to describe the current position of an airplane and its heading:

```
(at-segment ?a - airplane ?s - segment)
(facing ?a - airplane ?d - direction)
```

We need several predicates to describe the airport structure. All the following predicates are static; they will be set once in the initial state and never be changed.

```
(can-move ?s1 ?s2 - segment ?d - direction)
(can-pushback ?s1 ?s2 - segment ?d - direction)
(move-dir ?s1 ?s2 - segment ?d - direction)
(move-back-dir ?s1 ?s2 - segment ?d - direction)
(is-blocked ?s1 - segment ?t - airplanetype ?s2 - segment ?d - direction)
(is-start-runway ?s - segment ?d - direction)
```

The *can-move* predicate states that an airplane may move from segment *s1* to segment *s2* if its facing direction *d.* The *can-pushback* predicate describes the possible backward movement which is similar to the *can-move* predicate. In our encodings, the *can-move* predicate holds only for pairs of segments that belong to the *standard routes* on the airport – this is common practice in reality (as reroutes are likely to cause trouble or at least confusion), and yields much better planner performance.

The *move-dir* and *move-back-dir* predicates state the airplane's heading after moving from segment *s1* to segment *s2*. That means that in a correct airport domain fact file every *can-move* (*can-pushback*) predicate has its *move-dir* (*move-back-dir*) counterpart.

The *is-blocked* predicate is used to handle all blocking. It says that segment *s1* will be blocked by an airplane of type *t* at segment *s2* facing into direction *d*. We will see the use of this predicate in the move action's effect in detail.

The last predicate, *is-start-runway*, states that an airplane at segment *s* facing direction *d* is allowed to takeoff. This is an essential predicate as we cannot allow an airplane to takeoff wherever it (or better: the planner) wants.

Finally, we need two predicates to describe the current situation on the airport regarding blocked and occupied segments:

```
(occupied ?s - segment)
(blocked ?s - segment ?a - airplane)
```

3.1.1 Non-durative Actions.
Now we will look at the actions used in the non-durative ADL domain in detail.

The most important one is clearly the *move* action (see Figure 1). The parameters have the following meaning: an airplane *a* of type *t* facing direction *d1* on segment *s1* moves to segment *s2* and then faces direction *d2*. The first four predicates in the precondition make sure the airplane is in a proper state, meaning it is located in the right segment facing the right direction. Predicates five and six represent the airport structure as described above. The last two formulas are the really interesting ones as they deal with segment blocking. The first one makes sure that no other airplane blocks the segment our airplane is moving to. Here we use the full power of ADL to check for every airplane if it is blocking segment *s2*. Our moving airplane cannot block itself so we exclude it from the check. The second formula is used to make sure that none of the segments our airplane will block after the movement is occupied by another airplane. To achieve that we use the *is-blocked* predicate. Its instances give us the segments that will be blocked once our airplane has moved to segment *s2*. If we find such a segment we make sure its not occupied since a segment may not be occupied and blocked by different airplanes at the same time. We skip segment *s1* since it is always occupied by our airplane.

If all of these conditions apply, the *move* action may be executed. Most of the effects should be self-explanatory: updating of the occupied segment, changing the heading if necessary, and blocking the occupied segment. Again, the blocking is the part where full ADL is needed. We iterate over all segments to find those that are blocked from our airplane after the movement and those that were blocked before the movement. The latter ones need to be unblocked with exception of those blocked after the movement. Again, the *is-blocked* predicate is the central tool.

The *pushback* action differs only little from the *move* action. That is why we will skip a detailed description here and take a look at one of the more interesting actions used for performing the transitions of the airplane state.

```
(:action move
 :parameters (?a  - airplane
              ?t  - airplanetype
              ?d1 - direction
              ?s1 - segment
              ?s2 - segment
              ?d2 - direction)
 :precondition (and
              (has-type ?a ?t)
              (is-moving ?a)
              (at-segment ?a ?s1)
              (facing ?a ?d1)
              (can-move ?s1 ?s2 ?d1)
              (move-dir ?s1 ?s2 ?d2)
              (not (exists (?a1 - airplane) (and (not (= ?a1 ?a))
                                                 (blocked ?s2 ?a1))))
              (forall (?s - segment) (imply (and (is-blocked ?s ?t ?s2 ?d2)
                                                 (not (= ?s ?s1)))
                                            (not (occupied ?s)))
              ))
              )
 :effect      (and
              (at-segment ?a ?s2)
              (not (at-segment ?a ?s1))
              (occupied ?s2)
              (not (occupied ?s1))
              (when (not (= ?d1 ?d2))
                   (and (facing ?a ?d2)
                        (not (facing ?a ?d1))))
              (blocked ?s2 ?a)
              (when (not (is-blocked ?s1 ?t ?s2 ?d2))
                   (not (blocked ?s1 ?a)))
              (forall (?s - segment) (when (is-blocked ?s ?t ?s2 ?d2)
                                           (blocked ?s ?a)
              ))
              (forall (?s - segment) (when (and (is-blocked ?s ?t ?s1 ?d1)
                                                (not (= ?s ?s2))
                                                (not (is-blocked ?s ?t ?s2 ?d2))
                                           )
                                      (not (blocked ?s ?a))
              ))
              )
 )
```

Fig. 1. ADL *move* action.

The *startup* action (see Figure 2) represents the process of starting the airplane's engines after it has been pushed back from its park position and thus is clearly only needed for out-bound airplanes. That is why the preconditions contain the *is-pushing* predicate. The *startup* action represents the process of the airplane starting its engines. That means it begins blocking segments. So we need the exact same check for occupied segments as in the *move* action and also the blocking formula in the action's effect. Apart from that we only update the airplane state to *is-moving*.

The *park* action does the opposite of the *startup* action by unblocking all segments except the occupied one.

The takeoff action makes sure the airplane is completely removed from the airport meaning it does not block or occupy any segments anymore.

```
(:action startup
  :parameters (?a - airplane ?t - airplanetype ?s - segment ?d - direction)
  :precondition (and
                    (is-pushing ?a)
                    (has-type ?a ?t)
                    (at-segment ?a ?s)
                    (facing ?a ?d)
                    (forall (?s1 - segment)
                            (imply (and (is-blocked ?s1 ?t ?s ?d)
                                        (not (= ?s ?s1)))
                                   (not (occupied ?s1))
                    ))
                )
  :effect        (and
                    (not (is-pushing ?a))
                    (is-moving ?a)
                    (forall (?s1 - segment)
                            (when (is-blocked ?s1 ?t ?s ?d)
                                  (blocked ?s1 ?a)
                    ))
                )
)
```

Fig. 2. ADL *startup* action.

Definition 1. *A correct state of an airplane a is defined by the following facts:*

1. *a is at exactly one segment or is airborne.*
2. *a occupies exactly the segment it is at or is airborne.*
3. *If a is airborne it neither occupies nor blocks any segments.*
4. *a is facing in exactly one direction or is airborne.*
5. *If a is moving or being pushed it only blocks the segments determined by the is-blocked predicate and the one it occupies.*
6. *If a is parked it only blocks the segment it occupies.*
7. *a never blocks a segment occupied by another airplane.*
8. *a never occupies a segment blocked by another airplane.*

Proposition 1. *If all airplanes had a correct state before executing an action of the airport domain they also have correct states afterwards.*

The (straightforward) proof to Proposition 1 can be found in our TR [14].

3.1.2 Durative Actions. To obtain a domain with action durations, we enriched the above action encodings with the obvious "at start", "at end", and "over all" flags for the preconditions and effects. The duration of *move* and *pushback* actions is calculated as a function of segment length (airplane velocity is assumed as a fixed number). The duration of *startup* actions is calculated as a function of the number of engines. The *park* and the *takeoff* action's durations are both set to fixed values.

3.2 STRIPS

Most current PDDL planning systems can not handle full ADL, especially durative ADL. To work around this problem and make the airport domain accessible

```
(:action pushback_seg_pp_0_60_seg_ppdoor_0_40_south_south_medium
 :parameters    (?a - airplane)
 :precondition  (and
                  (has-type ?a medium)
                  (is-pushing ?a)
                  (facing ?a south)
                  (at-segment ?a seg_pp_0_60)
                  (not_occupied seg_ppdoor_0_40)
                  (not_blocked seg_ppdoor_0_40 airplane_CFBEG)
                  (not_blocked seg_ppdoor_0_40 airplane_DAEWH)
                )
 :effect        (and
                  (not (occupied seg_pp_0_60))
                  (not_occupied seg_pp_0_60)
                  (not (blocked seg_pp_0_60 ?a))
                  (not_blocked seg_pp_0_60 ?a)
                  (not (at-segment ?a seg_pp_0_60))
                  (occupied seg_ppdoor_0_40)
                  (not (not_occupied seg_ppdoor_0_40))
                  (blocked seg_ppdoor_0_40 ?a)
                  (not (not_blocked seg_ppdoor_0_40 ?a))
                  (at-segment ?a seg_ppdoor_0_40)
                )
)
```

Fig. 3. A STRIPS pushback action: pushing a medium airplane from seg_pp_0_60 to seg_ppdoor_0_40 heading south.

to most planning systems we need to remove the ADL constructs to create a STRIPS only version.

Due to the lack of quantified variables there is no way to determine which segments need to be unblocked and unoccupied when moving. In our context this difficulty can be tackled by pre-instantiating. We create one *move* (and *pushback*) action for every pair of segments, for every airplane type, and for every possible pair of directions associated to moving between the segments. We can then do the required state updates without the de-tour to conditions over the *is-blocked* predicate. (More formally, the conditional effects disappear because their conditions are all static.) We end up with a single non-instantiated parameter for the *move* and *pushback* actions: the particular airplane that is moved.

The *blocked* predicate depends on an airplane. In the ADL version a quantified precondition iterates over all airplanes to check if a segment is blocked. In STRIPS, instead we use a separate check for every airplane on the airport.

STRIPS does not allow negated preconditions. We need negated preconditions to test for unblocked and unoccupied segments, so we emulate their behavior using a standard translation approach. We introduce *not_blocked* and *not_occupied* predicates, and make sure that these always exhibit the intended behavior (i.e. they are assigned the inverse values initially, and every action effect is updated to affect them inversely).

Figure 3 shows an example of a non-durative STRIPS *pushback* action.

Now that we moved almost everything from the fact into the domain declaration it is obvious that we need a separate domain definition for each airport situation. The fact file merely defines the airplanes' starting state and the goal.

All airport layout is implicitly defined by the move actions. Thus we can drop the *is-blocked, can-move, move-dir, can-pushback,* and *move-back-dir* predicates. The STRIPS domain version can be enriched with durations exactly like the ADL version.

3.3 Time Windows

The controllers of most large airports in the world only control their fore-field but not the airspace above the airport. In particular, they can not change the landing times of airplanes, and independently of what they decide to do the respective runway will be blocked when a plane lands.

We have to model something like *segment s is blocked from time x to time y.* Clearly this can only be achieved with durative PDDL. The language for IPC-4, PDDL 2.2 [5], introduced *Timed Initial Literals,* which provide a very simple solution to the time-window problem. They allow the specification of a literal together with a time stamp at which the literal will become true. For example:

```
(at 119 (blocked seg_27 dummy_landing_airplane))
```

The above statement in the ":init" section of the fact file will make sure that segment seg_27 gets blocked at time 119. To unblock the segment after the landing we use a similar statement.

```
(at 119 (not (blocked seg_27 dummy_landing_airplane)))
```

Since the blocking predicate's second parameter is an airplane and we only simulate the landings but not the airplanes themselves, we use a dummy airplane for all landing actions. The dummy airplane is used nowhere else. (It does not have a correct state in the sense of Definition 1, but obviously this does not affect the correctness of our overall encoding.)

3.4 Optimization Criterion

We were not able to model the real optimization criterion of airport ground traffic control. The standard criterion in PDDL is to minimize the execution time, the *makespan,* of the plan. In our encoding of the domain this comes down to minimizing the arrival time of the last airplane. But the real objective is, as said above, to minimize the overall *summed up* travel time of all airplanes. There appears to be no good way of modeling this criterion in current PDDL. The difficulty lies in accessing the *waiting* times of the planes, i.e. the times at which they stay on a segment waiting for some other plane to pass. If one introduces an explicit waiting action then one must discretize time, in order to be able to tell the planner how long the plane is supposed to wait. For PDDL2.2, the introduction of a special fluent "current-time" was considered, returning the time point of its evaluation in the plan execution. Using such a "look on the clock", one could make each plane record its arrival time, and thus formulate the true optimization criterion in Airport. The IPC-4 organizing committee decided against the introduction of a "current-time" variable as it seems to be problematic from an algorithmic point of view (it implies a commitment to precise time points at planning time), and not relevant anywhere else but in the airport domain.

4   Results

To evaluate the performance of state-of-the-art planning systems in the Airport domain, we created five scaling example airports that we named "Minimal", "Mintoy", "Toy", "Half-MUC", and "MUC". The smallest of these airports is the smallest possible airport Astras can handle. The two largest airports correspond to one half of Munich Airport, MUC, respectively to the full MUC airport. Figure 4 shows sketches of the "Minimal" airport, and of the "MUC" airport.

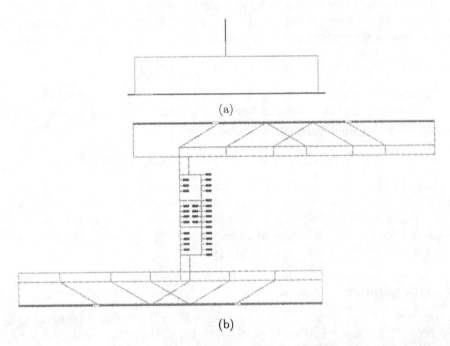

Fig. 4. Sketches of the "Minimal" (a) and "MUC" (b) airports. Park position segments are marked in black, while the segments airplanes can takeoff from are marked in white.

For each airport, we created a number of test examples that scaled by the number of airplanes to be moved, and by the number of time windows (if any). As indicated earlier in the paper, the test examples were generated by running an Astras simulation of the respective airport, then selecting various traffic situations during the simulation and putting them out in our different versions/encodings of the domain.

In our experiments, we ran the planners FF [9], IPP [10], MIPS [4], and LPG [7]. These planners are available online (programmed by one of the authors, in the cases of FF and IPP), and are suitable to represent the state-of-the-art in sub-optimal and (step-)optimal fully automated planning during the last 5 or 6 years, judging from the results of the international planning competitions. FF was the winner of the 2000 competition, and is able to handle non-durational ADL representations. MIPS was awarded a 2nd place at both the 2000 and 2002 competitions, and handles durational STRIPS as well as timed initial literals. LPG was the winner of the 2002 competition, and handles durational STRIPS representations. IPP is the only optimal planner in our collection; it is based on the Graphplan [2] approach, handles non-durational ADL representations, and finds plans with a provably smallest number of parallel time steps[2]. IPP won the ADL track of the 1998 competition.

The planners were run under Linux on a 6 GB RAM computer with 4 Xeon 3.06 GHz CPUs. We report total runtimes as put out by the systems. Whenever a planning system ran out of memory on an example, the respective table entry shows a "—". We used a runtime cutoff of 10 minutes, and examples not solved within that time are marked by ">>". We first give our results for the non-durational Airport domain, then for the durational domain without time windows, finally for the full durational domain with time windows. We then provide a brief summary of the results obtained for the airport domain in the 2004 competition.

4.1 Non-durational Results

In the non-durational domain, two of our tested systems – namely FF and IPP – could handle the original non-compiled ADL domain. We ran FF and IPP on both the ADL and STRIPS encodings of the domain, and we ran LPG and MIPS on the STRIPS encoding only. Table 1 shows the results. We only report runtimes, not plan quality. From a real-life perspective, talking about plan quality – summed up travel time – does not make much sense in a non-durational setting where actions don't take any time.

Instances with a number of airplanes not solved by any of our planners are not shown in the table. We observe the following. First, in the ADL encoding no planner is able to scale to the MUC airports. The failure is due to a memory explosion in the pre-processing routines of both FF and IPP, which ground out all actions[3]. Strangely, in those ADL instances that are feasible FF is a lot more efficient than in the corresponding STRIPS instances. We investigated this phenomenon but could not find an explanation for it. It appears to be due to the internal ordering of the action instances. Our second observation is that all planners scale reasonably well in the smaller artificial airports, but run into trouble on the real-life sized MUC airports. On the negative side, LPG and MIPS

---

[2] Of course, finding step-optimal movement sequences is a long way away from the real optimization criterion in controlling airport ground traffic. Nevertheless, we find it interesting to see how far an optimal planner scales in the domain.

[3] While grounding out the actions comes very close to what we did in the STRIPS compilation, FF and IPP do it in a general way and fail during the creation of the necessary thousands of 1st order formulas (i.e., pointer tree structures).

194   Sebastian Trüg, Jörg Hoffmann, and Bernhard Nebel

Table 1. Runtime results (in seconds) for the non-durational encodings of the Airport domain.

Airport	Nr. planes	ADL		STRIPS			
		FF	IPP	FF	IPP	LPG	MIPS
Minimal	1	0.03	0.02	0.01	0.01	0.02	0.09
Minimal	2	0.05	0.04	0.01	0.02	0.09	0.11
Mintoy	1	0.39	0.26	0.02	0.05	0.08	0.25
Mintoy	2	0.59	0.42	0.01	0.21	0.09	0.30
Mintoy	3	0.85	0.86	0.02	0.57	0.16	0.67
Mintoy	4	1.09	5.56	0.76	9.54	17.45	15.12
Toy	1	0.55	0.35	0.02	0.08	0.18	0.30
Toy	2	0.79	0.55	0.03	0.24	0.48	0.36
Toy	3	1.38	1.05	0.06	0.38	0.62	0.68
Toy	4	1.50	3.52	3.04	4.63	0.82	37.12
Toy	5	1.80	239.19	19.30	190.76	9.84	38.64
Toy	6	2.52	>>	5.57	>>	22.17	164.31
Toy	7	6.60	>>	>>	>>	—	>>
Half-MUC	2	—	—	0.25	8.96	>>	6.25
Half-MUC	3	—	—	0.37	18.73	—	13.51
Half-MUC	4	—	—	0.88	49.92	—	—
Half-MUC	5	—	—	1.34	61.14	—	—
Half-MUC	6	—	—	1.82	87.76	—	—
Half-MUC	7	—	—	3.59	131.13	—	—
Half-MUC	8	—	—	4.52	173.68	—	—
Half-MUC	9	—	—	5.60	240.01	—	—
Half-MUC	10	—	—	8.52	—	—	—
MUC	2	—	—	0.40	32.81	—	—
MUC	3	—	—	0.62	63.93	—	—
MUC	4	—	—	0.83	109.00	—	—
MUC	5	—	—	335.38	289.18	—	—

solve hardly any of the MUC instances – it is unclear if this is due to the size of the search spaces, or to implementational difficulties with the pre-compiled STRIPS encoding. On the positive side, FF and IPP can solve Half-MUC instances even with many airplanes, and scale up to 5 planes on the real-life MUC airport. It is interesting to note that the optimal planner IPP is competitive with the sub-optimal planner FF, and even outperforms LPG and MIPS – a very unusual phenomenon in today's planning landscape. Apparently, the heuristic function encoded in the planning graph is of high quality (comparable to the quality of heuristics based on ignoring the delete lists) in the airport domain. Altogether, it seems that planners are not too far away from real-life performance in the non-durational setting of this domain.

4.2 Durational Results

From the real-life perspective, of course the durational version of the Airport domain is the more interesting one, particularly the version including time windows for the landing airplanes. Of our tested systems, only LPG and MIPS can handle durations, and only MIPS can handle the timed initial literals necessary to encode the time windows. Both LPG and MIPS handle only STRIPS representations so we could not run the ADL encoding. See the results for the STRIPS encodings in Table 2. We only report runtime. The found plans are all optimal with respect to the summed up overall travel time, see the discussion below.

Table 2. Runtime results (in seconds) for the durational STRIPS encoding of the Airport domain, with and without time windows.

Airport	Nr. planes	No Time Windows LPG	MIPS	Time Windows MIPS
Minimal	1	0.03	0.15	0.18
Minimal	2	0.04	0.26	0.30
Mintoy	1	0.44	0.42	0.55
Mintoy	2	1.63	2.06	2.71
Mintoy	3	0.17	13.56	13.79
Mintoy	4	>>	74.88	19.45
Toy	1	0.10	0.50	1.16
Toy	2	0.37	2.41	13.77
Toy	3	0.24	13.65	83.59
Toy	4	2.76	101.51	102.68
Toy	5	3.46	>>	>>
Toy	6	5.48	>>	>>
Toy	7	>>	>>	>>
Half-MUC	2	>>	94.52	157.76
Half-MUC	3	—	405.19	497.93

As above, instances solved by none of the planners are not shown in the table. The obvious observation regarding runtime is that the durational domain is much harder for our planners than the non-durational domain – though as above it is unclear if LPG's and MIPS's inefficiency in the MUC airports is due to search complexity, or to the pre-compiled STRIPS encoding. LPG is generally more efficient than MIPS in the smaller airports, but fails completely in the larger Half-MUC airport.

Regarding plan quality, as said above already LPG and MIPS find the optimal plans in all cases they can handle, i.e. they return the plans with the smallest possible summed up overall travel time. We checked that by hand. While this is a good result, one should keep two things in mind. First, LPG and MIPS do not know about the real optimization criterion so it is largely a matter of chance if or if not the plan they find is optimal with respect to that criterion. Second, the instances shown here – those cases that LPG and MIPS can handle – are very simple. With just a few airplanes, there is not much potential for (possibly) harmful interactions between the intended travel routes of these planes. In the above examples, often it is the case that there is just one non-redundant solution (a solution that does not leave planes standing around waiting without reason), and that this solution is the optimal one. Specifically this is the case in the two Half-MUC instances solved by MIPS.

We also wanted to run Acore, the (sub-optimal) scheduler integrated with Astras, on the above instances (i.e. in the respective traffic situations during the simulation with Astras), and compare the results with those of our planners. This turned out to not be feasible. In the small airports, there are a lot of parking conflicts, i.e. cases where an in-bound airplane is headed for a parking position that is occupied by an out-bound airplane. Such situations do rarely occur in reality (in fact, the flight schedules try to avoid these situations), and Acore can't handle them. In the larger MUC airports, on the other hand, our planners could not solve many instances. In the two Half-MUC instances solved by MIPS, Acore finds the trivially optimal solutions just like MIPS does. Generally, concerning runtime Acore is vastly superior to our planners. Acore can solve instances with 50 planes and more on Frankfurt airport, which is far beyond the scalability of the tested planning systems.

4.3 IPC-4 Results

As mentioned in the Introduction, the IPC-4 results became available just a few days before the deadline for the version of this paper, and for this reason we cannot include a detailed discussion. Note that the IPC-4 results were obtained on the same machine that we used in the experiments above.

Some progress was made in the non-durational performance. Three planners ("Fast Downward", "SGPlan", and the new version of LPG) were able to solve Half-MUC with up to 12 planes within 100 seconds. Fast Downward even solved a MUC example with 15 planes within 200 seconds. The progress made on the durational performance is yet more impressive: even in the presence of time windows, the performance of LPG and "SGPlan" was very similar to that in the non-durational domain, easily (within 100 secs) solving Half-MUC examples with up to 11 planes, and solving MUC examples with up to 5 planes within 30 minutes. For optimal planners, not so much progress could be observed. The most efficient optimal planner in the non-durational domain, "SATPLAN04", was roughly as efficient as IPP in our own experiments. There were only three optimal planners that could handle durations, and only a singe Half-MUC instance (with two planes) got solved by them within 30 minutes.

5 Conclusion

The results show that today's PDDL planning systems are not quite yet powerful enough to handle the airport domain when it comes to real-life problems – for that, the planners would have to be able to, like Acore, generate good solutions to large airports (like Frankfurt) with many airplanes (roughly 50) in a few seconds. Nonetheless, the results, especially those obtained for the durational domain by the sub-optimal planners in IPC-4, are very encouraging. They definetely show that today's state-of-the-art planners are *a lot* closer to real-life applicability than they were some years ago. They even suggest that real-life applicability, at least in this particular domain, has come within close reach.

The core problem in controlling the ground traffic on an airport is to resolve the *conflicts* that arise when two planes need to cross the same airport segment [8]. In our PDDL encoding, this core problem is hidden deep in the domain semantics, and it seems likely that the automated planners spend most of their runtime unawares of the core difficulties. One can try to overcome this by not encoding in PDDL the physical airport, but only the conflicts and their possible solutions. Seeing if and how this is possible, ideally in connection with the real optimization criterion, is an important topic for future work.

Acknowledgement

This research was funded by DFG as part of the HEU-PLAN project.

References

1. Fahiem Bacchus. The AIPS'00 planning competition. *The AI Magazine*, 22(3):47–56, 2001.
2. Avrim L. Blum and Merrick L. Furst. Fast planning through planning graph analysis. *Artificial Intelligence*, 90(1-2):279–298, 1997.
3. Blai Bonet and Héctor Geffner. Planning as heuristic search. *Artificial Intelligence*, 129(1-2):5–33, 2001.
4. Stefan Edelkamp. Taming numbers and durations in the model checking integrated planning system. *Journal of Artificial Intelligence Research*, 20(195-238), 2003.
5. Stefan Edelkamp and Jörg Hoffmann. PDDL2.2: The language for the classical part of the 4th international planning competition. Technical Report 195, Albert-Ludwigs-Universität, Institut für Informatik, Freiburg, Germany, 2004.
6. Richard E. Fikes and Nils Nilsson. STRIPS: A new approach to the application of theorem proving to problem solving. *Artificial Intelligence*, 2:189–208, 1971.
7. A. Gerevini, A. Saetti, and I. Serina. Planning through stochastic local search and temporal action graphs in LPG. *Journal of Artificial Intelligence Research*, 20:239–290, 2003.
8. Wolfgang Hatzack and Bernhard Nebel. Solving the operational traffic control problem. In A. Cesta, editor, *Recent Advances in AI Planning. 5th European Conference on Planning (ECP'01)*, Toledo, Spain, September 2001. Springer-Verlag.
9. Jörg Hoffmann and Bernhard Nebel. The FF planning system: Fast plan generation through heuristic search. *Journal of Artificial Intelligence Research*, 14:253–302, 2001.
10. Jana Koehler, Bernhard Nebel, Jörg Hoffmann, and Yannis Dimopoulos. Extending planning graphs to an ADL subset. In S. Steel and R. Alami, editors, *Recent Advances in AI Planning. 4th European Conference on Planning (ECP'97)*, volume 1348 of *Lecture Notes in Artificial Intelligence*, pages 273–285, Toulouse, France, September 1997. Springer-Verlag.
11. Drew McDermott et al. *The PDDL Planning Domain Definition Language*. The AIPS-98 Planning Competition Comitee, 1998.
12. M.Fox and D.Long. The AIPS-2002 international planning competition. In *Proceedings of the 6th International Conference on Artificial Intelligence Planning Systems (AIPS-02)*. AAAI Press, Menlo Park, 2002.
13. Edwin P. D. Pednault. ADL: Exploring the middle ground between STRIPS and the situation calculus. In R. Brachman, H. J. Levesque, and R. Reiter, editors, *Principles of Knowledge Representation and Reasoning: Proceedings of the 1st International Conference (KR-89)*, pages 324–331, Toronto, ON, May 1989. Morgan Kaufmann.
14. Sebastian Trüg, Jörg Hoffmann, and Bernhard Nebel. Applying automatic planners to airport ground-traffic control. Technical Report 199, Albert-Ludwigs-Universität, Institut für Informatik, Freiburg, Germany, 2004.

Generalizing the Relaxed Planning Heuristic to Non-linear Tasks

Stefan Edelkamp

Computer Science Department
Baroper Str. 301
University Dortmund
stefan.edelkamp@cs.uni-dortmund.de

Abstract. The *relaxed planning heuristic* is a prominent state-to-goal estimator function for domain-independent forward-chaining heuristic search and local search planning. It enriches the state-space traversal of almost all currently available suboptimal state-of-the-art planning systems.
While current domain description languages allow general arithmetic expressions in precondition and effect lists, the heuristic has been devised for propositional, restricted, and linear tasks only. On the other hand, generalizations of the heuristic to non-linear tasks are of apparent need for modelling complex planning problems and a true necessity to validate software. Subsequently, this work proposes a solid extension to the estimate that can deal with non-linear preconditions and effects. It is derived based on an approximated plan construction with respect to intervals for variable assignments. For plan extraction, weakest preconditions are computed according to the assignment rule in Hoare's calculus.

1 Introduction

More and more successful forward-chaining planners apply variants of the *relaxed planning heuristic*, originally proposed by Hoffmann [22] as an extension to the estimated that was applied in the first heuristic search planning system HSP [2]. As one indicator, in the list of participants in the bianual series of the *international planning competition*[1], we observe a drastic increase of planners that incorporate the relaxed planning heuristic. In 2000, the planning systems *FF*, *STAN*, and *MIPS* at least partially applied a relaxed plan analysis. In 2002, the planners *Metric-FF*, *LPG*, *VHPOP*, *SimPlan*, *SAPA*, and *MIPS* implemented refinements and extensions to the heuristic. In 2004, the planners *SGPlan*, *Marvin*, *FAP*, *Fast Diogonally Downward*, *Crikey*, *Roadmapper*, *YAHSP*, *LPG-TD*, *Macro-FF*, and *P-MEP* refer to the notion of *relaxed plans* [12].

With Level(s) 2 (and 3) of PDDL2.1 [15] an agreed standard for metric (and temporal planning) has been introduced to allow richer and more flexible domain models. So-called *fluents* encode numerical quantities to express real-valued attributes. They call for numerical preconditions and effects. As a matter of fact, PDDL2.1 does not per se restrict arithmetic expressions in the precondition and effect lists.

One successful extension of the relaxed planning heuristic to planning problem with numerical state variables has been implemented in the planner Metric-FF [20]. The

---

[1] ipc.icaps-conference.org

S. Biundo, T. Frühwirth, and G. Palm (Eds.): KI 2004, LNAI 3238, pp. 198–212, 2004.

translation of the relaxation principle *ignoring the delete lists* to numeric state variables is involved and has been achieved by introducing negated variables in linear tasks[2]. As a feature, the heuristic can deal with repeated operator application in the relaxed plan. The algorithms presented in this paper shows that the relaxed planning heuristic is in fact more general. The changes we propose require a shift in the relaxation paradigm on how to represent and derive the approximation. Our extension contributes to the fact that, instead of propagating negated variables and introducing upper bounds, it is seemingly better to evaluate the heuristic based on upper *and* lower variable bounds.

The paper is structured as follows. First we introduce relaxed planning, and show where the current proposal for metric domains has its limitations. Next we generalize the relaxation scheme. The implementations base on a procedure that checks, if an operator can be applied with respect to a current vector of minimal and maximal numerical quantities, and on a procedure that adjusts the bounds accordingly. In both cases the combined vector of bounds is recursively evaluated in the expression for each operator. Backward extraction will have to determine weakest preconditions for variable assignments. We close with experiments, related work and concluding remarks.

2 Relaxed Planning

In propositional planning, we have a set of atomic propositions AP of which a subset is *true* in a given state. Planning operators modify the set of atomic propositions. As a prototype, consider STRIPS [14] operators $a = (pre(a), add(a), del(a))$. The application of a to a state S with $pre(a) \subseteq S$ yields the successor state $(S \setminus del(a)) \cup add(a)$.

2.1 Propositional Relaxed Planning

Since there are different ways to *relax* planning problems in order to approximate the state-to-goal distance, we briefly recall, what is meant with *relaxed* in this context. The *relaxed planning problem* for a STRIPS planning instance is constructed as follows [22]. The *relaxation* of an *operator* $a = (pre(a),add(a),del(a))$ is the tripel $(pre(a), add(a), \emptyset)$, so that the delete list is ignored. The *relaxation of a planning problem* is the one in which all operators are relaxed. It is not difficult to see that any solution that solves the original plan also solves the relaxed one, and that any goal can be established in the original task only if it can be achieved in the relaxed one [22].

Estimate h^+ is determined as the length of the shortest plan, that solves the relaxed problem. The heuristic is *consistent* by means that for all planning states u and v, with v being the successor of u, we have $h^+(u) \leq h^+(v)+1$: if plan with cost $h^+(v)$ has been established, it can be extended to a plan for u by adding the operator that leads from u to v, so that $h^+(u) \leq h^+(v) + 1$. Heuristic h^+ simplifies the state space graph by modifying edges to make it acyclic. The state space size, however, does not necessarily shrink. Unfortunately, the relaxed problem is still computationally hard.

Bylander has shown that propositional STRIPS planning is PSPACE complete [5]. By a simple reduction to 3-SAT, he also proved that minimizing the *sequential plan*

---

[2] Note that the term *non-linear task* has been used for other aspect in planning with a different meaning, e.g. *Pednault* refers to conditional effects as being non-linear.

procedure $\text{Relax}(\mathcal{C}, \mathcal{G})$
   $P_0 \leftarrow \mathcal{C}; t \leftarrow 0; A \leftarrow \emptyset$
   while $(\mathcal{G} \not\subseteq P_t)$
      $P_{t+1} \leftarrow P_t \cup \bigcup_{pre(a) \subseteq P_t} add(a)$
      if $(P_{t+1} = P_t)$ **return** ∞
      $t \leftarrow t+1$
   for $i \leftarrow t$ **downto** 1
      $G_i \leftarrow \{g \in \mathcal{G} \mid level(g) = i\}$
   for $i \leftarrow t$ **downto** 1
      for $g \in G_i$
         if $\exists a.\ g \in add(a)$ **and** $level(a) = i - 1$
         $A \leftarrow A \cup \{a\}$
         for $p \in pre(a)$
            $G_{level(p)} = G_{level(p)} \cup \{p\}$
   return $|A|$

Fig. 1. Propositional relaxed planning heuristic.

length for propositional relaxed tasks is in fact NP-complete. The corresponding plan existence problem, however, turns out to be computationally tractable, and an optimal *parallel plan* that solves the relaxed problem can be found in polynomial time. This has lead to an *approximation* of h^+, which counts the number of actions of a greedily extracted parallel plan in the unrolled relaxed planning graph.

Figure 1 provides an implementation in pseudo code. The planning goal $\mathcal{G}$ is provided as a set of atoms, while $\mathcal{C}$ denotes the current state. The set A that is constructed reflects the greedily extracted plan. The set of goal atoms in Layer i of the relaxed planning graph is denoted by G_i. Note that in difference to planning graphs in *Graphplan*, in the propositional relaxed planning graphs, atoms and operators are unique. In the sequel of this paper, with the term *relaxed planning heuristic* we will refer to the *approximation of* h^+. This approximation is efficient to compute, so that it is applied in forward-chaining planners to evaluate each expanded planning state.

This advantage, however, comes at a high price. Optimal parallel and optimal sequential plans may have different sets of operators, so that the approximation of h^+ is no longer *consistent* nor *admissible*, and thus fails to serve as a lower bound for the optimal sequential path length. Admissablity, however, is required, when standard heuristic search algorithms like A* [25] are applied to find optimal plans.

Therefore, the relaxed planning heuristic is usually employed in local search or hill climbing planners. Alternative designs of *admissible estimates* are the *max-atom* heuristic [2], defined as the maximal depth of a goal in the planning graph, the *max-pair heuristic* [17], which takes interactions of pairs of atoms into account, and the *pattern database heuristics* [7], that introduces *don't care* symbols in the state vector to relax the planning problem.

The h^+ heuristic and its approximation have been studied yielding an empirical validated [18] and theoretical founded [19] topology of the many benchmark domains.

2.2 Metric Planning

In a metric planning problem *conditions* are constraints of the form $exp = exp' \otimes exp''$, where $\otimes$ is a comparison symbol, and exp' and exp'' are arithmetic expressions over the set of variables and constants. *Assignments* in the effect lists are expressions $v \oplus exp$ with a *variable head* v, an arithmetic term exp, and an assignment operator $\oplus$. In grounded representation of a metric planning problem for some $k \in I\!N$ we have the state space

$$S \subseteq 2^{AP} \times I\!R^k,$$

where 2^{AP} is short for the power set of AP. Consequently a state $S \in \mathcal{S}$ is a pair (S_p, S_n) with propositional part $S_p \subseteq AP$ and numerical part $S_n \in I\!R^k$. For the ease of exposition we assume that all actions are in *normal form*, i.e. all propositional expressions satisfy STRIPS notation. All numerical condition and assignments refer to arithmetic expressions. Comparison operators $\otimes$ are selected from $\{\geq, \leq, >, <, =\}$ with common interpretation. Assignments have operators $\oplus$ in $\{\leftarrow, \uparrow, \downarrow, \nearrow, \searrow\}$, meaning variable *assignment, increase, decrease, scale-up,* or *scale-down,* respectively. This is not a limitation to general PDDL, since ADL constructs with object quantification, negated or disjunctive preconditions and conditional effects can be compiled away[16].

2.3 Numerical Relaxed Plans and Current Limitations

In brief terms, the *numerical extension to the relaxed planning heuristic* [20] generates and analyzes a layered graph, maintaining sets of propositional facts *and* arithmetic conditions in each layer. The planning graph *generation phase* applies relaxed operators until all goal conditions are established. In the backward *extraction phase*, goal propositions and conditions are selected and a greedy procedure selects either a proposition or a condition at a time. It searches for the corresponding operator of the forward phase, and marks its (numerical or propositional) preconditions in the *smallest possible layer* as still to be processed. The matching condition is deleted and the process repeats with the updated sets of propositions and conditions. The returned heuristic estimate is the number of operators in the relaxed plan. Multiple operator application is permitted by a special update option to the condition that has been met.

The heuristic is restricted to *linear tasks*, where expressions are of the form $a_0 v_0 + \ldots + a_k v_k$ for variables v_i and coefficients a_i. In case a coefficient a_i is negated, a surplus variable representing $-v_i$ is included into the state vector to approximate monotonicity in each variable. Many interesting planning tasks, however, include non-linear expressions. As a illustrative example consider the following domain, where a selection of numbers and arithmetic symbols is given, with the task to include the symbols into the sequence to compute a pre-specified target number. The domain has been invented by van der Krogt [28]. He observed that no current PDDL planning system can deal with this simple domain. An operator for introducing multiplication looks as follows.

```
(:action mul
 :parameters (?x ?y ?z - number)
 :precondition (and (active ?x) (active ?y) (non-active ?z))
 :effect (and (active ?z)
              (assign (value ?z) (* (value ?x) (value ?y)))))
```

Given an instance of three numbers $a = 1$, $b = 3$, and $c = 2$, the plan to generate value $e = 8$ is (add a b d) and (mul c d e). Breadth-first search exploration produces a plan while expanding 14 planning states. Included in A*, our variant of the numerical relaxed planning heuristic generates the above plan in the optimal number of 2 state expansions. Other examples are referred to in the experiments.

Beside extended planning benchmarks, some of which are possibly better dealt with constraint satisfaction techniques, our main motivation to deal with non-linear expressions in domain descriptions are *software verification domains*, where general expressions in form of variable assignments are by far more frequent.

2.4   Application Area for Non-linear Planning

Model checking [6] has evolved into one of the most successful software verification techniques. Examples range from mainstream applications such as *protocol validation* and *embedded systems verification* to exotic areas such as *business workflow analysis*, *scheduler synthesis* and *verification*. Automated software checking validates (mostly concurrent) code through an exploration of the space of system's states, consisting of propositional and numerical state variables [1]. Software model checking technology is also effective in automated test case generation.

There are two primary approaches to model checking. First, *symbolic model checking* [23] uses symbolic representations for the state sets based on binary decision diagrams [4]. Property validation in symbolic model checking amounts to symbolic fixpoint computation. *Explicit state model checking* uses a single-state representation for traversing the system's global state space graph. An explicit state model checker evaluates the validity of temporal properties over the model by interpreting its global state transition graph as an extended Kripke structure, and property validation amounts to a partial or complete exploration of the state space.

The success of model checking lies in its potential for *push-button* automation and in its error reporting capabilities. A model checker performs an automated complete exploration of the state space of a software model, commonly using a depth-first search strategy. When a property violating state is encountered the search stack contains an error trail that leads from an initial system state into the encountered state. This error trail greatly helps software engineers in interpreting validation results. The sheer size of the reachable state space of realistic software models imposes tremendous challenges on the algorithmics of model checking technology. Complete exploration of the state space is often impossible, and approximations are needed.

Recent advances have lead to a growth of interest in the use of the technology in AI. Heuristic and local search techniques can be directly integrated into existing model checkers. Different to heuristic search, which improves goal finding in action planning, *directed model checking* accelerates error detection [13]. With the *model checking as action planning* approach, software fragments are translated into a planning problem with planning operators for each source code line, having individual preconditions and effects [8]. However, model checking problems in software verification practice are more expressive, since complex source code instructions have to be dealt with. Therefore, it is apparent that a planning heuristic is applicable to existing model checking technology, only if it can handle non-linear expressions.

Procedure *Test*(*exp*, min, max)
    if (*op*(*exp*) = ≥ [>])
        return
                $Eval^+(left(exp), \min, \max) \geq [>]$
                $Eval^-(right(exp), \min, \max)$
    if (*op*(*exp*) = ≤ [<])
        return
                $Eval^-(left(exp), \min, \max) \leq [<]$
                $Eval^+(right(exp), \min, \max)$
    if (*op*(*exp*) = =)
        return
                $Eval^+(left(exp), \min, \max) \geq Eval^-(right(exp), \min, \max) \wedge$
                $Eval^-(left(exp), \min, \max) \leq Eval^+(right(exp), \min, \max)$

Fig. 2. Test if an expression is valid within the bounds.

3   Generalized Numerical Relaxed Plans

In the proposed alternative to the numerical planning heuristic, the planning graph is built and analyzed according to two main subroutines: *Test* and *Update*. The former procedure takes a vector of intervals for minimal and maximal variable bounds and tests if a given constraint is satisfied by at least one possible vector assignment. The latter procedure adjusts the bounds according to assignment effects in operators.

Both subroutines refer to function *Eval*(*exp*) that calculates the maximal and minimal value that an expression *exp* with variables v_i in $[\min^i, \max^i]$ can take. Function *Eval*(*exp*) is divided into two parts: $Eval^+(exp)$ computes the maximal value, and $Eval^+(exp)$ computes the maximal value of expression *exp*. Note that computing good bounds for an expression is not simple and refers to analyzing non-trivial functions. In our case *Eval* is itself an approximation that traverses the arithmetic tree in bottom-up fashion and uses constraint propergation rules to determine the bounds for the individual arithmetic operations. For example, for multiplying of two variables v_i and v_j we compute $Eval^-(v_i \cdot v_j)$ as $\min\{\min_i \cdot \min_j, \max_i \cdot \min_j, \min_i \cdot \max_j, \max_i \cdot \max_j\}$, and $Eval^+(v_i, v_j)$ as $\max\{\min_i \cdot \min_j, \max_i \cdot \min_j, \min_i \cdot \max_j, \max_i \cdot \max_j\}$. Unfortunately, this results in $Eval^-(v_i \cdot v_i) = -100$ for $v_i \in [-10, 10]$, where a refined study reveals that $Eval^-(v_i \cdot v_i) = 0$. Specialized techniques and refined bounds consistency algorithms can be applied to improve the inference of the bounds [24].

A *test* of a condition *exp* within the vector of variable bounds relaxes the requirement for accurate assignment information. If *any* assignment vector to the variables in the given ranges satisfies the conditions then the procedure returns *true*. In the pseudo-code in Figure 2 we perform a case study according to the comparison operator at the root of the expression *exp* and evaluate both subtrees for the maximal and the minimal possible value. It is not difficult to see, that if $Eval^{+[-]}(exp)$ calculates a maximal [minimal] value that an expression *exp* with variables v_i in $[\min^i, \max^i]$ can take, then *Test* returns *true* if there exist an assignment $a \in [\min, \max]$ to v that fulfills *exp*.

The observation is true for all options that we have devised. In each case we select the weakest condition for the set of variables that is available. E.g. for condition ≥ we

Procedure $Update(exp, \min', \max', \min, \max)$
  $v_{\min} \leftarrow Eval^-(\min', \max')$
  $v_{\max} \leftarrow Eval^+(\min', \max')$
  if $(op(exp) = \uparrow)$
    if $(v_{\min} < 0)$ $\min_{head(exp)} \uparrow v_{\min}$
    if $(v_{\max} > 0)$ $\max_{head(exp)} \uparrow v_{\max}$
  if $(op(exp) = \downarrow)$
    if $(v_{\min} > 0)$ $\min_{head(exp)} \downarrow v_{\min}$
    if $(v_{\max} < 0)$ $\max_{head(exp)} \downarrow v_{\max}$
  if $(op(exp) = \leftarrow)$
    if $(v_{\min} < \min_{head(exp)})$ $\min_{head(exp)} \leftarrow v_{\min}$
    if $(v_{\max} > \max_{head(exp)})$ $\max_{head(exp)} \leftarrow v_{\max}$

Fig. 3. Update according to a given expression.

determine if the maximum variable assignment on the left hand side is larger than the minimum variable assignment on the right hand side.

Figure 3 depicts the implementation for the *Update* procedure according the three main assignment operators $\leftarrow$, $\uparrow$, and $\downarrow$. First, the minimal and maximal evaluation values $v_{\min}$ and $v_{\max}$ are determined with respect to the old bounds. Then the new bounds are updated if the new evaluation exceeds the existing bounds.

If $Eval^{+[-]}(exp)$ calculates a maximal [minimal] value that an expression exp with variables v_i in $[\min^i, \max^i]$ can take, then *Update* adjusts the bounds so that each possible outcome of an assignment with variable values in $[\min', \max']$ is in $[\min, \max]$.

The operation modifies $[\min', \max']$ to $[\min, \max]$ given that $[\min, \max]$ is initialized with $[\min', \max']$. Since evaluation determines the lower and upper bound of variables in the expression tree, the three update rules we have devised, re-adjust the bounds conservatively. If, for example, we have an increase in variable h of a value of at least $v_{\min} < 0$ and of at most $v_{\max} > 0$, then the new interval $I = [\min_i + v_{\min}, \max_i + v_{\max}]$ ensures that the variable assignment to v_i will yield a value that is contained in I.

3.1 Relaxed Plan Generation

In Figure 4 we show the plan generation module to construct the relaxed planning graph. The presentation was chosen to be aligned with the one in [20]. For each layer t in the relaxed planning graph, a set of propositions and a vector $(\min_t, \max_t)$ of bounds for each variable is maintained, where C is the current state, G is the planning goal description, $p(\cdot)$ denotes the propositions true in a given state, and $v(\cdot)$ denotes the variable assignments with respect to a given state. To select the set of applicable actions A_t, we apply procedure *Test* to the vectors $\min_t$ and $\max_t$ with respect to the precondition expressions for each action. The process is continued until all propositional and all numerical goals are satisfied, or the relaxed problem proves to be unsolvable. We have not yet derived the latter criterion. Unfortunately, the simple fixpoint condition $P_t = P_{t+1}$ – as in the propositional case – together with $[\min_t, \max_t] = [\min_{t+1}, \max_{t+1}]$ may not be sufficient, since the growth of some numerical variables can be unbounded.

procedure Relax($\mathcal{C}, \mathcal{G}$)
  $P_0 \leftarrow p(\mathcal{C}); \forall i : \min_0^i \leftarrow \max_0^i \leftarrow v_i(\mathcal{C})$
  $t \leftarrow 0$
  while ($p(\mathcal{G}) \not\subseteq P_t$ **or** $\exists exp \in v(\mathcal{G}) : \neg Test(exp, \min_t, \max_t)$)
    $A_t = \{a \in A \mid pre(a) \subseteq P_t,$
                $\forall exp \in v(pre(a)) : Test(exp, \min_t, \max_t))\}$
    $P_{t+1} \leftarrow P_t \cup \bigcup_{pre(a) \subseteq P_t} add(a)$
    $[\min_{t+1}, \max_{t+1}] \leftarrow [\min_t, \max_t]$
    for $a \in A_t, exp \in v(eff(a))$
      $Update(exp, \min_t, \max_t, \min_{t+1}, \max_{t+1})$
    if (*relaxed problem unsolvable*) **return** ∞
    $t \leftarrow t + 1$

Fig. 4. Generating the problem graph for the *generalization of the relaxed planning heuristic*.

The option applied in [20] pre-computes bounds for *relevant variables*, by tracing the cone of influence for the variables and propositions in the goal description. The bounds are referred to as *max-need*. In our case, we would have have to extend the computation to *min-need$_i$*, so that the computation is terminated if $P_t = P_{t+1}$ and $[\min_{t+1}, \max_{t+1}] \not\subseteq [min\text{-}need, max\text{-}need]$.

The calculations can be performed recursively, initializing $[min\text{-}need_i, max\text{-}need_i]$ with $[-\infty, \infty]$ and further restricting the interval to the numerical conditions in the goal description and action preconditions. We recursively propagate the bounds through the numerical effect lists by determining the weakest preconditions that have to be satisfied if the given post-conditions are met. This will further restrict the intervals $[min\text{-}need_i, max\text{-}need_i]$. The process is continued until a fix-point is reached. *Irrelevant variables* are those in which $[min\text{-}need_i, max\text{-}need_i] = [-\infty, \infty]$ and can be omitted from the fixpoint requirement.

If algorithm *Relax* terminates with value ∞, then there is no solution to the original planning problem. The two aspects necessary to consider are: i) every plan for the original problem also solves the relaxed one and ii) if $P_t = P_{t+1}$ and $[\min_{t+1}, \max_{t+1}] \not\subseteq [min\text{-}need, max\text{-}need]$ once in the relaxed exploration process it will remain the same for all upcoming iterations. Part i) is true, since satisfying any numerical condition or any proposition will be preserved by the relaxation process. If condition *exp* or proposition p will be reachable in the original problem, so it will be in the relaxed one. For part ii) we observe that for all levels in the plan graph we have $P_t \subseteq P_{t+1}$ and $[\min_t, \max_t] \subseteq [\min_{t+1}, \max_{t+1}]$.

The complexity of the algorithm is proportional the size of the plan graph times the maximal length of the condition and effect lists and the maximal expression tree size to evaluate the vector in. Since operators can apply more that once, even in the case of bounded lists this does not necessarily imply polynomial complexity for deciding the relaxed task. In fact, the depth of the graph can be exponential in the binary encoding of the variables values in start and goal description. However, one may introduce so-called "∞ handling" rules as shown in [20] to match the result that deciding propositional relaxed PLANSAT is polynomial [5].

3.2   Relaxed Plan Extraction

For the extraction process as shown in Table 5, we first determine the minimal layers of the goal propositions and target arithmetic conditions in G to initialize the *pending queues* of requests. More precisely, in each layer in the planning graph we maintain two queues, one for the set of facts that have still to be processed and one for the set of constraints that have to be satisfied and propagated. In the procedure *Extract* the two queues are referred to as $p(G_i)$ and $v(G_i)$, with i being the smallest layer in which the propositions constraints are satisfied.

Next we greedily traverse the constructed graph backwards, layer by layer. To determine the set of matching operators A, for each layer i we process set A_i and reconstruct the vector $\min_{i+1}$ and $\max_{i+1}$ of lower and upper bounds to the variables, using the *Update* procedure. This will ease to determine which of the operators do match. There are two cases. Either the propositional *add* effect of an operator matches our propositional pending queue or a numerical constraint matches one in the arithmetic condition queue. In both cases we delete the matching condition from the queue and propagate the preconditions of the selected action a as yet to be established. The relaxed plan A is extended by action a. The minimal layer for each precondition, as denoted by the variable *level*, can be derived using additional information selected in the forward phase. Alternatively, the layer can be re-computed by applying procedure *Test* to the vectors $\min_j$ and $\max_j$ as computed for the level $j \in \{1, \ldots, i-1\}$.

The remaining pseudo-code fragment – starting with the line "**for** $exp' \in v(eff(a))$)" considers how to modify and propagate the numerical expression for which we have found a match, to allow repeated operator application. For instance, say that we have a lower bound on a variable of 10 units and an operator that increases the variable content by 2 units, then it is appropriate for the first application to denote that there are still 8 units to be produced. For the sake of simpler exposition, for the following we assume that we have updates only according to the uniform assignment operator "←". This is not a restriction, if we allow variables, that appear in the heads of an assignment to re-appear on the right hand side.

After selecting the numerical assignment that fires, we need to determine the associated *weakest preconditions* to be included in the pending queue in its individual smallest available layer. This is another precondition that has to be satisfied for the relaxed plan. In this case the (minimal) layer for the new goal *has to be* be computed using procedure *Test* and the vectors $(\min_j, \max_j)$ for increasing level index $j \in \{1, \ldots, i\}$. Note that the currently active Layer i is included in the range for j.

As a consequence, we need an option to derive the *weakest precondition* for a given *expression* with respect to an *assignment operator*. To solve this problem we go back to the early stages of verifying *partial correctness* of computer programs, namely to the *Hoare calculus*. In the calculus we have rules that are of the form

$$\frac{Premises}{Conclusion}.$$

Available rules are *skip* (the trivial operation) *assignment, composition, selection, iteration*, and *consequence*. For example, if S_1 and S_2 were programs and p, q, and r were conditions, then the *composition rule* says

Procedure *Extract*($\mathcal{G}$)

$A \leftarrow \emptyset$

for $i \in \{1, \ldots, t\}$

$\quad p(G_i) \leftarrow \{g \in p(\mathcal{G}) \mid level(g) = i\}$

$\quad$ **for** $exp \in v(\mathcal{G})$

$\quad\quad$ **if** *Test*($exp, \min_i \max_i$)

$\quad\quad\quad v(G_i) \leftarrow v(G_i) \cup \{exp\}; v(\mathcal{G}) \leftarrow v(\mathcal{G}) \setminus \{exp\}$

for $i \in \{t, \ldots, 1\}$

$\quad [\min_{i+1}, \max_{i+1}] \leftarrow [\min_i, \max_i]$

$\quad$ **for** $a \in A_i$

$\quad\quad$ **for** $exp \in v(\textit{eff}(a))$

$\quad\quad\quad$ *Update* $(exp, \min_i, \max_i, \min_{i+1}, \max_{i+1})$

$\quad\quad$ **for** $e \in add(a)$

$\quad\quad\quad$ **if** $e \in p(G_i)$

$\quad\quad\quad\quad A \leftarrow A \cup \{a\}; p(G_i) = p(G_i) \setminus add(a)$

$\quad\quad\quad\quad$ **for** $p \in p(pre(a))$:

$\quad\quad\quad\quad\quad p(G_{level(p)}) \leftarrow p(G_{level(p)}) \cup \{p\}$

$\quad\quad\quad\quad$ **for** $exp \in v(pre(a))$

$\quad\quad\quad\quad\quad v(G_{level(exp)}) \leftarrow v(G_{level(exp)}) \cup \{exp\}$

$\quad\quad$ **for** $exp \in v(G_i)$

$\quad\quad\quad$ **if** *Test*($exp, \min_{i+1}, \max_{i+1}$)

$\quad\quad\quad\quad A \leftarrow A \cup \{a\}; v(G_i) = v(G_i) \setminus \{exp\}$

$\quad\quad\quad\quad p(G_i) = p(G_i) \setminus add(a)$

$\quad\quad\quad\quad$ **for** $p \in p(pre(a))$

$\quad\quad\quad\quad\quad p(G_{level(p)}) \leftarrow p(G_{level(p)}) \cup \{p\}$

$\quad\quad\quad\quad$ **for** $exp \in v(pre(a))$

$\quad\quad\quad\quad\quad v(G_{level(exp)}) \leftarrow p(G_{level(exp)}) \cup \{exp\}$

$\quad\quad\quad\quad$ **for** $exp' \in v(\textit{eff}(a))$

$\quad\quad\quad\quad\quad h \leftarrow head(exp')$

$\quad\quad\quad\quad\quad exp \leftarrow exp[h \setminus exp']$

$\quad\quad\quad\quad\quad$ **for** $j \in \{1, \ldots, i\}$

$\quad\quad\quad\quad\quad\quad$ **if** ($Test(exp, \min_j, \max_j)$) $l \leftarrow j$

$\quad\quad\quad\quad\quad v(G_l) \leftarrow v(G_l) \cup \{exp\}$

return $|A|$

Fig. 5. Extracting the relaxed plan for the proposed *numerical relaxed planning heuristic*.

$$\frac{\{p\}\ S_1\ \{q\}; \{q\}\ S_2\ \{r\}}{\{p\}S_1; S_2\{r\}}.$$

The *selection rule* is written as

$$\frac{\{p \wedge B\}\ S_1\ \{q\}; \{q \wedge \neg B\}\ S_2\ \{r\}}{\{p\}\ \text{if } (B)\ \text{then } S_1\ \text{else } S_2\ \{q\}},$$

while the *iteration rule* is denoted as

$$\frac{\{p \wedge B\}\ S\ \{p\}}{\{p\}\text{while } (B)\ \text{do } S\ \{p \wedge \neg B\}}.$$

A proof of partial correctness starts with simple instructions and certified conditions on variable values. An analysis covers incrementally growing programm fragments, while maintaining respective pre- and postcondition lists. A program is *totally correct* if it is partially correct and terminating. Here we are only interested in the *assignment rule* to derive the weakest precondition of an assignment. It is denoted as

$$\{p[x \setminus t]\}\ x \leftarrow t;\ \{p\},$$

where x is a variable, p the postcondition of the assignment, and $[x \setminus t]$ is the substitution of t in x. As an example we take a program that merely consists of the assignment $u \leftarrow 3x + 17$, and a postcondition p of the form $u < 5x$. To find the weakest precondition for S with respect to p we have $t = 3x + 17$, so that $p[u \setminus t]$ is equal to $3x + 17 < 5x$, or equivalently $x > 8.5$.

The application in the program *Extract* is as follows. Suppose that we have an assignment of the form $h \leftarrow exp$ in one of the effects of the selected operator a and a postcondition of the form exp'. Both expressions exp and exp' are given in form of arithmetic trees. The weakest precondition is now found substituting each occurrence of h in exp' by exp. It will be simplified and inserted in the appropriate pending queue.

4   Experiments

To illustrate practical feasibility of our approach, we have implemented the heuristic estimate in our heuristic search forward chaining planner MIPS [9]. The planner has been extended to PDDL2.2 [11] to deal with timed initial literals and derived predicates [10]. For IPC-4 it has been used to check solvability especially temporal benchmark designs [21]. In our implementation we terminate relaxed planning graph construction, if the depth of the relaxed planning graph exceeds a pre-specified threshold. Since the relaxed planning graph reflects a simplified parallel execution of actions, goals for benchmark problems often appear in shallow depth.

Unfortunately, grounded and simplified benchmark problems in all planning competitions are at most linear. This lack of expressiveness is due to a compromise with respect to existing planning technology. Subsequently, we selected three different options for experimental evaluation: 1) problems that are non-linear by definition, 2) existing but modified benchmark domains, and 3) challenging linear domains. Although all problems agree with PDDL syntax, no other planning system can solve either of the domains. In the first two cases this is due to the lack in expressivity, while in the second case this is a due to a lack in performance[3].

First, we generated random instances to the *Arithmetic* domain with target value 24. As depicted in Table 1 the exploration efforts for A* and *breadth-first search* (BFS) are very small. A*'s exploration shows a considerable improvement to the uninformed one. Both algorithms found optimal solutions. In contrast, *enforced hill climbing* often fails to establish a plan.

---

[3] In the competition 2004, *SGPlan* turned out to be the only other system that solved entire *Settlers*, while *P-MEP* was announced to be a system that has non-linear expressivity.

Table 1. Number of expanded nodes in *Arithmetic* Domain.

id	1	2	3	4 5 6	7	8	9 10 11	12 13 14 15 16 17 18 19 20
A*	2	7	5	7 3 2	3 11 13	2 3 2 5 5 3 2 3 9 2 2
BFS	5 33 10 26 7 2 59 22 65 6 4 5 28 7 38 2 5 40 2 2

It is not difficult, to introduce non-linearities to existing benchmarks. In *ZenoTravel* we squared some preconditions, artificially making the domain non-linear. Since determining that variables are strictly positive can be as hard as the planning problem itself, actual planners will not be able to simplify the above formula. As shown to the left in Table 2, the planner solved all modified instances. The table is headed by problem *id*, the number of expanded *nodes*, the CPU search *time* on a 1.8 GHz Windows PC with 256 MB memory, the obtained solution *value*, and the *length* of the established plan.

We also conducted experiments in two domains provided by Amol Mali: one version of *Jugs*, where some pouring actions and goal constraints are non-linear, and *Karel, the Robot* domain, where the distance to move is non-linearly dependent to the current posistition, and some goal constraints are also non-linear. We could solve selected *Karel* domains, e.g. *Karel-2* required 98 expansions, 0.15s CPU time to produce a 5-step plan, while in *Jugs* the heuristic turns out to be too weak: complete jug fillings span the entire range for the *content* variables in the first layer of the relaxed planning graph.

Table 2 highlights that the approach is efficient in linear domains. On a slightly larger machine (2.66 GHz Linux PC with 512 MB memory) we could generate the first report in solving the entire problem suite of *Settlers*. Our planner also detects that Problem 8 is unsolvable; the goal requires a railway from *location6* to *location3*, in contrast to connectivity status of the two locations.

5   Conclusion

In this work we extended the mixed propositional and numerical relaxed planning heuristic [20], which itself is an extension to the propositional relaxed planning heuristic and the relaxed planning heuristic for restricted tasks. As the existing approach to translate *ignoring the delete lists* to numeric state variables restricts to at most linear tasks, the question was how to tackle non-linear expressions that are available in PDDL2.1 and do appear frequently in practice. In difference to the introduction of upper bounds and negated variables together with a transformation process beforehand, the proposed alternative applies upper and lower bounds. The algorithmic considerations of the generalization are tricky but base on simple subroutines. It enables to deal with complex problems and shows a way of understanding the heuristic in more detail.

The relaxed planning heuristic has been recently applied to *conformant planning problems* [3] and has also been integrated in a two stage scheduling approach for *temporal planning* [9]. In case of conformant planning, the planing graph construction is associated with an *implication graph* to derive information on atoms that are known to be true or false in a given level, while the temporal planning apporach parallelizes sequential plans with respect to action duration and action dependency. By *scheduling partial, relaxed and final plans*, non-linear expressions are universal for Level 1-3

Table 2. Results in *Modified Zeno Travel* (left) and in *Settlers* (right).

id	nodes	time	value	length		id	nodes	time	value	length
1	1	0.06	13,564	1		1	551	4.48	142	58
2	10	0.12	7,567	8		2	39	1.40	30	35
3	26	0.13	10,455	8		3	2,984	17.17	880	101
4	15	0.15	23,422	11		4	569	5.36	51	42
5	37	0.17	12,009	14		5	99	5.25	44	68
6	53	0.20	28,642	14		6	999	14.57	44	67
7	40	0.21	11,977	16		7	17	4.29	62	16
8	53	0.29	41,364	20		8	0	2.13	-	-
9	32	0.36	19,921	23		9	8,515	295.59	2,741	270
10	74	0.43	559,60	28		10	404	59.15	3,979	159
11	31	0.36	34,362	17		11	695	42.18	2,694	168
12	73	0.47	22,650	26		12	251	58.92	1,878	133
13	129	0.55	45,358	33		13	35,377	1,358	3,897	218
14	59	3.63	1,815	39		14	761	84.39	1,815	304
15	67	7.77	76,602	40		15	399	164.60	3,688	261
16	287	15.60	117,050	55		16	893	194.62	4,827	275
17	709	35.48	153,021	78		17	13,232	2,401	9,738	285
18	1,474	67.35	85,896	72		18	7,803	846.75	8,784	338
19	2,522	128.75	131,528	103		19	171,465	725.44	6,428	415
20	2,429	158.17	283,688	113		20	23,643	3,728.05	0	286

PDDL2.1 planning problems. Moreover, with relaxed plans for non-linear tasks we are not limited to PDDL2.1 planning. In concurrent work, we have extended our planning approach to PDDL2.2 [11] including *derived predicates* and *timed initial literals*. Our implementation solved relaxed non-linear problems in various domains that planners like *Metric-FF* cannot deal with.

In the context of the 2004 international planning competition, the forward state-space planner *(P-)MEP* [26], for *(parallel) more expressive planner*, is announced to handle PDDL2.1 expressivity and to apply a related technique of bounding intervals to generate a numerical relaxed planning graph and to extract a relaxed plan. Similar to MIPS it also supports ADL functionality and for Level 3 planning as it applies temporal reasoning to find a schedule after a sequential plan has been found. When comparing the two approaches we first realize that planning graph construction is similar in both cases. S-MEP [27] constructs the planning graph allowing each operator to apply at most once. In P-MEP – the participating planner in IPC-4 – this problem has been fixed. The refinement strategy merely reduces to relevant variables and is very different to the plan extraction phase we propose. The approach does not support weakest preconditioning. In some sense (P-)MEP truncates the planning graph of the forward phase, instead of greedily extracting plans as done in Metric-FF and MIPS. As IPC-4 has shown, P-MEP has efficiency deficies. For example, it cannot solve any of the instances in *Settlers*.

Although we proved that a generalization of the relaxed planning estimate is available for full PDDL, we strongly believe that there is much more efforts needed to make the tool appropriate e.g. for software model checking problems. Therefore, next we will address CSP techniques for evaluation and a fine-grained or mixed representation of the set of possible values that is available for a numerical variable. One option is to keep precise numeric information available until a certain threshold on the number values is exceeded. In this case we might swap back to finite constraint variable domains. We are certain that extending the approach is compatible with the *Test*-and-*Update* scheme for the construction of the relaxed planning graph and the extraction of the relaxed plan.

As the core motivation of the work is apply the relaxed planning heuristic to model checking, in future we may try implementing the estimate in an existing model checker.

Acknowledgments

The work is supported by *Deutsche Forschungsgemeinschaft* (DFG) in the projects *Heuristic Search* (Ed 74/3) and *Directed Model Checking* (Ed 74/2).

References

1. B. Bérard, A. F. M. Bidoit, F. Laroussine, A. Petit, L. Petrucci, P. Schoenebelen, and P. McKenzie. *Systems and Software Verification.* Springer, 2001.
2. B. Bonet and H. Geffner. Planning as heuristic search. *Artificial Intelligence*, 129(1–2):5–33, 2001.
3. R. Brafman and J. Hoffmann. Conformant planning via heuristic forward search: A new approach. In *International Conference on Automated Planning and Scheduling (ICAPS)*, 2004. 335-364.
4. R. E. Bryant. Symbolic boolean manipulation with ordered binary-decision diagrams. *ACM Computing Surveys*, 24(3):142–170, 1992.
5. T. Bylander. The computational complexity of propositional STRIPS planning. *Artificial Intelligence*, pages 165–204, 1994.
6. E. M. Clarke, O. Grumberg, and D. A. Peled. *Model Checking.* MIT Press, 1999.
7. S. Edelkamp. Planning with pattern databases. In *European Conference on Planning (ECP)*, 2001. 13-24.
8. S. Edelkamp. Promela planning. In *Workshop on Model Checking Software (SPIN)*, pages 197–212, 2003.
9. S. Edelkamp. Taming numbers and durations in the model checking integrated planning system. *Journal of Artificial Research (JAIR)*, 20:195–238, 2003.
10. S. Edelkamp. Extended critical paths in temporal planning. In *Proceedings ICAPS-Workshop on Integrating Planning Into Scheduling*, pages 38–45, 2004.
11. S. Edelkamp and J. Hoffmann. PDDL2.2: The language for the classical part of the 4th international planning competition. Technical report, University of Freiburg, 2003.
12. S. Edelkamp, J. Hoffmann, M. Littman, and H. Younes. *Proceedings Fourth International Planning Competition, International Conference on Automated Planning and Scheduling.* Jet Propulsion Laboratory, 2004.
13. S. Edelkamp, S. Leue, and A. Lluch-Lafuente. Directed explicit-state model checking in the validation of communication protocols. *International Journal on Software Tools for Technology (STTT)*, 2004.
14. R. Fikes and N. Nilsson. Strips: A new approach to the application of theorem proving to problem solving. *Artificial Intelligence*, 2:189–208, 1971.

15. M. Fox and D. Long. PDDL2.1: An extension to PDDL for expressing temporal planning domains. *Journal of Artificial Research (JAIR)*, 20:61–124, 2003.
16. B. C. Gazen and C. Knoblock. Combining the expessiveness of UCPOP with the efficiency of graphplan. In *European Conference on Planning (ECP)*, pages 221–233, 1997.
17. P. Haslum and H. Geffner. Admissible heuristics for optimal planning. In *Artificial Intelligence Planning and Scheduling (AIPS)*, pages 140–149, 2000.
18. J. Hoffmann. Local search topology in planning benchmarks: An empirical analysis. In *International Joint Conferences on Artificial Intelligence (IJCAI)*, pages 453–458, 2001.
19. J. Hoffmann. Local search topology in planning benchmarks: A theoretical analysis. In *Artificial Intelligence Planning and Scheduling (AIPS)*, pages 379–387, 2002.
20. J. Hoffmann. The Metric FF planning system: Translating "Ignoring the delete list" to numerical state variables. *Journal of Artificial Intelligence Research*, 20:291–341, 2003.
21. J. Hoffmann, S. Edelkamp, R. Englert, F. Liporace, and S. Thiebaux. Towards realistic benchmarks for planning: the domains used in the classical part of IPC-4. In *Proceedings Fourth International Planning Competition*, pages 8–15, 2004.
22. J. Hoffmann and B. Nebel. Fast plan generation through heuristic search. *Journal of Artificial Intelligence Research*, 14:253–302, 2001.
23. K. L. McMillan. Symbolic model checking. In M. K. Inan and R. P. Kurshan, editors, *Verification of Digital and Hybrid Systems*, pages 117–137. Springer, 1998.
24. K. Meriott and P. Stuckey. *Programming with Constraints*. MIT Press, 1998.
25. J. Pearl. *Heuristics*. Addison-Wesley, 1985.
26. J. Sanches, M. Tang, and A. D. Mali. P-MEP: Parallel more expressive planner. In *Proceedings Fourth International Planning Competition*, pages 53–55, 2004.
27. J. Sanchez and A. D. Mali. S-MEP: A planner for numeric goals. In *Proceedings IEEE International Conference Tools with Artificial Intelligence (ICTAI)*, pages 274–283, 2003.
28. R. van der Krogt, M. de Weerdt, and C. Witteveen. Exploiting opportunities using planning graphs. In *UK Planning and Scheduling SIG (PlanSig)*, pages 125–136, 2003.

Decision-Theoretic Planning
for Playing Table Soccer

Moritz Tacke, Thilo Weigel, and Bernhard Nebel

Institut für Informatik
Universität Freiburg
79110 Freiburg, Germany
{take,weigel,nebel}@informatik.uni-freiburg.de

Abstract. Table soccer (also called "foosball") is much simpler than real soccer. Nevertheless, one faces the same challenges as in all other robotics domains. Sensors are noisy, actions must be selected under time pressure and the execution of actions is often less than perfect. One approach to solve the action selection problem in such a context is decision-theoretic planning, i.e., identifying the action that gives the maximum expected utility. In this paper we present a decision-theoretic planning system suited for controlling the behavior of a table soccer robot. The system employs forward-simulation for estimating the expected utility of alternative action sequences. As demonstrated in experiments, this system outperforms a purely reactive approach in simulation. However, this superiority of the approach did not extend to the real soccer table.

1 Introduction

Playing *table soccer* (also called "foosball") is a task that is much simpler than playing real soccer. Nevertheless, one faces the same challenges as in other robotic domains. One has to interpret sensor signals and to select actions based on this interpretation. All this has to be done while keeping in mind that the sensor signals are noisy and the actuators are less than perfect.

One approach to solve the *action selection* problem is to use purely *reactive* methods. These are methods that select actions based on the current sensor input with only a minimum amount of computation. The action selection can be based on layered finite state automatons [4] or even simpler by using a simple decision tree. However, these purely reactive approaches have the disadvantage that they cannot anticipate changes in the environment caused by its own actions or by exogenous actions and for this reason might act sub-optimally.

Approaches such *behaviour networks* [5, 8] address this problem by modeling all possible actions, their consequences, and something similar to success likelihood. Based on this model, actions that promise to achieve the goals best are selected. As demonstrated by different robotic soccer teams [6, 9], this approach can be quite successful. However, it lacks theoretical foundation and, in fact, it is not clear under what circumstances the approach provably achieves its goals.

Decision-theoretic planning in contrast addresses the action selection problem by explicit deliberation about possible actions and aims at generating plans which promise

S. Biundo, T. Frühwirth, and G. Palm (Eds.): KI 2004, LNAI 3238, pp. 213–225, 2004.

to yield the *maximum expected utility* for an agent. This is achieved by explicitly considering the uncertain effects of the actions, the incomplete knowledge about the world and the possibly limited resources for carrying out a plan.

Decision theoretic planning can be implemented in various fashions. Using a classical refinement planner, it is possible to calculate the plan with the maximum expected utility by keeping ranges of possible utility values for partial plans [7]. A very popular way to realize decision-theoretic planning is the modeling of the planning problem as a Markov decision process [3]. Using such an approach, one could utilise techniques such as RTDP [1] or LRTDP [2] in order to approximate an optimal policy. We used instead a simple forward expanding tree-search, which allows us to simulate the physical behaviour and have a huge (potential) state space (defined by location, velocity, and direction) instead of having a small state space with very coarse states.

The main challenge in using such an approach is to simplify the model of the domain such that the computational costs are not prohibitive. For this reason, we do not consider e.g. all possible ways an action can fail, but distinguish only between successful execution and failure. Furthermore, we do not consider responses to successful ball interceptions but consider the plan as failed once the opponent has intercepted the ball. Finally, planning is carried out only to a limited depth and the utility of the resulting state is assessed using a heuristic measure.

The rest of the paper is structured as follows. In Section 2, the KiRo system is presented. Section 3 describes the implementation of a decision theoretic planning algorithm for KiRo. Experimental results are presented in Section 4 and a short conclusion and outlook is given in Section 5.

2   KiRo

KiRo is a table soccer robot, i.e., an automated table soccer table [10]. Its hardware consists of the following components (see Figure 1):

- a standard table soccer table, where all rods of one player are equipped with electro motors strong enough to shift and turn the rods fast,
- an overhead camera, and
- a standard PC, on which the control software runs.

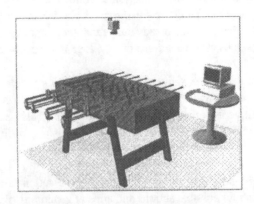

Fig. 1. The hardware setup.

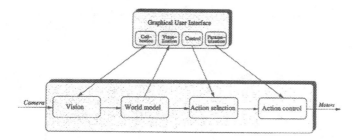

Fig. 2. One cycle of the control software.

The software executes a control cycle, as depicted in Figure 2:

1. During the *vision analysis phase*, the positions of the various items on the field are estimated (see Figure 3(a)).
2. These positions are combined with knowledge about former ones in order to build the new *world model*. The world model, shown in Figure 3(b), contains information about the positions and movements of all items on field. The field is represented by a coordinate system where the origin is in the middle of the field and the x-axis connects both goals.
3. Based on this world model, the best actions are chosen in the *action selection* phase.
4. *Action execution* translates the chosen actions into steering commands. These commands are sent to the actuators.

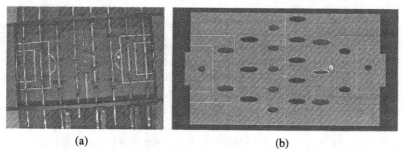

(a)   (b)

Fig. 3. (a) The camera picture and (b) the generated world state.

Since table soccer is a fast-paced game, the cycle duration has to be as short as possible in order to be able to react in time. KiRo works with a cycle time of 20 msec, which leads to strict bounds for the time available to select appropriate actions.

The first approach to action selection has been a purely reactive decision tree. The essence of this approach is depicted in Figure 4. Although very crude, this approach was able to beat 75% of a random sample of human opponents [10].

In contrast, the system presented in this paper selects the action that promises the best consequences. To identify this action, it is necessary to plan ahead and to simulate the change in the world state caused by the different actions. As this approach needed a different kind of action model, the action control had to be completely rewritten.

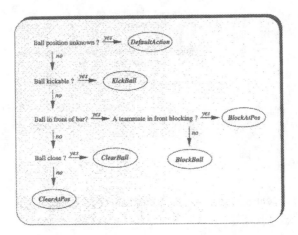

Fig. 4. The original action selection procedure.

3   Decision-Theoretic Planning for Table Soccer Playing

Table soccer does not seem to be well suited for decision-theoretic planning because it involves an opponent, which apparently means that we have to use game-solving methods, e.g., minimax search, instead of planning. However, the game is highly asymmetric. Only the player in possession of the ball, the *attacking player*, is able to decide on the future development of the game. The other player, the *defending player*, has to wait until the ball can be intercepted. For this reason, we can focus on a sub-game that is much easier to tackle.

We will consider the sub-game where the attacking player has continuous control of the ball. That means that this sub-game ends when the attacking player either scores a goal or looses control of the ball. This implies that the game tree can be pruned at nodes where the defending player intercepts the ball. Furthermore, all opponent actions that are unsuccessful in intercepting the ball do not influence the game at all. In summary, the defending player never needs to look ahead and just tries to intercept the current ball while the attacking player considers different possibilities of shooting the ball and takes the opponent into account only as a threat to the next action. So, we can indeed use decision-theoretic planning techniques to address the table soccer playing problem.

As a general strategy, KiRo uses a reactive positioning scheme when it is the defending player and employs decision-theoretic planning in the role of the attacking player. In what follows, we only consider the situation when KiRo is the attacking player.

3.1   Action and Forward Simulation

When planning, the attacking player can act all the time and the state changes continuously, because the ball is in motion most of time. Planning in such a setting is, of course, computationally infeasible. However, we do not have to consider all possible actions and all movements of the ball assuming that the following assumptions hold:

1. Most of the time, the movement of the ball and the rods is predictable, i.e., we have almost always full observability. The ball moves according to its inertia, the rods move in the way which is specified by the employed actions.
2. The movement of the ball and of the rods are fully independent apart from one case: One figure touching the ball. In this situation, the movement of the ball is influenced.
3. Whenever the movement of the ball changes, the actions of the rods are likely to change as both players react on the new situation.

Since these assumptions hold to a certain degree, we can interleave actions and physical simulations in a regular manner. Given a world state, an action of KiRo and a reaction of the opponent, we simulate the evolution of the world until the point of time at which one of both players can manipulate the ball again. At this moment is it necessary to stop the simulation and to evaluate the reactions of both players in the new situation.

3.2 One Iteration of Planning

For a given world state s, in which KiRo is playing the ball, all possible consequences of KiRo's actions as well as all possible reactions of the opponent are considered. For each combination among these, a new world state is constructed which is used as a base for further planning – provided that the opponent is not playing the ball in this state.

The search tree consists of three different kind of nodes which alternate in a given sequence. Each of theses types corresponds to a different planning step. The starting point of plan iteration is always a *state node* s corresponding to a game state s. The first step is to select a set of applicable actions $(a_1, \ldots, a_n)$. For each $a_i \in (a_1, \ldots, a_n)$ one *action node* a_i is created. As these nodes represent the different choices in state s, the utility value of the state node s is the maximum utility among its successors (once these are known):

$$utility(\mathbf{s}) = \max_{0 < i \leq n} utility(\mathbf{a}_i).$$

Figure 5 illustrates the generation of the action nodes.

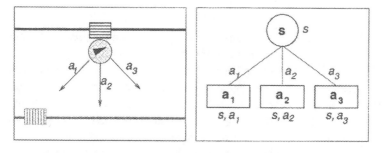

Fig. 5. The action choice and its representation within the tree.

The next step is the estimation of the opponent's reactions. Based on the world state s a set $\{(o_1, p(o_1)), \ldots, (o_m, p(o_m))\}$ of hypotheses is created where the o_j classify the reactions and the $p(o_j)$ the associated probabilities. Note, that we assume that these reactions depend only on s and are independent from the chosen action $\mathbf{a}_i$, which in fact is true in table soccer. There is usually no way an opponent can react to an the action of an attacking player.

For each action node $\mathbf{a}_i$, a set of successor *opponent nodes* $\{\mathbf{o}_{i1}, \ldots, \mathbf{o}_{im}\}$ is created. The value of $\mathbf{a}_i$ is the expected value over its successors:

$$utility(\mathbf{a}_i) = \sum_{j=1}^{m} p(o_j) \cdot utility(\mathbf{o}_{ij}).$$

In Figure 6 two possible reactions of the opponent and the formalization of this fact in the tree is depicted.

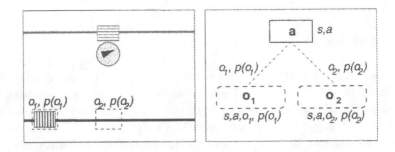

Fig. 6. The formalization of the opponent.

Every opponent node $\mathbf{o}_{ij}$ contains informations about the world state s as well as one specific action a_i and reaction $(o_j, p(o_j))$. To finish the planning step, the consequences $\{c_1, \ldots, c_q\}$ of a_i are estimated along with their probabilities $p(c_1), \ldots, p(c_q)$. The now gathered information $\langle s, a_i, o_j, c_k \rangle$ is used to estimate new world states s_{ijk} by means of a simulator. These states are used to build a new layer of *state nodes* $\mathbf{s}_{ijk}$.

The utility value of the precedent opponent node $\mathbf{o}_{ij}$ is calculated by

$$utility(\mathbf{o}_{ij}) = \sum_{k=1}^{q} p(c_k) \cdot utility(\mathbf{s}_{ijk}).$$

Figure 7 shows two different outcomes of an action and the use of the simulator to create a new world state based on the collected data.

After one iteration of planning, there exists a number of new state nodes containing the world state resulting from every possible action a_i, every possible reaction o_j and every possible consequence c_k of the action a_i. After the search tree has been built up to the leafs, those get evaluated using the utility function. These evaluations propagate backward through the tree until the root state node $\mathbf{s}$ is reached. The utility of $\mathbf{s}$ is the maximum expected utility among all selectable actions in world state s; the action a_i yielding this value is the one to be selected in s.

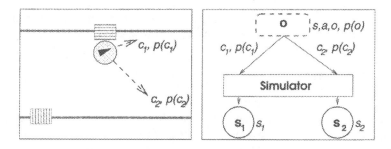

Fig. 7. The possible outcomes of an action.

3.3 Choosing an Applicable Action

Currently, KiRo's capabilities comprise the following actions for operating each of the four rods under his control:

- *KickBall*: Rotate the rod by 90° in order to kick the ball forward or diagonally to the left or right.
- *BlockBall*: Move the rod so that a figure intercepts the ball.
- *ClearBall*: Move to the same position as *BlockBall* but turn the rod to let the ball pass from behind.
- *StopBall*: Pen the ball in between figure and field.

Altogether, it is possible to assign a single rod one out of 6 different actions (three of them being kicks in different directions). Taking all four rods into account is it possible to create 24 different assignments of actions. In other words, our search tree would have a branching factor of 24. Fortunately, one can easily reduce this factor because only the rod close to the ball can kick and the others have a choice between the remaining three actions. We decided to assign statically *BlockBall* to all rods between the ball and the own goal in order to have a defence even when the ball is accidentally lost or reflected. Rods between the opponent's goal and the ball should not handicap the chances to score a goal. For that reason, they are assigned *ClearBall*.

With these static assignments, the branching factor is reduced to six while KiRo is playing the ball. If the opponent possesses the ball, a static defensive allocation of actions without any planning is employed. This reflects the already mentioned observation that planning in these situations is useless.

In some situations, performing a certain action might be useless (e.g. trying to stop an already stopped ball) or the chance of successful carrying out an action might become too low. In these cases, such actions are not evaluated in order to reduce the complexity further.

As the means the opponent is going to use in order to protect his goal are unknown, it is necessary to guess what his reactions will be. Each of these guesses is weighted by the probability that this reaction will occur. Currently, the opponent is always expected to either leave his rods unmoved or to protect his goal according to the scheme applied in the *BlockBall*-action. Each of these alternatives is weighted with a probability of

0.5. These probabilities are, of course, only a crude approximation and it is planned to replace this simple opponent model by a more sophisticated, experience-based one.

3.4   Calculating the Successor State

The last – and most important – step is to estimate the probability of a success of KiRo's actions and to create a new world state based on the data collected yet. The actions of KiRo can have two possible outcomes, success and failure. The probabilities of these depend on the encountered world state, e.g. a quickly moving ball is more difficult to kick than a static one. Based on the world state and on data about the effectiveness of the actions collected during earlier games, the success probability is estimated.

The means to create a new world state based on the informations about KiRo's actions, their success or failure and the opponent's reactions is a simple simulator. This simulator models the world based on the following principles:

- The angle of incidence and the angle of reflection are equal.
- Friction is ignored.

Additionally, the simulator has a model that allows to interpret the steering commands issued by both players. Of course, the real world is only very coarsely modeled by a simulator based on these principles. Further, since the input data is imperfect, the simulation is accumulating errors. The simulated span of time, however, is very short, so that the errors are still acceptable.

Simulation is performed in two steps: In the first one, the game is simulated until the point of time in which KiRo's action takes place. Afterwards, two successor states are generated: One of the resulting world states is a state according to the known consequences of the success of KiRo's action. The other state reflects the failure of the action. In this case, we have a new problem: The consequences of a successful action are known – in case of failure, anything can happen. The most frequent kind of failure is the inability of KiRo to hit the ball. For this reason, the failing case is simulated by letting the ball pass the failing rod without changing its movement parameters. The resulting world state is not used as a starting point for a new planning step; it is directly evaluated using the heuristic utility function (see Subsection 3.6).

3.5   Estimating the Success Probabilities

In order to estimate the success probability for a given action on a certain rod in a given world state, a Bayesian approach is employed. The first step is to classify the ball movements by a 4-tuple $\langle d_x, d_y, v_x, v_y \rangle$, where

- d_x is the distance in x-direction to the rod.
- d_y is the minimal distance in y-direction to a figure on this rod .
- v_x is the relative velocity in x-direction. "Relative" means in this context e.g. "approaching" or "departing"
- v_y is the relative velocity in y-direction.

Each of these values is discretized according to a seven step scale.

The task is now to calculate the success probability $P(S|d_x, d_y, v_x, v_y)$ of the action given this tuple. Using Bayes' rule yields

$$P(S|d_x, d_y, v_x, v_y) = \frac{P(d_x, d_y, v_x, v_y|S) \cdot P(S)}{P(d_x, d_y, v_x, v_y)}$$

In order to simplify the computation of the conditional probability, two independence assumptions are made:

1. $P(d_x, d_y, v_x, v_y) = P(d_x) \cdot P(d_y) \cdot P(v_x) \cdot P(v_y)$
2. $P(d_x, d_y, v_x, v_y|S) = P(d_x|S) \cdot P(d_y|S) \cdot P(v_x|S) \cdot P(v_y|S)$.

This "naive Bayes" assumption is clearly not met; this, however, is common practice in naive Bayes approaches (otherwise they would not be called "naive"). These assumption lead to the estimator

$$P_{NB}(S|d_x, d_y, v_x, v_y) \hat{=} \frac{P(d_x|S) \cdot P(d_y|S) \cdot P(v_x|S) \cdot P(v_y|S) \cdot P(S)}{P(d_x) \cdot P(d_y) \cdot P(v_x) \cdot P(v_y)}$$

These values are then normalized using

$$P_{NormNB}(S|d_x, d_y, v_x, v_y) = \frac{P_{NB}(S|d_x, d_y, v_x, v_y)}{P_{NB}(S|d_x, d_y, v_x, v_y) + P_{NB}(\neg S|d_x, d_y, v_x, v_y)}$$

3.6 The Utility Function

Table soccer poses a highly dynamic environment where only little time is available for selecting the most appropriate action. Due to the high uncertainties in sensing and acting, it is infeasible to create and carry out a complete plan for reaching the final aim of scoring a goal. It is necessary to plan with a limited horizon and to use an *utility function* for evaluating world states. Planning in this fashion is similar to depth-limited minimax search with a heuristic evaluation of the leafs of the game tree. The utility of inner nodes is estimated using a *rollback procedure* [3].

The heuristic utility function is used to estimate the world states contained in the leafs of the search tree – provided one has not reached a scored goal yet. The principles underlying this function are:

– If a goal is either scored or going to be scored (i.e. ball behind the keeper, moving towards the goal), a value of 100 is returned if it is the opponent's goal, otherwise 0.
– The closer the ball is to the opponent's goal wall, the better.
– If the distance between the ball and both front walls is equal, it is neither important who controls the ball nor whether the ball is on the left or right of the field. The closer it gets to one of the walls, the bigger the importance of these facts.

The resulting formula for the value V is as follows:

$$V = A + B \cdot \frac{x_b - c \cdot i \cdot |y_b|}{0.5 \cdot s} + C \cdot c \cdot k \tag{1}$$

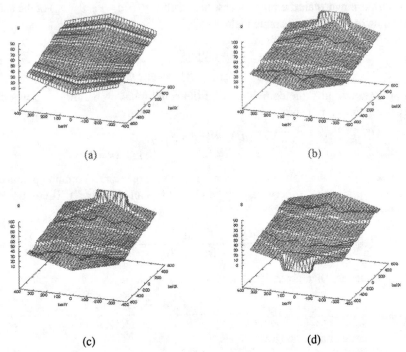

(a)   (b)

(c)   (d)

Fig. 8. Illustration of the utility function at different ball movements; all rods are at their center positions.

Where
- A is the base value, currently 50,
- B and C are the weights assigned to the position and the owner of the ball (Used values: $B = 40, C = 5$),
- s is the length of the field in x-direction, i.e. the distance between the goals,
- x_b, y_b are the coordinates of the ball in a coordinate system with the origin on the center of the field,
- i is the sign of x_b,
- c is the weighting factor calculated as $c = \frac{|x_b|}{0.5s}$,
- and k is the identity of the player to reach the ball next. If this is KiRo, k is 1, if the opponent reaches the ball next, k is -1, and 0 else. k depends on the positions and movements of the ball and the rods.

To illustrate this, Figure 8 shows the values over all ball positions. The figures differ only in the movement of the ball: In Figure 8(a), the ball doesn't move. In Figure 8(b), it moves straight in the direction of the opponent's front wall, in Figure 8(c) diagonally. Figure 8(d) shows a ball that is moving in the direction of KiRo's front wall.

3.7 Interleaving Planning and Action

Differently from conventional planning approaches, here we do not plan and then follow the plan step by step. Instead we execute the first action, the one with the highest expected utility, and then the plan is thrown away. The reason is that most likely the situation has developed in a somewhat different way and one has to plan from scratch in any way. This means that planning is used here more in order to get a reasonable estimate of the utility of an action than in order to develop a sequence of actions.

4   Results

The decision-theoretic planner has been fully implemented in the KiRo system and tested using a simulator and the real table soccer system.

4.1   Computational Costs

The implemented system runs on a 1.7 GHz AMD processor. On this processor, the vision analysis phase, the world modeling step and action execution (see Section 2) require together roughly 5 msec. With a cycle time of 20 msec, this gives us approximately 15 msec per cycle for planning.

Table 1 shows the worst case runtimes for different search depths. The search depth is in this case defined as the number of plan iterations. One planning step constructs a subtree of the depth 3; a search depth of x therefore corresponds to a tree depth of $3x$. The table shows that search depth values over 3 are clearly not feasible for KiRo with the current processor speeds. However, with newer, faster CPUs we might even be able to go to search depth of 3.

Table 1. Worst case runtimes.

Search depth	Runtime
1	0.3 msec
2	10 msec
3	23 msec
4	45 msec
5	80 msec

4.2   Performance Experiments

Two kinds of performance experiments have been conducted. The simulator has been used to compare the reactive and the decision-theoretic planning action selection directly by playing against each other. On the real table, games against human adversaries were performed to compare both approaches indirectly.

4.3   Results on the Simulator

Two kinds of experiments were conducted on the simulator: In a first run, the decision-theoretic planning procedure had a fixed search depth of two. Using this setting, a number of games were played. While the program using the reactive action selection scheme shot on average one goal in 10 minutes, the decision-theoretic approach scored once in 1.5 minutes.

As many of these goals were own goals by the reactive control system, a second criteria was employed: Field superiority. In this context, a team is called field superior if it is capable of keeping the ball in the opponent's half most of the time. The field superiority value of a team is therefore the percentage of time during which the ball was in the opponent's half of the field. Table 2 shows the results for the decision-theoretic planning approach, ordered by the employed search depth.

Table 2. Field superiority values for the decision-theoretic planning approach.

Search depth	Field superiority value
1	64%
2	72%
3	74%
4	57%

The decision theoretic planning approach is field superior. The field superiority increases with the search depth until the efficiency gets decreased due to the excessive time consumption.

4.4 Results on Physical Table Soccer System

The good results from the simulation experiments could not be replicated on the real table soccer system. Since we do not have a table with robot control for both sides, we had to conduct the tests indirectly by playing against humans. The setting of these experiments was as follows. Every opponent team consisted of two players. The teams were not allowed to switch their positions, and every team had to play four matches against the robot. During two of these, the reactive action selection was controlling the robot; the other two matches were performed by the planning approach. The order of the matches was randomly drawn and the human opponents did not know against which action selection they were playing. In total 12 human players took part in the experiment such that no one played more than eight games.

In 56 Matches, the reactive approach was on average able to shoot a goal in 0.6 minutes, while it took the human opponents 1.56 minutes to score. The planning approach hit the goal once in 0.84 minutes and admitted goals by the human teams on average every 1.19 minutes. One has to note, however, that the difference in defensive play between the planning and the reactive approach are (of course) not statistically significant on a 95% level, while the difference in offensive play between planning and reactive approach is statistically relevant.

5   Conclusion

We presented a decision-theoretic planning approach to play table soccer. The presented approach uses a forward-simulation scheme as well as an opponent model and a naive Bayesian approach to estimate the success probabilities of its own actions.

This approach was able to dominate a reactive action selection mechanism in direct matches performed on a simulator, but proved to be inferior in indirect comparisons playing on the real table soccer table against human teams. The main reason for the failure of the decision-theoretic planning approach seemed to be the noisy ball detection on the real table, especially if the ball is fully or partially covered by the players. A more recent hardware version detects the ball using a infrared camera located beneath the field; as this camera does not provide any information about the opponent's positions, therefore lacking one key information for the decision theoretic approach, we decided to perform the experiments on the real table with the inferior ball detection system.

While the result on the real table soccer table is disappointing, the simulation results have shown that the approach has potential. In particular, there are a number of parameters that appear to be worthwhile to be experimented with. The opponent model, for example, is currently very simple and could, e.g., be trained by recording real games. Furthermore, the success probability should also be adapted to the real table. Finally, the execution of actions themselves might be able to be enhanced. Summarizing, the decision-theoretic planning approach has shown promise but still has to live up to its expectations.

References

1. A. G. Barto, S. J. Bradtke, and S. P. Singh. Learning to act using real-time dynamic programming. *Artificial Intelligence*, 72(1-2):81–138, 1995.
2. B. Bonet and H. Geffner. Labeled RTDP: Improving the convergence of real-time dynamic programming. pages 12–21.
3. C. Boutilier, T. Dean, and S. Hanks. Decision-theoretic planning: Structural assumptions and computational leverage. *Journal of Artificial Intelligence Research*, 11:1–94, 1999.
4. R. A. Brooks. A robust layered control system for a mobile robot. *IEEE Journal of Robotics and Automation*, 2(1), 1986.
5. K. Dorer. Behavior networks for continuous domains using situation-dependent motivations. In *Proc. 16th Int. Joint Conf. on Artificial Intelligence (IJCAI)*, pages 1233–1238, Stockholm, Sweden, 1999.
6. K. Dorer. The magmaFreiburg Soccer Team. In M. Veloso, E. Pagello, and H. Kitano, editors, *RoboCup-99: Robot Soccer World Cup III*, Lecture Notes in Artificial Intelligence, pages 600–603. Springer-Verlag, Berlin, Heidelberg, New York, 2000.
7. P. Haddawy and M. Suwandi. Decision-theoretic refinement planning using inheritance abstraction. In K. Hammond, editor, *Proc. Second International Conference on Artificial Intelligence*. University of Chicago, Illinois, AAAI Press, 1994.
8. P. Maes. Situated agents can have goals. In P. Maes, editor, *Designing Autonomous Agents: Theory and Practice from Biology to Engineering and Back*, pages 49–70. MIT Press, Cambridge, MA, 1990.
9. T. Weigel, J.-S. Gutmann, A. Kleiner, M. Dietl, and B. Nebel. CS-Freiburg: Coordinating Robots for Successful Soccer Playing. *IEEE Transactions on Robotics and Automation*, 18(5):685–699, October 2002.
10. T. Weigel and B. Nebel. KiRo – An Autonomous Table Soccer Player. In *Proc. Int. RoboCup Symposium '02*, pages 119 – 127. Springer-Verlag, Fukuoka, Japan, 2002.

External A*

Stefan Edelkamp[1], Shahid Jabbar[1], and Stefan Schrödl[2]

[1] Computer Science Department
Baroper Str. 301
University Dortmund
{stefan.edelkamp, shahid.jabbar}@cs.uni-dortmund.de
[2] DaimlerChrysler Research and Technology Center
1510 Page Mill Road
Palo Alto, CA 94304
schroedl@rtna.daimlerchrysler.com

Abstract. In this paper we study *External A**, a variant of the conventional (internal) A* algorithm that makes use of external memory, e.g., a hard disk. The approach applies to implicit, undirected, unweighted state space problem graphs with consistent estimates. It combines all three aspects of best-first search, frontier search and delayed duplicate detection and can still operate on very small internal memory. The complexity of the external algorithm is almost linear in external sorting time and accumulates to $O(sort(|E|) + scan(|V|))$ I/O operations, where V and E are the set of nodes and edges in the explored portion of the state space graph. Given that delayed duplicate elimination has to be performed, the established bound is I/O optimal. In contrast to the internal algorithm, we exploit memory locality to allow blockwise rather than random access. The algorithmic design refers to external shortest path search in explicit graphs and extends the strategy of delayed duplicate detection recently suggested for breadth-first search to best-first search. We conduct experiments with sliding-tile puzzle instances.

1 Introduction

Often search spaces are so big that they don't fit into main memory. In this case, during the algorithm only a part of the graph can be processed at a time; the remainder is stored on a disk. However, hard disk operations are about a $10^5 - 10^6$ times slower than main memory accesses. Moreover, according to recent estimates, technological progress yields about annual rates of 40-60 percent increase in processor speeds, while disk transfers only improve by seven to ten percent. This growing disparity has led to a growing attention to the design of *I/O-efficient algorithms* in recent years.

Different variants of breadth-first and depth-first traversal of external graphs have been proposed earlier [3, 13]. In this paper we address A* search on secondary memory: in problems where we try to find the shortest path to a designated goal state, it has been shown that the incorporation of a heuristic estimate for the remaining distance of a state can significantly reduce the number of nodes that need to be explored [5].

The remainder of the paper is organized as follows. First we introduce the most widely used computation model, which counts I/Os in terms of transfers of blocks of

S. Biundo, T. Frühwirth, and G. Palm (Eds.): KI 2004, LNAI 3238, pp. 226–240, 2004.

records of fixed size to and from secondary memory. We describe some basic external-memory algorithms and some data structures relevant to graph search. Then we turn to the subject of external graph search that is concerned with breadth-first search in explicit graphs stored on disk. Korf's *delayed duplicate detection* algorithm [9] adapts Munagala and Ranade's algorithm [14] for the case of implicit graphs, and is presented next. Then we describe *External A**, which extends delayed duplicate detection to heuristic search. Internal and I/O complexities are derived followed by an optimality argument based on a lower bound for delayed duplicate detection. Finally, we address related work and draw conclusions.

2 Model of Computation and Basic Primitives

The commonly used model for comparing the performance of external algorithms consists of a single processor, a small internal memory that can hold up to M data items, and an unlimited secondary memory. The size of the input problem (in terms of the number of records) is abbreviated by N. Moreover, the *block size* B governs the bandwidth of memory transfers. It is often convenient to refer to these parameters in terms of blocks, so we define $m = M/B$ and $n = N/B$. It is usually assumed that at the beginning of the algorithm, the input data is stored in contiguous block on external memory, and the same must hold for the output. Only the number of block read and writes are counted, computations in internal memory do not incur any cost.

We can distinguish two general approaches to external memory algorithms: either we can devise algorithms to solve specific computational problems while explicitly controlling secondary memory access; or, we can develop general-purpose external-memory data structures, such as stacks, queues, search trees, priority queues, and so on, and then use them in algorithms that are similar to their internal-memory counterparts. The simplest operation is *external scanning*, which means reading a stream of records stored consecutively on secondary memory. In this case, it is trivial to exploit disk- and block-parallelism. The number of I/Os is $\Theta(\frac{N}{B}) = \Theta(n)$.

Another important operation is *external sorting*. *External Mergesort* converts the input into a number of elementary sorted sequences of length M using internal-memory sorting. Subsequently, a merging step is applied repeatedly until only one run remains. A set of k sequences $S_1, \ldots, S_k$ can be merged into one run with $O(N)$ operations by reading each sequence in block wise manner. In internal memory, k cursors p_k are maintained for each of the sequences; moreover, it contains one buffer block for each run, and one output buffer. Among the elements pointed to by the p_k, one with the smallest key, say p_i, is selected; the element is copied to the output buffer, and p_i is incremented. Whenever the output buffer reaches the block size B, it is written to disk, and emptied; similarly, whenever a cached block for an input sequences has been fully read, it is replaced with the next block of the run in external memory. When using one internal buffer block per sequence, and one output buffer, each merging phase uses $O(N/B)$ operations. The best result is achieved when k is chosen as big as possible, i.e., $k = M/B$. Then sorting can be accomplished in $O(\log_{M/B} \frac{N}{B})$ phases.

3 External BFS

Since heuristic search algorithms are often applied to huge problem spaces, it is an ubiquitous issue in this domain to cope with internal memory limitations. A variety of *memory-restricted search algorithms* have been developed to work under this constraint. A widely used algorithm is Korf's *iterative deepening A* (IDA*)* algorithm, which requires only space linear in the solution length [7], in exchange for an overhead in computation time due to repeated expansion. Various schemes have been proposed to reduce this overhead by flexibly utilizing additionally available memory. The common framework usually imposes a fixed upper limit on the total memory the program may use, regardless of the size of the problem space. Most of these papers do not explicitly distinguish whether this limit refers to internal memory or to disk space, but frequently the latter one appears to be implicitly assumed. On the contrary, in this section we introduce techniques that explicitly manage a two-level memory hierarchy.

3.1 Explicit Graphs

Under *external graph algorithms*, we understand algorithms that can solve the *depth-first search (DFS)*, *breadth-first search (BFS)*, or *single-source shortest path (SSSP)* problem for explicitly specified directed or undirected graphs that are too large to fit in main memory. We can distinguish between assigning (BFS or DFS) numbers to nodes, assigning BFS levels to nodes, or computing the (BFS or DFS) tree edges. However, for BFS in undirected graphs it can be shown that all these formulations are reducible to each other up to an edge-list sorting in $O(sort(|E|))$ I/O operations.

The input is usually assumed to be an unsorted edge list stored contiguously on disk. However, frequently algorithms assume an *adjacency list representation*, which consists of two arrays, one which contains all edges sorted by the start node, and one array of size $|V|$ which stores, for each vertex, its out-degree and offset into the first array. A preprocessing step can accomplish this conversion in time $O(\frac{|E|}{|V|}sort(|V|))$.

Naively running the standard internal-BFS algorithm in the same way in external memory will result in $\Theta(|V|)$ I/Os for unstructured accesses to the adjacency lists, and $\Theta(|E|)$ I/Os for finding out whether neighboring nodes have already been visited.

The algorithm of *Munagala and Ranade* [14] improves on the latter complexity for the case of undirected graphs, in which duplicates are constrained to be located in adjacent levels. The algorithm builds $Open(i)$ from $Open(i-1)$ as follows: Let $A(i) = N(Open(i-1))$ be the multi-set of neighbor vertices of nodes in $Open(i-1)$; $A(i)$ is created by concatenating all adjacency lists of nodes in $Open(i-1)$. Since after the preprocessing step the graph is stored in adjacency-list representation, this takes $O(|Open(i-1)| + |N(Open(i-1))|/B)$ I/Os. Then the algorithm removes duplicates by external sorting followed by an external scan. Hence, duplicate elimination takes $O(sort(A(i)))$ I/Os. Since the resulting list $A'(i)$ is still sorted, filtering out the nodes already contained in the sorted lists $Open(i-1)$ or $Open(i-2)$ is possible by parallel scanning, therefore this step can be done using $O(sort(|N(Open(i-1))|) + scan(|Open(i-1)| + |Open(i-2)|))$ I/Os. This completes the generation of $Open(i)$. The algorithm can record the nodes' BFS-level in additional $O(|V|)$ time using an external array. Figure 1 provides the implementation of the algorithm of Munagala and Ranade in

Procedure *External Breadth-First-Search*

$Open(-1) \leftarrow Open(-2) \leftarrow \emptyset; U \leftarrow V$
$i \leftarrow 0$
while $(Open(i - 1) \neq \emptyset \lor U \neq \emptyset)$
$\quad$ **if** $(Open(i - 1) = \emptyset)$
$\quad\quad$ $Open(i) \leftarrow \{x\}, where \ x \in U$
$\quad$ **else**
$\quad\quad$ $A(i) \leftarrow N(Open(i - 1))$
$\quad\quad$ $A'(i) \leftarrow remove \ duplicates \ from \ A(i)$
$\quad\quad$ $Open(i) \leftarrow A'(i) \setminus (Open(i - 1) \cup Open(i - 2))$
$\quad$ **foreach** $v \in Open(i)$
$\quad\quad$ $U \leftarrow U \setminus \{v\}$
$\quad$ $i \leftarrow i + 1$

Fig. 1. External BFS by Munagala and Ranade.

pseudo-code. A doubly-linked list U maintains all unvisited nodes, which is necessary when the graph is not completely connected. Since $\sum_i |N(Open(i))| = O(|E|)$ and $\sum_i |Open(i)| = O(|V|)$, the execution of external BFS requires $O(|V| + sort(|E|))$ time, where $O(|V|)$ is due to the external representation of the graph and the initial reconfiguration time to enable efficient successor generation.

The bottleneck of the algorithm are the $O(|V|)$ unstructured accesses to adjacency lists. The refined algorithm [12] consists of a preprocessing and a BFS phase, arriving at a complexity of $O(\sqrt{|V|} \cdot scan(|V| + |E|) + sort(|V| + |E|))$ I/Os.

3.2 Implicit Graphs

An *implicit graph* is a graph that is not residing on disk but generated by successively applying a set of operators to states selected from the search horizon. The advantage in implicit search is that the graph is generated by a set of rules, and hence no disk accesses for the adjacency lists are required.

A variant of Munagala and Ranade's algorithm for BFS-search in implicit graphs has been coined with the term *delayed duplicate detection for frontier search* [9]. Let $\mathcal{I}$ be the initial state, and N be the implicit successor generation function. The algorithm maintains BFS layers on disk. Layer $Open(i-1)$ is scanned and the set of successors are put into a buffer of size close to the main memory capacity. If the buffer becomes full, internal sorting followed by a duplicate elimination phase generates a sorted duplicate-free state sequence in the buffer that is flushed to disk[1].

In the next step, *external merging* is applied to unify the files into $Open(i)$ by a simultaneous scan. The size of the output files is chosen such that a single pass suffices. Duplicates are eliminated. Since the files were presorted, the complexity is given by the scanning time of all files. One also has to eliminate $Open(i - 1)$ and $Open(i - 2)$ from $Open(i)$ to avoid re-computations; that is, nodes extracted from the external

---

[1] Delayed internal duplicate elimination can be improved by using hash tables for the blocks before flushed to disk. Since the state set in the hash table has to be stored anyway, the savings by early duplicate detection are small.

Procedure *Delayed-Duplicate-Detection-Frontier-Search*
> $Open(-1) \leftarrow \emptyset, Open(0) \leftarrow \{\mathcal{I}\}$
> $i \leftarrow 1$
>   **while** $(Open(i-1) \neq \emptyset)$
>> $A(i) \leftarrow N(Open(i-1))$
>> $A'(i) \leftarrow$ *remove duplicates from* $A(i)$
>> $Open(i) \leftarrow A'(i) \setminus (Open(i-1) \cup Open(i-2))$
>> $i \leftarrow i+1$

Fig. 2. Delayed duplicate detection algorithm for BFS.

queue are not immediately deleted, but kept until after the layer has been completely generated and sorted, at which point duplicates can be eliminated using a parallel scan. The process is repeated until $Open(i-1)$ becomes empty, or the goal has been found.

The corresponding pseudo-code is shown in Figure 2. Note that the explicit partition of the set of successors into blocks is implicit in the Algorithm of Munagala and Ranade. Termination is not shown, but imposes no additional implementation problem.

As with the algorithm of Munagala and Ranade, delayed duplicate detection applies $O(sort(|N(Open(i-1))|) + scan(|Open(i-1)| + |Open(i-2)|))$ I/Os. However, since no explicit access to the adjacency list is needed, by $\sum_i |N(Open(i))| = O(|E|)$ and $\sum_i |Open(i)| = O(|V|)$, the total execution time is $O(sort(|E|) + scan(|V|))$ I/Os. In exploration problems where the branching factor is bounded, we have $|E| = O(|V|)$, and thus the complexity for implicit external BFS reduces to $O(sort(|V|))$ I/Os.

The algorithm applies $scan(|Open(i-1)| + |Open(i-2)|)$ I/Os in each phase. Does summing these quantities in fact yield $O(scan(|V|))$ I/Os, as stated? In very sparse problem graphs that are simple chains, if we keep each $Open(i)$ in a separate file, this would accumulate to $O(|V|)$ I/Os in total. However, in this case the states in $Open(i)$, $Open(i+1)$, and so forth are stored consecutively in internal memory. Therefore, I/O is only needed if a level has $\Omega(B)$ states, which can happen only for $O(|V|/B)$ levels.

Delayed duplicate detection was used to generate the first complete breadth-first search of the 2×7 sliding tile puzzle, and the Towers of Hanoi puzzle with 4 pegs and 18 disks. It can also be used to generate large pattern databases that exceed main memory capacity [10]. One file for each BFS layer will be sufficient. The algorithm shares similarities with the internal *Frontier search* algorithm [8, 11] that was used for solving multiple sequence alignment problems.

4   External A*

In the following we study how to extend external breadth-first-exploration in implicit graphs to *best-first* search. The main advantage of A* with respect to BFS is that, due to the use of a lower bound on the goal distance, it only has to traverse a smaller part of the search space to establish an optimal solution.

In A*, the *merit* for state u is $f(u) = g(u) + h(u)$, with g being the cost of the path from the initial state to u and $h(u)$ being the estimate of the remaining costs from u to the goal. In each step, a node u with minimum f-value is removed from *Open*, and the new value $f(v)$ of a successor v of u is updated to the minimum of its current value and $f(v) = g(v) + h(v) = g(u) + w(u,v) + h(v) = f(u) + w(u,v) - h(u) + h(v)$; in this case, it is inserted into *Open* itself.

In our algorithm, we assume a *consistent* heuristic, where for each u and its child v, we have $w(u,v) \geq h(u) - h(v)$, and a uniformly weighted undirected state space problem graph. These conditions are often met in practice, since many problem graphs in single agent search are uniformly weighted and undirected and many heuristics are consistent. BFS can be seen as a special case of A* in uniform graphs with a heuristic h that evaluates to zero for each state. Under these assumptions, we have $h(u) \leq h(v) + 1$ for every state u and every successor v of u. Since the problem graph is undirected this implies $|h(u) - h(v)| \leq 1$ and $h(v) - h(u) \in \{-1, 0, 1\}$. If the heuristic is consistent, then on each search path, the evaluation function f is non-decreasing. No successor will have a smaller f-value than the current one. Therefore, the A* algorithm, which traverses the state set in f-order, expands each node at most once.

Take for example sliding tile puzzles, where numbered tiles on a rectangular grid have to be brought into a defined goal state by successively sliding tiles into one empty square. The *Manhattan distance* is defined as the sum of the horizontal and vertical differences between actual and goal configurations, for all tiles. It is easy to see that it is consistent, since for two successive states u and v the the difference $h(v) - h(u)$ is either -1 or 1. Therefore, f-values of u and v are either the same or $f(v) = f(u) + 2$.

4.1 Buckets

Like external BFS, *External A*** maintains the search horizon on disk, possibly partitioned into main-memory-sized sequences. In fact, the disk files correspond to an external representation of Dial's implementation of a priority queue data structure that is represented as an array of buckets [4]. In the course of the algorithm, each bucket addressed with index i will contain all states u in the set *Open* that have priority $f(u) = i$. An external representation of this data structure will memorize each bucket in a different file.

We introduce a refinement of the data structure that distinguishes between states of different g-values, and designates bucket $Open(i,j)$ to all states u with path length $g(u) = i$ and heuristic estimate $h(u) = j$.

As with the description of external BFS, we do not change the identifier *Open* to separate *generated* from *expanded* states (traditionally denoted as the *Closed* list). During the execution of A*, bucket $Open(i,j)$ may refer to elements that are in the current search horizon or belong to the set of expanded nodes. During the exploration process, only nodes from one currently *active bucket* $Open(i,j)$ with $i + j = f_{min}$ are expanded, up to its exhaustion. Buckets are selected in lexicographic order for (i,j); then, the buckets $Open(i',j')$ with $i' < i$ and $i' + j' = f_{min}$ are *closed*, whereas the buckets $Open(i',j')$ with $i' + j' > f_{min}$ or with $i' > i$ and $i' + j' = f_{min}$ are *open*. For states in the active bucket the status can be either *open* or *closed*.

For an optimal heuristic, i.e., a heuristic that computes the shortest path distance f^*, A* will consider the buckets $Open(0, f^*), \ldots, Open(f^*, 0)$. On the other hand, if the heuristic is equal to zero, it considers the buckets $Open(0,0), \ldots, Open(f^*, 0)$. This leads to the hypothesis that the A* looks at f^* buckets. Unfortunately, this is not true.

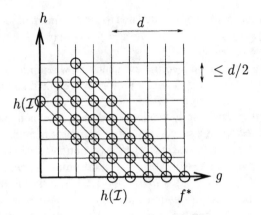

Fig. 3. The number of buckets selected in A*.

Consider Figure 3, in which the g-values are plotted with respect to the h-values, such that states with the same $f = g + h$ value are located on the same diagonal. For states that are expanded in $Open(g, h)$ the successors fall into $Open(g + 1, h - 1)$ $Open(g + 1, h)$, or $Open(g + 1, h + 1)$. The number of naughts for each diagonal is an upper bound on the number buckets that are needed. It is trivial to see that the number is bounded by $f^*(f^* + 1)/2$, since naughts only appear in the triangle bounded by the f^*-diagonal. We can, however, achieve a slightly tighter bound.

Lemma 1. *The number of buckets* Open(i, j) *that are considered by A* in a uniform state space problem graph with a consistent heuristic is bounded by* $(f^* + 1)^2/3$.

Proof. Let $d = f^* - h(\mathcal{I})$. Below $h(\mathcal{I})$ there are at most $d \cdot h(\mathcal{I}) + h(\mathcal{I})$ nodes. The *roof* above $h(\mathcal{I})$ has at most $1 + 3 + \ldots + 2(d/2) - 1$ nodes (counted from top to bottom). Since the sum evaluates to $d^2/4$ we need at most $d \cdot h(\mathcal{I}) + h(\mathcal{I}) + d^2/4$ buckets altogether. The maximal number $((f^*)^2 + f^* + 1)/3$ is reached for $h(\mathcal{I}) = (f^* + 2)/3$.

By the restriction for f-values in the sliding-tile puzzles only about half the number of buckets have to be allocated. Note that f^* is not known in advance, so that we have to construct and maintain the files on the fly.

As in the algorithm of Munagala and Ranade, we can exploit the observation that in undirected state space graph structure, duplicates of a state with BFS-level i can at most occur in levels i, $i - 1$ and $i - 2$. In addition, since h is a total function, we have $h(u) = h(v)$ if $u = v$. This implies the following result.

Lemma 2. *During the course of executing A*, for all* i, i', j, j' *with* $j \neq j'$ *we have that* Open$(i, j) \cap$ Open$(i', j') = \emptyset$.

Lemma 2 allows to restrict duplicate detection to buckets of the same h-value.

4.2   The Algorithm

For ease of presentation, we consider each bucket for the *Open* list as a different file. By Lemma 1 this accumulates to at most $(f^* + 1)^2/3$ files. For the following we therefore generally assume $(f^* + 1)^2/3 = O(scan(|V|))$ and $(f^* + 1)^2/3 = O(sort(|E|))$.

Procedure *External A**
$\quad Open(0, h(\mathcal{I})) \leftarrow \{\mathcal{I}\}$
$\quad f_{min} \leftarrow h(\mathcal{I})$
$\quad$**while** $(f_{min} \neq \infty)$
$\qquad g_{min} \leftarrow \min\{i \mid Open(i, f_{min} - i) \neq \emptyset\}$
$\qquad$**while** $(g_{min} \leq f_{min})$
$\qquad\quad h_{max} \leftarrow f_{min} - g_{min}$
$\qquad\quad Open(g_{min}, h_{max}) \leftarrow$ *remove duplicates from* $Open(g_{min}, h_{max})$
$\qquad\quad Open(g_{min}, h_{max}) \leftarrow Open(g_{min}, h_{max}) \backslash$
$\qquad\qquad\qquad (Open(g_{min} - 1, h_{max}) \cup Open(g_{min} - 2, h_{max}))$
$\qquad\quad A(f_{min}), A(f_{min} + 1), A(f_{min} + 2) \leftarrow N(Open(g_{min}, h_{max}))$
$\qquad\quad Open(g_{min} + 1, h_{max} + 1) \leftarrow A(f_{min} + 2)$
$\qquad\quad Open(g_{min} + 1, h_{max}) \leftarrow A(f_{min} + 1) \cup Open(g_{min} + 1, h_{max})$
$\qquad\quad Open(g_{min} + 1, h_{max} - 1) \leftarrow A(f_{min}) \cup Open(g_{min} + 1, h_{max} - 1)$
$\qquad\quad g_{min} \leftarrow g_{min} + 1$
$\qquad f_{min} \leftarrow \min\{i + j > f_{min} \mid Open(i, j) \neq \emptyset\} \cup \{\infty\}$

Fig. 4. *External A** for consistent and integral heuristics.

Figure 4 depicts the pseudo-code of the *External A** algorithm for consistent estimates and uniform graphs. The algorithm maintains the two values g_{min} and f_{min} to address the currently active bucket. The buckets of f_{min} are traversed for increasing g_{min} up to f_{min}. According to their different h-values, successors are arranged into three different horizon lists $A(f_{min})$, $A(f_{min} + 1)$, and $A(f_{min} + 2)$; hence, at each instance only four buckets have to be accessed by I/O operations. For each of them, we keep a separate buffer of size B; this will reduce the internal memory requirements to $4B$. If a buffer becomes full then it is flushed to disk. As in BFS, it is practical to presort buffers in one bucket immediately by an efficient internal algorithm to ease merging, but we could equivalently sort the unsorted buffers for one buckets externally.

Note that it suffices to perform the duplicate removal only for the bucket that is to be expanded next. The other buckets might not have been fully generated and hence we can save the redundant scanning of the files for every iteration of the inner most *while* loop. When merging the presorted sets with the previously existing *Open* buckets (both residing on disk), duplicates are eliminated, leaving the set $Open(g_{min}, h_{max})$, duplicate free. Moreover, bucket $Open(g_{min}, h_{max})$ is refined not to contain any state in $Open(g_{min} - 1, h_{max})$ or $Open(g_{min} - 2, h_{max})$. This can be achieved through a parallel scan of the presorted files.

Since *External A** simulates A* and changes only the order of elements to be expanded that have the same f-value, completeness and optimality are inherited from the properties shown for A* [15].

Theorem 1 (I/O performance of External A*). *The complexity for External A* in an implicit unweighted and undirected graph with a consistent estimate is bounded by* $O(sort(|E|) + scan(|V|))$ *I/Os.*

Proof. By simulating internal A*, the delayed duplicate elimination scheme looks at each edge in the state space problem graph at most once.

Each data item is I/O efficiently written once as a successor, once for external sorting, once for expansion and scanned twice for duplicate elimination.

More precisely, we have $O(sort(|N(Open(g_{min} - 1, h_{max}))| + |N(Open(g_{min} - 1, h_{max} - 1))| + |N(Open(g_{min} - 1, h_{max} + 1))|))$ I/Os for eliminating duplicates in the accumulated successor lists before expanding $(Open(g_{min}, h_{max}))$, since this operation is based on *external sorting*. While each state is expanded at most once, this yields an amount of $O(sort(|E|))$ I/Os for the overall run time.

File subtraction requires $O(scan(|N(Open(g_{min} - 1, h_{max}))| + |N(Open(g_{min} - 1, h_{max} - 1))| + |N(Open(g_{min} - 1, h_{max} + 1))|) + scan(|N(Open(g_{min} - 1, h_{max}))|) + scan(|N(Open(g_{min} - 2, h_{max}))|))$ I/Os. Therefore, subtraction add $O(scan(|V|) + scan(|E|))$ I/Os to the overall run time.

All other operation are available in scanning time of all reduced buckets.

If we additionally have $|E| = O(|V|)$, the complexity reduces to $O(sort(|V|))$ I/Os.

Internal costs have been neglected in the above analysis. All operation base on batched access, we can scale the internal memory requirements down to $O(1)$, namely 2-3 states, depending on the internal memory needs for external sorting. Since each state is considered only once for expansion, the internal time requirements are $|V|$ *times* the duration t_{exp} for successor generation, plus the efforts for internal duplicate elimination and sorting, if applied. By setting new edges weight $w(u, v)$ to $h(u) - h(v) + 1$, for consistent heuristics A* is a variant of Dijkstra's algorithm that requires internal costs of $O(C \cdot |V|)$, $C = \max\{w(u, v) \mid v \text{ successor of } u\}$ on a Dial. Due to consistency we have $C \leq 2$, so that, given $|E| = O(|V|)$, internal costs are bounded by $O(|V| \cdot (t_{exp} + \log |V|))$, where $O(|V| \log |V|)$ refers to the internal sorting efforts.

To reconstruct a solution path, we could store predecessor information with each state on disk, and apply backward chaining, starting with the target state. However, this is not strictly necessary: For a state in depth g, we intersect the set of possible predecessors with the buckets of depth $g - 1$. Any state that is in the intersection is reachable on an optimal solution path, so that we can recur. The time complexity is bounded by the scanning time of all buckets in consideration and surely in $O(scan(|V|))$.

In practice, to save disk space when expanding bucket $Open(g_{min}, h_{max})$, we can eliminate the bucket $Open(g_{min} - 2, h_{max})$ after file subtraction. In this case, solution path has to be reconstructed by regeneration or through divide-and-conquer strategy.

4.3   Non-uniformly Weighted Graphs

Up to this point, we have made the assumption of uniformly weighted graphs; in this section, we generalize the algorithm to small integer weights in $\{1, \ldots, C\}$. Due to consistency of the heuristic, it holds for every state u and every successor v of u that $h(v) \geq h(u) - w(u, v)$. Moreover, since the graph is undirected, we equally have $h(u) \geq h(v) - w(u, v)$, or $h(v) \leq h(u) + w(u, v)$; hence, $|h(u) - h(v)| \leq w(u, v)$. This means that the successors of the nodes in the active bucket are no longer spread across three, but over $3 + 5 + \ldots + 2C + 1 = C \cdot (C + 2)$ buckets.

For duplicate reduction, we have to subtract the $2C$ buckets $Open(i - 1, j), \ldots, Open(i - 2C, j)$ from the active bucket $Open(i, j)$ prior to its nodes' expansion. It can be shown by induction over $f = i + j$ that no duplicates exist in smaller buckets. The claim is trivially true for $f \leq 2C$. In the induction step, assume to the contrary that for some node $v \in Open(i, j)$, $Open(i', j)$ contains a duplicate v' with $i' < i - 2C$; let $u \in Open(i - w(u, v), j_u)$ be the predecessor of v. Then, by the undirectedness, there must be a duplicate $u' \in Open(i' + w(u, v), j_u)$. But since $f(u') = i' + w(u, v) + j_u \leq i' + C + j_u < i - C + j_u \leq i - w(u, v) + j_u = f(u)$, this is a contradiction to the induction hypothesis.

The derivation of the I/O complexity is similar to the uniform case; the difference is that each bucket is referred to at most $2C+1$ times for bucket subtraction and expansion.

Theorem 2 (I/O performance of External A* for non-uniform graphs). *The I/O complexity for External A* in an implicit and undirected graph, where the weights are in $\{1, \ldots, C\}$, with a consistent estimate, is bounded by $O(\text{sort}(|E|) + C \cdot \text{scan}(|V|))$.*

If we do not impose a bound C, or if we allow directed graphs, the run time increases to $O(sort(|E|) + f^* \cdot scan(|V|))$ I/Os. For larger edge weights and f^*-values, buckets could become sparse and should be handled more carefully, as we would be wasting a number of I/Os in accessing the buckets having fewer than B states. If we have $O((f^*)^2 \cdot B)$ main memory space, a plausible solution in this case would be to keep all the unfilled buffers in main memory. The space requirement can be reduced to $O(C \cdot f^* \cdot B)$, i.e., saving only the C layers that change between successive active buckets. In any case, our algorithm requires at least $\Omega(C^2 \cdot B)$ main memory, to be able to store the C^2 buffers into which a successor might fall.

5 Lower Bound

Is $O(sort(|V|))$ I/O-optimal? Aggarwal and Vitter [1] showed that external sorting has the above-mentioned I/O complexity of $\Omega\left(N \log \frac{N}{B} / B \log \frac{M}{B}\right)$ and provide two algorithms that are asymptotically optimal. As internal *set inequality*, *set inclusion* and *set disjointness* require at least $N \log N - O(N)$ comparisons, the lower bound on the number of I/Os for these problems is also bounded by $\Omega(sort(N))$.

Arge, Knudsen and Larsen [2] considered the duplicate elimination problem. A lower bound on the number of comparisons needed is $N \log N - \sum_{i=1}^{k} N_i \log N_i - O(N)$ where N_i is the multiplicity of record i. The authors argue in detail that after the duplicate removal, the total order of the remaining records is known. This corresponds to an I/O complexity of at most

$$\Omega\left(\max\left\{\frac{N \log \frac{N}{B} - \sum_{i=1}^{k} N_i \log N_i}{B \log \frac{M}{B}}, N/B\right\}\right).$$

The authors also give an involved algorithm based on Mergesort that matches this bound. For the sliding tile puzzle with two preceding buckets and a branching factor $b \leq 4$ we have $N_i \leq 8$. For general consistent estimates in uniform graphs, we have $N_i \leq 3c$, with c being an upper bound on the maximal branching factor. An algorithm performs *delayed duplicate bucket elimination*, if it eliminates duplicates within a bucket and with respect to adjacent buckets that are duplicate free.

Table 1. 15-puzzle instances used for experiments.

S. No.	Initial State	Initial Estimate	Solution Length
1	(0 2 1 3 5 4 6 7 8 9 10 11 12 13 14 15)	4	16
2	(0 1 2 3 5 4 7 6 8 9 10 11 12 13 14 15)	4	24
3	(0 2 1 3 5 4 7 6 8 9 13 11 12 10 14 15)	10	30
4 {12}	(14 1 9 6 4 8 12 5 7 2 3 0 10 11 13 15)	35	45
5 {16}	(1 3 2 5 10 9 15 6 8 14 13 11 12 4 7 0)	24	42
6 {14}	(7 6 8 1 11 5 14 10 3 4 9 13 15 2 0 12)	41	59
7 {60}	(11 14 13 1 2 3 12 4 15 7 9 5 10 6 8 0)	48	66
8 {88}	(15 2 12 11 14 13 9 5 1 3 8 7 0 10 6 4)	43	65

Theorem 3 (I/O Performance Optimality for External A*)). *If $|E| = \Theta(|V|)$, delayed duplicate bucket elimination in an implicit unweighted and undirected graph A* search with consistent estimates needs at least $\Omega(\text{sort}(|V|))$ I/O operations.*

Proof. Since each state gives rise to at most c successors and there at most 3 preceding buckets in A* search with consistent estimates in an uniformly weighted graph, given that previous buckets are mutually duplicate free, we have at most $3c$ states that are the same. Therefore, all sets N_i are bounded by $3c$. Since k is bounded by N we have that $\sum_{i=1}^{k} N_i \log N_i$ is bounded by $k \cdot 3c \log 3c = O(N)$. Therefore, the lower bound for duplicate elimination for N states is $\Omega(sort(N) + scan(N))$.

6   Experiments

We selected 15-Puzzle problem instances. Many instances cannot be solved internally with A* and the Manhattan distance. Each state is packed into 8 bytes.

Internal sorting is done by the built-in *Quicksort* routine. External merge is performed by maintaining the file pointers for every flushed buffer and merging them into a single sorted file. Since we have a simultaneous file pointers capacity bound imposed by the operating system, we implemented two-phase merging. Duplicate removal and bucket subtraction are performed on single passes through the bucket file. The implementation differs a little from the algorithm presented in this paper in that the duplicate removal within one bucket, as well as the bucket subtraction are delayed until the bucket is selected for expansion. The program utilizes an implicit priority queue. For sliding tile puzzles, during expansion, the successor's f value differs from the parent state by exactly 2. This implies that in case of an empty diagonal, the program terminates.

We performed our experiments on a mobile AMD Athlon XP 1.5 GHz processor with 512 MB RAM, running MS Windows XP. In Table 1 we give the example instances that we have used for our experiments. Some of them are adopted from Korf's seminal paper [7] (original numbers given in brackets). We chose some of the simplest and hardest instances for our experiments. The harder problems cannot be solved internally and were cited as the core reasons for the need of IDA*.

In Table 2 we show the diagonal pattern of states that is developed during the exploration for problem instance 1. The entry $x + y$ in the cell (i, j) implies that x

Table 2. States inserted in the buckets for instance 1.

g/h	1	2	3	4	5	6	7	8	9	10	11
0	-	-	-	1+0	-	-	-	-	-	-	-
1	-	-	-	-	2+0	-	-	-	-	-	-
2	-	-	-	0+4	-	2+0	-	-	-	-	-
3	-	-	-	-	7+3	-	4+0	-	-	-	-
4	-	-	-	0+7	-	13+4	-	10+0	-	-	-
5	-	-	-	-	5+15	-	24+10	-	24+0	-	-
6	-	-	-	0+6	-	12+26	-	46+28	-	44+0	-
7	-	-	-	-	9+10	-	20+51	-	99+57	-	76+0
8	-	-	-	0+8	-	15+25	-	48+137	-	195+0	-
9	-	-	-	-	4+17	-	45+52	-	203+0	-	-
10	-	-	-	0+3	-	13+49	-	92+0	-	-	-
11	-	-	-	-	2+19	-	46+0	-	-	-	-
12	-	-	-	0+5	-	31+0	-	-	-	-	-
13	-	-	0+2	-	10+0	-	-	-	-	-	-
14	-	0+2	-	5+0	-	-	-	-	-	-	-
15	0+2	-	5+0	-	-	-	-	-	-	-	-

Table 3. Effects on I/O performance due to different internal buffer sizes.

Initial State	B	I/O Reads	I/O Writes	Time (sec)
	10	5,214	6,525	2
2	25	3,086	3,016	1
	50	2,371	1,843	< 1
	100	2,022	1,265	< 1

and y number of states are generated from the expansion of $Open(i-1, j-1)$ and $Open(i-1, j+1)$, respectively.

The impact of internal buffer size on the I/O performance is clearly observable in Table 3. We show the I/O performance of two instances by varying the internal buffer size B. A larger buffer implies fewer flushes during writing, fewer block reads during expansion and fewer processing time due to internally sorting larger but fewer buffers. This I/O and time data are collected using the task manager of Windows XP.

In Table 4, we show the impact of duplicate removal and bucket subtraction. Note that we do not employ any pruning technique like hashing or predecessor elimination. As observable from the fourth entry, the gain is about 99% when duplicate removal and bucket subtraction are used. In the latter cases, we had to stop the experiment because of the limited hard disk capacity. These states are the number of states that are *generated* during the run and do not represent the total number of states that are actually *expanded*. The number of expanded states differs largely from the generated states because of the removal of duplicate states and generation of states of $(f^* + 2)$ diagonal.

Finally, we compare the node count of our algorithm to the node count of IDA* in Table 5. As is noticeable in the table that the problem instances 6,7, and 8 can not

238   Stefan Edelkamp, Shahid Jabbar, and Stefan Schrödl

Table 4. Impact of duplicate removal and bucket subtraction on generated states.

Initial State	N	N_{dr}	N_{dr+sub}
1	530,401	2,800	1,654
2	> 50,000,000	126,741	58,617
3	> 50,000,000	492,123	314,487
4	71,751,166	611,116	493,990
5	<out of disk space>	7,532,113	5,180,710
6	<out of disk space>	<out of disk space>	297,583,236
7	<out of disk space>	<out of disk space>	2,269,240,000
8	<out of disk space>	<out of disk space>	2,956,384,330

Table 5. Comparison of space requirement by IDA* and External A*.

Initial State	N_{IDA*} [7]	N_{ExA*}	S_{ExA*} (GB)	% gain
4	546,344	493,990	0.003	9.58
5	17,984,051	5,180,710	0.039	71.2
6	1,369,596,778	297,583,236	2.2	78.3
7	3,337,690,331	2,269,240,000	16.91	32
8	6,009,130,748	2,956,384,330	22	50.8

be solved internally, especially 7 and 8 whose memory requirements surpass even the address limits of current PC hardware.

7   Conclusion

In this work, we present an extension of external undirected BFS graph search to external A* search which can exploit a goal-distance heuristics. Contrary to some previous works in standard graph search, we are concerned with implicitly represented graphs. The key issue to efficiently solve the problem is a file-based priority queue matrix as a refinement to Dial's priority queue data structure. For consistent estimates in uniform graphs we show that we achieve optimal I/O complexity. On the other side of the memory hierarchy, through the achievement of better memory locality for access, the external design for A* seems likely to increase cache performance. Different from delayed duplicate detection, we start with the external BFS exploration scheme of Munagala and Ranade to give complexity results measured in the number of I/O operations that the algorithm executes.

There is a tight connection between the exploration of externally stored sets of states, and an efficient *symbolic* representation for sets of states with *Binary Decision Diagrams (BDDs)*. The design of existing symbolic heuristic search algorithms seems to be strongly influenced by the delayed duplication and external set manipulation. Another related research area are internal memory-restricted algorithms, that are mainly interested in oan early removal of states from the main memory. The larger space-efficiency of a breadth-first traversal ordering in heuristic search has lead to improved memory consumption for internal algorithms, with new algorithms entitled *breadth-first heuristic search* and *breadth-first iterative-deepening* [16]. One interesting feature of our approach from a practical point of view is the ability to pause and resume the program execution. For large problem instances, this is a desirable feature in case we reach the system bounds of secondary storage and after upgrading the system want to resume the execution. In near future we expect a practical relevant outcome of this research in application domains especially AI planning, model checking and route planning.

Very recently, there are two related but independent research results, considering external best-first exploration. On the one hand, Korf [6] has successfully extended delayed duplicate detection to best-first search and also considered omission of the visited list as proposed in *frontier search*. It turned out that any 2 of the 3 options were compatible: Breadth-first frontier search with delayed duplicate detection, best-first frontier search, and best-first with external but non-reduced visited list. For the latter Korf simulates the buffered traversal in a Dial priority queue. With respect to this work, we contribute an algorithm that can deal with all three approaches. As an additional feature, Korf showed how external sorting can be avoided, by a selection of hash functions that split larger files into smaller pieces which fit into main memory. As with the h-value in our case a state and its duplicate will have the same hash address.

Zhou and Hansen [17] incorporated a projection function that maps states into an *abstract* state space; this reduces the successor scope of states that have to be kept in main memory. Projections are state space homomorphisms, such that for each pair of consecutive abstract states there exist an original pair of consecutive original states. In the running example of the 15-puzzle, the projection was based on states that have the same blank position. Unfortunately, this state-space abstraction also preserves the additional property that the successor set and the expansion sets are disjoint, yielding no self-loops in the abstract state space graph. For this case a reduction similar to the 3-layer idea of Munagala and Ranade applies to the reduced graph. For multiple-sequence alignment the authors could define an abstract graph structure that works well together with the *Sweep-A** algorithm. The method is crucially dependent on the availability of suitable partition functions. If the remaining duplicate elimination scope fits into main memory, the authors provide an improved worst case bound of $O(n \cdot |E|)$ I/Os. By the additional assumption this does not contradict the lower bound provided. In contrast, we do not rely on any partitioning beside the h function and we do not require the duplicate scope to fit in main memory.

It seems that the other two approaches are quite compatible with our approach; e.g., by introducing the abstract state space concept, the spatial locality of the states can be further improved. Also, duplicate detection using external hashing within each of our buckets of the priority queue might result in better run-time of our algorithm, in practice. In summary, all three approaches have independent contributions and the future will show how they cooperate.

Acknowledgments

The work is supported by *Deutsche Forschungsgemeinschaft* (DFG) in the projects *Heuristic Search* (Ed 74/3) and *Directed Model Checking* (Ed 74/2).

References

1. A. Aggarwal and J. S. Vitter. Complexity of sorting and related problems. In *International Colloquim on Automata, Languages and Programming (ICALP)*, number 267 in LNCS, pages 467–478, 1987.
2. L. Arge, M. Knudsen, and K. Larsen. Sorting multisets and vectors in-place. In *Workshop on Algorithms and Data Structures (WADS)*, LNCS, pages 83–94, 1993.
3. Y.-J. Chiang, M. T. Goodrich, E. F. Grove, R. Tamasia, D. E. Vengroff, and J. S. Vitter. External memory graph algorithms. In *Symposium on Discrete Algorithms (SODA)*, pages 139–149, 1995.
4. R. B. Dial. Shortest-path forest with topological ordering. *Communication of the ACM*, 12(11):632–633, 1969.
5. P. E. Hart, N. J. Nilsson, and B. Raphael. A formal basis for heuristic determination of minimum path cost. *IEEE Trans. on on Systems Science and Cybernetics*, 4:100–107, 1968.
6. R. Korf. Best-first frontier search with delayed duplicate detection. In *National Conference on Artificial Intelligence (AAAI)*, 2004. To appear.
7. R. E. Korf. Depth-first iterative-deepening: An optimal admissible tree search. *Artificial Intelligence*, 27(1):97–109, 1985.
8. R. E. Korf. Divide-and-conquer bidirectional frontier search: First results. In *International Joint Conferences on Artificial Intelligence (IJCAI)*, pages 1184–1191, 1999.
9. R. E. Korf. Delayed duplicate detection. In *IJCAI-Workshop on Model Checking and Artificial Intelligence (MoChart)*, 2003.
10. R. E. Korf and A. Felner. *Chips Challenging Champions: Games, Computers and Artificial Intelligence*, chapter Disjoint Pattern Database Heuristics, pages 13–26. Elsevier, 2002.
11. R. E. Korf and W. Zhang. Divide-and-conquer frontier search applied to optimal sequence allignment. In *National Conference on Artificial Intelligence (AAAI)*, pages 910–916, 2000.
12. K. Mehlhorn and U. Meyer. External-memory breadth-first search with sublinear I/O. In *European Symposium on Algorithms (ESA)*, 2002.
13. U. Meyer, P. Sanders, and J. Sibeyn. *Memory Hierarchies*. Springer, 2003.
14. K. Munagala and A. Ranade. I/O-complexity of graph algorithms. In *Symposium on Discrete Algorithms (SODA)*, pages 87–88, 2001.
15. J. Pearl. *Heuristics*. Addison-Wesley, 1985.
16. R. Zhou and E. Hansen. Breadth-first heuristic search. In *International Conference on Automated Planning and Scheduling (ICAPS)*, pages 92–100, 2004.
17. R. Zhou and E. Hansen. Structured duplicate detection in external-memory graph search. In *National Conference on Artificial Intelligence (AAAI)*, 2004. To appear.

Combining Recurrent Neural Networks and Support Vector Machines for Structural Pattern Recognition

Brijnesh J. Jain, Peter Geibel, and Fritz Wysotzki

Methods of Artificial Intelligence, Sekr. Fr 5–8, Faculty IV, TU Berlin
Franklinstr. 28/29, D-10587 Berlin, Germany

Abstract. We apply support vector learning to attributed graphs where the kernel matrices are based on approximations of the Schur-Hadamard (SH) inner product by means of recurrent neural networks. We present and discuss experimental results of different classifiers constructed by a SVM operating on positive semi-definite (psd) and non-psd kernel matrices.

1 Introduction

In many application areas, Support Vector Machines (SVMs, [19, 17]) yield excellent learning results. SVMs are linear learning machines like the perceptron. If the non-linear discrimination of classes is required, the so called *kernel trick* is used. Using a kernel for learning corresponds to mapping the original input space to a feature space usually having a higher dimension.

SVM learning is based on maximizing a quadratic objective function (the dual Lagrangian) that depends on inner products for pairs of given feature vectors. The same holds true for the learned classification function where the inner product is computed for the so called support vectors and the example to be classified.

The required computations of the inner products can be replaced by applications of a two place *kernel function* that is defined as the inner product in the feature space to which the original input space is implicitly projected. Learning takes place without explicitly constructing or sometimes even knowing the transformation that is related to the chosen kernel.

In many application areas, the training examples cannot be represented by feature vectors without loss of structural information. Examples are the classification of chemical compounds (e.g. [2, 18]), and the classification of images. In such applications, graphs provide a natural representation of the data. In order to classify images – a typical pattern recognition task –, each image is described by its line or region adjacency graph. Learning on such a graphical representation yields classifiers that are invariant with respect of translations and rotations.

By providing an appropriate kernel function, the given domain of graphs is embedded into a linear space thus allowing the application of kernel based methods like the support vector machine.

S. Biundo, T. Frühwirth, and G. Palm (Eds.): KI 2004, LNAI 3238, pp. 241–255, 2004.

Since the kernel function defines the inner product in the feature space, it can be regarded as a *similarity measure* for graphs. In this article, we use a graph similarity that is based on the Schur-Hadamard inner product adapted for graphs in the SVM framework. The evaluation of the Schur-Hadamard inner product includes the computation of an optimal matching of the two graphs thus providing some insight in their similarity or dissimilarity.

Despite the fact that Schur-Hadamard inner product is not positive definite in general, we will show experimentally that nevertheless very good classification results can be obtained using a modified version of the SVMLight [14]. Additionally, we investigate the usage of similarity vectors constructed from the Schur-Hadamard inner product for learning as proposed in [6].

The computation of the Schur-Hadamard inner product requires the determination of optimal permutations for pairs of graphs. In order to solve this NP-complete task, a Hopfield-type network is employed. Thus this approach combines recurrent neural networks with SVMs. Similar combinations have been successfully applied to feed-forward and competitive neural networks [12, 13].

This article is structured as follows. Section 2 is a collection of basic notations and definitions. Section 3 discusses kernel functions for graphs. In section 4 we define the Schur-Hadamard inner product of graphs. Section 5 proposes a neural network approach to approximate the Schur-Hadamard inner product. In Section 6, we present experiments for a molecule classification task, and for the recognition of digits and letters. Section 7 concludes.

2   Terminology

Basic Notations and Definitions. Let S be a set. By $S^{[2]}$ we denote the set of all unordered 2-element subsets $\{i, j\} \subseteq S$. The set of real numbers is denoted by $\mathbb{R}$ and the set of non-negative real numbers by $\mathbb{R}_+$. We write $\mathcal{M}_n(S)$ for the set of all $(n \times n)$-matrices $\boldsymbol{A} = (a_{ij})$ with $a_{ij} \in S$. By $\boldsymbol{x}^T$ and $\boldsymbol{A}^T$ we denote the transpose of $\boldsymbol{x} \in \mathbb{R}^n$ and $\boldsymbol{A} \in \mathcal{M}_n(S)$, respectively.

Basic Graph Theory. Let $\mathcal{A}$ be an inner product space over $\mathbb{R}$, for example $\mathcal{A} = \mathbb{R}^m$. An *attributed graph* is a triple $Z = (V, E, \boldsymbol{Z})$ consisting of a finite set $V \neq \emptyset$, a set $E \subseteq V^{[2]}$, and a matrix $\boldsymbol{Z} = (z_{ij}) \in \mathcal{M}_{|V|}(\mathcal{A})$ such that

1. $\boldsymbol{Z}^T = \boldsymbol{Z}$
2. $\boldsymbol{z}_{ij} = \boldsymbol{0} \Leftrightarrow \{i, j\} \in V^{[2]} \setminus E$

The set V is the set of *vertices*, E is the set of *edges*, and $\boldsymbol{Z}$ is the (*attributed*) *adjacency matrix* of Z. The number of vertices of a graph Z is its *order*, written as $|Z|$. A *weighted graph* is an attributed graph $Z = (V, E, \boldsymbol{Z})$ with $\boldsymbol{Z} \in \mathcal{M}_n(\mathbb{R}_+)$. We call a weighted graph Z *normalized*, if $\boldsymbol{Z} \in \mathcal{M}_n([0, 1])$.

Two vertices i, j of Z are *adjacent*, if $\{i, j\} \in E$. The *degree* of a vertex i is the number δ_i of vertices adjacent to i. Its *co-degree* is the number $\delta_i^\perp = |Z| - 1 - \delta_i$.

If Z is a weighted graph, we define the *weighted degree* of i by

$$\delta_i^\omega = \sum_{j \neq i} z_{ij}.$$

The number $\delta = \max\{\delta_i : i \in V\}$ is the *degree* of Z and the number $\delta^\perp = \max\{\delta_i^\perp : i \in V\}$ its *co-degree*. If Z is weighted, then $\delta^\omega = \max\{\delta_i^\omega : i \in V\}$ denotes the *weighted degree* of Z.

Let $Z = (V, E, \mathbf{Z})$ be a weighted graph with non-negative adjacency matrix $\mathbf{Z}$. The *characteristic vector* of a subset U of V is a vector $\mathbf{x}_U = (u_1, \ldots, u_n)$ with

$$u_i = \begin{cases} 1 & : \quad \text{if } i \in U \\ 0 & : \quad \text{otherwise} \end{cases}$$

for all $i \in V$. The number

$$\omega(U) = \frac{1}{2} \mathbf{x}_U^T \mathbf{Z} \mathbf{x}_U \tag{1}$$

is the *weight* of subset U in Z.

A *clique* is a subset C of V such that $\{i, j\} \in E$ for all $i, j \in C$. A *maximal clique* is a clique C not contained in a clique C' with $|C'| > |C|$. A *maximum weighted clique* is a clique C with maximum weight $w(C)$. The *maximum weighted clique problem* asks for a clique with maximum weight. In the following let $\mathcal{C}_Z$ ($\mathcal{C}_Z^\times$, $\mathcal{C}_Z^*$) denote the set of all cliques (maximal cliques, maximum weighted cliques) of Z.

3   SVM

Support vector machines (SVM) [19, 17] have proven to be widely applicable and successful in data classification. Given a set $\{\mathbf{x}_1, \ldots, \mathbf{x}_M\} \subseteq \mathcal{X}$ of training objects from a domain $\mathcal{X}$ with corresponding labels $\{y_1, \ldots, y_M\} \subseteq \{+1, -1\}^M$, a SVM learns an optimal hyperplane to separate the training objects in a feature space $\mathcal{F}$ by solving the constrained optimization problem

$$\min_{\mathbf{w}, \xi} \frac{1}{2} \langle \mathbf{w}, \mathbf{w} \rangle + C \sum_{i=1}^{M} \xi_i$$
$$\text{subject to} \quad y_i \left(\langle \mathbf{w}, \phi(\mathbf{x}_i) \rangle + b \right) \geq 1 - \xi_i \tag{2}$$
$$\xi_i \geq 0, \ i = 1, \ldots, M$$

where $\phi : \mathcal{X} \longrightarrow \mathcal{F}$ is a transformation of the input space $\mathcal{X}$ to the feature space $\mathcal{F}$. The vector $\mathbf{w}$ and the bias b define a hyperplane in $\mathcal{F}$. The classification function is given by

$$f(\mathbf{x}) = \text{sign} \left(\langle \mathbf{w}, \phi(\mathbf{x}) \rangle + b \right) \tag{3}$$

Basically, an optimal hyperplane is determined such that each transformed example $\phi(\mathbf{x}_i)$ has a functional margin of at least 1 with respect to the hyperplane. In order to deal with non-separable datasets, the slack variables ξ_i are introduced. The slack variable ξ_i is zero for objects, that have a functional margin of more than 1. For objects with a margin less than 1, ξ_i expresses how much the object fails to have the required margin. It can be shown that $\sum_{i=1}^{M} \xi_i$ is an upper bound for the number of errors. The objective function of the minimization problem encompasses the maximization of the geometrical margin as well as the minimization of the number of misclassified objects. The regularization parameter C is used for weighting both criteria.

Solving (2) is accomplished through solving the Lagrangian dual problem

$$\max_{\alpha} \sum_{i=1}^{M} \alpha_i - \frac{1}{2} \sum_{i,j=1}^{M} \alpha_i \alpha_j y_i y_j \langle \phi(\boldsymbol{x}_i), \phi(\boldsymbol{x}_j) \rangle$$

$$\text{subject to } 0 \le \alpha_i \le C, \ i = 1, \ldots, M \tag{4}$$

$$\sum_i \alpha_i y_i = 0$$

where the α_i are Lagrangian multipliers. The function

$$k(\boldsymbol{x}, \boldsymbol{x}') = \langle \phi(\boldsymbol{x}), \phi(\boldsymbol{x}') \rangle$$

is called the *kernel*. The kernel k gives rise to a positive semi-definite (psd) *kernel matrix*

$$K = (k_{ij}) \qquad \text{with} \qquad k_{ij} = k(\boldsymbol{x}_i, \boldsymbol{x}_j). \tag{5}$$

For the solution $(\alpha_1^*, \ldots, \alpha_M^*)$ of (4), the dual form of the classification function in (3) is given by

$$f^*(\boldsymbol{x}) = \text{sign}\Big(\sum_i \alpha_i^* y_i k(\boldsymbol{x}_i, \boldsymbol{x}) + b \Big). \tag{6}$$

Now consider the case that we do not know the function ϕ, but a symmetrical two place function $k : \mathcal{X} \times \mathcal{X} \longrightarrow \mathcal{R}$ is given, where $\mathcal{R}$ is the set of real numbers. k is called a positive semi-definite kernel, iff the kernel matrix K is positive semi-definite for every training set $\boldsymbol{x}_1, \ldots, \boldsymbol{x}_M$, i.e. if

$$\sum_{i,j=1}^{M} c_i c_j k_{i,j} \ge 0 \tag{7}$$

holds for all $c_i \in \mathcal{R}$.

For a psd kernel function, there exists a mapping

$$\phi : \mathcal{X} \longrightarrow \mathcal{F}$$

into a Hilbert space $\mathcal{F}$ with $k(\boldsymbol{x}, \boldsymbol{x}') = \langle \phi(\boldsymbol{x}), \phi(\boldsymbol{x}') \rangle$. If we consider a training set of *graphs* $\boldsymbol{x}_i$, and if we do have a function k with the required property, then there exists an embedding ϕ of the domain of graphs $\mathcal{X}$ into an Euclidean space, and the SVM can be applied (e.g. [17]).

If a symmetric function k' is not psd, the following idea from [6] can be applied. Define the transformation $\phi(\boldsymbol{x}) = \boldsymbol{s}$, where the i-th component of $\boldsymbol{s}$

is given by $[s]_i = k'(x, x_i)$. This means that each example is described by the vector of similarities to the given training examples. The kernel function k is then defined by

$$k(x, x') = \sum_{l=1}^{M} k'(x, x_l) k'(x_l, x') \tag{8}$$

where the symmetry of k' was used.

Using this kernel function in (4) the optimal classifier defined in (6) amounts to

$$\text{sign}\left(\sum_i \alpha_i^* y_i \sum_{l=1}^{M} k'(x_i, x_l) k'(x_l, x) + b\right) = \text{sign}\left(\sum_{l=1}^{M} \beta_l k'(x_l, x) + b\right) \tag{9}$$

where $\beta_l = \sum_i \alpha_i^* y_i k'(x_i, x_l)$. I.e. a new example is classified by its similarities to *all* given examples, and not only to the support vectors as in (6).

If k is not positive semi-definite in general, it is still possible that the kernel matrix K is positive definite for the given training set. In this case it is possible to apply the SVM successfully. If the kernel matrix possesses small negative eigenvalues, it is possible to consider a modified matrix

$$K' = (K + \lambda I) \tag{10}$$

where $\lambda > 0$ is a constant and I is the identity matrix. If K has an eigenvalue c, K' has the eigenvalue $c + \lambda$. If c is the smallest negative eigenvalue of K, then K' is positive semi-definite for $\lambda \geq -c$, see also [17].

So far, most research on kernel methods has focused on learning from attribute value data. The investigation on kernel methods for attributed graphs, however, has recently started [3] and is still widely unexplored, though graphs are a more adequate representation of patterns in structured domains than feature vectors.

In this paper we propose the *Schur-Hadamard inner product* for support vector learning of attributed graphs. The SH inner product shares some properties of a kernel, but is in general not a kernel. In experiments we investigate the applicability of the SH inner product for support vector learning of graphs.

4   The Schur-Hadamard Inner Product

Assume that X and Y are attributed graphs of order n with adjacency matrices $X = (x_{ij})$ and $Y = (y_{ij})$. The *Schur-Hadamard inner product* of graphs is the maximum value of the following quadratic problem

$$\begin{aligned} \text{maximize} \quad & f(P) = tr\left(XPYP^T\right) \\ \text{subject to} \quad & P \in \Pi_n \end{aligned} \tag{11}$$

where tr denotes the trace of a matrix and Π_n is the set of all $(n \times n)$-permutation matrices. It is straightforward to extend (11) to graphs of different order by introducing additional dummy vertices with attribute $\mathbf{0}$.

Despite its name the SH inner product is not an inner product, since it is not bilinear. Nevertheless, the Euclidean norm induced by the SH inner product is a metric. In addition the SH inner product is symmetric, positive, and the Cauchy-Schwarz inequality holds [9, 10]. The SH inner product, however, shares some properties of a kernel, but it is in general not a kernel as can be shown by counterexamples.

Regardless whether the SH inner product σ is a kernel or not, its computation is an NP-complete problem, because it comprises the maximum common subgraph problem as a special case. Thus for large datasets of graphs computing the pairwise similarities might be intractable in a practical setting. One way around is to resort to heuristics which return approximate solutions within an acceptable time limit (see Section 5). But this may yield a non-psd kernel matrix.

Occasionally, non-psd matrices K are applied to (4). Examples include kernel matrices induced by the well known sigmoid kernel [19] or the tangent distance kernel [7]. If K is indefinite the primal-dual relationship does not exist. Thus, it is not clear what kind of classification problem we are solving. In addition, non-psd kernels may cause difficulties in solving (4). Surprisingly, non-psd matrices arising from kernels similar to the sigmoid kernel or tangent distance kernel have been applied successfully in several practical cases. According to [7] the experimental results show that the class of 'kernels' which produce accurate results is not restricted to *conditionally positive definite* (cpsd) *kernels*.

Nevertheless, theoretically sound solutions of support vector learning based on non-psd matrices have been proposed, for example the approach by Graepel et al. [6] where each pattern is described by the vector of proximities to all other patterns, see above.

5   Computing the SH Inner Product

The problem of computing the SH inner product is an NP complete graph matching problem (GMP). Due to its high computational complexity, execution times of exact algorithms which guarantee to return optimal solutions grow exponentially with the number of vertices of the graph. Therefore exact algorithms may be even useless for practical problems of moderate size. One way around is to resort to approximate solutions. In this section we suggest a neural network approach to approximately compute the SH inner product. We first transform the GMP to a maximum weighted clique problem (MWCP) given in terms of a zero-one integer quadratic problem. Next we provide an equivalent continuous formulation of the MWCP constrained over the unit hypercube. Finally, we propose a special Hopfield network for solving the continuous quadratic problem.

5.1   Transforming the GMP to a MWCP

Assume that X and Y are attributed graphs of order n with adjacency matrices $\boldsymbol{X} = (\boldsymbol{x}_{ij})$ and $\boldsymbol{Y} = (\boldsymbol{y}_{ij})$. An *inner product graph* $Z = X \diamond Y$ of X and Y is a weighted graph determined by the $(n^2 \times n^2)$-matrix $\boldsymbol{Z} = (z_{ij,kl})$ with entries

$$z_{ij,kl} = \begin{cases} x_{ij}^T y_{kl} + \varepsilon & : \quad \text{if } (i \neq j \wedge k \neq l) \vee (i = j \wedge k = l) \\ 0 & : \quad \text{otherwise} \end{cases}$$

The constant $\varepsilon > 0$ is chosen such that all vertex and edge weights are positive. Using Z, problem (11) can be formulated as a special quadratic assignment problem

$$\begin{aligned} \text{minimize} \quad & f(P) = -\tfrac{1}{2} x_P^T Z x_P \\ \text{subject to} \quad & P \in \Pi_n \end{aligned} \tag{12}$$

where x_P is the n^2-dimensional vector obtained by stacking the columns of matrix $P \in \Pi_n$. The next result establishes an one-to-one correspondence between the maximal cliques of Z and the permutation matrices of Π_n.

Theorem 1. *There is a bijective mapping*

$$\Phi : C_Z^\times \to \Pi_n, \quad C \mapsto P_C$$

such that

i. $\omega(C) = -f(P_C) + \tfrac{n}{2}\varepsilon$ *for all* $C \in C_Z^\times$

ii. $\omega(C) = -\min_P f(P) + \tfrac{n}{2}\varepsilon$ *for all* $C \in C_Z^*$.

Proof. Let C be a maximal clique of Z. Then $|C| = n$ by construction of Z. We define a $(n \times n)$-matrix $P_C = (p_{ij})$ with

$$p_{ij} = \begin{cases} 1 & : \quad \text{if } (i,j) \in C \\ 0 & : \quad \text{otherwise} \end{cases}$$

Since C is a clique and by definition of Z we find that P_C is a permutation matrix giving rise to a well-defined bijection $\Phi(C) = P_C$.

Next we show assertion (i). Let $P = P_C$ be the permutation matrix associated with C, let x_C be the characteristic vector of C, and let x_P be the vector representation of matrix P. Then we have

$$\begin{aligned} \omega(C) &= \frac{1}{2} x_C^T Z x_C \\ &= \frac{1}{2} x_P^T Z x_P \\ &= \frac{1}{2} tr\left(XPYP^T \right) + \frac{1}{2} tr\left(\varepsilon PP^T \right) \\ &= -f(P) + \frac{n}{2}\varepsilon. \end{aligned}$$

Finally, in light of (i), assertion (ii) is obvious. □

5.2   A Continuous Formulation of the MWCP

Let $Z = (V, E, Z)$ be a weighted graph of order n with adjacency matrix $Z = (z_{ij})$, let $D(Z) \in M_n(\mathbb{R}_+)$ be the diagonal matrix of Z, and let $d(Z) \in \mathbb{R}^n$

be the diagonal of Z. Without loss of generality we assume that Z is normalized[1]. The maximum weighted clique problem formulated as an integer quadratic minimization problem is of the form

$$\begin{aligned} \text{minimize} \quad & f(x) = -\tfrac{1}{2}x^T Q' x - c^T x \\ \text{subject to} \quad & x^T P x = 0 \\ & x \in \{0,1\}^n \end{aligned} \tag{13}$$

where $Q' = Z - D(Z)$, $c = \tfrac{1}{2}d(Z)$, and $P = (p_{ij})$ with entries

$$p_{ij} = \begin{cases} 1 & : \quad \text{if } \{i,j\} \in V^{[2]} \setminus E \\ 0 & : \quad \text{otherwise.} \end{cases}$$

By $S_f^\times$ (S_f^*) we denote the subset of all local (global) minima of f. We transform the zero-one integer quadratic program (13) to an equivalent indefinite quadratic problem over the unit hypercube

$$\begin{aligned} \text{minimize} \quad & f(x) = -\tfrac{1}{2}x^T Q x - c^T x \\ \text{subject to} \quad & x \in [0,1]^n \end{aligned} \tag{14}$$

where Q is any $(n \times n)$-matrix of the form $Q = Q' - \mu P$ with

$$\mu > \delta^\omega + \|c\|_\infty. \tag{15}$$

Recall that δ^ω is the weighted degree of Z and $\|c\|_\infty$ denotes the maximum norm. The next result establishes the equivalence of the MWCP and (14).

Theorem 2. *Consider the continuous quadratic problem (14). Then*

i. $C \in C_Z^* \Leftrightarrow x_C \in S_f^*$

ii. $C \in C_Z^\times \Leftrightarrow x_C \in S_f^\times$

iii. All minima of f in $[0,1]^n$ are strict.

Proof. [11].   □

Let $\lambda > 0$. Suppose that $Q_\lambda = \lambda Q$ and $c_\lambda = \lambda c$. Then the quadratic program

$$\begin{aligned} \text{minimize} \quad & f_\lambda(x) = -\tfrac{1}{2}x^T Q_\lambda x - c_\lambda^T x \\ \text{subject to} \quad & x \in [0,1]^n \end{aligned} \tag{16}$$

is equivalent to (14). Theorem 2 is valid for the non-linear program (16) with $Q_\lambda = \lambda Q' - \mu P'$ where $P' = \lambda P$ and

$$\mu > \lambda(\delta^\omega + \|c\|_\infty). \tag{17}$$

---

[1] If Z is not normalized, we can first transform Z to a normalized graph Z', compute the solution in Z', and back-transform the solution to Z.

5.3   Solving the MWCP Using Hopfield Networks

Following the seminal paper of Hopfield and Tank [8], the general approach to solve combinatorial optimization problems maps the objective function of the optimization problem onto an energy function of a neural network. The constraints of the problem are included in the energy function as penalty terms, such that the global minima of the energy function correspond to the solutions of the combinatorial optimization problem. Here the combinatorial optimization problem to be solved is given by the non-linear program (16).

The Hopfield clique network (HCN) comprises a fully interconnected system of n units. Unit i has an activation $x_i(t)$ and an output state $y_i(t)$. The activation $x_i(t)$ integrates an external input θ_i and the weighted sum of the outputs y_j from all other units. The weights w_{ij} determine the strength of the synaptic connection from unit j to unit i. The weights can be positive or negative corresponding to an excitatory or inhibitory synapse, respectively. The relationship between the activation x_i of unit i and its output y_i is determined by a non-decreasing transfer function $y_i = g_i(x_i)$. The mathematical model of the coupled discrete-time dynamics of a HCN is of the form

$$y_i(t+1) = g\left(x_i(t+1)\right)$$
$$x_i(t+1) = x_i(t) + \sum_{i=1}^{n} w_{ij} y_j(t) + \theta_i \tag{18}$$

We assume that the system (18) evolves in synchronous mode. For symmetric synaptic interactions satisfying $w_{ij} = w_{ji}$ let

$$E = -\frac{1}{2} \sum_{i=1}^{n} \sum_{j=1}^{n} w_{ij} y_i y_j - \sum_{i=1}^{n} \theta_i y_i \tag{19}$$

be the corresponding energy function of the network. In the following we show under which conditions the energy function E characterizes the dynamics (18) of the network in order to solve the maximum weighted clique problem as posed in terms of a non-linear program (16):

(E1) The weight matrix $W = (w_{ij})$ is of the form

$$W = \lambda Q' - \mu P'.$$

(E2) The external input θ is of the form

$$\theta = \lambda c.$$

(E3) The transfer function g is a bounded function satisfying the Lipschitz condition

$$|g(x') - g(x)| \le \frac{1}{\tau}|x' - x|$$

for all $x, x' \in \mathbb{R}$, where $\tau > 0$ is a constant independent of x and x'.

(E4) Excitatory weights are bounded by

$$\lambda < \frac{2\tau}{n - 1 + \delta^{\perp}(\delta^{\omega} + \|\boldsymbol{\theta}\|_{\infty} - 1)}. \tag{20}$$

(E5) Absolute values of inhibitory weights are bounded by

$$\mu > \lambda(\delta^{\omega} + \|\boldsymbol{\theta}\|_{\infty}). \tag{21}$$

Theorem 3. *Suppose that (E1)-(E5) hold. Then the discrete-time dynamics (18) decreases the energy function E for all $t \geq 0$*

$$E(t + 1) \leq E(t)$$

until convergence to an equilibrium point.

Proof. [11]. □

The weight matrix $\boldsymbol{W}$ and the external input $\boldsymbol{\theta}$ defined in *(E1)* and *(E2)* are of the same form as in the non-linear program (16). Hence, the energy function E of the network corresponds to the quadratic form f.

Since the transfer function g is bounded by *(E3)*, the energy function E is bounded and Theorem 3 proves convergence of the HCN to an equilibrium point, that is no oscillation or limit cycles occur. In particular, if g has lower and upper saturation limits $0 \leq g(x) \leq 1$, then the HCN operates on the n-dimensional hypercube $\mathcal{P}_n$ minimizing the non-linear program (16).

Bounding excitatory weights as demanded in *(E4)* enforces gradient descent of the energy function E as the HCN evolves according to its dynamical rule without violating the clique constraints after convergence to a vertex of $\mathcal{P}_n$. Note that excitatory weights are of the form λz_{ij} where $z_{ij} \in [0, 1]$. Hence, since $z_{ij} \leq \lambda$, the right hand side of (20) is in fact an upper bound of all excitatory weights in $\boldsymbol{W}$.

The bound on inhibitory weights μ formulated in *(E5)* ensures that convergence of the system (18) to a vertex of the hypercube $\mathcal{P}_n$ implies convergence to a characteristic vector of a maximal clique.

Finally note that the set of stable equilibrium points are the vertices of the unit hypercube corresponding to maximal cliques. No other stable equilibrium points exist. Unstable equilibria correspond to saddle points of the energy function. Due to their instability, imposing random noise or annealing the parameter τ shifts the output state into regions where the gradient is not zero.

6   Experiments

In all experiments we used the SVMLight [14] embedded into a 10-fold cross validation. We first computed the matrix $K = (k_{ij})$ of pairwise similarities with respect to the normalized SH inner product. The SH inner products were approximately solved according to the approach presented in Section 5. For computing the MWCP we applied the HCN dynamics (18) using the the piecewise limiter function

$$g(x) = \max(0, \min(1, \beta x))$$

with Lipschitz constant $\beta = 1$. Note that no parameter setting is required. Next we learned a support vector classifier using the following methods: (PPC) the pairwise proximities classifier as proposed by [6], (PPC–RBF) the PPC classifier with RBF kernel, (SH) support vector learning which directly operates on K, (SH-RBF$_N$) support vector learning using a RBF function on naive distances $d_{ij}^N = 1 - k_{ij}$, (SH-RBF$_E$) support vector learning using a RBF functions on Euclidean distances

$$d_{ij}^E = \sqrt{k_{ii}^2 - 2k_{ij} + k_{jj}^2} = \sqrt{2d_{ij}^N}.$$

6.1   Synthetic Characters

In our first experiment we investigated how a SVM can deal with both types of errors occuring in graph based representations, structural variations and noisy attributes.

We used synthetic data to emulate handwriting recognition of alphanumeric characters as it typically occurs in pen technology of small hand-held devices, for example PDAs. We do not apply additional on-line information. To simulate handwriting recognition as a classification task for structured objects, we draw two handwritten characters models $\mathcal{C} = \{'X', 'Y'\}$ using an X windows interface. The contours of each image were discretized and expressed as a set of points in the 2D plane. Both model images are shown in the first column of Figure 1.

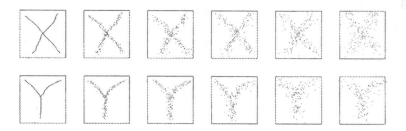

Fig. 1. Images of handwritten characters $'X'$ and $'Y'$. Explanation see text.

For each model character we generated 50 corrupted data characters as follows: First we randomly rotated the model image. Then to each point we added $N(0, \sigma)$ Gaussian noise with standard deviation $\sigma = 2, 4, 6, 8, 10$. Each point had 10% probability to be deleted. Columns 2-6 of Figure 1 show examples of corrupted data images for different standard deviations σ. For sake of presentation the graphics does not show the rotation of the images.

From each point set we randomly selected points such that the pairwise normalized distances between the chosen points is larger than a given threshold

θ. We transformed this point set $\mathcal{P}$ to a fully connected attributed graph. The vertices $v(\boldsymbol{p})$ represent the points $\boldsymbol{p} \in \mathcal{P}$, and the edges represent an abstract line between two points. To each vertex $v(\boldsymbol{p})$ we assigned a three dimensional attribute vector $\boldsymbol{a} = (a_1, a_2, a_3)$ where a_1 is the normalized distance of the point $\boldsymbol{p}$ to the center of gravity of the corrupted image, a_2 is the mean distance of the normalized distances from point $\boldsymbol{p}$ to all other points $\boldsymbol{q} \in \mathcal{P}$, and a_3 is the variance of the normalized distances between $\boldsymbol{p}$ an all other points $\boldsymbol{q} \in \mathcal{P}$. To each edge connecting vertex $v(\boldsymbol{p})$ and $v(\boldsymbol{q})$ we assigned a two dimensional attribute vector $\boldsymbol{b} = (b_1, b_2)$. The first attribute is the normalized distance between $\boldsymbol{p}$ and $\boldsymbol{q}$. The second attribute measures the normalized distance between the center of gravity of the corrupted image and the abstract line passing through $\boldsymbol{p}$ and $\boldsymbol{q}$. Thus each graph is a representation of a character, which is invariant to rotation, translation, and scaling.

The average order of the graphs for each standard deviation σ is 40.0 with variance 23.7. The smallest graph was of order 32 and the largest of order 50. Thus besides noise in the attributes there is a strong structural variation.

Table 1(a) summarizes the mean predictive accuracy for different noise levels σ. The results show that SVM with kernels based on the SH inner product can cope with both, noisy attributes and structural variation of the data. As expected, the performance decreases with the noise level though the recognition rate is very good even for highly corrupted and randomly rotated characters.

6.2   Handwritten Digits

In the second of our experiments we applied the SVM to classify handwritten digits invariant to rotation. We used the training set $\mathcal{T}$ of the well-known MNIST database containing $60,000$ gray-level images of handwritten digits [16]. We selected a subset of $\mathcal{T}$ consisting of 100 images of '0' and 100 images of '1'. We randomly rotated all 200 images as shown in Figure 2 for six examples. Each image was transformed into an attributed graph in a similar way as in the previous section to obtain a representation of the numbers '0' and '1', resp., which is invariant to rotation, translation, and scaling.

(a)   (b)   (c)   (d)   (e)   (f)

Fig. 2. Examples of rotated images of handwritten digits.

For the digits dataset we achieved an accuracy of 0.995 for PPC and PPC-RBF. The other variants performed slightly worse but were still better than 0.98.

6.3   Mutagenicity

The mutagenicity of a chemical compound is closely related to its cancerogenicity. A particular problem is to discover rules to predict mutagenicity in a database

Table 1. Estimated predictive accuracy.

(a) Synthetic handwritten letters

σ	2	4	6	8	10
PPC	1.0	1.0	0.94	0.92	0.71
PPC-RBF	1.0	1.0	0.96	0.94	0.77
SH	1.0	1.0	0.95	0.96	0.71
SH–RBF$_E$	1.0	1.0	0.95	0.96	0.80

(b) Mutagenesis dataset

dataset	188	42
RWK	0.90	-
DLK	0.89	-
IND	0.90	0.86
PPC	0.84	0.83
PPC-RBF	0.88	0.86
SH	0.85	0.86
SH-RBF$_N$	**0.92**	**0.90**
SH-RBF$_E$	0.90	0.86

of nitro aromatic compounds (e.g. [18]). The mutagenesis dataset is usually considered in two subsets containing 188 and 42 examples respectively.

Each compound in the dataset is described by its atoms and their bonds. An atom is described by its element symbol, its type (e.g. aromatic) and a partial electrical charge. There also exist some attributes that describe the molecule as a whole. For our experiments we have only used the structural information.

The estimated predictive accuracies are shown in Table 1(b). Surprisingly, the naive SH-RBF$_N$ approach outperforms all other algorithms reported in the literature. Although the 'kernel matrix' was indefinite, the SVMLight terminated for the optimal parameter setting while non-termination occurred for other parameter settings. The results for the random walk kernel (RWK) and the description logic kernel (DLK) are taken from [15] and [1], respectively. The learning system INDIGO [5] performs an explicit transformation of the graphs into feature vectors (row IND). Like the kernel approaches described in [4, 15] this transformation is also based on walks in the graphs.

For the naive SH-RBF$_N$ approach and the optimal parameter settings, 50 eigenvalues of the kernel matrix were negative. In the case of a non-positive definite kernel matrix, the dual Lagrangian becomes non-concave, i.e. there may be local minima and the objective function may even tend to $+\infty$. Despite of this, the SVMLIGHT terminated without problems though non-termination occurred for other parameter settings.

We also applied eq. (10) in order to obtain a positive definite kernel matrix K'. The usage of K' instead of K means that the value of the kernel function is increased for isomorphic graphs. For the choice $\lambda = 1.1$ the kernel matrix becomes positive definite, but the performance of SH-RBF$_N$ degrades from 0.92 to 0.90 which is still very good.

7   Conclusion

In this paper we have successfully applied support vector learning with kernels based on the SH inner product. We directly operated on non-psd matrices of approximated pairwise SH similarities and also considered different variants of the theoretical sound PPC approach. Though the latter approach works reasonably well, it is in general outperformed by the former approach. The results confirm that in practice the property of a kernel being cpsd is a sufficient but not necessary condition to learn an classifier with low error rate. Future work will focus on conditions when the SH inner product is a kernel.

References

1. C. Cumby and D. Roth. On kernel methods for relational learning. In T. Fawcett and N. Mishra, editors, *Proceedings of the Twentieth International Conference on Machine Learning*, pages 107–115. AAAI Press, 2003.
2. A. K. Debnath, L. de Compadre, G. Debnath, A. J. Shusterman, and C. Hansch. Structure-activity relationship of mutagenic aromatic and heteroaromatic nitro compounds. Correlation with molecular orbital energies and hydrophobicity. *J. Med. Chem.*, 34:786–797, 1991.
3. T. Gärtner. A survey of kernels for structured data. *SIGKDD Explorations*, 5(2):49–58, 2003.
4. T. Gärtner, P. A. Flach, and S. Wrobel. On graph kernels: Hardness results and efficient alternatives. In *Proceedings of the 16th Annual Conference on Computational Learning Theory and the 7th Kernel Workshop*, 2003. to appear.
5. P. Geibel and F. Wysotzki. Learning relational concepts with decision trees. In Lorenza Saitta, editor, *Machine Learning: Proceedings of the Thirteenth International Conference*, pages 166–174. Morgan Kaufmann Publishers, San Fransisco, CA, 1996.
6. T. Graepel, R. Herbrich, P. Bollmann-Sdorra, and K. Obermayer. Classification on pairwise proximity data. In *Advances in Neural Information Processing Systems 11*, pages 438–444, 1999.
7. B. Haasdonk and D. Keysers. Tangent distance kernels for support vector machines. In *ICPR 2002, International Conference on Pattern Recognition*, volume II, pages 864–868, 2002.
8. J.J. Hopfield and D.W. Tank. Neural computation of decisions in optimization problems. *Biological Cybernetics*, 52:141–152, 1985.
9. B.J. Jain and F. Wysotzki. Perceptron learning in the domain of graphs. In *Proc. of the International Joint Conference on Neural Networks, IJCNN'2003*, 2003.
10. B.J. Jain and F. Wysotzki. Central clustering of attributed graphs. *Machine Learning Journal. Special Issue: Theoretical Advances in Data Clustering*, 56(1-3):169–207, 2004.
11. B.J. Jain and F. Wysotzki. The maximum weighted clique problem and Hopfield networks. In M. Verleysen, editor, *Proc. of the 12th European Symposium on Artificial Neural Networks, ESANN'04*, pages 331–336. D-Facto, Brussels, 2004.
12. B.J. Jain and F. Wysotzki. Multi-layer perceptron learning in the domain of attributed graphs. In *In Proceedings of the International Joint Conference on Neural Networks IJCNN 2004. Accepted for publication*, 2004.
13. B.J. Jain and F. Wysotzki. Structural perceptrons for attributed graphs. In *Joint IAPR International Workshops on Structural and Syntactical Pattern Recognition and Statistical Pattern Recognition. Accepted for publication*, 2004.
14. T. Joachims. *Learning to Classify Text using Support Vector Machines: Machines, Theory and Algorithms*. Kluwer Academic Publishers, Boston, 2002.

15. H. Kashima, K. Tsuda, and A. Inokuchi. Marginalized kernels between labeled graphs. In T. Fawcett and N. Mishra, editors, *Proceedings of the Twentieth International Conference on Machine Learning*, pages 321–328. AAAI Press, 2003.
16. Y. LeCun. The MNIST Database of Handwritten Digits. NEC Research Institute, Princeton, NJ. URL = http://yann.lecun.com/exdb/mnist/, 2003.
17. B. Schoelkopf and A. J. Smola. *Learning with Kernels*. The MIT Press, Cambridge, MA, 2002.
18. A. Srinivasan, S. Muggleton, M. J. E. Sternberg, and R. D. King. Theories for mutagenicity: A study in first-order and feature-based induction. *Artificial Intelligence*, 85(1,2):227–299, 1996.
19. V. N. Vapnik. *The Nature of Statistical Learning Theory*. Springer, New York, 1995.

Genre Classification of Web Pages
User Study and Feasibility Analysis

Sven Meyer zu Eissen and Benno Stein

Paderborn University
Department of Computer Science
D-33095 Paderborn, Germany
{smze,stein}@upb.de

Abstract. Genre classification means to discriminate between documents by means of their form, their style, or their targeted audience. Put another way, genre classification is orthogonal to a classification based on the documents' contents. While most of the existing investigations of an automated genre classification are based on news articles corpora, the idea here is applied to arbitrary Web pages. We see genre classification as a powerful instrument to bring Web-based search services closer to a user's information need. This objective raises two questions:

1. What are useful genres when searching the WWW?
2. Can these genres be reliably identified?

The paper in hand presents results from a user study on Web genre usefulness as well as results from the construction of a genre classifier using discriminant analysis, neural network learning, and support vector machines. Particular attention is turned to a classifier's underlying feature set: Aside from the standard feature types we introduce new features that are based on word frequency classes and that can be computed with minimum computational effort. They allow us to construct compact feature sets with few elements, with which a satisfactory genre diversification is achieved. About 70% of the Web-documents are assigned to their true genre; note in this connection that no genre classification benchmark for Web pages has been published so far.

Keywords: Genre Classification, Machine Learning, User Study, Information Need, Information Retrieval, WWW

1 Introduction

People who search the World Wide Web usually have a clear conception: They know what they are searching for, and they know of which form or type the search result ideally should be. The former aspect relates to the content of a found document, the latter to the presentation of its content. Basically, each delivered document constitutes an HTML file; however, in consequence of the usability and the physical nature of the World Wide Web, several favorite specializations of HTML documents emerged. A document may contain many links (e. g. a link collection), a technical text (e. g. a research article), almost no text along with several pictures (e. g. an advertisement page), or a short answer to a particular question (e. g. a mail in a help forum).

S. Biundo, T. Frühwirth, and G. Palm (Eds.): KI 2004, LNAI 3238, pp. 256–269, 2004.

Clearly, it would be of much help if a search engine could deliver only documents of a desired – what is here called – "genre".

The paper is organized as follows. The remaining part of this section introduces genre classification and sketches out existing work. Section 2 discusses possible genre classes and ranks them with respect to a user study. Section 3 presents standard as well as new features to make genre classification amenable to machine learning. Section 4 provides some results from different genre classification experiments. In particular we apply discriminant analysis and learning with neural networks and support vector machines to construct a genre classifier.

1.1 What Does Genre Mean?

As pointed out by Finn and Kushmerick, the term "genre" is used frequently in our culture; e. g., in connection with music, with literature, or with entertainment [7]. Roussinov et al. argue that genre can be defined in terms of purpose or function, in terms of the physical form, or in terms of the document form. And, usually, a genre combines both purpose and form [14].

Here, we are interested in the genre of HTML documents. Several definitions for document genre have been given and discussed in the past [1, 8, 9]. Common to all is that document genre and document content are orthogonal, say, documents that address the same topic can be of a different genre: "The genre describes something about what kind of document it is rather than what the document is about." [7]. In this way, a genre classification scheme can be oriented at the style of writing, or at the presentation style. When analyzing newspaper articles for example, typical genres include "editorial", "letter", "reportage", "spot news".

1.2 What Does Genre Mean in the WWW?

In the literature on the subject there is more or less agreement on what document genre means and how different genre classes can be characterized. And, at first sight, it seems to be canonical to apply this common understanding to the World Wide Web: Certainly, "advertisement" seems to be a useful genre class, as well as "private homepage". On second sight, however, several difficulties become apparent: Where does a presentation of a company's mission end and where does advertisement begin? Or, does a scientific article on a private homepage belong to the same genre like a photo collection of mom's lovely pet?

Our proposed definition of genre classes for the World Wide Web is governed by two considerations:

– Usability from the standpoint of an information miner, which can be achieved by a what we call "positive" and "negative" filtering. With the former the need for a focused search can be satisfied, while the latter simply extends the idea of spam identification to a diversified genre scheme.
– Feasibility with respect to runtime and classification performance.

The first point means that we want to support people who use the World Wide Web as a huge database to which queries are formulated[1]. The second point states that automatic

---

[1] There are other groups of Internet users who use the Web for amusement, for example.

genre identification shall happen on the fly, in the form of a post-processing of the results of a search engine. This aspect prevents the computation of highly sophisticated features as well as the application of a fine-grained genre scheme[2]. To get an idea which genre classes are considered useful by search engine users, we conducted a user study that is described in detail in Section 2.

1.3   Existing Work

We distinguish the existing work for computer-based genre classification with respect to the underlying corpus, say, whether it is targeted to a particular document collection – like the Brown Corpus, for example – or to the World Wide Web. In the following we outline selected papers.

Corpus-specific genre classification has been investigated among others in [9, 15, 5, 7]. The existing work can further be distinguished with respect to the interesting genre classes and the types of features that have been evaluated. Kessler et al.'s work is based on the Brown Corpus. For the characterization of genre classes they employ so-called genre facets, which are quantified by linguistic and character-level features [9]. Stamatatos et al. use discriminant analysis based on the term frequencies to identify the most discriminative terms with respect to four newspaper genre classes [15]. Dewdney et al. concentrate on different learning approaches: Naive Bayes, C4.5, and support vector machines. They employ about three hundred features including part of speech, closed-class word sets, and stemmed document terms [5]. Rehm proposes a Web genre hierarchy for academic homepages and a classifier that relies on HTML metadata, presentation related tags and unspecified linguistic features. Finn and Kushmerick distinguish between the two genres "objective" and "subjective"; they investigate three types of features sets: the document vector containing the stemmed list of a document's terms without stop-words, features from a part of speech analysis, and easily computable text statistics [7].

Genre classification and navigation related to the World Wide Web is quite new, and only very few papers have been published on this topic. Bretan et al. propose a richer representation of retrieval results in the search interface. Their approach combines content-based clustering and genre-based classification that employs simple part-of-speech information along with substantial text statistics. The features are processed with the C4.5 algorithm; however, the authors give no information about the achieved classification performance [2]. Roussinov et al. present a preliminary study to automatic genre classification: Based on an explorative user study they develop a genre scheme that is in part similar to ours and that comprises five genre groups. However, their work describes an ongoing study, and no recognition algorithm has been implemented [14]. Dimitrova et al. describe how shallow text classification techniques can be used to sort the documents according to genre dimensions. Their work describes an ongoing study, and experience with respect to the classification performance is not reported [6]. Lee and Myaeng define seven genre types for classifying documents from the World Wide Web. Aside from the genre "Q&A" and "Homepage" Lee and Myaeng use also the newspaper-specific genres "Reportage" and "Editorial". The operationalized feature set is based on a list of about hundred document terms tailored to each genre class [10].

---

[2] Crowston and Williams identified about hundred genre classes on the World Wide Web [3].

2   User Study and Genre Selection

Although we have an idea of potentially useful genres, a user study should give insights into the importance of dedicated genre classes. Moreover, it can be used as a basis to select genres for building test collections. As a matter of course, selected genres influence feature selection for automatic classification.

2.1   User Study

As discussions with colleagues on the helpfulness of different Web page genre classes were manifold, we decided to interrogate a bigger number of search engine users. We developed a questionnaire that should shed light on search engine use, usefulness of genre classification, and usefulness of genre classes. In detail, we were interested in the following points.

1. *Frequency of Search Engine Use.* We expect that experienced search engine users have a clearer idea whether genre classification could be useful or not. We asked the interviewees how often they use search engines. Possible answers were "daily", "once or twice a week", "once or twice a month", and "never".
2. *Typical Topics for Queries.* As already pointed out, our target audience should use the Internet not only for entertainment, but also as information source. To get an idea what the interviewees search for on the Internet, we let them specify up to 3 typical search topics.
3. *Usefulness of Genre Classification.* With this question we wanted to figure out if genre filtering is considered as useful in general, i.e. if genre filtering helps to satisfy the user's information need. Possible answers were "very useful", "sometimes useful", "not useful", and "don't know".
4. *Favored Genre Classes.* We proposed ten genre classes that we found interesting: publications/articles, scholar material, news, shops, link collections, help and FAQ, private portrayals, commercial portrayals, discussion forums, and product presentations. For each of these genres, the interviewees could specify the usefulness in terms of "very useful", "sometimes useful", "not useful", and "don't know".
5. *Additional Useful Genre Classes.* We also wanted to find out which additional genre classes could be interesting for the users. Therefore, a set of up to three additional genre classes could be specified and classified into "very useful" and "sometimes useful".
6. *Comments.* We also gave the interviewees the possibility to comment on the idea of genre classification.

To give the respondents an idea of genre classification, we gave them a 2-minute introduction to genres and their use as positive and negative information filters. As we expect students to frequently use search engines, we asked 286 of them in our university to complete the proposed form. Figure 1 shows that we met the right audience: about three quarters of the students use search engines on a daily basis, and nearly the remaining quarter at least once a week.

The most frequently mentioned searches comprise scholar material, shopping and product information, help (discussions and troubleshooting), entertainment (music/

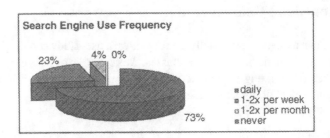

Fig. 1. Frequency of search engine use. About three quarters of the interrogated students use a search engine on a daily basis.

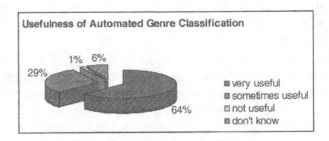

Fig. 2. Usefulness of genre classification.

games/films/humorous material/news), downloads, health, and programming (in this order). The fact that 64% of the students think that genre classification is very useful, and that another 29% find it sometimes useful shows that there is a strong need to post-process query results (cf. Figure 2).

To make up a ranked list of dedicated genre classes with respect to their usability, we assigned scores on the usefulness of each genre class: "very useful" scored 2 points, "sometimes useful" scored one point, "not useful" scored 0 points. We added the scores for each proposed genre and divided it by the number of interviewees that did not tick "don't know" on that genre class. The results are depicted in Figure 3: scholar material scores best, while private portrayals were not judged as very useful by the interviewees.

Additional genres that were significantly often proposed include Web page spam and download sites. As the given comments and some given specifications of spam let conclude, spam comprises in this context (a) paid links, (b) sites that try to install dialers, and (c) sites that are only used to improve a site's ranking in search engines. Other propositions included topics (and not genres) like pornography. The comments were encouraging and often asked for operationalization.

2.2 Genre Selection

An inherent problem of Web genre classification is that even humans are not able to consistently specify the genre of a given page. Take for example a tutorial on machine learning that could be either classified as scholar material or as article. In general, scholar material can be seen as a super-genre that covers help, article, and discussion

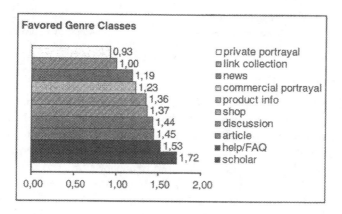

Fig. 3. The favored genre classes. Higher values indicate a greater expected usefulness.

pages; therefore scholar material was not chosen as a genre on its own. Another finding is that most product information sites are combined with a shopping interface, which renders a discrimination between shops and products impossible.

To cut a long story short, we finally ended up with the following eight genre classes:

1. *Help.* All pages that provide assistance, e. g. Q&A or FAQ pages.
2. *Article.* Documents with longer passages of text, such as research articles, reviews, technical reports, or book chapters.
3. *Discussion.* All pages that provide forums, mailing lists or discussion boards.
4. *Shop.* All kinds of pages whose main purpose is product information or sale.
5. *Portrayal (non-priv).* Web appearances of companies, universities, and other public institutions. I. e., home or entry or portal pages, descriptions of organization and mission, annual reports, brochures, contact information, etc.
6. *Portrayal (priv).* Private self-portrayals, i. e., typical private homepages with informal content.
7. *Link Collection.* Documents which consist of link lists for the main part.
8. *Download.* Pages on which freeware, shareware, demo versions of programs etc. can be downloaded.

Although not every document can be rigorously assigned to a single class, our scheme reflects the genre assessment of many human information miners: A scientific article or a link collection, for instance, is still distinguished as such, independently of the domain holder's form of organization where the document is hosted.

Finally, it should be noted that genre classification of Web pages is at its beginning. Upcoming research may concentrate on relations between genres, or even on the development of domain-specific genre ontologies [13].

3   Features for Genre Classification

With respect to the investigated features the existing literature on genre classification falls into three groups: Classifiers that rely on a subset of a document's terms (sometimes called bag-of-words, BOW) [15, 10], classifiers that employ linguistic features along with additional features relating to text statistics [9], or both [7]. This section gives an overview of these features. In particular we introduce new features that are based on the frequency class of a word.

3.1 Word Frequency Class

The frequency class of a word is directly connected to Zipf's law and can be used as an indicator of a word's customariness. Let C be a text corpus, and let $|C|$ be the number of words in C. Moreover, let $f(w)$ denote the frequency of a word $w \in C$, and let $r(w)$ denote the rank of w in a word list of C, which is sorted by decreasing frequency[3].

In accordance with [12] we define the word frequency class $c(w)$ of a word $w \in C$ as $\lfloor \log_2(f(w^*)/f(w)) \rfloor$, where w^* denotes the most frequently used word in C. In the Sydney Morning Herald Corpus [4], w^* denotes the word "the", which corresponds to the word frequency class 0; the most uncommonly used words within this corpus have a word frequency class of 19. The intuition to use the word frequency class as feature is the expectation that articles use a more specialized speech than e.g. shops. The complexity of speech is expected to be reflected in the average word class.

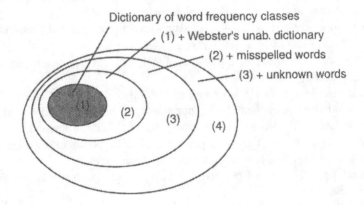

Fig. 4. The figure shows the inclusion relation of the used word sets. Note that the sets (3) and (4) are only implicitly defined, by means of the Levenshtein distance and the "not-found" predicate respectively.

Based on the Sydney Morning Herald Corpus, which contains more than 38,000 articles, word frequency classes for about one hundred thousand words have been computed. This dictionary is shown as set (1) in Figure 4. The other sets in the figure evolve in a natural manner as supersets of (1): Webster's unabridged dictionary (2), the set of misspelled words (3), and the set of unknown words (4). Observe that set (3) comprises all words from the sets (1) and (2) as well as words found in the Levenshtein distance of one [11]. We use these sets to define the following features:
- average word class
- average number of misspelled words
- average number of words not found in Webster's unabridged dictionary

---

[3] Zipf's law states that $r(w) \cdot f(w)$ is constant.

3.2   Syntactic Group Analysis

A syntactic group analysis yields linguistic features that relate to several words of a sentence. Such analyses quantify the use of tenses, relative clauses, main clauses, adverbial phrases, simplex noun phrases, etc. Since the identification of these features is computationally expensive, we have omitted them in our analysis. Dewdney et al., however, also include the transition in verb tense within a sentence in their analysis [5].

3.3   Part-of-Speech Analysis

Part-of-speech analysis groups the words of a sentence according to their function or word class. Part-of-speech taggers analyze a word's morphology or its membership in a particular set. In this connection one differentiates between so-called open-class word sets and closed-class word sets, where the former do not consist of a finite number; examples are nouns, verbs, adjectives, or adverbs. Examples for closed-class word sets are prepositions and articles. For our analysis we have employed the part-of-speech tagger of the University of Stuttgart [16]. Table 1 and 2 list the actually used word classes.

3.4   Other Closed-Class Word Sets

Aside from word classes that relate to grammatical function, we have also constructed other closed-class word sets that may be specific to a certain genre: currency symbols, help symbols ("FAQ", "Q&A", "support"), shop symbols, months, days, countries, first names, and surnames.

3.5   Text Statistics

Under the label "text statistics" we comprise features that relate to the frequency of easily accessible syntactic entities: clauses, paragraphs, delimiters, question marks, exclamation marks, or numerals. Counts for these entities are put in relation to the number of words of a document. Kessler et al. designate features of this type as "character-level cues" [9]; Finn and Kushmerick designate such features as "hand-crafted" [7].

3.6   Presentation-Related Features

This type of features relate to the appearance of a document. They include frequency counts as well as particular HTML-specific concepts and stylistic concepts. To the former we count the number of figures, tables, paragraphs, headlines, or captions. The latter comprises statistics related to the usage of colors, hyperlinks (anchor links, site-internal links, Internet links), URL specifications, mail addresses, etc.

3.7   Constructed Feature Sets

As our concern is genre classification of search results, the classification should be done "on the fly", as a post-processing step. Since a user usually waits actively for search results, the features must be computed quickly. We propose a split of the mentioned features with respect to computational effort as follows.

Table 1. Feature set A consists of 25 features. The averages are taken with respect to the total word count within a Web document.

	Feature type	Feature set A
(1)	Presentation related	avg. # of <p> tags
(2)		avg. # of <ul> tags
(3)		avg. # of tags
(4)		avg. # of anchor links
(5)		avg. # of links same domain
(6)		avg. # of links foreign domain
(7)		avg. # of mail links
(8)		avg. # of <img> tags
(9)		avg. # of <tr> tags
(10)	Closed word sets	avg. word frequency class
(11)		avg. # of currency symbols
(12)		avg. # of help symbols
(13)		avg. # of shop symbols
(14)		avg. # of date symbols
(15)		avg. # of first names
(16)		avg. # of surnames
(17)		avg. # of words that do not appear in Webster's dictionary
(18)	Text statistics	avg. # of question marks
(19)		avg. # of letters
(20)		avg. # of digits
(21)		avg. # of dots
(22)		avg. # of semicolons
(23)		avg. # of colons
(24)		avg. # of commas
(25)		avg. # of exclamation marks

1. *Features with Low Computational Effort.* These features comprise text statistics, which can be acquired at parse time through simple counters.
2. *Features with Medium Computational Effort.* All features that are word-related and that require dictionary lookups or non-trivial parsing. These are closed-class word sets, word frequency class and presentation related features.
3. *Features with Higher Computational Effort.* This class comprises features that rely on grammar analyses. Syntactic group analysis features and part-of-speech related features fall in this category.

It should be clear that feature category (1) is not powerful enough to discriminate between the genre classes solely. As a consequence, we built a feature set that comprises features of (1) and (2), and a feature set that makes use of all three feature classes. The Tables 1 and 2 show the details.

Table 2. Feature set B extends feature set A by ten additional features. The averages are taken with respect to the total word count within a Web document.

	Feature type	Feature set B
(1)-(25)		identical to feature set A
(1)	Part of speech	avg. # of nouns
(2)		avg. # of verbs
(3)		avg. # of rel. pronouns
(4)		avg. # of prepositions
(5)		avg. # of adverbs
(6)		avg. # of articles
(7)		avg. # of pronouns
(8)		avg. # of modals
(9)		avg. # of adjectives
(10)		avg. # of alphanumeric words

4 Experimental Setting and Analysis

Since no benchmark corpus is available for our concern, we compiled a new corpus with Web documents and analyzed statistical properties of the two feature sets with respect to them. We employed classifiers in the form of neural networks (MLP) and support vector machines to test the achievable classification performance. Moreover, we analyzed the classification performance for genre-specific searches and typical user groups. The following subsections outline our experiments.

4.1 Corpus Compilation

The compiled corpus of Web documents is described in Table 3. For the experiments, we used a subset of randomly drawn documents that is equally distributed over the aforementioned genres (100 documents each) and thus comprises about 800 documents.

Table 3. Composition of the Web document corpus.

Genre	# of Documents
link collection	204
help	136
shop	169
portrayal non-priv.	171
portrayal priv.	127
articles	123
download	152
discussion	127
sum	1209

Each element in the corpus represents a single HTML document; documents that are composed of frames and Flash elements were discarded. We then generated two distinct representations of each corpus according to the feature sets. The first feature set comprises 25 attributes (see Table 1), the second feature set extends the first by additional ten features (see Table 2).

4.2 Statistical Analyses

We conducted a discriminant analysis (linear model, incremental variable selection according to Wilks Lambda, a-priori probability uniformly distributed) to get an idea of the classification performance of the selected features. Table 4 shows a confusion matrix that belongs to feature set B. The results range from acceptable to very good – articles and download pages are detected with a very high precision, and shop, discussion, link collections as well as private portrayal documents are detected with a good performance. Only non-private portrayals and help loose roughly a bigger fraction to the other genres – the diversity of non-private portrayals is immense. However, about 70% classification performance for cross-validated data (ten-fold) on a huge corpus appears still very good to us.

The scatter plot in Figure 5 (left) shows that shopping sites, articles, and download pages can be separated quite well. Figure 5 (right) illustrates that help pages, non-private portrayals, and link collections overlap 5-11% each.

4.3 Classification Results

We split the corpus into test sets and training sets and, based on both feature sets, learned a classifier with both MLP neural networks and support vector machines. Table 5 comprises the classification results on the test sets. On average, for the one-against-all classification situation, which is reported in the first row of Table 5, support vector machines turned out to be better than neural networks.

It should be noted that official genre classification benchmarks for Web pages are not available. For this reason, but also to make our results reproducible for other researchers, we will make our corpus available on request.

Table 4. Ten-fold cross-validated confusion matrix. It shows the percentage of correctly classified documents on the diagonal and summarizes the percentage of misclassified documents with respect to other genres. The average classification performance is about 70%.

	Shop	Portrayal (priv)	Portrayal (non-priv)	Article	Link Collection	Help	Discussion	Download	total
Shop	66.9%	3.0%	11.2%	5.3%	7.7%	3.0%	1.2%	1.8%	100.0%
Portrayal (priv)	0.0%	67.7%	3.1%	8.7%	15.7%	2.4%	2.4%	0.0%	100.0%
Portrayal (non-priv)	7.0%	4.1%	57.9%	5.8%	18.1%	2.9%	2.3%	1.8%	100.0%
Article	0.0%	1.6%	3.3%	81.3%	8.1%	3.3%	0.8%	1.6%	100.0%
Link Collection	0.5%	4.4%	10.8%	11.3%	67.6%	1.0%	3.4%	1.0%	100.0%
Help	2.2%	2.2%	5.1%	19.1%	10.3%	55.1%	2.2%	3.7%	100.0%
Discussion	2.4%	0.0%	3.1%	5.5%	7.1%	7.9%	68.5%	5.5%	100.0%
Download	2.0%	1.3%	5.9%	5.3%	2.5%	1.3%	2.0%	79.6%	100.0 %

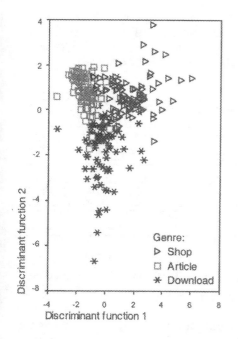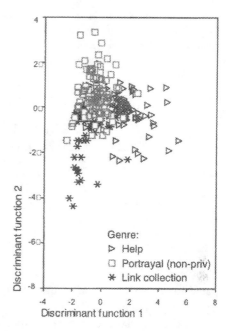

Fig. 5. The left figure shows a scatter plot of the genres Shop, Article, and Download, which can be separated quite well. The right figure refers to the genres Help, Portrayal (non-priv), and Link collection, which are much harder to become identified. The underlying feature set is B.

4.4   Specialized Classifiers

Aside from general classification performance, we are interested in the question how efficient classifiers for single genre classifications and typical user profiles can be built. Assumed that a user starts several queries on the same topic, an intelligent search assistant could figure out to which predefined user profile a user probably belongs and apply the corresponding classifier. We conducted classification experiments for the following three user profiles.

1. *Edu.* This profile is of educational nature and comprises articles, link collections, and help sites.
2. *Geek.* Geeks are mainly interested in downloads, discussions, articles, link collections, and help sites.
3. *Private.* This group comprises individuals that surf the net for shopping and for reading private portrayals.

The performance of the compiled classifiers with respect to both of the feature sets is given in Table 5.

Summary and Outlook

We see genre classification as a promising concept to improve the search efficiency and to address the information need of many users that use the World Wide Web as a

Table 5. The table shows the classification performance of specially crafted single-genre classifiers (first row) and three profile classifiers (remaining rows). The bigger boxes symbolize an aggregation of the genre classes that stand atop of them. Within a box, the upper value shows the classification performance for feature set A, while the lower value shows the performance for feature set B.

	Shop	Portrayal (priv)	Portrayal (non-priv)	Download	Discussion	Article	Link Collection	Help
Isolated Genre Identification	79.7% / 82.5%	78.0% / 77.5%	72.3% / 75.1%	83.4% / 87.5%	76.1% / 77.5%	70.7% / 72.7%	63.0% / 62.3%	68.2% / 72.5%
Profile "Edu"	75.5% / 77.8%					72.2% / 76.1%	78.7% / 81.8%	60.5% / 62.8%
Profile "Geek"	54.9% / 55.6%			60.6% / 62.9%	62.2% / 63.8%	58.4% / 61.2%	59.4% / 62.8%	74.3% / 77.2%
Profile "Private"	73.4% / 77.8%	80.1% / 82.9%	64.8% / 66.7%					

database. While in the past an automatic detection of genre classes has been demonstrated for newspaper corpora, there is the question whether genre classification can also be applied to the Internet.

A user study has shown the need for advanced page filtering and gave hints on the importance of dedicated Web genre classes. Taken the viewpoint of an Internet information miner we propose the following eight genres: help, article, discussion, shop, portrayals of companies and institutions, private portrayal, link collection, and download. We show that with a small set of features, which captures linguistic and presentation-related aspects, text statistics, and word frequency classes, acceptable classification results can be achieved: Our analysis reveals that about 70% of the documents are assigned correctly.

Users pointed out that there is a need for Web page spam filtering. Interesting questions here are what types of Web page spam exist and how they can be identified.

Currently we are developing a search engine that shall combine both topic search and genre search. Key questions here emerge in connection with the presentation of filtered results, say, the construction of a user friendly interface.

References

[1] D. Biber. The multidimensional approach to linguistic analyses of genre variation: An overview of methodology and findings. In *Computers and the Humanities*, volume 26, pages 331–345, 1992.

[2] I. Bretan, J. Dewe, A. Hallberg, and N. Wolkert. Web-specific genre visualization, 1999.

[3] K. Crowston and M. Williams. The effects of linking on genres of web documents. In *HICSS*, 1999.

[4] S. Dennis. The sydney morning herald word database. http://www2.psy.uq.edu.au/CogPsych/Noetica/OpenForumIssue4/SMH.html, 1995.

[5] N. Dewdney, C. VanEss-Dykema, and R. MacMillan. The form is the substance: Classification of genres in text. In *Proceedings of ACL Workshop on HumanLanguage Technology and Knowledge Management*, 2001.

[6] M. Dimitrova, A. Finn, N. Kushmerick, and B. Smyth. Web genre visualization. In *Proceedings of the Conference on Human Factors in Computing Systems*, 2002.

[7] A. Finn and N. Kushmerick. Learning to classify documents according to genre. In *IJCAI-03 WS on Computational Approaches to Style Analysis and Synthesis*, 2003.

[8] J. Karlgren and D. Cutting. Recognizing text genres with simple metrics using discriminant analysis. In *Proceedings of the 15th. International Conference on Computational Linguistics (COLING 94)*, volume II, pages 1071 – 1075, Kyoto, Japan, 1994.

[9] B. Kessler, G. Nunberg, and H. Schütze. Automatic detection of text genre. In P. R. Cohen and W. Wahlster, editors, *Proceedings of the Thirty-Fifth Annual Meeting of the Association for Computational Linguistics and Eighth Conference of the European Chapter of the Association for Computational Linguistics*, pages 32–38, Somerset, New Jersey, 1997. Association for Computational Linguistics.

[10] Y.-B. Lee and S. Myaeng. Text genre classification with genre-revealing and subject-revealing features. In *Proc. 25th annual international ACM SIGIR conference on Research and development in information retrieval*, pages 145–150. ACM Press, 2002. ISBN 1-58113-561-0.

[11] V. Levenshtein. Binary codes capable of correcting deletions insertions and reversals. *ISov Phys Dokl*, 6:707–710, 1966.

[12] U. of Leipzig. Wortschatz. http://wortschatz.uni-leipzig.de, 1995.

[13] G. Rehm. Towards Automatic Web Genre Identification. In *Proceedings of the 35th Hawaii International Conference on System Sciences (HICSS'02)*. IEEE Computer Society, Jan. 2002.

[14] D. Roussinov, K. Crowston, M. Nilan, B. Kwasnik, J. Cai, and X. Liu. Genre based navigation on the web. In *Proceedings of the 34th Hawaii International Conference on System Sciences*, 2001.

[15] E. Stamatatos, N. Fakotakis, and G. Kokkinakis. Text genre detection using common word frequencies. In *Proceedings of the 18th Int. Conference on Computational Linguistics*, Saarbrücken, Germany, 2000.

[16] University of Stuttgart. The decision tree tagger. http://www.ims.uni-stuttgart.de, 1996.

Integration of Statistical and Neural Methods to Design Classifiers in Case of Unequal Covariance Matrices

Šarūnas Raudys

Vilnius Gediminas Technical University
Saulėtekio 11, Vilnius, Lithuania
raudys@ktl.mii.lt

Abstract. The paper extends integration of statistical and neural approaches to design linear classifiers for situations where covariance matrices differ essentially. To ensure a good start for training of the single layer perceptron we perform special data shift and rotation. Here a difference between the covariance matrices of distinct pattern classes plays essential role. After the data transformation, we obtain a good linear classifier just after the first batch-mode training iteration. In small training set size cases, one needs utilize simplified estimates of covariance matrices.

1 Introduction

There exists a great variety of formal and heuristically based algorithms to design linear classifiers. Different types of assumptions and methods are used as design principles. Statistical and artificial neural network based methods are ones among most popular ones. In many research papers and scientific discussions, these methods from time to time are contradistinguished. In [1-6] a method to integrate both approaches was suggested and developed. New methodology is based on a fact that statistical methods are utilized to obtain good initialization of the network and early stopping helps to save information contained in starting weight vector. Practical applications of suggested methodology revealed high efficacy of suggested methodology, however, exposed also situations where it appeared ineffective.

If training sample size is too small, only very simple decision making algorithms can be useful. If distributions of input pattern vectors are multivariate Gaussian and covariance matrices of pattern classes, Σ_1, Σ_2, differ, optimal decision boundary is quadratic discriminant function (DF), Q [5, 7-10]. Quadratic classifier is asymptotically (as training set sizes tend to infinity) optimal for a number of more general models of multivariate distributions [9]. If pattern classes differ unimportantly, a hyperplane could substitute quadratic decision boundary successfully. Anderson and Bahadur [10] and a number of other authors [11-16] suggested ways how to find parameters of optimal hyperplane if $\Sigma_2 \neq \Sigma_1$ and pattern classes are Gaussian or belong to more general families of multivariate distributions. Such DF can be expressed as

$$g_{AB}(x) = x^T v_{AB} + v_0,$$ (1)

where

$$v_{AB} = (\Sigma_1 \alpha_1 + \Sigma_2 \alpha_2)^{-1}(\mu_1 - \mu_2) \text{ and } v_0 \text{ is a scalar,}$$ (2)

S. Biundo, T. Frühwirth, and G. Palm (Eds.): KI 2004, LNAI 3238, pp. 270–280, 2004.
© Springer-Verlag Berlin Heidelberg 2004

$\mu_1 - \mu_2$ is a difference in mean vectors of the classes, μ_1, μ_2, and "T" denotes a transpose operation. Unknown scalar coefficients α_1, α_2 and v_0 have to be found to minimize selected classification performance criteria.

If one assumes $\Sigma_2 = \Sigma_1 = \Sigma$, $\alpha = \beta = \frac{1}{2}$, $v_0 = -\frac{1}{2}(\mu_1 + \mu_2)^T v$, we have standard linear Fisher discriminant function, F. If $\alpha = \beta = 0$ (matrices Σ_1, Σ_2 are ignored, i.e. one supposes $(\Sigma_1 \alpha_1 + \Sigma_2 \alpha_2) = I$, identity matrix), then one obtains the Euclidean distance (nearest means) classifier, E (for a general introduction into statistical pattern recognition see e.g., [5, 7, 8]).

A dozen of other methods to obtain coefficients of linear decision boundary that minimizes a number of misclassifications in training set have been proposed in pattern recognition literature: a sequential random search procedure [17], utilization of the Kiefer-Wolfowitz stochastic approximation [18], linear programming [19], the algebraic method [20], sequential rejection of most distant incorrectly recognized training vectors [21], linear transformations of the co-ordinate system [22], window function technique [23]. Proper training of the SLP also can result the minimal empirical error classifier [1, 5]. Important feature of the SLP is that generalization error of properly trained SLP notably depends on a position of starting weights, $v_{(0)}$, $v_{0(0)}$ [24]. If initial weight vector is determined by a certain extent accurately and one stops training in a right time, *almost all information contained in $v_{(0)}$, $v_{0(0)}$ could be saved* [5, 24].

Truthful statistical hypothesis about a structure of distribution density functions of the pattern classes contains important information. Thus, one can start training SLP from weight vector of Fisher or Anderson-Bahadur classifiers (A-B). If $\Sigma_2 \neq \Sigma_1$, certain configuration of components of μ_1, μ_2, Σ_1 and Σ_2, utilization of the Fisher classifier can lead to much higher classification error as the Anderson-Bahadur solution. If data is multivariate Gaussian, the linear discriminant function is distributed according to the Gaussian law. Then one can calculate probabilities of misclassification of the linear discriminant functions analytically. For example, in 2D data model, where

$$\Sigma_1 = I, \Sigma_2 = \begin{bmatrix} 0.02\xi_1 & 0 \\ 0 & 0.02\xi_2 \end{bmatrix}, \mu_1 = -\mu_2 = \begin{bmatrix} 0.5 + 3\xi_3 \\ 0.5 + 3\xi_4 \end{bmatrix}$$

and all ξ_j ($j = 1, 2, 3, 4$) are independent uniformly in interval [0 1] distributed random variables, from 100 data generations we found that asymptotic error of optimal linear classifier, P_∞^{opt}, varied between 0.0015 and 0.223, while that of non-optimal linear Fisher classifier, P_∞^F, varied between 0.0043 and 0.237. In Fig. 1 we have 2D distribution of 75 smallest values selected out of 100 ones. We see that situations where A-B solution outperforms that of Fisher are not exceptional. In some cases, $P_\infty^F \gg P_\infty^{opt}$. In three cases, ratio $P_\infty^F / P_\infty^{opt}$ exceeds 10. In principle, one can construct the artificial data generation models with arbitrary ratio $P_\infty^F / P_\infty^{opt}$. While solving real world pattern recognition tasks, we also meet cases where $P_\infty^F \gg P_\infty^{opt}$. These results advocate that paying attention to dissimilarity of the covariance matrices sometimes may be very useful.

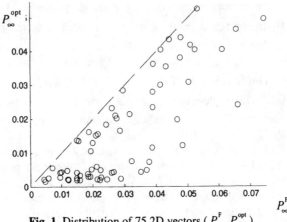

Fig. 1. Distribution of 75 2D vectors (P_{∞}^{F}, $P_{\infty}^{\mathrm{opt}}$)

For that reason, the previous data transformation technique based on the pooled co-variance matrix could lead to improper initialization of the perceptron in certain situations. For that reason, the integrated technique could become even harmful. An objective of present paper is to suggest a modification of data transformation technique to ensure that after the *first* batch-mode training iteration, we obtain weight vector ($w_{(1)}$, $w_{0(1)}$) with components proportional to weights of the A-B linear discriminant function.

2   Data Transformation When Covariance Matrices Are Different

2.1   Standard Data Transformation and SLP Training Procedures

While development of the method to integrate both approaches, in [1-6] it was supposed in an inexplicit way that the patterns are Gaussian and $\Sigma_2 = \Sigma_1 = \Sigma$. This "knowledge" was used to determine initial weights, $w_{(0)}$, $w_{0(0)}$. Instead of designing the Fisher classifier according to sample estimates, $\hat{\mu}_1$, $\hat{\mu}_2$ and $\hat{\Sigma}$, one subtracts data mean vector $\hat{\mu} = \frac{1}{2}(\hat{\mu}_1 + \hat{\mu}_2)$ and performs data whitening transformation

$$Y = T(X - \hat{\mu}), \tag{3}$$

where $T = \Lambda^{-1/2}\Phi^T$ and Λ, Φ^T are eigenvalues and eigenvectors of $\hat{\Sigma}$.
  Then one utilizes a sum of squares error criterion

$$cost = \sum_{i=1}^{2}\sum_{j=1}^{N_i} (f(w^T y_j^{(i)} + w_0) - t_j^{(i)})^2, \tag{4}$$

where $f(arg)$ is the activation function, $y_j^{(i)}$ stands for j-th p-dimensional training vector of i-th class in transformed feature space, w, w_0 are weights, $t_j^{(i)}$ stands for desired output and N_i is a number of training vectors of i-th class. If sigmoid activation function is used, one can choose: $t_j^{(1)} = t^{(1)} = 0.1$, $t_j^{(2)} = 1 - t_j^{(1)} = t^{(2)} = 0.9$.

In this paper we consider sigmoid function $f(arg)=1/(1+\exp(-arg)))$. In the integrated approach, one starts training from zero initial weights, i.e. $w_{0(0)} = 0$, $w_{(0)} = [0, 0, ..., 0]^T$. If $N_2 = N_1 = N$ and $t^{(2)} = 1 - t^{(1)}$, after the first batch-mode training iteration with learning step η, we obtain weight vector $(w_{(1)} \; w_{0(1)})$ which components are proportional to weights of the Euclidean distance classifier

$$ w_{(1)} = \frac{1}{4}\, \eta\, ((\,t^{(1)} - \frac{1}{2})N_1 \hat{\mu}_{Y1} + (\,t^{(2)} - \frac{1}{2})\, N_2 \hat{\mu}_{Y2}\,)), \; w_{0(1)} = 0, \qquad (5) $$

where $\hat{\mu}_{Yj} = T(X - \hat{\mu}_j)$, $j=1, 2$.

In original feature space, however, discriminant function obtained is identical to that of Fisher classifier F

$$ Y^T w_{(1)} = \frac{1}{8}\eta N\,(X - \hat{\mu}\,)^T T^T (T(\hat{\mu}_1 - \hat{\mu}\,) - T(\hat{\mu}_2 - \hat{\mu}\,)) $$

$$ = \frac{1}{8}\eta N\{X^T \hat{\Sigma}^{-1} (\hat{\mu}_1 - \hat{\mu}_2) - \frac{1}{2}(\hat{\mu}_1 + \hat{\mu}_2)^T \hat{\Sigma}^{-1} (\hat{\mu}_1 - \hat{\mu}_2)\}. \qquad (6) $$

Consequently, vector $(w_{(1)} \; w_{0(1)})$ serves as a good initial weight for further training. In many pattern classification problems, this approach resulted in significant improvement in comparison with statistical or neural network based methods [2-6].

2.2   New Data Transformation Procedure

To adjust the integrated approach to design the classifier for case where covariance matrices Σ_1, Σ_2 are supposed to be different, we will require that after the first batch-mode training iteration in linearly transformed space,

$$ Y = G(X - H), \qquad (7) $$

the classifier obtained would be equivalent to the A-B procedure in original, X, feature space. In Eq. (7), G stands for $p{\times}p$ transformation matrix and H stands for p-dimensional data shift vector. To ensure successful training later, both G and H have to determined in a proper way.

To find weights of A-B linear discriminant function (1), (2) we will use a criterion of minimal probability of misclassification for Gaussian data model expressed as

$$ P_{error}(\alpha_1, \alpha_2, w_0) = \sum_{i=1}^{2} q_i \Phi\,\{(-1)^{i+1}\, u_i / \sigma_i\}, \qquad (8) $$

where

$$ u_i(\alpha_1, \alpha_2, w_0) = \hat{\mu}_i^{\,T} \hat{w}(\alpha_1, \alpha_2) + w_0, \; \sigma_i^2 = (\hat{w}(\alpha_1, \alpha_2))^T \hat{\Sigma}_i \hat{w}(\alpha_1, \alpha_2) \qquad (9) $$

q_i is a prior probability of the i-th class and $\Phi\{c\}$ is a cumulative distribution function of Gaussian $N(0, 1)$ variable.

274   Šarūnas Raudys

To find coefficients α_1, α_2 and w_0 one minimizes probability of misclassification (8). Petterson and Mattson [11] expressed

$$w_{PM}(\alpha_1, \alpha_2) = (\Sigma_1 \alpha_1 - \Sigma_2 \alpha_2)^{-1}(\mu_1 - \mu_2) \quad (10)$$

with $\alpha_i = u_i / \sigma_i^2$ ($i = 1, 2$). In order to find w_0 they proposed heuristically based iterative procedure. Similarly to the back propagation training procedure, to find w_0 we suggest using gradient descent optimization

$$w_0(\text{new}) = w_0(\text{previous}) - \eta \frac{\partial P_{error}(w_0)}{\partial w_0}, \quad (11)$$

where, η is learning step,

$$\frac{\partial P_{error}(w_0)}{\partial w_0} = q_1 \exp(-\frac{1}{2} u_1^2 / \sigma_1^2) - q_2 \exp(-\frac{1}{2} u_2^2 / \sigma_2^2), \quad (12)$$

and Equations (9), (10) are used to recalculate components of w_{PM} after each iteration.

In real situations, mean vectors μ_1, μ_2 and matrices Σ_1, Σ_2 have to be estimated from training data. Moreover, in order to avoid numerous matrix inversions and speed up the calculations it is worth to perform standard linear transformation [7] of the data and make $\hat{\Sigma}_1 = I$ (identity matrix) and $\hat{\Sigma}_2 = D$ (diagonal matrix).

Suppose that above search procedure has been already executed and coefficients α_1, α_2 and w_0 were determined on basis of sample estimates of populations mean vectors $\hat{\mu}_1$, $\hat{\mu}_2$ and covariance matrices $\hat{\Sigma}_1, \hat{\Sigma}_2$. To have the Anderson-Bahadur solution just after the first back propagation iteration, we will require fulfill equality

$$Y^T w_{(1)} \equiv (X - H)^T G^T G(\hat{\mu}_1 - \hat{\mu}_2) = X^T(\hat{\Sigma}_1 \alpha_1 - \hat{\Sigma}_2 \alpha_2)^{-1}(\hat{\mu}_1 - \hat{\mu}_2) + w_0. \quad (13)$$

and choose transformation matrix G, and shift vector H from following equations

$$G^T G = (\hat{\Sigma}_1 \alpha_1 - \hat{\Sigma}_2 \alpha_2)^{-1}, \quad (14a)$$

$$H^T G^T G(\hat{\mu}_1 - \hat{\mu}_2) = -w_0. \quad (14b)$$

Then

$$G = L^{-1/2} F^T, \quad (15)$$

where L, F^T are eigenvalues and eigenvectors of matrix $\hat{\Sigma}_1 \alpha_1 - \hat{\Sigma}_2 \alpha_2$.

To determine shift vector H, we are assuming $H = c(\hat{\mu}_1 - \hat{\mu}_2)$, where c is a scalar. Then

$$c = \frac{w_0}{(\mu_1 - \mu_2)^T (\Sigma_1 \alpha_1 - \Sigma_2 \alpha_2)^{-1}(\mu_1 - \mu_2)} \quad \text{and}$$

$$H = -\frac{w_0}{(\mu_1 - \mu_2)^T (\Sigma_1 \alpha_1 - \Sigma_2 \alpha_2)^{-1}(\mu_1 - \mu_2)}(\hat{\mu}_1 - \hat{\mu}_2). \quad (16)$$

In comparison with the previous integrated technique, utilization of Eq. (15) and (16) in Eq. (7) ensures the better start if covariance matrices are different.

3 Small Sample Size Problems

Good starting position in perceptron training can help to reduce the generalization error. To save information contained in the good initial weight one needs stop training earlier before the minimum of the cost function will be found. Training until the minimum will abrogate positive influence of good initial weight vector. In analysis of regression task, it was shown that in order to find the best solution, the initial weight, w_0, and final one (where cost function is at its minimum), $\hat{w}_{\text{fin}}$, have to be weighted [24, 5]

$$\hat{w}_{new} = \gamma\, \hat{w}_{\text{fin}} + (1 - \gamma)\, w_0, \tag{17}$$

where optimal weighting factor γ depends on accuracies (cost function values) of initial and final weights, σ_0^2 and σ_{fin}^2

$$\gamma_{\text{opt}} = \sigma_0^2 / (\sigma_0^2 + \sigma_{\text{fin}}^2). \tag{18}$$

In SLP training, it is equivalent to early stopping: the more exact initial weight is, the earlier we have to stop training. In pattern recognition and regression, the accuracy of the statistical procedures depends on the data and complexity of decision making method. If data is multivariate Gaussian with common for both classes covariance matrix and Fisher linear discriminant function is utilized, the expected generalization error could be expressed as [5]

$$EP_N = \Phi\left(-\frac{1}{2}\delta\left(\left(1 + \frac{2p}{N\delta^2}\right)\frac{2N}{2N-p} \right)^{-1/2} \right), \tag{19}$$

where p is dimensionality of feature vector, δ is Mahalanobis distance between the pattern classes, and N is a number of training vectors of one pattern class.

In Eq. (19), term $2N/(2N-p)$ arises due to an inexact estimation of the covariance matrix, and term $1 + 2p/N\delta^2$ arises due to an inexact estimation of the mean vectors. Eq. (19) shows that if training set size is small, initial weight vector will be inexact. Consequently, in such case one cannot expect to obtain a gain in the integrated approach. In small sample size case, to improve the weight initialization one needs to use simplified estimates of the covariance matrix. For example, one can use some random process model to describe covariance matrix by small number of parameters [2, 3, 5]. Unfortunately, no theoretical results exist for the Anderson-Bahadur classification procedure. In the A-B procedure, in order to perform preliminary data transformation we estimate much more parameters of the data (two p-dimensional feature vectors and two $p{\times}p$ covariance matrices). It seems intuitively that here we could have more severe small sample problems.

To investigate small sample problems in application of the A-B procedure together with neural network training we performed a number of simulation experiments with multivariate Gaussian data. In Fig. 2 we have mean values of generalization errors obtained in 25 independent experiments with 100-dimensional spherically Gaussian data with $\Sigma = \mathbf{I}$ (identity matrix). After data transformation according to Eq (3) or (7), the SLP based classifier was trained starting from zero initial weight. To stop training in time, we used a pseudo-validation set formed from training set by means of a noise injection.

In order to reduce the data distortion we utilized a *colored noise* originally suggested by Duin [25, 26]. In this technique, we are forming pseudo-validation sets by adding many (say, ni) randomly generated vectors to each training vector. For each single training vector, $x_j^{(i)}$, one finds its k nearest neighbors, $x_{j1}^{(i)}$, $x_{j2}^{(i)}$, ... $x_{jk}^{(i)}$, from the same pattern class. Then one adds random zero mean Gaussian $N(0, \sigma_n^2)$ noise ni_{nn}, times in a subspace formed by k lines connecting vector $x_j^{(i)}$ and vectors $x_{j1}^{(i)}$, $x_{j2}^{(i)}$, ... $x_{jk}^{(i)}$. Three parameters have to be defined to realize noise injection procedure: k, the number of neighbors, ni_{nn}, the number of new, artificial vectors generated around vector $x_j^{(i)}$, and σ_n^2, the noise variance. We used: $\sigma_n^2 = 0.49$, $ni_{nn} = 10$ and $k = 3$ (three nearest neighbors).

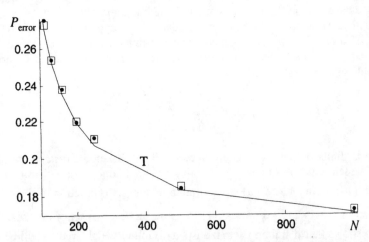

Fig. 2. Dependency of generalization error on sample size: T – theoretical estimate for Fisher rule (Eq. (19)); squares – SLP after standard data whitening transformation; bold points – new, the A-B procedure based, transformation by means of use of Eq. (15), (16) in Eq. (7).

Above experiment shows that after single layer perceptron training and optimal stopping, both procedures, the Fisher and the Anderson-Bahadur classifiers based, are equivalent. *No accuracy was lost* when initializing the perceptron with weight vector obtained by the procedure based on two different sample covariance matrices. In the case $\Sigma_2 = \Sigma_1$, both coefficients in Eq. (1) α_1 and α_2 were approximately equal. Thus,

the A-B procedure was similar to that of Fisher. Experimentation with different covariance matrices gave similar conclusion too (see next section).

4 Simulation Results

4.1 Simulation Experiment with High-Dimensional Artificial Gaussian and Non-Gaussian Data

Theoretical considerations indicate that new data transformation procedure could be
useful in situations where covariance matrices are different, data is non-Gaussian,
number of features and the number of training samples are high (it is easier to determine proper stopping moment in the large sample size case). In the experiments we
generated pairs of 100-dimensional data sets in a following way. First class: components $x_i \sim N(3, 1)$, $i = 1,...,100$; correlations between x_i and x_j $\rho = 0.01$; second class:
$x_i \sim N(3.2, 1)$, correlations between x_i and x_j, $\rho = -0.01$. As a result, the determinants
of covariance matrices Σ_1 and Σ_2, differ notably. Asymptotic error of Fisher classifier
$P_\infty^F = 0.1196$ and that of A-B procedure, $P_\infty^{opt} = 0.0567$. In Fig. 3 we plot mean values of generalization errors obtained in 25 independent experiments performed in the
same way as described above.

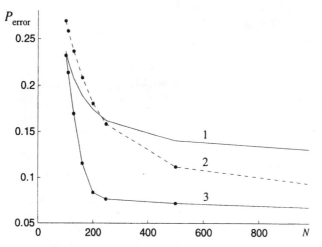

Fig. 3. Dependency of generalization error on sample size, N: 1 – theoretical estimate for Fisher
rule (Eq. (19)), 2 – SLP after standard data whitening transformation, 3 – new, the A-B procedure based, transformation. Correlated   100-dimensional Gaussian data. Covariance matrices
$\Sigma_2 \neq \Sigma_1$.

In case of correlated features and different covariance matrices, the A-B procedure
based data transformation lead to notably smaller generalization error. It is worth
mentioning that an increase in the generalization error of both classification procedures investigated is similar to that of the linear Fisher classifier.

In another series of the experiments in order to generate artificial non-Gaussian data, all variables were squared. Conclusions drawn from this series of the experiments, nevertheless, were the same.

4.2 Simulation Experiments with 199-Dimensional Machine Vibration Data

New data transformation method was tested with high dimensional real world data where *a priori* we knew that covariance matrices of two pattern classes differ remarkably. 405 electro motors were split into conditionally good and bad ones: two pattern classes, 200 motors in each of them, with intermediate five motors omitted from consideration. To discriminate the motors we used 199 spectral features. For training we used $N+N$ randomly selected vectors. Remaining 200-N vectors composed the test set of one pattern class.

In spite of equalizing the variances of all 199 features, high correlation between the spectral features ($\rho \approx 0.88$) resulted in zero determinants of the covariance matrices. As a result, without data rotation we did not succeed to train SLP at all. For small sample size values the number of training vectors was insufficient for reliable estimation of the covariance matrix. Therefore, we assumed that after reduction of data mean vector and the variance normalization of 199-dimensional input vector, the 199 features follow Markov process. We used this assumption to describe each single covariance matrix by $p=199$ variances and one single correlation parameter. The rest of experiment setup was the same as above. In Fig. 4 we have dependence of the generalization errors on the training set size.

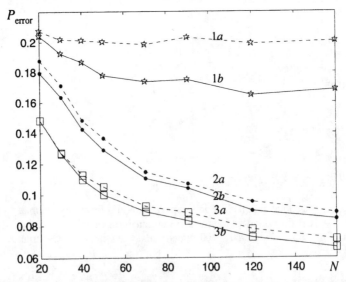

Fig. 4. Dependency of the generalization error on sample size, N: 1 – error of SLP after the first iteration (errors of Fisher and A-B classifiers), 2 – error of SLP if optimal stopping moment was determined from the pseudo-validation set, 3 – error of SLP if optimal stopping moment was determined from the test set; *a)* – Fisher classifier based data transformation, *b)* – the A-B procedure based, transformation. Machine vibration data.

In Fig. 3 we have more details: performance of initialization (graphs 1), classification errors obtained after using the test or the pseudo validation set to determine optimal stopping moment. According to theoretical considerations (Section 2) we have the Fisher or the A-B classification rules just after the first iteration.

Differences between the graphs 1 and 3 show a gain obtained in SLP training if absolutely optimal stopping moment would be found. Differences between the graphs 2 and 3 indicate a price we pay by not having real validation set. Nevertheless, we see notable difference between the graphs 1 and 2. It is the gain obtained due application of integration of statistical and neural network theories. Utilization of *a priori* knowledge that covariance matrices are different has made this gain even higher. The graphs in Fig. 4 are average values obtained in 100 experiments, each time after random permutation of the data.

5 Concluding Remarks

New data transformation method is aimed to perform data rotation, variance normalization and additional data shift to ensure a good starting point for training single layer perceptron based classifier in the two category and unequal covariance matrix case. The method is based on the Anderson-Bahadur linear discriminant function. The benefit of the new approach consists in the fact that in the new procedure we have good initial weights (Anderson-Bahadur decision). Then proper stopping of training process could save this supplementary information and lead to smaller generalization error. Besides, a good start, approximately equal eigenvalues of covariance matrices speed up the back propagation training process.

To make data rotation reliable in small sample – high dimensionality situations, we need to simplify the sample estimates of the covariance matrices. To save the computation time, for data shift we utilized analytical estimates of the classification error. To determine optimal stopping moments correctly one ought to have comparatively large amount of training data. Thus, the new data transformation method could be used in difficult pattern classification problems where the covariance matrices differ notably and both the data set size and number of features are high.

Acknowledgments

The author thanks Dr. R.P.W. Duin for providing machine vibration data for the experiments.

References

1. Raudys, S. Evolution and generalization of a single neurone. I. SLP as seven statistical classifiers. *Neural Networks*, 11:283–296, 1998.
2. Raudys S, Saudargiene A. Structures of the covariance matrices in the classifier design. *Lecture Notes in Computer Science*, 1451:583–92, 1998.
3. Saudargiene A. Structurization of the covariance matrix by process type and block diagonal models in the classifier design. *Informatica* 10(2):245–69, 1999.

4. Raudys, S. How good are support vector machines? *Neural Networks*, 13:9–11, 2000.
5. Raudys, S. *Statistical and Neural Classifiers: An integrated approach to design.* Springer, London, 2001.
6. Raudys, S. and Saudargiene A. First-order tree-type dependence between variables and classification performance. *IEEE Trans. on Pattern Analysis and Machine Intelligence*, 23: 233–239, 2001.
7. Fukunaga, K. *Introduction to Statistical Pattern Recognition.* 2nd ed. Academic Press, New York, 1990.
8. Duda, P.E., Hart, R.O. Stork, D.G. *Pattern Classification.* 2nd ed. Wiley, NY, 2000.
9. Day, N.E. Linear and quadratic discrimination in pattern recognition. *IEEE Trans. on Information Theory*, 15:419–420, 1969.
10. Anderson, T.W. and Bahadur, R.R. Classification into two multivariate normal distributions with different covariance matrices. *Annals of Mathematical Statistics*, 33:420–431, 1962.
11. Patterson D.W. and Mattson R.L. A method of finding linear discriminant functions for a class of performance criteria. *IEEE Trans. on Information Theory*, 12:380–387, 1966.
12. Smith F.W. Design of minimum-error optimal classifiers for patterns form distributions with Gaussian tails. *IEEE Trans. on Information Theory*, 17:701–707, 1971.
13. Malinovskij L.G. Discriminant analysis of normal populations represented by a large number of samples. *Problems of Transmission of Information.* Moscow Nauka, 11(1):64–71, 1975 (in Russian).
14. Zhezel. Y.N. A minimal essentially complete class of discriminant rules when the higher moments are unknown. *Theory of Probability and Applications*, 19:832–834, 1975.
15. Lipskaya V.A. An optimal decision rule for a problem of identification. *Theory of Probability and Mathematical Statistics*, Visha Shkola Publishers, Kiev, 24:91–102, 1981 (in Russian).
16. Bunke O. and Fisher K. Some fundamentals and procedures of distribution free and discrete discriminant analysis. *Preprint N 51, Neue Folge.* Humbolt Universitat zu Berlin, Sektion Matematik, Berlin, 1983.
17. Wolf A.C. The estimation of the optimum linear decision function with a sequential random method. *IEEE Trans. on Information Theory*, 12:312–315, 1966.
18. Yau S.S. and Schumpert J.M. Design of pattern classifiers with the updating property using stochastic approximation techniques. *IEEE Trans. Comp.*, 17:908–1003, 1968.
19. Ibaraki T. and Muroga S. Adaptive linear classifier by linear programming. *IEEE Transactions on Systems Science and Cybernetics*, 6:53–62, 1970.
20. Warmack R.E. and Gonzales R.C. An algorithm for optimal solution of linear inequalities and its application to pattern recognition. *IEEE Trans. on Computers*, 22:1065–75, 1973.
21. Vapnik V.N. and Chervonenkis D.Ya. *Theory of Pattern Recognition: Statistical learning problems.* Nauka, Moscow, 1974 (in Russian).
22. Miyake A. Mathematical aspects of optimal linear discriminant function. COMPSAC'79. *Proceedings of the IEEE Computer Society's 3rd International Computer Software and Applications Conference*, Chicago, Ill., pp. 161–166, 1979.
23. Do-Tu H. and Installe M. Learning algorithms for nonparametric solution to the minimum error classification problem. *IEEE Trans. on Computers*, 27:648–59, 1978.
24. Raudys S. and Amari S. Effect of initial values in simple perception. *Proceedings 1998 IEEE World Congress on Computational Intelligence, IJCNN'98*, Anchorage, Alaska, May 1998, pp. 1530–1535, 1998.
25. Duin R.P.W. Nearest neighbor interpolation for error estimation and classifier optimisation. In K.A. Hogda, B. Braathen, K. Heia (editors) *Proceedings of the 8th Scandinavian Conference on Image Analysis*, pp. 5–6. Tromso, Norway, 1993.
26. Skurichina M., Raudys S. and Duin R.P.W. K-nearest neighbors directed noise injection in multilayer perceptron training, *IEEE Trans. on Neural Networks*, 11: 504–511, 2000.

Semiring Artificial Neural Networks and Weighted Automata
And an Application to Digital Image Encoding

Sebastian Bader[1,*], Steffen Hölldobler[1], and Alexandre Scalzitti[2]

[1] International Center for Computational Logic, Technische Universität Dresden
[2] Institute of Theoretical Computer Science, Department of Computer Science
Technische Universität Dresden

Abstract. In their seminal paper [1] McCulloch and Pitts have shown the strong relationship between finite automata and so-called McCulloch-Pitts networks. Our goal is to extend this result to weighted automata. In other words, we want to integrate artificial neural networks and weighted automata. For this task, we introduce semiring artificial neural networks, that is, artificial neural networks which implement the addition and the multiplication of semirings. We present a construction of a semiring artificial neural network from a given weighted automaton, and back again. After that, we show how we can approach the problem of encoding an image into a weighted automaton by using a semiring artificial neural network in this process.

1 Introduction

In one of the first and most influential papers in the area of Artificial Neural Networks, McCulloch and Pitts have shown a strong relationship between finite automata and so-called McCulloch-Pitts networks [1] (see also [2]). In this paper we want to extend this correspondence to weighted automata.

Weighted automata are an extension of finite automata, obtained by assigning costs to the transitions, where the costs are taken from a semiring. These automata are well understood from a declarative point of view, i.e., we know what they do and what they are capable of (see e.g. [3,4]). Figure 1 shows a simple finite automaton and a simple weighted automaton, which will be explained in more detail in chapter 2.2.

Artificial neural networks are inspired by the information processing performed by animal or human brains. Typically, they are biologically plausible, massively parallel, robust, well-suited to learn and to adapt to new environments, and they degrade gracefully. In a nutshell an artificial neural network consists of a set of simple computational units which are connected (see Figure 2). Each unit receives inputs either externally or from other units, performs a simple operation and propagates the result via all its outgoing connections

---
* The first author is supported by the GK334 of the German Research Foundation.

S. Biundo, T. Frühwirth, and G. Palm (Eds.): KI 2004, LNAI 3238, pp. 281–294, 2004.

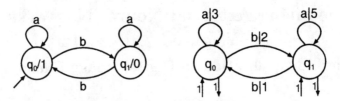

Fig. 1. A simple finite automaton as well as a simple weighted automaton with states q_0 and q_1 and transitions a and b. In case of a weighted automaton a certain cost is assigned to each transition.

to the successor units. The connections between the units are usually weighted, i.e., the input of a unit is weighted according to the connection via which it is transmitted. A unit can neither distinguish the units from which it receives information, nor the units it sends information to. If a unit does not have any incoming connections it will be called an input unit, since it needs to be activated from outside. A unit without outgoing connections will be called an output unit. By adjusting the weights of the connection the behaviour of the network can be changed; the network is said to be trained. See e.g. [5] for a detailed description of artificial neural networks.

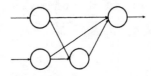

Fig. 2. A simple artificial neural network. Units are interconnected via directed arcs. Weights are omitted.

Artificial neural networks have been successfully applied to many tasks that involve function approximation. Unfortunately we usually have no direct access to the knowledge encoded in the (weights of the) connections of a given artificial neural network. This implies that we usually lack a declarative description of what is going on in an artificial neural network.

Our goal is to integrate both models of computation, weighted automata and artificial neural networks, in order to obtain a trainable system which has a declarative semantics. In this paper we want to generalize the well known relation between finite automata and McCulloch-Pitts networks [1,2] by introducing semiring artificial neural networks and showing their correspondence with weighted automata.

This paper is organized as follows. First we will briefly present the required background on semirings, weighted automata and artificial neural networks. We also define a new extension of artificial neural networks, namely semiring artificial neural networks. Thereafter, in Section 3 we will show a correspondence between weighted automata and semiring artificial neural networks. In Section 4, we will present an example where we apply our results to image encoding. Finally, in Section 5 we will review our findings and point to future work.

2   Background

2.1   Semirings and Formal Power Series

A *semiring* K is a structure $K = (K, \oplus, \odot, 0_K, 1_K)$ such that

1. $(K, \oplus, 0_K)$ is a commutative monoid, that is, $\oplus$ is a commutative associative binary operation on K and 0_K is the neutral element with respect to $\oplus$;
2. $(K, \odot, 1_K)$ is a monoid, that is, $\odot$ is an associative binary operation on K;
3. $\odot$ is both left and right distributive over $\oplus$, that is, for all x, y, $z \in K$ it holds that $x \odot (y \oplus z) = x \odot y \oplus x \odot z$ and that $(y \oplus z) \odot x = y \odot x \oplus z \odot x$ and
4. 0_K is absorbing with respect to $\odot$, that is, for all $x \in K$, it holds that $0_K \odot x = x \odot 0_K = 0_K$.

We call $\oplus$ and $\odot$ respectively the *addition* and the *multiplication* of the semiring K. We call 0_K *neutral element with respect to the addition* and 1_K *neutral element with respect to the multiplication.* Examples for semirings are

1. the boolean semiring $\mathbb{B} = (\{0, 1\}, \vee, \wedge, 0, 1)$ with $\vee$ acting as addition and $\wedge$ acting as multiplication;
2. the natural numbers $(\mathbb{N}, +, \cdot, 0, 1)$ with the usual addition and multiplication;
3. the real numbers $(\mathbb{R}, +, \cdot, 0, 1)$ with the usual addition and multiplication;
4. the real max-plus semiring $\mathbb{R}_{\max} = (\mathbb{R}_{\geq 0} \cup \{-\infty\}, \max, +, -\infty, 0)$ with max acting as addition and the usual addition of real numbers $+$ acting as multiplication. Moreover, $\mathbb{R}_{\geq 0} = [0, \infty)$ with the convention $-\infty + x = -\infty = x + -\infty$ for all $x \in \mathbb{R}_{\max}$;
5. stochastic semiring $([0, 1], \max, \cdot, 0, 1)$ with $[0, 1] \subseteq \mathbb{R}$ with max acting as addition and the usual multiplication $\cdot$ acting as multiplication;
6. distributive lattices: in this case, $\vee$ is interpreted as the semiring addition and $\wedge$ is interpreted as the semiring multiplication.

Let n be a positive integer. Let us consider the set $M^{n \times n}$ of all matrices of dimension $n \times n$ with entries taken from K. We define the addition $\oplus_M$ and the multiplication $\odot_M$ of $M^{n \times n}$ as follows. Let $A, B \in M^{n \times n}$. For $i, j \in \{1, \ldots, n\}$ we define

1. $(a \oplus_M b)_{ij} := (a)_{ij} \oplus (b)_{ij}$ and
2. $(a \odot_M b)_{ij} := \bigoplus_{k=1}^{n} a_{ik} \odot b_{kj}$.

The neutral element with respect to the addition $\oplus_M$ is the matrix 0_M such that all entries are 0_K and the neutral element with respect to the multiplication is the matrix 1_M such that its main diagonal has entries 1_K and the rest of 1_M

has entries 0_K. We observe that $M = (M^{n \times n}, \oplus_M, \odot_M, 0_M, 1_M)$ is a semiring. We also observe that we can compute, for example, $A_{p \times q} \odot_M B_{q \times r}$, with $1 \leq p, q, r \leq n$.

An *alphabet* is a non-empty finite set. Its elements are called *symbols* or *letters*. In further definitions in this paper we consider a fixed alphabet Σ. A *(finite) word* w over Σ is a finite sequence $a_1 a_2 \ldots a_n$ of symbols of Σ. We say that n is the *size* of w. If n is 0 then w is the *empty word* and we denote it by ε. We denote the set of words over Σ by Σ^*. We call a function $f : \Sigma^* \to K$ a *formal power series* with values in the semiring K.

2.2 Weighted Automata

In this section we will introduce an extension of finite automata by associating weights to the transactions.

Let K be a semiring. A *K-weighted automaton* $\mathcal{A}$ is a tuple (Q, T, c, λ, ρ) such that

1. Q is a non-empty finite set of *states*;
2. $T \subseteq Q \times \Sigma \times Q$ is a finite set of *transitions*;
3. $c : T \to K$ is a function which assigns costs to transitions;
4. $\lambda, \rho : Q \to K$ are cost functions for *entering* respectively *leaving* each state.

The underlying finite automaton is non-deterministic, i.e. there can be multiple transactions with the same label starting in a certain state, but for two states and one label there can be only one weighted transaction between these states. For the sequel of this paper we will treat c as a total function mapping every possible transaction, not only those contained in T to an element of K, by assuming that every non-included transaction will be mapped to 0_K.

Let $\mathcal{A}$ be a K-weighted automaton. A *finite path* P in $\mathcal{A}$ is a finite word over T of the form $(p_i, a_{i+1}, p_{i+1})_{i \in \{0, \ldots, n-1\}}$ for some positive integer n. The *label* of P is the finite word $w := a_1 a_2 \ldots a_n$. We also say that P is a *w-labeled path* from q_0 to q_n.

Let $P := (p_i, a_{i+1}, p_{i+1})_{i \in \{0, \ldots, n-1\}}$ be an arbitrary finite path in $\mathcal{A}$. The *running cost* of P in $\mathcal{A}$, denoted by $\mathrm{rcost}_{\mathcal{A}}(P)$, is defined by:

$$\mathrm{rcost}_{\mathcal{A}}(P) := \begin{cases} \odot_{i=0}^{n-1} c(p_i, a_{i+1}, p_{i+1}) & \text{if } n > 0, \\ 1_K & \text{if } n = 0. \end{cases}$$

The *cost* of P, denoted by $\mathrm{cost}_{\mathcal{A}}(P)$, is defined by:

$$\mathrm{cost}_{\mathcal{A}}(P) := \lambda(p_0) \odot \mathrm{rcost}_{\mathcal{A}}(P) \odot \rho(p_n).$$

The *behavior* of $\mathcal{A}$, denoted by $\|\mathcal{A}\|$, is the function $\|\mathcal{A}\| : \Sigma^* \to \mathbb{R}_{max}$ defined by

$$(\|\mathcal{A}\|, w) := \bigoplus \{ \mathrm{cost}_{\mathcal{A}}(P) \mid P \text{ is } w\text{-labeled path in } \mathcal{A} \},$$

where $w \in \Sigma^*$. We observe that if the above defined set is empty, then $(\|\mathcal{A}\|, w) := 0_K$.

In the sequel, we present an alternative representation of weighted automata which is very suitable for computations and can be easily implemented by an artificial neural network. Let $\mathcal{A} = (Q, T, c, \lambda, \rho)$ be a K-weighted automaton with n states. We say that $\mathcal{A}$ has a *matrix representation* if there are a row vector $I \in K^{1 \times n}$, a column vector $F \in K^{n \times 1}$, and for each $a \in \Sigma$ a matrix $W_a \in K^{n \times n}$ such that for every $w := a_1 a_2 \ldots a_k \in \Sigma^*$,

$$(\|\mathcal{A}\|, w) = I \odot_M W_{a_1} \odot_M W_{a_2} \odot_M \ldots \odot_M W_{a_k} \odot_M F.$$

Without going into the details and without showing the detailed proof we state the following lemma

Lemma 1. *For each weighted automaton there exists a matrix representation.*

Proof. To show the existence of this matrix representation we will construct the necessary vectors and matrices. We will consider the states to be ordered $(q_0, \ldots, q_n)$.

1. The initial weight vector I is constructed by applying λ to every state, i.e.
   $I := (\lambda(q_0), \ldots, \lambda(q_n))$
2. The final weight vector F is constructed by applying ρ to every state, i.e.
   $F := (\rho(q_0), \ldots, \rho(q_n))$
3. The weight matrices W_a for every $a \in \Sigma$ have the form:

$$W_a := \begin{pmatrix} c(q_0, a, q_0) & \ldots & c(q_0, a, q_n) \\ \vdots & \vdots & \vdots \\ c(q_n, a, q_0) & \ldots & c(q_n, a, q_n) \end{pmatrix}$$

Using this constructions it is easy to see, that the result is a matrix representation for the given weighted automaton. The details of the proof can be found in [6].

Example 1. We consider the weighted automaton shown in Figure 3. Its weights are taking from the semiring $(\mathbb{R}, +, \cdot, 0, 1)$ that is, the semiring of real numbers with usual addition and multiplication. The alphabet Σ in this case is $\{a, b\}$. We write

$$I := \begin{pmatrix} 1 & 1 \end{pmatrix}, W_a := \begin{pmatrix} 3 & 0 \\ 0 & 5 \end{pmatrix}, W_b := \begin{pmatrix} 0 & 2 \\ 1 & 0 \end{pmatrix}, F := \begin{pmatrix} 1 \\ 1 \end{pmatrix}.$$

2.3 Semiring Artificial Neural Networks

Within this section we want to introduce a new and very general type of artificial neural network. Instead of working on the real numbers only we will lift the mathematics to arbitrary semirings. Let $K = (K, \oplus, \odot, 0_K, 1_K)$ be such a semiring. The weights and activations of the connections and units, respectively, are taken from K. Using the operations provided by the semiring we can easily

286   Sebastian Bader, Steffen Hölldobler, and Alexandre Scalzitti

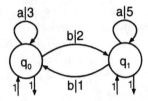

Fig. 3. An $\mathbb{R}$-weighted automaton with states q_0 and q_1 and transitions a and b.

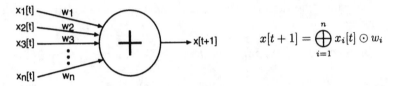

$$x[t+1] = \bigoplus_{i=1}^{n} x_i[t] \odot w_i$$

Fig. 4. Schematic plot and dynamics of $\oplus$-units.

define two new types of units called $\oplus$-*units* and $\odot$-*units* and shown in Figure 4
and Figure 5, respectively.

The unit shown in Figure 4 computes a weighted sum of the inputs, where
the activation of each unit is $\odot$-multiplied with the weight of the connection.
Thereafter the $\oplus$-sum of the weighted inputs is computed and propagated to the
successor units. Analogously, the unit shown in Figure 5 computes a weighted
product of its inputs.

Definition 1 *Let K be a fixed semiring. Let $\mathcal{N}$ be an artificial neural network
consisting of $\oplus$- and $\odot$-units, and K-weighted connections. Then we will call $\mathcal{N}$
a semiring artificial neural network.*

One should observe that such a network may be more abstract than the usual
artificial neural networks and, depending on the underlying semiring, $\oplus$- as well
as $\odot$-units may represent whole ensembles of standard units. For example, in
case of the natural or real numbers as semirings $\oplus$-units are simply computing
the weighted sum of their inputs with identity as output function, whereas in
case of the boolean semiring an $\oplus$-unit represents a McCulloch-Pitts network
consisting of and- and or-units.

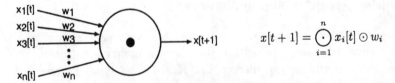

$$x[t+1] = \bigodot_{i=1}^{n} x_i[t] \odot w_i$$

Fig. 5. Schematic plot and dynamics of $\odot$-unit.

Definition 2 *Let $\mathcal{N}$ be a semiring neural network with n designated input neurons and exactly 1 output neuron. Then we will call $\mathcal{N}$ an $n-1$ semiring artificial neural network.*

In the following section we will show, that for each weighted automaton there exists an $n - 1$ semiring neural network, such that the input-output behaviour of both systems is equivalent.

3   Constructions

Theorem 3. *Let $\mathcal{A} := (Q, T, c, \lambda, \rho)$ be a K-weighted automaton. Then there exists an $n - 1$ semiring neural network $\mathcal{N}$ which simulates $\mathcal{A}$, i.e. for every word $w \in \Sigma^*$, $\mathcal{N}$ outputs $(\|\mathcal{A}\|, w)$.*

To proof the theorem we will first give a construction and thereafter show the equivalence. In what follows we will consider the weighted automaton $\mathcal{A}$ to be fixed. We will construct a network $\mathcal{N}$ simulating $\mathcal{A}$. This network has a very particular topology which consists of 4 layers as described below.

1. Input layer: it consists of σ-labeled units, where $\sigma \in \Sigma$, i.e., for each $\sigma \in \Sigma$ there is exactly one unit. The activation of each σ-labeled unit will be set from outside to 1_K if the current input symbol is σ and 0_K otherwise. For example, to input the word $w := a_1 a_2 \ldots a_n \in \Sigma^*$ to $\mathcal{N}$, in a first step the a_1-labeled unit is set to 1_K and the other input units is set to 0_K; in a second step a_2 is activated by 1_K and the other input units are set to 0_K, and so on.
2. Gate layer: it consists of $\odot$-units. For each pair (q, σ) there is a $\odot$-unit t and a connection with weight 1_K is drawn from the σ-unit of the input layer to t.
3. State layer: it consists of $\oplus$-units. For each $q \in Q$ there is an $\oplus$-unit. The gate and the state layer are fully connected with weights set according to the following rule:
   Let u be the $\odot$-unit of the gate layer of $\mathcal{N}$ which was associated with the pair (q, σ) and u' be the $\oplus$-unit associated to $q' \in Q$, in the state layer. The weight of the connection between u and u' is set to $c(q, \sigma, q')$ if $(q, \sigma, q') \in T$, and to 0_K otherwise.
   Moreover, a recurrent connection with weight 1_K from u' to each of the $\odot$-nodes of the gate layer labeled (q, σ) is added.
4. Output layer: it consists of a single $\oplus$-unit. For every state $q \in Q$, a connection with weight $\rho(q)$ from the $\oplus$-unit of the state layer which is associated with q and the $\oplus$-unit of the output layer is drawn.

The constructed network will consists of $|\Sigma| + |Q| \cdot |\Sigma| + |Q| + 1$ neurons. And, as shown below, it will compute the output for a word of length n in $2n + 1$ time steps, considering a complete update of the whole network as one step.

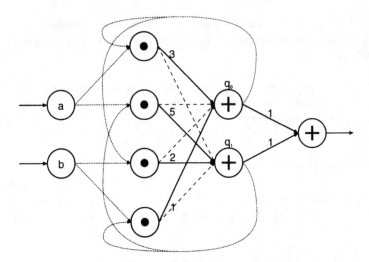

Fig. 6. The semiring artificial neural network corresponding to the weighted automata shown in Figure 3. It consists (from left to right) of the input, the gate, the state and the output layer. The dotted connections are fixed to 1_K and the dashed ones to 0_K.

Figure 6 shows the network constructed for the weighted automaton in Figure 3. This type of architecture is a mixture to the ones known as Elman- [7] and Jordan-networks [8] and possesses a similar dynamics.

In the sequel of this section we will describe the dynamics of the networks and show that the output of the network coincides with the output of the automaton for any given word w. Prior to running the network, we have to preset the activations of the state layer units to the corresponding λ-values.

Proof (of Theorem 3). Now we will show that the outputs of network and automaton coincide, i.e. $(\|\mathcal{A}\|, w) = \mathcal{N}(w)$ for all $w \in \Sigma^*$.

Let us assume that at time $t = 2n$ (after processing the word $w = a_1 \dots a_n$) the activation vector s of the state layer is $I \odot W_{a_1} \odot W_{a_2} \odot \dots \odot W_{a_n}$. It follows, that at time $t+1$ the output value will be $I \odot W_{a_1} \odot W_{a_2} \odot \dots \odot W_{a_n} \odot F$, which is the output $(\|\mathcal{A}\|, w)$ of the automaton, since the connections between state and output layer are weighted by ρ. Therefore, the output layer implements a vector multiplication of s and F.

By induction on the length n of w we will show that after $2n$ time steps the activation of the state layer actually is $I \odot W_{a_1} \odot W_{a_2} \odot \dots \odot W_{a_n}$. Let w be the empty word, i.e. $n = 0$. This case is trivial since we preset the activation to λ, as mentioned above.

For the induction step we assume that the activation of the state layer at time $t = 2n$ is $I \odot W_{a_1} \odot W_{a_2} \odot \dots \odot W_{a_n}$. Furthermore let the input layer be activated according to a_{n+1}. At time $t+1$ the activation of the gate layer will be 0_K almost everywhere, except for those neurons connected to the input neuron for a_{n+1}. The activation of those neurons will be a copy of the activation of the state layer at time t, since all the weights are set to 1_K, which is the neutral element with respect to multiplication. Since the weights between this neurons of the gate layer and the state layer implement $W_{a_{n+1}}$, we will have at time $t+2 = 2(n+1)$ that the activation of the state layer is exactly $I \odot W_{a_1} \odot W_{a_2} \odot \ldots \odot W_{a_n} \odot W_{a_{n+1}}$. This completes the proof. □

Figure 7 and Figure 8 show the activation scheme while processing the empty and non-empty word respectively.

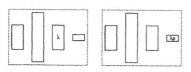

Fig. 7. The schema of a semiring artificial neural network processing the empty word.

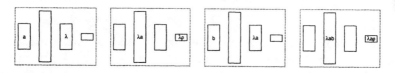

Fig. 8. The schema of a semiring artificial neural network processing a non-empty word.

So far we did show how to construct a network from a given automaton and showed the equivalence of both systems. Given a network and a set of input-output patterns, we want to adjust the weights, such that the behaviour of the network matches the patters. During the training process of the network only the weights between gate and state layer as well as between state and output layer as well as the initial activation of the state layer are adjusted, i.e. we keep the recurrent connections fixed to 1_K.

For certain semirings, e.g. $(\mathbb{R}, +, \cdot, 0, 1)$, this can be done using simple back-propagation through time as described in [7, 9]. In the following Section we will give an example of this process. Moreover, we can construct a network of this topology given an alphabet Σ and a number of states, without an automaton, by simply assigning random values to the weights between gate and state layer as well as state and output layer.

Proposition 4 *For each network of the type described above there exists a weighted automaton, such that both systems behave equivalently, i.e., for every word $w \in \Sigma^*$ we get the same output.*

Proof. The corresponding automaton can easily be extracted from the weight matrix between gate and state layer, which encodes the transactions of the automaton. □

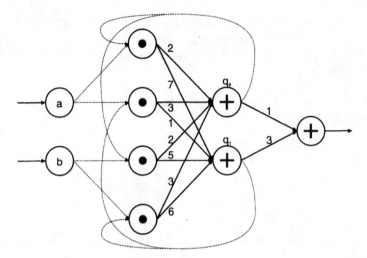

Fig. 9. A semiring artificial neural network.

Let us consider the network shown in Figure 9 and assume that $\lambda(q_0) = 2$ and $\lambda(q_1) = 3$ as result of a training process. We can easily extract the matrices shown in Figure 10. From the weights between gate- and state-layer we get the transaction matrices W_a and W_b and the values for ρ from the connections to the output layer. Given this matrices we can construct the automaton shown in Figure 11.

$$I := (2\ 3), \qquad W_a := \begin{pmatrix} 2 & 7 \\ 3 & 1 \end{pmatrix}, \qquad W_b := \begin{pmatrix} 2 & 5 \\ 3 & 6 \end{pmatrix}, \qquad F := \begin{pmatrix} 1 \\ 3 \end{pmatrix}.$$

Fig. 10. Transaction matrices of a weighted automaton extracted from the network shown in Figure 9.

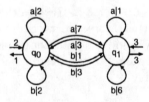

Fig. 11. A weighted automaton constructed from the matrices shown in Figure 10.

Other architectures are possible as well, but this one was chosen for several reasons. As mentioned above it is similar to well known architectures as Jordan- and Elman-networks. Furthermore, all recurrent connections have an associated weight of 1_K, which simplifies the training process.

4   An Example – Digital Images

In this section we want to discuss the problem of image encoding by weighted automata, that is, the problem of constructing a weighted automaton which computes for each pixel the color according to a given image.

First we define images. An *image* of resolution $r \times s$ for our purposes is a matrix of r rows and s columns of *pixels*. We can assign to each pixel a *gray-scale intensity*. Without loss of generality, we will consider images of resolution $2^n \times 2^n$ only, and for pixels we take gray-scale intensities in the interval $[0,1]$. Culik and Kari in [10] presented a first algorithm that constructs a weighted automaton which encodes a given image. The problem is that we cannot fix the number of states of this weighted automaton in advance. Culik and Kari in [11] and, later on, Katritzke in [12] proposed improvements of this algorithm which compute approximations of the image. In this section we want to use the results obtained in the last section to construct a weighted automaton by means of training a semiring artificial neural network.

But first, we need to introduce a method to address pixels of a given image. Let n be a natural number and let us consider an image of resolution $2^n \times 2^n$. We assign to each pixel a word of length n over the alphabet $\{0,1,2,3\}$ as follows.

1. If $n = 0$ then the image contains exactly one pixel which is addressed by the empty word ε.
2. If $n = 1$ then the image contains 2×2 pixels which can be addressed as shown in the left-hand side of Figure 12.
3. If $n = 2$ then the addresses are shown in the right-hand side of Figure 12.
4. The addresses for $n > 2$ are obtained inductively.

Roughly speaking, the pixel addressing method presented above provides us a set of finite words which can be interpreted as follows. Let w be a pixel address. If $w = v \cdot a$ with $a \in \Sigma$, then w addresses quadrant a of the sub-image addressed by v. To each address w we assign the average gray-scale c of the sub-image addressed by w, thereby we obtain a function $f : \Sigma^* \to [0,1]$.

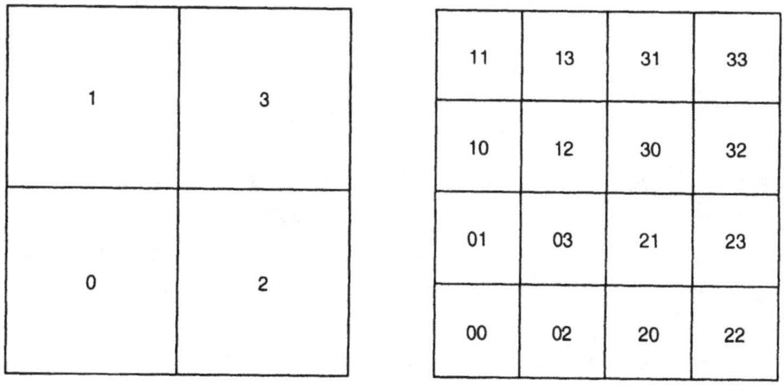

Fig. 12. Pixel addressing for $n = 1$ (left-hand side) and $n = 2$ (right-hand side).

Let $\mathcal{A}$ be an $\mathbb{R}$-weighted automaton and let $f_{\mathcal{A}}$ be its behavior. We decode the image $f_{\mathcal{A}}$ at resolution $2^k \times 2^k$ by computing $f_{\mathcal{A}}(w)$ for every $w \in \Sigma^*$ of length k.

We want to construct an automaton whose behaviour is f, or at least similar to f. To achieve this goal we constructed a randomly initialized semiring artificial neural network as described above. In addition, we extracted a set of training samples from a given image and used this samples to train the network using back-propagation through time, as described in [7]. Figure 13 shows a sample, the network output prior learning and the output after learning, each shown as a picture.

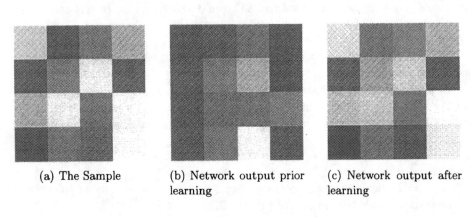

(a) The Sample   (b) Network output prior learning   (c) Network output after learning

Fig. 13. Sample and Network Output.

To create the example shown in Figure 13 we used a very simple implementation by the authors. The training procedure used was a standard backpropagation through time, without any improvements. Unfortunately we observed that the learning process for bigger examples ends very often in sub-optimal local minima. But we believe that this is due to our implementation, since backpropagation through time was shown to work for bigger data-sets [7]. The dynamics and limitations of the training will be subject to further investigations.

5 Conclusions and Future Work

In this paper we have introduced semiring artificial neural networks. These networks can be seen as a generalization of the so-called $\Sigma - \Pi$-networks (e.g. described in [13]) where the values as well as addition and multiplication are taken from an arbitrarily given semiring. We have shown that for each weighted automaton there exists such a network with identical input-output behaviour. We have thus extended the work by McCulloch and Pitts [1, 2]. In addition, we have shown by example of image encoding that back-propagation through time can be applied to train semiring artificial neural networks.

In Section 3 we have presented a construction method which receives as input a weighted automaton and outputs a $n-1$-semiring neural network of a particular topology. We can also do the inverse: given a $n-1$-semiring neural network of the particular topology as the outputs of the above mentioned construction method we can construct a weighted automaton with same behaviour. The conversion of arbitrary networks is still an open problem.

Let us review this application: The first algorithm of Culik and Kari in [10] receives as input an (possibly infinite) image and terminates if and only if the image is average preserving. This is a property which can be formulated in terms of linear dependence of a certain set of functions which can be constructed from the image. If the algorithm terminates, we have as output a weighted automaton which represents or encodes exactly the given image. Moreover, the number of states is exactly the dimension of the vector space whose basis is this set of functions mentioned above.

Depending on the number of states we may be interested in a weighted automaton with less states and which encodes an approximation of the given image. In our approach, we can construct a semiring artificial neural network with a fixed number of states and with the topology as discussed in Section 3. This network can be trained, and thereafter, be translated to a weighted automaton.

Taking a closer look at the transaction structure created by Kari's algorithm, we find that there are no loops of transactions, which might restrict the automaton. Please note that this is not true for the automata constructed using our approach. The consequences, regarding the expressive power need further investigations.

Culik and Kari [10] and later on Katritzke [12] made several improvements to the algorithm presented above. Particularly Katritzke implemented several algorithms concerning image encoding and compression in his software AutoPic. We intend to do a complexity comparison between AutoPic and our approach, and furthermore, extensive tests of the dynamics of the networks, including the training process.

References

1. McCulloch, W.S., Pitts, W.: A logical calculus and the ideas immanent in nervous activity. Bulletin of Mathematical Biophysics 5 (1943) 115–133
2. Arbib, M.A.: Brains, Machines, and Mathematics. 2nd edn. Springer (1987)
3. Schützenberger, M.P.: On the definition of a family of automata. Information and Control 4 (1961) 245–270
4. Droste, M., Vogler, H., eds.: Selected Papers of the Workshop Weighted Automata: Theory and Applications. Volume 8. (2003) Special issue of Journal of Automata, Languages and Combinatorics.
5. Hertz, J., Krogh, A., Palmer, R.G.: Introduction to the Theory of Neural Computation. Addison-Wesley Publishing Company (1991)
6. Eilenberg, S.: Automata, languages, and machines. Vol. A. Academic Press [A subsidiary of Harcourt Brace Jovanovich, Publishers], New York (1974) Pure and Applied Mathematics, Vol. 58.

7. Elman, J.L.: Finding structure in time. Cognitive Science **14** (1990) 179–211
8. Jordan, M.I.: Attractor dynamics and parallelism in a connectionist sequential machine. (1986) 531–546
9. Werbos, P.J.: Backpropagation through time: What it does and how to do it. In: Proceedings of the IEEE. Volume 78. (1990) 1550–1560
10. Culik, K., Kari, J.: Image-data compression using edge-optimizing algorithm for wfa inference. Journal of Information Processing and Management **30** (1994) 829–838
11. Culik, II, K., Kari, J.: Digital images and formal languages. In: Handbook of formal languages, Vol. 3. Springer, Berlin (1997) 599–616
12. Katritzke, F.: Refinements of data compression using weighted finite automata. PhD thesis, Universität Siegen, Germany (2002)
13. Rojas, R.: Theorie der neuronalen Netze. Springer (1993)

A New Method to Fit a Linear Regression Model for Interval-Valued Data

Francisco de A.T. de Carvalho,
Eufrasio de A. Lima Neto, and Camilo P. Tenorio

Centro de Informatica - CIn / UFPE, Av. Prof. Luiz Freire, s/n
Cidade Universitaria, CEP: 50740-540 - Recife - PE - Brasil
{fatc,ealn,cpt}@cin.ufpe.br

Abstract. This paper introduces a new approach to fit a linear regression model on interval-valued data. Each example of the learning set is described by a feature vector where each feature value is an interval. In the proposed approach, it is fitted two linear regression models, respectively, on the mid-point and range of the interval values assumed by the variables on the learning set. The prediction of the lower and upper bound of the interval value of the dependent variable is accomplished from its mid-point and range which are estimated from the fitted linear regression models applied to the mid-point and range of each interval values of the independent variables. The evaluation of the proposed prediction method is based on the estimation of the average behaviour of *root mean squared error* and of the *determination coefficient* in the framework of a Monte Carlo experience in comparison with the method proposed by Billard and Diday [3].

1 Introduction

Due the explosive growth in the use of databases new approaches have been proposed to discover regularities and summarize information stored in such large data sets. *Symbolic Data Analysis* (SDA) [1] has been introduced as a new domain related to multivariate analysis, pattern recognition and artificial intelligence in order to extend classical exploratory data analysis and statistical methods to symbolic data. Symbolic data allows multiple (sometimes weighted) values for each variable, and it is why new variable types (interval, categorical multi-valued and modal variables) have been introduced. These new variables allow to take into account variability and/or uncertainty present in the data.

This paper concerns the fitting of a linear regression model to an interval-valued data-set. The probabilistic assumptions that involve the linear regression model theory for classical data will not be considered in the case of symbolic data (interval variables), since this research's field is still open. Thus, the problem will be investigated as an optimization problem, in which we desire to fit the best straight line that minimizes an established criterion.

The classical model of regression for usual data had its origin in astronomic studies developed by Gauss between 1809 and 1821. It is a method which is

S. Biundo, T. Frühwirth, and G. Palm (Eds.): KI 2004, LNAI 3238, pp. 295–306, 2004.
© Springer-Verlag Berlin Heidelberg 2004

used to predict the behaviour of a dependent variable Y as a function of others independent variables that are responsible for the variability of variable Y. To fit this model on the data, it is necessary the estimation of a vector β of parameters from the data vector $\mathbf{Y}$ and the model matrix $\mathbf{X}$, supposed with complete rank p. The estimation using the *method of least square* does not require any probabilistic hypothesis on the variable Y. This method consists in minimize the sum of square of residuals. A detailed study of the linear regression models for classical data can be found in Scheffé [9], Draper and Smith [6], Montgomery and Peck [8], among others.

Billard and Diday [3] presented for the first time an approach to fitting a linear regression model to an interval-valued data-set. Their approach consist in fitting a linear regression model on the mid-point of the interval values assumed by the variables on the learning set and applies this model on the lower and upper bounds of the interval values of the independent variables to predict, respectively, the lower and upper bounds of the interval value of the dependent variable. Later, they presented other approaches to fit a linear regression model to the case of histogram-valued data [4], and to take into account taxonomic variables [2].

This paper introduces a new approach to fit a linear regression model for interval-valued data which improves the method proposed by Billard and Diday [3]. In the proposed approach, it is fitted two linear regression models, respectively, on the mid-point and range of the interval values assumed by the variables on the learning set. The prediction of the lower and upper bound of the interval value of the dependent variable is accomplished from its mid-point and range which are estimated from the fitted linear regression models applied to the mid-point and range of each interval values of the independent variables.

In order to show the usefulness of this approach, it is predicted, according to the proposed method and the method presented by Billard and Diday [3], based on independent test data sets , the lower and upper bound of the interval values of a variable which is linearly related to a set of independent interval-valued variables. The evaluation of the proposed prediction method is based on the estimation of the average behavior of the *root mean squared error* and of the *determination coefficient* in the framework of a Monte Carlo experience in comparison with the method proposed by Billard and Diday [3].

Section 2 presents the new approach to fit a linear regression model to interval-valued data. Section 3 describes the framework of the Monte Carlo simulations and presents experiments with artificial interval-valued data sets. Section 3 describes also an application of the proposed approach to a real interval-valued data set concerning a medical domain and section 4 gives the concluding remarks.

2   Linear Regression Models for Interval-Valued Data

Let $E = \{e_1, \ldots, e_n\}$ be a set of the examples which are described by $p + 1$ continuous quantitative variables: Y, and $X_1, \ldots, X_p$. Let us consider Y being a dependent variable and X_j $(j = 1, \ldots, p)$ being p independent predictor variables, related to Y according to a linear regression relationship:

$$Y = \beta_0 + \beta_1 X_1 + \ldots + \beta_p X_p + \epsilon \tag{1}$$

Each example $e_i \in E$ $(i = 1, \ldots, n)$ is represented as a continuous quantitative feature vector $\mathbf{z}_i = (x_{i1}, \ldots, x_{ip}, y_i)$ where $x_{ij} \in \Re$ $(j = 1, \ldots, p)$ and $y_i \in \Re$ are, respectively, the observed values of X_j and Y.

The complete linear regression model becomes then

$$y_i = (\mathbf{x}_i)^T \boldsymbol{\beta} + \epsilon_i \ (i = 1, \ldots, n) \tag{2}$$

where $(\mathbf{x}_i)^T = (1, x_{i1}, \ldots, x_{ip})$ and $\boldsymbol{\beta} = (\beta_0, \beta_1, \ldots, \beta_p)^T$.

In the matrix notation, the equation 2 becomes

$$\mathbf{y} = \mathbf{X}\boldsymbol{\beta} + \epsilon \tag{3}$$

where $\mathbf{y} = (y_1, \ldots, y_n)^T$, $\mathbf{X} = ((\mathbf{x}_1)^T, \ldots, (\mathbf{x}_n)^T)^T$ and $\epsilon = (\epsilon_1, \ldots, \epsilon_n)^T$.

The *method of least squares* selects $\boldsymbol{\beta}$ so as to minimize the sum of the squares of the residuals

$$S(\boldsymbol{\beta}) = \epsilon^T \epsilon = (\mathbf{y} - \hat{\mathbf{y}})^T (\mathbf{y} - \hat{\mathbf{y}}) =$$
$$= \sum_{i=1}^{n}(y_i - \hat{y}_i)^2 = \sum_{i=1}^{n}(y_i - \beta_0 - \beta_1 x_{i1} - \ldots - \beta_p x_{ip})^2 \tag{4}$$

If $\mathbf{X}$ has full rank $p + 1 \leq n$, the least squares estimates of $\boldsymbol{\beta}$ in equation 4 is given by

$$\hat{\boldsymbol{\beta}} = (\mathbf{X}^T \mathbf{X})^{-1} \mathbf{X}^T \mathbf{y} \tag{5}$$

Let $\hat{\mathbf{y}} = \mathbf{X}\hat{\boldsymbol{\beta}}$ denote the *fitted values* of $\mathbf{y}$ and $\hat{\epsilon} = \mathbf{y} - \hat{\mathbf{y}}$ denote the estimated *residuals*. Given a new example e, described by $\mathbf{z} = (x_1, \ldots, x_p, y)$, the value y of Y will be predicted by $\hat{y}$ according to

$$\hat{y} = (\tilde{\mathbf{x}})^T \hat{\boldsymbol{\beta}} \tag{6}$$

where $(\tilde{\mathbf{x}})^T = (1, x_1, \ldots, x_p)$ and $\hat{\boldsymbol{\beta}} = (\hat{\beta}_0, \hat{\beta}_1, \ldots, \hat{\beta}_p)^T$.

Here it was presented the classical linear regression model for continuous quantitative data. In the next sections, we will explain the method introduced by Billard and Diday [3] to fit a linear regression model on interval-valued data (here named *current method - CM*) and the method introduced in this paper (here named *new method - NM*).

2.1   Current Method (CM)

Let $E = \{e_1, \ldots, e_n\}$ be a set of the examples which are now described by $p + 1$ interval quantitative variables: Y, and $X_1, \ldots, X_p$. Each example $e_i \in E$ $(i = 1, \ldots, n)$ is represented as an interval quantitative feature vector $\mathbf{z}_i = (x_{i1}, \ldots, x_{ip}, y_i)$ where $x_{ij} = [a_{ij}, b_{ij}] \in \Im = \{[a, b] : a, b \in \Re, a \leq b\}$ $(j = 1, \ldots, p)$ and $y_i = [y_{Li}, y_{Ui}] \in \Im$ are, respectively, the observed values of X_j and Y.

Let us consider there exist a linear relationship between Y (the dependent variable) and X_j, $j = 1, \ldots, p$ (the p independent predictor variables). Given a new example e, described by $\mathbf{z} = (x_1, \ldots, x_p, y)$ where $x_j = [a_j, b_j]$ $(j = 1, \ldots, p)$ and $y = [y_L, y_U]$, the aim is to predict y from x_j $(j = 1, \ldots, p)$ through a linear regression model.

Billard and Diday [3] proposed to fit a linear regression model on the mid-point of the interval values assumed by the variables on the learning set and applies this model on the lower and upper bounds of the interval values of the independent variables to predict, respectively, the lower and upper bounds of the interval value of the dependent variable.

Formally, let us consider again the same set of examples $E = \{e_1, \ldots, e_n\}$ but they are now also described by $p+1$ continuous quantitative variables Y^{md}, and $X_1^{md}, \ldots, X_p^{md}$, which assume as value, respectively, the mid-point of the interval assumed by the interval-valued variables Y, and $X_1, \ldots, X_p$. This means that now each example $e_i \in E$ $(i = 1, \ldots, n)$ is represented as a continuous quantitative feature vector $\mathbf{w}_i = (x_{i1}^{md}, \ldots, x_{ip}^{md}, y_i^{md})$ where $x_{ij}^{md} = (a_{ij} + b_{ij})/2$ $(j = 1, \ldots, p)$ and $y_i^{md} = (y_{Li} + y_{Ui})/2$ are, respectively, the observed values of X_j^{md} and Y^{md}.

The fitted linear regression model is then

$$\mathbf{y}^{md} = \mathbf{X}^{md}\boldsymbol{\beta}^{md} + \boldsymbol{\epsilon}^{md} \tag{7}$$

where $\mathbf{y}^{md} = (y_1^{md}, \ldots, y_n^{md})^T$, $\mathbf{X}^{md} = ((\mathbf{x}_1^{md})^T, \ldots, (\mathbf{x}_n^{md})^T)^T$, $(\mathbf{x}_i^{md})^T = (1, x_{i1}^{md}, \ldots, x_{ip}^{md})$ $(i = 1, \ldots, n)$, $\boldsymbol{\beta}^{md} = (\beta_0^{md}, \ldots, \beta_p^{md})^T$ and $\boldsymbol{\epsilon}^{md} = (\epsilon_1^{md}, \ldots, \epsilon_n^{md})^T$.

If $\mathbf{X}^{md}$ has full rank $p+1 \leq n$, the least squares estimates of $\boldsymbol{\beta}^{md}$ in equation 7 is given by

$$\hat{\boldsymbol{\beta}}^{md} = ((\mathbf{X}^{md})^T\mathbf{X}^{md})^{-1}(\mathbf{X}^{md})^T\mathbf{y}^{md} \tag{8}$$

Given a new example e, described by $\mathbf{z} = (x_1, \ldots, x_p, y)$ and $\mathbf{z}^{md} = (x_1^{md}, \ldots, x_p^{md}, y^{md})$ where $x_j = [a_j, b_j]$ $(j = 1, \ldots, p)$, the value $y = [y_L, y_U]$ of Y will be predicted from the predicted value y^{md} of Y^{md} as follow:

$$\hat{y}_L = \hat{y}^{md} = (\mathbf{x}_L)^T\hat{\boldsymbol{\beta}}^{md} \text{ and } \hat{y}_U = \hat{y}^{md} = (\mathbf{x}_U)^T\hat{\boldsymbol{\beta}}^{md} \tag{9}$$

where $(\mathbf{x}_L)^T = (1, a_1, \ldots, a_p)$, $(\mathbf{x}_U)^T = (1, b_1, \ldots, b_p)$ and $\hat{\boldsymbol{\beta}}^{md} = (\hat{\beta}_0^{md}, \hat{\beta}_1^{md}, \ldots, \hat{\beta}_p^{md})^T$.

In the next section, we introduce a new method which improves the method of Billard and Diday [3].

2.2   The New Method (NM)

In the method proposed here, it is fitted two linear regression models, respectively, on the mid-point and range of the interval values assumed by the variables on the learning set. The prediction of the lower and upper bound of the interval value of the dependent variable is accomplished from its mid-point and range which are estimated from the fitted linear regression models applied to the mid-point and range of each interval value of the independent variables.

Let us consider again the same set of examples $E = \{e_1, \ldots, e_n\}$ but they are now also described by $p+1$ continuous quantitative variables Y^r, and $X_1^r, \ldots, X_p^r$ which assume as value, respectively, the range of the interval assumed by the interval-valued variables Y, and $X_1, \ldots, X_p$. This means that now each example $e_i \in E$ $(i = 1, \ldots, n)$ is represented as a continuous quantitative feature vector $\mathbf{r}_i = (x_{i1}^r, \ldots, x_{ip}^r, y_i^r)$ where $x_{ij}^r = (b_{ij} - a_{ij})$ $(j = 1, \ldots, p)$ and $y_i^r = (y_{Ui} - y_{Li})$ are, respectively, the observed values of X_j^r and Y^r.

The fitted linear regression model is then

$$\mathbf{y}^r = \mathbf{X}^r \boldsymbol{\beta}^r + \boldsymbol{\epsilon}^r \tag{10}$$

where $\mathbf{y}^r = (y_1^r, \ldots, y_n^r)^T$, $\mathbf{X}^r = ((\mathbf{x}_1^r)^T, \ldots, (\mathbf{x}_n^r)^T)^T$, $(\mathbf{x}_i^r)^T = (1, x_{i1}^r, \ldots, x_{ip}^r)$ $(i = 1, \ldots, n)$, $\boldsymbol{\beta}^r = (\beta_0^r, \ldots, \beta_p^r)^T$ and $\boldsymbol{\epsilon}^r = (\epsilon_1^r, \ldots, \epsilon_n^r)^T$.

If $\mathbf{X}^r$ has full rank $p + 1 \leq n$, the least squares estimates of $\boldsymbol{\beta}^r$ in equation 10 is given by

$$\hat{\boldsymbol{\beta}}^r = ((\mathbf{X}^r)^T \mathbf{X}^r)^{-1} (\mathbf{X}^r)^T \mathbf{y}^r \tag{11}$$

Given a new example e, described by $\mathbf{z} = (x_1, \ldots, x_p, y)$, $\mathbf{z}^{md} = (x_1^{md}, \ldots, x_p^{md}, y^{md})$ and $\mathbf{z}^r = (x_1^r, \ldots, x_p^r, y^r)$ where $x_j = [a_j, b_j]$, $x_j^{md} = (a_j + b_j)/2$ and $x_j^r = (b_j - a_j)$ $(j = 1, \ldots, p)$, the value $y = [y_L, y_U]$ of Y will be predicted from the predicted values y^{md} of Y^{md} and y^r of Y^r as follow:

$$\hat{y}_L = \hat{y}^{md} - (1/2)\hat{y}^r \text{ and } \hat{y}_U = \hat{y}^{md} + (1/2)\hat{y}^r \tag{12}$$

where $\hat{y}^{md} = (\tilde{\mathbf{x}}^{md})^T \hat{\boldsymbol{\beta}}^{md}$, $\hat{y}^r = (\tilde{\mathbf{x}}^r)^T \hat{\boldsymbol{\beta}}^r$, $(\tilde{\mathbf{x}}^{md})^T = (1, x_1^{md}, \ldots, x_p^{md})$, $(\tilde{\mathbf{x}}^r)^T = (1, x_1^r, \ldots, x_p^r)$, $\hat{\boldsymbol{\beta}}^{md} = (\hat{\beta}_0^{md}, \hat{\beta}_1^{md}, \ldots, \hat{\beta}_p^{md})^T$ and $\hat{\boldsymbol{\beta}}^r = (\hat{\beta}_0^r, \hat{\beta}_1^r, \ldots, \hat{\beta}_p^r)^T$.

3   The Monte Carlo Experiences

In order to show the usefulness of the approach proposed in this paper, experiments with simulated interval-valued data sets with different degrees of difficulty to fit a linear regression model are considered in this section as well as a cardiological data set.

3.1   Simulated Interval-Valued Data Sets

Initially, it is considered standard continuous quantitative data sets in $\Re^2$ and in $\Re^4$. Each data set (in $\Re^2$ or in $\Re^4$) has 375 points partitioned in a learning set (250 points) and a test set (125 points). Each data point, in $\Re^2$ or in $\Re^4$, belonging to a standard data set is a seed for an interval data set (a rectangle in $\Re^2$ or hypercube in $\Re^4$) and in this way, from these standard data sets it is obtained the interval data sets.

The construction of the standard data sets and of the corresponding interval data sets is accomplished in the following steps:

s1 Let us suppose that each random variables X_j^{md} ($j = 1$ if the data is in $\Re^2$ or $j = 1, 2, 3$ if the data is in $\Re^4$), which assume as value the midi-point of the interval value assumed by the interval-valued variables X_j ($j = 1, 2, 3$), is uniformly distributed in the interval $[a, b]$; at each iteration it is randomly selected 375 values of each variable X_j^{md}, which are the midi-points of these intervals;

s2 The random variable Y^{md}, which assume as value the midi-point of the interval value assumed by the interval-valued variable Y, is supposed to be related to variables X_j^{md} according to $Y = (\mathbf{X}^{md})^T \beta + \epsilon$, where $(\mathbf{X}^{md})^T = (1, X_1^{md})$ (if the data is in $\Re^2$) or $(\mathbf{X}^{md})^T = (1, X_1^{md}, X_2^{md}, X_3^{md})$ (if the data is in $\Re^4$), $\beta = (\beta_0 = 5, \beta_1 = 1.5)^T$ (if the data is in $\Re^2$) or $\beta = (\beta_0 = 5, \beta_1 = 1.5, \beta_2 = -2, \beta_3 = 0.5)^T$ (if the data is in $\Re^4$) and $\epsilon = U[c, d]$; the midi-points of these 375 intervals are calculated according this linear relation;

s3 Once obtained the midi-points of the intervals, let us consider now the range of each interval. Let us suppose that each random variable Y^r, X_j^r ($j = 1, 2, 3$), which assume as value, respectively, the range of the interval assumed by the interval-valued variables Y and X_j ($j = 1, 2, 3$), is uniformly distributed, respectively, in the intervals $[e, f]$ and $[g, h]$; at each iteration it is randomly selected 375 values of each variable Y^r, X_j^r, which are the range of these intervals;

s4 At each iteration, the interval-valued data set is partitioned in a learning (250 observations) and test (125 observations) set.

Table 1 shows nine different configurations for the interval data sets which are used to compare de performance of the **CM** method and **NM** method in different situations.

Table 1. Data set configurations.

C_1	$X_j^{md} \sim U[20, 40]$	$X_j^r \sim U[20, 40]$	$Y^r \sim U[20, 40]$	$\epsilon \sim U[-20, 20]$
C_2	$X_j^{md} \sim U[20, 40]$	$X_j^r \sim U[20, 40]$	$Y^r \sim U[20, 40]$	$\epsilon \sim U[-10, 10]$
C_3	$X_j^{md} \sim U[20, 40]$	$X_j^r \sim U[20, 40]$	$Y^r \sim U[20, 40]$	$\epsilon \sim U[-5, 5]$
C_4	$X_j^{md} \sim U[20, 40]$	$X_j^r \sim U[10, 20]$	$Y^r \sim U[10, 20]$	$\epsilon \sim U[-20, 20]$
C_5	$X_j^{md} \sim U[20, 40]$	$X_j^r \sim U[10, 20]$	$Y^r \sim U[10, 20]$	$\epsilon \sim U[-10, 10]$
C_6	$X_j^{md} \sim U[20, 40]$	$X_j^r \sim U[10, 20]$	$Y^r \sim U[10, 20]$	$\epsilon \sim U[-5, 5]$
C_7	$X_j^{md} \sim U[20, 40]$	$X_j^r \sim U[1, 5]$	$Y^r \sim U[1, 5]$	$\epsilon \sim U[-20, 20]$
C_8	$X_j^{md} \sim U[20, 40]$	$X_j^r \sim U[1, 5]$	$Y^r \sim U[1, 5]$	$\epsilon \sim U[-10, 10]$
C_9	$X_j^{md} \sim U[20, 40]$	$X_j^r \sim U[1, 5]$	$Y^r \sim U[1, 5]$	$\epsilon \sim U[-5, 5]$

These configurations take into account the combination of two factors (range and error on the mid-points) with three degrees of variability (low, medium and high): low variability range ($U[1, 5]$), medium variability range ($U[10, 20]$), high variability range ($U[20, 40]$, low variability error ($\epsilon \sim U[-5, 5]$), medium variability error ($\epsilon \sim U[-10, 10]$) and high variability error ($\epsilon \sim U[-20, 20]$).

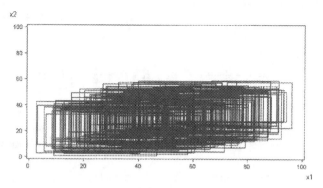

Fig. 1. Configuration C_1 showing a poor linear relationship between Y and X_1.

The configuration C_1, for example, represents observations with a high variability range and with a poor linear relationship between Y and X_1, X_2 and X_3 due the high variability error on the mid-points. Figure 1 shows the configuration C_1 when the data is in $\Re^2$.

In the other hand, the configuration C_9 represent observations with a low variability range and with a rich linear relationship between Y and X_1, X_2 and X_3 due the low variability error on the midi-points. Figure 2 shows the configuration C_9 when the data is in $\Re^2$.

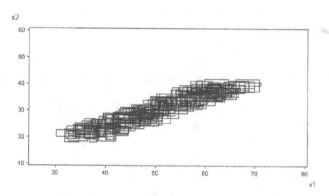

Fig. 2. Configuration C_9 showing a rich linear relationship between Y and X_1.

3.2   Experimental Evaluation

The evaluation of the performance of the linear regression models (**CM** approach and **NM** approach) is based on the following measures: the *lower bound root mean-squared error* $(RMSE_L)$, the *upper bound root mean-squared error* $(RMSE_U)$, the *lower bound determination coefficient* (R_L^2) and the *upper bound determination coefficient* (R_U^2).

These measures are obtained from the observed values $y_i = [y_{Li}, y_{Ui}]$ $(i = 1, \ldots, n)$ of Y and from their corresponding predicted values $\hat{y}_i = [\hat{y}_{Li}, \hat{y}_{Ui}]$. They are:

$$RMSE_L = \sqrt{\frac{\sum_{i=1}^{n}(y_{Li} - \hat{y}_{Li})^2}{n}} \text{ and } RMSE_U = \sqrt{\frac{\sum_{i=1}^{n}(y_{Ui} - \hat{y}_{Ui})^2}{n}} \quad (13)$$

$$R_L^2 = \frac{Cov(\mathbf{y}_L, \hat{\mathbf{y}}_L)}{S_{\mathbf{y}_L} S_{\hat{\mathbf{y}}_L}} \text{ and } R_U^2 = \frac{Cov(\mathbf{y}_U, \hat{\mathbf{y}}_U)}{S_{\mathbf{y}_U} S_{\hat{\mathbf{y}}_U}} \quad (14)$$

where: $\mathbf{y}_L = (y_{L1}, \ldots, y_{Ln})^T$, $\hat{\mathbf{y}}_L = (\hat{y}_{L1}, \ldots, \hat{y}_{Ln})^T$, $\mathbf{y}_U = (y_{U1}, \ldots, y_{Un})^T$, $\hat{\mathbf{y}}_U = (\hat{y}_{U1}, \ldots, \hat{y}_{Un})^T$, $Cov(\mathbf{y}_\bullet, \hat{\mathbf{y}}_\bullet)$ is the covariance between $\mathbf{y}_L$ and $\hat{\mathbf{y}}_L$ or between $\mathbf{y}_U$ and $\hat{\mathbf{y}}_U$, $S_{\mathbf{y}_\bullet}$ is the standard deviation of $\mathbf{y}_L$ or $\mathbf{y}_U$ and $S_{\hat{\mathbf{y}}_\bullet}$ is the standard deviation of $\hat{\mathbf{y}}_L$ or $\hat{\mathbf{y}}_U$.

These measures are estimated for both **CM** method and **NM** method in the framework of a Monte Carlo simulation with 100 replications for each independent test interval data set, for each of the nine fixed configurations, as well as for different numbers of independent variables in the model matrix. For each replication, a linear regression model is fitted on the training interval data set for each method (**CM** or **NM**) and these models are used to predict the interval values of the dependent variable Y on the test interval data set and these measures are calculated. Finally, it is calculated, for each measure, its average and standard deviation.

Table 2 presents the results of this Monte Carlo experience. This table shows that, in any considered situation and for all the measures considered, the **NM** method has an average performance higher than that of the **CM** method.

The comparison between these approaches is achieved by two statistical t-test for independent samples, at a significance level of 1% or a confidence level of 99%, applied to each measure considered. Concerning the $RMSE_L$ and $RMSE_U$ the hypotheses are: $H_0 : \mathbf{NM} = \mathbf{CM}$ versus $H_1 : \mathbf{NM} < \mathbf{CM}$. In the other hand, concerning R_L^2 and R_U^2 the hypotheses are $H_0 : \mathbf{NM} = \mathbf{CM}$ versus $H_1 : \mathbf{NM} > \mathbf{CM}$. Table 3 shows the observed values (and the corresponding p-values) of the test statistics following a Student's t distribution with 198 degrees of freedom.

From Table 3 we can see that the null hypothesis is rejected at a significance level of 1%, regardless the number of variables or the performance measure considered, for the following configurations: $C_1, C_2, C_3, C_4, C_5, C_6$ and C_9. In the configuration C_8, for the case of one independent variable, the methods are statistically equivalent according to their performance measured by the average value of R_L^2 and R_U^2. However, when the number of independent variables is 3, the null hypothesis is rejected at a significance level of 1% for all performance measures considered.

Only in the configuration C_7 the methods are statistically equivalent according to their performance measured by the average value of R_L^2 and R_U^2 regardless the number of independent variables considered, because this configuration represents an interval data with a low variability range and with a poor linear relationship due the high variability error on the midi-points.

Additionally, in all configurations, the increase of the number of independent variables produced an increase in the value of the T-Statistic. This means that the performance difference between **NM** method and **CM** method increases when the number of independent variables considered in the model increases.

Table 2. Average and standard deviation of each measure calculated from the 100 replications in the framework of a Monte Carlo experience.

Configuration	p	Statistic	$RMSE_L$		$RMSE_U$		R_L^2 (%)		R_U^2 (%)	
			CM	NM	CM	NM	CM	NM	CM	NM
1	1	$\bar{x}$	14.714	11.905	14.830	11.964	28.0	34.7	27.6	34.0
		S	1.287	0.516	1.260	0.518	6.5	6.2	5.7	6.5
	3	$\bar{x}$	21.010	11.984	20.737	12.022	47.2	59.3	47.1	59.2
		S	2.621	0.522	2.367	0.471	6.1	4.7	5.0	4.7
2	1	$\bar{x}$	10.714	6.469	10.691	6.480	51.5	63.9	51.4	64.2
		S	0.984	0.320	0.951	0.304	5.8	4.2	5.1	4.6
	3	$\bar{x}$	17.931	6.450	17.995	6.512	67.3	83.9	67.2	83.8
		S	1.754	0.313	1.748	0.304	4.8	2.4	4.0	2.2
3	1	$\bar{x}$	9.586	4.116	9.581	4.095	65.1	81.4	65.4	81.7
		S	0.622	0.208	0.589	0.215	3.6	1.9	3.9	2.1
	3	$\bar{x}$	17.224	4.102	17.390	4.151	74.3	92.8	74.5	92.8
		S	1.050	0.228	0.952	0.232	4.0	1.1	3.3	1.1
4	1	$\bar{x}$	12.418	11.615	12.371	11.589	33.4	35.7	34.6	36.4
		S	0.651	0.496	0.686	0.473	6.1	6.0	6.2	6.5
	3	$\bar{x}$	14.201	11.751	14.345	11.758	57.6	61.0	57.4	61.0
		S	1.093	0.504	1.226	0.490	4.7	4.5	4.9	4.4
5	1	$\bar{x}$	7.380	5.919	7.366	5.929	64.2	68.4	64.5	68.3
		S	0.491	0.283	0.491	0.253	4.5	4.4	4.7	3.9
	3	$\bar{x}$	10.299	5.977	10.388	6.003	80.7	85.7	80.6	85.6
		S	0.862	0.235	0.800	0.223	2.6	1.7	3.0	1.7
6	1	$\bar{x}$	5.428	3.228	5.515	3.265	82.6	87.9	82.5	87.7
		S	0.390	0.171	0.378	0.170	2.1	1.5	2.4	1.6
	3	$\bar{x}$	8.897	3.268	8.878	3.241	89.9	95.4	89.9	95.5
		S	0.570	0.168	0.566	0.158	1.6	0.7	1.4	0.6
7	1	$\bar{x}$	11.656	11.601	11.641	11.582	35.8	36.1	35.7	36.2
		S	0.472	0.449	0.441	0.440	6.0	6.1	6.1	6.1
	3	$\bar{x}$	11.765	11.581	11.763	11.572	60.5	61.1	60.5	61.1
		S	0.547	0.501	0.530	0.500	4.6	4.5	4.6	4.5
8	1	$\bar{x}$	5.940	5.820	5.913	5.811	68.1	68.9	68.4	69.0
		S	0.270	0.251	0.293	0.255	3.8	3.7	3.6	3.5
	3	$\bar{x}$	6.232	5.857	6.218	5.867	85.9	86.7	85.8	86.7
		S	0.264	0.194	0.257	0.199	1.8	1.7	1.9	1.7
9	1	$\bar{x}$	3.164	2.952	3.184	2.972	88.7	89.6	88.6	89.5
		S	0.152	0.128	0.171	0.126	1.1	1.1	1.4	1.2
	3	$\bar{x}$	3.589	2.960	3.638	2.957	95.2	96.1	95.0	96.1
		S	0.196	0.117	0.208	0.126	0.6	0.5	0.8	0.5

Now, comparing the configurations C_1, C_2, and C_3 that differ with respect to the error on the midi-points of the intervals, notice that when the variability of this error decreases, the value of the T-Statistics increases. This shows that, as much linear is the relationship between the variables as higher is statistically significant the difference between the methods. We reach the same conclusion comparing the configurations (C_4, C_5, C_6) and (C_7, C_8, C_9).

Table 3. Observed values (and corresponding p-values) of the test statistics following a Students's t distribution with 198 degrees of freedom.

Configuration	p	$RMSE_L$		$RMSE_U$		R_L^2 (%)		R_U^2 (%)	
		T	p-value	T	p-value	T	p-value	T	p-value
1	1	-20.26	0.0000	-21.04	0.0000	7.51	0.0000	7.37	0.0000
	3	-33.77	0.0000	-36.12	0.0000	15.66	0.0000	17.46	0.0000
2	1	-41.01	0.0000	-42.18	0.0000	17.10	0.0000	18.51	0.0000
	3	-64.44	0.0000	-64.72	0.0000	31.24	0.0000	36.70	0.0000
3	1	-83.45	0.0000	-87.57	0.0000	39.66	0.0000	36.84	0.0000
	3	-122.14	0.0000	-135.13	0.0000	44.30	0.0000	52.38	0.0000
4	1	-9.81	0.0000	-9.39	0.0000	2.57	0.0055	2.74	0.0034
	3	-20.35	0.0000	-19.59	0.0000	5.30	0.0000	5.47	0.0000
5	1	-25.78	0.0000	-26.02	0.0000	6.56	0.0000	6.09	0.0000
	3	-48.40	0.0000	-52.79	0.0000	16.05	0.0000	14.43	0.0000
6	1	-51.68	0.0000	-54.25	0.0000	20.20	0.0000	17.87	0.0000
	3	-94.70	0.0000	-95.90	0.0000	31.33	0.0000	36.36	0.0000
7	1	-0.83	0.2031	-0.95	0.1717	0.30	0.3805	0.52	0.3010
	3	-2.49	0.0068	-2.63	0.0047	0.86	0.1953	1.05	0.1485
8	1	-3.26	0.0007	-2.63	0.0046	1.51	0.0668	1.21	0.1136
	3	-11.43	0.0000	-10.81	0.0000	3.18	0.0008	3.57	0.0002
9	1	-10.63	0.0000	-9.98	0.0000	5.44	0.0000	4.90	0.0000
	3	-27.55	0.0000	-27.98	0.0000	11.10	0.0000	11.30	0.0000

In the other hand, comparing the configurations C_1, C_4 and C_7 that differ with respect to the variability on the range of the intervals, notice that when the interval's range decreases, the value of T-Statistics decreases too. This result is expected because if the range of the intervals approaches zero, we would have the **CM** method as an special case of the **NM** method. The same conclusion is reached comparing the configurations (C_2, C_5, C_8) and (C_3, C_6, C_9).

3.3   Cardiological Interval Data Set

This data set concerns the record of the pulse rate Y, the systolic blood pressure X_1 and diastolic blood pressure X_2 for each of eleven patients (see [3]). Table 4 shows this interval data set. The aim is to predict the interval values y of Y (the dependent variable) from x_j $(j = 1, 2)$ through a linear regression model.

Let Y^{md}, X_1^{md} and X_2^{md} continuous quantitative variable which assumes as value, respectively, the mid-points of the intervals assumed by the interval-valued variables Y, X_1 and X_2. According to the **CM** method, the fitted linear regression model on the mid-points is $Y_{md} = 21.1708 + 0.3289X_1^{md} + 0.1699X_2^{md}$. Given an example e of table 4, described by $z = ([a_1, b_1], [a_2, b_2], [y_L, y_U]$, the value $y = [y_L, y_U]$ of Y will be predicted from $\hat{y}_L = 21.1708 + 0.3289a_1 + 0.1699a_2$ and from $\hat{y}_U = 21.1708 + 0.3289b_1 + 0.1699b_2$

Let Y^r, X_1^r and X_2^r continuous quantitative variable which assumes as value, respectively, the range of the intervals assumed by the interval-valued variables

Table 4. Cardiological interval data set.

u	Pulse rate	Systolic blood pressure	Diastolic blood pressure
1	[44-68]	[90-100	[50-70]
2	[60-72]	[90-130]	[70-90]
3	[56-90]	[140-180]	[90-100]
4	[70-112]	[110-142]	[80-108
5	[54-72]	[90-100]	[50-70]
6	[70-100]	[130-160]	[80-110]
7	[63-75]	[60-100]	[140-150]
8	[72-100]	[130-160]	[76-90]
9	[76-98]	[110-190]	[70-110]
10	[86-96]	[138-180]	[90-110]
11	[86-100]	[110-150]	[78-100]

Y, X_1 and X_2. As described in section 2.2, the **NM** method fits two linear regression models, respectively, on the mid-points and range of the interval values assumed by the variable on the data set. The fitted linear regression model on the range is $Y_r = 20.2149 - 0.1467X_1^r + 0.3480X_2^r$. Given an example e of table 4, described by $z = ([a_1, b_1], [a_2, b_2], [y_L, y_U]$, the value $y = [y_L, y_U]$ of Y will be predicted from $\hat{y}_L = \hat{y}^{md} - (1/2)\hat{y}^r$ and $\hat{y}_U = \hat{y}^{md} + (1/2)\hat{y}^r$ where $\hat{y}_{md} = 21.1708 + 0.3289(a_1 + b_1)/2 + 0.1699(a_2 + b_2)/2$ and from $\hat{y}_r = 20.2149 - 0.1467(b_1 - a_1) + 0.3480(b_2 - a_2)$.

The performance of the **NM** method in comparison with the **CM** method is evaluated through the calculation of $RMSE_L$, $RMSE_U$, R_L^2 and R_U^2 measures on this cardiological interval data set. These measures evaluate the performance of the models identifying the best fit on the data set.

For the **CM** method, we have: $RMSE_L = 11.0942$, $RMSE_U = 10.4136$, $R_L^2 = 0.3029$, $R_U^2 = 0.5347$. For the **NM** method, we have: $RMSE_L = 9.8096$, $RMSE_U = 8.9414$, $R_L^2 = 0.4154$, $R_U^2 = 0.6334$. From this these results we can conclude the **NM** method outperforms **CM** method also on this cardiological interval data set.

4 Concluding Remarks

In this paper, we presented a new method to fit a linear regression model on interval-valued data. In the proposed approach, it is fitted two linear regression models, respectively, on the mid-point and range of the interval values assumed by the variables on the learning set. The prediction of the lower and upper bound of the interval value of the dependent variable is accomplished from its mid-point and range which are estimated from the fitted linear regression models applied to the mid-point and range of each interval values of the independent variables. Thus, with these two regression models it was possible the reconstruction of the intervals bounds in a more efficiency way.

The evaluation of the proposed prediction method is based on the estimation of the average behavior of *root mean squared error* and of the *determination coefficient* in the framework of a Monte Carlo experience in comparison with the method proposed by Billard and Diday [3].

The Monte Carlo simulations showed that the superiority of the method introduced in this paper, measured by the average behavior of the *root mean-squared error* and of the *determination coefficient*, when compared with the method proposed by Billard and Diday [3], was statistically significant. It was seen that the performance difference between **NM** method and **CM** method increases when the number of independent variables considered in the model increases. Additionally, we observed that as much linear is the relationship between the variables as higher is statistically significant the difference between the methods; also, these methods present an equivalent performance if the range of the intervals approaches zero. Finally, the **NM** method outperforms **CM** method also on cardiological interval data set.

Acknowledgments

The authors would like to thank CNPq and CAPES (Brazilian Agencies) for their financial support.

References

1. Bock, H.H. and Diday, E.: Analysis of Symbolic Data: Exploratory Methods for Extracting Statistical Information from Complex Data. Springer, Berlin Heidelberg (2000)
2. Alfonso, F., BIllard, L., Diday, E.: Régression Linéaire Symbolique avec Variables Taxonomiques. Actes des IVèmes journées d'Extraction et Gestion des Connaissance, EGC Clermont-Ferrand 2004, Hébrail et al. Eds, RNTI-E-2, Vol. 1 (2004) 205–210
3. Billard, L., Diday, E.: Regression Analysis for Interval-Valued Data. Data Analysis, Calssification and Related Methods: Proceedings of the Seventh Conference of the International Federation of Classification Societies, IFCS-2000, Namur (Belgium), Kiers, H.A.L. et al. Eds, Vol. 1 (2000), Springer, 369–374
4. Billard, L., Diday, E.: Symbolic Regression Analysis. Calssification, Clustering and Data Analysis: Proceedings of the Eighenth Conference of the International Federation of Classification Societies, IFCS-2002, Crakow (Poland), Jajuga, K. et al. Eds, Vol. 1 (2002), Springer, 281–288
5. Billard, L., Diday, E.: From the Statistics of Data to the Statistics of Knowledge: Symbolic Data Analysis. Journal of the American Statistical Association, Vol. 98 (2003) 470-487
6. Draper, N.R., Smith, H.: Applied Regression Analysis. John Wiley, New York (1981)
7. Marsaglia, G.: Uniform Random Number Generators. Journ. Assoc. for Computing Machin-ery, Vol. 12 (1965), 83-89
8. Montgomery, D.C., Peck, E.A.: Introduction to Linear Regression Analysis. John Wiley, New York (1982)
9. Scheffé, H.: The Analysis of Variance. John Wiley, New York, (1959)

Specifying Abnormal Action Qualifications with Sensing in FLUX

Yves Martin

Technische Universität Dresden
D-01062 Dresden, Germany
ym1@inf.tu-dresden.de

Abstract. Planning agents in real-world environments have to face the Qualification Problem, i.e., the failure of an action execution due to unexpected circumstances. Sensing actions are used to derive additional state knowledge. We present a high-level programming method to combine these two approaches in the agent programming language FLUX, which builds on the general action representation formalism of the Fluent Calculus. It is shown how this combination allows for an efficient reasoning about the causes of unexpected action failures. The explanations for an action failure help an agent to recover from unexpectedly failed plans.

1 Introduction

One of the major goals of Cognitive Robotics research is the design of autonomous agents, including robots, that explore partially known and dynamic environments and act sensibly under incomplete information. These demands require high-level cognitive capabilities of reasoning and planning. Using a mental model of the state of their environment allows for the agents to solve complex tasks. They can calculate in advance the outcome of different action sequences and then choose the best plan to execute for a specific goal in mind. During the execution of a plan, agents constantly update their internal world model to reflect the changes they have effected with their actions. Additionally, they can acquire and interpret sensor information and reason about the current status of their sensors in combination with previously observed facts.

Autonomous agents in real-world environments inevitably face the Qualification Problem: The executability of an action can never be predicted with absolute certainty; at any time, actions may fail due to unexpected circumstances [11]. Nevertheless, a planning agent would never get to really perform an action if it would reason about all conceivable causes for an action to fail. Rather, a rational agent needs to devise plans under the assumption that the world will behave as expected. On the other hand, an agent, which is aware of these assumptions, is able to reason about the explanations for unexpected failures encountered during the execution of a plan. In some cases, the knowledge of these default assumptions is not sufficient. If there is still uncertainty about the exact reason for the failure, an agent may use sensing actions to improve its state knowledge. In this

S. Biundo, T. Frühwirth, and G. Palm (Eds.): KI 2004, LNAI 3238, pp. 307–321, 2004.

way, the agent can further narrow the possible set of explanations. The use of the sensors should be efficient, i.e., with a minimum number of sensing actions a maximum number of possible explanations should be ruled out. Finally, with the newly acquired and integrated sensor information, the agent should search again to find a recovery plan.

Based on a formal account of the Qualification Problem [17], an approach to this problem in the high-level programming method FLUX has been developed and presented in [9, 8]. The high-level programming language FLUX (the Fluent Executor [18]) allows the design of intelligent agents that reason and plan on the basis of the Fluent Calculus which is a predicate logic formalism for reasoning about actions and change [15]. FLUX provides the crucial concept of an explicit state representation. Other existing agent programming methods like GOLOG [6] or the robot control language developed in [14] miss this concept and therefore have to regress the entire history of actions back to the initial situation to infer the current knowledge state of an agent. The computational effort for doing this will increase as the agent proceeds, so that the use of regression does not scale up well to long-term agent control [18]. Furthermore, these high-level programming languages and other planning systems, such as [10, 3], did not attempt to address the Qualification Problem. Other approaches, such as [1], can deal with noisy sensors and effectors but are not able to handle and reason about default assumptions.

In this paper, we present an approach which combines the generation of explanations in case of an unexpected action failure and the use of sensing actions to narrow the computed results to the most detailed explanation which can be obtained. We use a simplified method, compared with [9], to infer all possible explanations for an action failure. With the resulting set of possible explanations at hand, the agent searches for the shortest sequence of sensing actions which rules out the maximum number of conceivable explanations from this set. Afterwards, our agent program executes the sensing actions and integrates the resulting new information in the current knowledge state. Finally, the agent replans to reach the goal despite the abnormal circumstances and executes the computed sequence of actions, if there is any. As our system is based on formal methods in the Fluent Calculus, it provides a declarative approach to execution monitoring and troubleshooting. Being rooted in a logic formalism for reasoning about action and change, our approach allows to reason about more than a single state of the system. Instead, observations concerning a system's state prior, during, and after the execution of a series of actions can be taken into account. The formal basis in an action theory also helps towards fully determining the cause of an observed system failure with sensing actions.

The rest of the paper is organized as follows. In Section 2, the core concepts of the programming methodology FLUX are introduced. We then give very briefly the theoretical account of the Qualification Problem in the Fluent Calculus. In Section 4, we show the approach to the Qualification Problem and to sensing in FLUX. Section 5 describes the combination of both methods which provides for an efficient reasoning about possible explanations. In Section 6, we give a summary of our results.

The FLUX system and the example agent program are available for download at our web site: www.fluxagent.org

2 FLUX

The example agent program in this paper is set in the well-known artificial environment blocks-world. Here an autonomous robot equipped with a gripper and two sensors, one to check the status of the battery and one sensor to recognize the condition of a block, should shuffle around blocks. The robot is given the partially unknown initial situation and a partially specified goal situation. Using this information, the robot should solve the planning problem.

To develop an agent for this scenario, we use the high-level programming method FLUX, which is grounded in the action theory of the Fluent Calculus. The Fluent Calculus is a many-sorted predicate logic language with four standard sorts: FLUENT, STATE, ACTION, and SIT (for situations) [15]. States are composed of fluents (as atomic states) using the standard function $\circ$: STATE $\times$ STATE $\mapsto$ STATE and constant $\emptyset$: STATE (denoting the empty state). The program for our agent, for example, uses these two fluents: $On(x, y)$, representing that the block x stands on block y (for the sake of efficiency the *Table* is also considered to be a block), and $Clear(x)$, denoting that no other block stands on block x. Similarly as in the Situation Calculus [13], the constant S_0 denotes the initial situation and $Do(a, s)$ the situation after having performed action a in situation s. The state of a situation s is denoted by the standard function $State(s)$. For example, an initial state in the blocks-world may be axiomatized as[1]

$$(\exists z)\,(State(S_0) = On(A, D) \circ On(B, \mathit{Table}) \circ On(C, \mathit{Table}) \circ$$
$$On(D, \mathit{Table}) \circ Clear(A) \circ Clear(B) \circ Clear(C) \circ Clear(\mathit{Table}) \circ z \wedge \qquad (1)$$
$$(\forall x, y)\,\neg Holds(On(x, y), z))$$

The reader may notice that an incomplete state has been specified, i.e., the sub-STATE z may contain many more fluents, but no more On fluents. The foundational axioms of the Fluent Calculus ensure that the composition function "$\circ$" exhibits the properties of the union function for sets (with $\emptyset$ as the empty set), so that a state is identified with all the fluents that hold. On this basis, the macros $Holds(f, z)$ and $Holds(f, s)$ are defined as follows:

$$Holds(f, z) \overset{\text{def}}{=} (\exists z')\, z = f \circ z'$$
$$Holds(f, s) \overset{\text{def}}{=} Holds(f, State(s))$$

In our scenario, there is the action: $Move(r, u, v, w)$, denoting the movement of the block u from block v onto block w by robot r. The fundamental frame problem is solved in the Fluent Calculus by a so-called *state update axiom* for

---

[1] Predicate and function symbols, including constants, start with a capital letter whereas variables are in lower case. Free variables in formulas are assumed universally quantified. Variables of sorts FLUENT, STATE, ACTION, and SIT shall be denoted by letters f, z, a, and s, respectively. The function $\circ$ is written in infix notation.

each action, which describes the effects of the action in terms of the difference between the states before and after the execution of it. For example, the action $Move(r, u, v, w)$ can be specified as,

$$Poss(Move(r, u, v, w), s) \supset$$
$$w = Table \wedge State(Do(Move(r, u, v, w), s)) =$$
$$State(s) - On(u, v) + On(u, w) \circ Clear(v) \quad \vee \quad \text{(2)}$$
$$w \neq Table \wedge State(Do(Move(r, u, v, w), s)) =$$
$$State(s) - On(u, v) \circ Clear(w) + On(u, w) \circ Clear(v)$$

where "$-$" and "$+$" are macros for fluent removal and addition; and the macro $Poss(a, s) \overset{\text{def}}{=} Poss(a, State(s))$ denoting in the Fluent Calculus that action a is possible in state $State(s)$. Recall specification (1), and suppose, for the sake of argument, that $Poss(Move(Robot, B, Table, C), S_0)$. Then the state update axiom for $Move$ in (2) implies

$$State(Do(Move(Robot, B, Table, C), S_0)) = State(S_0) \circ On(B, C) \circ$$
$$Clear(Table) -$$
$$On(B, Table) \circ Clear(C)$$

Replacing $State(S_0)$ by an equal term according to (1) yields, after applying the macro for negative effects and performing simplification,

$$(\exists z) State(Do(Move(Robot, B, Table, C), S_0)) = On(A, D) \circ On(B, C) \circ \quad \text{(3)}$$
$$On(C, Table) \circ On(D, Table) \circ Clear(A) \circ Clear(B) \circ Clear(Table) \circ z$$

We have now obtained from an incomplete initial specification a still partial description of the successor state, which also includes fluents unaffected by the action. Moreover, knowledge specified in (1) as to which fluents do not hold in z applies to the new state, which includes z, just as well.

To reflect the incomplete knowledge of an agent about its environment, incomplete states are encoded in FLUX as open lists, that is, lists with a variable tail, of fluents [18]. These lists are accompanied by constraints both for negated and disjunctive state knowledge as well as for variable range restrictions. The constraints are of the form $NotHolds(f, z)$, indicating that fluent f does not hold in state z; $NotHoldsAll(f, z)$, indicating that no instance of f holds in z; and $Or\_Holds([f_1, \ldots, f_n], z)$, indicating that at least one of the fluents $f_1, \ldots, f_n$ holds in state z. In order to process these constraints, so-called declarative Constraint Handling Rules [4] have been defined and proved correct under the foundational axioms of the Fluent Calculus (for details see [18]).

Consider, for example, the initial state of (1) for our robot in FLUX:

```
init(Z0) :- Z0=[on(a,d),on(d,table),on(c,table),on(b,table),
            clear(a),clear(c),clear(b),clear(table)|_],
         consistent(Z0), duplicate_free(Z0).
```

The predicate $Consistent(z)$ verifies that all domain constraints[2] are fulfilled. For example, it would contain the constraint $NotHoldsAll(On(x, x), z)$ to account for

---

[2] Domain constraints formalize properties a state term must satisfy in order to represent a state that can actually occur in the world.

the impossibility of a block standing on itself in the real world. The auxiliary constraint $Duplicate\_Free(z)$ stipulates that list z does not contain multiple occurrences.

As in the Fluent Calculus, the effects of actions are encoded as state update axioms. For this purpose, the FLUX kernel provides a definition of the auxiliary predicate $Update(z_1, \vartheta^+, \vartheta^-, z_2)$. Its intuitive meaning is that state z_2 is the result of positive and negative effects ϑ^+ and ϑ^-, respectively, wrt. state z_1. In other words, the predicate encodes the state equation $z_2 = (z_1 - \vartheta^-) + \vartheta^+$. On this basis, the agent programmer can easily implement the update axioms by clauses which define the predicate $StateUpdate(z_1, a, z_2)$, as for example in the following encoding for the action $Move(r, u, v, w)$,

```
state_update(Z1,move(R,U,V,W),Z2)  :-
  W=table ->
  update(Z1,[on(U,W),clear(V)],[on(U,V)],Z2);
  update(Z1,[on(U,W),clear(V)],[on(U,V),clear(W)],Z2).
```

where the Eclipse-Prolog operator -> implements an if-then-else construction with an implicit cut.

Precondition axioms are realized in the Fluent Calculus by defining a macro $Poss(a, s)$ for each action. Consider, for example, the following axiom for our example action $Move(r, u, v, w)$ [3]:

$$Poss(Move(r, u, v, w), s) \equiv$$
$$u \neq w \wedge u \neq Table \wedge v \neq w \wedge Holds(On(u, v), s) \wedge$$
$$Holds(Clear(u), s) \wedge Holds(Clear(w), s) \wedge$$
$$\neg Holds(Ab(Movable(u)), s) \wedge \neg Holds(Ab(Functioning(Gripper\text{-}of(r))), s)$$
$$\tag{4}$$

The concept of knowing properties of the state is essential for the evaluation of conditions in agent programs under incomplete information. To account for this incomplete knowledge of an agent about its environment and still have a tractable implementation of knowledge, conditioning in FLUX is based on the foundational predicate $Knows(f, z)$, representing that the agent knows that fluent f holds in state z [16]. Thus, the precondition axiom (4) is implemented as follows:

```
poss(move(R,U,V,W),Z) :- robot(R), block(U),
 block(V), block(W), U\=W, U\=table, V\=W,
 knows(on(U,V),Z), knows(clear(U),Z),
 knows(clear(W),Z),\+ knows(ab(movable,U),Z),
 \+ knows(ab(functioning,R),Z).
```

The auxiliary predicates $Robot(r)$ and $Block(b)$ are used to denote the defined robots r or blocks b, respectively. The $Move$ action can only be executed if there are no abnormal circumstances regarding the moved block or the gripper of the robot. The fluents denoting abnormal qualifications, which are inferred to be not known using the standard Prolog operator for the principle of negation-as-failure, are explained in the next section.

---

[3] In the light of the approach to abnormal qualifications in Section 3, fluents denoting abnormal qualifications like $Ab(Movable(u))$ are already included in this axiom.

3   Qualifications in the Fluent Calculus

The theoretical account of the Qualification Problem introduces the special function $Ab(x)$ whose range is the sort FLUENT. The argument, x, denotes properties like $Movable(u)$, and $Functioning(Gripper\text{-}of(r))$, indicating that a block u cannot be moved by the gripper and that the gripper r is malfunctioning, respectively. Abnormalities are of sort FLUENT, because they represent properties of states that, once there, do not change unless by actions which effect such a change.

Instances of the general 'abnormality' fluent Ab are utilized to stand for the abnormal qualifications of actions. These qualifications are a priori unlikely to happen and therefore need to be assumed away by default in order to jump to the conclusion that the action is possible under normal circumstances. Thus, for an action to be executable, these obstacles should not be present and accordingly the precondition axiom for our example action $Move$ is specified as shown in Section 2.

Abnormal qualifications that are the result of the execution of an action and thus are caused by the agent himself are not assumed away by default. These fluents will occur as an (possibly indirect) effect of an action and therefore these abnormalities do not arise unexpectedly; this constitutes a solution to the general problem of anomalous models (for details see [17]).

To account for abnormal qualifications other than those caused by the agent, instances of Ab are allowed to become true during any situation transition as a side effect of the mere fact that the very transition takes place. For this reason, the Fluent Calculus employs the notion of causal relationships and ramifications. A causal relationship is formally specified with the help of the expression $Causes(\epsilon, \varrho, z, s)$ where ϵ (the *triggering effect*) and ϱ (the *ramification*, i.e., indirect effect) are possibly negated atomic fluent formulas and z is a state and s a situation. The intuitive meaning is that the change to ϵ causes the change to ϱ in state z and situation s. Additional causal relationships allow for instances of $Ab(x)$ to occur as indirect effects of actions, which are not conditioned on any direct effects but only on the predicate $AbCaused(x, s)$. This predicate models abnormalities other than those caused by the agent, and it indicates that in the current situation the property x is the result of an exogenous cause:

$$AbCaused(x, s) \wedge \neg Holds(Ab(x), z) \supset Causes(\epsilon, Ab(x), z, s)$$

This is to say, whenever the predicate $AbCaused(x, s)$ is true for a property, for example $Movable(A)$, in situation s, and the abnormality fluent $Ab(Movable(A))$ is not already part of state z, then during the ramification this fluent would become true as a side-effect of the action. Due to space restrictions, the reader is referred to [17, 9] for details.

Whenever abnormal qualifications are not caused by an action, they should be minimized. This assumption of normal circumstances has to be realized by a non-monotonic theory, that means, appropriate default rules in the sense of [12] are used in the formal approach to the Qualification Problem. In this way, the Fluent Calculus gets embedded into a default theory. Formally, 'unexpected' abnormalities are minimized by default rules of the following form, which is prerequisite-free and normal,

$$\frac{:\neg AbCaused_{(x,s)}}{\neg AbCaused_{(x,s)}} \tag{5}$$

A second default assumption concerns abnormalities of any kind in the initial situation:

$$\frac{:\neg Holds(Ab(x),S_0)}{\neg Holds(Ab(x),S_0)} \tag{6}$$

If, for example, the observations suggest no abnormalities initially, then the underlying default theory admits a unique extension (in the sense of [12]), which includes $(\forall x) \neg Holds(Ab(x), S_0)$. If later on an observation contradicts this assumption, the default theory grants different extensions, each of them leading to an explanation for the action failure [17].

Besides abnormalities, which are persistent qualifications, the formal account of the Qualification Problem also introduces accidents. Accidents are considered to be failures which do not normally recur and therefore, do not persist. They are denoted by $Acc(c, s)$ where c represents a function symbol of sort ACCIDENT. Consider, for example, $Acc(Grasp(x), s)$, indicating an accident while trying to grasp block x in situation s. Accidents are only postulated in retrospect and never predicted to persist: It is always rational for an agent to assume that actions have their intended effects as long as the observations are in line with this assumption. Accidents are assumed away by defaults of the following form,

$$\frac{:\neg Acc_{(x,s)}}{\neg Acc_{(x,s)}} \tag{7}$$

and only used when there is a need to explain unexpected observation. For such cases, accidents are specified in state update axioms to denote that the normal effects of an action do not materialize. Consider, for example, the following partially specified state update axiom for $Move$,

$$Poss(Move(r, u, v, w), s) \supset$$

$$\begin{aligned}
&\cdots \\
&w \neq Table \wedge \\
&(\neg Acc(Grasp(u), s) \wedge State(Do(Move(r, u, v, w), s))) = \\
&\quad State(s) - On(u,v) \circ Clear(w) + On(u,w) \circ Clear(v) \\
&\vee \\
&Acc(Grasp(u), s) \wedge State(Do(Move(r, u, v, w), s)) = \\
&\quad State(s) - On(u,v) + On(u, Table) \circ Clear(v))
\end{aligned} \tag{8}$$

where the second disjunct describes what happens if an accident occurs. In this case, block u is removed from block v but instead of landing on block w it ends up on the table. The possibility to explain unexpected effects as accidents may help a planning agent quickly recover from an observed action failure. If an accident is assumed to be the explanation, then the agent can predict that it will succeed with simply retrying the crucial action.

4   Sensing and Qualifications in FLUX

In the first subsection, the FLUX approach to sensing actions is briefly reca-
pitulated (for details we refer to [16]). In the second subsection, we present a
simplified approach to the Qualification Problem based on [9]. We show that our
method works for strong qualifications, i.e., where action cannot be executed at
all as well as for weak qualifications, i.e., where the execution of actions do not
achieve all intended effects. For this paper, we make the assumption that the
sensors of our agent function properly and therefore all observations are correct.

4.1   Sensing Actions in FLUX

Reasoning about actions which involve sensing is specified in FLUX by so-called
knowledge update axioms [16]. These axioms are defined just like ordinary state
update axioms having an additional argument, which encodes sensor information. Thus, the first part of the update, the physical effect, is inferred exactly in
the way as discussed in Section 2. Afterwards, the second part of the update, involves the evaluation of the sensing result. For this evaluation, knowledge update
axioms are formulated in such a way that they restrict the possible states after
the integration of a sensing result so as to agree with the actual state of the world
on the sensed properties. Take, for example, the sensing action $Sense(r, Battery)$
to check if the battery of the robot is low. This pure sensing action has no physical effect but if, say, the action delivers the sensing result $True$, this entails the
abnormality $Ab(Functioning(Gripper\text{-}of(r)))$. In FLUX, the knowledge update
is encoded as follows, where abnormalities are encoded in FLUX in a flattened
form to ensure the correct treatment by the FLUX constraint solver:

```
state_update(Z1,sense(R,battery),Z1,[Bat]) :-
 Bat==true, holds(ab(function_gripper,R),Z1);
 Bat==false, not_holds(ab(function_gripper,R),Z1).
```

The last argument transfers the perceived sensor information with which the new
state has to agree. If, for example, the sensor indicates a low battery, the predicate *Holds*, which is defined in the FLUX kernel [18], ensures that the current
state includes the abnormal qualification fluent $Ab(Functioning(Gripper\text{-}of(r)))$.
The sensor information is generated by the environment (in our example scenario
by a simulator).

4.2   Constructing Extensions

For our FLUX approach, all accidents and abnormalities other than those caused
by the agent, are assumed away by default for the initial state and during planning. Therefore, our agent devises its plan by assuming that the world will behave
as expected during the plan execution later on. To reflect this, only the standard
predicate *StateUpdate* is used in planning.

    If one of the action in the planned sequence nonetheless unexpectedly fails
during the execution, extensions of the underlying default theory have to be constructed. For the sake of efficiency, the arising of an abnormality is not actually

inferred by ramification in FLUX but simply asserted. This is possible because
the progression of the internal world model ensures that this assertion does not
have an effect on the past, where this abnormality has been assumed away by
default when checking preconditions. For an efficient encoding of state update
axioms with unusual effects, the standard predicate *StateUpdate* is accompanied
by a new predicate *AbStateUpdate*, by which accidental effects of an action or
abnormalities regarding the execution of an action are specified. Writing state
update axioms in this fashion avoids the explicit encoding of the underlying default theory. Instead, the SLDNF-resolution with backtracking as the standard
inference mechanism of the used Eclipse-Prolog system yields all possible extensions (for details see [8, 7]). The order of alternative explanations implicitly
given in a state update axiom defines a preference ordering among accidents and
abnormalities. Exploiting the fixed computation strategy of Prolog allows for an
efficient implementation and avoids the explicit encoding of so-called *prioritized
defaults* [2, 17]. Take, for example, the instance of *AbStateUpdate* for the action
Move which is implemented as follows:

```
ab_state_update(Z1,move(R,U,V,_),Z2,[S]):-
 S=false,
 ((V\=table ->
     update(Z1, [acc(grasp,U),on(U,table),clear(V)],[on(U,V)],Z2);
     update(Z1, [acc(grasp,U)], [], Z2));
 holds(ab(movable,U),Z1), Z2=Z1;
 holds(ab(function_gripper, R),Z1), Z2=Z1).
```

An accident concerning the block u will be generated as the first explanation,
only afterwards abnormalities regarding block u and the gripper of robot r will
be assumed. In order to distinguish between normal and the unusual updates
for the action *Move*, the axiom has been extended by a sensing component. The
last parameter denotes the execution status of the action, if it was successful or
not. If the sensing result indicates an 'abnormal' execution, then the predicate
AbStateUpdate will be used.

During the execution of a plan, observations, i.e., sensing results, are obtained
by the predicate $Perform(a, \boldsymbol{y})$, denoting the execution of action a with perceived
sensor values $\boldsymbol{y}$ in the simulator. These observations are evaluated against the
internal model whenever this clause is applied,

```
execute(A,Z1,Z2)  :-
 perform(A,Y)    ->
   (Z1=[sit(S)|Z], ! ; S=[], Z=Z1 ),
   (state_update(Z,A,Z3,Y); ab_res([(A,Y)|S],Z3)),
   !, Z2=[sit([(A,Y)|S])|Z3].
```

where the predicate $Execute(a, z_1, z_2)$ denotes the execution of plan a in state z_1
reaching state z_2. The sensing values $\boldsymbol{y}$, which are the result of performing action
a, are integrated in the internal world model when resolving $StateUpdate(z_1, a,$
$z_2, \boldsymbol{y})$. If the observation contradicts the world model, then $StateUpdate$ fails. The
inconsistency has to be resolved and therefore, the predicate $AbRes$ is executed
and generates explanations which bring the new unexpected observation into
accord with world model again. To this end, each action and its corresponding

observation is recorded and added to the world model using the special fluent sit as shown above.

The predicate *AbRes* infers explanations which explain the observations and is implemented as:

```
ab_res([],Z) :- init(Z).
ab_res([(A,Y)|S],Z) :- ab_res(S,Z1),
 (state_update(Z1,A,Z,Y); ab_state_update(Z1,A,Z,Y)).
```

The first argument of this predicate is a sequence of pairs $(a_n, y_n), \ldots, (a_1, y_1)$ such that the situation $Do(a_n, \ldots, Do(a_1, S_0))$ is the one that contradicts the world model by an unexpected observation, and $y_1, \ldots, y_n$ encode the sensing results obtained in the course of this action history. An instance $AbRes(\sigma, z)$ is true if the state z is reached from the initial state by a sequence of updates according to the actions and observations in $\sigma = (a_n, y_n), \ldots, (a_1, y_1)$. The order of the alternative updates as specified in the clauses of *AbRes* determines a preference relation. The first computed answer of *AbRes* will assume a normal execution, using just regular updates via *StateUpdate*. Only if this is inconsistent with the observation, the computed answer will postulate accidents or abnormalities using the predicate *AbStateUpdate*, where later qualifications are generally preferred. Additionally, the ordering also respects the minimality requirement of extensions, only if one accident or abnormality is not sufficient to explain the observation, then larger explanations are generated.

Let N be the total number of actions performed so far, and let the maximum number of possible accidents or abnormalities for one action be k. Then at worst, our algorithm will take time $O(N^{k+1})$ for computing one explanation. In practice we have found that an average of 3 accidents or abnormalities per action is almost always sufficient, in which case the algorithm remains polynomial in complexity, $O(N^4)$ in fact. Furthermore, errors are more likely to occur at the end of the action history and our algorithm works backwards from the end, so that the computation is very fast.

5   Combining the Methods

In this section, we combine the approach to the Qualification Problem and to sensing actions in a concise and modular way. The explanation of unexpected action failures and the search for the shortest sensing action sequence to make this explanation more precise is carried out on the basis of the same techniques which are used in planning. There is no need of any special theorem prover. We also demonstrate our approach with the help of an example.

The robot begins by defining the initial state and the verification that this state is consistent wrt. the domain constraints. Afterwards, the goal state is defined and the planning algorithm is put into execution to solve the planning problem. During the planning process all qualifications are assumed away by default. Thus, the robot devises its plans under the assumption that the world will behave as expected. We use a forward-chaining planner where iterative deepening is applied as search strategy. Some simple heuristics are applied to cut down the search space.

After the planning algorithm has computed a plan, this sequence of actions is executed step by step. The execution of each action is monitored. If all actions can be executed without abnormal circumstances then the goal state will be reached and no additional computations are needed. In this case, our approach will behave like any other system without the ability to react to unexpected action failures.

If an action surprisingly fails then an abnormal qualification must have occurred. If so, the approach in Subsection 4.2 is used to compute the set of all possible explanations for this unexpected observation. For the intended applications of the system, we assume that all explanations have the same prior probabilities or it is impractical to determine the differences beforehand. When the generation of explanations is completed, the resulting set of different explanations is logically a big disjunction, each disjunct corresponding to one extension of the underlying default theory. This new disjunctive state knowledge is added to the current state. In our system, the constraint *Or_Holds* is used, which encodes the set of possible explanations as a list of disjuncts. The implementation is as follows,

```
findall(Z,ab_res([(A,Y)|S],Z),ZL),
transform(ZL,LE), or_holds(LE,Z0)
```

where the predicate *FindAll* is a built-in Prolog predicate and computes a set of solutions. The result is a list l_1 of different states containing each one possible explanation, and the auxiliary predicate $Transform(l_1, l_2)$ simply extracts only the explanations to a new list l_2.

At this point, the robot is planning a sequence of sensing actions which would render the new disjunctive state knowledge more precise. Taking the current state and this new state knowledge into account, the planning algorithm is searching for sensing actions. These actions should be of such kind that would rule out the maximum number of possible explanations in order to obtain a short plan. In this search process it is assumed that the currently considered sensing action in question will not point out any abnormalities and thus eliminates possible explanations. Recall, for example, the sensing action $Sense(r, Battery)$ of Subsection 4.1. If one assumes that the sensing result of this action yields $False$, then this would render one explanation, namely, $Ab(Functioning(Gripper\text{-}of(r)))$ impossible. On the other hand, if in the real execution of a sensing action later on the sensing result implies an abnormal qualification, then the appropriate explanation is found immediately. The search process for this sequence of sensing actions is again based on the same action specifications and state update axioms as in the planning to reach a goal. For the former, the difference lies only in the restriction to sensing actions and the use of a different heuristic, i.e., the reduction of disjunctive knowledge. This process is encoded using the predicate $FindSense(z_0, s, n)$, denoting the sequence of sensing actions s that would rule out n explanations from the disjunctive state knowledge in state z_0:

```
findall([N,S],findsense(Z0,S,N),L), select(L,P)
```

The auxiliary predicate $Select(l, s)$ takes the resulting list l, where each element is a list of a sequence of sensing actions s together with the corresponding number of eliminated explanations n, and selects the best plan p with the highest number.

Afterwards, the robot executes the selected plan of sensing actions. This is realized by the predicate $Execute$. The perceived sensor information is integrated in the current state using knowledge update axioms as explained in Subsection 4.1. After the sensing has finished, the set of possible explanations has been reduced, and the current state has becomes the new initial state for the altered planning problem. Then, the planning algorithm is executed to find a new plan despite the encountered abnormality. The determined explanation for the action failure helps this planning process. If a new plan has been found it is executed again step by step.

The following results of our experiments in a blocks-world scenario have shown that our approach is able to generate a set of explanations for unexpected action failures, to restrict this set to one abnormality and to recover from the failure of the action in the end.

For the initial state we take the state term specified in Section 2. As a partially specified goal state we use the list `[on(a,b),on(b,c)]`, denoting as a goal the existence of a tower of blocks where block A is on the top and block C is the lowest block. With this information the planning algorithm of the robot has devised the following correct plan:

`[move(robot,b,table,c), move(robot,a,d,b)]`

Thus, our robot wants to move block B from the $Table$ onto block C at first. Afterwards, it would like to move block A from block D onto block B which would solve the planning problem.

At this point, the robot executes the two actions one after the other in our blocks-world simulator. The first action is completed successfully. The second action does not execute normally in the simulator. How is this observation explained in the Fluent Calculus? Let $S_1 = Do(Move(Robot, B, Table, C), S_0)$ and $State(S_1)$ be given by equation (3). If the observation $\neg Poss(Move(Robot, A, D, B), S_1)$ is added, then together with precondition axiom (4) the underlying default theory admits two kinds of extensions. In one extension all defaults are applied except for instance $AbCaused(Movable(A), S_1)$ of (5) while the other extension is obtained by applying all defaults except the instance of (5) with substitution $\{x/Functioning(Gripper\text{-}of(Robot)), y/S_1\}$. On the other hand, if the observation suggests a weak qualification, formally expressed as $Holds(On(A, Table), Do(Move(Robot, A, D, B), S_1))$, then the default theory together with state update axiom (8) has a unique extension, where all defaults are part of the extension except for the instance $Acc(Grasp(A), Do(Move(Robot, A, D, B), S_1))$ of (7).

In our approach in FLUX, the same explanations are now inferred as in the Fluent Calculus. The computation proceeds on the same techniques used in the planning algorithm and without the explicit need to calculate default extensions or ramifications:

```
?- init(Z0), execute(move(robot,b,table,c),Z0,Z1),
   findall(Z,ab_res([(move(robot,a,d,b),[false]),
```

```
                      (move(robot,a,d,b),[true])], Z), ZL),
   transform(ZL,LE),or_holds(LE,Z1).
```

```
LE = [acc(grasp,a),ab(movable,a),ab(function_gripper,robot)]
```

The resulting set contains three possible qualifications which are: Either block
A could not have been moved or the gripper did not function properly or an
accident has happened while being grasped by the gripper. The reader may
notice that the two abnormalities are strong qualifications in the sense that the
last action could not be executed, i.e., had no effect at all. For the accident as
explanation it is a weak qualification because block A was not moved onto block
B but an unexpected effect happened, i.e., it fall from block D onto the *Table*.

The robot is now searching for an sensing action which would rule out as
much as possible of the above qualifications in case that its execution shows
no abnormalities. The robot has two sensors and two general sensing actions at
its disposition. $Sense(r, Battery)$ was defined above. If this check of the battery
status would show a normal battery then this result would preclude the explanation $Ab(Functioning(Gripper\text{-}of(Robot)))$ from the above list. Another possible
sensing action is $Sense(r, Block(x))$, delivering the position and the status of
block x. It is encoded as:

```
state_update(Z1,sense(_,block(X)),Z1,[Mov,Grasp]) :-
 Mov==true, Grasp==true, holds(ab(movable,X), Z1),holds(acc(grasp,X),Z1);
 Mov==true, Grasp==false, holds(ab(movable,X), Z1);
 Mov==false, Grasp==true, holds(acc(grasp,X), Z1);
 not_holds(ab(movable,X), Z1), not_holds(acc(grasp,X), Z1).
```

If this generic action applied with instance $\{x/A\}$ would show no abnormalities,
the explanations $Ab(Movable(A)), Acc(Grasp(A))$ could not be true in the real
world. This sensing action would specify the explanation for the state z_1 above
in the most precise way and therefore our robot selects it for execution:

```
?- findall([N,S],findsense(Z1,S,N),L), select(L,P), execute(P,Z1,Z2).
```

```
P = [sense(robot, block(a))]
```

```
Simulator: Mov==false, Grasp==true      (acc(grasp,a) true)
New plan:   [move(robot,a,table,b)]
```

```
Simulator: Mov==false, Grasp==false     (ab(function_gripper,robot) true)
New plan:   [charge(robot,battery),move(robot,a,d,b)]
```

Now the real sensing result of this sensing action depends on the simulator.
Above, we have shown two possible runs, one after the other. For the first run,
the accident $Acc(Grasp(A))$ has occurred in the real world. The robot uses this
information to find a recovery plan where he just looks for block A on the *Table*
and moves it onto block B. As an accident is not a persistent qualification, it
is assumed to not recur. The second experiment shows that sensing the block A
resulted in no qualifications and therefore the battery must have been low. The
robot uses the instance $Charge(Robot, Battery)$ of action $Charge(r, b)$ to resolve
this problem, where the action is encoded as:

```
state_update(Z1,charge(R,B),Z2,[]):-cancel(ab(function_gripper,R),Z1,Z2).
```

The predicate *Cancel* is provided by the flux kernel and used to cancel partial information about a fluent which is no longer entailed by the state specification at hand [18]. Here, it has the effect that the abnormality will no longer be known, but it is not explicitly false so that later on it can be asserted again if the observations suggest so.

In both cases, our robot is able to recover from the action failure and can finally solve the planning problem.

6   Discussion

We have presented an approach in the agent programming language FLUX which is able to cope with unexpected failures of action during the execution of a plan. Our method constitutes a combination of an approach to the Qualification Problem in FLUX and the realization of state knowledge and sensing actions in FLUX.

Our method allows for the generation of plans under the assumption that actions succeed as they normally do, and to reason about these assumptions in order to recover from unexpected action failures. For this reasoning process our system is able to generate sets of possible explanations and to find the shortest possible sequence of sensing actions that renders this disjunctive state knowledge about the possible explanations more precise. Furthermore, our agent program can integrate this new knowledge into its internal world model and deliver a recovery plan, if there is one.

While other agent programming methods have been extended by execution monitoring in the past, e.g., [5], our system is the first which is based on a formal approach to the Qualification Problem. It thus provides a declarative approach to troubleshooting.

The crucial advantage of our approach is that both the search for explanations for unexpected action failures and the search for sensing actions to explain the observation in more detail are carried out on the basis of the same action specification and reasoning techniques which are used in planning.

Although our approach can reason about very general abnormalities, suitable for all environments, to be of greater help for the replanning agent our method should be combined with ontology learning for explanations in the future.

Acknowledgements

I want to thank my supervisor Michael Thielscher, Yi Jin and all members of the FLUX Group at Technische Universität Dresden for many fruitful discussions about this work. Three anonymous reviewers provided helpful comments on this article for which I am grateful.

References

1. Fahiem Bacchus, Joseph Y. Halpern, and Hector J. Levesque. Reasoning about Noisy Sensors and Effectors in the Situation Calculus. Artificial Intelligence, 111(1–2):171–208, 1999.

2. Gerhard Brewka. Adding priorities and specificity to default logic. In C. MacNish, D.Pearce, and L.M. Pereira, editors, Proceedings of the European Workshop on Logics in AI (JELIA), volume 838 of LNAI, pages 247–260, York, UK, September 1994, Springer.
3. Patrick Doherty, Joakim Gustafsson, Lars Karlsson, and Jonas Kvarnstrom. Temporal action logics (TAL): Language specification and tutorial. Electronic Transactions on Artificial Intelligence, 2(3–4):273–306, 1998. URL: http://www.ep.liu.se/ea/cis/1998/015/.
4. Thom Fr-uhwirth. Theory and practice of constraint handling rules. Journal of Logic Programming, 37(1–3):95–138, 1998.
5. Giuseppe De Giacomo, Ray Reiter, and Mikhail Soutchanski. Execution monitoring of high-level robot programs. In Cohn, Schubert, and Shapiro, editors, Proceedings of the International Conference on Principles of Knowledge Representation and Reasoning (KR), pages 453–464, Trento, Italy, June 1998.
6. Hector J. Levesque, Raymond Reiter, Yves Lesperance, Fangzhen Lin, and Richard B. Scherl. GOLOG: A logic programming language for dynamic domains. Journal of Logic Programming, 31(1–3):59–83, 1997.
7. John W. Lloyd. Foundations of Logic Programming. Series Symbolic Computation. Springer, second, extended edition, 1987.
8. Yves Martin. Solving the Qualification Problem in FLUX. Master's thesis, TU Dresden, Germany, March 2001. URL: http://www.cl.inf.tu-dresden.de/ yves.
9. Yves Martin and Michael Thielscher. Adressing the qualification problem in FLUX. In F. Baader, G. Brewka, and T. Eiter, editors, Proc. of the Joint German/Austrian Conference on AI, volume 2174 of LNAI, pages 290–304, Vienna, Austria, September 2001. Springer.
10. Norman McCain and Hudson Turner. Satisfiability planning with causal theories. In A. G. Cohn, L. K. Schubert, and S. C. Shapiro, editors, Proceedings of the International Conference on Principles of Knowledge Representation and Reasoning (KR), pages 212–223, Trento, Italy, June 1998. Morgan Kaufmann.
11. John McCarthy. Epistemological problems of artificial intelligence. In Proceedings of the International Joint Conference on Artificial Intelligence (IJCAI), pages 1038–1044, Cambridge, MA, 1977. MIT Press.
12. Ray Reiter. A logic for default reasoning. Artificial Intelligence, 13:81–132, 1980.
13. Raymond Reiter. Logic in Action. MIT Press, 2001.
14. Murray Shanahan and Mark Witkowski. High-level robot control through logic. In C. Castelfranchi and Y. Lesperance, editors, Proceedings of the International Workshop on Agent Theories Architectures and Languages (ATAL), volume 1986 of LNCS, pages 104–121, Boston, MA, July 2000. Springer.
15. Michael Thielscher. From Situation Calculus to Fluent Calculus: State update axioms as a solution to the inferential frame problem. Artificial Intelligence, 111(1–2):277–299, 1999.
16. Michael Thielscher. Inferring implicit state knowledge and plans with sensing actions. In F. Baader, G. Brewka, and T. Eiter, editors, Proc. of the Joint German/Austrian Conference on AI, volume 2174 of LNAI, pages 366–380, Vienna, Austria, September 2001. Springer.
17. Michael Thielscher. The qualification problem: A solution to the problem of anomalous models. Artificial Intelligence, 131(1–2):1–37, 2001.
18. Michael Thielscher. FLUX: A logic programming method for reasoning agents. Theory and Practice of Logic Programming, 2004. To appear.

On-Line Decision-Theoretic Golog
for Unpredictable Domains

Alexander Ferrein, Christian Fritz, and Gerhard Lakemeyer

Computer Science Department, RWTH Aachen, D-52056 Aachen
{ferrein,fritz,lakemeyer}@cs.rwth-aachen.de

Abstract. DTGolog was proposed by Boutilier et al. as an integration of
decision-theoretic (DT) planning and the programming language Golog.
Advantages include the ability to handle large state spaces and to limit
the search space during planning with explicit programming. Soutchanski developed a version of DTGolog, where a program is executed on-line
and DT planning can be applied to parts of a program only. One of the
limitations is that DT planning generally cannot be applied to programs
containing sensing actions. In order to deal with robotic scenarios in unpredictable domains, where certain kinds of sensing like measuring one's
own position are ubiquitous, we propose a strategy where sensing during
deliberation is replaced by suitable models like computed trajectories so
that DT planning remains applicable. In the paper we discuss the necessary changes to DTGolog entailed by this strategy and an application
of our approach in the ROBOCUP domain.

1   Introduction

Boutilier et al (2001) proposed DTGolog, an integration of Markov Decision
Processes (MDPs) [13] and the programming language Golog [9], which is based
on Reiter's variant of the situation calculus [14]. Golog is equipped with familiar
control structures like sequence and while-loops, but also nondeterminism, which
allow for complex combinations of actions operating on fluents (predicates and
functions changing over time). DTGolog extends Golog by adding familiar MDP
notions like stochastic actions and rewards. Moreover, decision-theoretic planning is incorporated in the form of an MDP-style optimization method, which
takes a program ρ and computes a policy (another program), which follows the
controls of ρ except that it chooses among nondeterministic actions in order to
maximize expected utility up to a given horizon of actions. The advantage over
traditional MDP's is that the state space need not be represented explicitly and
that the search space can be narrowed effectively by Golog's control structures.

One serious limitation of DTGolog is that it does not account for sensing
actions[1]. The reason for this limitation is that DTGolog operates in an off-line
modus, that is, it computes a policy for the whole program, which is then handed

---

[1] The only exception are sensing actions which are introduced by the optimizer to
determine the state after a stochastic action.

S. Biundo, T. Frühwirth, and G. Palm (Eds.): KI 2004, LNAI 3238, pp. 322–336, 2004.
© Springer-Verlag Berlin Heidelberg 2004

to an execution module. When the program contains actions sensing fluents that can take on a large, perhaps infinite number of values, finding a policy quickly becomes infeasible, if not impossible. For this reason Soutchanski [16] introduced an on-line version of DTGolog, which interleaves policy optimization and execution. The main idea is that a user can specify for which parts of the program an MDP-style policy is to be computed. As an example, consider the program $optimize(\rho_1); sense(\phi);$ if ϕ then ρ_2 else ρ_3. The idea is, roughly, that first a policy is computed for the subprogram ρ_1, which is then executed, followed by an action sensing the truth value of ϕ. Finally, depending on the outcome either ρ_2 or ρ_3 is executed, both of which may themselves contain further occurrences of $optimize$.

In order to see that Soutchanski's approach is problematic for decision making in highly dynamic domains, it is useful to distinguish two very different forms of sensing, which we refer to as *active* and *passive* sensing. An example of active sensing is an automatic taxi driver asking a customer for her destination. Typically, this form of sensing happens only occasionally and should be part of the robot's control program. An example of passive sensing is keeping track of one's own position, which happens frequently, often in the order of tens of milliseconds. It would make little sense to explicitly represent such passive sensing actions in the robot's control program, for these would make up the bulk of the program and render reasoning about the program all but impossible. While Soutchanski does not say so explicitly, he clearly is concerned only with active sensing, as all his sensing actions are part of the control program.

In highly dynamic domains, passive sensing is ubiquitous as a robot has to constantly monitor its own position and its environment. The aim of this paper is to show how decision-theoretic planning can be adapted to account for this form of sensing. The starting point for our investigations is the work by Grosskreutz and Lakemeyer [6], who integrated passive sensing into Golog. The idea is, roughly, that when reasoning about a program (e.g. projecting its outcome) one uses *models* of how fluents like the robot's position change. (To model the movement of a robot they use simple linear functions of time to approximate the robot's trajectories.) During actual execution these models are replaced by passive sensing actions which are represented as so-called exogenous actions, which periodically update fluents like the position of the robot and which are inserted by the interpreter of the program.

Assuming we have appropriate models of how the relevant fluents change during deliberation, could we then simply adopt Soutchanski's approach or even the original DTGolog if we ignore active sensing? The answer, in short, is No. What is missing in both cases is that, after a policy has been computed, its execution must be carefully *monitored*. This is because the model of the world used during deliberation is only a rough approximation of the real world and things may very well turn out differently and may even result in aborting the current policy. For example, when a driver initiates passing a car and another vehicle suddenly appears speeding from behind, it may be advisable to let the other car pass first. Monitoring then means to compare assumptions made by the model of the world (such as computed agent trajectories) with the actual values obtained by sensing during execution. As we will see, this can be achieved by annotating the policy with appropriate information.

Given that we are motivated by robots operating in highly dynamic and unpredictable domains, deliberation and decision making should happen quickly, preferably in less than a second. For arbitrary Golog programs this clearly cannot be guaranteed[2]. Here we are concerned with control programs for robots that operate continuously over longer periods of time. In such scenarios it makes little sense to find optimal policies for the robot's actions from start to finish, since it is impossible to predict what the world will be like after even a few seconds. Instead one is content to peek into the future to plan perhaps only a handful of actions with highest utility, like passing another car. As we will demonstrate at the end of the paper, under these assumptions, efficient decision-theoretic planning is achievable and can lead to overall good performance.

Since an application like an automatic taxi driver is currently still out of reach, we have chosen robotic soccer, in particular, the ROBOCUP MIDDLE SIZE LEAGUE as a benchmark. While the environment is still fairly controlled (a fixed playing field with four mobile robots on each team), game situations are nevertheless challenging due to their dynamics and unpredictability. To keep things simple, we only consider the case of passive sensors, that is, Golog programs as supplied by a user do not contain explicit sensing actions.

In sum, this paper shows how on-line decision theoretic Golog can be adapted to deal with passive sensing. Technically, this involves remembering the outcome of tests during policy generation and monitoring whether the same outcomes obtain during the execution of the policy. Last, but not least, we also report on an empirical evaluation of this method in the robotic soccer domain with tight real-time constraints.

In related work, Poole [12] incorporates a form of decision-theoretic planning into his independent choice logic. While he also distinguishes passive from active sensing, he does not consider the issue of on-line DT planning. Other action logics addressing uncertainty include [15], where abduction is the focus, and [7], which addresses symbolic dynamic programming and which itself is based on [2]. Finally, [8] also discuss ways of replacing sensing by models of the environment during deliberation.

The rest of the paper is organized as follows. First, we give a brief overview of DTGolog and its underlying semantics. Then we describe our approach to on-line decision-theoretic planning, followed by a discussion of applying decision-theoretic to ROBOCUP's MIDDLE SIZE LEAGUE and some concluding remarks.

2   The Situation Calculus and DTGolog

2.1   The Situation Calculus

Golog is based on Reiter's variant of the Situation Calculus [14, 11], a second-order language for reasoning about actions and their effects. Changes in the world

---

[2] In the coffee-delivery example in [3], the robot needed several seconds or even minutes to find a policy.

are only due to actions so that a situation is completely described by the history of actions since the initial situation S_0. Properties of the world are described by *fluents*, which are predicates and functions with a situation term as their last argument. For each fluent the user defines a successor state axiom describing precisely when a fluent value changes or does not change after performing an action. These, together with precondition axioms for each action, axioms for the initial situation, and foundational axioms as well as unique names and domain closure assumption, form a so-called *basic action theory* [14].

2.2   Off-Line DTGolog

DTGolog uses basic action theories to give meaning to primitive actions and it inherits Golog's programming constructs such as sequence, if-then-else, while-loops, and procedures, as well as nondeterministic actions. From MDPs DTGolog borrows the notion of *reward*, which is a real number assigned to situations indicating the desirability of reaching that situation, and *stochastic actions*. To see what is behind the latter, consider the action of intercepting a ball in robotic soccer. Such an action routinely fails and we assign a low probability (0.2) to its success. To model this in DTGolog, we define a stochastic action *intercept*. It is associated with two non-stochastic or deterministic actions *interceptS* and *interceptF* for a successful and failed intercept, respectively. Instead of executing *intercept* directly, nature chooses to execute *interceptS* with probability 0.2 and *interceptF* with probability 0.8. For the purpose of projection, the effect of *interceptS* can be as simple as setting the robot's position to the position of the ball. The effect of *interceptF* can be to teleport the ball to some arbitrary other position and setting the robot's position to the old ball position[3].

While the original Golog merely looks for any sequence of primitive actions that corresponds to a successful execution of a program, DTGolog takes a program and converts it into another simplified program, called a policy, which is a tree of conditional actions. This policy, roughly, follows the advice of the original program in case of deterministic actions and settles on those choices among nondeterministic actions which maximize expected utility. The search for the right choices is very similar to the search for an optimal policy in an MDP. One advantage of using Golog compared to a regular MDP is that the search can be arbitrarily constrained by restricting the number of nondeterministic actions.

DTGolog is defined in terms of a macro $BestDo(p, s, h, \pi, v, pr)$, which ultimately translates into a situation calculus expression. Given a program p and a starting situation s, $BestDo$ computes a policy π with expected utility v and probability pr for a successful execution. h denotes a finite horizon, which provides a bound on the maximal depth of any branch in the policy. For space reasons we only consider the definition of $BestDo$ for nondeterministic choice and stochastic actions. (See [3] for more details.)

---

[3] While this model is certainly simplistic, it suffices in most real game situations, since all that matters is that the ball is not in the robot's possession after a failed intercept.

Suppose a program starts with a nondeterministic choice between two programs p_1 and p_2, written as $(p_1|p_2)$, followed by the rest of the program p. (We use ";" to denote sequential execution.) Then

$$BestDo((p_1|p_2); p, s, h, \pi, v, pr) \overset{def}{=}$$
$$\exists \pi_1, v_1, pr_1.BestDo(p_1; p, s, h, \pi_1, v_1, pr_1) \wedge$$
$$\exists \pi_2, v_2, pr_2.BestDo(p_2; p, s, h, \pi_2, v_2, pr_2) \wedge$$
$$((v_1, p_1) \geq (v_2, p_2) \wedge \pi = \pi_1 \wedge pr = pr_1 \wedge v = v_1) \vee$$
$$(v_1, p_1) < (v_2, p_2) \wedge \pi = \pi_2 \wedge pr = pr_2 \wedge v = v_2)$$

Here $BestDo$ commits the policy to the best choice among the two alternatives, where "best" is defined in terms of a multi-objective optimization of expected value and success probability. See [3] for an example of how $(v_i, p_i) \geq (v_j, p_j)$ can be defined.

Now suppose that a is a stochastic action with nature's choices $n_1, n_2, \ldots, n_k$.

$$BestDo(a; p, s, h, \pi, v, pr) \overset{def}{=}$$
$$\exists \pi'.BestDoAux(\{n_1, \ldots, n_k\}, p, s, h, \pi', v, pr) \wedge$$
$$\pi = a; senseEffect(a); \pi'.$$

Here the policy is $a; senseEffect(a); \pi'$ where π' is computed by $BestDoAux$ below. The action $senseEffect(a)$ is inserted in order to maintain the MDP assumption of full observability. Its job is to make sure that after performing a the robot gathers enough information to distinguish between the outcomes n_i. In the case of $intercept$, the sensing would involve finding out whether the robot has the ball denoted by the fluent $haveBall(s)$.

$$BestDoAux(\{n_1, \ldots, n_k\}, p, s, h, \pi, v, pr) \overset{def}{=}$$
$$\neg Poss(n_1, s) \wedge BestDoAux(\{n_2, \ldots, n_k\}, p, s, h, \pi, v, pr) \vee Poss(n_1, s) \wedge$$
$$\exists \pi', v', pr'.BestDoAux(\{n_2, \ldots, n_k\}, p, s, h, \pi', v', pr') \wedge$$
$$\exists \pi_1, v_1, pr_1.BestDo(n_1, do(n_1, s), h - 1, \pi_1, v_1, pr_1) \wedge$$
$$\pi = if(\varphi_1, \pi_1, \pi') \wedge$$
$$v = v' + v_1 \cdot prob(n_1, s) \wedge$$
$$pr = pr' + pr_1 \cdot prob(n_1, s)$$
$$BestDoAux(\{\}, p, s, h, \pi, v, pr) \overset{def}{=} \pi = Stop \wedge v = 0 \wedge pr = 0$$

Note that $BestDoAux$ produces a policy of the form $if(\varphi_1, \pi_1, if(\varphi_2, \pi_1, \ldots))$ accounting for all outcomes of nature's choices. The φ_i are user-defined tests which allow the robot to distinguish between them. In our intercept example, these could be $haveBall(s)$ for $interceptS$ and $\neg haveBall(s)$ for $interceptF$. A policy contains $Stop$ if in the respective branch no further actions can be executed, i.e. an action was not possible.

2.3   On-Line DTGolog

The original version of DTGolog, which we just described, operates in an off-line modus, that is, it first computes a policy for the whole program and only then initiates execution. As was observed already in [5], this is not practical for large programs and certainly not for applications with tight real-time constraints such as ROBOCUP. In the extreme one would only want to reason about the next action of a program, execute it and then continue with the rest of the program. This is the basic idea of an on-line interpretation of a Golog program [5]. To make this work, a so-called transition semantics is needed, which takes a configuration consisting of a program and a situation and turns it into another configuration. Formally, one introduces a predicate $Trans(\delta, s, \delta', s')$, which first appeared in [4], expressing a possible transition of program δ in situation s to the program δ' leading to situation s' by performing an action. For space reasons we only consider the case of while-loops.

$$Trans(while(\varphi, p), s, \delta', s') \equiv$$
$$\exists \delta''. Trans(p, s, \delta'', s') \wedge \varphi[s] \wedge \delta' = \delta''; while(\varphi, p)^4$$

Given such definitions for all constructs, the execution of a complete program can be defined in terms of the reflexive and transitive closure of $Trans^5$.

A nice feature of on-line interpretation is that the step-wise execution of a program can easily be interleaved with other exogenous actions or events, which are supplied from outside. This is how we handle periodic sensor updates for position estimation, for example. (See [6] for details of how this can be done in Golog.)

With the basic transition mechanism in hand, it is, in principle, not hard to reintroduce off-line reasoning for parts of the program. In the case of DTGolog, Soutchanski proposed for that purpose an interleaving of off-line planning and on-line execution. We show an excerpt of his interpreter implemented in Prolog. We only consider the case of executing deterministic and sensing actions, leaving out stochastic actions:

```
online(E,S,H,Pol,U) :-
  incrBestDo(E, S, ER, H, Pol1, U1, Prob1),
  ( final(ER, S, H, Pol1, U1), Pol=Pol1, U=U1  ;
    reward(R, S), Pol1 = (A : Rest),
    ( agentAction(A), doReally(A), !,        %% deterministic action
      online(ER, do(A,S), H, PolFut, UFut),
      Pol = (A : PolFut), U is R + UFut ;
      senseAction(A), doReally(A), !,        %% sensing action
      online(ER, do(A,S), H, PolFut, UFut),
      Pol=(A: PolFut), U is R + UFut ;
    ...
    )
).
```

---

[4] $\varphi[s]$ denotes the situation calculus formula obtained from φ by restoring situation variable s as the suppressed situation argument for all fluent names mentioned in φ. Also note that free variables are universally quantified in the following formulas.

[5] One also needs the notion of a final configuration, an issue we ignore here for simplicity.

Roughly, the interpreter *online* calculates a policy π for a given program e up to a given horizon h, executes its first action $(doReally(a))$ and recursively calls the interpreter with the remaining program again.

To control the search while optimizing Soutchanski proposes an operator *optimize* defined by the following macro:

$$IncrBestDo(optimize(p_1); p_2, s, p_r, h, \pi, u, pr) \stackrel{def}{=}$$
$$\exists p'.IncrBestDo(p_1; Nil, s, p', h, \pi, u, pr) \wedge$$
$$(p' \neq Nil \wedge p_r = (optimize(p'); p_2) \vee$$
$$p' = Nil \wedge p_r = p_2).$$

This has the effect that p_1 is optimized and the resulting policy is executed before p_2 is even considered. As mentioned already in the introduction, one advantage is that a user can deal with explicit (active) sensing actions by restricting *optimize* to never go beyond the next sensing action. Note that the predicate *IncrBestDo* does the same as the *BestDo* in [3], namely calculating the policy for the given program.

Nevertheless the approach has a number of shortcomings. First note that, in the definition of the interpreter *online*, after executing only one action of a computed policy, the optimizer is called again. This means that large parts of the program are re-optimized over and over again, which is computationally too expensive for the kind of real-time decision making which we have in mind. While it would not be that difficult to modify the interpreter so that a complete policy is executed before computing the next one, the main problem has to do with sensing. As we remarked in the introduction, Soutchanski's approach only addresses active sensing, where it is reasonable to assume that there usually are a number of non-sensing actions happening between two sensing actions. With passive sensing, which is the focus of this paper, this is not the case. As shown in [6], one way to deal with this kind of ubiquitous sensing is to keep it in the background and not even refer to it in the robot control program. Adopting this idea for DTGolog has two consequences. For one, policy generation needs to work with a suitable model of how the world evolves. For another, during policy execution it needs to be monitored whether the way the world actually evolves is compatible with the model assumptions. This is what Soutchanski and, for that matter, the original DTGolog neglect to do. As an indication of this note that, when Soutchanski's interpreter executes an action a from the policy $(doReally(a))$, it is tacitly assumed that a is still executable, which may not be the case. Perhaps more seriously, the whole policy may become obsolete due to unforeseen developments in the world, and this needs to be detected as well.

In the next section, we will show how such mechanisms can be integrated into on-line DTGolog. The main ideas are (a) to remember during policy generation the assumptions used for following a certain course of actions (Section 3.1) and (b) to monitor during policy execution whether these assumptions are still valid (Section 3.2).

3   On-Line DTGolog for Passive Sensing

As the re-optimization of a remaining program is generally not feasible in real-time environments[6], our first modification of on-line DTGolog is to make sure that the whole policy and not just the first action is executed. For this purpose we introduce the operator $solve(p, h)$ for a program p and a fixed horizon h.

$$Trans(solve(p, h), s, \delta', s') \equiv$$
$$\exists \pi, v, pr.BestDo(p, s, h, \pi, v, pr)$$
$$\wedge \; \delta' = applyPol(\pi) \wedge s' = s.$$

The predicate $BestDo$ first calculates the policy for the whole program p. For now the reader may assume the definition of the previous section, but we will see below that it needs to be modified. This policy is then scheduled for execution as the remaining program. However, as discussed before, the policy is generated using an abstract model of the world to avoid sensing, and we need to monitor whether π remains valid during execution. To allow for this special treatment, we use the special construct $applyPol$, whose definition is deferred until later.

3.1   Annotated Policies

In order to see why we need to modify the original definition of $BestDo$ and, for that matter, the one used by Soutchanski, we need to consider, in a little more detail, the idea of using a model of the world when planning vs. using sensor data during execution. The following fragment of the control program of our soccer robots might help to illustrate the problem:

> **while** $game\_on$ **do** ... ;
>> $solve(...;$
>>> **if** $\exists x, y(ball\_pos(x, y) \wedge reachable(x, y))$
>>> **then** $intercept$
>>> **else** ... ; ... , $h)$
> **endwhile**

While the game is still on, the robots execute a loop where they determine an optimal policy for the next few (typically less than six) actions, execute the policy and then continue the loop. One of the choices is intercepting the ball which requires that the ball is reachable, which can be defined as a clear trajectory between the robot and the ball. Now suppose $BestDo$ determines that the if-condition is true and that $intercept$ has the highest utility. In that case, since $intercept$ is a stochastic action, the resulting policy π contains ... $intercept$; $senseEffect(intercept)$; .... Note, in particular, that the if-condition of the original program is not part of the policy. And this is where the problem lies. For

---

[6] But see, for example, [1] for an approach to re-optimization using learning techniques.

during execution of the policy it may well be the case that the ball is no longer reachable because an opponent is blocking the way. In that case *intercept* will fail and it makes sense to abort the policy and start planning for the next moves. For that, the if-condition should be re-evaluated using the most up-to-date information about the world provided by the sensors and compared to the old value. Hence we need to make sure that the if-condition and the old truth value are remembered in the policy.

In general, this means we need to modify the definition of *BestDo* for those cases involving the evaluation of logical formulas. Here we consider if-then-else and test actions. While-loops are treated in a similar way.

$$BestDo(if(\varphi, p_1, p_2); p, s, h, \pi, v, pr) \stackrel{def}{=}$$
$$\varphi[s] \land \exists \pi_1.BestDo(p_1; p, s, h, \pi_1, pr) \land$$
$$\pi = \mathfrak{M}(\varphi, true); \pi_1 \lor$$
$$\neg \varphi[s] \land \exists \pi_2.BestDo(p_2; p, s, h, \pi_2, v, pr) \land$$
$$\pi = \mathfrak{M}(\varphi, false); \pi_2$$

The only difference compared to the original *BestDo* is that we prefix the generated policy with a marker $\mathfrak{M}(\varphi, true)$ in case φ turned out to be true in s and $\mathfrak{M}(\varphi, false)$ if it is false. The treatment of a test action $?(\varphi)$ is even simpler, since only the case where φ is true matters. If φ is false, the current branch of the policy is terminated, which is indicated by the *Stop* action.

$$BestDo(?(\varphi); p, s, h, \pi, v, pr) \stackrel{def}{=}$$
$$\varphi[s] \land \exists \pi'.BestDo(p, s, h, \pi', v, pr) \land$$
$$\pi = \mathfrak{M}(\varphi, true); \pi' \lor$$
$$\neg \varphi[s] \land \pi = Stop \land pr = 0 \land v = reward(s)$$

In the next subsection, we will see how our annotations will allow us to check at execution time whether the truth value of conditions in the program at planning time are still the same and what to do about it when they are not. Before that, however, it should be mentioned that explicit tests are not the only reason for a possible mismatch between planning and execution. To see that note that when a primitive action is entered into a policy, its executability has been determined by *BestDo*. Of course, it could happen that the same action is no longer possible at execution time. It turns out that this case can be handled without any special annotation.

3.2   Execution and Monitoring

Now that we have modified *BestDo* so that we can discover problems at execution time, all that is left to do is to define the actual execution of a policy. Given our initial definition of $Trans(solve(p, h), s, \delta', s')$, this means that we need to define

Trans for the different cases of *applyPol*(π). To keep the definitions simple, let us assume that every branch of a policy ends with *Stop* or *nil*, where *nil* represents the empty program.

$$Trans(applyPol(Nil), s, \delta', s') \equiv s = s' \wedge \delta' = nil$$
$$Trans(applyPol(Stop), s, \delta', s') \equiv s = s' \wedge \delta' = nil$$

Given the fact that configurations with *nil* as the program are always final, that is, execution may legally terminate, this simply means that nothing needs to be done after *Stop* or *nil*.

In case a marker was inserted into the policy we have to check the test performed at planning time still yields the same result. If this is the case we are happy and continue executing the policy, that is, *applyPol* remains in effect in the successor configuration. But what should we do if the test turns out different? We have chosen to simply abort the policy, that is, the successor configuration has *nil* as its program. While this may seem simplistic, it seems the right approach for applications like RoboCup. As an example, consider the case of an intercept. If we find out that the path is blocked, the intercept will likely fail and all subsequent actions in the policy become meaningless. Moreover, a quick abort will enable immediate replanning according to the control program, which is not a bad idea under the circumstances.

$$Trans(applyPol(\mathfrak{M}(\varphi, v); \pi), s, \delta', s') \equiv s = s' \wedge$$
$$(v = true \wedge \varphi[s] \wedge \delta' = applyPol(\pi) \vee$$
$$v = false \wedge \neg\varphi[s] \wedge \delta' = applyPol(\pi) \vee$$
$$v = true \wedge \neg\varphi[s] \wedge \delta' = nil \vee$$
$$v = false \wedge \varphi[s] \wedge \delta' = nil)$$

If the next construct in the policy is a primitive action other than a stochastic action or a *senseEffect*, then we execute the action and continue executing the rest of the policy. As discussed above, due to changes in the world it may be the case that *a* has become impossible to execute. In this case we again abort the rest of the policy with the successor configuration $\langle nil, s \rangle$.

$$Trans(applyPol(a; \pi), s, \delta', s') \equiv$$
$$\exists\delta''. Trans(a; \pi, s, \delta'', s') \wedge \delta' = applyPol(\delta'') \vee$$
$$\neg Poss(a[s], s) \wedge \delta' = nil \wedge s' = s$$

If *a* is a stochastic action, we obtain

$$Trans(applyPol(a; senseEffect(a); \pi), s, \delta', s') \equiv$$
$$\exists\delta''. Trans(senseEffect(a); \pi, s, \delta'', s') \wedge \delta' = applyPol(\delta''))$$

Note the subtlety that *a* is ignored by *Trans*. This has to do with the fact that stochastic actions have no direct effects according to the way they are modeled in DTGolog. Instead one needs to perform *senseEffect* to find out about the actual effects. Therefore *senseEffect* is handled separately as case (3) of the *icpxeq* predicate in our interpreter (see below). The action *a* is executed (*execute(Act)*). Then the interpreter waits until new sensor updates arrive (*wait_for_next_update*) to determine the outcome of action *a* which was chosen by nature.

Finally, if we encounter an *if*-construct, which was inserted into the policy due to a stochastic action, we determine which branch of the policy to choose and go on with the execution of that branch.

$$Trans(applyPol(if(\varphi, \pi_1, \pi_2)), s, \delta', s') \equiv$$
$$\varphi[s] \wedge Trans(applyPol(\pi_1), s, \delta', s') \vee$$
$$\neg\varphi[s] \wedge Trans(applyPol(\pi_2), s, \delta', s')$$

We end this section with a few notes about the implementation of our on-line decision-theoretic interpreter called Readylog[7].

We begin with a (very) rough sketch of the main loop of the interpreter.

```
/******** Interpreter mainloop ******/
/* (1)- exogenous action occured (e.g. passive sensing)*/
icpgo(E,H) :- exog_occurs(Act,H), exog_action(Act),!,icpgo(E,[Act|H]).

/* (2) - performing a step in program execution */
icpgo(E,H) :- trans(E,H,E1,H1),icpxeq(H,H1,H2),!, icpgo(E1,H2).

/* (3) - program is final -> execution finished */
icpgo(E,H) :- final(E,H).

/* (4) - waiting for an exogenous action to happen */
icpgo(E,H) :- wait_for_exog_occurs, !, icpgo(E,H).

/******** Executing actions ******/
/* (1) - No action was scheduled for execution so nothing to do */
icpxeq(H,H,H).

/* (2) - The action is not a sense effect action: simply execute it */
icpxeq(H,[Act|H],H1):-not Act=senseEffect(_),execute(Act,_,H),H1=[Act|H].

/* (3) - The action is a sense effect action: wait for next update */
icpxeq(H,[Act|H],H1):- Act = senseEffect(_), execute(Act, _, H),
                       wait_for_next_update, H1=[Act|H].
```

First, it checks whether an exogenous event occurred and if so inserts it into the history. Next, it is checked if a transition to a new configuration can be made executing the next possible action. If there is no successor configuration reachable a test for a final configuration is conducted. In case (4) where none of the previous cases apply the interpreter waits until some exogenous event occurs, e.g. the robot has reached a certain position.

For the actual execution the predicate *icpxeq* exists. It checks whether there is an action to execute (added to the situation term by the last call to *Trans*) and if so, executes it in case it is not a sense effect action, or, otherwise, waits for the next (passive) sensory update. Here we assume that the information provided by passive sensing suffices to determine the outcome of any stochastic action.

We put a lot of effort into tuning the performance of the interpreter. One major speed-up was achieved by integrating a progression mechanism for the

---

[7] Readylog stands for "real-time dynamic Golog".

internal database in the spirit of Lin and Reiter [10]. For space reasons we leave out all details except to say that this is indispensable for maintaining tractability because the action history would otherwise grow beyond control very quickly. We also omitted progression in the interpreter code above.

Additional speed-ups were obtained by using a Readylog preprocessor. It takes a complete domain axiomatization as input and generates optimized Prolog code, i.e. run-time invariants like static conditions are evaluated at compile-time to save the time of evaluating them many times at run-time.

4   Empirical Results in RoboCup

We used the described version of Readylog for our ROBOCUP MIDDLE SIZE robot team at the world championships 2003 in Padua, Italy, and at the German Open 2004 in Paderborn. In this Section we show some details of the implementation of our soccer agent and present some results of the use of decision-theoretic planning in Golog in the soccer domain.

Among the basic actions we used the most important were $goto\_pos(x, y, \theta)$, $turn(\theta)$, $dribble\_to(x, y, \theta)$, $intercept$, $kick(power)$, and $move\_and\_kick(x, y, \theta)$.

While the goalie was controlled without Readylog in order to maintain the highest possible level of reactivity, all other players of our team had an individual Readylog procedure for playing. We assigned fixed roles to the three field players: defender, supporter, and attacker. Only the best positioned player to the ball started to deliberate, i.e. solved the MDP given by the program in Fig. 1, otherwise it performed a program according to its role like defending the team's goal.

The set of alternatives made up from the *bestInterceptor* program is best described by Figure 2. In line 3 of Fig. 1 the choice is between a dribbling to the free goal corner or to dribble thereto but finishing the action with a shot as soon as the goal is straight ahead. In line 6 the agent decides among four angles to turn to in order to push the ball to either side where it can be intercepted by a teammate, using the *pickBest* construct.

Figure 3 shows an example decision tree made up from this program. For readability we pruned some similar branches. The root node stands for the situation were the agent switched to off-line mode, i.e., the current situation. The boxes denote agent choices, i.e. the agent can decide which of the alternatives to take. The circles are nature's choices, denoting the possible outcomes of stochastic actions. Numbers of outgoing edges in these nodes are the probabilities for the possible outcomes. The numbers in the boxes are the rewards for the corresponding situation. The actually best policy in the situation of the example is marked by a thick line.

Indispensable for a successful acting agent using decision-theoretic planning is a reasonable reward function. For this scenario, however, we used a rather primitive reward function based solely on the velocity, relative position and distance of the ball towards the opponents goal. In future work this could be refined for improving the overall play.

```
    solve(nondet(
     [kick(ownNumber, 40),
       dribble_or_move_kick(ownNumber),
       dribble_to_points(ownNumber),
  5    if(isKickable(ownNumber),
           pickBest(var_turnAngle, [-3.1, -2.3, 2.3, 3.1],
              [turn_relative(ownNumber, var_turnAngle, 2),
                nondet([[intercept_ball(ownNumber, 1),
                    dribble_or_move_kick(ownNumber)],
 10                [intercept_ball(no_ByRole(supporter), 1),
                      dribble_or_move_kick(no_ByRole(supp.))]])]),
           nondet([[intercept_ball(ownNumber, 1),
                dribble_or_move_kick(ownNumber)],
                intercept_ball(ownNumber, 0.0, 1)]) ) ]), 4)
 15
    proc(dribble_or_move_kick(Own),
          nondet([[dribble_to(Own, oppGoalBestCorner, 1)],
                  [move_kick(Own, oppGoalBestCorner, 1)]])).

 20 proc(dribble_to_points(Own),
          pickBest(var_pos, [[2.5, -1.25], [2.5, -2.5],
                  [2.5, 0.0], [2.5, 2.5], [2.5, 1.25]],
                  dribble_to(Own, var_pos, 1))).
```

Fig. 1. The *bestInterceptor* program performed by an offensive player. Here, *nondet*(Σ) denotes the nondeterministic choice of actions.

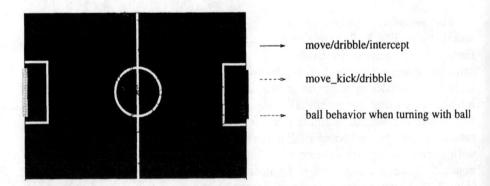

Fig. 2. The set of alternatives for the attacker when it is in ball possession. The red boxes denote opponents, the black ones are teammates. Everything else are field markings.

Naturally, the time a player spent deliberating depended highly on the number of alternatives that were possible. In this respect, whether or not the ball was kickable made the most difference (all times in seconds):

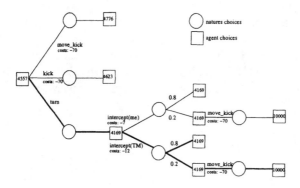

Fig. 3. A (pruned) example decision tree for the *bestInterceptor* program.

	examples	min	avg	max
without ball	698	< 0.01	0.094	0.450
with ball	117	0.170	0.536	2.110

The hardware used was an on-board Pentium III-933. With the described decision making method we shot 13 goals at the world championships and scratched the final round by one goal. During the recent GermanOpen 2004 Championships we were able to advance to the quarter finals.

5   Conclusion

In this paper, we proposed a novel method of on-line decision-theoretic planning and execution in Golog, which is particularly suited for robotic applications with frequent sensor updates like measuring one's own position and that of other agents and objects. We overcame the problem of Soutchanski's approach, which cannot plan past the next sensing action, by eliminating explicit sensor updates of the above kind from a robot control program altogether and replacing them instead with models that allow the approximate calculation of otherwise sensed values during planning. However, this also required annotating policies with information about the models so that discrepancies with the real world could be detected while executing the policy. Our approach was applied in the RoboCup domain with encouraging results.

The strategy for the execution monitoring is to discard all plans where the model assumptions fail in real world execution. Not using least commitment for executing actions could end up in numerous invalid plans. We therefore use symbolic action arguments which are resolved in the low-level execution system.

One weakness of the current implementation is that rewards are assigned manually in a rather ad-hoc manner. In the future we hope to employ learning methods to improve the overall performance.

Acknowledgments

This work was supported by the German National Science Foundation (DFG) in the Priority Program 1125, *Cooperating Teams of Mobile Robots in Dynamic Environments*. We would like to thank the anonymous reviewers for their valuable comments.

References

1. M. Beetz, T. Schmitt, R. Hanek, S. Buck, F. Stulp, D. Schröter, and B. Radig. The AGILO 2001 robot soccer team: Experience-based learning and probabilistic reasoning in autonomous robot control. *Autonomous Robots*, 2004.
2. C. Boutilier, R. Reiter, and B. Price. Symbolic dynamic programming for first-order MDPs. In *IJCAI*, pages 690–700, 2001.
3. C. Boutilier, R. Reiter, M. Soutchanski, and S. Thrun. Decision-theoretic, high-level agent programming in the situation calculus. In *Proc. of AAAI-00*, pages 355–362. AAAI Press, July 30– 3 2000.
4. G. De Giacomo, Y. Lésperance, and H. J. Levesque. ConGolog, A concurrent programming language based on situation calculus. *Artificial Intelligence*, 121(1–2):109–169, 2000.
5. G. De Giacomo and H. Levesque. An incremental interpreter for high-level programs with sensing. In H. J. Levesque and F. Pirri, editors, *Logical Foundation for Cognitive Agents: Contributions in Honor of Ray Reiter*, pages 86–102. Springer, Berlin, 1999.
6. H. Grosskreutz and G. Lakemeyer. On-line execution of cc-Golog plans. In *Proc. of IJCAI-01*, 2001.
7. A. Großmann, S. Hölldobler, and O. Skvortsova. Symbolic dynamic programming with the Fluent Calculus. In *Proc. IASTED (ACI-2002)*, pages 378–383, 2002.
8. Y. Lespérance and H.-K. Ng. Integrating planning into reactive high-level robot programs. In *Proc. 2nd Int. Cognitive Robotics Workshop*, pages 49–54, 2000.
9. H. J. Levesque, R. Reiter, Y. Lesperance, F. Lin, and R. B. Scherl. GOLOG: A logic programming language for dynamic domains. *Journal of Logic Programming*, 31(1-3):59–83, 1997.
10. F. Lin and R. Reiter. How to progress a database. *Artificial Intelligence*, 92(1-2):131–167, 1997.
11. J. McCarthy. Situations, actions and causal laws. Technical report, Stanford University, 1963.
12. D. Poole. The independent choice logic for modelling multiple agents under uncertainty. *Artificial Intelligence*, 94(1-2):7–56, 1997.
13. M. Puterman. *Markov Decision Processes: Discrete Dynamic Programming*. Wiley, New York, 1994.
14. R. Reiter. *Knowledge in Action*. MIT Press, 2001.
15. M. Shanahan. The event calculus explained. *Lecture Notes in Computer Science*, 1600, 1999.
16. M. Soutchanski. An on-line decision-theoretic golog interpreter. In *Proc. IJCAI-2001*, Seattle, Washington, August 2001.

Relation Variables
in Qualitative Spatial Reasoning

Sebastian Brand

National Research Institute for Mathematics and Computer Science (CWI)
P.O. Box 94079, 1090 GB, Amsterdam, The Netherlands
Sebastian.Brand@cwi.nl

Abstract. We study an alternative to the prevailing approach to modelling qualitative spatial reasoning (QSR) problems as constraint satisfaction problems. In the standard approach, a relation between objects is a constraint whereas in the alternative approach it is a variable.
By being declarative, the relation-variable approach greatly simplifies integration and implementation of QSR. To substantiate this point, we discuss several specific QSR algorithms from the literature which in the relation-variable approach reduce to the customary constraint propagation algorithm enforcing generalised arc-consistency.

1 Introduction

Qualitative spatial representation and reasoning (QSR) [6] lends itself well to modelling by constraints. In the standard approach, a spatial object, such as a region, is described by a variable, and the qualitative relation between spatial objects, such as a topological relation between two regions, contributes a constraint. For many QSR calculi, it is known that if all the constraints represent definite (base) relations and path-consistency (PC) holds, then this description of a spatial scene is consistent. If the relation is not fully specified, the corresponding constraint is a disjunction of basic constraints. By establishing PC, such a disjunctive constraint is refined in view of the constraints with which it shares a variable. A combination of PC with search over the disjunctive constraints decides the consistency of indefinite scene descriptions.

We examine here an alternative constraint-based formulation of QSR. In this approach, a spatial object is a constant, and the relation between spatial objects is a variable. We call this the *relation-variable* approach, in contrast to the conventional *relation-constraint* approach above. Although modelling QSR with relation variables is not original, see [27], it is mentioned very rarely. This fact surprises in view of the advantages of this approach. In particular, the following two important issues are tackled successfully:

Integration. Space has several aspects that can be characterised qualitatively, such as size, shape, orientation. These aspects are interdependent, but no convenient canonical representation exists that provides a link (the role of time points in temporal reasoning). Spatial reasoning problems in practice

S. Biundo, T. Frühwirth, and G. Palm (Eds.): KI 2004, LNAI 3238, pp. 337–350, 2004.

are also not likely to occur in pure form. They may be embedded into a non-spatial context, or contain application-specific side constraints. The relation-variable approach to QSR is declarative in a strict sense and is thus well-suited for these integration problems.

Systems. Typical current constraint solving platforms focus on domain reduction, and accordingly provide convenient access to variable domains. Modifying the constraint network, on the other hand, is usually difficult. This task is, however, required for enforcing PC.

A formulation of QSR according to the relation-variable approach means that generic domain-reducing propagation algorithms and conventional constraint solving platforms can be used instead of dedicated spatial reasoning systems.

Plan of the paper. We begin by introducing briefly the necessary constraint solving concepts and methods, and qualitative spatial reasoning, using the example of the RCC-8 calculus. The next section presents in-depth the two modelling approaches for constraint-based QSR. In the following sections, we discuss several aspects of space and contrast the relation-variable and relation-domain approach. We finally mention some new modelling options, and end with a summary.

1.1   Constraint Satisfaction

Recent coverage of the field can be found in [1, 8, 12].

Consider a sequence $X = x_1, \ldots, x_m$ of pairwise different variables with respective domains $D_1, \ldots, D_m$. By a *constraint* C on X, written $C(X)$, we mean a subset of $D_1 \times \cdots \times D_m$. The arity of C is m. A *constraint satisfaction problem (CSP)* consists of a finite sequence of variables $X = x_1, \ldots, x_n$ with respective domains $\mathcal{D} = D_1, \ldots, D_n$, and a finite set $\mathcal{C}$ of constraints, each on a subsequence of X. We write it as $\langle \mathcal{C}; x_1 \in D_1, \ldots, x_n \in D_n \rangle$, or shorter as $\langle \mathcal{C}; X \in \mathcal{D} \rangle$. Given an element $d = d_1, \ldots, d_n$ of $D_1 \times \ldots \times D_n$ and a subsequence $Y = x_{i_1}, \ldots, x_{i_\ell}$ of X we denote by $d[Y]$ the sequence $d_{i_1}, \ldots, d_{i_\ell}$; in particular, we have $d[x_k] = d_k$. A *solution* to $\langle \mathcal{C}; X \in \mathcal{D} \rangle$ is an element $d \in \mathcal{D}$ such that for each constraint $C \in \mathcal{C}$ on the variables Y we have $d[Y] \in C$.

Constraint Propagation. One method to establish satisfiability of CSPs when the search space is finite is systematic search for a solution. For reducing the search space and overall search effort, constraint propagation is often very useful; the principle is to replace a given CSP by another one that is equivalent with respect to the solutions but that is easier to solve. Constraint propagation is typically characterised by the resulting *local consistency*. The two notions most relevant for this paper are:

Path Consistency (PC): A CSP of binary constraints is path-consistent [24] if for every triple of variables x, y, z

$$C(x, z) = \{ (a, c) \mid b \text{ exists s.t. } (a, b) \in C(x, y) \text{ and } (b, c) \in C(y, z) \}.$$

It is assumed here that a unique constraint $C(u, w)$ for each pair of variables u, w exists, and that $C(u, w) = C^{-1}(w, u)$.

Generalised Arc-Consistency (GAC): A constraint $C(X)$ is generalised arc-consistent [23] if for all $x_k \in X$ and all $a \in D_k$

$$d \in C(X) \quad \text{exists such that} \quad d[x_k] = a.$$

In short, every domain value must participate in a local solution.
A CSP is generalised arc-consistent if each of its constraints is.

For example, the CSP $\langle x + y = z; \ x, y, z \in \{1, 2, 3\}\rangle$ can be reduced to $\langle x + y = z; \ x, y \in \{1, 2\}, z \in \{2, 3\}\rangle$ which is GAC.

Enforcing PC means reducing constraints but not domains, whereas enforcing GAC means reducing domains but not constraints.

A number of generic methods to establish GAC for a constraint are known, and many constraint solving systems have implementations. One example is the *GAC-schema* [3] available in ILOG Solver [16].

1.2 Qualitative Spatial Reasoning

The topological calculus RCC-8 [25] is one of the best-known formalisations in spatial reasoning. We use it to illustrate a number of concepts. In RCC-8 one distinguishes 8 topological relations between two regions, see Fig. 1: *disconnected, externally connected, partially overlapping, equal, tangential proper part, non-tangential proper part*, and inverses of the latter two. These are denoted DC, EC, PO, EQ, TPP, NTPP, TPPi, NTPPi, respectively; together they form a set that we call RCC8.

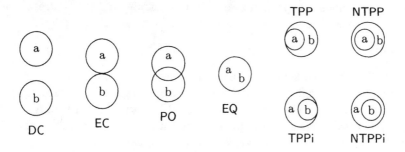

Fig. 1. RCC-8 relations (2D example).

Jointly exhaustive and pairwise disjoint. Any two spatial regions are in one and exactly one of the RCC-8 relations to each other.

Composition table. Considering the triple $R_{a,b}, R_{b,c}, R_{a,c}$ of relations between regions a, b, c, one finds that not all triples of RCC-8 relations are semantically feasible. The consistent triples are collected in the RCC-8 composition table. It contains 193 relation triples, such as (NTPP, EC, DC). Bennett [2] proved that compositional consistency entails global consistency: if for all triples of regions the relations between them respect the composition table then this topological scenario is consistent.

Converse relation table. In analogy to the composition table, it is helpful to think of a converse relation table consisting of the 8 pairs (R, Ri) of RCC-8 relations such that Ri is the converse of R. It contains for example (EQ, EQ) and (TPP, TPPi). If we agree on (EQ) for the relation of a region with itself then the converse relation table follows from the composition table.

2   Approaches to Constraint-Based QSR

A spatial topological scenario consists of a set of region names denoted by *Regions*, and possibly some restrictions on the topological relation for regions pairs. A scenario is fully specified if for each region pair exactly one RCC-8 relation is given.

We examine now how scenarios can be modelled as constraint satisfaction problems. We continue using topology with RCC-8 as an example, but most of the concepts below are immediately transferable to other spatial aspects.

2.1   Relations as Constraints

In this conventional approach, *Regions* is considered to be a set of region variables. Their infinite domain is the set of all spatial regions in the underlying topological space; for example, if we model 2D space then a region variable represents a set of points in the plane. Information about the topological relation between two regions is expressed as a binary constraint *Rel* that corresponds to a subset of RCC8. One usually writes this in infix notation as

$$\text{constraint} \quad x \; Rel \; y \quad \text{where} \quad Rel \subseteq \text{RCC8} \quad \text{and} \quad x, y \in Regions.$$

Such a CSP describes a possibly partially specified scenario. Whether a corresponding fully specified and satisfiable scenario exists is checked by path-consistency and search over the relations. A PC-enforcing algorithm revises the constraints between regions according to the converse relation and composition tables of RCC-8, and search branches over disjunctive constraints.

Establishing satisfiability of a scenario processes only the constraints, for compositional consistency. The variables remain unassigned.

2.2   Relations as Variables

Here we interpret every element of *Regions* as a constant. The topological relation between two regions is a variable with a subset of RCC8 as its domain. Such a relation variable exists for each ordered pair of regions, and we collect all these variables in an array *Rel*. We write an individual relation as

$$\text{variable} \quad Rel[a, b] \quad \text{where} \quad Rel[a, b] \subseteq \text{RCC8} \quad \text{and} \quad a, b \in Regions.$$

Integrity Constraints. Relation converse and composition in this setting are captured at the constraint level. The binary constraint conv represents the converse relation table:

$$\text{conv}(\ Rel[a,b],\ Rel[b,a]\ ) \qquad \text{for all} \quad \{a,b\} \subseteq Regions.$$

The composition table is represented by the ternary constraint comp, with

$$\text{comp}(\ Rel[a,b],\ Rel[b,c],\ Rel[a,c]\ ) \qquad \text{for all} \quad \{a,b,c\} \subseteq Regions.$$

In presence of

$$Rel[a,a] = \text{EQ} \qquad \text{for all} \quad a \in Regions$$

and a conv constraint for all pairs of different regions, one comp constraint per three different regions suffices.

2.3 Comments

By modelling the items of interest as variables and static information as constraints, the relation-variable approach yields plain finite-domain CSPs in which the solutions (i. e., assignments) are relevant. There is a straightforward correspondence between a solution and a fully specified, consistent scenario. Obtaining the latter from a partially specified scenario amounts to the standard task of solving a finite-domain CSP.

Constructing a relation-variable model means finding integrity constraints that embody the intended semantics. Once that has been established, the origin or meaning of the constraints is irrelevant. For example, a constraint solver can ignore whether comp represents the composition operation in a relation algebra; we also discuss examples below in which other restrictions on the relations must be satisfied. There is thus a clear distinction between specification and execution. The relation-variable approach is declarative in a strict sense.

Constraint Propagation. The relation-variable approach is independent of the particular constraint solving method. We could, however, choose a solver based on search and propagation, and furthermore we could choose a GAC-enforcing propagation algorithm.

Path consistency in the relation-constraint approach and generalised arc-consistency in the relation-variable approach simulate each other. This can be seen by analysing, in both approaches, the removal of one topological relation from the disjunctive constraint $a\ Rel\ b$, or from the domain of the variable $Rel[a,b]$, respectively. The reason in both cases must be the lack of supporting relations between a,c and b,c, for some third region c; that is, compositional consistency.

Complexity. It is perhaps not surprising but useful to mention that establishing the respective local consistency in either approach (i. e., PC and GAC) requires the same computational effort. Let n denote the number of regions. Enforcing PC by an algorithm as the one given in [21] requires time in $O(n^3)$ [22]. For this, one assumes that one PC step, restricting a Rel c by a Rel b and b Rel c, takes constant time.

Analogue reasoning entails that GAC can be enforced in constant time on a single comp($Rel[a, b]$, $Rel[b, c]$, $Rel[a, c]$) constraint – observe that the three variables have domains of size at most eight. In this way, the overall time complexity depends only on the number of such constraints, and is thus in $O(n^3)$.

Previous Work. Tsang [27] describes the relation-variable approach in qualitative temporal reasoning, a field similar to QSR. The idea appears not to have caught on, however. One reason is probably that integration in temporal reasoning is simpler because the canonical representation of time points on the real line exists. By referring to its end points, a time interval can directly be related to its duration or another time interval. Space, in contrast, has no such convenient canonical representation – but many aspects to be integrated.

In QSR, the possibility of the relation-variable approach is mentioned occasionally in passing, but without examining its potential. For actually modelling and solving QSR problems using relation variables I am only aware of [1, pages 30-33], which deals with a single aspect (topology) only.

3   Relation Variables in Use

An essential advantage of the relation-variable approach is that the relevant information is available in variables. This means that linking pieces of information reduces to merely stating additional constraints on the variables. In that way, embedding a QSR problem into an application context or adding side restrictions, for example, can be dealt with easily and declaratively.

We illustrate the issue of composite models with the case of aspect integration.

3.1   Combining Topology and Size

Following Gerevini and Renz [13], we study scenarios combining topological and size information. We collect information about both these aspects and their link in one CSP.

Let n be the number of regions.

Topological Aspect. As in Section 2.2, the

$$n \times n \text{ array } TopoRel$$

of RCC-8 relation variables stores the topological relation between two regions. The integrity constraints conv_{RCC8}, comp_{RCC8} need to hold.

Size Aspect. Relative size of regions is captured by one of $\{<, =, >\}$, as in [13]. The

$$n \times n \text{ array } SizeRel$$

of variables stores the relative sizes of region pairs. The converse relation and composition tables are straightforward; the integrity constraints are

$$\mathsf{conv}_{\mathsf{Size}} = \{ (<, >), (=, =), (>, <) \}, \quad \text{and}$$
$$\mathsf{comp}_{\mathsf{Size}} = \{ (<, <, <), (<, =, <), \ldots \} \quad (13 \text{ triples}).$$

Linking the Aspects. The topological relation between two regions is dependent on their relative size. A table with this information is given in [13], it contains rules such as the following:

$$TopoRel[x, y] = \mathsf{TPP} \quad \text{implies} \quad SizeRel[x, y] = (<),$$
$$SizeRel[x, y] = (=) \quad \text{implies} \quad TopoRel[x, y] \in \{\mathsf{DC}, \mathsf{EC}, \mathsf{PO}, \mathsf{EQ}\}.$$

In [13], these rules represent a meta constraint. Here, we infer the linking constraint

$$\mathsf{link}_{\mathsf{Topo\&Size}} = \{ (\mathsf{TPP}, <), (\mathsf{DC}, =), \ldots \} \quad (14 \text{ pairs})$$

which is to be stated as

$$\mathsf{link}_{\mathsf{Topo\&Size}}(\; TopoRel[a, b], \; SizeRel[a, b] \;)$$

for all regions a, b.

Example. Let us pick up the combined scenario from [13, p. 14]. Five regions, denoted by $\{0, \ldots, 4\}$, are constrained by

$$TopoRel[0, 2] \in \{\mathsf{TPP}, \mathsf{EQ}\} \qquad\qquad SizeRel[0, 2] \in \{<\}$$
$$TopoRel[1, 0] \in \{\mathsf{TPP}, \mathsf{EQ}, \mathsf{PO}\} \qquad SizeRel[3, 1] \in \{<, =\}$$
$$TopoRel[1, 2] \in \{\mathsf{TPP}, \mathsf{EQ}\} \qquad\qquad SizeRel[2, 4] \in \{<, =\}$$
$$TopoRel[4, 3] \in \{\mathsf{TPP}, \mathsf{EQ}\}$$

Independently, the topological and the size scenarios are consistent while the combined scenario is not. It is pointed out in [13] that naive propagation scheduling schemes do not suffice to detect inconsistency.

A formulation of this scenario as a combined topological & size CSP in the relation-variable approach is straightforward. The resulting CSP can be entered into a constraint programming platform such as ECL^{i}PS^e [28]. ECL^{i}PS^e is focused on search and domain-reducing propagation; in particular, it offers a GAC-enforcing propagation algorithm for user-defined constraints. Given our CSP in ECL^{i}PS^e, solely executing GAC-propagation for all constraints yields failure, which proves that this CSP is inconsistent. □

For the same purpose but within the relation-constraint approach, Gerevini and Renz proposed a new algorithm called BIPATH-CONSISTENCY [13]. Its principle is the computation of path-consistency for both types of relations in an interleaved fashion while taking into account the interdependency. The link$_{\text{Topo\&Size}}$ constraint is in essence treated as a *meta constraint* on the algorithm level. Moreover, the BIPATH-CONSISTENCY algorithm fixes in part the order of propagation.

The relation-variable method, on the other hand, is declarative; all information is in the five types of constraints. They are handled by repeated, interleaved calls to the same GAC-enforcing algorithm. The actual propagation order is irrelevant for the result.

BIPATH-CONSISTENCY is restricted to combining two types of relations (e. g., two aspects of space). In contrast, the relation-variable approach is compositional in the sense that adding a third aspect, such as morphology [7] or orientation, is straightforward. It amounts to formulating integrity constraints (e. g., conv, comp), linking constraints to each of the already present aspects, and a constraint linking all three aspects. Some of these constraints may be logically redundant.

3.2 Combining Cardinal Directions and Topology

In orientation, another important aspect of space, one studies the relation of two objects, the primary and the reference object, with respect to a frame of reference. It is thus inherently a ternary relation, but by agreeing on the frame of reference, a binary relation is obtained.

The binary relation approach is realised in the cardinal direction model [9], based on the geographic (compass) directions. Points as well as regions have been studied as the objects to be oriented. The point-based models can be cast in the relation-variable approach analogously to topology, Section 2.2. For instance, Frank [9] distinguishes the jointly exhaustive and pairwise disjoint relations N, NW, W, ... for points; denoting North, Northwest, West, and so on. Ligozat [20] gives a composition table.

Orienting Regions. Goyal and Egenhofer [15] and Skiadopoulos and Koubarakis [26] study a more expressive model, in which the oriented objects are regions. The exact shape of the primary region is taken into account, and a ninth atomic relation B exists, describing overlap of the primary region and the axes-parallel minimum bounding box of the reference region. *Sets* of the atomic relations are then used to describe directional information. In this way, for example, the position of South America for an observer located in Ecuador can be fully described by the set {B, N, NE, E, SE, S}.

Relation variables for directional information are thus naturally *set variables*: they take their value from a set of sets of constants, unlike relation variables for topology and size whose domain is a set of atomic constants.

For each pair a, b of regions, the direction is a relation variable

$$DirRel[a, b] \in \mathcal{P}(\text{Dir}) \qquad \text{where} \quad \text{Dir} = \{\text{B, N, NW}, \ldots, \text{NE}\}.$$

$\mathcal{P}$ denotes the power set function.

Integrity Constraints. A restriction on the set values that $DirRel[a, b]$ can take arises if a, b are internally connected regions, which is often assumed. Only 218 of the 512 subsets of Dir are then semantically possible. This knowledge can be represented in a unary integrity constraint, which for example allows $\{N, NE, E\}$ but excludes $\{N, S\}$. The usual integrity constraints comp and conv can be derived from studies of composition [26] and converse [5].

Integration with Topology. Let us briefly consider linking directional information to topology. The relevant knowledge could be expressed by rules as

$$TopoRel[x, y] \in \{EQ, NTPP, TPP\} \quad \text{implies} \quad DirRel[x, y] = \{B\},$$
$$TopoRel[x, y] \in \{NTPPi, TPPi\} \quad \text{implies} \quad DirRel[x, y] \supseteq \{B\},$$

from which a constraint $link_{Topo\&Dir}$ can be defined. It is to be stated as

$$link_{Topo\&Dir}(\ TopoRel[a, b],\ DirRel[a, b]\ )$$

for all regions a, b. We now have the necessary components of a combined cardinal directions & topology model. It can be given to any sufficiently expressive constraint solver, which in particular would provide constraints on set variables.

Constraint solving with set variables is discussed in [14]. Many contemporary constraint programming systems support set variables.

3.3   Cyclic Ordering of Orientations with Relation Variables

From the several formalisations of orientation with an explicit frame of reference let us examine Isli and Cohn's approach to cyclic ordering of 2D orientations [19]. At its root is the qualitative classification of an angle α by

$$Or(\alpha) = \begin{cases} e & \text{(equal)} & \text{if } \alpha = 0, \\ l & \text{(left)} & \text{if } 0 < \alpha < \pi, \\ o & \text{(opposite)} & \text{if } \alpha = \pi, \\ r & \text{(right)} & \text{if } \pi < \alpha < 2\pi. \end{cases}$$

Let a, b, c be three points in the plane. The angle between the directed lines $\overrightarrow{ba}$ and $\overrightarrow{bc}$ is denoted by $\sphericalangle(ba, bc)$. We consider the triple

$$\langle\ Or(\sphericalangle(ac, ab)),\ Or(\sphericalangle(bc, ab)),\ Or(\sphericalangle(bc, ac))\ \rangle.$$

Of all 4^3 triples over $\{e, l, o, r\}$ only 24 combinations are geometrically possible; we denote this set by Cyc. It contains for instance $\langle e, e, e \rangle$ and $\langle l, r, r \rangle$.

Such cyclic ordering information can be expressed within the relation-variable approach in a ternary array $CycRel$. Thus, we have a relation variable

$$CycRel[a, b, c] \in Cyc$$

for every three points a, b, c. The integrity constraints now have the form

$$\text{conv}(\ CycRel[a, b, c],\ CycRel[a, c, b]\ ),$$
$$\text{rotate}(\ CycRel[a, b, c],\ CycRel[c, a, b]\ ),\quad \text{and}$$
$$\text{comp}(\ CycRel[a, b, c],\ CycRel[a, c, d],\ CycRel[a, b, d]\ ).$$

Details and definitions can be found in [19]. Working within the relation-constraint approach, Isli and Cohn construct a new algorithm called $s4c$ that enforces 4-consistency [11] on the ternary relation constraints that correspond to $CycRel$. They are able to prove that $s4c$ decides consistency (i. e., 2D geometric feasibility) of fully specified scenarios. The $s4c$ algorithm uses exactly the information that we represent in the conv, rotation, comp constraints. Consequently, we conclude that in our relation-variable model these constraints guarantee geometric consistency.

We hypothesise further that $s4c$ in the relation-constraint model propagates as much information as a GAC-enforcing algorithm does in our relation-variable model. For reasons of space and focus, we dispense here with a detailled analysis of this issue, as well as of the question whether the integrity constraints must be stated on *every* pair/triple of points, or whether some are logically redundant.

3.4   Combining Cardinal Direction with Relative Orientation

Isli [17, 18] studies the problem of exchanging information between a cardinal direction model for pairs of points as in Section 3.2, and a relative orientation model for triples of points, derived from Freksa and Zimmermann's formalisation [10]. This problem is again similar to combining topology and size, Section 3.1. Isli works with the relation-constraints and proposes a new algorithm for this integration issue.

We formulate a relation-variable model. The cardinal direction subproblem can straightforwardly be expressed in this approach; we omit the obvious details here. The relative orientation subproblem leads to a model similar to that of orientations in the preceding section; in particular, it is based on a ternary array. The arrays in the combined model are:

$$n \times n \times n \text{ array } ROrientRel, \text{ and}$$
$$n \times n \text{ array } CDirRel,$$

if we assume n points.

For linking the two models, Isli [18] devises functions for both directions of the information transfer. They can be transformed into the two constraints

$$\text{link}_{\text{CD}\rightarrow\text{RO}}(\ CDirRel[a, b],\ CDirRel[b, c],\ ROrientRel[a, b, c]\ ),$$
$$\text{link}_{\text{CD}\leftarrow\text{RO}}(\ ROrientRel[a, b, c],\ CDirRel[a, b],\ CDirRel[b, c],\ CDirRel[a, c]\ ).$$

For the relation-constraint model it is necessary to treat the information in $\text{link}_{\text{CD}\rightarrow\text{RO}}, \text{link}_{\text{CD}\leftarrow\text{RO}}$ as meta-constraints, embedded inside an algorithm that moreover integrates $s4c$ of [19] and a path-consistency algorithm.

Using relation variables, it suffices to state the constraints and provide a generic GAC-enforcing algorithm. Also, for a given triple of points, the first constraint $\mathsf{link}_{\mathrm{CD}\rightarrow\mathrm{RO}}$ should just be the restriction of the second constraint $\mathsf{link}_{\mathrm{CD}\leftarrow\mathrm{RO}}$ in which the variable $CDirRel[a,c]$ is projected away. The former constraint is then redundant, and we just need one constraint

$$\mathsf{link}_{\mathrm{CD\&RO}}(\ ROrientRel[a,b,c],\ CDirRel[a,b],\ CDirRel[b,c],\ CDirRel[a,c]\ ).$$

On the grounds that both the relation-variable and the relation-constraint approach are based on the same semantic information, for one embedded in an algorithm, for the other in constraints, we conclude that both accept exactly the same point configuration scenarios.

4   Extensions

Variables Ranging over Spatial Objects. In the relation-variable model, spatial objects are denoted by constants. An *object variable*, whose domain is the set of object constants, has thus a different meaning than in the relation-constraint approach. This issue is best demonstrated by an example. Suppose we wish to identify two regions among all given regions such that

- the first is smaller than the second, and
- they are disconnected or externally connected.

We use topological and size information, formalised as in Section 3.1, so we have arrays *SizeRel* and *TopoRel* recording the qualitative relations. Let *Regions* be the set of the n region constants. We define the

region variables x_1, x_2

whose domain is the set *Regions*, and constrain them by

$$SizeRel[x_1, x_2] = (<), \tag{C_1}$$
$$TopoRel[x_1, x_2] \in \{\mathsf{DC}, \mathsf{EC}\}. \tag{C_2}$$

C_1 is a constraint on the variables x_1, x_2 and on all size relation variables in the array *SizeRel*. Namely, region constants $r_1, r_2 \in Regions$ must be assigned to x_1, x_2 such that the size relation variable $SizeRel[r_1, r_2]$ is assigned a '$<$'.

We call such constraints, in which arrays are indexed by variables instead of constants, *array constraints*. They are a generalisation of the better-known element constraint, which corresponds to a one-dimensional array indexed by a variable. Constraint propagation to establish GAC for array constraints is studied in [4]. The constraint programming system ILOG Solver [16] accepts and propagates array constraints.

Reasoning About Spatial Change. It is not difficult to augment a relation-variable model with temporal information. It suffices to add a new time index to each array of qualitative relations, and to link the new time-annotated scenarios appropriately. We extend Rel from a binary to a ternary array such that

$$Rel[a, b, t]$$

is a variable specifying the relation between the spatial objects a and b at time t. Suppose we view time as linear and discrete, such that only atomic relational changes can occur between subsequent time points. We can specify these atomic changes (the so-called conceptual neighbourhood) by pairs of qualitative relations and define accordingly a new binary constraint neighbour. For example, the pair (DC, EC) in the constraint neighbour$_{Topo}$ indicates that the topological relation *disconnected* between two regions may change in one time step to *externally connected*. The neighbour constraint is then stated on all variable pairs $(Rel[a, b, t], Rel[a, b, t'])$ where t directly precedes t' temporally.

5   Summary

We have presented an alternative formulation of qualitative spatial reasoning problems as constraint satisfaction problems. Contrary to the conventional approach, we model qualitative relations as variables. Uncertain relational information is naturally expressed by variables with domains; consistency of this information is naturally expressed by static constraints. The propagation of these constraints is a well-understood issue in research on constraint programming, and corresponding generic algorithms are provided by many constraint solving systems.

While the principle of the relation-variable approach is not new, the advantages of applying it to QSR, especially for integration tasks, have so far very rarely been realised. We have argued that several algorithms that are custom-designed for integrating spatial aspects become unnecessary if a relation-variable model and a generic GAC-establishing constraint propagation algorithm is used: the BIPATH-CONSISTENCY algorithm of [13], the $s4c$ algorithm of [19], the algorithm combining $s4c$ and a path-consistency algorithm of [18]. We have shown how the relation-variable approach can accommodate composite qualitative relations as investigated in [5, 26] with the help of set variables and constraints. We have indicated that extending or combining a relation-variable model often consists mainly in defining appropriate constraints, contrary to what is the case in the relation-constraint approach where new algorithms must be designed.

Finally, we remark that the strictly declarative model that results from using relation-variables can be solved by any sufficiently expressive solver of CSPs. This includes typical CP systems based on search and propagation, but also for example solvers based on stochastic local search.

References

1. K. R. Apt. *Principles of Constraint Programming.* Cambridge University Press, 2003.
2. B. Bennett. Determining consistency of topological relations. *Constraints*, 2:213–225, 1998.
3. C. Bessière and J.-C. Régin. Arc consistency for general constraint networks: preliminary results. In *Proc. of 15th International Joint Conference on Artificial Intelligence (IJCAI'97)*, pages 398–404, 1997.
4. S. Brand. Constraint propagation in presence of arrays. In K. R. Apt, R. Barták, E. Monfroy, and F. Rossi, editors, *Proc. of 6th Workshop of the ERCIM Working Group on Constraints*, 2001.
5. S. Cicerone and P. Di Felice. Cardinal directions between spatial objects: The pairwise-consistency problem. *Information Sciences*, to appear.
6. A. G. Cohn and S. M. Hazarika. Qualitative spatial representation and reasoning: An overview. *Fundamenta Informaticae*, 46(1-2):1–29, 2001.
7. M. Cristani. The complexity of reasoning about spatial congruence. *Journal of Artificial Intelligence Research*, 11:361–390, 1999.
8. R. Dechter. *Constraint Processing.* Morgan Kaufmann, 2003.
9. A. U. Frank. Qualitative spatial reasoning about distance and directions in geographic space. *Journal of Visual Languages and Computing*, 3:343–373, 1992.
10. C. Freksa and K. Zimmermann. On the utilization of spatial structures for cognitively plausible and efficient reasoning. In *Proc. of IEEE International Conference on Systems, Man, and Cybernetics*, pages 18–21. IEEE, 1992.
11. E. C. Freuder. Synthesizing constraint expressions. *Communications of the ACM*, 21(11):958–966, 1978.
12. T. Frühwirth and S. Abdennadher. *Essentials of Constraint Programming.* Springer, 2003.
13. A. Gerevini and J. Renz. Combining topological and size constraints for spatial reasoning. *Artificial Intelligence*, 137(1-2):1–42, 2002.
14. C. Gervet. Interval propagation to reason about sets: Definition and implementation of a practical language. *Constraints*, 1(3):191–244, 1997.
15. R. K. Goyal and M. J. Egenhofer. The direction-relation matrix: A representation of direction relations for extended spatial objects. In *Proc. of UCGIS Annual Assembly and Summer Retreat*, 1997.
16. ILOG S.A. *Solver 5.1 Reference Manual*, 2001.
17. A. Isli. Combining cardinal direction relations and relative orientation relations in qualitative spatial reasoning. Technical report, University of Hamburg, Dept. of Informatics, 2003.
18. A. Isli. Combining cardinal direction relations and other orientation relations in QSR. In *Proc. of 8th International Symposium on Artificial Intelligence and Mathematics (AI&M'04)*, 2004.
19. A. Isli and A. G. Cohn. A new approach to cyclic ordering of 2D orientations using ternary relation algebras. *Artificial Intelligence*, 122(1-2):137–187, 2000.
20. G. Ligozat. Reasoning about cardinal directions. *Journal of Visual Languages and Computing*, 9(1):23–44, 1998.
21. A. K. Mackworth. Consistency in networks of relations. *Artificial Intelligence*, 8(1):118–126, 1977.
22. A. K. Mackworth and E. C. Freuder. The complexity of some polynomial network algorithms for constraint satisfaction problems. *Artificial Intelligence*, 25:65–74, 1985.

23. R. Mohr and G. Masini. Good old discrete relaxation. In Y. Kodratoff, editor, *Proc. of European Conference on Artificial Intelligence (ECAI'88)*, pages 651–656. Pitman publishers, 1988.
24. U. Montanari. Networks of constraints: Fundamental properties and applications to picture processing. *Information Science*, 7:95–132, 1974.
25. D. A. Randell, Z. Cui, and A. G. Cohn. A spatial logic based on regions and connection. In B. Nebel, C. Rich, and W. R. Swartout, editors, *Proc. of 2nd International Conference on Principles of Knowledge Representation and Reasoning (KR'92)*, pages 165–176. Morgan Kaufmann, 1992.
26. S. Skiadopoulos and M. Koubarakis. Composing cardinal direction relations. In C.S. Jensen, M. Schneider, B. Seeger, and V.J. Tsotras, editors, *Proc. of 7th International Symposium on Advances in Spatial and Temporal Databases (SSTD'01)*, volume 2121 of *LNCS*, pages 371–386. Springer, 2001.
27. E. P. K. Tsang. The consistent labeling problem in temporal reasoning. In K. S. H. Forbus, editor, *Proc. of 6th National Conference on Artificial Intelligence (AAAI'87)*, pages 251–255. AAAI Press, 1987.
28. M. G. Wallace, S. Novello, and J. Schimpf. ECLiPSe: A platform for constraint logic programming. *ICL Systems Journal*, 12(1):159–200, 1997.

Default Reasoning
over Domains and Concept Hierarchies

Pascal Hitzler

Department of Computer Science, Dresden University of Technology

Abstract. W.C. Rounds and G.-Q. Zhang have proposed to study a
form of disjunctive logic programming generalized to algebraic domains
[1]. This system allows reasoning with information which is hierarchically
structured and forms a (suitable) domain. We extend this framework to
include reasoning with *default negation*, giving rise to a new nonmonotonic reasoning framework on hierarchical knowledge which encompasses
answer set programming with extended disjunctive logic programs. We
also show that the hierarchically structured knowledge on which programming in this paradigm can be done, arises very naturally from formal concept analysis. Together, we obtain a default reasoning paradigm
for conceptual knowledge which is in accordance with mainstream developments in nonmonotonic reasoning.

1 Introduction

In [1], Rounds and Zhang propose to study a form of clausal logic generalized to
algebraic domains, in the sense of domain theory [2]. In essence, they propose
to interpret finite sets of compact elements as clauses, and develop a theory
which links corresponding logical notions to topological notions on the domain.
Amongst other things, they establish a sound and complete resolution rule and a
form of disjunctive logic programming over domains. A corresponding semantic
operator turns out to be Scott-continuous.

We will utilize this proposal as a link between the formerly unrelated areas
of formal concept analysis, on the one hand, and nonmonotonic reasoning, in the
form of answer set programming, on the other. The relationships thus worked
out serve a threefold purpose, namely (1) to obtain a sound domain-theoretic
perspective on answer set programming, (2) to provide a formal link between
domain logics and formal concept analysis for the purpose of cross-transfer of
methods and results, and (3) to devise a reasoning paradigm which encompasses
two formerly unrelated formalisms for commonsense reasoning, namely formal
concept analysis, and answer set programming.

So in this paper, we will extend the logic programming paradigm due to
Rounds and Zhang to include reasoning with default negation. We are motivated
by the gain in expressiveness through the use of negation in artificial intelligence
paradigms related to nonmonotonic reasoning. This approach, using ideas from
default logic [3], treats negation under the intuition that the negation of an item
shall be believed if there is no reason to believe the item itself. This perspective

S. Biundo, T. Frühwirth, and G. Palm (Eds.): KI 2004, LNAI 3238, pp. 351–365, 2004.
© Springer-Verlag Berlin Heidelberg 2004

on negation has recently led to the development of applications in the form of nonmonotonic reasoning systems known as *answer set programming*, the two most popular probably being dlv and smodels [4, 5]. We will indeed see that the extension of the approach by Rounds and Zhang by default negation is a natural generalization of answer set programming with extended disjunctive logic programs [6].

On the other hand, building on the work reported in [7], we establish a strong connection between the clausal logic on algebraic domains mentioned above, and fundamental notions from formal concept analysis [8]. More precisely, we will see that in certain cases the formation of formal concepts from formal contexts can be recast naturally via the notion of logical consequence in Rounds' and Zhang's clausal logic. Our default reasoning paradigm on domains can therefore be reinterpreted as a reasoning paradigm over conceptual knowledge, with potential applications to symbolic data analysis.

To the best of our knowledge, the results in this paper constitute the first proposal for a default reasoning paradigm on conceptual knowledge which is compatible with mainstream research developments in nonmonotonic reasoning. We focus on laying foundations for this, but will not pursue questions of applicability to data analysis at this stage. This will be done elsewhere.

The plan of the paper is as follows. In Section 2 we recall main notions and results on the clausal logic of Rounds and Zhang, and its extension to a logic programming paradigm. In Section 3 we will add a notion of default negation, and in Section 4 we will see that it naturally extends answer set programming for extended disjunctive programs. Section 5 is devoted to the study of conceptual knowledge related to our paradigm. Related work is being discussed in Section 6, while we will conclude and discuss further work in Section 7.

Proofs have been omitted for lack of space; they can be found on the author's webpage.

2   Clausal Logic and Logic Programming in Algebraic Domains

The study of domain theory from a logical perspective has a long tradition, and originates from [9], where a logical characterization (more precisely, a categorical equivalence) of bounded complete algebraic cpo's (with Scott continuous functions as morphisms) was given. Rounds and Zhang [1] have recently devised a similar characterization of Smyth powerdomains. They use a clausal logic for this purpose, and have also shown that it extends naturally to a disjunctive logic programming paradigm. We recall necessary notation and terminology in order to make this paper self-contained.

A *partially ordered set* is a pair $(D, \sqsubseteq)$, where D is a nonempty set and $\sqsubseteq$ is a reflexive, antisymmetric, and transitive relation on D. A subset X of a partially ordered set is *directed* if for all $x, y \in X$ there is $z \in X$ with $x, y \sqsubseteq z$. Note that the empty set is directed. An *ideal* is a directed and downward closed set. A *complete partial order*, *cpo* for short, is a partially ordered set $(D, \sqsubseteq)$

with a least element $\perp$, called the *bottom element* of $(D, \sqsubseteq)$, and such that every directed set in D has a least upper bound, or supremum, $\bigsqcup D$. An element $c \in D$ is said to be *compact* or *finite* if whenever $c \sqsubseteq \bigsqcup L$ with L directed, then there exists $e \in L$ with $c \sqsubseteq e$. The set of all compact elements of a cpo D is written as $K(D)$. An *algebraic cpo* is a cpo such that every $e \in D$ is the directed supremum of all compact elements below it. For $a, b \in D$ we write $a \mathbin{\not\kern-0.3em Y} b$ if a and b are *inconsistent*, i.e. if there does not exist a common upper bound of a and b.

A set $U \subseteq D$ is said to be *Scott open*, or just *open*, if it is upward closed and for any directed $L \subseteq D$ we have $\bigsqcup L \in U$ if and only if $U \cap L \neq \emptyset$. The *Scott topology* on D is the topology whose open sets are all Scott open sets. An open set is *compact open* if it is compact in the Scott topology. A *coherent algebraic cpo* is an algebraic cpo such that the intersection of any two compact open sets is compact open. We will not make use of many topological notions in the sequel. So let us just note that coherency of an algebraic cpo implies that the set of all minimal upper bounds of a finite number of compact elements is finite, i.e. if $c_1, \ldots, c_n$ are compact elements, then the set $\mathsf{mub}\{c_1, \ldots, c_n\}$ of minimal upper bounds of these elements is finite. As usual, we set $\mathsf{mub}\,\emptyset = \{\perp\}$, where $\perp$ is the least element of D.

In the following, $(D, \sqsubseteq)$ will always be assumed to be a coherent algebraic cpo. We will also call these spaces *domains*. All of the above notions are standard and can be found e.g. in [2].

The following notions are taken from [1].

Definition 1. *Let D be a coherent algebraic cpo with set $K(D)$ of compact elements. A* clause *is a finite subset of $K(D)$. We denote the set of all clauses over D by $\mathcal{C}(D)$. If X is a clause and $w \in D$, we write $w \models X$ if there exists $x \in X$ with $x \sqsubseteq w$, i.e. X contains an element below w. A* theory *is a set of clauses, which may be empty. An element $w \in D$ is a* model *of a theory T, written $w \models T$, if $w \models X$ for all $X \in T$ or, equivalently, if every clause $X \in T$ contains an element below w. A clause X is called a* logical consequence *of a theory T, written $T \models X$, if $w \models T$ implies $w \models X$. If $T = \{E\}$, then we write $E \models X$ for $\{E\} \models X$. Note that this holds if and only if for every $w \in E$ there is $x \in X$ with $x \sqsubseteq w$. For two theories T and S, we say that $T \models S$ if $T \models X$ for all $X \in S$. In order to avoid confusion, we will throughout denote the empty clause by $\{\}$, and the empty theory by $\emptyset$. A theory T is* closed *if $T \models X$ implies $X \in T$ for all clauses X. It is called* consistent *if $T \not\models \{\}$ or, equivalently, if there is w with $w \models T$.*

The clausal logic introduced in Definition 1 will henceforth be called the *logic RZ* for convenience.

A main technical result from [1], where the notions from Definition 1 were introduced, shows that the set of all consistent closed theories over D, ordered by inclusion, is isomorphic to the collection of all non-empty Scott-compact saturated subsets of D, ordered by reverse inclusion – and the latter is isomorphic to the Smyth powerdomain of D. This result rests on the Hofmann-Mislove theorem [10]. It is also shown that a theory is logically closed if and only if it is an ideal[1], and also that a clause is a logical consequence of a theory T if and only if it is a logical consequence of a finite subset of T. The latter is a compactness theorem for clausal logic in algebraic domains.

Example 1. In [1], the following running example was given. Consider a countably infinite set of propositional variables, and the set $\mathbb{T} = \{\mathbf{f}, \mathbf{u}, \mathbf{t}\}$ of truth values ordered by $\mathbf{u} \leq \mathbf{f}$ and $\mathbf{u} \leq \mathbf{t}$. This induces a pointwise ordering on the space $\mathbb{T}^\mathcal{V}$ of all interpretations (or *partial truth assignments*). The partially ordered set $\mathbb{T}^\mathcal{V}$ is a coherent algebraic cpo[2] and has been studied e.g. in [11] in a domain-theoretic context, and in [12] in a logic programming context. Compact elements in $\mathbb{T}^\mathcal{V}$ are those interpretations which map all but a finite number of propositional variables to $\mathbf{u}$. We denote compact elements by strings such as $pq\bar{r}$, which indicates that p and q are mapped to $\mathbf{t}$ and r is mapped to $\mathbf{f}$. Clauses in $\mathbb{T}^\mathcal{V}$ can be identified with formulae in disjunctive normal form, e.g. $\{pq\bar{r}, \bar{p}q, r\}$ translates to $(p \wedge q \wedge \neg r) \vee (\neg p \wedge q) \vee r$.

In [1], it was shown that the logic RZ is compact. A proof theory for it was also given. An alternative version was reported in [13, 14].

The logic RZ provides a framework for reasoning with disjunctive information on a lattice which encodes background knowledge. Indeed it was shown [7] that it relates closely to formal concept analysis, which in turn has been applied successfully in data mining, and we will expand on this point later on in Section 5. Moreover, the system can be extended naturally to a disjunctive logic programming paradigm, as presented next, following [1].

Definition 2. *A (disjunctive logic) program over a domain D is a set P of rules of the form $Y \leftarrow X$, where X, Y are clauses over D. An element $e \in D$ is said to be a* model *of P if for every rule $Y \leftarrow X$ in P, if $e \models X$, then $e \models Y$. A clause Y is a* logical consequence *of P if every model of P satisfies Y. We write* cons(P) *for the set of all clauses which are logical consequences of P. If T is a theory, we write* cons(T) *for the set of all clauses which are logical consequences of T, i.e.* cons(T) *is the logical closure of T.*

Note that the notions of logical consequence differ for theories and programs. However, given a theory T, we have cons$(T) =$ cons(P_T), where $P_T = \{X \leftarrow \{\perp\} \mid X \in T\}$.

The *(clause) propagation*[3] *rule*

$$\frac{X_1 \quad \dots \quad X_n; \quad a_i \in X_i \ (\text{all } i); \quad Y \leftarrow Z \in P; \quad \mathsf{mub}\{a_1, \dots, a_n\} \models Z}{Y \cup \bigcup_{i=1}^n (X_i \setminus \{a_i\})},$$

denoted by $\mathsf{CP}(P)$, for given program P, was studied in [1]. Applying this rule, we say that $Y \cup \bigcup_{i=1}^n (X_i \setminus \{a_i\})$ is a $\mathsf{CP}(P)$-consequence of a theory T if $X_1, \dots, X_n \in$

---

[1] An ideal with respect to the *Smyth preorder* $\sqsubseteq^\sharp$, where $X \sqsubseteq^\sharp Y$ if and only if for every $y \in Y$ there exists some $x \in X$ with $x \sqsubseteq y$.

[2] In fact it is also bounded complete.

[3] This rule was called the *hyperresolution rule determined by P* in [1].

T. The following operator is based on the notion of $\mathsf{CP}(P)$-consequence and acts on logically closed theories. Let T be a logically closed theory over D and let P be a program and define

$$\mathcal{T}_P(T) = \mathsf{cons}\left(\{Y \mid Y \text{ is a } \mathsf{CP}(P)\text{-consequence of } T\}\right).$$

In [1], it was shown that $\mathcal{T}_P$ is a Scott-continuous function on the space of all logically closed theories under set-inclusion, hence has a least fixed point $\mathsf{fix}(\mathcal{T}_P) = \bigsqcup\{\mathcal{T}_P \uparrow n\}$, where $\mathcal{T}_P \uparrow 0 = \mathsf{cons}(\{\{\bot\}\})$ and recursively $\mathcal{T}_P \uparrow (n+1) = \mathcal{T}_P(\mathcal{T}_P \uparrow n)$. It was also shown that $\mathsf{fix}(\mathcal{T}_P) = \mathsf{cons}(P)$.

3   Default Negation

We intend to add a notion of default negation to the logic programming framework presented above. The extension is close in spirit to mainstream developments concerning knowledge representation and reasoning with nonmonotonic logics.

Definition 3. *Let D be a coherent algebraic domain. An* extended clause *is a pair (C,N) of clauses over D, which we also write as "$C, \sim N$". An extended clause (C,N) is called* trivially extended *if $N = \{\}$, and we may omit N in this case. A (trivially)* extended rule *is of the form $Y \leftarrow X$, where Y is a clause and X is a (trivially) extended clause. An (extended disjunctive)* program *consists of a set of extended rules. If $Y \leftarrow C, \sim N$ is an extended rule, then we call (C,N) the* body *of the rule and Y the* head *of the rule.*

Informally, we read an extended rule $Y \leftarrow C, \sim N$ as follows: If C holds, and N does not, then Y shall hold. This intuition gives rise to the following notions, akin to the answer set semantics [6], a point which we will discuss further in Section 4.

Definition 4. *Let D be a coherent algebraic domain, let P be an extended disjunctive program, and let $w \in D$. We define P/w to be the (non-extended) program obtained by applying the following two transformations: (1) Replace each body (C,N) of a rule by C if $w \not\models N$. (2) Delete all rules with a body (C,N) for which $w \models N$. An element $w \in D$ is an* answer model *of P if it satisfies $w \models \mathsf{fix}\left(\mathcal{T}_{P/w}\right)$. An element $w \in D$ is a* min-answer model *of P if it is minimal among all v satisfying $v \models \mathsf{fix}\left(\mathcal{T}_{P/w}\right)$.*

Note that every min-answer model is an answer model. Recall also from [1] that the set of all models of a theory is compact saturated, hence is the upper closure of its minimal elements.

Example 2. Consider the (finite) domain D depicted in Figure 1. This example is taken from [7] and encodes restaurant menues via formal concept analysis, a point which will be discussed in more detail later on in Section 5. We can now encode the wishes of a customer by programs, e.g. as follows.

$$\{d\} \leftarrow \{\perp\}$$
$$\{2,3,4\} \leftarrow \{\perp\}$$
$$\{rw\} \leftarrow \{\perp\}, \sim\{ww\}$$

Informally, the first rule states that the customer definitely wants a dessert. The second rule states that the customer wants one of the set meals 2, 3 or 4. The third rule states that the customer will choose red wine in all cases in which he does not have a good reason to choose white wine.

The element $4 \in D$ is a min-answer model for P, since $P/4$ consists of the clauses $\{d\} \leftarrow \{\perp\}$, $\{2,3,4\} \leftarrow \{\perp\}$, and $\{rw\} \leftarrow \{\perp\}$, and 4 is a minimal model of $\{\{d\}, \{2,3,4\}, \{rw\}\}$. Likewise, $3 \in D$ is a min-answer model since $P/3$ consists of the first two clauses from above and 3 is a minimal model of these. $7 \in D$ is an answer model of P, but not a min-answer model.

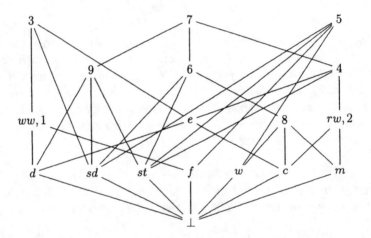

Fig. 1. Figure for Example 2. Abbreviations are: *sd* salad, *st* starter, *f* fish, *m* meat, *rw* red wine, *ww* white wine, *w* water, *d* dessert, *c* coffee, *e* expensive. Numbers 1 to 9 stand for set meals.

4   Answer Set Programming

Answer set programming is an artificial intelligent reasoning paradigm which was devised in order to capture some aspects of commonsense reasoning. More precisely, it is based on the observation that humans constantly tend to *jump to conlusions* in real-life situations, and on the idea that this imprecise reasoning mechanism (amongst other things) allows us to deal with the world effectively. Formally, *jumping to conclusions* can be studied by investigating supraclassical logics, see [15], where *supraclassicality* means, roughly speaking, that under such a logic more conclusions can be drawn from a set of axioms (or knowledge base) than could be drawn using classical (e.g. propositional or first-order) logic. Answer set programming, as well as the related default logic [3], is also non-monotonic, in the sense that a larger knowledge base does not necessarily yield a larger set of conclusions.

We next describe the notion of answer set for extended disjunctive logic programs, as proposed in [6]. It forms the heart of answer set programming systems like dlv [4], which have become a standard paradigm in artificial intelligence.

Let $\mathcal{V}$ denote a countably infinite set of propositional variables. A *rule* is an expression of the form

$$L_1, \ldots, L_n \leftarrow L_{n+1}, \ldots, L_m, \sim L_{m+1}, \ldots, \sim L_k,$$

where each of the L_i is a literal, i.e. either a propositional variable or of the form $\neg p$ for some $p \in \mathcal{V}$. Given such a rule r, we set $\texttt{Head}(r) = \{L_1, \ldots, L_n\}$, $\texttt{Pos}(r) = \{L_{n+1}, \ldots, L_m\}$, and $\texttt{Neg}(r) = \{L_{m+1}, \ldots, L_k\}$.

In order to describe the answer set semantics, or stable model semantics, for extended disjunctive programs, we first consider programs without $\sim$. Thus, let P denote an extended disjunctive logic program in which $\texttt{Neg}(r)$ is empty for each rule $r \in P$. A subset X of $\mathcal{V}^{\pm} = \mathcal{V} \cup \neg\mathcal{V}$ is said to be *closed by rules* in P if, for every $r \in P$ such that $\texttt{Pos}(r) \subseteq X$, we have that $\texttt{Head}(r) \cap X \neq \emptyset$. The set $X \in 2^{\mathcal{V}^{\pm}}$ is called an *answer set* for P if it is a minimal subset of $\mathcal{V}^{\pm}$ such that the following two conditions are satisfied.

1. If X contains complementary literals, then $X = \mathcal{V}^{\pm}$.
2. X is closed by rules in P.

We denote the set of answer sets of P by $\alpha(P)$. Now suppose that P is an extended disjunctive logic program that may contain $\sim$. For a set $X \in 2^{\mathcal{V}^{\pm}}$, consider the program P/X defined as follows.

1. If $r \in P$ is such that $\texttt{Neg}(r) \cap X$ is not empty, then we remove r i.e. $r \notin P/X$.
2. If $r \in P$ is such that $\texttt{Neg}(r) \cap X$ is empty, then the rule r' belongs to P/X, where r' is defined by $\texttt{Head}(r') = \texttt{Head}(r)$, $\texttt{Pos}(r') = \texttt{Pos}(r)$ and $\texttt{Neg}(r') = \emptyset$.

The program transformation $(P, X) \mapsto P/X$ is called the *Gelfond-Lifschitz transformation* of P with respect to X.

It is clear that the program P/X does not contain $\sim$ and therefore $\alpha(P/X)$ is defined. We say that X is an *answer set* or *stable model* of P if $X \in \alpha(P/X)$. So, answer sets of P are fixed points of the operator $\texttt{GL}_P$ introduced by Gelfond and Lifschitz in [6], where $\texttt{GL}_P(X) = \alpha(P/X)$. We note that the operator $\texttt{GL}_P$ is in general not monotonic, and call it the *Gelfond-Lifschitz operator* of P.

Now consider the coherent algebraic cpo $\mathbb{T}^{\mathcal{V}}$ from Example 1, and call an extended program over $\mathbb{T}^{\mathcal{V}}$ a *propositional program* if for each rule $Y \leftarrow (C, N)$ in P we have that Y, C and N contain only atoms in $\mathbb{T}^{\mathcal{V}}$ or $\bot$, i.e. propositional variables or their negations (with respect to $\neg$) or $\bot$, Y does not contain $\bot$, and C is a singleton clause.

Now if P is a propositional program, then let P' be the extended disjunctive logic program obtained from P by transforming each rule

$$\{p_1, \dots, p_n\} \leftarrow \{q_1 \dots q_m\}, \sim\{r_1, \dots, r_k\}$$

from P into the rule

$$p_1, \dots, p_n \leftarrow q_1, \dots, q_m, \sim r_1, \dots, \sim r_k,$$

in P', where p_i, q_j, r_l are atoms in $\mathbb{T}^{\mathcal{V}}$, i.e. literals over $\mathcal{V}$. If $q_1 \dots q_m = \bot$, then it is omitted. If $r_i = \bot$ for some i, then the rule will never play a role, so we can assume without loss of generality that this does not occur. This transformation can obviously be reversed. We say that P and P' are *associated with each other*.

Theorem 1. *Let P be a propositional program and P' be its associated extended disjunctive logic program. Then $w \in \mathbb{T}^{\mathcal{V}}$ is a min-answer model of P if and only if $w' = \{p \in \mathcal{V}^{\pm} \mid w \models \{p\}\}$, i.e. the set of all atoms for which w is a model, is an answer set for P'. Conversely, if $X \subseteq \mathcal{V}^{\pm}$ is an answer set for P' which does not contain complementary literals, then $x = \bigsqcup X \in \mathbb{T}^{\mathcal{V}}$ exists and is a min-answer model of P. If $\mathcal{V}^{\pm}$ is an answer set for P' (and hence the only answer set of P'), then P does not have any min-answer models.*

Theorem 1 shows that reasoning (or programming) with min-answer models encompasses answer set programming with extended disjunctive logic programs. More precisely, we obtain the classical answer set programming paradigm by restricting our attention to the domain $\mathbb{T}^{\mathcal{V}}$. What do we gain through this more general framework? One the one hand, we improve in conceptual clarity: Our results open up the possibility of a domain-theoretical (and domain-logical) treatment of answer set programming in the basic paradigm, and possibly also for some extensions recently being studied. On the other hand, we gain flexibility due to the possible choice of underlying domain, which we like to think of as background knowledge on which we program or which we query. The choice of $\mathbb{T}^{\mathcal{V}}$ corresponds to the language of propositional logic, and all order structures satisfying the requirements of being coherent algebraic cpos are suitable. These requirements are rather weak from a computational perspective, because among the computationally relevant order structures studied in domain theory, coherent algebraic cpos form a rather general class. In particular, they encompass all finite partial orders, and all complete algebraic lattices.

In Section 5 we will actually propose a very general way – using formal concept analysis – of obtaining suitable order structures.

The following theorem is an immediate corollary from Theorem 1.

Theorem 2. *Let P be a propositional program not containing $\sim$ and P' be its associated extended disjunctive program. If $w \in \mathbb{T}^{\mathcal{V}}$ is a minimal model of P then $w' = \{p \in \mathcal{V}^{\pm} \mid w \models \{p\}\}$ is minimally closed by rules in P'. Conversely, if $X \subseteq \mathcal{V}^{\pm}$ is minimally closed by rules in P' and does not contain complementary literals, then $x = \bigsqcup X \in \mathbb{T}^{\mathcal{V}}$ exists and is a minimal model of P. If $\mathcal{V}^{\pm}$ is minimally closed by rules in P' (and thus is the only answer set of P'), then P does not have any models.*

In particular, Theorem 1 shows that the minimal model semantics for definite logic programs [16] can be recovered using the original approach from [1] without default negation. Likewise, the same holds for the stable model semantics for normal logic programs [17], which are non-disjunctive ones without negation ¬.

5   Formal Concept Analysis

Formal concept analysis is a powerful lattice-based approach to symbolic data analysis. It was devised in the 1980s [18] and was originally inspired by ideas from philosophy, more precisely by *Port Royal Logic*, which describes a *concept* as consisting of a set of objects (the *extent* of the concept) and a set of attributes (the *intent* of the concept) such that these objects share exactly all these attributes and vice-versa. In the meantime, an active community is driving the field, covering mathematical foundations, logical aspects, and applications in data mining, ontology engineering, artificial intelligence, and elsewhere.

The formation of concepts can be viewed as logical closure in the sense that a set of attributes B implies an attribute m (which may or may not be contained in B), if all objects which fall under all attributes in B also share the attribute m. This will be made more precise below. We thus obtain a notion of logical consequence on attribute sets, respectively a natural implicative theory, which corresponds to so-called *association rules* in data mining. This implicative theory is intimately related to the logic RZ, a point which we mentioned earlier and will study formally in the following. The strong correspondence between the logic RZ and the formation of formal concepts from formal contexts has already been reported in [7] for the case of finite contexts. We will now supplement these results by a theorem which treats the case of infinite contexts.

We first introduce the notions of formal context and concept as used in formal concept analysis. We follow the standard reference [8].

A *(formal) context* is a triple (G, M, I) consisting of two sets G and M and a relation $I \subseteq G \times M$. Without loss of generality, we assume that $G \cap M = \emptyset$. The elements of G are called the *objects* and the elements of M are called the *attributes* of the context. For $g \in G$ and $m \in M$ we write gIm for $(g, m) \in I$, and say that g *has the attribute* m.

For a set $A \subseteq G$ of objects we set $A' = \{m \in M \mid gIm \text{ for all } g \in A\}$, and for a set $B \subseteq M$ of attributes we set $B' = \{g \in G \mid gIm \text{ for all } m \in B\}$. A *(formal) concept* of (G, M, I) is a pair (A, B) with $A \subseteq G$ and $B \subseteq M$, such that $A' = B$ and $B' = A$. We call A the *extent* and B the *intent* of the concept (A, B). For singleton sets, e.g. $B = \{b\}$, we simplify notation by writing b' instead of $\{b\}'$.

The set $\mathcal{B}(G, M, I)$ of all concepts of a given context (G, M, I) is a complete lattice with respect to the order defined by $(A_1, B_1) \leq (A_2, B_2)$ if and only if $A_1 \subseteq A_2$, which is equivalent to the condition $B_2 \subseteq B_1$. $\mathcal{B}(G, M, I)$ is called the *concept lattice* of the context (G, M, I).

Remark 1. For every set $B \subseteq M$ of attributes we have that $B' = B'''$, so that (B', B'') is a concept. Hence, the concept lattice of a context (G, M, I) can be identified with the set $\{B'' \mid B \subseteq M\}$, ordered by reverse subset inclusion.

Furthermore, if $m \in M$ is an attribute, then we call $(m', m'') = (\{m\}', \{m\}'')$ an *attribute concept*. Dually, if $g \in G$ is an object, then we call $(g'', g') = (\{g\}'', \{g\}')$ an *object concept*. The subposet L of $\mathcal{B}(G, M, I)$ consisting of all attribute and object concepts is called the *Galois subhierarchy* or *AOC* associated with (G, M, I). By abuse of notation, we denote members of L by elements from $G \cup M$. This is justified by the obvious possibility to identify the set L with $(G \cup M)/_{\sim}$, where $\sim$ is the equivalence relation identifying each two elements in $G \cup M$ whose associated concepts coincide. We denote the induced order on L by $\leq$.

Theorem 3. *Let (G, M, I) be a formal context, $\mathcal{B}(G, M, I)$ be the corresponding formal concept lattice, and $(L, \leq)$ be the Galois subhierarchy associated with (G, M, I). Let $(D, \sqsubseteq)$ be a coherent algebraic cpo and $\iota : L \to D$ be an order-reversing injective function which covers all of $K(D)$, i.e. for each $c \in K(D)$ there exists some $a \in L$ with $\iota(a) = c$. Furthermore, let $A = \{m_1, \ldots, m_n\} \subseteq M$ such that $\iota(m_i) \in K(D)$ for all i. Then*

$$A'' = \{m \mid \{\{\iota(m_1)\}, \ldots, \{\iota(m_n)\}\} \models \{\iota(m)\}\}.$$

We remark that Theorem 3 applies to all finite contexts since the Galois subhierarchy of a finite context is always (and trivially) a coherent algebraic cpo where all elements are compact; a bottom element may have to be added, though. This finite case is also a corollary from [7, Theorem 3], taking Example 1 and Proposition 1 from [7] into account.

Table 1. Formal context for Example 3.

	salad	starter	fish	meat	red wine	white wine	water	dessert	coffee	expensive
1			×			×		×		
2		×		×					×	
3	×		×			×		×	×	×
4		×		×				×	×	×
5	×	×	×				×			
6	×	×		×			×		×	
7	×	×		×	×		×	×	×	×
8				×			×	×		
9	×	×					×			

The following example is taken from [7]; it complements Example 2.

Example 3. Consider the formal context given in Table 1. It shall represent, in simplified form, a selection of set dinners from a restaurant menu. The Galois subhierarchy of its formal concept lattice is depicted in Figure 1. Concepts in this setting correspond to types of dinners, e.g. one may want to identify the concept with extent $\{4, 6, 7\}$ and intent $\{st, m, c\}$, using the abbreviations from Figure 1, to be the *heavy* meals, while the *expensive* ones are represented by the attribute concept of e, and turn out to always include coffee. Using the logic RZ, we can for example conclude that a customer who wants salad and fish will choose one of the meals 3 or 5, since these elements of the poset are exactly those which are both objects and models of the theory $\{\{sd\}, \{f\}\}$. Also, he will always get a starter or a dessert, formally $\{\{sd\}, \{f\}\} \models \{st, d\}$. To give a slightly more sophisticated example, suppose that a customer wants salad or a starter, additionally fish or a dessert, and drinks water. From this we can conclude that in any case he will get both a salad and a starter. Formally, we obtain $\{\{sd, st\}, \{f, d\}, \{w\}\} \models \{sd\}$ and $\{\{sd, st\}, \{f, d\}, \{w\}\} \models \{st\}$. A little bit of reflection on the context makes it clear that these inferences are indeed natural ones.

Let us stop for a moment and dwell on the significance of Theorem 3. We note first of all that the hypothesis is not very strong from a domain-theoretic perspective: we encompass all concept lattices for which some corresponding Galois subhierarchy forms at least an abstract basis for a coherent algebraic cpo. One could argue that such or similar conditions have to be satisfied in any case if one intends to perform computation on an infinite order structure. The conclusion of the theorem then says that concept closure (or in other words, the underlying implicative theory) basically coincides with consequence in RZ, restricted to finite sets of singleton clauses, which can be interpreted as conjunctions of elements or items from $G \cup M$. The logic RZ then lifts concept closure to become part of disjunctive reasoning, in a natural and intuitively appealing way. From this perspective we can say that the logic RZ *is* the implicative theory obtained from concept closure, naturally extended with a notion of disjunction.

What we gain from this perspective is not only a tight relationship between formal concept analysis and domain theory, but also a non-monotonic reasoning paradigm on conceptual knowledge, by utilizing our results in Section 4. Formal contexts can now be interpreted as providing *background knowledge* in elementary form, which can be queried, or programmed on, by using disjunctive logic programs with default negation, as described in Section 4. From this, we obtain a clear distinction between the (monotonic!) background knowledge or underlying database, and the program written on top of it, allowing for a clear separation of the nonmonotonic aspects which are diffcult to deal with efficiently and effectively.

6   Related Work

Logical aspects of formal concept analysis have certainly received ample attention in the literature, see e.g. [19, 20]. In particular, the *contextual attribute logic* due to Ganter and Wille [19] is closely related to our results in Section 5, and for the finite case this was spelled out in [7].

The study of relationships between formal concept analysis and domain theory has only recently received attention. Zhang and Shen [21, 22] approach the issue from the perspective of Chu spaces and Scott information systems. A category-theoretical setting was developed from these investigations in [23]. The work just mentioned has a different focus than our result in Section 5 and [7], but develops along similar basic intuitions and is mainly compatible with ours. Its flavour is more category-theoretical and targets categorial constructions which may be used for ontology engineering.

Osswald and Petersen [24, 25] study an approach to encoding knowledge in order structures which is inspired from linguistics. They obtain a framework which is more flexible than formal concept analysis, and appears to be compatible with our results in Section 5 and [7]. They also propose a default reasoning paradigm, but it remains to be worked out how it relates to ours.

Relationships between domain theory and nonmonotonic reasoning have hardly been studied in the literature, except from series of papers by Rounds and Zhang, e.g. [1, 26, 27], and Hitzler and Seda, e.g. [28–30]. This is remarkable since domain theory has become a respected paradigm in the theory of computing with widespread applications. We believe that this relationship deserves much more attention in order to understand the theoretical underpinnings of nonmonotonic reasoning and other artificial intelligence paradigms.

Default reasoning on concept hierarchies has also been studied before, for example in the form of default reasoning in semantic networks, e.g. [31], and as nonmonotonic reasoning with ontologies, e.g. [32, 33]. Since ontology creation is a currently evolving area of application for formal concept analysis, we expect that our paradigm will also be useful for similar purposes. Another related paradigm is logic programming with inheritance [34], where the underlying order structures are is-a hierarchies, which do not have a similarly rich logical structure as the logic RZ or Galois subhierarchies of formal concept lattices.

7   Conclusions and Further Work

The work presented in this paper touches domain theory, nonmonotonic reasoning, and symbolic data analysis. The contribution should mainly be considered as an inspiration for further investigations which grow naturally out of our observations. There are several starting points for such work, and some of them bear potential for full research projects which are interesting in their own right.

Concerning the relations worked out between the logic RZ and nonmonotonic reasoning, we have described a general reasoning framework which encompasses answer set programming with extended disjunctive programs as a special case, namely with the domain restricted to $\mathbb{T}^\mathcal{V}$. This opens up new ways for domain-theoretic analysis for nonmonotonic reasoning in this paradigm, with the hope that e.g. decidability aspects could be tackled – an issue which has so far received only little attention in the nonmonotonic reasoning community. On the other hand, by substituting $\mathbb{T}^\mathcal{V}$ by other domains, it should be possible to lift answer set programming out of the restricted syntax provided by the fragment of first-order logic usually considered.

Concerning the relations between the logic RZ and formal concept analysis displayed in Section 5, we can understand the logic RZ as a means of reasoning with conceptual knowledge, related to the approach presented in [19], as already mentioned in [7]. Indeed, the choice of $\mathbb{T}^\mathcal{V}$ as underlying domain relates to answer set programming, while the choice of other domains can be motivated by formal concept analysis. Of particular interest are also the infinitary aspects of this, and the potential of the domain-theoretic approach to deal with questions of computability and query-answering even on infinite contexts. From this perspective, it should be investigated under which conditions a context satisfies the hypotheses of Theorem 3. It would also be important to relate this result to those of [21], where domain theory and formal concept analysis are being related by means of Chu space theory, and [24, 25], where a general approach encompassing formal concept analysis is described for obtaining order structures carrying hierarchical knowledge.

Finally, we would like to emphasize that the results presented here lead to a nonmonotonic reasoning paradigm on conceptual knowledge. More precisely, starting from a given (and possibly infinite) context, we have provided means for doing nonmonotonic reasoning on the Galois subhierarchy of the context. Since the logic RZ captures the notion of concept closure, we obtain a reasoning paradigm dealing with conceptual knowledge in a way very natural to formal concept analysis. On the other hand, the nonmonotonic reasoning paradigm thus put in place is very close in spirit to mainstream developments in answer set programming, and can thus benefit from the experience gained within this field of research.

We believe that the resulting nonmonotonic reasoning paradigm with conceptual knowledge bears potential for applications. One could envisage background knowledge in the form of formal contexts, and sophisticated queries or planning tasks expressed by programs. We are not aware of any other work which proposes a default reasoning paradigm on conceptual knowledge compatible with mainstream research developments in nonmonotonic reasoning.

Acknowledgements

This work was supported by a fellowship within the Postdoc-Programme of the German Academic Exchange Service (DAAD) and carried out while the author was visiting the Department of Electrical Engineering and Computer Science at Case Western Reserve University, Cleveland, Ohio. I am grateful for inspiring discussions with Rainer Osswald, Matthias Wendt, and Guo-Qiang Zhang, and for the feedback of some anonymous referees on an earlier version of this paper.

References

1. Rounds, W.C., Zhang, G.Q.: Clausal logic and logic programming in algebraic domains. Information and Computation **171** (2001) 156–182
2. Abramsky, S., Jung, A.: Domain theory. In Abramsky, S., Gabbay, D., Maibaum, T.S., eds.: Handbook of Logic in Computer Science. Volume 3. Clarendon, Oxford (1994)
3. Reiter, R.: A logic for default reasoning. Artificial Intelligence **13** (1980) 81–132

4. Eiter, T., Leone, N., Mateis, C., Pfeifer, G., Scarcello, F.: A deductive system for nonmonotonic reasoning. In Dix, J., Furbach, U., Nerode, A., eds.: Proceedings of the 4th International Conference on Logic Programming and Nonmonotonic Reasoning (LPNMR'97. Volume 1265 of Lecture Notes in Artificial Intelligence., Springer, Berlin (1997)

5. Simons, P., Niemelä, I., Soininen, T.: Extending and implementing the stable model semantics. Artificial Intelligence (200x) To appear.

6. Gelfond, M., Lifschitz, V.: Classical negation in logic programs and disjunctive databases. New Generation Computing **9** (1991) 365–385

7. Hitzler, P., Wendt, M.: Formal concept analysis and resolution in algebraic domains. In de Moor, A., Ganter, B., eds.: Using Conceptual Structures – Contributions to ICCS 2003, Shaker Verlag, Aachen (2003) 157–170

8. Ganter, B., Wille, R.: Formal Concept Analysis – Mathematical Foundations. Springer, Berlin (1999)

9. Scott, D.S.: Domains for denotational semantics. In Nielsen, M., Schmidt, E.M., eds.: Automata, Languages and Programming, 9th Colloquium, July 1982, Aarhus, Denmark, Proceedings. Volume 140 of Lecture Notes in Computer Science., Springer, Berlin (1982) 577–613

10. Hofmann, K.H., Mislove, M.W.: Local compactness and continuous lattices. In Banaschewski, B., Hofmann, R., eds.: Continuous Lattices, Proceedings. Volume 871 of Lecture Notes in Mathematics., Springer-Verlag (1981) 209–248

11. Plotkin, G.: T^ω as a universal domain. Journal of Computer and System Sciences **17** (1978) 209–236

12. Fitting, M.: A Kripke-Kleene-semantics for general logic programs. The Journal of Logic Programming **2** (1985) 295–312

13. Hitzler, P.: A resolution theorem for algebraic domains. In Gottlob, G., Walsh, T., eds.: Proceedings of the 18th International Joint Conference on Artificial Intelligence, Acapulco, Mexico, August 2003, Morgan Kaufmann Publishers (2003) 1339–1340

14. Hitzler, P.: A generalized resolution theorem. Journal of Electrial Engineering, Slovak Academy of Sciences **55** (2003) 25–30

15. Makinson, D.: Bridges between classical and nonmonotonic logic. Logic Journal of the IGPL **11** (2003) 69–96

16. Lloyd, J.W.: Foundations of Logic Programming. Springer, Berlin (1988)

17. Gelfond, M., Lifschitz, V.: The stable model semantics for logic programming. In Kowalski, R.A., Bowen, K.A., eds.: Logic Programming. Proceedings of the 5th International Conference and Symposium on Logic Programming, MIT Press (1988) 1070–1080

18. Wille, R.: Restructuring lattice theory: An approach based on hierarchies of concepts. In Rival, I., ed.: Ordered Sets. Reidel, Dordrecht-Boston (1982) 445–470

19. Ganter, B., Wille, R.: Contextual attribute logic. In Tepfenhart, W.M., Cyre, W.R., eds.: Conceptual Structures: Standards and Practices. Proceedings of the 7th International Conference on Conceptual Structures, ICCS '99, July 1999, Blacksburgh, Virginia, USA. Volume 1640 of Lecture Notes in Artificial Intelligence., Springer, Berlin (1999) 377–388

20. Wille, R.: Boolean judgement logic. In Delugach, H., Stumme, G., eds.: Conceptual Structures: Broadening the Base, Proceedings of the 9th International Conference on Conceptual Structures, ICCS 2001, July 2001, Stanford, LA, USA. Volume 2120 of Lecture Notes in Artificial Intelligence., Springer, Berlin (2001) 115–128

21. Zhang, G.Q.: Chu spaces, concept lattices, and domains. In: Proceedings of the Nineteenth Conference on the Mathematical Foundations of Programming Semantics, March 2003, Montreal, Canada. Volume 83 of Electronic Notes in Theoretical Computer Science. (2003)
22. Zhang, G.Q., Shen, G.: Approximable concepts, Chu spaces, and information systems. Theory and Applications of Categories (200x) To appear.
23. Hitzler, P., Zhang, G.Q.: A cartesian closed category of approximable concept structures. In Pfeiffer, H., Wolff, K., eds.: Proceedings of the International Conference On Conceptual Structures, Huntsville, Alabama, USA. Lecture Notes in Computer Science, Springer (2004) To appear.
24. Osswald, R.: Assertions, conditionals, and defaults. In: Proceedings of the 1st Workshop on Conditionals, Information, and Inference. Lecture Notes in Artificial Intelligence (200x) To appear.
25. Osswald, R., Petersen, W.: A logical approach to data driven classification. In Günter, A., Kruse, R., Neumann, B., eds.: KI-2003: Advances in Artificial Intelligence. Volume 2821 of Lecture Notes in Artificial Intelligence., Springer (2003) 267–281
26. Zhang, G.Q., Rounds, W.C.: Reasoning with power defaults (preliminary report). In Dix, J., Furbach, U., Nerode, A., eds.: Proceedings of the Fourth International Conference on Logic Programming and Non-Monotonic Reasoning, LPNMR'97, Dagstuhl, Germany. Volume 1265 of Lecture Notes in Computer Science., Springer (1997) 152–169
27. Zhang, G.Q., Rounds, W.C.: Semantics of logic programs and representation of Smyth powerdomains. In Keimel, K., et al., eds.: Domains and Processes. Kluwer (2001) 151–179
28. Hitzler, P., Seda, A.K.: Some issues concerning fixed points in computational logic: Quasi-metrics, multivalued mappings and the Knaster-Tarski theorem. In: Proceedings of the 14th Summer Conference on Topology and its Applications: Special Session on Topology in Computer Science, New York. Volume 24 of Topology Proceedings. (1999) 223–250
29. Hitzler, P., Seda, A.K.: Generalized metrics and uniquely determined logic programs. Theoretical Computer Science **305** (2003) 187–219
30. Seda, A.K., Hitzler, P.: Topology and iterates in computational logic. In: Proceedings of the 12th Summer Conference on Topology and its Applications: Special Session on Topology in Computer Science, Ontario, August 1997. Volume 22 of Topology Proceedings. (1997) 427–469
31. Shastri, L.: Default reasoning in semantic networks: A formalization of recognition and inheritance. Artificial Intelligence **39** (1989) 283–355
32. Baader, F., Hollunder, B.: Embedding defaults into terminological representation systems. J. Automated Reasoning **14** (1995) 149–180
33. Donini, F.M., Nardi, D., Rosati, R.: Description logics of minimal knowledge and negation as failure. ACM Trans. Comput. Logic **3** (2002) 177–225
34. Buccafurri, F., Leone, N.: Disjunctive logic programs with inheritance. Theory and Practice of Logic Programming **2** (2002) 293–321

Improving Fault Localization of Programs by Using Labeled Dependencies

Rong Chen[1,2], Daniel Köb[1], and Franz Wotawa[1]

[1] Technische Universität Graz, Institut for Software Technology
Inffeldgasse 16b/2, A-8010 Graz, Austria
[2] Institute of Software Research, Zhongshan University
Xingangxilu 135, 570215 Guangzhou, China
{chen,koeb,wotawa}@ist.tugraz.at

Abstract. In this paper we present a new model of Java programs. We show how a program can be compiled into the model. The model can be directly used by a model-based diagnosis engine in order to determine the set of possible causes for a detected misbehavior. The new model is based on the concept of dependencies between variables of a program but leads to improvements with respect to the quality of diagnosis results. First experimental results show the improvements of the presented approach.

1 Introduction

Computer-aided software debugging can help to reduce time to market and the overall costs for software development. For that purpose, model-based diagnosis has been adopted for debugging programs to support automatic fault localization (see [13, 16, 18]).

Model-based software debugging (MBSD) starts from a description of a working piece of software. This description can be automatically extracted from the software and captures its structure and behavior. Using this model, one can make predictions in terms of values of variables under certain circumstances. If any of these values contradict the test case (i.e., the software does not behave as expected), the diagnostic system will isolate which statement or expression accounts for this contradiction.

There is a great variability of techniques for inferring program behavior models: finite state machine model [2], application interfaces [17], constraints over variables [7], functional dependency model (FDM) [11] and value-based model [12]. Using these models, one can find the sources of errors/bugs in various cases. However, the inferred models may lead to unsatisfactory results because of the richness and variety of errors in programs. For example, the FDM yields many bogus bug diagnoses if programs contain object accesses within control flow statements. Another dependency-based approach was introduced by Jackson in [9]. In his Aspect system, automatically-extracted dependencies are compared with user-specified dependencies. Hence, Aspect is a verification system and not a system for fault localization.

In this paper, these problems are avoided by using a new model. The model is extracted from the input programs with the aim to employ two-tiered dependencies augmented with conditions and types. A two-tiered dependency has a

---

[1] Authors are listed in alphabetical order.

S. Biundo, T. Frühwirth, and G. Palm (Eds.): KI 2004, LNAI 3238, pp. 366–380, 2004.
© Springer-Verlag Berlin Heidelberg 2004

two-leveled structure, consisting of a main dependency and a set of auxiliary dependencies. From this model, we can derive enriched logical rules of various types (compared with the previous work [10, 11]). Several case studies suggest that it can release the power of the underlying diagnosis engine and we are on the right way towards better bug diagnoses. Moreover, we also discuss one limitation of our framework and suggest a solution.

In the rest of the paper, we first give a short introduction to model-based diagnosis for software debugging in Section 2. Then we present a new model and the conversion algorithm in Section 3, where we distinguish four types of dependencies, and we keep their structure and track path condition to keep them precise. After that, in Section 4 we show how to convert almost-strong dependencies into logical rules, which can be directly used by a standard model-based diagnosis engine. In Section 5, we evaluate the diagnosis results achieved by our algorithm. Finally, we summarize and discuss our method in Section 7.

2   Model-Based Diagnosis for Software Debugging

The development and improvement of consistency-based diagnosis techniques are built on the strict logical foundations provided by Reiter (in [14]) and others (see [8]). Since the MBSD follows this framework, we rephrase the standard methodology in the setting of software debugging.

A consistency-based diagnosis system is a tuple $(SD, STMNTS, SPEC)$, where SD is a system description modeling the program's structure and behavior, $STMNTS$ denotes a set of statements (the artifacts that are assumed to be either correct or faulty), and $SPEC$ is a set of test cases. A diagnosis problem arises when the prediction made by the diagnostic system contradicts a test case. It is clear that correctly working statements contribute to the prediction. If we use $\neg AB(S)$ to denote the assumption about a correctly working statement S, we can figure out the contradiction is supported by one or more sets of $\neg AB(S)$-like assumptions. We call these sets of assumptions conflicts. Formally, a set $CO \subseteq STMNTS$ is a conflict if and only if $SD \cup SPEC \cup \{\neg AB(S)|S \in CO\} \vdash \bot$.

Therefore, to avoid the contradiction, we cannot assume that all the statements in CO work correctly at the same time. For example, suppose a conflict CO compromising n statements $S_1, S_2, .., S_{n-1}, S_n$, i.e., $\neg AB(S_1) \wedge \neg AB(S_2) \wedge ... \wedge \neg AB(S_{n-1}) \wedge \neg AB(S_n)$, we should assume that at least one of the assumptions should be false; that is, there must be a statement S_i $(1 \le i \le n)$ such that $AB(S_i)$ is true. Thus for resolving the contradiction, a set of diagnostic candidates is generated by identifying sets of statements covering all conflicts. Formally, a diagnosis Δ is a minimal subset of all assumptions such that $SD \cup STMNTS \cup \{\neg AB(S)|S \in STMNTS - \Delta\} \cup \{AB(S)|S \in \Delta\}$ is consistent. This concept means that some subset of statements must be assumed to work incorrectly in order to avoid the contradiction (see [14] for the algorithm of the computation of diagnoses).

3   Generating Program Models

In this section, we briefly introduce the concepts of programs in the static single assignment forms (see [1]), points-to relations and their corresponding points-to

```
            class Ticket{
                int price;
                Ticket(){ price = 0; }
                ...
            }
            class TicketFor12Days extends Ticket{
                ...
                int price(boolean ageOver26) {
                    if (ageOver26) price = 266;
                        else price = 182;
                    return price
                    }
            }
            class TestTicket{
                Ticket ticket;
                static int test(boolean ageOver26, int nFull, int nHalf) {
                    int fullPrice, halfPrice;
1                   ticket = New TicketFor12Days();
2                   ticket.price(ageOver26);
3                   fullPrice = ticket.price * nFull;
4                   if ( nHalf > 0) {
4.1                     halfPrice = ticket.price * nHalf − 2;} //faulty
4.2                     else halfPrice = 0;
5                   return fullPrice + halfPrice;
                    }
            }
```

Fig. 1. A Small Java Program.

graph (see [6]). Then we define dependencies with path conditions. Using these concepts, we finally show how precise dependencies can be extracted from the source code.

3.1 Handling Program Variables

Since there may be many assignments to the same variable, we adopt Ananian's static single form to distinguish various occurrences; that is, we assign a unique index to all definition points of variables (see [1] for more detail). For example, statement $x = x + y$ is mapped to $x_1 = x_0 + y_0$, by associating unique index 1 to variable x. Henceforth, we write programs in the static single form directly.

To deal with the features of Java language, *Locations* are used to represent the run-time objects. For example, a pointer assignment, *ticket = new Ticket-For12Days()* (see statement 1 in the *test* method in Figure 1), introduces an abstract location 1 to represent the run-time object referenced by *ticket*. Here we assume that all abstract locations are positive integers, i.e., 0, 1, 2, etc..

Since object variables are mapped to locations, their attributes are mapped to the content of locations, represented by internal indexed variables. In our example, internal variable $1 :: price_1$, created for location 1 as a side effect of the above-mentioned pointer assignment, corresponds to the *price* attribute of object variable *ticket*.

In our discussion, a *points-to relation* is a binary relation that relates object variables and their locations. In our example, the pointer assignment $ticket = new$ $TicketFor12Days()$ produces a pair $(ticket_1, 1)$ in a points-to relation. Points-to relations are created at pointer assignments, where the (internal) variables (represent the left-hand-side expression) point to the target locations accessed by right-hand-side expression. When points-to relations are considered as edges, their elements as nodes, they are also called a *points-to graph* (see [6]).

3.2   Dependencies with Path Conditions

We say a statement i **influences** statement j if values computed at i have some effect on either the values computed at j or the mere execution of j. Sometimes influences are indirect, so we manage them by considering conditions under which they may happen.

Definition 1 (Path Condition)
A path condition P is a condition over indexed variables which is necessary for influences.

That is, a certain influence is possible if there exist values for the indexed variables such that the path condition becomes true. In our discussion, a **program state** is an environment containing the run-time values of variables. We say a **program execution** t, denoted by (S', t^s, t^e), comprises of a sequence of statements S' executed in program S, a starting state t^s, and an ending state t^e. With these conceptions, we further consider the possible influences among program variables, which is captured by the following definition:

Definition 2 (Weak Dependency)
Let x be a program variable, M_x a set of indexed variables, P a path condition, and S a program. Let $t_1 = (S_1, t_1^s, t_1^e)$ be a program execution of S. Suppose t is a state, we use $t(x)$ to denote the value of variable x in state t. A weak dependency with respect to x is a notation $M_x \{P\} S \{x\}$, which has the following interpretation:

1. If the execution of S starts from state t_1^s satisfying P, then it is terminated in state t_1^e, and
2. There exist a program execution $t_2 = (S_2, t_2^s, t_2^e)$, which starts from state t_2^s satisfying P and terminates in state t_2^e such that (1) $S_1 \cap S_2 \neq \emptyset$, and (2) $t_1^s(y) \neq t_2^s(y)$ holds for some variable $y \in M_x$, $t_1^s(z) = t_2^s(z)$ holds for any variable $z \in M_x - \{y\}$, but $t_1^e(x) \neq t_2^e(x)$.

Furthermore, if $M_x \{P\} S \{x\}$ is a dependency, we call M_x the dependency set of x.

Intuitively, we say that x *depends on* y if and only if under some condition P, a change of the value of y may result in a change of the value of x. Note that a weak dependency collapses into the functional dependency defined in [10], if the path condition is *true*. Moreover, we put symbol $\top$ in the dependency set in case the variable is assigned with a constant.

Example 1 Given a program fragment $S =$:

1   $x_1 = x_0 + y_0$;
2   $x_2 = x_1 - y_0$;
3   $y_1 = 8$;

A good example of weak dependencies is $\{x_0, x_1, y_0\} \{true\} S \{x\}$, which means the value of x is influenced by the values of variables x_0 and x_1. Another example is $\{\top\} \{x_0 \geq 100\} S \{y\}$, which means the value of y is changed (by constant 8) if $x_0 \geq 100$ is satisfied.

Note that dependency can be rephrased as a binary relation:

Definition 3 (Dependency Relation)
Let $M_x \{P\} S \{x\}$ be a (weak) dependency, and $M = \{(x_i, \top) \mid M_x$ is empty, and i is the highest index of x in $S\} \cup \{(x_i, v_j) \mid$ for any $v_j \in M_x^l \subseteq M_x$, where M_x^l is the dependency set of x on statement $S_l \in S$, and i is the highest index of x in $S_l\}$. Then (M, P) is s dependency relation with respect to S.

Furthermore, for any $(x_i, v_j) \in M$, x_i's level is defined as follows:

$$level(x_i) = \begin{cases} max\{level(v_j) + 1\} & \text{for all } (x_i, v_j) \in M \\ 0 & \text{there is no } (v_j, y_k) \text{ in } M \end{cases}$$

For the program in Example 1, we have dependency relation $(\{(x_1, x_0), (x_1, y_0), (x_2, x_1), (x_2, y_0)\}, true)$, where each pair (x_i, v_j) is read as "variable x_i has a weak dependency on variable v_j".

Now it is straightforward to define the transitive closure of dependency if we consider all pairs in the dependency relation M for (x, M_x, P). Thus we denote by $trans(M)$ the transitive closure of the target dependency (x, M_x, P).

Note that the combination of two weak dependencies possibly introduces variables that have no influence. For example, let $\{x_0, x_1, y_0\} \{true\} S \{x\}$ be a union of dependencies before statement 3 in Example 1, but we can see that variable y_0 is bogus, since it does not affect the value of variable x. Therefore, to achieve better diagnosis result, we should keep dependencies precise (or almost-strong) if possible.

3.3   Constructing Almost-Strong Dependencies

To construct dependencies, we keep the history of indexed variable occurrences of a method. Provided with the points-to graph G, an indirect memory access can easily mapped into a direct access by means of internal variable. For example, $v.f$ is mapped to an internal variable $i :: f$ by checking points-to relations ($i \in Pt(G, v)$) and therefore attaching field name f. So function $Pt(G, v)$ returns the locations that object variable v might reference to. In addition, we denote the working environment for computing the indexed (internal) variables by ENV, and by $ENV.G$ the points-to graph G stored in ENV). Moreover, function $ENV(v)$ denotes the indexed variable for v with the highest index in ENV.

In our model, we use a two-tiered dependency comprising a main dependency and a set of auxiliary dependencies, which are pictured in Figure 2 (where nodes are variables, and edges are dependency relations). Since a certain variable in

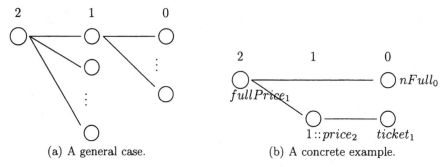

(a) A general case. (b) A concrete example.

Fig. 2. Pictures of Two-tiered Dependencies.

the dependency set of the main dependency occurs in the auxiliary dependency, the main dependency possibly is one-level higher than its auxiliary dependencies (see Figure 2(a) for a general case with dependency levels 2, 1 and 0). In our algorithm care is taken to avoid flattening the two-tiered structure in the union of dependencies.

In addition, we distinguish four types of dependencies:

- **Functional dependency** (labeled by $FUNC$). Functional dependency (fully discussed in [10]) is a weak dependency with a trivial path condition, $true$.
- **Conditional dependency** (labeled by $COND$). Conditional dependency is a weak dependency with non-trivial path condition (i.e. different from $true$), arising from the union of two dependencies with inconsistent path conditions.
- **Scope dependency** (labeled by $SCOPE$). Scope dependency is an auxiliary dependency for an indexed variable and its scope variables. Scope dependency is always used for assisting other non-scope dependencies.
- **Points-to dependency** (labeled by $PNTO$). Points-to dependency is a two leveled functional dependency that is used for handling object variables and their locations.

Typically a path condition is constructed from conditions associated with an if- or while-statement, and it is possibly inconsistent. To union dependencies with inconsistent path conditions, we possibly create three dependency sets, some of them might hold under a non-trivial path condition, and their corresponding dependencies are labeled by $COND$. This distinguishes our work from the summarize function used in [10].

Now we in the point to define the union of two dependencies, which is one of the operations frequently used by our algorithm.

Definition 4 (Union of Dependencies)
Let (M_1, P_1) and (M_2, P_2) be two dependency relations with respect to program S_1 and S_2 respectively, and l an integer. Suppose $D = \{y_k \mid \text{any } (x_i, y_k) \in trans(M_1 \cup M_2)$, such that (x_i, y_k) has a level not larger than $l\}$, and j is a fresh index for variable x. The union of the two dependencies for $S_1; S_2$ with respect to l is defined as follows:

$$union^l_{\{S_1;S_2\}} = \begin{cases} \{(M, P_1 \wedge P_2)\} & P_1 \text{ and } P_2 \text{ are consistent} \\ \{(M, true), (M_1 - M, P_1), (M_2 - M, P_2)\} & \text{otherwise} \end{cases}$$

where $M = \{(x_j, y) \mid y \in D \text{ and } \top \notin D\} \cup \{(x_j, \top) \mid \top \in D\}$.
Moreover, we call l a *union level*.

Example 2 Given a program fragment taken from Figure 1 (rewritten by using indexed variables):

```
4     if (nHalf₀ > 0){
4.1      halfPrice₁ = 1 :: price₂ * nHalf₀ − 2; }
4.2      else halfPrice₂ = 0;
```

and suppose the union level l is 1.

The dependencies on statements 4.1 and 4.2 are $(M_{4.1}, nHalf_0 > 0)$ and $(M_{4.2}, nHalf_0 \leq 0)$ respectively, where $M_{4.1} = \{(halfPrice_1, 1 :: price_2), (halfPrice_1, nHalf_0)\}$ and $M_{4.2} = \{(halfPrice_2, \top)\}$. Here the fresh index for variable $halfPrice$ is 3, so one of the combined dependencies is $(M, true)$, where $M = \{(halfPrice_3, \top)\}$.

Since their path conditions are inconsistent, there are some other dependencies. $M_{4.1} - M_{4.2} = M_{4.1}$, it is not empty, so we have another combined dependency $(M_{4.1}, nHalf_0 > 0)$, which means that $halfPrice$ is influenced by $1 :: price_2$ and $nHalf_0$ when $nHalf_0 > 0$ holds. So we have the final union of dependencies: $union^1_{\{4\}} = \{(\{(halfPrice_3, \top)\}, true), (\{(halfPrice_1, 1 :: price_2), (halfPrice_1, nHalf_0)\}, nHalf_0 > 0)\}$.

Now we are going to define scope variables which are collected by our algorithm. Variables and scope variables are different in terms of influences; scope variables have a larger influence range, variables have a smaller influence range because they represent the 'content' of their scope variables.

Definition 5 (Scope Variables)
Let $v_0.v_1. \cdots .v_n.f$ be an object access expression. Suppose $ENV(v_0.v_1. \cdots .v_n.f)$ return $i :: f_j$. Scope variable(s) for $v_0.v_1. \cdots .v_n.f$ is a set of indexed (internal) variables, $ENV(v_0) \cup ENV(v_0.v_1) \cdots \cup ENV(v_0.v_1. \cdots .v_n)$, denoted by $ENV^\star(v_0.v_1. \cdots .v_n.f)$.

For example, let $Pt(ENV.G, ticket) = \{0\}$ (i.e., $ticket$ currently points to location 0), and $ENV(ticket) = ticket_1$ (i.e., the current index for $ticket$ is 1). Then the scope variable for $ticket.price$ is $ticket_1$, which means the content of location 0 (referenced by $ticket_1$) can be accessed by $ticket.price$ (indeed $ENV(ticket.price)$ returns $0 :: price_1$).

When it comes to points-to dependencies and scope dependencies, we consider the program in Figure 1.

Example 3 Statement 1 of the *test* method in Figure 1 produces a functional dependency $(1 :: price_1, \{\}, true)$ (as a side effect of object creation) and two points-to dependencies: $(ticket_0, \{ticket_1\}, true)$, and $(ticket_1, \{\}, true)$.

Note that they also cause the ENV updating, that is, adding a new points-to relation $(tickt_1, 1)$ to $ENV.G$ (where 1 is a fresh location). By checking the updated ENV, the field access $ticket.price$ on statement 3, is mapped to an indexed variable, $1 :: price_1$. Since its scope variable is of $ticket_1$, we have a two-tiered dependency:

$(fullPrice_1, \{1::price_2, nFull_0\}, true)$ (main dependency)
$(1::price_2, \{ticket_1\})$ (auxiliary dependency)

Indeed they make a two-tiered dependency (see Figure 2(b)); the main dependency is at level 2, and its auxiliary dependency at level 1.

Our algorithm follows the framework in [10, 11]; that is, classes and methods in the input Java program are converted successively by applying a function *conv* to each statement and expression and the output program models are built on dependencies defined over indexed variables. In our algorithm (Figure 3), we are working on programs without exceptions and threads. The algorithm starts from a local working environment *env*, which is a copy of the current *ENV*, and the functions for *ENV* are also applicable to *env* (e.g., $env(v)$ and $env.G(v)$ etc.). The function *conv* returns a sequence of diagnosis components $[c_1, \cdots, c_n]$ corresponding to the statements in the target method. In conversion, attributes of diagnosis components store the dependencies *wd*, the type *type*, and possibly sets of subcomponents (depending on its type).

In Figure 3, we assume that v possibly represents an expression involving object variables (e.g., an object field access). Note that the modeling of method invocations and loops has been discussed in [10]. In case of a method call, its dependencies are first combined, then incorporated into the caller's environment (see Example 4).

In addition, we use the following auxiliary functions:

- Function *addwd* is used to add dependencies to *env* or to a component.
- Function *env.addPt* is used to add points-to relations into the working environment *env*.
- Function $env.wd(v)$ always returns the two-tiered points-to dependencies for variable v of reference type. (if such a structured dependency does not exist, we assume $env.wd(v)$ would create a new two-tiered dependency for v). For simplicity, $env.mainWD(v)$ denotes the main dependency.
- Function $env.var(v)$ denotes the (internal) variable that represents v.
- $Expr(env)$ denotes the set of indexed variables for variables occurring in $Expr$.
- $Expr(env.v)$ denotes a set of scope variables for the variable v in $Expr(env)$.
- *merge* denotes the summary function for combining dependencies, formally defined in Definition 4

Now we illustrate how the conversion algorithm in Figure 3 works:

Example 4 We consider the small Java example in Figure 1. Since statement 1 is an object creation statement, a diagnosis component $c1$ is created with the type *ASSIGN*. The (internal) variable *olhs* for *ticket* is itself (i.e. *olhs* = $env.var(ticket) = ticket$). So we create a new two-tiered points-to dependency with type *PNTO* (See Example 3 for more details), together with dependency $(1::price_1, \{\}, true)$ (as a side effect of object creation.

Statement 2 invokes a method call *price(boolean)*. The conversion algorithm calls $price.conv(env')$ (with a fresh working environment env') to convert the *price* method. Within this method, the statement to be converted is a if-statement, a new diagnosis component is created with the type *IF*. After that, the statement *price* = 266 in the *then* branch is processed. Again the

ObjectCreation ::= $\quad v = \text{new } C$	FUNCTION $ObjectCreation.conv(env)$ $c := new(DiagnosisComponent)$; $c.type := ASSIGN$ $olhs := env.var(v)$; $c.wd := \{(olhs_0, \{olhs_1\}), (olhs_1, \{\})\}$; $c.wd.type :=$ $PNTO$; $env.addwd(c.wd)$; $index := env(olhs) + 1$; $env(olhs) := index$; $env.addPt((olhs, i))$; (where i is a fresh location)

ObjectAssignment ::= $\quad v = w$ (v is of reference type)	FUNCTION $ObjectAssignment.conv(env)$ $c := new(DiagnosisComponent)$; $c.type := ASSIGN$ $olhs := env.var(v)$; $orhs := env.var(w)$; LET $env.mainWD(olhs) = (olhs_{i_0}, \{olhs_{i_1}, \cdots, olhs_{i_k}\})$; LET $env.mainWD(orhs) = (orhs_{j_0}, \{orhs_{j_1}, \cdots,$ $orhs_{j_n}\})$; FOR all indices $l(1 \leq l \leq k)$ and $l'(1 \leq l' \leq n)$ $\quad$IF $Pt(env.G, olhs_l) \equiv Pt(env.G, orhs_{l'})$ $\quad\quad$THEN $\quad\quad index := env(olhs) + 1$; $\quad\quad c.addwd((olhs_{i_0}, \{olhs_{i_1}, \cdots, olhs_{i_k}, olhs_{index}\} -$ $\quad\quad \{olhs_l\}))$; $\quad\quad c.addwd((olhs_{index}, \{olhs_l, orhs_{l'}\}))$; $\quad\quad env(olhs) := index$; $\quad\quad$ELSE $\quad\quad c.addwd((olhs_{i_0}, \{olhs_{i_1}, \cdots, olhs_{i_k}, olhs_{l'}\}))$; $\quad\quad env.addPt((olhs, Pt(env.G, orhs_{l'})))$; $env.addwd(c.wd)$;

SimpleAssignment ::= $\quad v = Expr$; (v is not of reference type)	FUNCTION $SimpleAssignment.conv(env)$ $c := new(DiagnosisComponent)$; $c.type := ASSIGN$ $olhs := env.var(v)$; $index := env(olhs) + 1$; $c.wd := \{(olhs_{index}, Expr(env))\}$; FOR each variable $v \in Expr(env)$ $\quad$IF $Expr(env.v)notempty$ $\quad\quad c.addwd((v, Expr(env.v)))$; $env.addwd(c.wd)$; $env(olhs) := index$;

IfStatement ::= $\quad$if Expr $\quad\quad$Statements$_{then}$ $\quad$else $\quad\quad$Statements$_{else}$	FUNCTION $IfStatement.conv(env)$ $c := new(DiagnosisComponent)$; $c.type := IF$ $c.then := Statements_{then}.conv(env)$; $c.else := Statements_{else}.conv(env)$; $c.addwd(merge(c.then, c.else, Expr, env))$; $env.addwd(c.wd)$;

Fig. 3. Algorithm for converting Java methods.

conversion for simple assignment starts, and the dependency we have got is $(\{(0::price_1, \{\})\}, true)$. Then from the *else* branch we get $(\{(0::price_2, \{\})\}, true)$. Since there are dependencies for $0::price$ in both branch, the merged dependency becomes $(\{(0::price_3, \{\})\}, true)$. The *return* statement is rewritten as an assignment, and therefore its dependencies can be handled by the conversion algorithm. Since $(\{(0 :: price_3, \{\})\}, true)$ is the only dependency, visible to the caller at the call site. So it is renamed and incorporated in the caller's working environment as a side-effect component $c2$, so $c2.wd = \{(1 :: price_2, \{ageOver26_0\}, true), (1 :: price_2, \{ticket_1\}, true)\}$ (because $Pt(env.G, ticket_1) = 1$, and $env(1 :: price)$ returns $1 :: price_2$).

Next statement 3 calls the conversion for simple assignment, which creates a new assignment component $c3$. For clarity, let $Expr_{3.rhs}$ denotes the expression, $ticket.price*nFull$, on the right hand side of statement 3. Since $ticket.price$ is an object access occurring in the expression $Expr_{3.rhs}$, an invoked function call $Expr_{3.rhs}.vars(env)$ in this conversion returns two sets:

$Expr_{3.rhs}(env) = \{nFull_0, 1 :: price_2\}$

$Expr_{3.rhs}.(env.1 :: price_2) = \{ticket_1\}$

So we have $c3.wd = \{(fullPrice_1, \{1 :: price_2, nFull_0\}, true), (1 :: price_2, \{ticket_1\}, true))\}$ (where the second one is a scope dependency).

The conversion continues in this way. Finally we get a sequence of diagnosis components $[c1, c2, c3, c4, c5]$, corresponding to each statement. Note that $c4.type = IF$, and $c4.wd = \{(halfPrice_3, \{1 :: price_3, nHalf_0\}, nHalf_0 > 0), (1 :: price_3, \{ticket_1\}, nHalf > 0)), (halfPrice_3, \{\}, true)\}$.

4   Diagnosing with Logical Rules

Our model-based diagnosis engine uses a theorem prover to find conflict sets and thus to compute diagnoses. Since it requires a logical representation, we use the following rules to convert each dependency wd of all diagnosis components:

$$< wd = (x, M_x, P), wd.type = FUNC > \quad \neg Ab(i) \wedge \bigwedge_{y \in M_x} ok(y) \rightarrow ok(x) \quad (1)$$
$$< wd = (x, M_x, P), wd.type = PNTO > \quad \neg Ab(i) \wedge \bigwedge_{y \in M_x} ok(y) \rightarrow ok(x) \quad (2)$$
$$< wd = (x, M_x, P), wd.type = COND > \quad \neg Ab(i) \wedge \bigwedge_{y \in M_x} ok(y) \wedge \neg ok(x) \quad (3)$$
$$\rightarrow \bot$$
$$< wd = (x, M_x, P), wd.type = SCOPE > \bigwedge_{y \in M_x} ok(y) \rightarrow ok(x) \quad (4)$$

Fig. 4. Generation rules for various dependencies.

Note that the path condition should be checked before applying Rule (3). Rules (1) $\sim$ (4) characterize the logical meaning of weak dependencies of various types. For example, Rules (1) and (2) are read as "if the current statement i works correctly and variables in x's dependency set are OK, then x is also OK" (because there is no further variable affecting x). The intended meaning of Rule (3) is that the dependencies on focus hold under a condition, if the path condition is satisfied but variable x is not OK, we cannot assume that the statement i is correct and variables in x's dependency set are OK. Rule (4) is sound because scope variables here are not defined but used, thus if they are OK, their contents (presented by variables) are also OK.

How these rules are used for diagnosing is discussed in the following example:

Example 5 We consider diagnosis components $[c1, c2, c3, c4, c5]$, obtained from Example 4.

For the functional dependency and points-to dependencies stored in $c1.wd$, we apply rules (2) and (1) and have:

$$\neg AB(1) \wedge ok(ticket_1) \rightarrow ok(ticket_0) \tag{4.1}$$

$$\neg AB(1) \rightarrow ok(ticket_1) \tag{4.2}$$

$$\neg AB(1) \rightarrow ok(1::price_1) \tag{4.3}$$

Component $c2$ has a functional dependency and a scope dependency, we use rules (1) and (4) and get logical rules:

$$\neg AB(2) \wedge ok(ageOver26_0) \rightarrow ok(1::price_1) \tag{4.4}$$

$$ok(ticket_1) \rightarrow ok(1::price_2) \tag{4.5}$$

Component $c3$ has a scope dependency (same as before) and a functional dependency, so rule (4) is used (the result is omitted). By using rule (1), we have:

$$\neg AB(3) \wedge ok(1::price_2) \wedge ok(nFull_0) \rightarrow ok(fullPrice_1) \tag{4.6}$$

At component 4, we assume here that we cannot check a certain path condition (e.g., $nHalf_0 > 0$) is satisfied or not. So we can use Rule (3) to convert the conditional dependency $(halfPrice_3, \{\ \}, true)$. So we have:

$$\neg AB(4) \wedge ok(halfPrice_3) \rightarrow \bot \tag{4.7}$$

By applying rule (1), we get a logical rule for $c5.wd$:

$$\neg AB(5) \wedge ok(halfPrice_3) \wedge ok(fullPrice_1) \rightarrow ok(\_return) \tag{4.8}$$

If the test case says that $ok(fullPrice_1)$ and $\neg ok(halfPrice_3)$. By calling the diagnosis engine, we get one conflict set $\{\neg AB(4)\}$. Then we can compute a single-fault diagnosis: $\{4\}$. It is easy to see that this diagnosis isolates the right cause for a bug on statement 4.1, which introduce a wrong arithmetic operator. In contrast, the previous work [10, 11] would list all statements as diagnosis candidates.

Moreover, if we check all path conditions in the conversion of logical rules, we can achieve more precise bug diagnosis. For example, suppose the test case is $\{nHalf_0 = 1, ageOver26_0 = false, nFull_0 = 2\}$. In this case, the logical rules are the same except for component $c4$. Here we only convert the conditional dependency $(halfPrice_3, \{1::price_3, nHalf_0\}, nHalf_0 > 0)$ because $nHalf_0 > 0$ is $true$. So we have:

$$\neg AB(4.1) \wedge ok(1::price_1) \wedge ok(nHalf_0) \wedge ok(halfPrice_3) \rightarrow \bot \tag{4.9}$$

If we now observe that $ok(fullPrice_1)$ and $\neg ok(halfPrice_3)$ is valid. By calling the diagnosis engine, we get one conflict set $\{\neg AB(1), \neg AB(4.1)\}$. Then can compute 2 single-fault diagnosis candidates: $\{1\}$ and $\{4.1\}$. Here we get a precise bug diagnosis $\{4.1\}$.

5   Experimental Results

The proposed algorithm has been implemented in Smalltalk using VisualWorks 7.1 non-commercial. In this section we present the experiments that evaluate two-tiered dependencies with path conditions. Experiments are performed on a sun Ultra 60 workstation (model 2450, 2.0 GB memory, 450MHz CPU speed), running Solaris 8 operating system. The results are reported in the following tables.

Table 1 lists the benchmarks and methods that we use to measure our model-based debugger's performance. All programs listed involved various control flows (shown by the column N-if&Loop, which represents the number of if-statements and while-statements, and possibly some of them are embedded), virtual method invocation (shown by the rightmost column), and object-oriented language notations, such as multiple objects, class creation, instance method calls, class and instance variables, etc (shown by the rightmost column).

Table 1. Benchmarks and debugged methods.

Program	Main Methods	Lines [num.]	N-If&Loop[2] [num.,num.]	Object Accesses [num.]
LinkedList	insert, remove findOrNil, findMax, findMin	136	6, 5	50
LinkedStack	put, remove, countEntries getValue, getPredecessor, test	157	2, 4	22
Ticket	Ticket, price, test asTicket, halfPrice	200	20, 2	20
Library	Library, addBook getNumberOfBooks, demo	174	1, 1	25
Adder	and, or, not, demo	69	5, 0	0
SumPowers	power, sumPowers	36	1, 2	0

To evaluate the debugger's capability, we intensionally inject a single fault into the method of a certain benchmark, and thus create several faulty version of the correct program. A set of diagnosis candidates is assumed to be sound if they can cover this fault. Moreover, the smaller is the size of diagnosis set, the better diagnosis we have achieved.

Table 2 shows our debugger's performance. It reports the versions of the program analyzed, the time for generating models and making diagnoses, and the number of diagnosis candidates. The results show the faulty statements of all programs can be covered by the diagnosis candidates. Compared with the FDM (the rightmost column in Table 2), the size of diagnosis candidates is indeed reduced for the first four programs because they involve intensive object accesses, and our new model can eliminate much more irrelevant statements. In fact, it is clear that method calls, selection statements and loop statements would raise context-sensitive dependency relations. In this case, induced dependencies become bogus. Therefore, the FDM-based debugger fail to isolate the real cause of program errors.

---

[2] Some loop statements and if statements are embedded.

Table 2. Debugger's performance for model generation and diagnosis correctness.

Program	Faulty Version	M-Generation [sec.]	T-Diagnosing [sec.]	N-Diagnosis [num.]	FDM N-Diagnosis
LinkedList	f1	1.2	0.5	3	6
LinkedStack	f1	0.6	0.4	6	10
	f2	0.5	0.4	5	11
Ticket	f1	2.1	0.3	1	5
	f2	2.1	0.3	2	5
Library	f1	1.3	0.5	4	20
Adder	f1	0.1	0.0	9	9
	f2	0.1	0.0	9	9
SumPowers	f1	0.0	0.0	5	5
	f2	0.0	0.0	4	4

6   Related Work

Several automatic debugging approaches have been proposed so far to help programmers solving the debugging task.

In [9] Jackson proposes to use abstract dependencies as the specification and check the required dependencies against those implied by the source code. This approach is good at catching errors of missing variables.

The PREfix tool [3] detects anomalies by symbolic execution of code. It uses path-sensitive analysis to explore multiple execution paths in a function, with the goal of finding path conditions under which undesirable properties like null pointers hold. Carefully heuristics are needed to detect errors without generating too many spurious reports.

Zeller's Delta Debugging [19] is a technique for minimizing error trails that works by conducting a modified binary search between a failing and a succeeding run of a program.

The ESC [5] uses a powerful tailored theorem prover to check code against user-supplied annotations. It has been successfully applied to find faults such as out-of-bounds array access, null pointer dereferencing and unsound use of locks. However error reports can be spurious. More remarkably, omission of error reports does not imply correctness.

In the last years our colleagues have developed two categories of models for debugging Java programs: (1) the functional dependency model (FDM) [10, 11], and (2) the value-based model(VBM) [12]. Since the construction of dependencies is simple, compositional and automated, the FDM scales up well to large-sized programs, as is shown in [18].

Basically, our algorithm for handling dependencies is an extension of the conversion algorithm presented in [10]. While the original conversion algorithm is fast and it guaranteed to terminate in a polynomial time, it might generate many spurious dependencies because the union operation makes summarized dependencies weaker and weaker. In our model, this is improved by tracking path and relevant context to gain almost-strong dependencies, and Example 5 is a good example to see the weakness of the FDM and the improvement of our model. Moreover, the summary function *merge* of our algorithm combine dependencies at the union level 2. In contrast, the algorithm in [10] do the combination at the union level 1.

Another line of research is to apply model checking technology to detect program errors. Using program slicing and shape analysis, the Bandera project [4] is developing a toolkit that extracts finite state machines from code, which can thus be used by model checkers. The SLAM project has developed a strategy that combines symbolic execution and model checking. They make use of a model checker to produce error traces in order to localize the fault in the source code [2].

7   Discussion and Conclusion

In this paper, we try to find the tradeoff between exact dependencies and cost of modeling. Our approach is to use a two-tiered dependency, which consists of a main dependency and a set of auxiliary dependencies, augmented with path condition and types. Moreover care is taken to merge dependency from different (possibly inconsistent) sources. The experimental results show our approach can achieve better diagnosis results.

But a limitation of our current framework is that we are not considering structural faults (e.g., wrong objects are used at some program points. see [16] for more). The main reason is that automatically generated model is not the program specification but the implementation. One solution under investigation is the process-oriented modeling proposed by Struss and Heller in [15]. The goal of our diagnostic reasoning is to satisfy the test cases (denoted by $GOAL$). We suggest to use a set of test cases to train the generated model. The training process forces the model to be aware of statements necessary for the correct runs (i.e., any syntactic modification over them will lead to an incorrect run). In the meantime, we identify the program points where the dependencies in the initial model can be reduced/increased/removed by a syntactic modification (e.g., a slight modification of if- and while-condition, alias information, etc.). Here we denote these modifications by $ACTIONS$. So the initial model can be revised by taking one of the $ACTIONS$ and assuming that the corresponding relevant program point is abnormal. Afterwards, we validate the current action by checking whether the running against all test cases are correct (i.e., our $GOAL$ is achieved).

Acknowledgments

The work presented in this paper was funded by the Austrian Science Fund (FWF) P15265-N04, and partially supported by the National Natural Science Foundation of China (NSFC) Project 60203015 and the Guangdong Natural Science Foundation Project 011162. The authors like to thank Bernhard Peischl and Roderick Bloem for their comments on the manuscript.

References

1. C. Scott Ananian. The static single information form. Master's thesis, Massachusetts Institute of Technology, Sep. 1990.
2. T. Ball, M. Naik, and S.K. Rajamani. From symptom to cause: localizing errors in counterexample traces. In *Proc. of the 30th ACM SIGPLAN-SIGACT symposium of programming languages (POPL)*, pages 97–105. ACM Press, 2003.

3. William R. Bush, Jonathan D. Pincus, and David J. Sielaff. A static analyzer for finding dynamic programming errors. *Software Practice and Experience*, 30(7):775–802, June 2000.
4. James C. Corbett. Using shape analysis to reduce finite-state models of concurrent Java programs. *ACM Transactions on Software Engineering and Methodology*, 9(1):51–93, January 2000.
5. David L. Detlefs, K. Rustan M. Leino, Greg Nelson, and James B. Saxe. Extended static checking. Technical Report SRC-RR-159, Hewlett Packard Laboratories, December 18 1998.
6. Maryam Emami, Rakesh Ghiya, and Laurie J. Hendren. Context-sensitive inter-procedural points-to analysis in the presence of function pointers. In *Proceedings of the ACM SIGPLAN 1994 conference on Programming language design and implementation*, pages 242–256. ACM Press, 1994.
7. Michael D. Ernst, Jake Cockrell, William G. Griswold, and David Notkin. Dynamically discovering likely program invariants to support program evolution. *IEEE Trans. Softw. Eng.*, 27(2):99–123, 2001.
8. W. Hamscher, Luca Console, and Johan de Kleer, editors. *Readings in Model-Based Diagnosis*. Morgan Kaufmann, 1992.
9. Daniel Jackson. Aspect: Detecting Bugs with Abstract Dependences. *ACM Transactions on Software Engineering and Methodology*, 4(2):109–145, April 1995.
10. Cristinel Mateis, Markus Stumptner, and Franz Wotawa. Debugging of Java programs using a model-based approach. In *Proceedings of the Tenth International Workshop on Principles of Diagnosis*, Loch Awe, Scotland, 1999.
11. Cristinel Mateis, Markus Stumptner, and Franz Wotawa. Modeling Java Programs for Diagnosis. In *Proceedings of the European Conference on Artificial Intelligence (ECAI)*, Berlin, Germany, August 2000.
12. Cristinel Mateis, Markus Stumptner, and Franz Wotawa. A Value-Based Diagnosis Model for Java Programs. In *Proceedings of the Eleventh International Workshop on Principles of Diagnosis*, Morelia, Mexico, June 2000.
13. Wolfgang Mayer, Markus Stumptner, Dominik Wieland, and Franz Wotawa. Can ai help to improve debugging substantially? debugging experiences with value-based models. In *Proceedings of the European Conference on Artificial Intelligence (ECAI)*, pages 417–421, Lyon, France, 2002. IOS Press.
14. Raymond Reiter. A theory of diagnosis from first principles. *Artificial Intelligence*, 32(1):57–95, 1987.
15. Peter Struss and Ulrich Heller. Process-oriented modeling and diagnosis - revising and extending the theory of diagnosis from first principles. In *Proceedings of the Ninth International Workshop on Principles of Diagnosis*, pages 110–117, Cape Cod, Massachusetts, USA, May 1998.
16. Markus Stumptner, Dominik Wieland, and Franz Wotawa. Comparing two models for software debugging. In *Proceedings of the Joint German/Austrian Conference on Artificial Intelligence (KI)*, Vienna, Austria, 2001.
17. John Whaley, Michael Martin, and Monica Lam. Automatic extraction of object-oriented component interfaces. In Phyllis G. Frankl, editor, *Proc. of the ACM SIG-SOFT 2002 International Symposium on Software Testing and Analysis (ISSTA-02)*, volume 27, 4, pages 221–231, New York, July 22–24 2002. ACM Press.
18. Franz Wotawa. Debugging VHDL Designs using Model-Based Reasoning. *Artificial Intelligence in Engineering*, 14(4):331–351, 2000.
19. Andreas Zeller and Ralf Hildebrandt. Simplifying and isolating failure-inducing input. *IEEE Transactions on Software Engineering*, 28(2), feb 2002.

Improving the Scalability of Rule Base Verification Using Binary Decision Diagrams: An Empirical Study

Christophe Mues[1,2] and Jan Vanthienen[1]

[1] K.U.Leuven
Naamsestraat 69, B-3000 Leuven, Belgium
{Christophe.Mues,Jan.Vanthienen}@econ.kuleuven.ac.be
[2] University of Southampton, School of Management
Southampton, SO17 1BJ, UK

Abstract. As their field of application has evolved and matured, the importance of verifying knowledge-based systems is now widely recognized. Nevertheless, some problems have remained. In recent work, we have addressed the poor scalability to larger systems of the ATMS-inspired computation methods commonly applied to rule-chain anomaly checking. To tackle this problem, we introduced a novel anomaly checking method based on binary decision diagrams (BDDs), a technique emanating originally from the hardware design community. In this paper, we present further empirical evidence of its computational efficiency on real-life rule bases. In addition, we will investigate the issue of BDD variable ordering, and its impact on the efficiency of the computations. Thereby, we will also assess the utility of dynamic reordering.

1 Introduction

As knowledge-based systems (KBS) technology is being deployed in business settings where errors may have serious financial consequences or cause considerable damage, the importance of ensuring the quality and reliability of those systems is now widely recognized. As a result, verification and validation (V&V) have become key activities in the KBS development cycle. What's more, with the growing attention that the business rules paradigm is currently receiving from information systems practitioners, the potential scope of application for V&V techniques and tools developed in the KBS realm has broadened even more in recent years.

Especially during the late eighties and early nineties, the traditional view on the V&V of KBS was established. In fact, many of the techniques and tools commonly accepted today can be traced back to that period. Nevertheless, some problems have remained. In this paper, we will address one such outstanding issue: the scalability of the computation methods applied to rule-chain anomaly checking towards larger-scale systems.

Checking for logical anomalies in a given knowledge description (most often a rule base) is a widely applicable KBS verification method. In general, an *anomaly* involves a particular use or rather abuse of the applied formalism that may

S. Biundo, T. Frühwirth, and G. Palm (Eds.): KI 2004, LNAI 3238, pp. 381–395, 2004.

indicate a mistake on the part of the human expert or knowledge engineer – in other words, anomalies should be interpreted not as errors, but as symptoms of possible errors. According to a popular classification by Preece & Shinghal [7], four main classes of rule base anomalies can be distinguished:

- *redundancy*: a rule can be omitted without affecting the system's inferences;
- *conflict*: incompatible inferences can be made from valid initial data;
- *circularity*: an inference depends on itself;
- *deficiency*: no useful conclusions are produced for some valid input set.

To detect the most complex class of anomalies, i.e., those occurring over inference chains, arguably the predominant computation technique at present is rooted in de Kleer's assumption-based truth maintenance system (ATMS) [2]. Its core idea is to represent the input conditions under which an output is true as a set (*label*) of valid input sets (*environments*) [3, 8, 9]. In order to detect anomalies, the computed labels (which are essentially disjunctive normal form expressions) are to be checked against each other. In theory however, the required unfolding process can easily result in an exponential number of environments, with the exponent being in the depth of the reasoning induced by the rule base. In practice, the – albeit rather scarce – reports of case studies on real-world rule bases indeed tend to reveal a rapid increase in the number of generated environments for inference spaces of a larger scale. For example, in [3], the unfolding of knowledge bases of approximately 50, 150 and 370 rules in size took about 700, 4000 and 35000 environments, respectively. Hence, the actual deployment of many of the proposed verification techniques and tools has so far suffered from their limited scalability from toy example to practice [12].

In order to deal with this scalability issue, we have recently introduced a novel KBS anomaly detection technique, which uses *binary decision diagrams* (BDDs) to encode and analyze KBS behavior [6]. BDDs provide a canonical class of rooted, acyclic digraph representations of Boolean functions, accompanied by a set of graph algorithms implementing operations on these functions [1]. Until now, they have to a great extent been studied and applied by the hardware design community, where they contributed to a breakthrough in the scale of digital systems eligible for automatic optimization and verification. There are, on the other hand, a smaller but growing number of reported applications in the domain of artificial intelligence (e.g. [4, 11]), while their use for rule anomaly checking has, to our knowledge, not been proposed before.

The organization of this paper is as follows. Firstly, ATMS-derived checks will be discussed in Sect. 2. In Sect. 3, the BDD representation will be explained. Next, Sect. 4 will illustrate how the latter can be used to check a rule-based system for anomalies. Next, Sect. 5 discusses the results of three experiments addressing the efficiency of this approach on a set of real-world test cases, as well as the impact of variable ordering. Sect. 6 concludes the paper.

2   Rule Base Anomaly Detection: ATMS-Based Methods

Several specialized computation methods have been devised that verify a rule base by converting it into some specific representation where certain anomalies become more explicit and thus easier to check for. The required algorithms however generally fall within three main theoretical complexity categories [7]. Firstly, a linear-complexity class of *integrity checks* over inputs, rules and goals must be capable of revealing the absence of certain cross-references: unsatisfiable conditions, unusable rule consequents, and unused inputs – all of them concerned with the 'connectivity' of the rule base – are detected in this manner. Secondly, *rule pair checks* search for redundant or conflicting rule pairs by comparing each rule against all other rules. Their complexity is quadratic, viz. $O(n^2)$, where n is the number of rules. Thirdly, *rule chain checks* are to detect the most general types of redundant, conflicting, circular and missing rule anomalies. To that end, they have to systematically explore the inference space induced by the rule base, by tracing and analyzing chains of rules. Here, theoretical complexity generally is $O(b^d)$, where b and d denote the breadth and depth of that search space, respectively. Clearly, these algorithms face the risk of combinatorial explosion as the problem size increases. For that reason, and because the earlier two classes are essentially concerned with special cases of anomalies whose detection can be incorporated into rule-chain checking procedures as well, we have chosen to focus on the latter class.

Ginsberg [3] and Rousset [9] were the first to propose a rule-chain checking technique rooted in ATMS label calculus. Their systems were named KB-Reducer and COVADIS, respectively. Further developments were implemented in Preece's COVER tool (e.g. [8]). The core idea of the approach is to unfold the rule base into a series of so-called *labels*, which explicitly state the dependencies between the inputs and outputs of the reasoning. The label of an output is basically a set of *environments* (the latter being defined as valid sets of input facts that may be supplied to the system), from (a superset of) each of which the output can be inferred. Each label is computed by forward (cf. [3]) or backward (cf. [8,9]) chaining through the rule base, substituting intermediate hypotheses in partial labels until only inputs remain. During this process, these labels are checked against each other for anomalies. A path of rules is associated with each environment for reporting purposes.

Let us illustrate this using the following example rule base for determining a person's academic status (for a more detailed explanation, we refer to [8]):

$$univMember(X) \wedge enrolled(X) \rightarrow student(X) \qquad (\mathrm{r}1)$$
$$student(X) \wedge \neg hasDegree(X, bSc) \rightarrow undergraduate(X) \qquad (\mathrm{r}2)$$
$$student(X) \wedge hasDegree(X, bSc) \rightarrow graduate(X) \qquad (\mathrm{r}3)$$
$$enrolled(X) \wedge \neg hasDegree(X, bSc) \rightarrow undergraduate(X) \qquad (\mathrm{r}4)$$
$$\neg student(X) \rightarrow staff(X) \qquad (\mathrm{r}5)$$

Let $univMember(a)$, $enrolled(a)$, $hasDegree(a, bSc)$ be the possible inputs to the system. Accordingly, let $undergraduate(a)$, $graduate(a)$ and $staff(a)$ be (mutually incompatible) goal outputs.

In order to check this rule base, we build labels for its respective outputs. For example, $undergraduate(a)$ can be inferred via two different inference paths:

Table 1. ATMS labels for the academic rule base.

goal	label	rule paths
$undergraduate(a)$	$\{\{enrolled(a), \neg hasDegree(a, bSc)\}\} \vee$ $\{\{univMember(a), enrolled(a), \neg hasDegree(a, bSc)\}\}$ $= \{\{enrolled(a), \neg hasDegree(a, bSc)\}\}$	$(r_4),$ (r_1, r_2)
$graduate(a)$	$\{\{univMember(a), enrolled(a), hasDegree(a, bSc)\}\}$	(r_1, r_3)
$staff(a)$	$\{\{\neg univMember(a)\}, \{\neg enrolled(a)\}\}$	(r_1, r_5)

either directly from rule r_4, resulting in a first environment, viz. $\{enrolled(a),$ $\neg hasDegree(a, bSc)\}$, or using r_1 and r_2, that is, through the intermediate hypothesis $student(a)$. By substituting the literal $student(a)$ in the antecedent of r_2 by the antecedent of r_1, we are able to trace back the firing of the latter path to a certain combination of inputs, viz. $\{univMember(a), enrolled(a),$ $\neg hasDegree(a, bSc)\}$. Both sets can then be joined as members of a tentative label for $undergraduate(a)$. At that point however, we observe that the second set is a superset of the first one, so it can as well be eliminated in the final label (cf. Table 1). Accordingly, the rule path (r_1, r_2) does not contribute to the reasoning of (r_4), and is thus found redundant. Apart from this redundancy, the rule base also contains a case of conflict, as the conjunction of the labels for $staff(a)$[1] and $undergraduate(a)$ includes the valid combination $\{enrolled(a),$ $\neg hasDegree(a, bSc), \neg univMember(a)\}$.

The efficiency of such an approach clearly depends on the compactness of these generated label expressions. It is however well known that these may require exponential size, with the exponent being in the depth of the rule set (we refer to [5] for a detailed treatment on the issues of decidability and complexity). Therefore, we have investigated a potentially more time- and space-efficient representation for the functional behavior of a KBS, viz. binary decision diagrams.

3   Binary Decision Diagrams

OBDD Representation. A *binary decision diagram* (BDD) is a rooted, directed acyclic graph, with two sink nodes labelled by the constants 0 and 1, and whose internal nodes are of out-degree two. Each internal node v is labelled by a binary variable $var(v) = x_i$ $(i = 1, ..., n)$. Its two outgoing edges are labelled by 0 and 1, and are usually depicted as dotted and solid lines, respectively. Let the two corresponding successor nodes of v be denoted by $low(v)$ and $high(v)$, respectively. A BDD is *ordered* (OBDD), iff, on all paths through the graph, the variables respect a given linear order $x_1 \prec x_2 \prec ... \prec x_n$; i.e., for each edge leading from a node labelled by x_i to a node labelled by x_j, it holds that $x_i \prec x_j$.

---

[1] In the example, negation is assumed to be decided by the notion of *negation-as-failure* (i.e., the inference engine will assume $\neg student(a)$ when all rules that might infer $student(a)$ have failed).

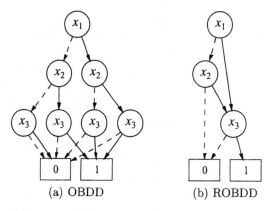

(a) OBDD (b) ROBDD

Fig. 1. BDD examples.

An OBDD is meant to represent an n-variable Boolean function, $\{0,1\}^n \rightarrow \{0,1\}$. For a given assignment to the variables, the function value is determined by tracing a path from the root to a sink, thereby following the edges indicated by the values assigned to the variables. The label of the sink node specifies the function value assigned for that input case. Fig. 1a displays an example of an OBDD for a three-variable function given by the Boolean formula $(x_1 + x_2) \cdot x_3$, with respect to the variable order $x_1 \prec x_2 \prec x_3$.

Reduced OBDDs. Up to here, OBDDs are not yet uniquely determined for each function. However, by further restricting the representation, a canonical form of BDDs is obtained, namely *reduced* OBDDs (ROBDD). An OBDD is said to be reduced, iff it does not contain a node v whose successor nodes are identical (i.e., $low(v) = high(v)$), and no two distinct nodes u, v exist such that the subgraphs rooted in u and v are isomorphic, i.e., for which: $var(u) = var(v)$, $low(u) = low(v)$, and $high(u) = high(v)$. In Fig. 1b, the ROBDD representation is depicted that can be obtained from Fig. 1a. For a given variable ordering, the ROBDD representation of any function is uniquely determined (up to isomorphism), so that several properties (e.g., functional equivalence, constant functions, etc.) become easily testable. Conceptually, a reduced diagram can be interpreted as the result of the repeated application of two types of transformations: one reduction rule is to bypass and delete redundant nodes (*elimination rule*), the other is to share isomorphic subgraphs (*merging rule*). Note that, from here on, we will use the term 'BDD' to denote ROBDDs in particular.

Variable Ordering. When using BDDs to represent a (set of) function(s), some total ordering of the input variables must be selected. Since the size of a BDD is very sensitive to this choice, finding a suitable ordering is critical: inability to do so will in general lead to unacceptable running times or even memory overflow. Several exact minimization algorithms have been proposed, but, considering that finding an optimal order is an NP-hard problem, they are often too costly for larger problem instances. Hence, many applications select some ordering at the outset, based on a heuristic analysis of available input information (such as the topology of a given hardware circuit). Alternatively, local search techniques have been developed, such as Rudell's *sifting* algorithm [10], which aim at improving a given order of variables. They repeatedly seek a better position for a variable (or an entire group of variables in the case of a variant known as *group sifting*) at which level the BDDs are at their widest, by moving it up and down the current order. Interestingly, the reordering may be invoked automatically in the background, during the course of computations. Therefore, they are often called *dynamic reordering* algorithms.

Basic BDD Manipulations. A number of operations on Boolean functions can be implemented as graph algorithms applied to their corresponding BDDs. For example, binary operations such as the Boolean sum and product can be implemented by the same general procedure, APPLY, which takes as arguments two BDDs representing functions f and g, and a binary operator op, and which produces the BDD representing the function f op g. It operates by traversing the argument graphs in a depth-first manner, returning a node of the result graph at every recursive call. Apart from APPLY, other typical operations include: taking the complement of a function (COMPLEMENT); the restriction of a certain variable to 0 or 1 (RESTRICT); the composition operation, where a function is substituted for a variable of an other function (COMPOSE); finding a satisfying input assignment for the represented function (SATISFY_ONE). Importantly, the devised algorithms are such that, during the computations, the size of the BDD under construction remains bounded, as a reduced form is produced directly, not in a separate step. In fact, all operations listed above have time and space complexities that are at most polynomial in the sizes of their operand graphs.

Over the years, several highly efficient BDD packages have been implemented, which provide interfaces for the manipulation of BDDs. In our experiments (cf. infra, Sect. 5), we have applied David Long's package, developed at Carnegie Mellon University (http://www-2.cs.cmu.edu/~modelcheck/bdd.html).

4   Rule Base Verification Using Binary Decision Diagrams

In [6], we have applied BDDs to the problem of checking a rule-based system for anomalies. The presented approach involves:

- encoding the system's input space into binary form;
- traversing the rule base, thereby constructing BDDs (instead of ATMS labels) that describe the input/output dependencies of the system;
- checking these BDD labels against each other, and reporting any anomalies.

Revisiting the academic rule base, e.g., one can choose to represent its input space by a three-bit encoding, letting x_1, x_2, x_3 denote the presence (value 1) or absence (value 0) of the inputs $univMember(a)$, $enrolled(a)$ and $hasDegree(a, bSc)$, respectively. One can then traverse the inference space, either by forward or backward chaining through the rule base, and, using the selected encoding scheme, compute BDD labels for every hypothesis. For every rule instance in the inference space, a BDD, referred to as the rule label, is constructed using the BDD labels of the literals in its antecedent, and the APPLY or COMPOSE operation (cf. Sect. 3). The label of the corresponding hypothesis is obtained by computing the Boolean sum (again by means of the APPLY operation) of the rule labels of all rule instances having that hypothesis as a consequent. If a backward strategy is applied, the required subgoal labels of the rule's antecedent literals are recursively constructed using the same method; this process stops at any input literal, whose (trivial) label derives its BDD from the agreed input encoding. In contrast, a forward strategy starts at the other end of the inference space, computing rule labels that can be readily built from inputs solely. Then, it typically advances through the rule base on a level-by-level basis, making sure that the labels of all subgoals whereupon the computation of a new rule label depends, are completed beforehand. For the example rule base, either of these processes results in the BDD labels depicted in Fig. 2.

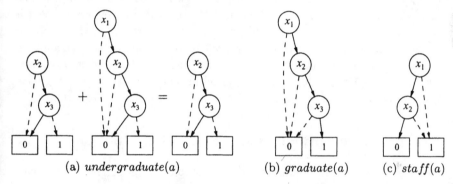

$$(a) \; undergraduate(a) \qquad\qquad (b) \; graduate(a) \qquad (c) \; staff(a)$$

Fig. 2. BDD labels for the academic rule base.

During and after the BDD label computations, various checks can be applied to detect anomalies; only now, we are using BDDs, not ATMS labels, to perform these analyses. For example, checking for the general case of redundant rules again involves a test for label containment, which can be implemented by applying the Boolean implication operation to two argument BDDs (e.g., the labels for rules r_2 and r_4) and verifying whether the result reduces to the single-node BDD $\boxed{1}$ (representing the tautology function). Similarly, we can establish that the incompatible outputs $undergraduate(a)$ and $staff(a)$ can be simultaneously inferred, by computing the Boolean product of their corresponding BDD labels, again using the APPLY procedure. Since the outcome is different from the single-node BDD $\boxed{0}$, a conflict is indicated for the input combinations encoded by the satisfying input assignments of the result BDD (cf. Fig. 3).

A more detailed explanation of the suggested approach, including its handling of (domain-specific) input constraints (through which semantically incompatible sets of inputs may be declared, whose encoding combinations should be treated as *'don't care'*s in the tests for anomalies), as well as its options for the treatment of negation (which determines whether extra variables are needed to distinguish between the absence of certain inputs and falsity), is provided in [6]. Note here that it is not our intent to provide a (logically complete) BDD-based reasoning

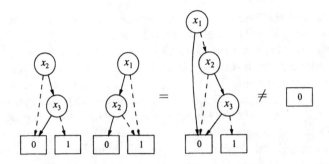

Fig. 3. Checking for conflict: *undergraduate*(a) vs. *staff*(a).

system of our own, but to closely mirror the type of reasoning that will be performed by a subsequent KBS implementation (which, in many of the systems currently applied in a business context, can be logically characterized using a form of modus ponens). The closer the assumptions adhered to in the symbolic evaluation of the rule base reflect the actual inference engine mechanism, the more likely the anomalies thus identified correspond to actual errors. However, as pointed out in [3, 8], useful analyses can often still be provided in situations where the inference engine does not entirely conform to these assumptions.

5   Computational Efficiency: Empirical Evaluation

In this section, we will empirically assess the computational efficiency and scalability advantages of the proposed BDD-based approach over a representative ATMS-inspired procedure, viz. COVER's rule chain check. To conduct our experiments, we selected three real-life rule bases, largely on account of availability:

- Tapes (3M Corp, help-desk);
- DMS1 (Bell Canada, fault diagnosis/repair);
- Handirules (K.U.Leuven, legal advice system).

The former two are public-domain knowledge bases that have served as test cases before in the V&V literature [7] – they were verified using the COVER tool. The third rule base originates from a development effort that involved our own modelling and verification tool environment, PROLOGA [13]. The most relevant statistics regarding their input, goal and rule space are listed in Table 2. Note that, in the number of input attributes[2] and rules shown, unused attributes and rules are omitted from the count, as they do not affect the actual label computations. Additionally, a convenient input space size measure used in the table is the number of bits necessary to represent an input case. If all attributes are binary (e.g., yes/no-attributes), the number of bits is simply equal to the number of attributes. More generally, this measure is the sum of: (1) the log

---

[2] In these systems, rule expressions were constructed using attribute/value-pairs; attributes have determinable types and ranges, and may be designated as *input* attributes (to be supplied by the user) or *goal* attributes (pursued reasoning outputs).

Table 2. Characteristics of the rule bases being verified.

			Tapes	DMS1	Handirules
input space	# input attributes		16	164	125
	mean values per attribute		4.94	2.36	2.11
	# bits		32	219	137
goal space	# goal attributes		1	1	2
	# goal hypotheses		21	1	2
rule space	# rules		101	405	264
	avg. antecedent size		3.57	5.64	4.39
	mean rules per consequent		3.16	12.66	2.56
	depth of reasoning	min.	0	0	1
		avg.	1.84	1.05	8.55
		max.	6	2	11
	# reasoning paths		95	838	419517

to the base 2 of the cardinalities of the value sets of ordinary single-valued attributes; (2) the cardinalities of the value sets for set-valued attributes. Finally, the provided reasoning depth measures are derived from the length of inference paths (i.e., the number of consecutive rule instances minus 1). A flat rule base thus has zero depth.

5.1   Experiment 1: Comparing Time and Space Requirements

The first experiment that we conducted was to run the ATMS-inspired rule chain check for redundancy and conflict implemented in COVER, as well as a BDD-based check, and to compare their performance on the three aforementioned rule bases in terms of running times and memory consumption.

Firstly, as far as the input encoding method for the BDD-based procedure is concerned, we have, in all three cases, applied a compact encoding using as many binary variables as indicated by the '# bits' entries in Table 2. Specifically, yes/no-attributes were encoded by a single variable (1 for yes, 0 for no). To other single-valued attributes with any set of (discrete) values, a *logarithmic* encoding variant was applied in which spare code points (occurring if the cardinality of this set is not a power of two) were dissolved by taking together some of the adjacent higher-end combinations (for an example, see Fig. 4a). Set-valued attributes, finally, were encoded by standard *positional* notation (i.e., allocating one variable per value, cf. Fig. 4b).

Secondly, a relatively simple static variable ordering scheme is adopted, based on goal-oriented, depth-first rule dependency graph traversal, whereby the encoding variables for a certain input attribute are added to the order as soon as the attribute is encountered for the first time in some visited rule's antecedent. This order can be readily obtained during COVER's initial integrity-checking phase, during which the rule dependency graph is built. No additional heuristic for sorting alternatives was implemented: intermediate hypotheses are pursued in the (textual) order by which they appear in rule antecedents. The experiment was conducted on an IBM SP2 workstation. Table 3 shows the running times, together with the aggregate label size at the end of the process.

subs1 (Tapes)	encoding
hasValue upvc	$(0,0,0,0,0)$
hasValue glass	$(0,0,0,0,1)$
hasValue pain_wood	$(0,0,0,1,0)$
hasValue oth_rubbr	$(0,0,0,1,1)$
hasValue lam_chip	$(0,0,1,0,0)$
hasValue cloth	$(0,0,1,0,1)$
hasValue acetal	$(0,0,1,1,0)$
hasValue paint_met	$(0,0,1,1,1)$
hasValue absacryl	$(0,1,0,0,0)$
hasValue sm_se_con	$(0,1,0,0,1)$
hasValue unpaint_m	$(0,1,0,1,0)$
hasValue cc_steel	$(0,1,0,1,1)$
hasValue oth_plas	$(0,1,1,0,0)$
hasValue poly_eth	$(0,1,1,0,1)$
hasValue suit_plas	$(0,1,1,1,*)$
hasValue plywood	$(1,0,0,0,*)$
hasValue p_propyle	$(1,0,0,1,*)$
hasValue ppvc	$(1,0,1,*,*)$
hasValue bare_wood	$(1,1,*,*,*)$

(a) log. encoding example

Trouble_Report (DMS1)	encoding
includes RINGS_DOES_NOT_ANSWER	$(1,*,*,*,*,*,*)$
includes NOISE	$(*,1,*,*,*,*,*)$
includes RINGS_TRIPS	$(*,*,1,*,*,*,*)$
includes CUTS_OFF	$(*,*,*,1,*,*,*)$
includes NO_DIAL_TONE	$(*,*,*,*,1,*,*)$
includes FALSE_DIALING	$(*,*,*,*,*,1,*)$
includes CANNOT_BREAK_DIAL_TONE	$(*,*,*,*,*,*,1)$

(b) positional encoding example

Fig. 4. Input attribute encoding examples. The '*' sign is used to indicate that the corresponding binary variable can take either value (0 or 1) under the shown encoding.

First of all, one must be cautious in interpreting the presented running times, since they are produced by very different implementations. Specifically, COVER is for the most part written in Prolog, whereas the BDD package is composed of highly efficient C-code. Furthermore, there is no common measurement unit available with regard to label size (number of environments versus number of nodes). Therefore, rather than at the absolute figures, one should mainly look at the relative differences in requirements over the three sample rule bases.

In so doing, probably the most striking result is COVER's breakdown on the Handirules case, set against the relative performance of the BDD-based procedure on the same case. More in particular, when compared to the DMS1 case, COVER's performance deteriorates to the point of failure to complete within 24 hours, whereas the BDD-based computations are in fact roughly three times faster on Handirules than they are on DMS1. This result shows that the scalability concerns expressed earlier were warranted. The ATMS procedure indeed turns out to be infeasible on the deepest (cf. Table 2) of the three rule bases, whereas there is considerably less performance variability, both in terms of running time and label size, on the part of the BDD-based procedure. For example,

Table 3. Time & space requirements for ATMS- vs. BDD-based checks.

rule base	running time		label size	
	ATMS-based	BDD-based	ATMS-based	BDD-based
Tapes	0 min. 26.9 sec.	0 min. 0.3 sec.	167 environments	996 nodes
DMS1	3 min. 10.9 sec.	0 min. 3.6 sec.	1626 environments	2492 nodes
Handirules	> 24 hrs.	0 min. 1.1 sec.	> 28532 environments	8863 nodes

while the BDD node count scales up nicely from 996 nodes for Tapes, over 2492 for DMS1, to 8863 for Handirules, the corresponding increase in the number of ATMS label environments is much more prominent (note that, although it could not be obtained, the ultimate environment count for Handirules will most likely lie well above 28532, which is the last reported figure).

5.2   Experiment 2: Growth Analysis of Computed Labels

In the second experiment, we were interested in the evolution of ATMS- vs. BDD-label size in the course of computations. More specifically, we considered the number of environments and BDD nodes, respectively, after processing each rule. In theory, we may apply any rule processing order, but in order to make a fair comparison, we should at least apply the same rule order in both instances. In addition, to provide an insightful picture of how label growth relates to reasoning depth in specific, we have chosen to partition the rules into levels according to the inference dependencies among them, and then use a forward strategy that processes the rules level by level. This has been done for both the ATMS- and BDD-computations. As could be expected, for Tapes and DMS1, being rather 'flat' rule bases[3], the perceived trends for both methods were not too disparate. The results for the more involved Handirules case are plotted in Fig. 5.

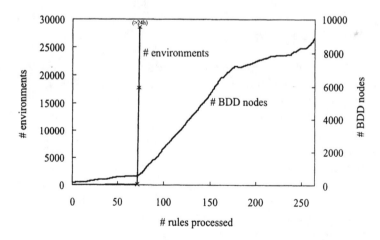

Fig. 5. Handirules: ATMS- vs. BDD-label growth plot.

Upon closer inspection of the latter, COVER runs over a CPU time limit set at 24 hours after having processed 74 out of a total of 264 rules. After a slow initial build-up, an abrupt increase in the growth rate (indicated by a sharp knee in the plot) is observed when the ATMS label computations enter inference level 3. The BDD node count, on the other hand, appears less affected. Roughly

---

[3] For example, a typical inference chain in DMS1 consists of no more than two rule instances (cf. Table 2), while 200 of the 405 rules conclude the system's sole goal hypothesis.

around the same point, the BDD size curve becomes steeper as well, but this change in the slope is far less dramatic than that of the ATMS curve. Moreover, after this bend, the graph reassumes a more or less linear trajectory.

5.3   Experiment 3: BDD Variable Ordering

In a third experiment, we now investigate to what extent the achieved efficiency results depend on the BDD variable ordering. In addition, we will evaluate the usability of a representative dynamic reordering method based on Rudell's sifting algorithm. Firstly, to give an indication of the performance degradation of the earlier outlined BDD label computation and checking procedure in the absence of a well-informed static variable ordering method, we generated ten random orders for the input attributes of each rule base. In the left part of Table 4, the minimum, average and maximum running times and node counts for the matching BDD variable orders are set against the earlier reported results using the depth-first strategy, without any dynamic reordering. The presented running times refer again to an IBM SP2 workstation. Next to the final node count after sweeping up unused BDD nodes, we have also included the number before garbage collection, put between brackets. In the experiment, an upper size limit was set at 10 000 000 nodes.

Next, in the two columns at the right, test results are listed regarding the use of sifting as a dynamically invoked reordering method. On the one hand, sifting may be applied as the sole ordering method, the performance of which has again been assessed using each of the ten aforementioned random permutations as a starting order. On the other hand, we also consider the time and space consumption of a combined approach that starts with the initial order provided by the former depth-first method (cf. 'initial variable order' column), and applies sifting after that. In both instances, the sifting parameters were set to their package defaults, with no extra sifting cycle being called at the end of each run.

Firstly, by comparing the results for the null-method (no static or dynamic ordering algorithm) against the other, one can see that the investigated methods unmistakably improve the performance in nearly all instances. The larger and the more complex the rule base is, the bigger their utility becomes. For example, under none of the ten random attribute orders did the computations for the Handirules rule base succeed without further reordering.

Secondly, the results show that, in comparison with the applied one-time ordering method, (dynamic) sifting is able to find better orderings for the examined rule bases, but at the expense of higher total running times. Since our goal is to obtain not the best, but an acceptable order, we need to consider the trade-off between the additional time spent to find a better order, and the actual application savings of finding one. In this case, the reduced efforts required to manipulate and check such smaller BDD labels do not outweigh the increased time taken by the sifting itself.

Thirdly, our experimental evaluation does not seem to provide evidence in support of a combined approach. Although the total running times turn out to be somewhat lower when sifting starts from the – already fairly good – depth-

Table 4. BDD variable ordering experiment: results.

rule base	initial variable order		no dynamic reordering		sifting	
			run time	# nodes	run time	# nodes
Tapes	depth-first		0m 00.3s	996 (2909)	0m 00.3s	996 (2909)
	random	min.	0m 00.3s	973 (3955)	0m 00.3s	855 (1064)
		avg.	0m 00.5s	1354 (6610)	0m 00.5s	1250 (5930)
		max.	0m 00.8s	1895 (8530)	0m 00.9s	1813 (8530)
DMS1	depth-first		0m 03.6s	2492 (6580)	0m 03.6s	2492 (6580)
	random	min.	0m 03.7s	2464 (8565)	0m 03.7s	1735 (4677)
		avg.	0m 53.0s	3198 (57589)	0m 06.1s	2073 (7380)
		max.	2m 38.8s	5877 (167154)	0m 08.3s	2640 (10637)
Handirules	depth-first		0m 01.1s	8863 (16034)	0m 12.7s	5634 (9794)
	random	min.	N/A	> 10 000 000	0m 10.9s	2758 (5790)
		avg.	N/A	> 10 000 000	0m 16.3s	3711 (7623)
		max.	N/A	> 10 000 000	0m 23.9s	4886 (8854)

first order (at least relative to an average random initial order), there is no clear advantage with respect to the final size of the BDDs. Of course, results may vary depending on the specific parameter settings of the sifting subroutine and on the timing of its last call, but they do tell us that sifting is reasonably robust to whatever variable order happens to be supplied at the outset.

Fourthly, as far as the amount of BDD nodes prior to garbage collection is concerned (cf. the numbers between brackets), we would like to draw the reader's attention to the relatively high numbers reported for the 10 random DMS1-runs. These figures are indicative of the space consumption by the (numerous) redundancy checks involving goal-level rules. As these checks may well be looked upon as an added level of operations to the system's inference structure, these figures hint at the much bigger impact that the variable ordering might have if the rule base were to include an additional level of inference. More directly, the fact that there are quite a lot of rule labels to check against each other also provides an explanation as to why it takes longer to verify DMS1 than it does to verify Handirules (cf. Sect. 5.1).

To conclude this section, Fig. 6 plots against each other the respective label evolution in the course of three Handirules-runs: one employing the one-time depth-first ordering strategy, a second one adhering to a representative random order, and a third one applying sifting to the latter starting order. The depicted data series can be intuitively interpreted as follows. For the first few levels, the respective growth in the number of nodes roughly coincides. After that, at inference level 3, the random-order curve rapidly takes off, whereas the depth-first curve holds out nicely. The sifting graph, on the other hand, rises for a certain time, together with the random graph, but recovers at the point where the original order is abandoned in favor of a better, reshuffled variable order. The effect of a second successful reordering can be observed near the end.

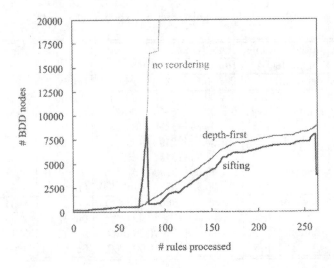

Fig. 6. Handirules: variable ordering methods – growth plot / example runs.

6   Conclusions and Future Work

In this paper, we have presented empirical evidence of the computational efficiency of a novel rule-chain anomaly checking method for KBS verification, based on binary decision diagrams (BDDs). For this study, a test set of real-life rule bases was used, on which we carried out three types of experiments. Firstly, we compared the time and space consumption of an ATMS- and a BDD-based procedure for detecting general redundant or conflicting rule anomalies. Here, we found that the ATMS-derived tool failed to terminate on the 'deepest' of the three rule bases, whereas the BDD-based procedure showed relatively little performance variability over the three test cases. In the second experiment, the respective growth of the ATMS- and BDD-labels during these computations was examined. This analysis showed that the generated ATMS-labels, unlike their BDD-counterparts, rapidly blow up beyond a certain level in the inference structure. Thirdly, the practical importance of the applied BDD variable ordering method was demonstrated. Our comparison of the performance of the heuristic strategy used in the first experiment with (dynamically invoked) sifting and a null-strategy showed that: (1) sifting was able to find better variable orders for the examined rule bases, but at the expense of higher total running times; (2) both methods were clearly superior to a random ordering. Hence, the presented results suggest that BDDs provide an efficient technique for anomaly checking, which scales up well to knowledge bases with a deeper inference structure.

Although, on our present set of rule bases, we have already obtained satisfactory results using the former heuristic variable ordering method, there is of course no guarantee that this method will perform equally well on other, possibly more complex rule bases. Therefore, an interesting topic for further research would be to expand our study and investigate the utility of other ordering methods. More specifically, alternative incremental search techniques, such as *group* sifting (cf. Sect. 3), and other (static) heuristic methods (as in [11]) might be considered. For example, as far as group sifting is concerned, we suspect that the ability to identify groups of variables that should always be moved together, might be particularly relevant in our research context, since the required binary encoding of general discrete attributes easily results in highly cohesive variable subsets, which would otherwise cause the reordering to get stuck in local minima.

References

1. R.E. Bryant. Graph-based algorithms for Boolean function manipulation. *IEEE Transactions on Computers*, C-35(8):677–691, 1986.
2. J. de Kleer. An assumption-based TMS. *Artificial Intelligence*, 28(2):127–162, 1986.
3. A. Ginsberg. Knowledge-base reduction: a new approach to checking knowledge bases for inconsistency & redundancy. In *Proc. of the 7th National Conf. on Artificial Intelligence (AAAI-88)*, pages 585–589, 1988.
4. T. Horiyama and T. Ibaraki. Ordered binary decision diagrams as knowledge-bases. *Artificial Intelligence*, 136(2):189–213, 2002.
5. A. Levy and M.-C. Rousset. Verification of knowledge bases based on containment checking. *Artificial Intelligence*, 101(1-2):227–250, 1998.
6. C. Mues. *On the Use of Decision Tables and Diagrams in Knowledge Modeling and Verification*. PhD thesis, K.U.Leuven, Dept. of Applied Econ. Sciences, 2002.
7. A. Preece and R. Shinghal. Foundation and application of knowledge base verification. *Intl. Journal of Intelligent Systems*, 9(8):683–701, 1994.
8. A. Preece, R. Shinghal, and A. Batarekh. Principles and practice in verifying rule-based systems. *The Knowledge Engineering Review*, 7(2):115–141, 1992.
9. M.-C. Rousset. On the consistency of knowledge bases: the COVADIS system. *Computational Intelligence*, 4:166–170, 1988.
10. R. Rudell. Dynamic variable ordering for ordered binary decision diagrams. In *Proc. of the 1993 IEEE/ACM Intl. Conf. on Computer-Aided Design (ICCAD-93)*, pages 42–47. IEEE Computer Society Press, 1993.
11. P. Torasso and G. Torta. Computing minimum-cardinality diagnoses using OB-DDs. In A. Günter, R. Kruse, and B. Neumann, editors, *Proc. of the 26th German Conf. on Artificial Intelligence (KI-2003)*, volume 2821 of *Lecture Notes in Computer Science*, pages 224–238. Springer, 2003.
12. W.-T. Tsai, R. Vishnuvajjala, and D. Zhang. Verification and validation of knowledge-based systems. *IEEE Transactions on Knowledge and Data Engineering*, 11(1):202–211, 1999.
13. J. Vanthienen, C. Mues, and A. Aerts. An illustration of verification and validation in the modelling phase of KBS development. *Data and Knowledge Engineering*, 27(3):337–352, 1998.

Modeling of Tutoring Processes in Intelligent Tutoring Systems

Alke Martens and Adelinde M. Uhrmacher

University of Rostock
Department of Computer Science and Electrical Engineering
18051 Rostock, Germany
martens@informatik.uni-rostock.de

Abstract. In this paper, a formal tutoring process model for case-based Intelligent Tutoring Systems is described. Case-based training necessitates flexibility and adaptability in an Intelligent Tutoring System. Training cases can be developed in different levels of guidance, reflecting the intensity of support given to the learner. The tutoring process model is described as an abstract tutoring process model. Based on the abstract tutoring process model, the basic tutoring process model and the adaptive tutoring process model are realized. The basic tutoring process model contains no learner model and thus is not able to adapt to the learner. It can be used for the design and the steering of simple training cases. The adaptive tutoring process model contains a learner model and adaptation possibilities. Adaptation takes place as adaptation to the learner and adaptation to the training case's development.

1 Introduction

The 'Intelligent Tutoring System' (ITS) can look back on a tradition of more than 30 years. Combining methods of Artificial Intelligence and Cognitive Science, ITS research has contributed to both areas. Examples are insights into usability of AI techniques resulting from the usage of planning (e.g. [11]), agent technology (e.g. [18]), and modeling and simulation (e.g. [9]) in ITS, and insights into human learning resulting from specifically designed ITS (e.g. [2], [15]).

Over the years, brought forward by systems like GUIDON [3], a common agreement has been reached about the main components of the ITS architecture many years ago (e.g. [1], [3], [7], for more details see [13]). Regarding this agreement, the ITS architecture consists of the main components 'expert knowledge model', 'pedagogical knowledge model', 'learner model', and 'user interface'. This ITS architecture is called the classical ITS architecture. Sometimes, an additional component, called the 'exercise generator', is embedded in the architecture (see [7]). Because this component is rarely usable in case-based training, it will be left out in the following.

In contrast to the agreement about the ITS components, the usage and the interpretation of the role of each component in the ITS is quite heterogeneous.

S. Biundo, T. Frühwirth, and G. Palm (Eds.): KI 2004, LNAI 3238, pp. 396–409, 2004.

The component's realization and implementation seems to be application dependent and also domain dependent (see [12]). The effects of the heterogeneous usage of the components are: rarely comparable ITS, hardly comparable results of evaluations regarding the underlying learning theory, and not reusable components. These deficiencies can be met by formal methods and by development of fundamental theories for ITS. The lack of formal description has been mentioned by J. Self in an interview several years ago [19]. However, no efforts have been made toward formalization and development of theories yet.

In the last years many approaches have been made toward development of standards and meta-data for teaching and training systems, like the Learning Technology Systems Architecture LTSA [5] or the Learning Object Metadata (LOM) [8]. Standards and meta-data descriptions are helpful for unifying development processes and naming of components, for facilitating communication about systems and exchange of data between systems. However, when it comes to system development, standards like LTSA necessarily have a lack of detail and require additional descriptions. Thus, also in combination with standards and with integrated use of meta-data descriptions of contents, a formal approach is useful supplement.

The 'tutoring process model' is one attempt toward formalization in case-based ITS. It formally describes training cases and the central steering of flexible and adaptive training cases. Integrated in the classical ITS architecture, the 'tutoring process model' interacts with the traditional components 'expert knowledge model', 'pedagogical knowledge model', 'learner model', and 'user interface'. Based on the 'tutoring process model', a centralization of the flow control in the ITS is reached. As a side effect, this has led to clarification of the description of the role and functionality of the other ITSs components. 'Expert knowledge model' and 'pedagogical knowledge model' are released of steering and interaction tasks. They now function as information sources. The 'tutoring process model' takes the information provided by the 'expert knowledge model' and the 'pedagogical knowledge model' and adapts the training case contents to the entries in the learner model. The adapted contents are then shown to the learner via the user interface.

The 'tutoring process model' is realized in the project Docs 'n Drugs – The virtual polyclinic [10] [13], which has been developed at the University of Ulm. Docs 'n Drugs is part of the medical curriculum at the University of Ulm since the year 2000 (see www.docs-n-drugs.de).

The 'tutoring process model' has been developed for case-based ITS. Thus, in the following, a short introduction to case-based training and the three dimensions of adaptation is given. Afterward, the 'tutoring process model' is described. The description starts with the abstract 'tutoring process model' and the training cases. Then, the 'basic tutoring process model' is introduced. Next, the extension with the learner model leads to the 'adaptive tutoring process model'. To complete the approach described, the notion of paths and partial paths in the training case is sketched. The paper concludes with a discussion and outlook.

2   Case-Based Training

Case-based training is used traditionally in domains like education in law science, business science, and in medical science (see [12] [14]). Case-based training can only be realized with flexible and adaptable contents. Whereas in human-human interaction, flexibility in the interaction and adaptation of the provided contents comes naturally, in human-computer interaction this is not so easy to realize. To adapt to the learner's abilities and to the learner's choice of steps, and at the same time to stay logical coherent in the provided story line, requires a large amount of flexibility of the ITS.

There exist three dimensions of adaptation [6]:

- Object of adaptation:
  What has to be adapted?
- Object of influence:
  What leads to the adaptation? Why is an adaptation required?
- Time of adaptation:
  When should the adaptation take place?

In case-based training, the objects of the adaptation are the training case contents and the training case navigation, i.e. the actions available to the learner. Generally, training cases can be categorized similar to methods of instruction [4]. Guided training cases, half guided training cases and unguided or free training cases can be distinguished (see Figure 1):

- Guided training cases:
  The guided training case has a linear case structure. The learner interacting with such a training case has no choice of next steps. Thus, he has no scope of actions and no freedom of decision-making. This kind of training case can also be used in a traditional presentation in a lecture. It is suitable for beginners in the application domain. The training case contents can be adapted. An adaptation of navigation can only take place in advance, e.g. via determining the sequence of actions to be taken by a learner.
- Half guided training cases:
  In half guided training cases the information is offered in an unstructured way. These cases contain correct facts or correct and wrong facts. Another dimension of complexity can be added to half guided training cases by integrating different final states. According to this spectrum, the required expertise of the learner depends on the training case's complexity. Adaptation of contents and adaptation of navigation takes place.
- Unguided training cases:
  The unguided or free training case equals the free exploration space. Each training case contains correct and wrong facts and a set of final states. These training cases are only suitable for experts. Adaptation of contents and of navigation can take place, however the number of actions available to the learner and the amount of information provided should not be restricted.

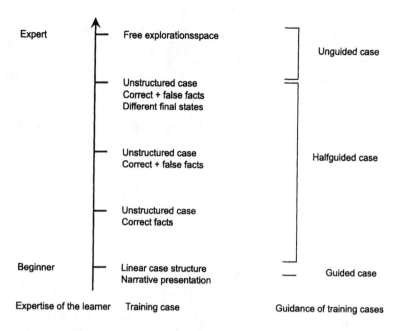

Fig. 1. Levels of guidance in case-based training.

The object influencing the adaptation can be the learner and the information provided in the training case. Learner-related adaptation of the training case is based on the learner model. The training case must be adapted to the learner's capabilities, his knowledge in the training domain, and also to the learner's choice of next step. Thus, the training case must be adaptable in following ways:

1. Adaptation to the learner model:
   Taking temporal aspects into account, two types can be distinguished in this learner related adaptation: initial adaptation and adaptation at runtime.
   - Inital adaptation: The training case should initially be adapted to the learner model. This adaptation should take into account e.g. the learner's expertise, his knowledge in the application domain, and his success in former training cases.
   - Adaptation at runtime: The training case should be adapted to the learner model at runtime. This adaptation should take into account e.g. the learner's increasing knowledge during interaction with the training case, and his success in the current training case.
2. Adaptation to the learner's choices:
   The training case development should reflect the learner's choice of steps. Additionally, the training case must be logical coherent, thus taking content-related adaptation into account.

Last but not least, the different different times when adaptation can take place shall be explicated. Adaptation can take place initially and at runtime, or as a combination of both. Initial adaptation without adaptation at runtime takes place for example in guided training cases. Here, the object influencing the adaptation is the learner model. A combination of both will usually be performed in half-guided training cases. Here, adaptation should take the learner model, changes in the learner model, and the training case's development into account.

To allow for adaptation in the described way, the training case must be flexible and variably structured. However, it is hardly possible to develop a realistic training case in all its complexity. In developing training cases, the training case's author has to make some didactical decisions in advance. These didactical decisions concern the competence in the application domain required by the learner, the guidance the system should provide for supporting the learner, and also the answer to the question what should be learned with the training case. The author's decisions are reflected in the didactically elaborated training case contents and in the overall structure of the training case.

3   The 'Tutoring Process Model'

The 'tutoring process model' is a formal description of the new established ITS component, which allows for adaptation in all three dimensions described in the last section. In centralizing the 'tutoring process model', the classical ITS architecture has been changed (see Figure 2). The term 'tutoring process model' is intentionally constructed and consists of the terms 'tutoring process' and 'process model'. 'Tutoring process' is used in instead of 'teaching process' or 'learning process'. 'Teaching process' denotes the process of knowledge transfer by a teacher. 'Learning process' can be seen as the process of learning and knowledge acquisition by the learner. The term 'tutoring process' has its origins in 'Intelligent Tutoring System' and thus can be interpreted as the knowledge transfer by an ITS. The role of the tutor is taken over by the ITS. In contrast to the human teacher, the software-tutor has only a part of the teacher's knowledge available. The tutor's knowledge is represented in the ITS in the 'expert knowledge model' and in the 'pedagogical knowledge model'.

Even if the developed 'tutoring process model' is not a kind of social science model, a classification of models described by Troitsch [20] can be used to classify the 'tutoring process model'. According to Troitsch, a classification of model classes differentiates between static models and process models. The process model describes a sequence of actions in a state space. Due to this description, the 'tutoring process model' is a process model. In each step, the learner has the possibility to select one action out of a set of actions. Via selection of actions, the learner initiates state changes, thus he moves from one state to another. The selection of actions by the learner is also described as navigation in the training case.

The abstract 'tutoring process model' is a structure (see [12]):

$$TPM = \langle C, show, enable \rangle \tag{1}$$

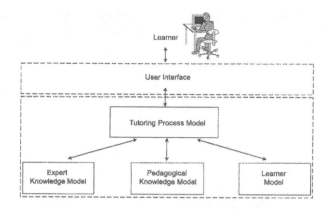

Fig. 2. ITS architecture with central 'tutoring process model'.

with:
C training case
show   show state function
enable enable action function

The training case C is a structure itself, consisting of:

$$C = \langle Q, A, q_0, F, B, \delta, select, allow \rangle \tag{2}$$

with:
Q finite set of states
A finite set of actions
$q_0 \in Q$ start state
$F \subset Q$ finite set of final states
B finite set of bricks
δ state transition function
select   select brick function
allow   select action function

The abstract formal 'tutoring process model' consists of a training case C and the functions *show* and *enable*. The training case C is also a structure, consisting of a set of states Q and a set of actions A. An action always leads to exactly one state. Each training case has only one start state $q_0 \in Q$ but can have multiple final states $f \in F$.

States Q and F contain the elements displayed to the learner on the monitor. To achieve flexibility in constructing this display, each state consists of a set of bricks B. Bricks are the parts that actually contain the information that shall be displayed to the learner, e.g. text, pictures, or composed interaction elements. For example, in Figure 3, one text brick and two picture bricks are displayed. Adaptation of contents can take place via selecting bricks. Regarding the first dimension of adaptation described in Section 2, the first 'object of adaptation'

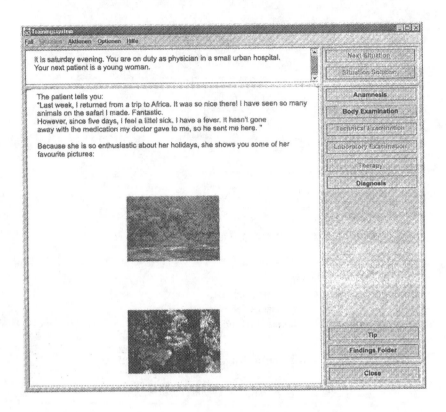

Fig. 3. Example of a display [12].

are the bricks. Accordingly, bricks play their main role in the 'adaptive tutoring process model' and thus will be described in detail in Section 5.

Regarding the display on the monitor (see Figure 3), actions A are available for the learner as the elements of the navigation. Elements of the navigation can be available, i.e. they are active and can be chosen by the learner (e.g. 'Anamnesis' in Figure 3), or not available, i.e. they are displayed in gray and cannot be chosen (e.g. 'Therapy' in Figure 3). Via adaptation of the amount of available actions in each step of the training case, the levels of guidance are realized. If in each step exactly one action is available, the training case is guided – the learner has no choice of next steps. The contrast is the unguided or free training case, where always all actions are available. In-between is the half guided training case. Only a subset of all actions is available in each step. The amount of available actions is adapted at runtime. Regarding the first dimension of adaptation in Section 2, the second 'object of adaptation' are the actions. This adaptation requires the 'adaptive tutoring process model', described in Section 5.

The state transition function δ determines the transition from one state to another, depending on the action chosen by the learner. The function *select* selects the bricks associated with each state. The function *allow* is responsible for the selection of the actions associated with the new state. The functions *select* and *allow* do not constitute the new display for the learner. Another selection step has to take place, performed by the 'tutoring process model' functions *show* and *enable*.

The functions *show* and *enable*, which are not part of the training case, have to be extended in the 'basic tutoring process model' and in the 'adaptive tutoring process model'. The function *show* is responsible for determining the bricks that shall be displayed to the learner. As input, the function uses the set of bricks determined by *select*. The function *enable* is responsible for selecting the action, which shall be displayed after the new state is determined. These selected actions constitute the new navigation displayed to the learner together with the new page. As input, the function uses the set of actions determined by *allow*.

4   'Basic Tutoring Process Model'

The 'basic tutoring process model' $TPM_{basic} = \langle C, show, enable \rangle$ specifies the functions *show* and *enable* in a way that allows the construction of simple training cases without adaptation. The development of these training cases is easy compared to the development of adaptive training cases. The navigation is usually less complex in not adaptive training cases. The 'basic tutoring process model' works without a learner model. An initial adaptation of a training case, e.g. to the learner's expertise, might be possible, but is not part of the formal description. Another kind of adaptation is not taking place.

The show state function *show* determines exactly the bricks for display that are derived by the select brick function *select*:

$$\forall q \in Q : show(q) \equiv select(q)$$

The enable action function *enable* works in a similar way:

$$\forall q \in Q : enable(q) \equiv allow(q)$$

i.e. exactly the set of actions, which are determined by the select action function *allow* will constitute the new navigation.

5   'Adaptive Tutoring Process Model'

To realize adaptation with the 'tutoring process model', an extension of the model and the integration of a learner model are necessary. A simple learner model is introduced. Regarding the second dimension of adaptation in Section 2, the learner model is an 'object of influence' for the adaptation. At the current state, the learner model represents the minimal information required for adaptation and should be extended in future work. The learner model should at least consist of two parts. The first part is the learner's profile LP, which can be perceived as 'knowledge about the learner'. It can contain information like the learner's expertise, his name, his experience etc. The second part is the 'knowledge of the learner' LW. It can for example contain information about the facts the learner has acquired during interaction with the training case. Thus, regarding again the dimensions of adaptation in Section 2, the learner model contains static information for the initial adaptation (i.e. the learner's profile LP), and dynamic information for continuous adaptation (i.e. the learner's knowledge LW). It might be discussed that the learner's profile could change at runtime. However, this is part of future work and will be left out in the following.

The learner model is a structure

$$LM = \langle LP, LW \rangle \tag{3}$$

Here, LP is a structure $LP = \langle id, expertise \rangle$, and LW is a structure $LW = \langle id, Lpath, Lresult, Lacq \rangle$
LP's components are:

$$\begin{array}{ll} id & \text{identification of the learner} \\ expertise & \text{the learner's expertise} \end{array}$$

LW's components are:

$$\begin{array}{ll} id & \text{identification of the training case} \\ Lpath & \text{the partial path} \\ Lresult & \text{set of results} \\ Lacq & \text{set of facts} \end{array}$$

An actualization of the learner model has to take place after each selection of an action by the learner, to allow for an adaptation during runtime that takes changes in the learner model into account. The basis for this actualization is the definition of paths $path$ and partial paths $part$, as sketched in Section 6.

The 'adaptive tutoring process model' now contains the learner model LM described above:

$$TPM_{adapt} = \langle C, LM, show, enable \rangle \tag{4}$$

$$\begin{array}{ll} \text{with:} \\ C & \text{training case} \\ LM & \text{learner model} \\ show & \text{show state function} \\ enable & \text{enable action function} \end{array}$$

In the 'adaptive tutoring process model', bricks and actions are now represented as structures themselves, to allow for a finer grained adaptation strategy.

The bricks $b \in B$ contain a pre-condition PRE, which is used to evaluate whether the brick will be selected to be part of the display or not. Additionally, bricks contain facts, noted as post-conditions $POST$, which become part of the learner's knowledge LW if the brick is displayed to the learner. Thus, each brick from the set of bricks $b \in B$ is a structure:

$$b = \langle id, con, PRE, POST \rangle \tag{5}$$

with:
id   identification of the brick
con   list of content elements
PRE set of preconditions
$POST$ set of postconditions

The list of content elements can be distinguished in information elements, providing only information that does not require any further action by the learner, and interaction elements, where the learner has to perform any kind of interaction like answering questions (see [12]).

Actions $a \in A$ also contain pre-conditions PRE. Same as the brick's pre-condition, the action's pre-condition determines whether the action will be available to the learner or not. In contrast to bricks, actions have no post-conditions. However, the action itself will be recorded in the learner model after selection by the learner. This information can be used for evaluation of the learner's knowledge (see [12] and [11]). An action $a \in A$ is a structure:

$$a = \langle id, name, PRE \rangle \tag{6}$$

with:
id   identification of the action
name   (display) name
PRE set of preconditions

The functions *show* and *enable*, both of which had no real functionality in the 'basic tutoring process model', are now extended.

The show state function *show* is now responsible for the selection of the bricks that should be displayed in a certain training case C, given the learner model LM of the learner currently interacting with the training case. Thus, *show* derives a subset of the bricks, determined by *select*:

$$show : 2^B \times LP \times LW \longrightarrow 2^B$$

with:

$$show(B_q, expertise, Lacq) = B_a$$

where B_q is the set of bricks determined by *select*, i.e. the bricks associated with the state Q. *expertise* is the entry in the learner's profile, and $Lacq$ is the amount of facts the learner has acquired so far. $B_a \neq \emptyset$, i.e. there must be at least one brick to be displayed.

The enable action function *enable* is now responsible for the selection of the actions that constitute the learner's navigation in the new page. As input, *enable* takes the set of actions determined by *allow*, and adapts them to the learner model, i.e. selects a subset.

$$enable : 2^A \times LP \times LW \longrightarrow 2^A$$

with:

$$enable(A_q, expertise, Lacq) = A_a$$

where A_q is the set of actions determined by *allow*, *expertise* and *Lacq* are the same as described above. There should be at least one action that meets the preconditions, i.e. with $a \in A_a$ and $pre_a \in PRE_a$ it is:

$(A_a \subseteq A_q \subseteq A) \wedge \forall a \in A_a . (pre_a \in Lacq \vee pre_a = expertise \vee PRE_a = \emptyset)$

As can be seen above, the set of pre-conditions PRE of an action $a \in A$ can also be the empty set – then, the action is always active.

By constructing the pre-conditions, the author of a training case can make sure, that the training case is adapted in a way that meets the required level of expertise by the learner. Regarding the third dimension of adaptation of Section 2, the 'time of adaptation', the 'adaptive tutoring process model' uses the pre-conditions for adaptation at runtime. The entries in the learner model can additionally be used for an initial adaptation of the training case.

6   The Notion of Paths

The brick's structure together with the structure of actions, as described above, allows itself to model paths in the training case. Paths and partial paths are currently used to track and record the learner's chosen sequence of steps in the training case. Being close to the notion of AI plans, the paths and the partial paths can be used to evaluate the learner's performance, and, possibly, to reason about the learner's mental plans, as suggested in [11]. This, however, is work in progress and requires the close interaction with cognitive science research.

A path in the training case, called *path*, is a sequence

$$path = (q_0, a_1, a_2, ..., a_{n-1}, a_n, q_f) \tag{7}$$

with the start state $q_0 \in Q$, the actions $a_i \in A$ with $0 < i < n$, with the action leading to a final state $a_n \in A$, and with the final state $q_f \in F$.

Each path has to start with a start state $q_0 \in Q$ and has to end with a final state $q_f \in F$. Thus, the shortest path possible is: $path = (q_0, a_n, q_f)$

Usually, due to the adaptation of the navigation, a training case provides multiple paths. The only exception might be the guided training case, as described above. This kind of training case can be developed with exactly one path for exactly one type of learner. For all the other training cases, the set of paths is given by:

$PATH_C = \{p|p \text{ is an allowed path } path\}$

with: $PATH_C \neq \emptyset \wedge |PATH_C| \geq 1$.

The tracking of the learner's way through the training case in *Lpath* requires the definition of partal paths. A partial path is called *part* and can be described as:

part is an allowed partial path

$\Leftrightarrow ((part = (q_0, a_1) \wedge a_1 \in allow(q_0) \wedge a_1 \notin A_F)$

$\vee (part = part' \circ a_i \wedge path' = (q_0, a_1, ..., a_{i-1})$ is allowed partial path

$\wedge a_i \in allow(q_{i-1}) \wedge a_i \notin A_F))$

with:

$q_0 \in Q$ start state

$a_1, a_i, a_{i-1} \in A$ actions with $0 < i < n$

$a_n \in A$ action leading to a final state

A_F set of actions leading to a final state

After every time, the learner has selected an action, the partial path is actualized. The actualization is performed by a function described in [12].

7 Discussion and Outlook

In this paper, the 'tutoring process model' with its two extensions as 'basic tutoring process model' and 'adaptive tutoring process model' is introduced. The 'tutoring process model' has been developed as part of the ITS Docs 'n Drugs: the ITSs central steering component has been implemented based on the 'tutoring process model'. The implementation of the 'tutoring process model' in Java and a description of the 'tutoring process model' in EBNF (Extended Backus-Naur-Form) is given in [16]. The 'tutoring process model' should not be perceived as automata for describing training cases in all their complexity, but as the formal basis for an ITS implementation. Thus, it shall not be used by an author to construct the training case, but by the system's developer. From this perspective, it provides an alternative approach to descriptions or standards-in-development like the LTSA (Learning Technology Systems Architecture) [12].

In the first development of the 'tutoring process model' as the core of an ITS, a workflow-management based approach has been investigated. Based on these thoughts, a workflow editor has been developed [17]. During the development of the system, it became clear that the intended functionality of the 'tutoring process model' cannot be met by workflow management. However, the workflow approach still seems to be promising in steering the interaction in multi-user settings like CSCW (Computer Supported Collaborative Work). This has not been realized in Docs 'n Drugs, yet. It might be interesting to investigate, whether and how workflow and 'tutoring process model' can interact.

The realization of a tutoring process based on petri-nets has been considered. Based on the fact that the 'tutoring process model' does not need the petri-nets main functionalities, i.e. concurrency and synchronization, this approach has not been chosen.

The formal description of the 'tutoring process model' is on an advanced level, not all aspects have been described in this paper (see [12]). However, some aspects still have to be developed. One aspect of future work should be the development of an extended learner model and the integration of this learner model in the 'tutoring process model'. An extensive learner model can be used to evaluate and investigate the learner's progress. Thus, it can be used in a twofold way: on one hand, it would allow for a finer grained adaptation of training cases, on the other hand, it would allow for learning psychological evaluations of learner progress with ITS.

Due to the fact, that the 'tutoring process model' is domain independent, it can be re-used in different systems. The mathematical description should make the 'tutoring process model' language independent. Thus, the model should allow and facilitate communication about ITS and comparison of ITS. Based on the 'basic tutoring process model', even not-intelligent learning systems might be developed. However, this has not been investigated, yet. Another aspect of investigation can be, whether it is possible to apply the 'tutoring process model' to other than case-based training scenarios. It suggests itself, that the 'tutoring process model' is usable for problem-based learning. Work in progress investigates the usage of the model in a modeling and simulation environment for teaching and training.

Main drawback of the case-based approach, described in this paper, is the large amount of authoring work required for the development of an adaptive training case. Thus, the development of an authoring system that supports the authoring process is an important aspect of realizing an ITS. The usage of the 'tutoring process model' as part of an authoring system has not been realized, but seems to be promising. The 'tutoring process model' can be used as central steering component in an authoring system. It might also support the authoring process via controlling and verifying the author's navigation. Extended by a kind of learner simulation, the author might let the authoring system virtually interact with the training case, to see how a learner's work might look like. This can be part of future work.

References

1. Anderson, J. R., Boyle, C. F.,Reiser, B. J.: Intelligent Tutoring Systems. Science, 28, 4698, (1985) 456–462
2. Anderson, J.R., Corbett, A.T., Koedinger, K., Pelletier, W.: Cognitive Tutors: Lessons Learned. Journal of Learning Sciences, 4, (1995) 167–207
3. Clancey, W. J.: Knowledge-Based Tutoring – The GUIDON Program. The MIT Press, Cambridge, Massachusetts, 2nd printing,(1987)
4. Einsiedler, W.: Lehrmethoden. Urban & Schwarzenberg, Wien, Baltimore, (1981)
5. Farance, F., Tonkel, J: LTSA Specification – Learning Technology Systems Architecture, Draft 8. http://www.edutool.com/ltsa, (2001)
6. Harrer, A., Martens, A.: Adaptivitaet in eLearning-Standards – ein vernachlaessigtes Thema?. to appear in: Proc. of the DeLFI conference, Paderborn, Germany, (2004)
7. Lelouche, R.: Intelligent Tutoring Systems from Birth to Now. KI – Kuenstliche Intelligenz, 4, (1999) 5–11
8. LOM Working Group: Draft Standard for Learning Object Metadata, Final Draft Standard, Proposed IEEE Standard. IEEE Learning Technology Standards Committee, (2002)
9. Martens, A., Uhrmacher, A. M.: Modeling Tutoring as a Dynamic Process – A Discrete Event Simulation Approach. Proc. of the European Simulation Multiconference ESM'99, SCS, Warsaw, Poland, (1999) 111–119

10. Martens, A., Bernauer, J., Illmann, T., Seitz, A.: Docs 'n Drugs – The Virtual Poly-clinic An Intelligent Tutoring System for Web-Based and Case-Oriented Training in Medicine. Proc. of the American Medical Informatics Conference 2001, AMIA 01, (2001)

11. Martens, A., Uhrmacher, A.: Adaptive Tutor Prozesses and Mental Plans. Proc. of ITS02, Conf. on Intelligent Tutoring Systems, ITS 02, (2002) 71–80

12. Martens, A.: Ein Tutoring Prozess Modell für Intelligente Tutoring Systeme. PhD thesis, University of Rostock, Germany, DISKI Series 281, (2003)

13. Martens, A.: Discussing the ITS Architecture. Proc. of the GI Workshop 'Ex-pressive Media and Intelligent Tools for Learning', 26th German Conference on Artificial Intelligence KI-2003, (2003)

14. Merseth, K.: The Early History of Case-Based Instruction. Journal of Teacher Education, 42, 4, (1991) 243–249

15. Möbus, C.: Towards an Epistemology of Intelligent Problem Solving Environments: The Hypothesis Testing Approach. Proc. of the World Conf. on AI in Education AI-ED 95, AACE, Washington D.C., (1995) 138–145

16. Volz, E.: Konzeption und Implementierung eines effizienten Ausführungssystems für variable Lehrprozesse. Master thesis, University of Ulm, Germany, (2002)

17. Reichmann, D.: Visual Workflow – Ein Java-Beans basiertes Werkzeug zur grafis-chen Workflowmodellierung. Master thesis, University of Ulm, Germany, (2000)

18. Rickel, J., Johnson, W. L.: STEVE: A Pedagogical Agent for Virtual Reality. Proc. of the 2th Int. Conf. on Autonomous Agents, Minneapolis, St. Paul, ACM Press, (1998)

19. Self, J.: Interview with Prof. Dr. John Self, by C. Peylo at the AI-ED'99. KI – Kuenstliche Intelligenz, 4, (1999) 47–49

20. Troitsch, K. G.: Modellbildung und Simulation in den Sozialwissenschaften. West-deutscher Verlag GmbH, (1990)

A New Method for Asynchronous Multisensor Information Fusion

Kejun Zhang and Jianbo Su

Department of Automation & Research Center of Intelligent Robotics
Shanghai Jiaotong University
Shanghai, China
kejunzh@sjtu.edu.cn

Abstract. This paper presents a novel method for asynchronous multisensor information fusion (AMIF), which is real-time, model free and can provide the capability of reconfiguring sensors. The method is motivated by the idea that the information fusion is a procedure that the data of some sensors complement the data of others. The system computes the complements between the sensors. These complements are used to adjust the measurement at the moment of the fusion with a fuzzy inference system. The detailed principles are first described and the algorithm is then implemented in a calligraphic robot, which includes three asynchronous sensors, image sensor, tactile sensor and sonar sensor.

1 Introduction

Multisensor fusion system (MFS) integrates information from multiple sources to obtain precise description of the environment. The potential advantages, such as redundancy, complementary, timeliness, and cost of the information, allow MFS being applied in many fields including military, satellites, aircraft navigation, robots, and industrial assembly [1-5]. Normally, to increase sorts of information that can be sensed, an MFS often involves many dissimilar sensors. Hereafter, the system should consider not only the problem of sensor measurement missing, but also the coordination between sensors, such as different sampling rates and different communication delays. Accordingly, the asynchronous multisensor information fusion (AMIF) problem becomes common in real applications.

Many methods have been developed to deal with this problem. They can be classified into three categories: Kalman filter, interpolation method and sliding window method.Kalman filter [13, 14] provides an optimal solution in the mean square sense. The Kalman filter bases on the statistic model. When the sensor's model is known and the frequency of the fusion is fixed, the data of sensor in the next fusion time can be obtained by propagating forward the sensor data from the current observation using Kalman filters. However, in dynamic environment, the precise statistic models of the sensors are difficult to achieve. The interpolation method is firstly proposed in [11] and extended in [12]. By integrating all the fast sensor data between two measurements of the slow sensor, the asynchronous multisensor information fusion becomes synchronous one. In

S. Biundo, T. Frühwirth, and G. Palm (Eds.): KI 2004, LNAI 3238, pp. 410–423, 2004.

this method, the fusion is performed when the slow sensor measurement is observed. Therefore, in dynamic environment, this method may fail the real-time requirement. Sliding window method is proposed in [15]. This method is used for multitarget tracking. The system associates the last frames of the image measurement with the track list. Each track is updated to the time of the window tail. The real-time requirement is also a problem in this method.

The above methods have been applied in many cases, however they are limited in dynamic environment for the real time and model free features. In this paper, a novel method is presented to deal with the AMIF problem considering this features. In this method, information fusion is considered as a procedure that the data of some sensors complement the data of others in order to get a precise description of the environment. The system obtains the complements between the data from slow sensors and those from the fast sensor when the slow sensor data are obtained. Then, a fuzzy inference system (FIS) uses these complements to adjust the measurement of the fast sensor at the fusion time. Besides the capability of dealing with uncertainty, FIS is convenient for the reconfiguration of the MFS. It allows adding or deleting a sensor at any time without affecting the entire MFS structure [19]. As the fusing operation is at the time moment that aligns with the measurement of the fastest sensor and does not require any sensor models , this method can satisfy the real-time and model-free features of the dynamic environment. A calligraphic robot system is designed and developed including three asynchronous sensors: image sensor, tactile sensor and sonar sensor. Experiments in this test bed show the feasibility of the proposed method.

This paper is organized as follows. Section 2 analyzes the problem of asynchronous fusion. Section 3 describes the detailed principle and an algorithm implementation of the proposed method. Section 4 provides an application in a calligraphic robot. The final section provides a conclusion of our work and proposed future work.

2 Analysis of the Problem

The asynchronous fusion problem is illustrated in Fig. 1. The system is assumed to include n. At the fusion time: T, the available measurements from n sensors are $D_i(T - l_i), (i = 1, 2, ..., n)$, where $l_i(i = 1, 2, ..., n)$ is the time delay for sensor measurements. In asynchronous fusion problems, every l_i is different. This is not only due to different sampling rate of sensors and the different communication delays, but also due to measurement missing. For instance, in some applications including image occlusions, the image sensor cannot obtain the measurements of the current scene. In that sense, the image data cannot synchronize with other sensors' measurements. In the time-variant environment, every $D_i(T - l_i)$ is the measurement of the different scene. The system cannot obtain a well fusion result by integrated these measurements directly.

In dynamic environment, AMIF problem is more complex. Besides resolving the basic problem: time aligning between measurements, the AMIF method

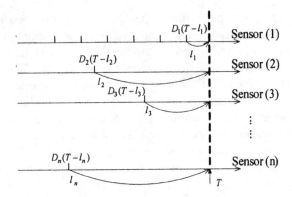

Fig. 1. The condition of the asynchronous fusion.

should realize real-time, model free and provide the capability of sensor reconfiguring.

The real-time is a significant feature of dynamic MFS. The data sampling, processing and fusion must be finished in time. Then, the system can keep up with the changing of the environment. That is to say, the real-time characteristic is an important factor for the availability of whole system. The agent methods in [11][15] do not care it. In these methods, as the fusion results are not time aligned with the latest measurement, the real-time failures may occur.

The model free characteristic is another one. It is caused by many reasons, such as environment changing or unexpected events occurring. The measurement missing is also an important but unattended reason. For example, in the conditions including the image occlusion, the image sensor cannot observe the interested information of the current scene. If the time of the occlusion is long, the image information of the current environment cannot be predicted from the former measurements. In these conditions, the existing methods based on model, such as Kalman filters [18], are not valid.

In the dynamic environment, working conditions often change. Accordingly, the information required to finish a certain task are variant. In some conditions, the system may need additional information to finish the task. In other conditions, some information is not necessary. It means that system should have the ability to reconfigure sensors dynamically. For example, the system can add or subtract sensors dynamically. This kind of capability can not only save the cost of information processing, such as the energy and the time, but also aid the system to accomplish the fusion task. The dynamic AMIF method should also have the capability to reconfigure sensors conveniently.

3 Principle and Algorithm Implementation

Multisensor information fusion can be considered as an information processing procedure that the data of some sensors complement the data of others [12]. In an AMIF system, the complements between n sensors are asynchronous. Accordingly, the focus of asynchronous fusion problem is that how the system gets the complements to the measurement at the fusion time moment. Considering the features of the dynamic environment, a new method is presented in the sequel.

There are two assumptions in the method. One is that the communication delay of each sensor is fixed. The problem with the arbitrary communication delay is not involved in this method. This assumption can be satisfied by most application except for some sensor systems communicating by internet. Another is that there is a fastest sensor among all sensors. The number of this sensor measurement achieved by the system in a time unit is the most. Then, the fusion time moment can be assumed equal to the latest measurement time of this sensor.

The method consists of two parts. In the first part, the system computes the complements between sensors. In the second part, the system associates these complements to adjust the measurement at the fusion moment by the FIS and obtains the fusion result.

3.1   Computing Complements Between Sensors

This part is illustrated in Fig. 2 for $n = 3$ sensors. The sensor with the fastest rate and communication is set to be sensor(1). The fusion time is t. The fastest sensor is set to be sensor(1). The $t1$, S_2 and S_3 are the reversal first, second and fifth measurement time of this sensor, respectively. $D_i(t_j)$ is the measurement of sensor(i) at t_j. According to the second assumption, the fusion time: t is equal to the time: t_1. Then, at the fusion time, the fusion module receives these measurements, $D_1(t_1)$, $D_2(t_2)$ and $D_3(t_3)$. According to the section2, the $D_1(t_1), D_2(t_2)$ and $D_3(t_3)$ cannot be fused directly. While, in Fig. 2, it can be noted that the time of S_2 and S_3 are near to the t_2 and t_3. In that sense, the $D_1(S_2)$ and $D_2(t_2)$ can be considered as the measurements of the same scene. Therefore, they can be associated. For the same reason, the $D_1(S_3)$ and $D_3(t_3)$ can be associated. In our method, the association result of $D_1(S_2)$ and $D_2(t_2)$ is a complement $P(2)$ of sensor(2) to sensor(1). The association result of $D_1(S_3)$ and $D_3(t_3)$ is a complement $P(3)$ of sensor(3) to sensor(1). Since the communication delays are fixed, the S_2 and S_3 can be achieved. The system fuses $P(2)$, $P(3)$ and the latest measurement $D_1(t_1)$ to obtain the fusion result by the FIS. In this part, the fusing procedure focuses on the latest measurement of the fastest sensor. The real-time feature of the dynamic asynchronous MFS can be satisfied. As the method has not to predict the sensor measurements at the fusion moment, it can satisfy the model free feature.

3.2   Fuzzy Interference System

FIS is involved to achieving the complement of the $D_1(t_1)$ from $P(2)$ and $P(3)$. The core of the FIS is the fuzzy theory addressed by Zadeh [6]. It is based on the fuzzy set where every individual has a degree of membership ranging over a continuum of values, rather than 0 or 1. FIS can deal with uncertainty with the

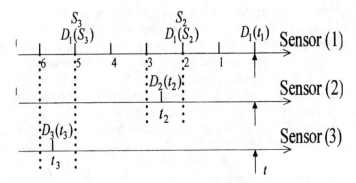

Fig. 2. The asynchronous fusion of three sensors.

subjective decisions of experts. It contains four basic elements: fuzzifier, fuzzy knowledge-base, fuzzy inference engine, and defuzzifier [8]. In this case, the inputs of fuzzifier is the $P(2)$ and $P(3)$. They are partitioned by the fuzzy set. Normally, the accuracy of the output is affected by the number of the fuzzy set. The more numbers of fuzzy sets the system made, the more accuracy of output the system got. However, more numbers of fuzzy sets leads to complicated computation expense. In applications, the number of fuzzy sets will be decided by experience. For example, each crisp input is specified as three fuzzy sets NL, ZO, PL. The linguistic terms NL, ZO and PL correspond to negative large, zero and positive large. It is shown in Fig. 3. The fuzzy sets of the output are the same with the fuzzy sets of inputs. With the input and output defined above, the fuzzy knowledge-base is assumed as the following rule-base structure:

IF $P(2)$ is ... AND $P(3)$ is ... THEN P is ....
IF $P(2)$ is ... AND $P(3)$ is ... THEN P is ....

......

IF $P(2)$ is ... AND $P(3)$ is ... THEN P is .... The fuzzy inference engine

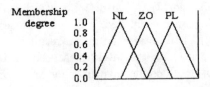

Fig. 3. Example of fuzzy sets.

uses Min-Max method proposed in [9]. The gravity center method is used as the "defuzzification" method. An example is shown in Fig. 4 for the case above. FIS is used to obtain the complement to the latest measurement. For the incoming of FIS, the system can reconfigure the MFS conveniently. For example, if the system subtracted some sensors, the changing of the method is only to remove

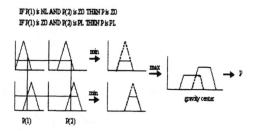

IF R(1) is NL AND R(2) is ZO THEN P is ZO
IF R(1) is ZO AND R(2) is PL THEN P is PL

Fig. 4. An example of FIS.

the corresponding fuzzy sets and fuzzy rules of the FIS. The rest parts of the method, such as other sensors' fuzzy sets, fuzzy rules, fuzzy inference engine and defuzzifier can be unchanged.

3.3 Algorithm Implementation

Assuming there are n sensors in the system, $S(i), (i = 2, ..., n)$ is the communication delay of the sensor(i) according to the sensor(1). The unit is the sampling period of sensor(1). Let $L = max(S(i))$. Build a buffer, $B(i), (i = 1, ..., S)$, to store the measurements of sensor(1). The length of the buffer, S, is greater than or equal to L. Let $P(i), (i = 2, ..., n)$ be the component of sensor(i) to sensor(1). When a measurement, $D_i(t_j)$ of the i sensor at the time t_j, is received, the algorithm is carried out as follows.

1. If the buffer is not full, the system does not carry out the data fusion. The system will wait for the next measurement of sensor(1). The data rate of the sensor(1) is the fastest, thus it will not take a long time to fill the buffer.
2. If the measurement is not from sensor(1), the system takes out the $B(S - S_i)$ and carries out the difference between the $B(S - S_i)$ and the $D_i(t_j)$. The difference is the tentative component of the sensor(i) to sensor(1). It is denoted by $R(i)$. The $R(i)$ is used to update the $P(i)$ by the follows.

$$P^{(n+1)}(i) = \beta(i) * P^{(n)}(i) + (1 - \beta(i)) * R(i) \qquad (1)$$

where the $\beta(i)$ is the weight corresponding to strength of the $R(i)$.
If the measurement is from sensor(1), all the measurements of the buffer are shifted to the left, i.e., the data in $B(2)$ is pushed into $B(1)$, the data in $B(1)$ is lost. The new measurement of sensor(1) is pushed into $B(S)$.
3. If the system needs the fusion result now, the $P(i)$ is passed to the FIS. If the system does not need the fusion, proceed to step 5. In the procedure of the fusion, the FIS gets the degree of membership of $P(i)$ according to the fuzzy set of each input. By using the fuzzy rules and fuzzy inference engine, the output by the FIS is obtained. The Gravity Centre method is used to get the scalar value of the output: P.

4. The fusion procedure will be carried out by follows.

$$fusion = \alpha * D_1(t) + (1 - \alpha) * P \qquad (2)$$

where α is the weight parameter.
5. The system initiates the $R(i)$ and waits for another measurement.

The above five steps describe the implementation of our algorithm used to deal with the asynchronous fusion. To clarify this approach, it is illustrated schematically in Fig. 5.

The algorithm implementation of the proposed method considers the features of the dynamic MFS. Table1 is a summarization of these features and the solutions of the algorithm.

Table 1. The features of the dynamic MFS and solutions of the algorithm.

Features of the dynamic MFS	Solutions of the algorithm
Real-time	The algorithm focuses on the latest measurement of the fastest sensor.
Model free	The algorithm does not need to predict the sensors' measurements of the fusion time. The complements to the latest measurement are achieved by fuzzy inference system.
Dynamical reconfiguration of MFS	The fuzzy inference system allows adding or subtracting the sensor at anytime without affecting the entire MFS.

4   Application

The proposed method in our paper is utilized and verified in a calligraphic robot system, shown in Fig. 6. The objective of the system is to control the robot to write Chinese characters with the help of feedback information of AMFS.

4.1   Experimental System of the Calligraphic Robot

The calligraphic robot system is composed of a robot and an AMFS. The robot is an Adept One robot arm that is an assembly manipulator with four degree-of-freedoms. AMFS includes three asynchronous sensors: a camera, sonar and a tactile sensor. They are located as Fig. 7. A writing brush is connected with the tactile sensor. The tactile sensor and sonar are fixed at the end of the robot. The camera is located over the robot workspace. The sonar is fixed vertically to the paper. The three sensors have the different data rates. The sample rate of the tactile sensor is the fastest and the sample rate of the sonar is the slowest. During the procedure of writing, the Chinese characters are achieved from a man/machine interface. The AMFS of the calligraphic robot works as follows.

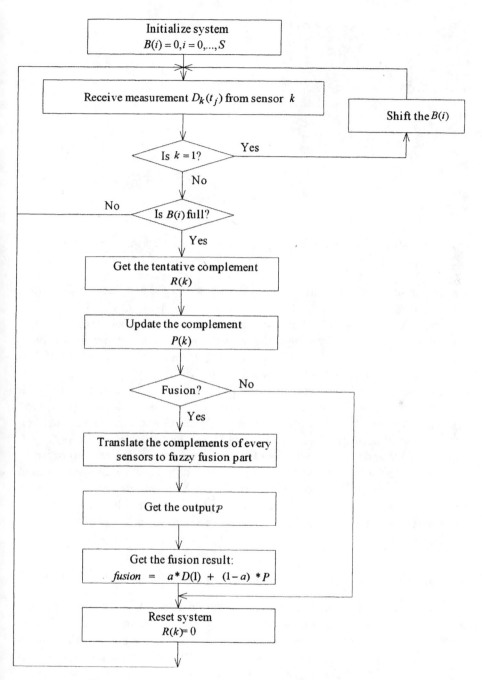

Fig. 5. Asynchronous fusion algorithm implementation.

The camera observes the image of Chinese characters and extracts the width of the current stroke. The sonar measures the distance from brush's end to paper. The width of stroke is wider with the distance shorter. Therefore, the system can extract the width of the stroke from the data of the distance. The tactile

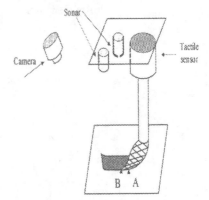

Fig. 6. Calligraphic robot hardware.   **Fig. 7.** Schematic structure.

sensor measures the pressure of brush during writing. The width of the stroke is proportional to the pressure. The width of current point of the stroke can be extracted from the pressure. Three widths coming from three sensors are fused to get a more precise one. By comparing with the width of the stroke in database, the system computes the next coordinate of x, y, z and passes it to robot. Then the robot is driven to finish the movement prescribed.

A decentralized framework of AMFS is used in this robot, shown in Fig. 8. The measurements of three sensors are passed to processing modules (PM) that are run independently. The outputs of each PM are passed to the fusion module as the inputs. The output by the fusion module is a more precise width: $Woutput$. The $Woutput$ and the $Winput$ from Chinese character library are compared to achieve w. The w is mapped to z that is the robot arm moving distance of Z direction. The robot arm moving of the X and Y directions are exacted from Chinese character library. The sensor management part decides which sets and what patterns of the sensors should be used in the different stage of the writing procedure.

4.2   Implementation of the Algorithm in the Calligraphic Robot

For the different data rates and communication delays of three sensors, the outputs by three processing modules are asynchronous. Moreover, for the occlusion of the brush, when the tactile and sonar sensor measures the point A, the camera can only observe the image of point B (in Fig.7). Obviously, if the fusion part of the system used the information of the three sensors directly, the result will be erroneous. In this case, our asynchronous fusion method is used to deal with the problem. According to the section3, the tactile sensor is set to be the sensor(1). The sonar is the sensor(2) and camera is the sensor(3). By experience, the S_2 is 5 and the S_3 is 18. It means the communication delay of sensor(2) to sensor(1) is 5 periodic times of sensor(1). The communication delay of sensor(3) to sensor(1) is 18 periodic times of sensor(1). The length of the buffer: S is 20.

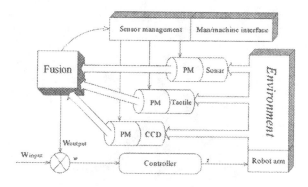

Fig. 8. Framework of the calligraphic robot.

The crisp inputs $P(2)$ and $P(3)$ and the crisp output are specified as seven fuzzy sets NL, NM, NS, ZO, PS, PM and PL. These linguistic terms correspond to negative large, negative middle, negative small, zero, positive small, positive middle and positive large. The FIS includes 26 rules. Min-Max method is used in the fuzzy inference engineer. The gravity center method is used as the defuzzification method. The FIS is shown in the Fig. 9.

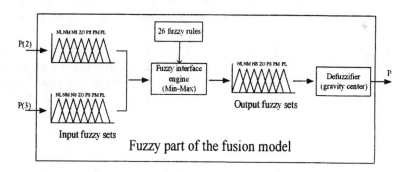

Fig. 9. Fuzzy part of the fusion module.

4.3   Experiment Results

A Chinese character "Yong" is written by the calligraphic robot, shown in Fig. 10. "Yong" includes eight kinds of skills in the writing of the Chinese character. The writing of this word is considered as the basic training of the calligraphy.

To test the proposed method, we do a series of comparison experiments. Firstly, the necessity of asynchronous fusion method in the calligraphic robot is proofed. Secondly, the necessity of the decentralized framework and FIS incoming in the method is proofed.

Fig. 10. Chinese character of "Yong".

Comparison Experiments About Asynchronous Fusion Problem. First-ly, the system used the information of the three sensors directly to write a stroke: "Heng". Then, the same stroke was write again by the system using the proposed asynchronous data fusion (ADF) method. The fusion results are shown in Fig. 11. In the figure, the line is the standard width of the stroke. The "o" points are the fusion results using ADF case. The "+" points are the results without using ADF. Obviously, the values of the ADF results are more approximate the standard values.

The two strokes are shown in Fig. 12. The above one is the result without using ADF. Another is the case using ADF. In the writing procedure without using ADF, the fluctuation of the fusion result is too large. It leads the value of the control is unstable. Then, the stroke cannot be smooth as shown in the figure.

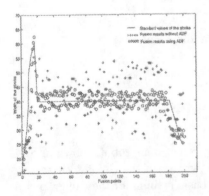

Fig. 11. Comparison experiments.

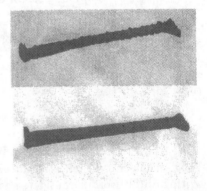

Fig. 12. Comparison of the two strokes.

Necessity of the Decentralized Framework and FIS. The incoming of decentralized framework and FIS is convenient to deal with sensor management problem. The sensor management is to change sensor combination and configuration dynamically to achieve the given sensing goals optimally [16]. Because of aiding to sensor data fusion, it has been used in many dynamic MFS applications [17]. In the calligraphic robot system, the sensor management is necessary. In this case, three different kinds of sensors are integrated. In many conditions, not all the measurements of each sensor are valid. For example, in the connecting and overlaying parts of strokes, the system cannot exact a right stroke width from image data. As shown in Fig. 13, it is a middle stage of writing a Chinese character. Now, it is writing the third stroke: "Shu". The stroke starts at the middle of the first stroke and goes through the second one. In the connecting part (I) with the first stroke and in the overlaying part (II) with the second stroke, from the image, the valid width of "Shu" cannot be extracted. We should stop the image sensor in both parts and restart it when the brush passed them. To illustrate the effect of the sensor management, we do a comparison experiment. In Fig. 14(a), the system did not use sensor management. In Fig. 14(b), the sensor management is used. We can find the part in dotted circle is too large

Fig. 13. The middle stage of writing a Chinese character.

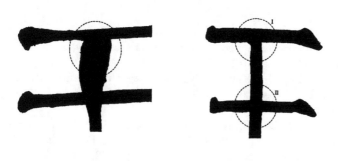

(a): Without sensor management   (b): Using sensor management

Fig. 14. Comparative experiments.

and not smooth in Fig. 14(a). The data of image sensor do bad effects to the fusion result in this part. The part (I) and part (II) in Fig. 14(b) is better.

The conditions of connecting and overlaying of strokes often occur. They appear in various locations of Chinese characters. Thus, the system must meet the requirement of easily performing the sensor management. The decentralized framework and FIS can satisfy this requirement very well. In this framework, the sensor sampling module and data processing module of different sensors are independent. Moreover, FIS allows conveniently reconfiguring sensors. Therefore, stopping or restarting of image sensor can be easily performed and have little effect to tactile or sonar sensor.

5   Conclusion

The problem of the asynchronous fusion is very common in MFS. Considering the features of the dynamic MFS, we present a new method to deal with this problem. In this method, multisensor information fusion is considered as a procedure that the data of one sensor are complemented by the data of others. The method includes two parts. The first part is to compute the complements between asynchronous sensors. The second part is to integrate these complements and the latest measurement to obtain the fusion result by FIS.

The method is applied in a calligraphic robot. This robot has 3-D moving comparing with existed works [10]. It includes three asynchronous sensors: a camera sensor, a tactile sensor and sonar. Experiments lead to the conclusion that the method can deal with the asynchronous fusion problem very well.

In this paper, the method is used as an asynchronous filter. It seems, however, that the method can be applied in other fusions, such as feature fusion and decision fusion. In the future works, we will extend the applying range of this method.

References

1. Ren C. Luo, Chih-Chen Yih, and Kuo Lan Suk, "Multisensor fusion and integration–approaches, applications, and future research directions", IEEE SENSORS JOURNAL, vol. 2, APRIL 2002.
2. Ren C. Luo, Michael G.Kay, "Multisensor Integration and Fusion in Intelligent Systems", IEEE Transaction on Systems, Man and Cybernetics, vol.19(5), pp.901-931, 1989.
3. Luo, R.C., Kay, M.G. and Lee, W.G., "Future Trends in Multisensor Integration and Fusion, Industrial Electronics", 1994. Symposium Proceedings, ISIE '94, 1994 IEEE International Symposium on, vol.25-27, pp.7 -12, May 1994.
4. P. K. Varshney, "Multisensor Data Fusion", Electron. Commun. Eng. J. pp.245-253, 1997.
5. David L. Hall. Mathematical Techniques in Multisensor Data Fusion. ARTECH HOUSE, INC. 1992.
6. L.A. Zadeh, "Fuzzy Sets and Systems", North-Holland, Amsterdam, 1978.

7. Fabrizio Russo, "A Fuzzy Approach to Digital Signal Processing: Concepts and Applications", Instrumentation and Measurement Technology Conference, pp.640-645, May 1992.
8. Y.M. Chen, H.C. Huang, "Fuzzy Logic Approach to Multisensor Data Association", Mathematics and Computers in Simulation. vol.52, pp.399-412, 2000.
9. E.H. Mamdani, "Application of Fuzzy Logic to Approximate Reasoning Using Linguistic Synthesis", IEEE Trans. Comput., C-26 (1977).
10. Potkonjak, V., Tzafestas, S., Kostic D., Djordjevic, G. and Rasic, M, "The handwriting problem [man-machine motion analogy in robotics]", Robotics & Automation Magazine, IEEE, vol.10, pp.35-46, March 2003.
11. Blair, W. D., T. R. Rice, A. T. Alouani, and P. Xia, "Asynchronous Data Fusion for Target Tracking with a Multi-tasking Radar and Optical Sensor", SPIE International Society for Optical Engineering, vol. 1482, 1991.
12. A. T. Alouani and T.R.Rice, "On Asynchronous Data Fusion", Proceeding of the Annual Southeastern Symposium on System Theory, Athens, 1994, pp.143-146.
13. A. T. Alouani and T. R. Rice, "On Optimal Asynchronous Track Fusion",ADFS '96., First Australian , 21-22 Nov. 1996, pp. 147-152.
14. Eduardo M. Nebot and Hugh Durrant-Whyte, "A High Integrity Navigation Architecture for Outdoor Autonomous Vehicles", Robotics and Autonomous Systems, 1999, pp.81-97.
15. T. Kirubarajan, H.Wang, Y, Bar-Shalom, K. R. Pattipati, "Efficient Multisensor Fusion Using Multidimensional Data Association", IEEE Transactions on Aerospace and Electronic Systems, vol. 37(2), April 2001, pp. 386-398.
16. Sukhan Lee and Xiaoming Zhao, "A New Sensor Planning Paradigm and its Application to Robot Self-localization", Intelligent Robots and Systems 95. 'Human Robot Interaction and Cooperative Robots', Proceedings. 1995 IEEE/RSJ International Conference on , vol.2, pp.462 -467, 5-9 Aug. 1995.
17. Adrian, R.A. "Sensor Management", Digital Avionics Systems Conference, pp.32 -37, 1993. 12th DASC., AIAA/IEEE , 25-28 Oct. 1993.
18. Eduardo M. Nebot, Mohammad Bozorg, Hugh F. Durrant-whyte, "Decentralized Architecture for Asynchronous Sensors", Autonomous Robots, 6, pp.147-164, 1999.
19. Ajay Mahajan, Kaihong Wang, and Probir Kumar Ray, "Multisensor Integration and Fusion Model that Uses a Fuzzy Inference System", IEEE/ASME Trans. On Mechatronics. vol.6 (2), June, 2001, pp.188-196.

Adaptive Vision for Playing Table Soccer

Thilo Weigel, Dapeng Zhang, Klaus Rechert, and Bernhard Nebel

Institut für Informatik
Universität Freiburg
79110 Freiburg, Germany
{weigel,zhangd,rechert,nebel}@informatik.uni-freiburg.de

Abstract. For real time object recognition and tracking often color-based methods are used. While these methods are very efficient, they usually dependent heavily on lighting conditions. In this paper we present a robust and efficient vision system for the table soccer robot *KiRo*. By exploiting knowledge about invariant characteristics of the table soccer game, the system is able to adapt to changing lighting conditions dynamically and to detect relevant objects on the table within a few milliseconds. We give experimental evidence for the robustness and efficiency of our approach.

1 Introduction

For real-time object recognition and tracking often color-based methods are used. While these methods are very efficient, they are also very sensitive to differing lighting conditions. Adjusting the color classes by hand is usually a tedious task and sometimes unfeasible when the color and the brightness of the environmental light change over time. For this reason, *robust* vision systems, which either automatically adapt the relevant color classes or which don't rely on color labeling at all, are desirable.

In this paper we consider the problem of designing an efficient and robust vision system for the autonomous table soccer robot *KiRo* [1]. KiRo allows humans to play table soccer on a regular table against a machine. It observes the playing field with an overhead camera and controls the four rods of one team according to its observations and pre-defined tactics. In many test games KiRo showed to be a competitive challenge for average human players [1]. The original version of the system used a simple, efficient and straightforward color segmentation method, however, it was very sensitive to changing lighting conditions.

One possible solution for dealing with such conditions is to first extract illumination independent descriptions of an image's surface colors [2]. For the analysis of sports videos, using parallel color spaces and detecting players based on histogram similarities has been proposed [3]. In the context of robotic soccer, many approaches for robust color region finding have been developed. For instance, the work by Jüngel et al. [4] proposes a method for an auto-adjusting vision system using color classes defined by their relative position to a reference class. Dahm et al. [5] describe a color space transformation that is guided by an evolutionary algorithm, and Wyeth et al. [6] describe how to remove the image background based on color histograms.

S. Biundo, T. Frühwirth, and G. Palm (Eds.): KI 2004, LNAI 3238, pp. 424–438, 2004.

Inspired by these approaches, we designed two robust methods for detecting the field lines, the players, and the ball. Both methods exploit a number of invariant characteristics of the table soccer setup for guiding the vision process. In particular, for each rod, the location of its axis, the number of corresponding playing figures and the distance between the figures are known. Since we use a yellow ball, it is also known that there is at most one yellow object on the playing surface.

The first method is based on color classifiers which are automatically adapted using a heuristic search in the space of color classifiers. In contrast, the second method doesn't rely on explicit color classes, but rather exploits the contrast beween the objects of interest as an illumination independent descriptor. As the two methods are based on fundamentally different principles, we were particularly interested in a direct comparison between them.

The rest of this paper is structured as follows. In Section 2 we give an overview of KiRo's vision system and describe the invariants that can be expoited. In Section 3 we describe the adaptive color classification method and in Section 4 we present the method based on illumination independent color descriptors. These two approaches are evaluated in Section 5 and we conclude with Section 6.

2   The Vision System

KiRo detects the postions of the ball and the playing figures from color images delivered by a camera overlooking the table. The images are in YUV-format which has the advantage that a pixel's luminance and chrominance values are encoded in separate channels. By processing each half-frame individually, we achieve a frame rate of 50 Hz with an image resolution of 384x288 pixels. Figure 1(a) shows an example of a camera image.

Since the colors of the different players and the yellow ball are easy to distinguish, a straightforward way for detecting the objects is to segment the image regarding predefined color classes and to form regions of pixels which belong to the same class. Each region can then be associated with an object of interest on the table. Using for example the *CMVision* library [7] this can be done efficiently within a few milliseconds.

In order to estimate the real world coordinates of a detected object, the image coordinates have to be transformed to real world coordinates. A suitable transformation matrix can be determined by examining the field lines and finding both the center circle and the center line using a simple template matching method. The circle's center yields the position of the table, the angle of the straight line its orientation and the circle radius the zoom factor [1].

Knowing the table's posture in the camera image allows to mask out the background and to exclusively focus on objects inside the table when detecting the ball and playing figures. Figure 1(b) shows the camera image of Figure 1(a) after calibrating, segmenting and removing the background.

Since the table soccer setup is well defined, a lot of invariant facts can be taken into account for improving the performance of the vision proceess. In particular, the following observations hold throughout a game:

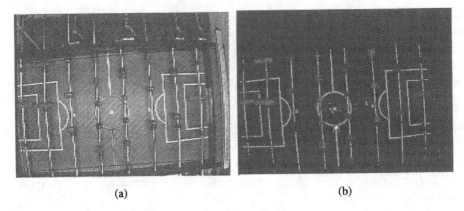

(a)   (b)

Fig. 1. (a) An original camera image with the black circle and line indicating the result of the calibration step. (b) The same image after segmenting and removing the background.

1. There is a total of eleven playing figures of the same color for each team.
2. The field lines are fixed and bright white.
3. The ball is the only yellow object inside the playing field.
4. For each rod, the location of its axis, the number of corresponding playing figures and the distance between the figures is known.

By exploiting the first three very general observations, it is possible to automatically find appropriate classifiers for the field lines, the players and the ball. In Section 3 we describe how the classifiers can be obtained by a heuristic search in the space of color bounds.

By utilzing also the fourth, more specialized observation, it is possible to obtain the position of the playing figures without relying on explicit color classes. In Section 4 we describe, how the field lines, the playing figures and the ball can be found based on the contrast to the green playing field.

3   Determining Color Classifiers by Heuristic Search

A color class is a particular subset of the color space. If one is lucky, the class can be approximated by a cube in the color space and can be described by the upper and lower bounds for each channel of the color space. Working on images in the YUV-format we define a color class as

$$C = \{y_{min}, y_{max}, u_{min}, u_{max}, v_{min}, v_{max}\},$$

and say that a pixel belongs to a color class if its values for y, u and v lie between the respective minima and maxima. As it turns out, for our purposes it is enough to specify just one of these six limits in order to describe the colors relevant for table soccer.

As the y-channel encodes a pixel's luminance, the color class "white" can be defined with all bounds set to their maximum and minimum values, except the lower y-bound:

$$C_{white} = \{y_{min}, 255, 0, 255, 0, 255\}.$$

The typical setup of the table soccer game features blue and red playing figures. Since high values for u correlate with the blue color and high values for v correlate with the red color, we are able to classify the players sufficiently by also only adjusting one relevant bound while leaving the others fixed:

$$\mathcal{C}_{blue} = \{0, 255, u_{min}, 255, 0, 255\}$$
$$\mathcal{C}_{red} = \{0, 255, 0, 255, v_{min}, 255\}.$$

Also the yellow ball can be sufficiently classified by only adjusting one bound, namely the upper u-bound:

$$\mathcal{C}_{yellow} = \{0, 255, 0, u_{max}, 0, 255\}.$$

3.1 Field-Line Identification

Figure 2 shows, how changing the lower y-bound affects the classification of "white" pixels.

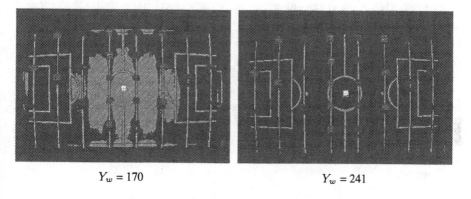

$Y_w = 170$ $Y_w = 241$

Fig. 2. $\mathcal{C}_{white}$ for two different values of y_{min}.

Let N denote the total number of pixels in a camera image and let t_w denote the total number of pixels which are classified as "white" with respect to a particular classifier. Then, the percentage of "white" pixels in the image is given by $p_w = \frac{t_w}{N}$. Now, the important observation is, that if the classifier is adjusted to capture just the field lines and nothing else, p_w is a constant for a fixed N. Therefore, the process of calibrating the field lines can be expressed as the search for the lower y-bound which yields the p_w closest to the known fixed percentage. In other words, as p_w is a function of y_{min}, the appropriate y_{min} for classifying the field-line can be obtained by minimizing

$$f_w(y_{min}) = |p_w(y_{min}) - P_w|, \tag{1}$$

where P_w denotes the constant percentage which can be easily determined empirically.

A simple binary search can be used for minimizing f. Since the field-lines can be covered more or less by the playing figures, the actual percentage of "white" pixels in the camera image may vary. However, classifying the field lines is usually tolerant against deviations in the exact value for p_w.

As the table's posture in the camera image is not known prior to assessing the transformation matrix (which in turn requires an appropriate classifier), white objects outside the table may render the described method completely unusable. However, such "noise" can usually be filtered out reliably by discarding all "white" regions whose width and height makes them very unlikely to correspond to a field-line.

In order to cope with such conditions, the previously found value for y_{min} is revised by adapting P_w according to the identified noise: With n_w denoting the number of pixels which are considered to be noise, a new P'_w is calculated as $P'_w(y_{min}) = \frac{n_w}{N} + P_w$. Now, we seek to minimize an enhanced version of f_w:

$$f'_w(y'_{min}) = |p_w(y'_{min}) - P'_w(y_{min})|. \tag{2}$$

Again, this can be done by a simple binary search. However, as P'_w is a function of y_{min} we need to repeat the search with P'_w re-calculated according to the newly found y'_{min}. This process is iterated until $P'_w(y_{min})$ converges such that the absolute difference between two consecutive P'_w's is smaller than some ϵ.

The described method can either be run on one camera frame until the calibration is completed or be used in an *anytime-fashion*. While the first is usually appropriate for an initial calibration step, the latter is advantageous for adapting the system to changing lighting conditions during a game where only a limited amount of time is available for the vision process in each control cycle.

When the calibration is updated in an *anytime-fashion* we usually allow about 5 msec in each cycle for the vision process. Then, the currently considered values for y'_{min} and $P'_w(y_{min})$ are saved for continuing the search with a new frame in the next cycle. As sudden brightness changes between consecutive frames can change the wanted value for y'_{min} considerably, a linear search is used in these cases in order to assure completeness of the search.

3.2   Identifying Blue and Red Players

As the sizes of the player-regions change considerably when a rod is rotated, a fixed percentage value can't be used to guide the search for the appropriate classifiers of the blue and red players. Figure 3 illustrates the effect of applying the same method as for the field lines by using a fixed target percentage. If all the playing figures are positioned horizontally, an appropriate classifier is found. But if the figures are facing downwards, the resulting classifier produces too much noise which will hamper the correct detection of the rod's posture.

However, we know that there is a fixed total of eleven playing figures of the same color for each team and we also know the possible minimum and maximum size of the regions corresponding to a playing figures. Furthermore, it is now possible to examine only image pixels which correspond to the inside of the table since its posture in the camera image has been previously determined using the field lines.

Exploiting this knowledge, we are able to find the optimal blue and red classifier by searching for the lower u- and v-bound which yield the best *noise ratios* $r_b(u_{min})$ and

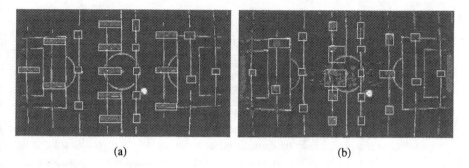

(a)   (b)

Fig. 3. The same target percentage resulting in an appropriate classifier (a) or a too noisy one (b). The bounding boxes indicate the estimated player dimensions.

$r_r(v_{min})$. With N_{table} being the total amount of pixels belonging to the table, the ratios are calculated as

$$r_b(u_{min}) = \frac{n_b(u_{min})}{N_{table}} \quad \text{and} \quad r_r(v_{min}) = \frac{n_r(v_{min})}{N_{table}},$$

where n_b and n_r are the number of "blue" and "red" pixels which are considered as noise. With empirically determined target percentages P_b and P_r, the search for the optimum classifiers can now be described as minimizing the following equations:

$$f_b(u_{min}) = |r_b(u_{min}) - P_b| \qquad (3)$$
$$f_r(v_{min}) = |r_r(v_{min}) - P_r|. \qquad (4)$$

Of course, the distinction between noise and correctly classified pixels is crucial for this approach. However, with the aid of our domain knowledge, this can be accomplished in a rule-based manner:

- If there are less than eleven regions and no region has dimensions larger than the possible maximum, then there is no noise.
- If there is a region larger than the possible maximum size, then all its pixels are considered to be noise.
- if there are more than eleven regions, all but the eleven biggest ones are considered to be noise.

Considering these "rules", the search can be guided to increase or decrease the lower u- and v-bounds such that f_b and f_r converge to a minimum value.

As for the field lines, a binary search can be used if the calibration is done on one frame only. In general, though, a linear search is applied for being able to interrupt and resume the search arbitrarily.

The current values for u_{min} and v_{min} can now be used for classifying the image. Subsequently, the position of a playing figure is calculated from the center of gravity of its corresponding bounding box and the player's angle is estimated from its size [1].

3.3   Identifying the Ball

Since the ball is the only yellow object on the table, estimating the ball color is very similar to estimating the color of the players. We now seek to minimize the following:

$$f_y(u_{max}) = |r_y(u_{max}) - P_y|,\qquad(5)$$

where $r_y(u_{max}) = \frac{n_y(u_{max})}{N_{table}}$ and $n_y(u_{max})$ is the number of pixels which are considered as noise with respect to the yellow classifier.

The decision if a pixel has to be considered as noise is made in a similar way as for the players – with the only difference that there is only one target region now. Interestingly, this approach also copes with situations where the ball is not visible because it is either outside the table or hidden by a playing figure or a rod: As "yellow" noise arises during the search at many places simultaneously, f_y usually converges in such a case to an absolute value greater than the required ϵ. As a consequence, the ball detection can be suspended until an appropriate classifier is found once the ball is back in play.

In order to cope with situations where the ball is partially covered by a rod or a playing figure a more elaborate approach than for the players is used to estimate' it's position on the table. At all possible ball locations squares of the expected blob size are examined and the pixels which correspond to the ball, the players or the rods are counted. By selecting the square with the "best" ratio between the number of pixels of the different color classes, the ball's center can usually be estimated reliably even if it is only partially visible [1].

4   Detecting Objects by Contrast

An alternative to region finding using explicit color classes is to detect objects of interest based on the contrast between them. By searching along scan-lines we are able to identify the object positions directly. However, for being able to determine the coordinate transform for both approaches in the same way, we explicitly calculated the lower y-bound of the field lines.

4.1   Field-Line Identification

Currently, the method for determining the coordinate transformation requires the lower y-bound y_{fl}^- of the field lines. As this bound needs to separate the field lines from the background, it can also be considered as the upper y-bound y_r^+ of all the *remaining* color-classes: $y_{fl}^- = y_r^+$.

In the following, a *scan-line* is defined as a horizontal scan along the image which only considers the y-channel of the YUV image data. Figure 4(a) shows a raw scan-line. The peaks usually mark the locations of the field lines and the rods but may also be caused by image noise. Therefore, y_r^+ can be obtained by filtering out these peaks.

For this, along the scan-line the positive and negative difference between the actual y-value and its predecessor is computed as

$$\delta_i^+ = \left\{ \begin{array}{l} \delta_i, \text{if } \delta_i > 0 \\ 0, \text{else} \end{array} \right. \qquad \delta_i^- = \left\{ \begin{array}{l} \delta_i, \text{if } \delta_i < 0 \\ 0, \text{else}, \end{array} \right. \qquad(6)$$

where $\delta_i = y_i - y_{i-1}$ and $i \in [1, n-1]$. By averaging δ_i^+ and δ_i^-, an upper ($\bar{\delta}^+$) and lower ($\bar{\delta}^-$) threshold can be calculated as

$$\bar{\delta}^- = \frac{1}{n^-} \sum_{i=1}^{n-1} \delta_i^- \qquad\qquad \bar{\delta}^+ = \frac{1}{n^+} \sum_{i=1}^{n-1} \delta_i^+, \qquad (7)$$

where $n^- = |\{\delta_i | \delta_i < 0\}|$ and $n^+ = |\{\delta_i | \delta_i > 0\}|$. Figure 4(b) shows the calculated δ-values and the two averages.

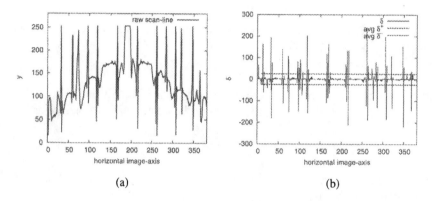

(a)   (b)

Fig. 4. (a) A horizontal scan-line and (b) its corresponding δ-distribution.

After removing y-values with a δ-value above $\bar{\delta}^+$ or below $\bar{\delta}^-$, the scan-line represents the y-color distribution of the *remaining* color-classes and could in principle be used for defining y_{fl}^-. However, the scan-line may still contain plateaus at positions of larger white regions, e. g. at the field's center point. Figure 5(a) shows the filtered scan-line with one remaining plateau.

Plateaus are characterized by a a series of y-values which lie between a sharp ascent and descent of the y-values along the scan line. In order to filter them out, the ascent and descent are detected in a similar way as the peaks were detected and the values between are removed. However, more elaborate δ-values are now used, since $\bar{\delta}^+$ and $\bar{\delta}^-$ are not suited for discriminating between the background and white areas in very bright images. An additional threshold which depends on the general image brightness is computed, and the thresholds for filtering the plateaus are computed from both as:

$$\bar{\delta}'^+ = min(2 * \bar{\delta}^+, \frac{y_{max} - y_{r_{max}}}{2}) \qquad (8)$$

$$\bar{\delta}'^- = min(2 * \bar{\delta}^-, \frac{y_{max} - y_{r_{max}}}{2}), \qquad (9)$$

where $y_{r_{max}}$ denotes the current maximum y-value along the scan-line which doesn't belong to a plateau.

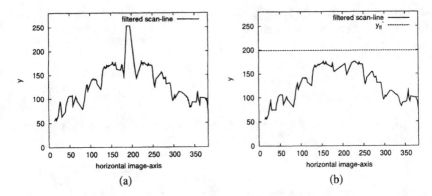

Fig. 5. (a) The scan-line from Figure 4(a) with the peaks removed and and (b) the same scan-line with the plateau removed and resulting y_{fl}^-.

After futher removing from the scan-line all y-values with a δ-value above $\bar{\delta}'^+$ or below $\bar{\delta}'^-$, the upper bound of the non-white color classes can now be obtained as:

$$y_r^+ = \max_{y \in \mathbf{S}} y, \qquad (10)$$

where $\mathbf{S}$ is the set of all the y-values along the scan-line which haven't been filtered out in the previous steps. In principle, y_r^+ could be directly used as the lower y-bound for classifying the field-lines. However, in order to achieve a clear and robust separation between the color class for the field-lines and the remaining color classes, we define y_{fl}^- by adding an offset as

$$y_{fl}^- = y_r^+ + \epsilon. \qquad (11)$$

In relatively dark environments the contrast between white regions and the background (with respect to the lower y-bound) is larger than in brighther environments. Consequently, ϵ should be larger in darker environments. Sine the general brightness level is reflected in y_r^+, we define ϵ depending on y_r^+ as $\epsilon = \frac{y_{max} - y_r^+}{P}$, where $y_{max} = 255$. It turned out that a good value for ϵ is 10% of the distance between y_r^+ and y_{max} ($P = 10$). Figure 5(b) shows the resulting y_{fl}^-.

4.2 Identifying Blue and Red Players

For detecting the playing figures we use the knowledge of the fixed axis of their corresponding rods. With the known transformation from world coordinates to image coordinates we compute a scan line for each rod which corresponds to its location in the camera image. The playing figures can then be found by searching for the contrast between them and the background along the scan-lines. However, this search only yields an approximate position and needs to be refined in a second step.

For the search we exploit the fact, that the chrominance values u and v of the playing figures differ significantly while the respective values are usually very similar for the rods and the green field. In Figure 6 it can be seen how three men cause significant peaks along the scan-line.

As the chrominance values are usually independent from lighting conditions, a linear combination of both chrominance channels is a robust feature to distinguish the playing figures from the rod along the scan-line. Empirically, we determined the linear combinations such that they have a local maximum at the positions of the blue or red player's playing figures:

$$f_{blue}(i) = u_i + |u_i - v_i| \qquad\qquad f_{red}(i) = v_i + |u_i - v_i|. \qquad (12)$$

Here, i denotes a position along the scan-line. Finding the N playing figures of a rod can now be considered as finding the N maxima of f. In Figure 6 it can be seen, how f_{blue} produces three clearly distinguishable peaks at the playing figure's positons.

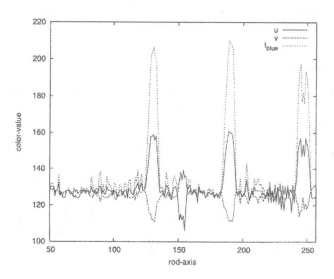

Fig. 6. Scan along a rod with three men.

In order to make the search more robust, we exploit the knowledge of the fixed distance D between the rod's playing figures. This allows us to consider in parallel N points on the scan-line being D pixels apart. Thus, we aim at finding the maximum of the following functions:

$$f'_{blue}(i) = \sum_{n=0}^{N-1} f_{blue}(i + n * D) \qquad f'_{red}(i) = \sum_{mn0}^{N-1} f_{red}(i + n * D) \qquad (13)$$

The position of the nth playing figure i_n along the scan-line can then be obtained as:

$$i_n = \arg\max_i (f'(i + n * D)). \qquad (14)$$

Starting with the estimated man position, the man's exact position can be found by expanding the position to an area equal to the man's width. This is done by an *hill-climbing* algorithm, which finds the man's most likely position: Starting with an initial interval, which only contains the approximated position, the interval is grown until its length reaches the man width M. The interval is grown by comparing the f-values to the left and the right of the interval and growing the interval towards the direction of the larger value.

For determining the angle of a playing figure, several scans are done parallel to the rod axis around the figure's position. Using the same functions f, these scans check in an interval $[-M, M]$ for the presence of the playing figure. As the scans are moved in both directions away from the rod center, a sudden change in the maximum values of f indicates, that the figure's bounds are reached. Since the playing figure's maximum possible length (when aligned horizontally) is known, the search-scans can be limited to the area around the rod defined by the maximum possible figure's length.

Once a figure's length is known, it's angle can be estimated from this information in a straightforward way [1].

4.3   Identifying the Ball

For detecting the ball, a priori knowledge of its radius and color is utilized. Finding the ball's exact position is done in a similar way as finding the men's positions with a linear combination defined as

$$f_{ball}(i, j) = (255 - u_{ij}) + |u_{ij} - v_{ij}| \tag{15}$$

where i and j now denote coordinates on the table. Since we have to scan the whole field we speed up the search by searching along scan-lines which are the ball's radius apart from each other. This way, first an approximate of the ball's position is found at the global maximum of f_{ball}. Starting at this position, a *hill-climbing* algorithm, similar to the one used for the playing figures, finds the exact area which covers the ball.

5   Results

In order to evaluate the techniques described in the previous sections, we took a log-file consisting of images taken by the camera during a 90 second period. While the log-file was taken, we continuously altered lighting conditions by turning on and off different environmental light sources and changing the camera's shutter speed and gain. We also changed the position and angle of the playing figures and the position of the ball between well known positions. The real world coordinates of these poses were measured by hand and served as the *ground truth* for the evaluation process. While the positions were changed the log file taking was stopped for a moment. Figure 7 shows screen shots of four different stages of the log file.

For each frame of the log file we computed the resulting position and angle estimates of the two dynamic methods and one additional static approach. The static classifier for the players and the ball was adjusted once at the beginning of the log file and tremained fixed during the log file

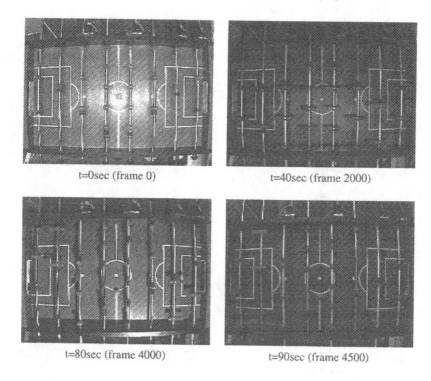

t=0sec (frame 0)   t=40sec (frame 2000)

t=80sec (frame 4000)   t=90sec (frame 4500)

Fig. 7. Camera images from different positions of the log file.

For a rough comparison of the results, we also calculated color classifiers for the contrast method based on the color distributions at the found object positions. As can be seen in Figure 8, the two dynamic approaches produced similar color classificators and – unlike the static classifier – reflect the changes in illumination.

More interesting is, of course, how the different features on the field are estimated. The results are plotted in Figures 9–11, whereby the deviations are averaged over 20 frames. When a method couldn't perceive a feature, the difference values for the respective object were set to a maximum of 40mm and 50°.

As one can see, all methods produced similar good estimates at the beginning of the log file where lighting conditions were best. Considering, that at the current image resolution one pixel corresponds to 3mm on the table, a position deviation of less than 4mm seems very acceptable. Also the angle estimates are satisfying since usually only the rough orientation of a playing figure needs to be known. Considering, that the angles have to be calculated from the observed length of the playing figures it would certainly be hard to obtain more accurate estimates.

However, when lighting conditions changed and got more difficult, the static classifier lost the object positions frequently while the adaptive methods continued to give accurate position and angle estimates. The heuristic search approach sometimes needed a couple of frames for recovering from drastic brightness changes but turned out to be slightly more accurate than the contrast approach, especially for the ball. The contrast approach, however, showed a clearly better worst case performance.

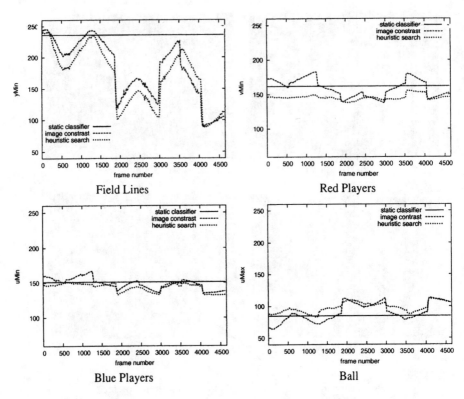

Fig. 8. Change in classifiers for the different methods.

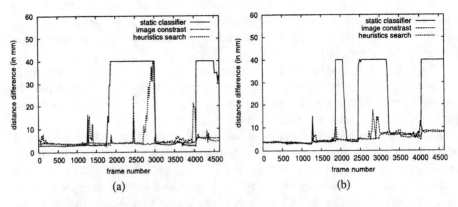

Fig. 9. Deviation of the (a) the red player's positions and (b) the blue player's positions with respect to the ground truth.

Figure 12 displays the averaged position and angle devitations with respect to the ground truth. Please note, that the means for the static classifier strongly depend on the pre-set worst case values for unrecognized objects. Nevertheless, it becomes clear, that the two adaptive approaches are superior to the static variant. Even though the

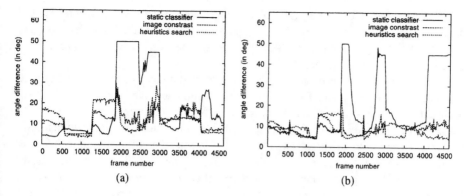

Fig. 10. Deviation of the (a) the red player's angle and (b) the blue player's anle with respect to the ground truth.

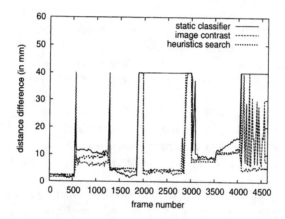

Fig. 11. Deviation of the ball positions with respect to the ground truth.

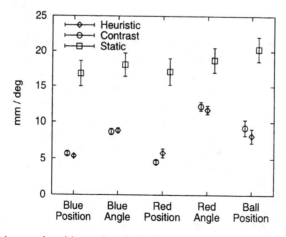

Fig. 12. Averaged position and angle deviations with 95% confidence intervals.

color information in YUV-images is robust against some brightness variations, the two dynamic approaches were far more often capable of adapting to the changed conditions. Interestingly, the performance of two dynamic approaches was very similar and the differences almost not significant.

An important difference between the two dynamic methods are the computational resources required by them. The heuristic search approach may need up to 211 msec (on a 2.6 GHz CPU) to recover the classifiers after illumination changed drastically. However, on average only 12.5 msec are needed for this task. This allows to distribute the adaptive calibration over a series of frames. Limiting the processing time to 5 msec per frame, on average 3 frames are needed for adapting the classifiers. Nevertheless, the approach based on image contrast is far more efficient. It needs less than 2 msec per frame since only a few scan-lines have to be followed and evaluated.

6   Conclusion and Outlook

We presented two methods for efficient and robust object recognition and tracking for the autonomous table soccer robot *KiRo*. Both methods heavily exploit domain knowledge. The first method is based on a heuristic search in the space of color classifiers, while the second uses mainly image contrast information and knowledge about the geometry of the table.

Both methods are much better than static color classification and give comparable results. The percentage values required by the heuristic search method are easy to obtain, but the method can be very expensive compuationally. The contrast method is a lot more efficient. However, the functions for discriminating the features may be more difficult to obtain.

In the future, we will evaluate the possibility of learning the percentage values and the color discriminating functions. We will also address the problem of non-uniform lighting conditions.

References

1. Weigel, T., Nebel, B.: KiRo – An Autonomous Table Soccer Player. In: Proc. Int. RoboCup Symposium '02. Springer-Verlag, Fukuoka, Japan (2002) 119 – 127
2. Barnhard, K., Finlayson, G., Funt, B.: Colour Constancy for Scenes with Varying illumination. Computer Vision and Image Understanding (1997) 311–321
3. Ekin, A., Tekalp, A.M., Mehrotra, R.: Automatic Soccer Video Analysis and Summarization. IEEE Transactions on Image Processing (to appear)
4. Jüngel, M., Hoffmann, J., Lötzsch, M.: A Real-Time Auto-Adjusting Vision System for Robotic Soccer. In: Proc. Int. RoboCup Symposium '03. (2004)
5. Dahm, I., Deutsch, S., Hebbel, M., Osterhues, A.: Robust color classification for robot soccer. In: Proc. Int. RoboCup Symposium '03. (2004)
6. Wyeth, G., Brown, B.: Robust Adaptive Vision for Robot Soccer. Mechatronics and Machine Vision in Practice (2000) 41–48
7. Bruce, J., Balch, T., Veloso, M.: Fast and inexpensive color image segmentation for interactive robots. In: Proc. Int. Conf. on Intelligent Robots and Systems (IROS), Takamatsu, Japan (2000) 2061–2066

Shape-Based Robot Mapping

Diedrich Wolter[1], Longin J. Latecki[2], Rolf Lakämper[2], and Xinyui Sun[2]

[1] Universität Bremen
[2] Temple University

Abstract. We present a novel geometric model for robot mapping suited for robots equipped with a laser range finder. The geometric representation is based on shape. Cyclic ordered sets of polygonal lines are the underlying data structures. Specially adapted shape matching techniques originating from computer vision are applied to match range scan against the partially constructed map. Shape matching respects for a wider context than conventional scan matching approaches, allowing to disregard pose estimations. The described shape based approach is an improvement of the underlying geometric models of todays SLAM implementations. Moreover, using our object-centered approach allows for compact representations that are well-suited to bridge the gap from metric information needed in robot motion and path planning to more abstract, i.e. topological or qualitative spatial knowledge desired in complex navigational tasks or communication.

Keywords: cognitive robotics, robot mapping, shape matching

1 Motivation

The problems of self-localization, i.e. localizing the robot within its internal map, and robot mapping, i.e. constructing the internal map autonomously, are of high importance to the field of mobile robotics [18]. Coping with unknown or changing environments requires to carry out both tasks simultaneously, therefore this has been termed the SLAM problem: Simultaneous Localization and Mapping [5] – it has received considerable attention [5, 8, 18]. Successful stochastical approaches have been developed that tackle representation and handling of uncertain data which is one key point in SLAM. As todays stochastical models are powerful, even linking them to a simple geometric representation like reflection points measured by a range sensor already yields impressive results. Advances in stochastical means have improved the overall performance leaving the basic spatial representation untouched. As the internal geometric representation is a foundation for these sophisticated stochastical techniques, shortcomings on the level of geometric representation affect the overall performance.

We claim that an improved geometric representation enhances the overall performance dramatically. A compact, object oriented representation based on shape is an universal yet slender one. It can outperform often-used occupancy grids in storage as well as in computational resources, since smaller sets of data

S. Biundo, T. Frühwirth, and G. Palm (Eds.): KI 2004, LNAI 3238, pp. 439–452, 2004.
© Springer-Verlag Berlin Heidelberg 2004

need to be processed. Object-centered representations have been judged necessary to represent dynamic environments [18]. Moreover, a more comprehensive spatial representation can allow to mediate between different aspects of spatial information that are desired or even necessary in applications. We propose a shape representation of the robot's surrounding that grants access to metric information as needed in robot motion or path planning alongside with more abstract, qualitative or topological knowledge which is desired in navigational tasks and a well-suited foundation for communication.

2   Related Work

Any approach to master the SLAM problem can be decomposed into two aspects: handling of map features (extraction from sensor data and matching against the (partially) existing map) and handling of uncertainty.

To address uncertainty mainly statistical techniques are used, e.g., particle filters, the extended Kalman filter, a linear recursive estimator for systems described by non-linear process models and/or observation models, are used in most current SLAM algorithms [17, 18, 8]. As this paper focusses exclusively on the map's geometric representation, we now review related aspects in detail.

Typically, map features extracted from sensor data (esp. range finder data) are either the positions of special landmarks [5], simple geometric features, especially lines [12, 13, 3], or range finder data is used rather directly [18].

Direct use of data, that is without further interpretation despite noise filtering, results in constructing a bitmap-like representation of the environment termed occupancy grid [6]. The simplicity of this approach causes its strength, namely universality: It may be used in unstructured, unprepared environments. However, harmful features show off as well. First, the crucial method of matching a scan against the map in order to localize the robot is formulated as a minimization [12, 18, 8]. Therefore, a good estimation of the robot's pose is required to prevent minimization getting stuck in local minima. Second, occupancy grids grow with the environment's size, not its complexity. As grids need to fine, using these maps can easily end up in handling large data sets. This is not only a problem of storage, but, far more important, it affects run-time of algorithms handling the map as huge amounts of data need to be processed. To keep path planning in a once constructed map feasible, a topological representation can be coupled with the metric one [16].

To maintain a map at manageable size from the beginning, representations based on features or landmarks provide excellent means. These so-called object maps represent only position of landmarks and their distinctive features. Thus, these maps grow with the environment's complexity (i.e. the number of landmarks visible). This allows for an efficient processing. Using natural landmarks is of special interest as environments do not need to be prepared, like, e.g., by installing beacons [5]. For example, mapping based on line segments has been shown to improve performance in office environments [13]. A key point in feature-based approaches is a matching of perceived features against the ones represented in the map. Wrong matchings result in incorrect, hence, useless maps. Complex features help to prevent a mixup when matching the robot's perception against its map. As features' presence is required, application is often limited to special environments only. On the contrary, choosing simple, omnipresent features can easily inhibit a reliable matching of perceived features against the map. Unreliable feature extraction, e.g. extracting line segments from round objects causes problems, too, as additional noise gets introduced. As noise gets propagated, it sums up and can cause inconsistent maps.

To overcome these problems, we propose a shape based representation that is (a) universal as employed shape features can be extracted in any environment, but (b) features provide distinctive information as shape respects a wide spatial context. Matching of features is, thus, based on a shape matching which has received much attention in the context of computer vision.

The idea of applying shape matching in the context of robot mapping is not new. In the fundamental paper by Lu & Milios [12], scan matching has already been considered similar to model-based shape matching. Thrun considers this connection underexploited [18]. Recent advances in shape matching provide a good starting point to bring these fields together. Our approach utilizes a model based similarity measure.

In the domain of robot mapping mainly two key aspects dictate to the applicability of shape descriptors, namely partial shape retrieval and the ability to deal with simple shapes. Firstly, as only partial observations of the environment can be made, any approach to shape representation that cannot handle partial shapes renders itself unemployable. This includes, for example, encoding by feature vectors like Fourier or momenta spectra. Secondly, any robot's working environment must be representable in the framework of the chosen shape descriptor. Besides these confinements, investigating into shape information available in typical indoor environments displays another feature required: Much shape information perceivable is often rather poor, like for instance straightaway walls with small protrusions only. Therefore, shape recognition processes must be very distinctive, even on rather featureless shapes.

Structural approaches represent shape as a colored graph representing metric data alongside configurational information. Amongst these so-called skeleton based techniques, especially shock graphs (cp. [15]) are worth consideration[1]. Though primarily structural approaches may very well bridge the gap from metric to more abstract qualitative or topological information (cp. [16]), recognizing shapes lacking of a rich structure of configuration, has not yet proven feasible. Moreover, a robust computation and matching of a skeleton in the presence of noise has not yet been solved.

Therefore, we propose the utilization of a boundary based approach. Considering the discrete structure provided by sensors, using polygonal lines to represent the boundaries of obstacles may be achieved easily. Related techniques for matching rely on a so-called similarity measure. Various measures, often metrics, have been developed. Arkin et al. ([1]) accumulates differences in turning angle

---

[1] Skeleton based approaches relate closely to Voronoi based spatial representations used in the field of robotics (cp. [16, 15]).

in straightforward manner; it fails to account for noise, esp. if not uniformly distributed, adequately. Basically all improvements in similarity measures, thus, employ a matching of boundaries to establish a correspondence prior to summing up dissimilarities of corresponding parts. Basri et al. propose a physically motivated deformation energy ([2]). More recently, an alignment-based deformation measure has been proposed by Sebastian et al. which considers the process of transforming one outline into another ([14]). However, common to these approaches is that an equal sampling rate of the outlines is required. The emerging problem of comparing two, let us assume identical outlines with different sample points, can be illustrated easily: Computing a correspondence of either points or line-segments introduces large deformations due to mismatches in point correspondence, hence, underestimating similarity dramatically. Considering shape information obtained by a range sensor, scanning the same object from different positions generates this effect.

An improved performance in similarity measures for closed contours has been achieved by Latecki & Lakämper who consider a matching on basis of a a priori decomposition into maximal arcs (cp. [10]). We will formulate the presented approach on this basis. However, it is adapted such that it is tailored to deal with any kind of open polyline and addresses the problem of noisy data in a direct manner. The representation is complemented by a structural representation of robust ordering information. Applicability of the elementary shape similarity measure has been shown in [11].

3   Structural Shape Representation

Shape information can directly be derived from sensor readings obtained by a range sensor, typically a laser range finder (LRF). Shape is represented as a structure of boundaries. Polygonal lines, called *polylines*, serve as the basic entity.

Polylines represent obstacles' boundaries. Much of the spatial information represented in the map can be captured by individual polylines which form visual parts (cp. [10]). The variety of perceivable shapes in a regular indoor scenario already yields a more reliable matching than other feature-based approaches, as mixups in determining corresponding features are more unlikely to occur. At the same time, we are able to construct a compact representation for an arbitrary environment. However, we exploit even more context information than represented by a single polyline considering shape as a structure of polylines. This allows us with basically no extra effort to cope with environments displaying mostly simple shapes. The structure captured is ordering information. For any given viewpoint, perceivable objects can be ordered in a counter-clockwise manner. Thus, for a map containing polylines the structure of ordering can be expressed as a mapping from a point (the robot's position in the map) to a vector of polylines. Given a polygonal map, computing the vector of visible polylines can be achieved by applying a sweep line algorithm used in computational geometry to determine visibility [4]. A first step in the presented approach, however, is to extract shape information, i.e. polylines from data acquired by the LRF.

3.1   Grouping and Simplification of Polylines

Let us assume that the range data is mapped to locations of reflection points in the Euclidean plane, using a local coordinate system. Now, these points are segmented into individual polylines which represent visual parts of the scan. For this grouping a simple heuristic may be employed: Traversing the reflection points in the (cyclic) order as measured by the LRF, an object transition is said to be present wherever two consecutive points are farer apart than a given distance threshold. For obtaining the experimental results we used a threshold of 20cm, however the precise choice is not important, as differences in grouping are accounted for (cp. section 4.2).

Polylines extracted this way still carry all the information (and noise) retrieved by the sensor. To make the representation more compact and to cancel out noise, we employ a technique called Discrete Curve Evolution (DCE) introduced by Latecki & Lakämper ([9]) to (a) make the data more compact without loosing valuable shape information and (b) to cancel out noise. DCE is a context-sensitive process that proceeds iteratively: *Irrelevant* vertices get removed until no irrelevant ones remain. Though the process is context-sensitive, it is based on a local relevance measure for a vertex v and its two neighbor vertices u, w:[2]

$$K(u, v, w) = |d(u, v) + d(v, w) - d(u, w)| \tag{1}$$

Hereby, d denotes the Euclidean distance. The process of DCE is very simple and proceeds in straightforward manner. The least relevant vertex is removed until least relevance exceeds a given simplification threshold. Proceeding this way we obtain a cyclic ordered vector of polylines. Consequently, as no relevance measure is assigned to end-points, they remain fixed. The choice of a specific simplification threshold is not crucial, since only the overall shape needs to be preserved. The precise classification of noise will done in the context of corresponding polylines (cp. section 4.1). Exemplary results for applying DCE to LRF data are shown in Figure 1; Figure 2 demonstrates suitability for curved boundaries.

4   Matching of Shapes

To match two shapes means to match two ordered set of polylines against each other. Whereas one shape has been extracted from a sensor reading, the other is determined by the partially built map. Based on an estimation of the robot's position in its internal map, the shape perceivable according to the map is computed. To localize the robot and update its map, visual parts perceived by the sensor need to be matched against those extracted from the map. Hence, we need to seek for the *best* correspondence of individual polylines that preserves the shapes' structure, i.e. which does not violate their order. Shape similarity is the key point to quantify quality of a correspondence.

---

[2] Context is respected as in the course of simplification the vertices' neighborhood changes.

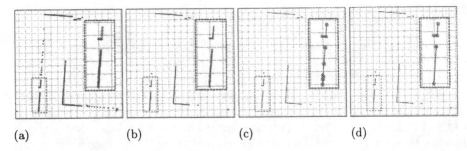

Fig. 1. Extracting polylines from a scan. Raw scan points (a) are grouped to polylines (b), then simplified by means of DCE. The threshold used in (c) is 1.0 and 5.0 in (d). The two additional rectangles show magnifications of marked parts. The grid denotes 1 meter distance.

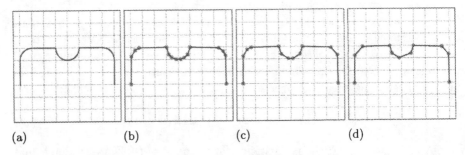

Fig. 2. Extracting shape information from curved synthetic data by DCE. The original data is shown in (a), (b) displays the result using 1.0 as stop threshold. A threshold of 2.5 was used in (c) and 5.0 in (d) (cp. Figure 1 for real LRF data). The grid denotes 1 meter distance.

4.1   Similarity of Polylines

The similarity measure utilized in our approach is based on a measure introduced by Latecki & Lakämper which we first will summarize very briefly and indicate changes made as it is necessary in this context; for details refer to [10].

To compute the basic similarity measure between two polygonal curves, we establish the best possible correspondence of maximal left- or right-arcuated arcs[3]. To achieve this, we first decompose the polygonal curves into maximal subarcs which are likewise bent. Since a simple one-to-one comparison of maximal arcs of two polylines is of little use, due to the fact that the curves may consist of a different number of such arcs and even similar shapes may have different small features, we allow for 1-to-1, 1-to-many, and many-to-1 correspondences of maximal arcs. The main idea here is that we have at least on one of the contours a maximal arc that corresponds to a part of the other contour composed of adjacent maximal arcs. The best correspondence can be computed using Dynamic Programming, where the similarity of the corresponding visual

---

[3] The original work is based on convex and concave arcs respectively. As we deal with open polylines here, the terms convex or concave would be meaningless.

parts is as defined below. The similarity induced from the optimal correspondence of polylines C and D will be denoted $S(C, D)$.

Basic similarity of arcs is defined in tangent space, a multi-valued step function representing angular directions and relative lengths of line-segments only. It was previously used in computer vision, in particular, in [1]. Denoting the mapping function by T, the similarity gets defined as follows:

$$S_a(C, D) = (1 + (l(C) - l(D))^2) \cdot \int_0^1 (T_C(s) - T_D(s) + \Theta_{C,D})^2 ds \qquad (2)$$

where $l(C)$ denotes the arc length of C. The constant $\Theta_{C,D}$ is chosen to minimize the integral (cp. [10]) (it respects for different orientation of curves) and is given by

$$\Theta_{C,D} = \int_0^1 T_C(s) - T_D(s) ds. \qquad (3)$$

Obviously, the similarity measure is a rather a dissimilarity measure as the identical curves yield 0, the lowest possible measure. This measure differs from the original work in that it is affected by an absolute change of size rather than a relative one. It should be noted that this measure is based on shape information only, neither the arcs' position nor orientation are considered. This is possible due to the large context information of polylines.

A problem of comparing polylines extracted from LRF data is that often the amount of noise and the size of shape features present is challenging. Applying DCE to a degree that would certainly remove all noise would remove many valuable shape features as well. DCE makes vertex removal decisions in the context of a single object. A better noise identification can made in the context of comparing corresponding polylines. Therefore, we encapsulate the basic similarity measure S in another process that masks out noise in the context of corresponding polylines. It is similar to the initial curve evolution employed. When comparing a polyline C perceived by the sensor and a polyline D extracted from the map, C might still contain extra vertices caused by noise. Therefore, we continue evolving polyline C if the resulting similarity measure improves. The maximal similarity obtained this way, i.e. the lowest value of $S(C, D)$, is denoted $S^*(C, D)$. To make this process robust against local minima, a small lookahead is used. This means that evolution is continued as long as removing the next 3 vertices according to the simplification rule yields a gain in similarity. The reason for delaying the final curve evolution steps to the matching is to enable the exploitation of even small shape features. Already starting the DCE process on sensor data, on the contrary, allows to benefit from DCE's lower computational complexity. Proceeding this way, only a few simplification steps need to be carried out during the matching. An example is depicted in Figure 3. To enhance presentation, the preceding DCE has been left out. When comparing the two polylines shown in Figure 3 (a) and (b), vertices from the perceived contour (b) are removed in the order of vertex (ir-)relevancy while the shape similarity improves. The similarity values in the course of the evolution and the resulting, simplified polyline are shown.

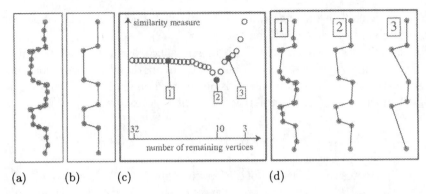

Fig. 3. Computation of the model based similarity measure. A perceived, distorted polyline (a) is compared with one extracted from the robot's internal map (b). Curve evolution of distorted polyline is continued as long as the similarity between the two polylines improves. The development of similarity values in the course of the simplification is given in (c), the X axis represents simplification stages (decreasing number of remaining vertices). The evolution would stop at the position marked 2, the best similarity. (d) Different stages in the evolution process marked in (c). The polyline resulting from the model based evolution is marked 2.

4.2   Matching of Polylines

Computing the actual matching of two structural shape representations extracted from scan and map is performed by finding the *best* correspondence of polylines which respects the cyclic order. For the ease of description, let us assume that no information about the robot's movement since the last matching is available. Consequently, the shape is extracted from the map according to the last view point determined (cp. 5.1). Shape similarity is the key to measure quality of a matching. Additionally, we must take into account that (a) not all polylines may get matched as features' visibility changes and (b) that due to grouping differences (cp. section 3.1) not necessarily 1-to-1 correspondences exist. Noise or change of view point, for example, may lead to a different grouping. Moreover, since every correspondence of polylines induces an alignment that would align scan and map, we demand all induced alignments to be very similar. This criterion is helpful to correctly match featureless shapes, e.g. short segments like obtained when scanning a chairs' legs. The clue in our approach is exploiting correspondence of salient visual parts to correctly identify featureless ones even if no a priori alignment is available (cp. [8]).

An estimation of the alignment, or equivalently: the robot's position in the internal map, is necessary to utilize an efficient matching algorithm. We will show in (Section 4.3) how to compute it using shape similarity. Clearly, it can be derived from odometry if odometry data is available.

Let us now assume that such an estimation exists. Let us further assume that $B = (B_1, B_2, \ldots, B_b)$ and $B' = (B'_1, B'_2, \ldots, B'_{b'})$ are two cyclic ordered vectors of polylines. Denoting correspondence of B_i and B'_j [4] by relation $\sim$, the task can formulated as minimization.

$$\sum_{(B_i, B'_j) \in \sim} (S^\star(B_i, B'_j) + D(B_i, B'_j)) + \sum_{B \in \tilde{B}} P(B) + \sum_{B' \in \tilde{B}'} P(B') \overset{!}{=} \min \quad (4)$$

Hereby, $\tilde{B}$ (rsp. $\tilde{B}'$) denotes the set of polylines not belonging to any matching. P denotes a penalty function for not matching a polyline. This is necessary, as not establishing any correspondence would otherwise yield the lowest possible similarity 0. The penalty function is chosen to linearly grow with the polyline's size modeling a higher likelihood for smaller polylines to appear or disappear[5]. D denotes the aforementioned alignment measure quantifying the deviation of the estimated alignment from the one induced by the correspondence $B_i \sim B'_j$. The best correspondence can so be computed by applying an extended Dynamic Programming scheme. The extension regards the ability to detect 1-to-many and many-to-1 correspondences of polylines. The basic idea here is to consider in each step of the computation if it is advantageous to establish a grouping with the latest correspondence determined so far, i.e. if the summed up (dis-)similarity values and skipping penalties can be decreased. This results in a linear extra effort such that the overall complexity for matching two vectors of n polylines each is $O(n^3)$ – low enough that our prototypical implementation on a standard computer can process several scans per second.

4.3 Matching in the Absence of Odometry

The outlined matching is already capable of tracking complex shapes even if no estimate of the induced alignment is available, because shape similarity is very distinctive. We will detail now on obtaining an alignment estimation purely by shape similarity.

If we had two corresponding polylines, hence, the induced alignment, we could use this as the estimation in the matching. Observing that many shapes can be matched only in consideration of shape similarity, the matching can be employed to obtained this correspondence[6]. Thus, the matching can be computed in a two pass process. Within the first matching pass the consideration of induced alignments' similarity is ineffective. Then, the *most reliable* correspondence is selected. Finally, the actual matching is computed using the alignment induced by the selected matching. To quantify reliability, a measure based on shape similarity and shape complexity has been proposed [11]. A polyline's shape complexity may be expressed by summing up inner points' relevance measures

---

[4] To be more precise: correspondences of either B_i and $\{B'_j, B'_{j+1}, \ldots, B'_{j'}\}$ or $\{B_i, B'_{i+1}, \ldots, B'_{i'}\}$ and B'_j since we consider correspondences of types 1-to-many and many-to-1, too.

[5] When comparing likewise noisy polylines, similarity values grow linearly with the polylines' size, too.

[6] As there are not necessarily 1-to-1 correspondences, it might not be sufficient to only consider individual similarities.

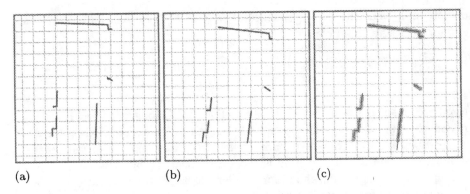

(a)   (b)   (c)

Fig. 4. Exemplary results of the shape based matching. Shape perceived by the LRF (a) is matched against the shape extracted from the map (b). Shapes are matched in a two step process. In the first step, only the most reliable matching (marked $\star$ in (c)) is used to align perception and map. In the second step, the final matching is computed and the perception is aligned. (c) Shows the alignment of (a) and (b), using thick lines for the map shape and thin lines for the perceived shape. The grid in the illustrations denotes 1m distance.

(cp. equation 1). If a polyline has no inner points, complexity is given by half the Euclidean distance of its end points. Terming this complexity measure C, the reliability is defined as

$$Q(P,Q) = C(P) + C(Q) - S^\star(P,Q). \quad (5)$$

The idea is expressing reliability as high similarity of complex shapes (cp. [11] for details). An exemplary result is presented in Figure 4 where a scan is matched against the shape extracted from the map (a). Based on the most reliable correspondence the estimated alignment, i.e. the position of the robot within the map, is computed. Accordingly aligned scan and map excerpt is shown together with the computed matching in (b). The presented technique can cope with differences in position estimates of more than 1m; rotational changes that retain the visibility of most salient objects are mastered, too. Observe, that this is a dramatical improvement compared to the precision required by standard scan matching approaches which typically rely on a hill climbing strategy (cp. [8]).

5   Map Update

Once the shape extracted from the map and the shape perceived by the sensor have been matched, the internal map can be updated. The first step is to align perceived shape and map. Next, corresponding polylines can be merged to obtain a single polyline in the map comprising existing map and new shape information. Perceived polylines not corresponding to a polyline in the map are considered to be a newly emerged features. Thus, they are added to the map.

5.1   Alignment and Localization

To localize a robot within its map, the perceived scan needs to be aligned with the internal map. This yields the position of scan's origin in the map's frame of reference, hence, provides the localization. To align perceived scan and map, we adapt a scan matching technique originally developed by Cox [3] and improved by Gutmann [7].

The adapted approach is based on a scan point to line matching, i.e. reflection points measured by the LRF are matched against model lines represented in the map. Distance of scan points and model lines is minimized by aligning the scan. Given a correspondence of points and lines, the optimal alignment, i.e. a rotation around the scan's origin and a translation, can be computed in a closed form (cp. [7]). The correspondence, however, might not be correct from the beginning, since it is based on rather simple rule. The idea to overcome this problem is carrying out several steps of matching and aligning iteratively, to allow convergence of correspondences and, thus, alignment. Limitations of this procedure are due to the rather simple matching rule which considers no large spatial context than a simple line. A good a priori alignment are therefore a prerequisite for successful operation. Even with small distortions, some scan points may get matched to the wrong model line. This can cause the process to get trapped in a local minima.

To apply the method of Cox, we need to improve the matching of points and model lines. The knowledge of matching shapes is the key here. Only correspondences between corresponding shapes are considered in the alignment process. For each perceived shape sample points are determined. To obtain the experimental results in this paper, we used a sampling of 10 cm. Additionally, we ensured that at least one sampling point lies on each of the polyline's line segments. Using these sampling points, corresponding line segments of corresponding shapes are determined based on proximity. For every sampling point the nearest point contained in the corresponding polyline is computed and the scan is aligned. The procedure is repeated until convergence is reached, i.e. the alignment does not change significantly any more. Experiments show that this rather simple, straightforward adaption already yields good results.

5.2   Merging of Polylines

After perceived shape and map have been aligned, we need to merge corresponding polylines to obtain a single, comprehensive one. This way, newly detected features can be added to a polyline. Moreover, it can be mediated between differing perceptions of the same polyline. We need to account that due to change of visibility only some parts of the polylines may actually correspond. Hence, we first decompose each polyline into *head*, *body*, and *tail* (cp. Figure 5). The body part refers to the corresponding part of the polyline. Head and tail denote the remaining parts.

To obtain the merged polylines, the merged body parts are appended with head and tail parts. Note that there exists at most one head and one tail. To determine the body parts of corresponding polylines, the shortest distance between a polyline's end points and the other polyline are computed. This induced

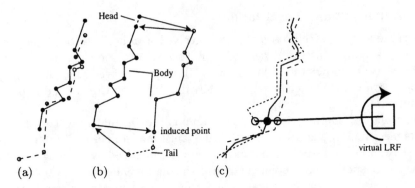

Fig. 5. Illustration of the merging process. (a) Two aligned polylines (solid and dashed lines) are the starting point. (b) End points are mapped to nearest points on the other polyline (For illustration purposes the lines have been shifted apart). The nearest points induced determine beginning of head and tail parts. (c) To average the corresponding body parts, a laser scanner is simulated. The solid line shows the result of averaging the two dashed lines which show a magnified excerpt from the body parts shown in (b).

two additional points on the other polyline. The body parts are said to be determined by the points whose nearest points not coincide with an end point. Refer to Figure 5 for illustration.

To merge the body parts, we use a simple technique. A laser range finder located at the robot's current position in the map is simulated. It scans both body parts simultaneously. Averaging the distances measured yields a new, comprehensive body part. To obtain a more sophisticated mediation between newly perceived shape and map, a weighted average can be used. For example, as a polyline in the map may result from many measurements, a single new measurement should not change the polyline dramatically any more. Since this closely relates to handling of uncertainty and stochastical models which have been masked out in this paper, this issue is not detailed any further here.

6   Experimental Results

In our experiments, we have processed data obtained from SICK LMS laser range finders mounted on a Pioneer-2 robot or on the Bremen autonomous wheelchair [13]. Figure 6 shows the resulting map from processing 450 scans taken at a rate of aprox. 15 scans per second. The average robot speed was 0.5 m/sec. No odometry information has been used to obtain the results.

7   Conclusion and Outlook

We have presented a comprehensive geometric model for robot mapping based on shape information. A shape matching has been specially tailored to match

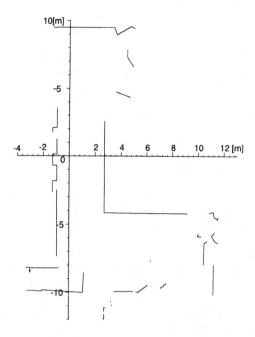

Fig. 6. A shape based map consisting of only a few polygonal lines. It has been constructed autonomously from processing 450 laser range finder scans recorded at University of Bremen. The unit size is 1m.

shape perceived by a laser range finder against a partially existing polygonal map. The matching is powerful enough to disregard any pose information and cope with scans significantly differing from the map. Based on corresponding shapes, the process of localization and map update have been detailed.

We are aware that statistical methods are needed to guarantee robust performance, but did not include any as we concentrated on geometric models exclusively. So, future work comprises the coupling with a state-of-the-art stochastical model. Since object centered approaches are judged well-suited to handle dynamics and shape matching enables us to identify corresponding objects, explicit handling of dynamics within our architecture is of great interest to us. Additionally, as we believe that our shape based approach is particularly promising in attacking the problem of cycle detection, we plan to investigate into this topic.

Acknowledgment

This work was carried out in the framework of the SFB/TR 8 Spatial Cognition, project R3 [Q-Shape]. Financial support by the Deutsche Forschungsgemeinschaft is gratefully acknowledged. Additionally, this work was supported in part by the National Science Foundation under grant INT-0331786 and the grant 16 1811 705 from Temple University Office of the Vice President for Research and Graduate Studies. Thomas Röfer is acknowledged for providing scan data.

References

1. M. Arkin, L.P. Chew, D.P. Huttenlocher, K. Kedem, and J. S. B. Mitchell. An efficiently computable metric for comparing polygonal shapes. *IEEE Transactions on Pattern Analysis and Machine Intelligence*, 13, 1991.
2. Ronen Basri, Luiz Costa, Davi Geiger, and David Jacobs. Determining the similarity of deformable shapes. *Vision Research*, 38, 1998.
3. Ingemar J. Cox. Blanche: Position estimation for an autonomous robot vehicle. In Ingemar J. Cox and G.T. Wilfong, editors, *Autonomous Robot Vehicles*, pages 221–228. Springer-Verlag, 1990.
4. Mark de Berg, Marc van Kreveld, Mark Overmars, and Otfried Schwarzkopf. *Computational Geometry. Algorithms and Applications*. Springer-Verlag, 2000.
5. G. Dissanayake, P. Newman, S. Clark, H.F. Durrant-Whyte, and M. Csorba. A solution to the simultaneous localization and map building (SLAM) problem. *IEEE Transactions of Robotics and Automation*, 2001.
6. A. Elfes. *Occupancy Grids: A Probabilistic Framework for Robot Perception and Navigation*. PhD thesis, Department of Electrical and Computer Engineering, Carnegie Mellon University, 1989.
7. Jens-Steffen Gutmann. *Robuste Navigation autonomer mobiler Systeme*. PhD thesis, University of Freiburg, 2000. (in German).
8. D. Hähnel, D. Schulz, and W. Burgard. Map building with mobile robots in populated environments. In *In Proceedings of International Conference on Intelligent Robots and Systems (IROS'02)*, 2002.
9. L. J. Latecki and R. Lakämper. Convexity rule for shape decomposition based on discrete contour evolution. *Computer Vision and Image Understanding*, 73, 1999.
10. L. J. Latecki and R. Lakämper. Shape similarity measure based on correspondence of visual parts. *IEEE Trans. Pattern Analysis and Machine Intelligence*, 22(10), 2000.
11. Longin Jan Latecki, Rolf Lakämper, and Diedrich Wolter. Shape similarity and visual parts. In *Proceedings of the 11th International Conference on Disrecte Geometry for Computer Imagery (DGCI), Naples, Italy*, November 2003.
12. F. Lu and E. Milios. Robot pose estimation in unknown environments by matching 2D range scans. *Journal of Intelligent and Robotic Systems*, 1997.
13. T. Röfer. Using histogram correlation to create consistent laser scan maps. In *Proceedings of the IEEE International Conference on Robotics Systems (IROS-2002)*, 2002.
14. Thomas B. Sebastian, Philip N. Klein, and Benjamin B. Kimia. On aligning curves. *IEEE Transactions on Pattern Analysis and Machine Intelligence*, 25(1):116–125, 2003.
15. K. Siddiqi, A. Shokoufandeh, S. J. Dickinson, and S. W. Zucker. Shock graphs and shape matching. *International Journal of Computer Vision*, 35(1):13–32, 1999.
16. S. Thrun. Learning metric-topological maps for indoor mobile robot navigation. *Artificial Intelligence*, 99(1):21–71, 1998.
17. S. Thrun. Probabilistic algorithms in robotics. *AI Magazine*, 21(4):93–109, 2000.
18. S. Thrun. Robotic mapping: A survey. In G. Lakemeyer and B. Nebel, editors, *Exploring Artificial Intelligence in the New Millenium*. Morgan Kaufmann, 2002.

Vision-Based
and Eye Gaze Tracking System

Kang Ryoung Park

Division of Media Technology, SangMyung University
7 Hongji-Dong, JongRo-Gu, Seoul, Republic of Korea

Abstract. Gaze detection is to locate the position (on a monitor) where a user is looking. Previous researches use one wide view camera, which can capture a whole user's face. However, the image resolution is too low with such a camera and the fine movements of user's eye cannot be exactly detected. So, we propose the new gaze detection system with dual cameras (a wide and a narrow view camera). In order to locate the user's eye position accurately, the narrow-view camera has the functionalities of auto focusing/panning/tilting based on the detected 3D eye positions from the wide view camera. In addition, we use the IR-LED illuminators for wide and narrow view camera, which can ease the detecting of facial features, pupil and iris position. To overcome the problem of specular reflection on glasses by illuminator, we use dual IR-LED illuminators for wide and narrow view camera and detect the accurate eye position, which is not hidden by the specular reflection. Experimental results show that the gaze detection error between the computed positions and the real ones is about 2.89 cm of RMS error.

Keywords: Gaze Detection, Dual Cameras, Dual IR-LED Illuminators

1 Introduction

Interacting with the computer through the head and eye gaze is natural for human-machine interaction since this involves sensing the human gestures of the face that can be recognized without any discomfort for the user [1]. Gaze detection system is important in many applications such as the view control in 3D simulation programs, virtual reality and video conferencing. In addition, they can help the handicapped to use computers and are also useful for those whose hands are busy controlling other menus on the monitor [19]. Most Previous studies were focused on 2D/3D head rotation/translation estimation [2][15], the facial gaze detection [3-9][16][17][19][23] and the eye gaze detection [10-14][18][24-29]. Recently, the gaze detection considering both head and eye movement has been researched. Ohmura and Ballard et al. [5][6]'s methods have the disadvantages that the Z distance between camera and facial feature points should be measured manually and they takes much time (over 1 minute) to compute the gaze direction vector. Gee et al. [7] and Heinzmann et al. [8]'s methods only compute gaze direction vector whose origin is located between two eyes in the head coordinate and do not obtain the gaze position on a monitor. In addition, if

S. Biundo, T. Frühwirth, and G. Palm (Eds.): KI 2004, LNAI 3238, pp. 453–465, 2004.
© Springer-Verlag Berlin Heidelberg 2004

3D rotation and translation of the head happen simultaneously, they cannot estimate the accurate 3D motion due to the complexity of their least-square fitting algorithm. Rikert et al. [9]'s method has the constraints that the Z distance between a face and the monitor must be maintained unchanged during training and testing procedures, which can give much inconvenience to user. In the methods of [11][13][14][16][17], a pair of glasses having marking points is required to detect facial features, which can be also inconvenient to a user. The researches of [3][4][20] show the gaze detection methods only considering head movements and have the limits that the gaze errors are increased in case that the eye movements happen. To overcome such problems, the research of [21] shows the gaze detection considering both head and eye movements, but uses only one wide view camera, which can capture the whole face of user. In such case, the eye image resolution is too low and the fine movements of user's eye cannot be exactly detected. Wang et al. [1]'s method provides the advanced approaches that combines head pose determination with eye gaze estimation by a wide view camera and a panning/tilting narrow camera. However, their method supposes that they know the 3D distance between two eyes and that between both lip corners. and there is no individual variation for the 3D distances. In addition, they suppose that they know the 3D diameter of eye ball and there is no individual variation for that. Based on the assumptions, they compute the gaze position on a monitor. However, our preliminary experiments show that there are much individual variations for the 3D distances/3D diameter and such cases can increase much gaze errors. To overcome above problems, we propose the new method of computing gaze position. In order to implement practical gaze system based on our method, we use dual cameras (a wide view and a narrow view camera). In order to track the positions of user's eye changed by head movements, the narrow view camera has the functionalities of auto focusing/panning/tilting based on the detected 3D eye positions from the wide view camera. In addition, we use IR-LED illuminators for wide and narrow view camera, which can ease the detecting of facial features, pupil and iris position. To overcome the problem of specular reflection on glasses by illuminator, we use dual IR-LED illuminators for wide and narrow view camera.

2   Localization of Facial Features in Wide View Image

In order to detect gaze position on a monitor, we first locate facial features (both eye centers, eye corners, nostrils) in wide view images. There have been many researches for detecting facial features. One of them is to use facial skin color [22], but their performance can be affected by the environmental light or race, etc. To overcome such problems and detect the facial features robustly in any environment, we use the method of detecting specular reflection on the eyes. For that, we implement the gaze detection system as shown in Fig. 1.

As shown in Fig. 1, the IR-LED(1) is used to make the specular reflections on eyes. The IR pass filter(2) in front of camera lens can only pass the infrared light (over 800 nm) and the brightness of input image is only affected by the

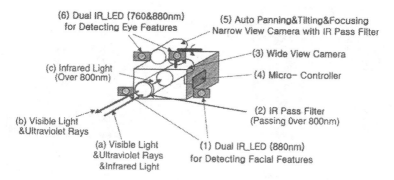

Fig. 1. The gaze detecting system.

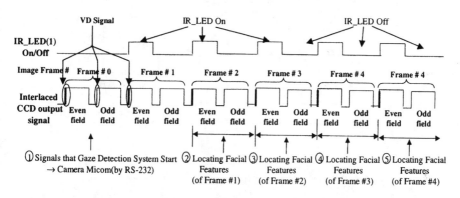

Fig. 2. The on/off controlling of IR-LED illuminator for detecting eye features.

IR-LED(1) excluding external illumination. We use a wide view(3) and a narrow view(5) CCD camera (interlaced scan mode). The reason of using IR-LED(1) of 880nm is that human eye can only perceive the visible and the near infrared light (below about 880nm) and our illuminators do not make dazzling to user's eye, consequently. When a user starts our gaze detection S/W in PC, the starting signal is transmitted to the micro-controller(4) in camera via the RS-232C. Then, the micro-controller turns on the illuminator(1) synchronized with the even field of CCD signal and turns off it synchronized with the next odd field of CCD signal successively, as shown in Fig. 2 [21]. Here, the VD(Vertical Drive) signal means the starting signal of the even and odd field. From that, we can get a difference image between the even and the odd image as shown in Fig. 3 and the specular reflection points on both eyes can be easily detected because their image gray level are higher than other regions [21]. In addition, we use the Red-Eye effect and the method of changing Frame Grabber decoder value in order to detect more accurate eye position [21]. We implement a 2 channel Frame Grabber to convert the camera output signal (NTSC analog signal) into digital image. The decoder chip in the conventional Frame Grabber has the functionality of A/D (analog to digital) conversion for the camera output signal.

Specular points of both eyes from IR_LED(1) in Fig.1

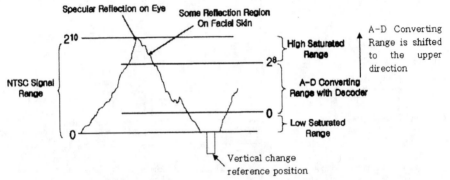

(a)   (b)

Fig. 3. The even and odd images of frame #1 (a)Even field image (b)Odd field image.

Fig. 4. The NTSC signal range vs. AD conversion range.

In general, the NTSC signal has high resolution $(0 \sim 2^{10} - 1)$, but the range of A/D conversion by conventional decoder is low resolution $(0 \sim 2^8 - 1)$. So, the NTSC signal in high saturated range is represented as 255 $(2^8 - 1)$ gray level of image and both the specular reflection on eye (cornea) and the some reflection region on facial skin can be represented as same image level $(2^8 - 1)$, which makes it difficult to discriminate the corneal specular reflection only by image processing algorithm. However, the NTSC signal level of corneal specular reflection is higher than that of other reflection due to the reflectance rate. So, if we make the decoder brightness value lower (we can control it by the device driver S/W) as shown in Fig. 4, then the A/D conversion range of decoder can be shifted to the upper direction. In such case, there is no high saturated range and the corneal specular reflection and the other reflection can be discriminated, easily. Around the detected corneal specular reflection points, we determine the eye candidate region of 30*30 pixels and locate the accurate eye (iris) center by the circular edge detection method [30]. Because the eye localization is performed in the restricted region, it can be done in real-time (below 3 ms in Pentium-III 866MHz). After locating the eye center, we detect the eye corner by using eye corner shape template and SVM (Support Vector Machine) [21]. We get 2000 successive image frames (100 frames × 20 persons in various sitting positions) for SVM training. From that, 8000 eye corner data (4 eye corners × 2000 images) are obtained

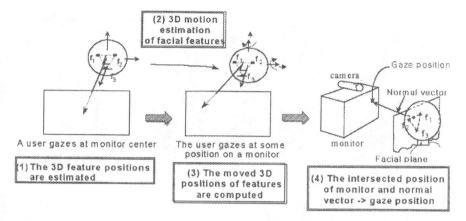

Fig. 5. 4 steps in order to compute a facial gaze position on a monitor.

and additional 1000 (50 frames × 20 persons in various sitting positions) images are used for testing. Experimental results show the classification error for training data is 0.11% (9/8000) and that for testing data is 0.2% (8/4000) and our algorithm is also valid for the users with glasses or contact lens. In comparing experiments, MLP (Multi-Layered Perceptron) shows the worse performance (the error of 1.58% for training data and 3.1% for testing data). The classification time of SVM is so small as like 8 ms in Pentium-III 866MHz. After locating eye centers and eye corners, the positions of nostrils can be detected by anthropometric constraints in a face and SVM. In order to reduce the effect by the facial expression change, we do not use the lip corners for gaze detection. Experimental results show that RMS error between the detected feature positions and the actual positions (manually detected positions) are 1 pixel (of both eye centers), 2 pixels (of both eye corners) and 4 pixels (of both nostrils) in 640×480 pixels image. From them, we use 5 feature points (left/right eye corners of left eye, left/right eye corners of right eye, nostril center) in order to detect facial gaze position.

3   4 Steps for Computing Facial Gaze Position

After feature detection, we take 4 steps in order to compute a facial gaze position on a monitor as shown in Fig. 5 [3][4][21]. At the 1st step, when a user gazes at 5 known positions on a monitor ((1),(6),(12),(18),(23) of Fig. 11), the 3D positions (X, Y, Z) of initial 5 feature points (detected in the section 2) are computed automatically [3][4]. In Fig. 5 and 10(b), we only depict 3 feature points for convenience. At the 2nd step and 3rd step, when the user rotates/translates his head in order to gaze at one position on a monitor, the new (changed) 3D positions of those 5 features can be computed from 3D motion estimation. Considering many limitations of previous motion estimation researches, we use the EKF (Extended Kalman Filtering) [2] for 3D motion estimation and the

Calibration Panel   2D position of Calibration Points

Fig. 6. The calibration panel of the internal/external camera parameters.

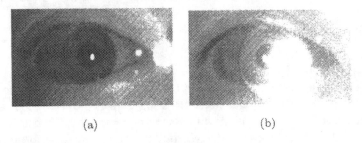

(a)   (b)

Fig. 7. The eye image having specular reflection on glasses (a)Eye image with left illuminator (b)Eye image with right illuminator.

new 3D positions of those features can be computed by the EKF and affine transform [3][21]. The estimation accuracy of the EKF is compared with 3D position tracking sensor [32]. Experimental results show the RMS errors are about 1.4 cm and 2.98° in translation and rotation. In addition, the experimental results show that the RMS error of between the changed(estimated) 3D positions of 5 features and the actual ones (measured by 3D position tracking sensor) is 1.15 cm (0.64cm in X axis, 0.5cm in Y axis, 0.81cm in Z axis) for 20 person data which were used for testing the feature detection performance. At the 4th step, one facial plane is determined from the new (changed) 3D positions of the 5 features and the normal vector (whose origin exists in the middle of the forehead) of the plane shows a gaze vector by head (facial) movements. The gaze position on a monitor is the intersection position between a monitor and the gaze vector [3][4] as shown in Fig. 10(b).

4   Auto Panning/Tilting/Focusing of Narrow View Camera

Based on the new (changed) 3D positions of the 5 feature points (which are computed at the 2nd and 3rd step as mentioned in section 3), we can pan and tilt the narrow view camera in order to capture the eye image. For that, we also perform the coordinate conversion between monitor and narrow view camera using the internal/external camera parameters, which are obtained at initial calibration stage. Such calibration method is same to that between the wide view camera and the monitor and it uses the calibration panel as shown in Fig. 6. Detail accounts can be referred in [3]. When the user rotates his head severely, one of his eyes may disappear in camera view. So, we track only one visible eye with auto panning/tilting narrow view camera. Conventional narrow view camera has small DOF (Depth of Field) and there is the limitation of increasing the DOF with the fixed focal camera. So, we use the auto focusing narrow view camera in order to capture clear eye image. For auto focusing, the Z distance between the eye and the camera is required and we can obtain the Z distance at the 2nd and 3rd step (as mentioned in section 3). In order to compensate the focusing error due to the inaccurate Z distance measure, we use an additional focus quality checking algorithm [33]. That is, the auto focusing for eye image is accomplished based on the computed Z distance and the captured eye image is transmitted to PC. With that, the focus quality checking algorithm computes the focus quality. If the quality does not meet our threshold (70 of the range ($0 \sim 100$)), then we perform additional focusing process by sending the moving command of focus lens to camera micro-controller. In this stage, we should consider the specular reflection on glasses. The surface of glasses can make the specular reflection, which can hide the whole eye image. In such case, the eye region is not detected and we cannot compute the eye gaze position. So, we use dual IR-LED illuminators like Fig. 1(6). When the large specular reflection happens from one illuminator (right or left illuminator), then it can be detected from image. As mentioned in section 2, the NTSC analog level of specular reflection region is higher than any other region and they can be detected by changing decoder brightness setting. When the large specular region proves to exist with the changed decoder brightness value, then our gaze detection system change the illuminator (from left to right or right to left) as shown in Fig. 7 and the specular reflection on glasses does not happen, consequently.

5   Localization of Eye Features in Narrow View Image

After we get the focused eye image, we perform the localization of eye features as shown in Fig. 8 and 9. We detect $P_1 \sim P_4'$ in right eye image as shown in Fig. 8 and also detect $P_5 \sim P_8'$ in left eye image as shown in Fig. 9 for computing eye gaze detection. Here, the P_1 and P_1' show the pupil center and the P_2 and P_2' does the iris center. J. Wang et al. [1] uses the method that detects the iris outer boundary by vertical edge operator, morphological "open" operation and elliptical fitting. However, the upper and lower region of iris outer boundary tend to be covered by eyelid and inaccurate iris elliptical fitting happens due to the lack of iris boundary pixels. In addition, their method computes eye gaze position by checking the shape change of iris when a user gazes at monitor positions. However, our experimental results show that the shape change amount of iris is very small and it is difficult to detect the accurate eye gaze position only by that information. So, we use the positional information of both pupil

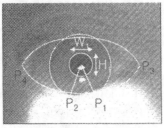
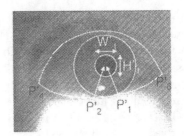

| (a) Gazing at Center | (b) Gazing at Left Uppermost |
| Position of Monitor | Position of Monitor |

$$f_1 = \frac{P'_3(x) - P'_1(x)}{P_3(x) - P_1(x)} \quad f_2 = \frac{P'_4(x) - P'_1(x)}{P_4(x) - P_1(x)} \quad f_3 = \frac{P'_3(x) - P'_2(x)}{P_3(x) - P_2(x)} \quad f_4 = \frac{P'_4(x) - P'_2(x)}{P_4(x) - P_2(x)}$$

$$f_5 = \frac{P'_3(y) - P'_1(y)}{P_3(y) - P_1(y)} \quad f_6 = \frac{P'_4(y) - P'_1(y)}{P_4(y) - P_1(y)} \quad f_7 = \frac{P'_3(y) - P'_2(y)}{P_3(y) - P_2(y)} \quad f_8 = \frac{P'_4(y) - P'_2(y)}{P_4(y) - P_2(y)}$$

$$f_9 = \frac{P'_1(x) - P'_2(x)}{P_1(x) - P_2(x)} \quad f_{10} = \frac{P'_1(y) - P'_2(y)}{P_1(y) - P_2(y)} \quad f_{11} = \frac{H'_1 / W'_1}{H_1 / W_1}$$

Fig. 8. The features for eye gaze detection from right eye.

and iris. Also, we use the information of shape change of pupil, which does not tend to be covered by eyelid. In general, the IR-LED of short wavelength (700nm $\sim$ 800nm) makes the high contrast between iris and sclera. On the other hand, that of long wavelength (800nm $\sim$ 900nm) makes the high contrast between pupil and iris [34]. Based on that, we use the IR-LED illuminator of multi-wavelength (760nm and 880nm) as shown in Fig. 1(6). As shown in Fig. 8(b) and 9(a), the shapes of iris and pupil are almost ellipse, when the user gazes at a side position of monitor. So, the method of circular edge detection [30] cannot be used. Instead, we use the canny edge operator to extract edge components and a 2D edge-based elliptical Hough transform [31]. From that, we can get the center positions and the major/minor axes of iris/pupil ellipses. In order to detect the eye corner position, we detect the eyelid as shown in Fig. 8 and 9. That is because the upper and lower eyelids meet on two eye corner positions. To extract the eyelid region, we use the region-based template deformation and masking method [35]. In detail, we make the eyelid edge image with canny edge operator and apply the deformable template as the eyelid mask. Here, we use 2 deformable templates (parabolic shape) for upper and lower eyelid detection. From that, we can detect the accurate eye corners as shown in Fig. 8 and 9. Experimental results show that RMS errors between the detected eye feature positions and the actual ones (manually detected) are 2 pixels (of iris center), 1 pixel (of pupil center), 4 pixels (of left eye corner) and 4 pixels (of right eye corner).

Based on the detected eye features, we select the 22 feature values ($f_1 \sim f_{11}$ are used in case that right eye image can be captured by narrow view camera as shown in Fig. 8 and $f_{12} \sim f_{22}$ are used in case that left eye image can be captured as shown in Fig. 9). With those feature values, we can compute eye gaze position on a monitor as shown in Fig. 10(a). Detail accounts are shown in section 6.

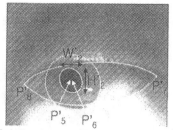
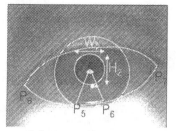

(a) Gazing at Right Lowermost
Position of Monitor

(b) Gazing at Center
Position of Monitor

$$f_{12} = \frac{P'_7(x) - P'_5(x)}{P_7(x) - P_5(x)} \quad f_{13} = \frac{P'_8(x) - P'_5(x)}{P_8(x) - P_5(x)} \quad f_{14} = \frac{P'_7(x) - P'_6(x)}{P_7(x) - P_6(x)} \quad f_{15} = \frac{P'_8(x) - P'_6(x)}{P_8(x) - P_6(x)}$$

$$f_{16} = \frac{P'_7(y) - P'_5(y)}{P_7(y) - P_5(y)} \quad f_{17} = \frac{P'_8(y) - P'_5(y)}{P_8(y) - P_5(y)} \quad f_{18} = \frac{P'_7(y) - P'_6(y)}{P_7(y) - P_6(y)} \quad f_{19} = \frac{P'_8(y) - P'_6(y)}{P_8(y) - P_6(y)}$$

$$f_{20} = \frac{P'_7(x) - P'_6(x)}{P_7(x) - P_6(x)} \quad f_{21} = \frac{P'_7(y) - P'_6(y)}{P_7(y) - P_6(y)} \quad f_{22} = \frac{H'_2 / W'_2}{H_2 / W_2}$$

Fig. 9. The features for eye gaze detection from left eye.

6   Detecting the Gaze Position on a Monitor

In section 3, we explain the gaze detection method only considering head movement. As mentioned before, when a user gazes at a monitor position, both the
head and eyes tend to be moved simultaneously. So, we compute the additional
eye gaze position with the detected 22 feature values (as mentioned in section 5)
and a neural network (multi-layered perceptron) as shown in Fig. 10(a). Here,
the input values for neural network are normalized by the distance between the
iris/pupil center and the eye corner, which are obtained in case of gazing at
monitor center. That is because we do not use a zoom lens in our camera. That
is, the more the user approaches the monitor (camera), the larger the eye size
becomes and the farther the distance between the pupil/iris and the eye corner
becomes, consequently. After detecting eye gaze position based on the neural
network, we can determine a final gaze position on a monitor by head and eye
movements based on the vector summation of each gaze position (face and eye
gaze) as shown in Fig. 10(b).

7   Performance Evaluations

The gaze detection error of the proposed method is compared to that of our
previous methods [3][4][19][21] as shown in Table 1. The researches [3][4] compute facial gaze position not considering the eye movements. The research [19]
calculates the gaze position by mapping the 2D facial feature position into the
monitor gaze position by linear interpolation or neural network without 3D computation and considering eye movements. The method [21] computes the gaze

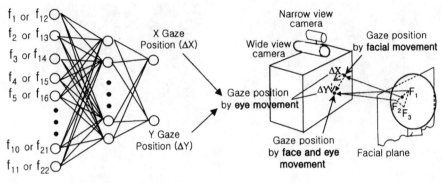

(a) Neural network for detecting
eye gaze position

(b) Gaze position detection by
face and eye movement

Fig. 10. The neural network for eye gaze detection and gaze position detection by face
and eye movement.

positions considering both head and eye movements, but uses only one wide view
camera. The test data are acquired when 10 users gaze at 23 gaze positions on a
19" monitor as shown in Fig. 11. Here, the gaze error is the RMS error between
the actual gaze positions and the computed ones. Shown in Table 1, the gaze
errors are calculated in two cases. The case I shows that gaze error about test
data including only head movements and the case II does that the gaze error
including head and eye movements.

Table 1. Gaze error about test data (cm).

Method	Linear interpol.[19]	Single neural net[19]	Combined neural nets[19]	[3] method	[4] method	[21] method	Proposed method
case I	5.1	4.23	4.48	5.35	5.21	3.40	2.24
case II	11.8	11.32	8.87	7.45	6.29	4.8	2.89

Shown in Table 1, the gaze error of the proposed method is the smallest
in any case. Fig. 11 shows an example of the gaze detection errors on a 19"
monitor. The reference positions are marked as "black circle" and the computed
gaze positions are shown as "X". From the Fig. 11, we can know the gaze errors
are more increased in lower region of the monitor. That is because two cameras
are positioned on the monitor as shown in Fig. 10(b) and fine movement of head
and eye cannot be seen in case of gazing at the lower positions of the monitor,
consequently. At the 2nd experiment, the points of radius 5 pixels are spaced
vertically and horizontally at 1.5" intervals on a 19" monitor with the screen
resolution of 1280×1024 pixels as such Rikert's research [9]. The RMS error
between the real and calculated gaze position is 2.85 cm and it is much superior to
Rikert's method (almost 5.08 cm). Our gaze error is correspondent to the angular

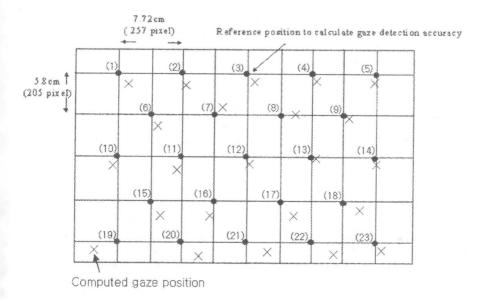

Fig. 11. An example of gaze detection errors on a 19" monitor.

error of 2.29 degrees on X axis and 2.31 degrees on Y axis. In addition, we tested the gaze errors according to the Z distance (55, 60, 65cm). The RMS errors are 2.81cm at 55cm, 2.85cm at 60cm, 2.92cm at 65cm. It shows that the performance of our method is not affected by the user's Z position. Last experiment for processing time shows that our gaze detection process takes about 500ms in Pentium-III 866MHz and it is much smaller than Rikert's method (1 minute in alphastation 333MHz). Our system only requires the user to gaze at 5 known monitor positions at the initial calibration stage (as shown in the section 3) and can track/compute the user's gaze position without any user's intervention at real-time speed. The research [1] shows the angular error of below 1 degree, but their method supposes that they know the 3D distance between two eyes and that between both lip corners and there is no individual variation for the 3D distances. In addition, they suppose that they know the 3D diameter of eye ball and there is no individual variation for that. However, our preliminary experiments show that there are much individual variations for the 3D distances/3D diameter and such cases can increase much gaze errors (the angular error of more than 4 degree). The material cost of our system is below 100 dollars and we can mass-produce our gaze detection system with below 300 dollars excluding the price of computer.

8   Conclusions

This paper describes a new gaze detecting method. In future works, we have plans to research the method of capturing higher resolution eye image with zoom lens and it will increase the accuracy of final gaze detection. In addition, the method to increase the auto panning/tilting/focusing speed of narrow view camera should be researched to decrease total processing time.

Acknowledgement

This work was supported by Korea Science and Engineering Foundation (KOSEF) through Biometrics Engineering Research Center(BERC) at Yonsei University

References

1. J. Wang and E. Sung, 2002. Study on Eye Gaze Estimation, IEEE Transactions on System, Man and Cybernatics, Vol. 32, No. 3, pp.332-350
2. A. Azarbayejani., 1993, Visually Controlled Graphics. IEEE Transactions on Pattern Analysis and Machine Intelligence, Vol. 15, No. 6, pp. 602-605
3. K. R. Park et al., Apr 2000, Gaze Point Detection by Computing the 3D Positions and 3D Motions of Face, IEICE Transactions on Information and Systems, Vol. E.83-D, No.4, pp.884-894
4. K. R. Park et al., Oct 1999, Gaze Detection by Estimating the Depth and 3D Motions of Facial Features in Monocular Images, IEICE Transactions on Fundamentals, Vol. E.82-A, No. 10, pp. 2274-2284
5. K. OHMURA et al., 1989. Pointing Operation Using Detection of Face Direction from a Single View. IEICE Transactions on Information and Systems, Vol. J72-D-II, No.9, pp. 1441-1447
6. P. Ballard et al., 1995. Controlling a Computer via Facial Aspect. IEEE Transactions on System, Man and Cybernatics, Vol. 25, No. 4, pp. 669-677
7. A. Gee et al., 1996. Fast visual tracking by temporal consensus, Image and Vision Computing. Vol. 14, pp. 105-114
8. J. Heinzmann et al., 1998. 3D Facial Pose and Gaze Point Estimation using a Robust Real-Time Tracking Paradigm. Proceedings of International Conference on Automatic Face and Gesture Recognition, pp. 142-147
9. T. Rikert, 1998. Gaze Estimation using Morphable Models. Proceedings of International Conference on Automatic Face and Gesture Recognition, pp.436-441
10. A.Ali-A-L et al., 1997, Man-machine Interface through Eyeball Direction of Gaze. Proceedings of the Southeastern Symposium on System Theory, pp. 478-482
11. A. TOMONO et al., 1994. Eye Tracking Method Using an Image Pickup Apparatus. European Patent Specification-94101635
12. Eyemark Recorder Model EMR-NC, NAC Image Technology Cooperation
13. Porrill-J et al., Jan 1999, Robust and Optimal Use of Information in Stereo Vision. Nature. vol.397, no.6714, pp.63-6
14. Varchmin-AC et al., 1998, Image based Recognition of Gaze Direction Using Adaptive Methods. Gesture and Sign Language in Human-Computer Interaction. Proceedings of International Gesture Workshop. Berlin, Germany, pp. 245-257.
15. J. Heinzmann et al., 1997. Robust Real-time Face Tracking and Gesture Recognition. Proceedings of International Joint Conference on Artificial Intelligence, Vol. 2, pp. 1525-1530

16. Matsumoto-Y, et al., 2000, An Algorithm for Real-time Stereo Vision Implementation of Head Pose and Gaze Direction Measurement. Proceedings of International Conference on Automatic Face and Gesture Recognition. pp. 499-504
17. Newman-R et al., 2000, Real-time Stereo Tracking for Head Pose and Gaze Estimation. Proceedings of International Conference on Automatic Face and Gesture Recognition, pp. 122-128
18. Betke-M et al., 1999, Gaze Detection via Self-organizing Gray-scale Units. Proceedings of International Workshop on Recognition, Analysis and Tracking of Faces and Gestures in Real-Time System. pp. 70-76
19. K. R. Park et al., 2000. Intelligent Process Control via Gaze Detection Technology. Engineering Applications of Artificial Intelligence, Vol. 13, No. 5, pp. 577-587
20. K. R. Park et al., 2002. Gaze Position Detection by Computing the 3 Dimensional Facial Positions and Motions. Pattern Recognition, Vol. 35, No.11, pp. 2559-2569
21. K. R. Park et al., 2002, Facial and Eye Gaze detection. Lecture Notes in Computer Science, Vol.2525, pp. 368-376
22. Jie Yang and Alex Waibel, 1996, A Real-time Face Tracker, Proceedings of Workshop on Applications of Computer Vision, pp. 142-147
23. Y. Matsumoto, 2000. An Algorithm for Real-time Stereo Vision Implementation of Head Pose and Gaze Direction Measurement, Proceedings of International Conference on Automatic Face and Gesture Recognition, pp.499-505
24. http://www.iscaninc.com
25. http://www.seeingmachines.com
26. B Wolfe, D. Eichmann, 1997. A Neural Network Approach to Tracking Eye Position, International Journal of Human Computer Interaction, Vol. 9, No.1, pp. 59-79
27. David Beymer and Myron Flickner, 2003. Eye Gaze Tracking Using an Active Stereo Head, IEEE Computer Vision and Pattern Recognition
28. J. Zhu et al., 2002. Subpixel Eye Gaze Tracking, Proceedings of International Conference on Automatic Face and Gesture Recognition
29. R. Stiefelhagen, J. Yang, and A. Waibel, 1997. Tracking Eyes and Monitoring Eye Gaze, Proceedings of Workshop on Perceptual User Interfaces, pp. 98-100
30. J. Daugman, 2003. The Importance of Being Random: Statistical Principles of Iris Recognition, Pattern Recognition, vol. 36, no. 2, pp. 279-291
31. Ramesh Jain, 1995, Machine Vision, McGraw-Hill International Edition
32. http://www.polhemus.com
33. Kang-Sun Choi et al., 1999, New Auto-focusing Technique Using the Frequency Selective Weight Median Filter for Video Cameras, IEEE Transactions on Consumer Electronics, Vol.45, No.3, pp.820-827
34. Vogel, 1991, Optical Properties of Human Sclera and Their Consequences for Trans-scleral Laser Applications, Lasers in Surgery & Medicine, 11(4), pp.331-340
35. J. Deng et al., 1997, Region-based Template Deformation and Masking for Eye Feature Extraction and Description, Pattern Recognition, 30(3), pp.403-419

Author Index

Lecture Notes in Artificial Intelligence (LNAI)